Commonsense Reasoning

Commonsense Reasoning

Commonsense Reasoning

An Event Calculus Based Approach

Second Edition

Erik T. Mueller

IBM Watson Group and IBM Research

Acquiring Editor: Steve Elliot

Editorial Project Manager: Kaitlin Herbert Project Manager: Punithavathy Govindaradjane

Designer: Matthew Limbert

Morgan Kaufmann is an imprint of Elsevier 225 Wyman Street, Waltham, MA, 02451, USA

Copyright © 2015, 2006 Elsevier Inc. All rights reserved.

No part of this publication may be reproduced or transmitted in any form or by any means, electronic or mechanical, including photocopying, recording, or any information storage and retrieval system, without permission in writing from the publisher. Details on how to seek permission, further information about the Publisher's permissions policies and our arrangements with organizations such as the Copyright Clearance Center and the Copyright Licensing Agency, can be found at our website: www.elsevier.com/permissions.

This book and the individual contributions contained in it are protected under copyright by the Publisher (other than as may be noted herein).

Notices

Knowledge and best practice in this field are constantly changing. As new research and experience broaden our understanding, changes in research methods, professional practices, or medical treatment may become necessary.

Practitioners and researchers must always rely on their own experience and knowledge in evaluating and using any information, methods, compounds, or experiments described herein. In using such information or methods they should be mindful of their own safety and the safety of others, including parties for whom they have a professional responsibility.

To the fullest extent of the law, neither the Publisher nor the authors, contributors, or editors, assume any liability for any injury and/or damage to persons or property as a matter of products liability, negligence or otherwise, or from any use or operation of any methods, products, instructions, or ideas contained in the material herein.

Library of Congress Cataloging-in-Publication Data

Mueller, Erik T.

Commonsense reasoning : an event calculus based approach / Erik T. Mueller. – Second edition. pages cm

Includes bibliographical references and index.

ISBN 978-0-12-801416-5 (paperback)

Commonsense reasoning-Automation.
 Artificial intelligence-Mathematics.
 Logic, Symbolic and mathematical-Data processing.
 Title.

Q338.85.M84 2015 153.4'3-dc23

2014029954

British Library Cataloguing-in-Publication Data

A catalogue record for this book is available from the British Library.

ISBN: 978-0-12-801416-5

For information on all Morgan Kaufmann publications visit our web site at www.mkp.com

Contents

Praise for C	omn	nonsense Reasoning	xvii
Foreword to	the	First Edition	xix
Preface			xxi
About the A	utho	or	xxvii
		nts to the First Edition	
Acknowled	gmen	nts to the Second Edition	xxxi
New to the	Seco	nd Edition	xxxiii
		The state of the s	
CHAPTER		Introduction	
	1.1	What is Commonsense Reasoning?	1
	1.2	Key Issues of Commonsense Reasoning	2
		1.2.1 Summary	6
	1.3	Brief History of Commonsense Reasoning	
		1.3.1 Logical Methods	
		1.3.2 Nonlogical Methods	
	1.4	The Event Calculus	9
		1.4.1 Events, Fluents, and Timepoints	
		1.4.2 A Simple Example	10
		1.4.3 Automated Event Calculus Reasoning	
	Bib	liographic Notes	12
PART I	FO	UNDATIONS	
CHAPTER	2	The Event Calculus	19
		First-Order Logic	
	2.1	2.1.1 Syntax of First-Order Logic	
		2.1.2 Semantics of First-Order Logic	20
		2.1.3 Proof Theory	20
		2.1.4 Many-Sorted First-Order Logic	20
		2.1.5 Notational Conventions	
	22	Event Calculus Basics	
		2.2.1 Event Calculus Sorts	
		2.2.2 Event Calculus Predicates	
		2.2.3 States of a Fluent	
	2.3	Event Calculus Axiomatizations	23
		2.3.1 EC	
		2.3.2 DEC	
		2.3.3 Choosing Between EC and DEC	27
	21	Reification	28
	2.7		
	2.4	2.4.1 Unique Names Axioms	

	2.6	Circumscription	30
		2.6.1 Computing Circumscription	31
		2.6.2 Example: Circumscription of Happens	31
		2.6.3 Example: Circumscription of Initiates	32
	2.7	Domain Descriptions	32
		2.7.1 Example: Sleep	34
		2.7.2 Inconsistency	36
	2.8	Reasoning Types	
		2.8.1 Deduction and Temporal Projection	37
		2.8.2 Abduction and Planning	
		2.8.3 Example: Sleep Abduction	
		2.8.4 Postdiction	
		2.8.5 Model Finding	39
		liographic Notes	
	Exe	rcises	46
	_	a patrimonical section of the disconnection of the	
PART II	C	OMMONSENSE PHENOMENA	
CHAPTER	3	The Effects of Events	
Olini ILIK		Positive and Negative Effect Axioms	
	5.1	3.1.1 Example: Telephone	
	32	Effect Axiom Idioms	
		Preconditions	
	5.5	3.3.1 Fluent Preconditions	
		3.3.2 Action Preconditions	
		3.3.3 Example: Walking Through a Door	
	3.4	State Constraints	
	0.1	3.4.1 Example: Telephone Revisited	
	Rib	liographic Notes	62
		rcises	
CHAPTER			
CHAPIER	-	The Triggering of Events	
	4.1	Trigger Axioms	
	4.0	4.1.1 Example: Alarm Clock	
	4.2	Preventing Repeated Triggering	70
	4.0	4.2.1 Example: Bank Account Service Fee	
		Triggered Fluents	
		liographic Notes	
		rcises	
CHAPTER	_	The Commonsense Law of Inertia	
	5.1	Representation of the Commonsense Law of Inertia	77
		5.1.1 Frame Problem	77
		5.1.2 Classical Frame Axioms	78
		5.1.3 Explanation Closure Axioms	78

		5.1.4 Minimizing Event Occurrences	.79
		5.1.5 Introduction of <i>Initiates</i> Predicate	
		5.1.6 Minimizing Event Effects	
		5.1.7 Introduction of <i>Terminates</i> Predicate	.80
		5.1.8 Discussion	.80
	5.2	Representing Release from the Commonsense Law of Inertia	
		5.2.1 Example: Yale Shooting Scenario	
		5.2.2 Releasing from Inertia	. 82
		5.2.3 Restoring Inertia	. 83
		5.2.4 Explanation Closure Axioms for <i>ReleasedAt</i>	
		5.2.5 Example: Russian Turkey Scenario	.84
	5.3	Release Axioms	.85
	Bibl	liographic Notes	.86
	Exe	rcises	. 89
CHAPTER	6	Indirect Effects of Events	.91
		Effect Axioms	
	• • •	6.1.1 Example: Carrying a Book	
		6.1.2 Discussion	
	6.2	Primitive and Derived Fluents	
	0.2	6.2.1 Example: Device	
	6.3	Release Axioms and State Constraints	.96
	0.0	6.3.1 Example: Carrying a Book Revisited	.96
	64	Effect Constraints	98
	0.4	6.4.1 Example: Carrying a Book Revisited	99
	65	Causal Constraints	
	0.0	6.5.1 Example: Thielscher's Circuit	102
	66	Trigger Axioms	
	0.0	6.6.1 Example: Thielscher's Circuit with Delays	105
		6.6.2 Example: Shanahan's Circuit with Delays	
	Dik	liographic Notes	
	Evo	rcises	115
CHAPTER		Continuous Change	
	7.1	Trajectory Axioms	
		7.1.1 Example: Falling Object	117
		7.1.2 Example: Falling Object with Events	
		7.1.3 Introduction of <i>Trajectory</i> Predicate	
	7.2	AntiTrajectory Axioms	
		7.2.1 Example: Hot Air Balloon	
	7.3	Using AntiTrajectory Instead of Releases	
		7.3.1 Example: Falling Object with AntiTrajectory	123
	Bib	liographic Notes	125
		rcises	

CHAPTER	8	Concurrent Events	127
		Restricting Concurrency	
		8.1.1 State Constraints	
		8.1.2 Event Occurrence Constraints	128
		8.1.3 Discussion	129
	8.2	Cumulative and Canceling Effects	129
		8.2.1 Example: Camera with Flash	
		8.2.2 Example: Moving Robot	
		ographic Notes	
	Exer	cises	136
CHAPTER	9	Nondeterministic Effects of Events	139
		Determining Fluents	
		9.1.1 Example: Roulette Wheel	
		Disjunctive Event Axioms	
		9.2.1 Example: Running and Driving	142
	Bibli	ographic Notes	143
		cises	
PART III	CO	DMMONSENSE DOMAINS	
CHAPTER	10	Space	147
	10.1	Relational Space	
		10.1.1 Basic Representation	
		10.1.2 Extended Representation	
		10.1.3 Example: Moving a Newspaper and a Box	150
	10.2	10.1.3 Example: Moving a Newspaper and a Box	
	10.2	Metric Space	153
			153 154
		Metric Space	153 154 160 160
	10.3	Metric Space	153 154 160 160 162
	10.3 Bibli	Metric Space	153 154 160 160 162 163
	10.3 Bibli	Metric Space	153 154 160 160 162 163
CHAPTER	10.3 Bibli Exer	Metric Space 10.2.1 Example: Two Baseballs Colliding. Object Identity 10.3.1 Example: One Screen 10.3.2 Example: Two Screens ographic Notes cises	153 154 160 160 162 163 164
CHAPTER	Bibli Exerci	Metric Space	153 154 160 160 162 163 164
CHAPTER	Bibli Exerci	Metric Space 10.2.1 Example: Two Baseballs Colliding. Object Identity 10.3.1 Example: One Screen 10.3.2 Example: Two Screens ographic Notes cises	153 154 160 160 162 163 164 167
CHAPTER	Bibli Exerc	Metric Space. 10.2.1 Example: Two Baseballs Colliding. Object Identity. 10.3.1 Example: One Screen 10.3.2 Example: Two Screens. ographic Notes. cises. The Mental States of Agents Beliefs, Goals, and Plans.	153 154 160 160 162 163 164 167 167
CHAPTER	Bibli Exerc	Metric Space 10.2.1 Example: Two Baseballs Colliding. Object Identity 10.3.1 Example: One Screen 10.3.2 Example: Two Screens ographic Notes cises The Mental States of Agents Beliefs, Goals, and Plans 11.1.1 Reactive Behavior	153 154 160 160 162 163 164 167 167 167
CHAPTER	10.3 Bibli Exer 11 11.1	Metric Space. 10.2.1 Example: Two Baseballs Colliding. Object Identity. 10.3.1 Example: One Screen 10.3.2 Example: Two Screens. ographic Notes. cises. The Mental States of Agents Beliefs, Goals, and Plans. 11.1.1 Reactive Behavior. 11.1.2 Goal-Driven Behavior. 11.1.3 Formalization. 11.1.4 Example: Hungry Cat Scenario.	153 154 160 162 163 164 167 167 167 167 168 170
CHAPTER	10.3 Bibli Exer 11 11.1	Metric Space 10.2.1 Example: Two Baseballs Colliding. Object Identity 10.3.1 Example: One Screen 10.3.2 Example: Two Screens ographic Notes cises. The Mental States of Agents Beliefs, Goals, and Plans 11.1.1 Reactive Behavior 11.1.2 Goal-Driven Behavior 11.1.3 Formalization	153 154 160 162 163 164 167 167 167 167 168 170
CHAPTER	10.3 Bibli Exer 11 11.1	Metric Space 10.2.1 Example: Two Baseballs Colliding. Object Identity 10.3.1 Example: One Screen 10.3.2 Example: Two Screens ographic Notes cises The Mental States of Agents Beliefs, Goals, and Plans 11.1.1 Reactive Behavior 11.1.2 Goal-Driven Behavior 11.1.3 Formalization 11.1.4 Example: Hungry Cat Scenario Emotions 11.2.1 Emotion Theory	153 154 160 160 162 163 164 167 167 167 168 170 184 184
CHAPTER	10.3 Bibli Exer 11 11.1	Metric Space 10.2.1 Example: Two Baseballs Colliding. Object Identity 10.3.1 Example: One Screen 10.3.2 Example: Two Screens ographic Notes cises The Mental States of Agents Beliefs, Goals, and Plans 11.1.1 Reactive Behavior 11.1.2 Goal-Driven Behavior 11.1.3 Formalization 11.1.4 Example: Hungry Cat Scenario Emotions	153 154 160 162 163 164 167 167 167 168 170 184 184 185

	Biblio	The Epistemic Functional Event Calculus 11.3.1 FEC Basics 11.3.2 FEC Axiomatization 11.3.3 EFEC Basics 11.3.4 EFEC Axiomatization ographic Notes cises	196 196 197 197 199
PART IV	DE	FAULT REASONING	
CHAPTER	12	Default Reasoning	205
	12.1	Atemporal Default Reasoning	
		Temporal Default Reasoning	
		12.2.1 Event Occurrences	206
		12.2.2 Event Effects	
		12.2.3 Using Minimized Events and Effects	
		Default Reasoning Method	
	12.4	Defaults and the Qualification Problem	
		12.4.1 Example: Device Revisited	
		12.4.2 Example: Broken Device	
		12.4.3 Strong and Weak Qualifications	
	40.5	12.4.4 Example: Erratic Device	
	12.5	Default Events and Properties	
		12.5.1 Default Events	
	D'1.1'	12.5.2 Default Properties	
		ographic Notes	
	Exerc	alses	210
PART V	PR	OGRAMS AND APPLICATIONS	
CHAPTER	13	The Discrete Event Calculus Reasoner	221
	13.1	Discrete Event Calculus Reasoner Architecture	221
	13.2	Encoding Satisfiability Problems	221
		Simple Examples	
		13.3.1 Deduction	
		13.3.2 Abduction	
		13.3.3 Postdiction	
		13.3.4 Model Finding	
		Example: Telephone	
		Discrete Event Calculus Reasoner Language	
		ographic Notes	
	Exerc	cises	231

CHAPTER	14	Applications	233
	14.1	Business Systems	
		14.1.1 Payment Protocols	
		14.1.2 Workflow Modeling	
	14.2	Natural Language Understanding	
		14.2.1 Story Understanding	
	14.3	Vision	
	Bibli	ographic Notes	245
		cises	
CHAPTER	15	Commonsense Reasoning Using Answer Set	
		Programming	. 249
	15.1	Answer Set Programming	
		15.1.1 Syntax of Answer Set Programs	
		15.1.2 Semantics of Answer Set Programs	
		15.1.3 Stable Models: Example 1	
		15.1.4 Stable Models: Example 2	
		15.1.5 Stable Models: Example 3	
		15.1.6 Choice Rules	
	15.2	Event Calculus in Answer Set Programming: Theory	
		15.2.1 SM	
		15.2.2 Relation Between SM and Stable Models	256
		15.2.3 Relation Between SM and Circumscription	257
		15.2.4 Use of SM for Event Calculus Reasoning	
		15.2.5 EC2ASP	259
		15.2.6 Correctness of EC2ASP	260
	15.3	Event Calculus in Answer Set Programming: Practice	261
		15.3.1 Writing the Domain Description	261
		15.3.2 Running the Solver	. 262
		15.3.3 Example: Running and Driving	. 264
		15.3.4 Example: Carrying a Book	. 265
		F2LP	
		\mathcal{E}	
		ographic Notes	
	Exerc	cises	. 269
PART VI	LO	GICAL AND NONLOGICAL METHODS	
CHAPTER	16	Logics for Commonsense Reasoning	273
JIM IEK	16.1	그렇게 그렇게 되었다.	
	10.1	16.1.1 Relational and Functional Fluents	
		16.1.2 Actions.	
		16.1.3 Action Effects	
		16.1.4 Action Preconditions	

		16.1.5 Equivalence of the Situation Calculus and	
		the Event Calculus	
		16.1.6 Discussion	
	16.2	The Features and Fluents Framework	
		16.2.1 Temporal Action Logics	
	16.3	Action Languages	279
		16.3.1 C+	280
	16.4	The Fluent Calculus	
		16.4.1 States	
		16.4.2 Plus and Minus Macros	286
		16.4.3 State Update Axioms	286
		16.4.4 Nondeterministic Effects	286
		16.4.5 Concurrent Actions	286
		16.4.6 Discussion	287
	16.5	Discussion and Summary	287
		ographic Notes	
		ises	
CHAPTER	17	Nonlogical Methods for Commonsense	
CHAPTER	1 /	Passaning	207
		Reasoning	291
	17.1	Qualitative Reasoning	
	47.0	17.1.1 QSIM	
	17.2	Analogical Processing	
		17.2.1 Structure-Mapping Engine	
	17.3	Probabilistic Reasoning	
		17.3.1 Probability and Action	
		17.3.2 Bayesian Networks	
	17.4	Society of Mind	
		17.4.1 ThoughtTreasure	
		17.4.2 Polyscheme	
		17.4.3 EM-ONE	
		ographic Notes	
	Exerc	rises	312
CHAPTER	18	Commonsense Reasoning Using Unstructured	
Olive TER		Information	315
	18 1	Natural Language as a Programming Language	
	10.1	18.1.1 SAFE	
		18.1.2 OWL	
	18 2	Reasoning with Restricted Natural Language	
	10.2	18.2.1 Montagovian Syntax	
		18.2.2 Attempto Controlled English	
	10 2		
		Reasoning Directly with Natural Language	321
	10.4	Walson	341

		18.4.1 Watson Architecture	. 321
		18.4.2 Question Analysis	. 322
		18.4.3 Primary Search	
		18.4.4 Answer Lookup	
		18.4.5 SKB	
		18.4.6 Candidate Generation	. 324
		18.4.7 Supporting Evidence Retrieval	
		18.4.8 Term Matching	
		18.4.9 Term Weighting	
		18.4.10 Answer Scoring	
		18.4.11 Final Merging and Ranking	
		18.4.12 WatsonPaths	
		18.4.13 WatsonPaths for Commonsense Reasoning	
		18.4.14 The AdaptWatson Methodology	
	18.5	Comparison	
		ographic Notes	
		cises	
PART VII	K	NOWLEDGE ACQUISITION	
CHAPTER	10	Agguinition of Commoncence Vnewledge	220
CHAPTER		Acquisition of Commonsense Knowledge	
	19.1	Manual Acquisition of Commonsense Knowledge	
		19.1.1 Cyc	
		19.1.2 WordNet	
	100	19.1.3 ThoughtTreasure	
	19.2	Crowdsourcing Commonsense Knowledge	
		19.2.1 Open Mind Common Sense	
		19.2.2 Learner	
		19.2.3 Open Mind Commons and ConceptNet	
	10.2	19.2.4 AnalogySpace	
	19.3	Games for Acquisition of Commonsense Knowledge	
		19.3.1 ANIMAL	
		19.3.2 Game for Interactive Open Mind Improvement	
		19.3.3 Verbosity	
	10.4	19.3.4 Common Consensus	
	19.4	Mining Commonsense Knowledge	
		19.4.1 Mining Relation Instances From Text	
	10 5	19.4.2 Mining Implicit Knowledge From Text	. 333
	19.5	Event Calculus Reasoning Over Acquired Commonsense	257
	10.6	Knowledge	
		Comparison of Acquisition Methods	
		How Big is Human Common Sense?	
		ographic Notes	
	Exerc	eises	363

PART VIII	CONCLUSION	- 193
CHAPTER 20	Conclusion	367
20.	1 What Was Accomplished?	367
	20.1.1 What is the Event Calculus?	
	20.1.2 How is the Event Calculus Used?	
20.	2 Where is this Leading?	368
20.	3 Closing Remarks	369
Bib	bliographic Notes	369
PART IX	APPENDICES	
APPENDIX A	Logical Foundations	373
A.1	Relations	373
A.2	Inductive Definitions	374
A.3	First-Order Logic	374
	A.3.1 Syntax of First-Order Logic	374
	A.3.2 Semantics of First-Order Logic	
	A.3.3 Herbrand Structures and Models	377
	A.3.4 Proof Theory	
A.4	Many-Sorted First-Order Logic	
	A.4.1 Syntax of Many-Sorted First-Order Logic	
	A.4.2 Semantics of Many-Sorted First-Order Logic	380
A.5	Second-Order Logic	
	Datatypes	
	A.6.1 Real Numbers	381
	A.6.2 Lists	382
A.7	Circumscription	
	A.7.1 Definition of Circumscription	383
	A.7.2 Example: Circumscription of $P(A)$	384
	A.7.3 Parallel Circumscription	384
A.8	SM	
Bibl	liographic Notes	385
APPENDIX B	Equivalence of EC and DEC	387
APPENDIX C	Events with Duration	
	Bibliographic Notes	
	The Discrete Event Calculus with Branching Time	
	LDEC	
	BDEC	
	Relationship of BDEC and LDEC	
	Relationship of BDEC and the Situation Calculus	
RID	AUDITATION INCHES	

APPENDIX E	The Event Calculus and Temporal Action Logics.	409
	The Event Calculus and TAL	
	E.1.1 TALA Axiomatization	412
	E.1.2 ECA Axiomatization	413
E.2	Lack of Equivalence Between TALA and ECA	
	ECB Axiomatization	
E.7	Equivalence of TALAS and DECA	418
	Translation from TAL 1.0 $\mathcal{L}(ND)$ to $\mathcal{L}(FL)$	
APPENDIX F	Answers to Selected Exercises	423
Cha	pter 2	423
Cha	pter 3	423
Cha	pter 4	424
	age of the second of the secon	
Bibliography		429
E.5 E.6 E.7 E.8 APPENDIX F Cha Cha Cha Cha Cha Cha Author Index	Lack of Equivalence Between TALA and ECB. General Action Type Specifications Restriction to Single-Step Actions. Equivalence of TALAS and DECA. Translation from TAL 1.0 \(\mathcal{L}(ND) \) to \(\mathcal{L}(FL) \). Answers to Selected Exercises. pter 2 pter 3 pter 4 pter 5 pter 6 pter 8	417 418 421 423 423 424 424 426 427 429 429

Praise for Commonsense Reasoning

A comprehensive exposition of reasoning about actions and change using the circumscription-based Event Calculus. The book has an excellent up-to-date bibliography on actions and change.

Chitta Baral, Arizona State University

Central to the idea of Artificial Intelligence is getting computers to understand simple facts about people and everyday life-what we call Common Sense. Amid the technical discussions about inference algorithms and knowledge representation, a larger question arises: What have we actually learned in the past 30 years about how to put Commonsense knowledge in computers? Look no further than Erik Mueller's Commonsense Reasoning for a deep and insightful survey of the state of the art in this topic. Some say that Commonsense defies logic; here Mueller shows that logic, at least, can put up a good fight.

Henry Lieberman, MIT Media Laboratory

Erik Mueller has given the most thorough treatment of commonsense knowledge and reasoning yet to appear.

John McCarthy, Stanford University

The strength of this book is that it uses a uniform representation formalism, the event calculus, to solve a variety of commonsense reasoning problems. Researchers will find the book an inspiring tool which provides many ideas for applications of action formalisms. Thanks to both the exemplary presentation style and numerous examples, the book is also well-suited for teachers and students alike.

Michael Thielscher, Dresden University of Technology

Developing systems that can perform actions and deal with change is a major challenge in intelligent system design, because it requires the construction of sophisticated models for knowledge representation and reasoning. This book provides important ideas and methods which can be used to model commonsense reasoning about events in complex and dynamic environments. The content is well thought out, and difficult topics are presented in highly accessible ways. The author tells a compelling story that highlights the utility of event calculus for applications that require commonsense models of action and change.

Mary-Anne Williams, University of Technology, Sydney, and Knowledge Representation and Reasoning Inc.

Praise for Commonsense Reasoning

redit jako jene tan serence more maneren iran apen evienaden, eta iran redig gened I sir ji gene I kurra eta ezak ordanti. Ilasko bis iranen enengingiroa iran ordan errorea

Children Paragi Birge of Son Private Co

contribution of the contribution tensor services of some off tenders of the contribution of the contributi

role langua de la TW- general esta esta en

First Municipality and interpretable to the partnership at the countries of the contract of th

victorial inches 2 dischild cons

The storaging it was based in the reasonable on the meaning material and the first storage of the first continuence of the storage materials and the second process of the secon

일입니다 그 내가 가는 그리지만 그렇게 없었다는데 한 다시 나무로 내가 없었다는데

The stands to the control of the standard of t

to beauty apple Wildiams, it investly in commonly full by which and the wireless Representations and American

Foreword to the First Edition

An eminent professor of logic once said to me, "Why do you bother devising all those little predicate calculus theories? We already know that first-order predicate calculus is capable of expressing almost anything, so what is the point?" This question typifies the attitude of a certain breed of logician, for whom the quintessence of intellectual endeavour is the study of the metalevel properties of various formalisms—their expressive power, their computational limitations, and the relationships between one formalism and another. Without doubt such work is, from an academic point of view, noble and worthwhile. So I did wonder, for several minutes, whether the eminent logician was perhaps right. But then it occurred to me that no one ever says, "Why do you bother giving your undergraduates all those little programming exercises? We already know that Turing machines can compute almost anything, so what is the point?"

The point, of course, is that the gap between believing something to be possible and knowing how to achieve it is very wide indeed. There is an art to programming, and learning how to do it well takes many years. If the eminent logician had not retired to his office before allowing me a return blow, I would have replied that what goes for programming also goes for logic: There is an art to the use of logic for knowledge representation, and learning it requires much practise. So it is surprising that more books aimed at teaching this art do not exist. Fortunately, we can now add to this small corpus the admirable volume by Erik Mueller that you are hopefully about to read. But this book is more than just a guide to building complex representations of knowledge in logic because its target is an area that might be thought of as the nemesis of artificial intelligence, namely common sense.

One of the starkest lessons of AI research in the twentieth century was that it is those aspects of human behavior that we most take for granted that are the hardest to emulate on a computer. A two-year-old child who finds a chocolate bar hidden in his mother's bag is performing a feat of common sense that our most sophisticated AI systems would be utterly incapable of matching. It is true that we now have programs that can defeat chess grandmasters—but only at chess. To a cognitive scientist, the most remarkable thing about a chess grandmaster is that, having played a great game of chess, she can then go and make a cup of tea. The very same biological apparatus that has mastered chess had long beforehand mastered the everyday physical world of solids, liquids, gravity, surfaces, and shapes, not to mention the everyday social world of interaction with her peers.

What is the right way to approach the daunting problem of endowing computers and robots with common sense? There's no shortage of opinions on this question among AI researchers and cognitive scientists. Perhaps we should be inspired by biology. Perhaps we should imitate evolution. Perhaps we should eschew nature and instead embrace mathematical formalisms such as logic. If we were empirical scientists, there would be a right and a wrong answer, whether or not we yet knew

which was which. But insofar as we are engineers, there can be many right answers. With a mere half century of thinking behind us—a very short time in the history of ideas—we still do not know how far the symbolic approach exemplified by this book can take us towards human-level artificial intelligence. But we do know that the symbolic approach makes for elegant designs with provable properties in a wide range of application areas where systems with a little extra intelligence have the edge. So Erik Mueller's book is necessary and timely, and I hope it gains the wide readership it deserves.

Murray Shanahan Imperial College London July 2005

Preface

Commonsense reasoning is the sort of reasoning we all perform about the everyday world. We can predict that, if a person enters a kitchen, then afterward the person will be in the kitchen. Or that, if someone who is holding a newspaper walks into a kitchen, then the newspaper will be in the kitchen. Because we make inferences such as these so easily, we might get the impression that commonsense reasoning is a simple thing. But it is very complex.

Reasoning about the world requires a large amount of knowledge about the world and the ability to use that knowledge. We know that a person cannot be in two places at once, that a person can move from one location to another by walking, and that an object moves along with a person holding it. We have knowledge about objects, events, space, time, and mental states and can use that knowledge to make predictions, explain what we observe, and plan what to do.

This book addresses the following question: How do we automate commonsense reasoning? In the last few decades, much progress has been made on this question by artificial intelligence researchers. This book provides a detailed account of this progress and a guide to automating commonsense reasoning using logic. We concentrate on one formalism, the event calculus, that incorporates many of the discoveries of the field. Although the event calculus is defined by a handful of classical predicate logic axioms, it enables reasoning about a wide range of commonsense phenomena.

WHY COMMONSENSE REASONING?

Why study commonsense reasoning? The first reason for studying commonsense reasoning is practical. Automated commonsense reasoning has many applications ranging from intelligent user interfaces and natural language processing to robotics and vision. Commonsense reasoning can be used to make computers more human-aware, easier to use, and more flexible.

The second reason for studying commonsense reasoning is scientific. Commonsense reasoning is a core capability of intelligence that supports many other high-level capabilities. The ability to understand what is happening in a story, for example, crucially involves commonsense reasoning. By studying commonsense reasoning we can gain a greater understanding of what intelligence is.

APPROACH

The approach to commonsense reasoning taken in this book is not shared by all researchers. My approach can be characterized by the following assumptions.

I assume, along with most cognitive scientists, that commonsense reasoning involves the use of representations and computational processes that operate on those representations.

I assume, along with researchers in symbolic artificial intelligence, that these representations are symbolic.

I assume, along with researchers in logic-based artificial intelligence, that commonsense knowledge is best represented declaratively rather than procedurally.

I use the declarative language of classical many-sorted predicate logic with equality.

I do not claim that the methods for commonsense reasoning presented in this book are the methods used by humans. This book presents one way of automating commonsense reasoning. How humans perform commonsense reasoning is an interesting topic, but it is not the topic of this book. There is evidence both for and against the use of logic in human reasoning.

INTENDED AUDIENCE

This book is intended for use by researchers and students in the areas of computer science, artificial intelligence, mathematics, and philosophy. It is also intended for use by software designers wishing to incorporate commonsense reasoning into their applications. The book can be used as a graduate-level textbook for courses on commonsense reasoning and reasoning about action and change, as well as a reference work for researchers working in these areas. It will be of interest to those using logic as their primary technique, as well as those using other techniques. This book can also be used as a supplementary graduate-level or advanced undergraduate textbook for courses on knowledge representation and artificial intelligence. I assume the reader has some familiarity with predicate logic, although reviews of predicate logic are provided in Chapter 2 and Appendix A.

ROADMAP

This book consists of 20 chapters and six appendices. The chapters are organized into eight parts.

Part I describes the foundations of the event calculus.

Part II deals with various commonsense phenomena. Chapter 3 discusses the effects of events. Chapter 4 discusses the triggering of events by conditions. Chapter 5 discusses the commonsense law of inertia. Chapter 6 discusses the indirect effects of events. Chapter 7 discusses continuous change. Chapter 8 discusses concurrent events. Chapter 9 discusses nondeterministic effects of events.

Part III deals with important commonsense domains. Chapter 10 presents axiomatizations of relational and metric space, and discusses reasoning about object identity, space, and time. Chapter 11 presents axiomatizations of the mental states of agents, including beliefs, goals, plans, and emotions. Part IV discusses default reasoning.

Part V deals with programs and applications. Chapter 13 discusses the Discrete Event Calculus Reasoner program used to solve event calculus reasoning problems, Chapter 14 discusses several real-world applications, and Chapter 15 discusses the use of answer set programming for commonsense reasoning. Part VI reviews logical and nonlogical methods for commonsense reasoning and discusses their relationship to the event calculus. Chapter 16 reviews logical methods, Chapter 17 reviews nonlogical methods, and Chapter 18 discusses the use of unstructured information for commonsense reasoning.

Part VII discusses the acquisition of commonsense knowledge.

Part VIII presents my conclusions.

MATERIAL COVERED

The skills that make up human commonsense reasoning are complex, and the body of research related to it is large. Because no book can realistically cover every aspect of commonsense reasoning, a choice had to be made about what this book would cover. The coverage of this book was determined by the following considerations.

Most instances of commonsense reasoning involve action and change because action and change are pervasive aspects of the world. It is crucial for any method for commonsense reasoning to deal with action and change. Therefore, a large part of this book is devoted to this topic. In addition to reasoning about action and change, or the domain of time, this book covers two other significant domains of commonsense reasoning: space and mental states, including emotions, goals, plans, and beliefs. This book also covers default reasoning and reasoning about object identity.

Over the last few decades, researchers have developed a number of logics for commonsense reasoning. It would take much time and space to cover all of these in detail. Hence, this book concentrates on one logic, the event calculus, which incorporates many of the features of the other logics. The reader who understands the event calculus will be well equipped to understand the other logics. They are closely related to the event calculus, and some are provably equivalent to the event calculus—see Appendices D and E. Chapter 16 compares the event calculus with other logics, and detailed Bibliographic notes throughout the book discuss research performed using other logics.

Several types of commonsense reasoning are not covered by this book. Commonsense reasoning using probability theory is not covered because this is not a well-developed area. But this book does cover nondeterminism, and some work on the use of probability theory for commonsense reasoning is reviewed (in Section 17.3). Although this book covers most features of the event calculus, it does not cover

continuous change described using differential equations; this book does, however, cover continuous change described by closed-form expressions.

SUPPLEMENTAL MATERIALS WEB SITE AND REASONING PROGRAMS

The book web site at decreasoner.sourceforge.net contains additional material related to this book. This includes links to tools that can be downloaded, such as the Discrete Event Calculus Reasoner program discussed in Chapter 13 and answer set programming tools discussed in Chapter 15.

EXERCISES AND SOLUTIONS

Exercises are provided at the end of Chapters 2 through 19. Solutions to selected exercises are provided in Appendix F. Solutions to further exercises are available online to instructors who have adopted this text. Register at www.textbooks.elsevier.com for access.

TEXT AND FIGURE ACKNOWLEDGMENTS

Portions of the book, *The Snowman*, by Raymond Briggs, courtesy of Random House. Portions of the book, *Solving the Frame Problem*, by Murray Shanahan, courtesy of MIT Press.

Portions of the article "A Logic of Actions" by Patrick J. Hayes, in *Machine Intelligence*, Vol. 6, courtesy of Edinburgh University Press.

Portions of the article, "Event Calculus Reasoning Through Satisfiability" by Erik T. Mueller, in *Journal of Logic and Computation*, courtesy of *Journal of Logic and Computation* and Oxford University Press.

Portions of the article, "Story understanding through multi-representation model construction" by Erik T. Mueller, in *Text Meaning: Proceedings of the HLT-NAACL 2003 Workshop*, courtesy of Association for Computational Linguistics.

Portions of the article, "Discrete event calculus with branching time" by Erik T. Mueller, in *Logical Formalizations of Commonsense Reasoning: Papers from the AAAI Spring Symposium*, courtesy of the Association for the Advancement of Artificial Intelligence.

Portions of the article, "Event calculus and temporal action logics compared" by Erik T. Mueller, in *Artificial Intelligence*, courtesy of Elsevier.

Portions of the discussion, "[Protocol of online discussion about the article A logical account of the common sense informatic situation for a mobile robot]" by Murray Shanahan, courtesy of "Electronic News Journal on Reasoning about Actions and Change."

Figure, "Shanahan's Circuit," reprinted from *Proceedings of the Sixteenth International Joint Conference on Artificial Intelligence*, by Murray Shanahan, "The ramification problem in the event calculus," p. 145, 1999, with permission from Elsevier.

Figure, "Thielscher's Circuit," reprinted from "Ramification and Causality," by Michael Thielscher, p. 19, 1996, with permission from Berkeley, CA: International Computer Science Institute.

Angures "Soun and the all repended from the control of Surveying the surveying the negligible of Conference on Arthoritical Services and Managery and Arthoritical Research non-incommentation and the control of the Conference of the Arthoritical C

Jaguna (Tiber cher der einemit beginnter fram 18. m.c. der der schrieb by Michael Thiele from p. 18. 1 Orthwich permission from der der der der der George Pompmer Science bestake

About the Author

Erik T. Mueller is a Research Staff Member at IBM Watson Group and IBM Research. He is a member of the IBM team that developed Watson,™ a natural language question answering system that won a two-game Jeopardy! match against two Jeopardy! grand champions. His previous books include *Daydreaming in Humans and Machines* and *Natural Language Processing with ThoughtTreasure*. He received an S.B. in Computer Science and Engineering from the Massachusetts Institute of Technology and an M.S. and Ph.D. in Computer Science from the University of California, Los Angeles. He is currently developing WatsonPaths, a reasoning system based on Watson, and Watson for Healthcare, which will help healthcare professionals diagnose, treat, and manage patients.

nontuA antituodA

Linkert Minches and Asserts Sinh Weight on the Constant Minches and Indi-Resourced by a constant of the Constant of the Constant of the Constant of Constant of

Acknowledgments to the First Edition

It is my great pleasure to acknowledge the people who have contributed to this book, although space constraints do not permit me to refer to everyone by name. I am particularly indebted to the inventors of the event calculus. This book owes its existence to the pathbreaking work of Robert A. Kowalski, Marek J. Sergot, Murray Shanahan, Rob Miller, and other researchers in the field of reasoning about action and change.

I am privileged to work in the academically stimulating environment of the IBM T. J. Watson Research Center. Special thanks are due to Doug Riecken, the creator of the Commonsense Computing department in which I work. I am grateful for the support of Guruduth S. Banavar, Arthur C. Ciccolo, Thomas A. Cofino, Paul Horn, Charles W. Lickel, Alfred Spector, John Turek, Jürg von Känel, and Ellen J. Yoffa. Over the years, I have learned a great deal about formal knowledge representation from Leora Morgenstern. My research benefited immensely from many conversations with Tessa A. Lau, Daniel Oblinger, and David Canfield Smith. Other colleagues who helped in a number of ways were Rangachari Anand, Karen Appleby, Richard J. Cardone, David Ferrucci, Leiguang Gong, Robert Hoch, Xuan Liu, Mark Podlaseck, Moninder Singh, Vugranam Sreedhar, Malgorzata Stys-Budzikowska, and Christopher Welty.

I feel very fortunate to receive continuing inspiration from the faculty, staff, and students of the MIT Media Laboratory. I particularly value the support and friendship of Marvin Minsky and Push Singh, who made it possible for me to begin to work seriously in the area of commonsense reasoning by inviting me to spend 6 months as a research scientist at the Media Lab. Both Marvin and Push have helped improve my thinking about this area in innumerable ways. Other people from the Media Lab who have helped me in my work are Barbara A. Barry, Walter Bender, Nicholas L. Cassimatis, Timothy Chklovski, Glorianna Davenport, Robert W. Lawler, Henry Lieberman, Xinyu Hugo Liu, Betty Lou McClanahan, Nicholas Negroponte, Deb Roy, Warren Sack, Oliver G. Selfridge, and Ted Selker.

Other researchers have been very generous in assisting me. Conversations with Benjamin Kuipers helped me to define a research strategy for commonsense reasoning. The excellent paper of Murray Shanahan and Mark Witkowski on event calculus planning through satisfiability sparked my interest in this technique. My work has vastly improved as a result of the helpful comments and criticism I received from those who served as anonymous referees of my papers on the event calculus. I am grateful to John McCarthy for his ongoing support. I thank Geoff Sutcliffe for his collaboration on the use of automated theorem proving for event calculus reasoning. Discussions with Srini Narayanan have also been helpful.

I also acknowledge the reviewers, Chitta Baral, Arizona Stata University; Patrick Hayes, Florida Institute for Human and Machine Cognition; Michael Thielscher,

Technische Universität Dresden; Mary-Anne Williams, University of Technology, Sydney; and an anonymous reviewer, who took the time to read the entire manuscript and provide me with feedback. Vladimir Lifschitz's helpful comments significantly improved the section on the $\mathcal{C}+$ action language.

I have had the good fortune to work with an extremely talented group of people at Morgan Kaufmann and Elsevier. Special thanks go to Denise E. M. Penrose, publisher, whose strong support for this project has never faltered. The editorial and production process was a smooth and efficient experience thanks to the excellent work of Valerie Witte, editorial assistant, and of Dawnmarie E. Simpson, project manager. I also thank Julie F. Nemer for copyediting the book, and Dartmouth Publishing for producing many of the figures.

I am grateful for the support and friendship of Alexandra Guest, Anne-Marie Hainault, Karen M. Kensek, Lo-Ann Lai, Christopher A. Perez, Joseph E. Pingree, Lorenzo A. Sadun, and Uri Zernik. My thanks also go to Eyal Amir, Patrick Doherty, Jeffrey Epstein, Dov M. Gabbay, Douglas B. Lenat, Jane Spurr, and Jeff Wolfers, who assisted this project in many ways.

My greatest debt is to my family. I especially thank my parents, Diana E. Mueller and Robert E. Mueller, for their love and enthusiasm for my work. I am grateful for the love and moral support of my sister, Rachel A. G. Mueller-Lust, and brother-in-law, Andrew D. Mueller-Lust. I thank my in-laws, David Hackett Fischer and Judith H. Fischer, who read the manuscript and provided helpful feedback. My thanks also go to Ilus Lobl, John H. Fischer, Victor Lobl, Anne W. Fischer, Frederick C. Turner, and Althea W. Turner. Sophie and Nicole Fischer provided welcome distractions. Words cannot express my love and gratitude to my wife, Susanna F. Fischer, and our son, Matthew E. Mueller, for the happiness we share.

Erik T. Mueller July 2005

Acknowledgments to the Second Edition

I would like to thank all those at Elsevier who made the second edition happen. Special appreciation goes to Steve Elliot, publisher, for suggesting a second edition and for his editorial help. Kaitlin Herbert, editorial project manager, and Punitha Govindaradjane, project manager, made the publishing process enjoyable.

I would like to thank the reviewers of parts of this book. Joohyung Lee and Ravi Palla provided useful comments on the chapter about commonsense reasoning using answer set programming. Catherine Havasi and Rob Speer gave helpful suggestions on the chapters about commonsense reasoning using unstructured information and acquisition of commonsense knowledge.

I am grateful to Michael Dyer, Douglas Metzler, Rob Miller, Murray Shanahan, and Stuart C. Shapiro for their helpful input on the second edition. I thank Henry Lieberman for fruitful discussions about AnalogySpace.

This work would not be possible without the kind support of Jennifer Chu-Carroll, Eric W. Brown, and the entire Watson Group at IBM.

I am so happy to be in the delightful company of my wife Susanna and our son Matthew.

Erik T. Mueller September 2014

Acknowledgments to the Second Edition

t designed tille til flamen som store store som en store for the security of the designed to the designed to the security of t

Control of the control of the form of the form of the control of t

and sense of the medical of the first transport of the sense of the se

akon territoria en la companya de l Medical de la companya de la company

in gant a pain all prive to be en a confuncion affine de la japa o me

than the first that the

New to the Second Edition

There has been intense activity in the field of commonsense reasoning since the first edition of this book, which was published in 2006. I have added three chapters to cover three areas that have blossomed since the first edition:

Chapter 15 discusses the use of answer set programming for efficient commonsense reasoning using the event calculus.

Chapter 18 discusses the use of unstructured information for commonsense reasoning, including the Watson system.

Chapter 19 discusses the acquisition of commonsense knowledge through crowdsourcing, text mining, and other techniques.

I have also added several sections and appendices:

- Section 11.3 discusses the epistemic functional event calculus.
- Appendix D discusses the discrete event calculus with branching time.
- Appendix E discusses the relation between the event calculus and temporal action logics.

New to the Second Edition

Figure has been interest in a viter in the treld of commencer are executing a community of the final real and the community of the first of the community of th

Chapter 15 throuse. The transfer set program up to be cellicles

an aing mayo ait garag ga maggo banbenonmas

Chipter (8 discusses — c of uit innound internal inferior innound in annual inclusion of Victorian in the control of the contr

- Chapter 19, discusses the authorities in common easily forest equipment of the section of the

Jimong has known and button one was I

- The first of the event and a single property of the contract of the extraction of th
- and the company of th
- isani, espesi na manjave digaska tiplintara, masisa Aydanoq.

Introduction

1

This book is about commonsense reasoning, the sort of reasoning people perform in daily life. Here are some examples of commonsense reasoning:

- 1. In the living room, Lisa picked up a newspaper and walked into the kitchen. Where did the newspaper end up? It ended up in the kitchen.
- 2. Kate set a book on a coffee table and left the living room. When she returned, the book was gone. What happened to the book? Someone must have taken it.
- 3. Jamie walks to the kitchen sink, puts the stopper in the drain, turns on the faucet, and leaves the kitchen. What will happen as a result? The water level will increase until it reaches the rim of the sink. Then the water will start spilling onto the floor.
- **4.** Kimberly turns on a fan. What will happen? The fan will start turning. What if the fan is not plugged in? Then the fan will not start turning.
- **5.** A hungry cat saw some food on a nearby table. The cat jumped onto a chair near the table. What was the cat about to do? The cat was about to jump from the chair onto the table in order to eat the food.

This book is concerned with understanding and describing commonsense reasoning to such a level of detail that it can be *automated*, or performed automatically by a machine such as a computer. It reviews methods for commonsense reasoning and describes in detail a method for commonsense reasoning using the event calculus, which is based on classical predicate logic.

1.1 WHAT IS COMMONSENSE REASONING?

Commonsense reasoning is a process that involves taking information about certain aspects of a scenario in the world and making inferences about other aspects of the scenario based on our commonsense knowledge, or knowledge of how the world works. Commonsense reasoning is essential to intelligent behavior and thought. It allows us to fill in the blanks, to reconstruct missing portions of a scenario, to figure out what happened, and to predict what might happen next. Commonsense reasoning stands in contrast to various types of expert reasoning such as economic, legal, mathematical, medical, and scientific reasoning.

1.2 KEY ISSUES OF COMMONSENSE REASONING

Although commonsense reasoning comes naturally to us and appears to be simple, it is actually a complex process. In this section, we examine the previously mentioned examples of commonsense reasoning in detail. We introduce fundamental concepts and point out some of the key issues that must be addressed by any method for commonsense reasoning.

Consider the first scenario.

Representation

In the living room, Lisa picked up a newspaper ...

In order to automate commonsense reasoning about a scenario such as this, we must first build a representation of the scenario. A *representation* is something that resembles something else. For the purpose of automating commonsense reasoning, the representation should be a data structure or a sentence of a language defined by a formal syntax, and the representation should facilitate automated reasoning.

Objects, properties, events, and time

Several fundamental entities must be represented. First, we must represent objects in the world and agents such as persons and animals; we must represent Lisa, the newspaper, and the living room. Second, we must represent properties of the world that change over time; we need to represent the time-varying locations of Lisa and the newspaper. Third, we must represent events or actions that occur in the world; we need to represent the event of Lisa picking up the newspaper. Fourth, we must represent time; we must represent that Lisa picked up the newspaper when she and the newspaper were in the living room.

Object identity

We must represent the identities of objects; we must represent the fact that Lisa and the newspaper are not the same object.

Reasoning

Having formed a representation of the scenario, we can then perform commonsense *reasoning* or *inference*. Because our goal is automation, the method of reasoning should be expressed as an algorithm or formal rule that takes representations as input and produces representations as output.

Representations of commonsense knowledge

We must construct representations of commonsense knowledge that can be used by the reasoning method to reason about this scenario as well as other scenarios.

Effects of events

We must be able to represent and reason about the effects of events on world properties. We must be able to reason from a specific event and general knowledge about the effects of events to the specific effects of the specific event. We should be able to represent that, if a person picks up an object, then the person will be holding that object. Given that Lisa picked up the newspaper, and this piece of commonsense knowledge, we should be able to infer that Lisa was then holding the newspaper.

Context-sensitive effects

We must be able to represent and reason about the context-sensitive effects of events. We should be able to represent that, if a person picks up a slippery object and is not careful, then the person will not be holding the object.

Nondeterministic effects

We must also be able to represent and reason about events with nondeterministic effects. We should be able to represent that, if a person picks up a slippery object, then the person may or may not be holding the object.

Concurrent events

We must be able to represent and reason about concurrent events. We should be able to represent that certain concurrent events are impossible; for example, a person cannot walk into two rooms simultaneously. We must be able to reason about concurrent events with cumulative or canceling effects. For example, if a shopping cart is pushed, it moves forward. If it is pulled, it moves backward. But, if it is simultaneously pulled and pushed, then it moves neither forward nor backward; instead, it spins around.

Space

...and walked into the kitchen.

In order to automate commonsense reasoning, we must be able to deal with space. We must represent the knowledge that, after a person walks into a room, the person will be in that room. From this knowledge and the fact that Lisa walked into the kitchen, we should be able to infer that afterward Lisa was in the kitchen.

Indirect effects

Where did the newspaper end up? It ended up in the kitchen.

In order to make this inference, we must be able to reason about the indirect effects or ramifications of events. We know that, if a person is holding an object, then the object moves along with the person.

Next, we consider the second scenario.

Kate set a book on a coffee table ...

We must represent the effect of setting an object on another object, and we should be able to reason that, after Kate set the book on the coffee table, the book was on the coffee table.

Preconditions

We should also be able to infer that before Kate set the book on the table, she was holding the book and she was near the table; we must be able to represent and reason

about the preconditions of actions or events. We need to represent two preconditions of a person placing an object onto a surface: (1) the person must be holding the object, and (2) the person must be near the surface.

... and left the living room.

We should be able to infer that, after Kate left the living room, she was no longer in the living room.

Commonsense law of inertia

We should also be able to infer that the book was still on the table in the living room after she left.

When she returned. ...

We should be able to infer that, after Kate returned, the book was probably still on the table in the living room. That is, unless a person or animal moved the book, or some natural phenomenon such as an earthquake occurred, the book was where Kate left it. This property of the commonsense world, that things tend to stay the same unless affected by some event, is known as the *commonsense law of inertia*.

But we learn that the book was no longer in the living room:

...the book was gone.

In this case we should be able to infer that someone took the book out of the room (or a natural phenomenon occurred):

What happened to the book? Someone must have taken it.

Next, we consider the third scenario.

Delayed effects and continuous change

Jamie walks to the kitchen sink, puts the stopper in the drain, turns on the faucet, and leaves the kitchen.

We have so far seen that it is necessary for us to be able to represent and reason about the immediate effects of events, such as putting a stopper in a drain and turning on a faucet. Thus, we should be able to infer that the stopper is in the drain, the faucet is running, and the sink is filling. In addition, we should be able to represent and reason about the delayed effects of events:

What will happen as a result? The water level will increase until it reaches the rim of the sink. Then the water will start spilling onto the floor.

Making these inferences involves representing and reasoning about continuous change. We should be able to represent that, if a faucet is turned on with the stopper in place, then the water level will increase with time.

Release from the commonsense law of inertia

Recall that the commonsense law of inertia states that things stay the same unless affected by some event. But notice that the water level continues to change after the event of turning on the faucet. Therefore we must be able to represent that, after the faucet is turned on, the water level is released from the commonsense law of inertia and is permitted to vary. We must further represent that the water level is proportional to the time elapsed since the faucet was turned on.

Triggered events

In order to reason about this scenario, we must also be able to represent and reason about triggered events. The water level does not increase endlessly. When a sink is filling and the water reaches the rim of the sink, the sink will overflow. We should be able to represent and reason that, when a sink overflows, the water starts spilling onto the floor and the water level stops increasing. At this point, the water level will again be subject to the commonsense law of inertia.

Consider the fourth scenario.

Default reasoning

When we perform commonsense reasoning, we rarely have complete information. We are unlikely to know the state of affairs down to the last detail, everything about the events that are occurring, or everything about the way the world works. Therefore, when we perform commonsense reasoning, we must jump to conclusions. Yet, if new information becomes available that invalidates those conclusions, then we must also be able to take them back. Reasoning in which we reach conclusions and retract those conclusions when warranted is known as *default reasoning*. In the fourth scenario,

Kimberly turns on a fan. What will happen? The fan will start turning.

How can the method for commonsense reasoning conclude that the fan will start turning? In fact, the fan might not start turning if the fan is broken, if the fan is not plugged in, and so on. The world is filled with exceptions such as these. The method must be able to assume that things are as normal and conclude that the fan will start turning. If it is later learned that the fan is not plugged in, then the conclusion should be revised:

What if the fan is not plugged in? Then the fan will not start turning.

Two special cases of default reasoning are required for reasoning about events. First, although we are told that a fan is turned on, we do not know what other events occur. We do not know whether, for example, some other person is simultaneously attempting to turn off the fan. The method for commonsense reasoning must assume that this is not the case; that is, it must be assumed by default that unexpected events do not occur.

Second, although we know that a fan will start turning after it is turned on, we do not know what the other results of turning on the fan might be. Perhaps turning

on the fan also unlocks a nearby door. The method for commonsense reasoning must assume by default that events do not have unexpected effects.

Next, we consider the fifth scenario.

Mental states

A hungry cat saw some food on a nearby table.

We must represent the piece of commonsense knowledge that, if an agent has an unsatisfied goal, then the agent will form a plan to achieve that goal. In this case, if an animal has the goal to eat and has the belief that food is nearby, then the animal will form the plan to go to the food and eat it.

The cat jumped onto a chair near the table.

We must further represent that agents act on their plans. We should be able to infer that jumping onto a chair is part of the cat's plan to eat.

What was the cat about to do? The cat was about to jump from the chair onto the table in order to eat the food.

Based on the knowledge that agents act on their plans, we should be able to infer that the cat will complete the plan. After the cat eats the food, we should infer that the plan is completed. We may also then infer that the goal to eat is satisfied.

Reasoning types

A method for automated commonsense reasoning must support several types of commonsense reasoning. The first is *temporal projection* or *prediction*, in which we start with an initial state and some events and then reason about the state that results from the events. The examples of Lisa walking into the kitchen, the kitchen sink overflowing, and the cat eating the food all involve temporal projection. The second type of reasoning is *abduction*, in which we start with an initial state and a final state and then reason about the events that lead from the initial state to the final state. The example of Kate's book disappearing involves abduction. The third type of reasoning is *postdiction*, in which we start with some events that lead to a state and then reason about the state prior to the events. If we are told that Lisa picked up a newspaper and was then holding the newspaper, we may reason that Lisa was not previously holding the newspaper.

1.2.1 SUMMARY

Any method for automated commonsense reasoning must address the following.

Representation. The method must represent scenarios in the world and must represent commonsense knowledge about the world.

Commonsense entities. The method must represent objects, agents, time-varying properties, events, and time.

Commonsense domains. The method must represent and reason about time, space, and mental states. The method must deal with object identity. Commonsense phenomena. The method must address the commonsense law of inertia, release from the commonsense law of inertia, concurrent events with cumulative and canceling effects, context-sensitive effects, continuous change, delayed effects, indirect effects, nondeterministic effects, preconditions, and triggered events.

Reasoning. The method must specify processes for reasoning using representations of scenarios and representations of commonsense knowledge. The method must support default reasoning, temporal projection, abduction, and postdiction.

1.3 BRIEF HISTORY OF COMMONSENSE REASONING

Artificial intelligence researchers have been trying to invent ways of automating commonsense reasoning since the inception of the field in 1956. Work on commonsense reasoning can be divided into two categories: logical and nonlogical. Logical methods are reviewed in Chapter 16, and nonlogical methods are reviewed in Chapters 17–19. In this section, we present a brief history of work on logical and nonlogical methods.

1.3.1 LOGICAL METHODS

In 1958, John McCarthy proposed to use logic to give computer programs common sense. In the 1960s, he and Patrick J. Hayes introduced the situation calculus, a logical formalism for commonsense reasoning. In the 1970s, the crucial role of defaults in commonsense reasoning was recognized, and researchers began to formalize methods for default reasoning. Important formalisms for default reasoning such as circumscription and default logic appeared around 1980.

Taking their inspiration from the situation calculus, Robert Kowalski and Marek Sergot introduced the event calculus in 1986. In the late 1980s, several other logical formalisms began to appear, including the features and fluents framework, action languages, and the fluent calculus.

Since the early 1990s, logic-based commonsense reasoning has been the focus of intense activity. Researchers proposed a number of benchmark problems designed to expose issues of commonsense reasoning not yet addressed by the available formalisms. This led to a considerable evolution of the formalisms.

In this book, we use a version of the event calculus developed in the 1990s by Murray Shanahan and Rob Miller, which we call EC, and a version that is equivalent for integer time, called the discrete event calculus (DEC). The event calculus has benefited enormously from the investigation of benchmark problems. Table 1.1 shows some of the benchmark problems that led to the addition of features to the event calculus.

Table 1.1 Benchmark Problems Leading to the Addition of Features to the Event Calculus

Benchmark Problem	Commonsense Phenomena	Event Calculus Features Added
Bus ride scenario	Nondeterministic	Disjunctive event axioms
(Kartha, 1994)	effects	(Shanahan, 1997b)
Chessboard scenario	Nondeterministic	Determining fluents
due to Raymond Reiter (Kartha & Lifschitz, 1994)	effects	(Shanahan, 1997b)
Commuter scenario (Shanahan, 1999a)	Compound events	Three-argument Happens
Kitchen sink scenario	Continuous change,	Trajectory axioms,
(Shanahan, 1990)	triggered events	trigger axioms
Russian turkey scenario	Nondeterministic	Release axioms
(Sandewall, 1994)	effects	(Shanahan, 1997b)
Shopping outlet scenario (R. Miller, Morgenstern, & Patkos, 2013)	Knowledge	Possible worlds
Soup bowl scenario	Concurrent events	Cumulative effect axioms
(Gelfond, Lifschitz,	Concurrent events	(R. Miller & Shanahan, 1999)
& Rabinov, 1991)		(11. Willief & Shaharlanan, 1999)
Stolen car scenario	Explanation	Abduction
(Kautz, 1986)	Explanation	(Shanahan, 1997b)
Stuffy room scenario	Indirect effects	State constraints,
(Ginsberg & Smith, 1988a)	I I I I I I I I I I I I I I I I I I I	primitive and derived fluents
,	EF To Talentin	(Shanahan, 1997b)
Thielscher's circuit	Indirect effects	Causal constraints
(Thielscher, 1996)		(Shanahan, 1999b)
Walking turkey scenario	Indirect effects	Effect constraints
due to Matthew L. Ginsberg (Baker, 1991)		(Shanahan, 1997b)
Yale shooting scenario	Commonsense	Circumscription,
(Hanks & McDermott, 1987)	law of inertia	forced separation
	aha shohumda i	(Shanahan, 1997b)

1.3.2 NONLOGICAL METHODS

Starting in the early 1970s, Roger Schank, Robert Abelson, and their colleagues and students developed a number of knowledge structures and inference methods for use in natural language understanding systems. A notation known as conceptual dependency (CD) was proposed for representing actions and states. Knowledge structures called scripts were introduced to represent stereotypical activities such as

attending a birthday party. A taxonomy of human plans and goals was developed, and representations for the themes of stories were introduced.

Starting in the late 1970s, researchers working in the area of qualitative reasoning developed techniques for automated reasoning about physical mechanisms such as bathtubs, clocks, electrical circuits, pressure regulators, sliding blocks, and water tanks. Physical devices are described using a modeling language, and simulation algorithms are used to perform reasoning. These techniques are useful for commonsense reasoning in the physical domain. Some of the techniques have been recast in first-order logic.

Beginning in the early 1980s, researchers developed methods for analogical processing. These methods can be used to find an analogy between a familiar domain and a novel domain and then to use the analogy to generate candidate inferences about the novel domain. Analogical processing is not a complete method for commonsense reasoning, because candidate inferences must still be evaluated and repaired using other commonsense reasoning techniques.

Probability theory has a long history and is well suited to default reasoning. Since the late 1980s, some work has been performed on using probabilistic reasoning for reasoning about action and change, but this approach is not as well developed as the logical approach. The logical and probabilistic approaches are closely related, and the integration of logic and probability theory is an active area of research.

Starting in the early 1970s, the society of mind theory was developed by Marvin Minsky and his colleagues and students. This theory views human common sense as a vast collection of skills involving multiple representation and reasoning techniques. Unlike most other approaches, this approach places a great emphasis on procedural representations of knowledge and on the ways that procedures can monitor and influence one another.

In the 2000s, after Push Singh's introduction of the Open Mind Common Sense knowledge base and Marti A. Hearst's publication of influential papers on mining WordNet relations from text, there was much activity on crowdsourcing commonsense knowledge and mining commonsense knowledge. In 2011, IBM's Watson system won a Jeopardy! television game show match against two Jeopardy! grand champions, which demonstrated the power of using unstructured information and machine learning for solving difficult artificial intelligence problems.

1.4 THE EVENT CALCULUS

The event calculus addresses all the key issues of commonsense reasoning described in Section 1.2. Using the event calculus we can represent commonsense knowledge, represent scenarios, and use the knowledge to reason about the scenarios.

1.4.1 EVENTS, FLUENTS, AND TIMEPOINTS

The basic notions of the event calculus are as follows. An *event* represents an event or action that may occur in the world, such as a person picking up a glass. We use the words *event* and *action* interchangeably. A *fluent* represents a time-varying

property of the world, such as the location of a physical object. A *timepoint* represents an instant of time, such as 9:30 AM Greenwich Mean Time on November 13, 2017. The event calculus uses *linear time*, in which time is considered to be a line, rather than the *branching time* of the situation calculus, in which time is considered to be a tree.

An event may occur or happen at a timepoint. A fluent has a truth value at a timepoint or over a timepoint interval; the possible truth values are true and false. After an event occurs, the truth values of the fluents may change. We have commonsense knowledge about the effects of events on fluents. Specifically, we have knowledge about events that initiate fluents and events that terminate fluents. For example, we know that the event of picking up a glass initiates the fluent of holding the glass and that the event of setting down a glass terminates the fluent of holding the glass. We represent these notions in first-order logic as follows.

HoldsAt(f, t) represents that fluent f is true at timepoint t.

Happens(e, t) represents that event e occurs at timepoint t.

Initiates (e, f, t) represents that, if event e occurs at timepoint t, then fluent f will be true after t.

Terminates(e, f, t) represents that, if event e occurs at timepoint t, then fluent f will be false after t.

1.4.2 A SIMPLE EXAMPLE

Here is a simple example of how the event calculus works. We use a simplified version of the event calculus, consisting of the following single axiom:

$$(Happens(e, t_1) \land Initiates(e, f, t_1) \land t_1 < t_2 \land$$

$$\neg \exists e, t (Happens(e, t) \land t_1 < t \land t < t_2 \land Terminates(e, f, t))) \Rightarrow$$

$$HoldsAt(f, t_2)$$

$$(1.1)$$

This axiom states that, if an event occurs and the event is known to initiate a particular fluent, then that fluent will be true from just after the moment the event occurs, until and including the moment an event occurs that is known to terminate the fluent.

Now let us see how this axiom can be used to solve a simple commonsense reasoning problem, using one event and one fluent. The event WakeUp(p) represents that person p wakes up, and the fluent Awake(p) represents that person p is awake. Our commonsense knowledge consists of the following.

If a person wakes up, then the person will be awake:

$$Initiates(e, f, t) \Leftrightarrow \exists p (e = WakeUp(p) \land f = Awake(p))$$
 (1.2)

If a person falls asleep, then the person will no longer be awake:

$$Terminates(e, f, t) \Leftrightarrow \exists p \ (e = FallAsleep(p) \land f = Awake(p)) \tag{1.3}$$

Now suppose we have the following scenario. Nathan is not awake at timepoint 0:

$$\neg HoldsAt(Awake(Nathan), 0)$$
 (1.4)

The only known event is that Nathan wakes up at timepoint 1:

$$Happens(e,t) \Leftrightarrow e = WakeUp(Nathan) \land t = 1$$
 (1.5)

From this commonsense knowledge and scenario, and event calculus axiom (1.1), we can prove that Nathan is awake at timepoint 3:

$$(1.1) \land (1.2) \land (1.3) \land (1.4) \land (1.5) \vdash HoldsAt(Awake(Nathan), 3)$$

The proof runs as follows. From (1.3) and (1.5), we have $\neg \exists e, t \ (Happens(e, t) \land 1 < t \land t < 3 \land Terminates(e, Awake(Nathan), t))$. From this, (1.1), (1.2), (1.5), and 1 < 3, we have HoldsAt(Awake(Nathan), 3), as required.

Adding commonsense knowledge and event occurrences to this formalization requires us to modify (1.2), (1.3), and (1.5). Later, in Sections 2.6 and 2.7, we show how circumscription allows us to add commonsense knowledge and event occurrences simply by adding axioms.

1.4.3 AUTOMATED EVENT CALCULUS REASONING

In the logic-based approach to commonsense reasoning, knowledge is represented declaratively as logical formulas rather than procedurally as computer code. Using a declarative knowledge representation has two main advantages. First, the same knowledge can be used for different types of commonsense reasoning such as temporal projection, abduction, and postdiction. If a procedural knowledge representation is used, knowledge must often be duplicated for each type of commonsense reasoning. Second, using a declarative knowledge representation allows us to use the latest, off-the-shelf, automated theorem-proving techniques to solve reasoning problems. If a procedural knowledge representation is used, reasoning techniques must often be built from scratch or reinvented.

Of course, entailment in first-order logic is *undecidable*: There is no algorithm that, given arbitrary formulas of first-order logic ψ and π , will eventually respond "yes" if ψ entails π and "no" if ψ does not entail π . First-order logic entailment is only *semidecidable*: There are algorithms that, given arbitrary formulas of first-order logic ψ and π , will respond "yes" if ψ entails π ; if ψ does not entail π , the algorithms may eventually respond "no" or may never terminate. It turns out, however, that many real-world reasoning problems in the event calculus can be solved efficiently by computer programs.

Automated reasoning in the event calculus can be performed using several programs, as listed in Table 1.2. The Discrete Event Calculus Reasoner is discussed in Chapter 13. The F2LP program is discussed in Chapter 15. These programs rely on various solvers and provers, namely, satisfiability (SAT) solvers, logic programming languages, answer set grounders and solvers, and first-order automated theorem provers. Improving the efficiency of these solvers and provers is a major focus of activity. As better solvers and provers are developed, they can be plugged into event calculus reasoning programs.

The SAT approach is particularly effective. A SAT solver takes as input a set of Boolean variables and a propositional formula over those variables and produces as output zero or more models or satisfying truth assignments, truth assignments for the

Table 1.2 Event Calculus Reasoning Programs

Description	Technique	Reasoning Types
Event calculus planner (Shanahan, 2000)	Abductive logic programming	Abduction
Event calculus planner (Shanahan & Witkowski, 2004)	Propositional satisfiability	Abduction
Discrete Event Calculus Reasoner	Propositional	Deduction,
(Mueller, 2004a, 2004b)	satisfiability	abduction, postdiction,
Discrete event calculus theorem prover	First-order logic automated theorem	model finding Deduction
(Mueller & Sutcliffe, 2005b, 2005a; Sutcliffe & Suttner, 2014)	proving	Le de la grant description
F2LP	Answer set	Deduction,
(Kim, Lee, & Palla, 2009; Lee & Palla, 2012)	programming	abduction, postdiction, model finding

variables such that the formula is true. SAT solvers take a propositional formula in conjunctive normal form: a conjunction of clauses where each clause is a disjunction of literals and where each literal is a variable or a negated variable. In order to use a SAT solver to solve an event calculus problem, formulas of predicate logic must be transformed into formulas of propositional logic. This is accomplished by restricting the problem to a finite universe. Although entailment in propositional logic is decidable, it is *NP-complete*, or believed in the worst case to take a number of steps that is exponential on the size of the problem. But, in practice, large real-world SAT problems, some with as many as tens of millions of clauses and variables, can be solved efficiently.

BIBLIOGRAPHIC NOTES

Commonsense reasoning

People have long sought to describe and capture commonsense reasoning. Logic was developed to characterize valid reasoning (Kneale & Kneale, 1962, pp. 738 and 739). The advent of computers led to the field of artificial intelligence and to a call by McCarthy (1959) to use logic to build computer programs with common sense. Computer science and artificial intelligence drove the development of new logics (Gabbay & Guenthner, 2001, p. vii). Crevier (1993), Russell and Norvig (2009), and McCorduck (2004) provide histories of the field of artificial intelligence.

Book-length treatments of commonsense reasoning are provided by Hobbs and Moore (1985), Minsky (1986), E. Davis (1990), Lenat and Guha (1990), Lifschitz (1990a), Thanassas (1992), Reiter (2001), and Thielscher (2005a, 2008). Books on the related area of knowledge representation are by Reichgelt (1991), Baral (2003), Brachman and Levesque (2004), and van Harmelen, Lifschitz, and Porter (2008). Textbooks on artificial intelligence are by Nilsson (1998) and Russell and Norvig (2009).

The ability to perform commonsense reasoning starts to develop early in life. Several-month-old infants are able to reason using pieces of commonsense knowledge such as that a moving object must follow an unbroken path over time, an object cannot pass through another object, the parts of an object move together, and unsupported objects fall (Baillargeon, 1995; Spelke, Vishton, & von Hofsten, 1995).

Thagard (1996) reviews the basic notions of representations and computational processes that operate on those representations. Our list of key issues of commonsense reasoning follows those of other researchers. McCarthy (1984b, pp. 131-135) presents important aspects of commonsense capability. He considers reasoning about action and change to be a central aspect, writing that "the most salient commonsense knowledge concerns situations that change in time as a result of events" (p. 131). McCarthy also mentions other key aspects: knowledge about knowledge; knowledge about objects, space, beliefs, goals, intentions, and commonsense physics; logical inference; obtaining facts by observation; and default reasoning. For E. Davis (1990), the important areas are plausible reasoning, quantities and measurements, time, space, physics, minds, plans and goals, and society.

Logic and commonsense reasoning

The assumptions of logic-based artificial intelligence are elaborated by Nilsson (1991). Whether logic is the right approach to commonsense reasoning has been hotly debated (Birnbaum, 1991; Ginsberg, 1991; Hayes, 1977; Israel, 1985; Kolata, 1982; McCarthy & Lifschitz, 1987; McDermott, 1987; Minsky, 1974, 1986, 1991b; R. C. Moore, 1982; Nilsson, 1991). The following advantages of logic have been pointed out:

- Logic can be used to represent any domain (R. C. Moore, 1982, p. 430).
- Via model theory, logic provides an account of the meaning of logical formulas (Hayes, 1977, pp. 559-561; Nilsson, 1991, pp. 34-40).
- Logic allows the representation of incomplete information (R. C. Moore, 1995, p. 7).

The following alleged disadvantages of logic have been pointed out:

 Logic focuses on deductive reasoning, and not all reasoning is deductive (Birnbaum, 1991, pp. 59, 70 and 71; McDermott, 1987, pp. 151 and 152). But note that deduction is not the only type of reasoning that can be performed with logic; other types of reasoning such as abduction can be performed (Shanahan, 1997b, pp. xxxii and xxxiii).

- Logic is preoccupied with consistency, and anything can be deduced from a contradiction (Birnbaum, 1991, p. 63; Hewitt, 1987, pp. 185 and 186; Minsky, 1974, pp. 76-78). But note that logics have been developed without this property, such as paraconsistent logic (Priest, 2002) and active logic (Elgot-Drapkin & Perlis, 1990; Elgot-Drapkin, Kraus, Miller, Nirkhe, & Perlis, 1999). Also note that a logical theory can be revised by subtracting axioms as well as adding them (Hayes, 1979, pp. 54 and 55; Israel, 1980, p. 101; 1985, pp. 436 and 437). See also the discussion of Bibel and Nicolas (1989, pp. 18-22).
- Logical reasoning is computationally inefficient (Birnbaum, 1991, p. 72; Minsky, 1974, p. 76). But note that the efficiency of theorem-proving systems is constantly being improved (Balint, Belov, Heule, & Järvisalo, 2013; Sutcliffe, 2013).

The role of logic in human reasoning has been vigorously debated. Henle (1962), Braine (1978), Rips (1983, 1994), Braine and O'Brien (1998), and others argue that humans use a *mental logic* in which inference rules similar to those of the natural deduction of formal logic are applied, and they present experimental evidence supporting this theory. Other researchers disagree. Johnson-Laird (1983, 1993) proposes and presents experimental evidence for a *mental models* approach in which humans reason by building, updating, and evaluating models in the mind.

Logical methods for commonsense reasoning

McCarthy (1963, 1968) and McCarthy and Hayes (1969) introduced the situation calculus. Kowalski and Sergot (1986) introduced the original event calculus within the framework of logic programming (Kowalski, 1979). The event calculus was reformulated in classical predicate logic by Shanahan (1995a, 1996, 1997b, 1999a, 1999b). R. Miller and Shanahan (1999, 2002) introduced several alternative formulations of the classical logic event calculus. Mueller (2004a) introduced the discrete event calculus. Introductions to the classical logic event calculus are provided by Shanahan (1999a) and Mueller (2009). Symposia on logical formalizations of commonsense reasoning are regularly held (Kakas, 2013), as are conferences on knowledge representation and reasoning (Eiter, 2014). The Winograd Schema Challenge is a competition for commonsense reasoning. ¹

Benchmark problems

Lifschitz (1989) created a list of commonsense reasoning benchmark problems, following a suggestion by John McCarthy. E. Davis (1990, pp. 4-12) presents a methodology for formalization of commonsense reasoning based on the use of benchmark problems. Sandewall (1994) proposes a systematic methodology for assessing entailment methods, which we discuss in the Bibliographic notes of Chapter 16. McCarthy (1983, 1998a) argues that the field of artificial intelligence needs an equivalent to drosophilae, the fruit flies biologists use to study genetic mutations

¹http://commonsensereasoning.org/winograd.html

because of their short generation time. A list of unsolved benchmark problems and a few solved ones is maintained by Leora Morgenstern (Morgenstern & Miller, 2014).

The kitchen sink scenario is from Shanahan (1990; 1997b, pp. 326-329; 1999a, pp. 426-428). This scenario can be traced back to Siklóssy and Dreussi (1973, pp. 426, 429) and Hendrix (1973, pp. 149, 159-167), who used the example of filling a bucket with water. McDermott (1982, pp. 129-133, 135-138) used the example of water flowing into a tank, and Hayes (1985, pp. 99-103) used the example of filling a bath. The shopping cart example is from Shanahan (1997b, pp. 302-304). The hungry cat scenario is from Winikoff, Padgham, Harland, and Thangarajah (2002).

Nonlogical methods for commonsense reasoning

Conceptual dependency, scripts, plans, goals, and themes are discussed by Schank and Abelson (1977), Schank and Riesbeck (1981), Abelson (1981), Schank (1982), and Dyer (1983). Singh (2002) and Singh et al. (2002) describe Open Mind Common Sense, which was part of the larger Open Mind Initiative (Stork, 1999). Hearst (1992, 1998) describes methods for mining WordNet relations from text. WordNet is described by Fellbaum (1998). Watson is described by Ferrucci et al. (2010). Bibliographic notes for nonlogical methods are provided in Chapters 17–19.

Declarative/procedural distinction

The distinction between declarative and procedural (or imperative) knowledge representation is discussed by McCarthy (1959, pp. 79 and 80), Winograd (1975), Hayes (1977), Winston (1977, pp. 390-392), and Genesereth and Nilsson (1987, pp. 2-4). Winograd (1975, p. 186) and McCarthy (1988, p. 299) suggest that declarative representations are more flexible. They point out that a fact represented declaratively can be used for many purposes, even unanticipated ones, whereas a fact represented procedurally has to be represented differently for each purpose.

Automated reasoning and SAT

Automated theorem proving is treated in detail by Robinson and Voronkov (2001a, 2001b).

The undecidability of first-order logic entailment, satisfiability, and validity is due to Church (1936/2004) and Turing (1936/2004). The semidecidability of first-order logic entailment, unsatisfiability, and validity is due to Gödel (1930/1967). It is useful to keep in mind the following relationships among entailment, satisfiability, and validity:

- ψ entails π if and only if $\psi \wedge \neg \pi$ is unsatisfiable.
- ψ entails π if and only if $\neg \psi \lor \pi$ is valid.
- ψ entails π if and only if $\psi \Rightarrow \pi$ is valid.
- ψ is valid if and only if $\neg \psi$ is unsatisfiable.

Satisfiability (SAT) solvers are discussed by Du, Gu, and Pardalos (1997), Gomes, Kautz, Sabharwal, and Selman (2008), and Biere, Heule, van Maaren, and Walsh

(2009). Automated theorem-proving system competitions (Sutcliffe, 2013), SAT system competitions (Balint, Belov, Heule, & Järvisalo, 2013), and answer set programming system competitions (Calimeri, Ianni, & Ricca, 2014), are regularly held. The use of SAT solving for planning was proposed by Kautz and Selman (1992, 1996). The use of SAT solving in the event calculus was introduced by Shanahan and Witkowski (2004). Runtime statistics for the solution of some event calculus reasoning problems using SAT are given by Mueller (2003, 2004b, 2004c). NP-completeness is discussed by Garey and Johnson (1979). The NP-completeness of propositional satisfiability was proved by Cook (1971) and Levin (1973). The growth in the capabilities of SAT solvers is discussed by Selman, Kautz, and McAllester (1997), Kautz and Selman (2003), and Dechter (2003, pp. 186-188). The satisfiability of the post-cbmc-zfcp-2.8-u2-noholes problem, which has 10,950,109 variables and 32,697,150 clauses, was proved in under 30 s by several solvers (SAT Competition, 2011).

Foundations

Foundations

The Event Calculus

In this chapter, we present the foundations of the event calculus, a formalism for commonsense reasoning. We review first-order logic and describe some notational conventions. We discuss the basics of the event calculus, and we present two axiomatizations of the event calculus: EC and DEC. We discuss how to choose which axiomatization to use. We present reification, which is needed to represent statements about events and fluents in first-order logic. We discuss unique names axioms, conditions, circumscription, and domain descriptions, and we describe the types of reasoning that can be performed using the event calculus.

2.1 FIRST-ORDER LOGIC

The event calculus is based on first-order logic, which consists of a syntax, semantics, and proof theory. The version of first-order logic used in this book is described in detail in Appendix A. Here we provide a summary.

2.1.1 SYNTAX OF FIRST-ORDER LOGIC

A language \mathcal{L} of first-order logic is specified by disjoint sets of constants, function symbols, predicate symbols, and variables. Each predicate and function symbol has an arity. If the arity of a symbol is n, then we say that the symbol is n-ary.

A *term* is a constant, a variable, or, recursively, $\phi(\tau_1, \dots, \tau_n)$, where ϕ is an *n*-ary function symbol and τ_1, \dots, τ_n are terms.

An *atom* is $\rho(\tau_1, ..., \tau_n)$, where ρ is an *n*-ary predicate symbol and $\tau_1, ..., \tau_n$ are terms, or $\tau_1 = \tau_2$, where τ_1 and τ_2 are terms.

A *formula* is an atom, or, recursively, $\neg \alpha$, $\alpha \land \beta$, $\alpha \lor \beta$, $\alpha \Rightarrow \beta$, $\alpha \Leftrightarrow \beta$, $\exists \nu_1, \ldots, \nu_n \alpha$, or $\forall \nu_1, \ldots, \nu_n \alpha$, where α and β are formulas and ν_1, \ldots, ν_n are variables.

The *scope* of the quantifier \exists in the formula $\exists \nu \alpha$ is α , and the scope of \forall in $\forall \nu \alpha$ is α . An occurrence of a variable ν in a formula Γ that is within a formula of the form $(\exists \nu \alpha)$ or $(\forall \nu \alpha)$ in Γ is *bound*; otherwise, it is *free*. A *sentence* is a formula that contains no free occurrences of variables.

For example, suppose we specify a language with the predicate symbols *Walk* (arity 3), *Happy* (arity 1), and *Sad* (arity 1); the function symbol *Cos* (arity 1); the

constants Lisa, Kitchen, Living Room, 0, and 1; and the variable a. Then 0, Cos(0), and Cos(Cos(0)) are terms; Walk(Lisa, Kitchen, Living Room) and Cos(0) = 1 are atoms; and $Happy(a) \Rightarrow \neg Sad(a)$ is a formula. The following are sentences:

$$Walk(Lisa, Kitchen, LivingRoom)$$

 $Cos(0) = 1$
 $\forall a (Happy(a) \Rightarrow \neg Sad(a))$

2.1.2 SEMANTICS OF FIRST-ORDER LOGIC

The semantics of a language \mathcal{L} of first-order logic defines the meaning of a formula of \mathcal{L} as the set of models of the formula or the set of structures in which the formula is true. For example, one model of the formula $P(A,B) \wedge P(B,C)$ is the structure consisting of the following:

- the domain {A, B, C}
- the mapping from constants to elements of the domain $A \mapsto A$, $B \mapsto B$, $C \mapsto C$
- the mapping from predicate symbols to relations $P \mapsto \{(A, B), (B, C)\}$

The set $\{\langle \mathbf{A}, \mathbf{B} \rangle, \langle \mathbf{B}, \mathbf{C} \rangle\}$ is called the *extension* of P in the structure. If a formula π is true in all models of a formula ψ , then we write $\psi \models \pi$ and say that ψ *entails* π .

2.1.3 PROOF THEORY

The proof theory defines a proof of a formula π given a formula ψ as a sequence of formulas such that

- The last formula is π.
- Each formula is either a logical axiom, ψ, or a formula derived from previous formulas using an inference rule.

An example of an inference rule is *modus ponens*, which states that, from α and $\alpha \Rightarrow \beta$, we may derive β . We write this inference rule as

$$\frac{\alpha \quad \alpha \Rightarrow \beta}{\beta}$$

If a proof of a formula π given a formula ψ exists, then we write $\psi \vdash \pi$ and say that π is *provable* from ψ .

2.1.4 MANY-SORTED FIRST-ORDER LOGIC

The event calculus uses an extension of first-order logic called many-sorted first-order logic. We specify a set of sorts, and for each sort, a possibly empty set of subsorts. We specify the sort of each constant, variable, and function symbol and the sort of each argument position of each predicate and function symbol. Every term, atom, formula, and sentence must satisfy the sort specifications.

For example, suppose we specify the following. We have agent, person, and room sorts. The person sort is a subsort of the agent sort. The sort of *Lisa* is the person sort, and the sorts of *Kitchen* and *LivingRoom* are the room sort. The sort of the first argument position of *Walk* is the agent sort, and the sorts of the second and third argument positions of *Walk* are the room sort. Then the following is a formula and sentence:

We assume a real number sort and appropriate functions and predicates such as *Plus* (+) and *LessThan* (<). See Section A.6.1 for details.

2.1.5 NOTATIONAL CONVENTIONS

In this book we use several notational conventions.

Case conventions

Predicate symbols, function symbols, and nonnumeric constants start with an uppercase letter. Examples of predicate symbols are *Walk* and *InRoom*, examples of function symbols are *Distance* and *Cos*, and examples of constants are *Lisa*, *Nathan*, -4, 1, and π . Variables start with a lowercase letter. Examples of variables are a, b, b_1 , and b_2 .

Implicit universal quantification

Free variables are implicitly universally quantified. For example, $P(x, y, z) \land \exists u \, R(u, x)$ is an abbreviation for $\forall x, y, z \, (P(x, y, z) \land \exists u \, R(u, x))$.

Conjunctions and disjunctions

The expression $\bigwedge_{i=1}^n \Gamma_i$ stands for $\Gamma_1 \wedge \cdots \wedge \Gamma_n$, and $\bigvee_{i=1}^n \Gamma_i$ stands for $\Gamma_1 \vee \cdots \vee \Gamma_n$.

Running exclusive or (XOR) notation

The expression $\alpha_1 \dot{\vee} \alpha_2 \dot{\vee} \alpha_3$ means that exactly one of α_1, α_2 , and α_3 is true, which is equivalent neither to $(\alpha_1 \dot{\vee} \alpha_2) \dot{\vee} \alpha_3$ nor to $\alpha_1 \dot{\vee} (\alpha_2 \dot{\vee} \alpha_3)$. In general, $\alpha_1 \dot{\vee} \cdots \dot{\vee} \alpha_n$ stands for the conjunction of $\alpha_1 \vee \cdots \vee \alpha_n$ and $\alpha_i \Rightarrow \neg \alpha_j$ for every $i, j \in \{1, \dots, n\}$ such that $i \neq j$. Thus, $\alpha_1 \dot{\vee} \alpha_2 \dot{\vee} \alpha_3$ stands for

$$(\alpha_1 \lor \alpha_2 \lor \alpha_3) \land$$

$$(\alpha_1 \Rightarrow \neg \alpha_2) \land (\alpha_1 \Rightarrow \neg \alpha_3) \land$$

$$(\alpha_2 \Rightarrow \neg \alpha_1) \land (\alpha_2 \Rightarrow \neg \alpha_3) \land$$

$$(\alpha_3 \Rightarrow \neg \alpha_1) \land (\alpha_3 \Rightarrow \neg \alpha_2)$$

Definitions of abbreviations

The notation $\Gamma_1 \stackrel{\text{def}}{\equiv} \Gamma_2$ defines Γ_1 as an abbreviation for Γ_2 . That is, $\Gamma_1 \stackrel{\text{def}}{\equiv} \Gamma_2$ means that all occurrences of the expression Γ_1 are to be replaced with the expression Γ_2 .

2.2 EVENT CALCULUS BASICS

This section discusses the sorts and predicates of the event calculus, and the possible states of a fluent.

2.2.1 EVENT CALCULUS SORTS

The event calculus uses the following sorts:

- an event sort, with variables e, e_1 , e_2 , ...
- a fluent sort, with variables f, f_1, f_2, \ldots
- a timepoint sort, which is a subsort of the real number sort, with variables t, t_1, t_2, \ldots

2.2.2 EVENT CALCULUS PREDICATES

The predicates of the event calculus are as follows.

Happens(e, t): Event e happens or occurs at timepoint t.

HoldsAt(f, t): Fluent f is true at timepoint t. If $\neg HoldsAt(f, t)$, then we say that f is false at t.

ReleasedAt(f, t): Fluent f is released from the commonsense law of inertia at timepoint t. If $\neg ReleasedAt(f, t)$, then we say that f is not released from the commonsense law of inertia at t. The commonsense law of inertia states that a fluent's truth value persists unless the fluent is affected by an event. When a fluent is released from this law, its truth value can fluctuate. We discuss the commonsense law of inertia in detail in Chapter 5.

Initiates (e, f, t): Event e initiates fluent f at timepoint t. If e occurs at t, then f will be true and not released from the commonsense law of inertia after t. If Happens(e, t) and Initiates(e, f, t), then we say that f is initiated by an event e that occurs at t.

Terminates (e, f, t): Event e terminates fluent f at timepoint t. If e occurs at t, then f will be false and not released from the commonsense law of inertia after t. If Happens(e, t) and Terminates(e, f, t), then we say that f is terminated by an event e that occurs at t.

Releases (e, f, t): Event e releases fluent f at timepoint t. If e occurs at t, then fluent f will be released from the commonsense law of inertia after t. If Happens(e, t) and Releases(e, f, t), then we say that f is released by an event e that occurs at t.

Trajectory(f_1, t_1, f_2, t_2): If fluent f_1 is initiated by an event that occurs at timepoint t_1 , and $t_2 > 0$, then fluent f_2 will be true at timepoint $t_1 + t_2$.

AntiTrajectory (f_1, t_1, f_2, t_2) : If fluent f_1 is terminated by an event that occurs at timepoint t_1 , and $t_2 > 0$, then fluent f_2 will be true at timepoint $t_1 + t_2$.

2.2.3 STATES OF A FLUENT

In any given model, a fluent f can be in one of the following four states at a timepoint t:

true and released $HoldsAt(f,t) \land ReleasedAt(f,t)$ true and not released $HoldsAt(f,t) \land \neg ReleasedAt(f,t)$ false and released $\neg HoldsAt(f,t) \land ReleasedAt(f,t)$ false and not released $\neg HoldsAt(f,t) \land \neg ReleasedAt(f,t)$

2.3 EVENT CALCULUS AXIOMATIZATIONS

This section presents and describes two axiomatizations of the event calculus: EC and DEC. We give a short explanation of each axiom or definition as it is presented. Much of the remainder of the book is devoted to exploring the behavior and uses of these axioms and definitions in detail.

2.3.1 EC

EC consists of 17 axioms and definitions. We divide them into several groups.

Clipped, declipped, stopped, and started

Some abbreviations relating to the initiation and termination of fluents are defined. **Definition EC1.** A fluent is *clipped* between timepoints t_1 and t_2 if and only if the fluent is terminated by some event that occurs at or after t_1 and before t_2 .

$$Clipped(t_1, f, t_2) \stackrel{\text{def}}{\equiv} \exists e, t \ (Happens(e, t) \land t_1 \leq t < t_2 \land Terminates(e, f, t))$$

Definition EC2. A fluent is *declipped* between timepoints t_1 and t_2 if and only if the fluent is initiated by some event that occurs at or after t_1 and before t_2 .

$$Declipped(t_1, f, t_2) \stackrel{\text{def}}{\equiv} \exists e, t \ (Happens(e, t) \land t_1 \le t < t_2 \land Initiates(e, f, t))$$

Definition EC3. A fluent is *stopped* between timepoints t_1 and t_2 if and only if the fluent is terminated by some event that occurs after t_1 and before t_2 .

$$StoppedIn(t_1, f, t_2) \stackrel{\text{def}}{\equiv} \exists e, t \ (Happens(e, t) \land t_1 < t < t_2 \land Terminates(e, f, t))$$

Definition EC4. A fluent is *started* between timepoints t_1 and t_2 if and only if the fluent is initiated by some event that occurs after t_1 and before t_2 .

$$StartedIn(t_1, f, t_2) \stackrel{\text{def}}{\equiv} \exists e, t \ (Happens(e, t) \land t_1 < t < t_2 \land Initiates(e, f, t))$$

Trajectory and AntiTrajectory

The behavior of trajectories is defined.

Axiom EC5. If $Trajectory(f_1, t_1, f_2, t_2)$, $0 < t_2$, f_1 is initiated by some event that occurs at t_1 , and f_1 is not stopped between t_1 and $t_1 + t_2$, then f_2 is true at $t_1 + t_2$.

$$Happens(e, t_1) \wedge Initiates(e, f_1, t_1) \wedge 0 < t_2 \wedge$$

$$Trajectory(f_1, t_1, f_2, t_2) \land \neg StoppedIn(t_1, f_1, t_1 + t_2) \Rightarrow HoldsAt(f_2, t_1 + t_2)$$

Axiom EC6. If $AntiTrajectory(f_1, t_1, f_2, t_2)$, $0 < t_2, f_1$ is terminated by some event that occurs at t_1 , and f_1 is not started between t_1 and $t_1 + t_2$, then f_2 is true at $t_1 + t_2$.

$$Happens(e, t_1) \land Terminates(e, f_1, t_1) \land 0 < t_2 \land AntiTrajectory(f_1, t_1, f_2, t_2) \land \neg StartedIn(t_1, f_1, t_1 + t_2) \Rightarrow HoldsAt(f_2, t_1 + t_2)$$

Inertia of HoldsAt

24

The commonsense law of inertia is enforced for the truth values of fluents.

Definition EC7. A fluent *persists* between timepoints t_1 and t_2 if and only if the fluent is not released from the commonsense law of inertia at any timepoint after t_1 and at or before t_2 .

$$PersistsBetween(t_1, f, t_2) \stackrel{\text{def}}{\equiv} \neg \exists t \ (ReleasedAt(f, t) \land t_1 < t \leq t_2)$$

Definition EC8. A fluent is *released* between timepoints t_1 (inclusive) and t_2 if and only if the fluent is released by some event that occurs at or after t_1 and before t_2 .

ReleasedBetween
$$(t_1, f, t_2) \stackrel{\text{def}}{\equiv} \exists e, t \ (Happens(e, t) \land t_1 \le t < t_2 \land Releases(e, f, t))$$

Axiom EC9. If a fluent is true at timepoint t_1 and the fluent persists and is not clipped between t_1 and some later timepoint t_2 , then the fluent is true at t_2 .

$$HoldsAt(f, t_1) \land t_1 < t_2 \land PersistsBetween(t_1, f, t_2) \land \neg Clipped(t_1, f, t_2) \Rightarrow HoldsAt(f, t_2)$$

Axiom EC10. If a fluent is false at timepoint t_1 and the fluent persists and is not declipped between t_1 and some later timepoint t_2 , then the fluent is false at t_2 .

$$\neg HoldsAt(f, t_1) \land t_1 < t_2 \land PersistsBetween(t_1, f, t_2) \land \\ \neg Declipped(t_1, f, t_2) \Rightarrow \neg HoldsAt(f, t_2)$$

Inertia of ReleasedAt

A form of inertia is also enforced for *ReleasedAt*.

Axiom EC11. If a fluent is released from the commonsense law of inertia at timepoint t_1 and the fluent is neither clipped nor declipped between t_1 and some later timepoint t_2 , then the fluent is released from the commonsense law of inertia at t_2 .

$$ReleasedAt(f, t_1) \land t_1 < t_2 \land \neg Clipped(t_1, f, t_2) \land \neg Declipped(t_1, f, t_2) \Rightarrow ReleasedAt(f, t_2)$$

Axiom EC12. If a fluent is not released from the commonsense law of inertia at timepoint t_1 and the fluent is not released between t_1 (inclusive) and some later timepoint t_2 , then the fluent is not released from the commonsense law of inertia at t_2 .

$$\neg ReleasedAt(f, t_1) \land t_1 < t_2 \land \neg ReleasedBetween(t_1, f, t_2) \Rightarrow \neg ReleasedAt(f, t_2)$$

Influence of events on fluents

Event occurrences influence the states of fluents.

Definition EC13. A fluent is *released* between timepoints t_1 (not inclusive) and t_2 if and only if the fluent is released by some event that occurs after t_1 and before t_2 .

$$ReleasedIn(t_1, f, t_2) \stackrel{\text{def}}{\equiv} \exists e, t \ (Happens(e, t) \land t_1 < t < t_2 \land Releases(e, f, t))$$

Axiom EC14. If a fluent is initiated by some event that occurs at timepoint t_1 and the fluent is neither stopped nor released between t_1 (not inclusive) and some later timepoint t_2 , then the fluent is true at t_2 .

$$Happens(e, t_1) \land Initiates(e, f, t_1) \land t_1 < t_2 \land \neg StoppedIn(t_1, f, t_2) \land \neg ReleasedIn(t_1, f, t_2) \Rightarrow HoldsAt(f, t_2)$$

Axiom EC15. If a fluent is terminated by some event that occurs at timepoint t_1 and the fluent is neither started nor released between t_1 (not inclusive) and some later timepoint t_2 , then the fluent is false at t_2 .

$$Happens(e, t_1) \land Terminates(e, f, t_1) \land t_1 < t_2 \land \neg StartedIn(t_1, f, t_2) \land \neg ReleasedIn(t_1, f, t_2) \Rightarrow \neg HoldsAt(f, t_2)$$

Axiom EC16. If a fluent is released by some event that occurs at timepoint t_1 and the fluent is neither stopped nor started between t_1 and some later timepoint t_2 , then the fluent is released from the commonsense law of inertia at t_2 .

$$Happens(e, t_1) \land Releases(e, f, t_1) \land t_1 < t_2 \land \neg StoppedIn(t_1, f, t_2) \land \neg StartedIn(t_1, f, t_2) \Rightarrow ReleasedAt(f, t_2)$$

Axiom EC17. If a fluent is initiated or terminated by some event that occurs at timepoint t_1 and the fluent is not released between t_1 (not inclusive) and some later timepoint t_2 , then the fluent is not released from the commonsense law of inertia at t_2 .

$$Happens(e, t_1) \land (Initiates(e, f, t_1) \lor Terminates(e, f, t_1)) \land$$

 $t_1 < t_2 \land \neg ReleasedIn(t_1, f, t_2) \Rightarrow$
 $\neg ReleasedAt(f, t_2)$

We use EC to mean the conjunction of the axioms EC5, EC6, EC9, EC10, EC11, EC12, EC14, EC15, EC16, and EC17. The definitions EC1, EC2, EC3, EC4, EC7, EC8, and EC13 are incorporated into EC.

Note that we distinguish between definitions and axioms. EC1, for example, is called a definition and not an axiom because *Clipped* is not a predicate symbol of the first-order language. EC1 merely defines $Clipped(t_1, f, t_2)$ as an abbreviation for $\exists e, t \ (Happens(e, t) \land t_1 \leq t < t_2 \land Terminates(e, f, t))$. An axiomatization that supports event occurrences with duration is presented in Appendix C.

2.3.2 DEC

26

DEC restricts the timepoint sort to the integers. It consists of 12 axioms and definitions.

Stopped and started

The definitions of StoppedIn and StartedIn are the same as in EC.

Definition DEC1.

$$StoppedIn(t_1, f, t_2) \stackrel{\text{def}}{\equiv} \exists e, t \ (Happens(e, t) \land t_1 < t < t_2 \land Terminates(e, f, t))$$

Definition DEC2.

$$StartedIn(t_1, f, t_2) \stackrel{\text{def}}{\equiv} \exists e, t \ (Happens(e, t) \land t_1 < t < t_2 \land Initiates(e, f, t))$$

Trajectory and AntiTrajectory

The axioms for trajectories are the same as in EC.

Axiom DEC3.

$$Happens(e, t_1) \land Initiates(e, f_1, t_1) \land 0 < t_2 \land$$

$$Trajectory(f_1, t_1, f_2, t_2) \land \neg StoppedIn(t_1, f_1, t_1 + t_2) \Rightarrow$$

$$HoldsAt(f_2, t_1 + t_2)$$

Axiom DEC4.

$$Happens(e, t_1) \land Terminates(e, f_1, t_1) \land 0 < t_2 \land$$

 $AntiTrajectory(f_1, t_1, f_2, t_2) \land \neg StartedIn(t_1, f_1, t_1 + t_2) \Rightarrow$
 $HoldsAt(f_2, t_1 + t_2)$

Inertia of HoldsAt

The commonsense law of inertia is enforced for *HoldsAt*.

Axiom DEC5. If a fluent is true at timepoint t, the fluent is not released from the commonsense law of inertia at t + 1, and the fluent is not terminated by any event that occurs at t, then the fluent is true at t + 1.

$$HoldsAt(f,t) \land \neg ReleasedAt(f,t+1) \land \neg \exists e (Happens(e,t) \land Terminates(e,f,t)) \Rightarrow HoldsAt(f,t+1)$$

Axiom DEC6. If a fluent is false at timepoint t, the fluent is not released from the commonsense law of inertia at t + 1, and the fluent is not initiated by any event that occurs at t, then the fluent is false at t + 1.

$$\neg HoldsAt(f,t) \land \neg ReleasedAt(f,t+1) \land \\ \neg \exists e (Happens(e,t) \land Initiates(e,f,t)) \Rightarrow \\ \neg HoldsAt(f,t+1)$$

Inertia of ReleasedAt

Inertia is enforced for ReleasedAt.

Axiom DEC7. If a fluent is released from the commonsense law of inertia at timepoint t and the fluent is neither initiated nor terminated by any event that occurs at t, then the fluent is released from the commonsense law of inertia at t + 1.

$$ReleasedAt(f,t) \land \\ \neg \exists e \ (Happens(e,t) \land (Initiates(e,f,t) \lor Terminates(e,f,t))) \Rightarrow \\ ReleasedAt(f,t+1)$$

Axiom DEC8. If a fluent is not released from the commonsense law of inertia at timepoint t and the fluent is not released by any event that occurs at t, then the fluent is not released from the commonsense law of inertia at t + 1.

$$\neg ReleasedAt(f,t) \land \neg \exists e (Happens(e,t) \land Releases(e,f,t)) \Rightarrow \neg ReleasedAt(f,t+1)$$

Influence of events on fluents

Event occurrences influence the states of fluents.

Axiom DEC9. If a fluent is initiated by some event that occurs at timepoint t, then the fluent is true at t + 1.

$$Happens(e, t) \land Initiates(e, f, t) \Rightarrow HoldsAt(f, t + 1)$$

Axiom DEC10. If a fluent is terminated by some event that occurs at timepoint t, then the fluent is false at t + 1.

$$Happens(e, t) \land Terminates(e, f, t) \Rightarrow \neg HoldsAt(f, t + 1)$$

Axiom DEC11. If a fluent is released by some event that occurs at timepoint t, then the fluent is released from the commonsense law of inertia at t + 1.

$$Happens(e, t) \land Releases(e, f, t) \Rightarrow ReleasedAt(f, t + 1)$$

Axiom DEC12. If a fluent is initiated or terminated by some event that occurs at timepoint t, then the fluent is not released from the commonsense law of inertia at t+1.

$$Happens(e,t) \land (Initiates(e,f,t) \lor Terminates(e,f,t)) \Rightarrow \neg ReleasedAt(f,t+1)$$

We use DEC to mean the conjunction of the axioms DEC3 through DEC12. The definitions DEC1 and DEC2 are incorporated into DEC. DEC is logically equivalent to EC if we restrict the timepoint sort to the integers. A proof of the equivalence of DEC and EC for integer time is provided in Appendix B.

2.3.3 CHOOSING BETWEEN EC AND DEC

In this book we freely alternate between EC and DEC. We offer the following guidance for choosing between EC and DEC when we are attempting to solve a given commonsense reasoning problem:

- 28
- DEC can be used in most cases (as can EC).
- If integer time is sufficient to model the problem, then DEC can be used.
- If continuous time is required to model the problem, then EC must be used.
- If continuous change is being modeled, then EC must be used, although DEC can be used to model the discrete version of continuous change known as gradual change. For details, see Chapter 7.
- If the truth values of fluents are to be determined at every timepoint in {0, 1, 2, ..., n} for some n ≥ 0, then it is convenient to use DEC, which proceeds timepoint by timepoint except in the case of gradual change.
- If the truth values of fluents are to be determined only at a few timepoints in $\{0, 1, 2, ..., n\}$, then it is convenient to use EC, which facilitates the application of the commonsense law of inertia to a span of timepoints.

It should be pointed out that DEC restricts the timepoint sort only to the integers. Other sorts are not restricted in this fashion. Notably, the real number sort may be used in DEC (but not in the Discrete Event Calculus Reasoner or answer set programming implementations of DEC).

2.4 REIFICATION

In first-order logic, we express the atemporal proposition that Nathan is in the living room using an atom such as

InRoom(Nathan, LivingRoom)

In the event calculus, we wish to write a temporal proposition, such as

$$Holds(InRoom(Nathan, LivingRoom), 1)$$
 (2.1)

But for (2.1) to be a formula of first-order logic, InRoom(Nathan, LivingRoom) must be a term and not an atom.

We therefore use the technique of *reification*, which in general consists of making a formula of a first-order language \mathcal{L}_1 into a term of another first-order language \mathcal{L}_2 . We make atoms of \mathcal{L}_1 into terms of \mathcal{L}_2 . We treat a predicate symbol in \mathcal{L}_1 such as InRoom as a function symbol in \mathcal{L}_2 whose sort is fluent. Then in \mathcal{L}_2 , InRoom(Nathan, LivingRoom) is a term.

Similarly we would like to represent temporal propositions involving events such as

We treat *PickUp* as a function symbol whose sort is event. Then *PickUp* (*Nathan*, *Glass*) is a term.

Definition 2.1. A *fluent term* is a term whose sort is fluent, an *event term* is a term whose sort is event, and a *timepoint term* is a term whose sort is timepoint.

2.4.1 UNIQUE NAMES AXIOMS

Consider the following event terms:

PickUp(Nathan, Glass) SetDown(Ryan, Bowl)

Nothing says that these do not denote the same event. But we would like them to denote distinct events, because *PickUp* and *SetDown* represent different types of actions. Further, consider the following event terms:

PickUp(Nathan, Glass1) PickUp(Nathan, Glass2)

Again, nothing says that these do not denote the same event. In fact, they *might* denote the same event if *Glass1* and *Glass2* denote the same physical object.

We formalize our intuitions about when fluent and event terms denote distinct objects using *unique names axioms*. These are defined using the following U notation. **Definition 2.2.** If ϕ_1, \ldots, ϕ_k are function symbols, then $U[\phi_1, \ldots, \phi_k]$ is an abbreviation for the conjunction of the formulas

$$\phi_i(x_1,\ldots,x_m)\neq\phi_j(y_1,\ldots,y_n)$$

where m is the arity of ϕ_i , n is the arity of ϕ_j , and x_1, \ldots, x_m and y_1, \ldots, y_n are distinct variables such that the sort of x_l is the sort of the lth argument position of ϕ_i and the sort of y_l is the sort of the lth argument position of ϕ_j , for each $1 \le i < j \le k$, and the conjunction of the formulas

$$\phi_i(x_1,\ldots,x_m) = \phi_i(y_1,\ldots,y_m) \Rightarrow x_1 = y_1 \wedge \cdots \wedge x_m = y_m$$

where m is the arity of ϕ_i , and x_1, \ldots, x_m and y_1, \ldots, y_m are distinct variables such that the sort of x_l and y_l is the sort of the lth argument position of ϕ_i , for each $1 \le i \le k$.

Definition 2.3. If ϕ_1, \ldots, ϕ_n are function symbols, then $U[\phi_1, \ldots, \phi_n]$ is a *unique names axiom*.

2.5 CONDITIONS

We use conditions within many types of event calculus formulas such as action precondition axioms, effect axioms, state constraints, and trigger axioms.

Definition 2.4. If τ_1 and τ_2 are terms, then $\tau_1 < \tau_2$, $\tau_1 \le \tau_2$, $\tau_1 = \tau_2$, $\tau_1 \ge \tau_2$, $\tau_1 > \tau_2$, and $\tau_1 \ne \tau_2$ are *comparisons*.

Definition 2.5. A *condition* is defined inductively as follows:

- A comparison is a condition.
- If β is a fluent term and τ is a timepoint term, then $HoldsAt(\beta, \tau)$ is a condition.
- If γ is a condition, then $\neg \gamma$ is a condition.
- If γ_1 and γ_2 are conditions, then $\gamma_1 \wedge \gamma_2$ and $\gamma_1 \vee \gamma_2$ are conditions.
- If ν is a variable and γ is a condition, then $\exists \nu \gamma$ is a condition.

- If ρ is an *n*-ary predicate symbol and τ_1, \ldots, τ_n are terms, then $\rho(\tau_1, \ldots, \tau_n)$ is a condition.
- Nothing else is a condition.

(Inductive definitions are explained in Section A.2.) Atoms of the form $\rho(\tau_1, \ldots, \tau_n)$ can be used in a condition when it is necessary to incorporate general truths. Examples in this book include $Arc(s, a_1, a_2)$, which represents that the appearance of shape s can change from a_1 to a_2 by shifting the viewing angle (Section 14.3), and ElementOf(x, l), which represents that x is an element of list l (Section A.6.2).

2.6 CIRCUMSCRIPTION

In the event calculus, we use logical formulas such as the following to describe the effects of events and the events that occur:

$$Initiates(SwitchOn, LightOn, t)$$
 (2.2)

$$Terminates(SwitchOff, LightOn, t)$$
 (2.3)

$$Happens(SwitchOn, 3)$$
 (2.4)

But these formulas say nothing about which effects events do not have and about which events do not occur. For example, the following could also be the case:

$$Initiates(SwitchOn, WaterBoiling, t)$$
 (2.5)

$$Happens(SwitchOff, 6)$$
 (2.6)

As mentioned in Chapter 1, we must be able to assume by default that there are no such unexpected effects and that no such unexpected events occur. To do this, the event calculus uses a technique introduced by John McCarthy called circumscription. Specifically, the event calculus uses circumscription to minimize the extension of predicates such as *Happens*, *Initiates*, and *Terminates*.

The circumscription of *Initiates* in (2.2), written *CIRC*[(2.2); *Initiates*], is

$$(e = SwitchOn \land f = LightOn) \Leftrightarrow Initiates(e, f, t)$$
 (2.7)

CIRC[(2.3); Terminates] is

$$(e = SwitchOff \land f = LightOn) \Leftrightarrow Terminates(e, f, t)$$
 (2.8)

CIRC[(2.4); Happens] is

$$(e = SwitchOn \land t = 3) \Leftrightarrow Happens(e, t)$$
 (2.9)

Circumscription is defined using second-order logic as described in Section A.7.

Nonmonotonic reasoning

First-order logic entailment is *monotonic*: If $\psi \models \pi$, then $\psi \land \psi' \models \pi$ for every ψ' ; also, if $\psi \vdash \pi$, then $\psi \land \psi' \vdash \pi$ for every ψ' . Circumscription allows us to perform *nonmonotonic reasoning*: If the circumscription of ψ entails π , then it is not necessarily the case that the circumscription of $\psi \land \psi'$ entails π .

Suppose that the only known event occurrence is given by (2.4). Then from (2.7)–(2.9), and other appropriate axioms, we can conclude that the light is on at timepoint 7:

Now suppose that, in addition to (2.4), the event (2.6) is known to occur. The circumscription $CIRC[(2.4) \land (2.6); Happens]$ is

$$(e = SwitchOn \land t = 3) \lor (e = SwitchOff \land t = 6) \Leftrightarrow Happens(e, t)$$

From this, (2.7), and (2.8), we can no longer conclude that the light is on at timepoint 7. In fact, we can conclude that the light is *not* on at that timepoint.

2.6.1 COMPUTING CIRCUMSCRIPTION

The algorithms for computing circumscription in general are complex. In many cases, however, we can compute circumscription by applying the following two theorems. The first theorem provides a method for computing circumscription using *predicate completion*.

Theorem 2.1. Let ρ be an n-ary predicate symbol and $\Delta(x_1, \ldots, x_n)$ be a formula whose only free variables are x_1, \ldots, x_n . If $\Delta(x_1, \ldots, x_n)$ does not contain ρ , then the basic circumscription $CIRC[\forall x_1, \ldots, x_n (\Delta(x_1, \ldots, x_n) \Rightarrow \rho(x_1, \ldots, x_n)); \rho]$ is equivalent to $\forall x_1, \ldots, x_n (\Delta(x_1, \ldots, x_n) \Leftrightarrow \rho(x_1, \ldots, x_n))$.

Proof. See the proof of Proposition 2 of Lifschitz (1994).

Thus, we may compute circumscription of ρ in a formula by (1) rewriting the formula in the form

$$\forall x_1, \dots, x_n (\Delta(x_1, \dots, x_n) \Rightarrow \rho(x_1, \dots, x_n))$$

where $\Delta(x_1, \ldots, x_n)$ does not contain ρ , and (2) applying Theorem 2.1.

The second theorem provides a method for computing parallel circumscription or the circumscription of several predicates. First a definition is required.

Definition 2.6. A formula Δ is *positive* relative to a predicate symbol ρ if and only if all occurrences of ρ in Δ are in the range of an even number of negations in an equivalent formula obtained by eliminating \Rightarrow and \Leftrightarrow from Δ . We eliminate \Rightarrow from a formula by replacing all instances of $(\alpha \Rightarrow \beta)$ with $(\neg \alpha \lor \beta)$. We eliminate \Leftrightarrow from a formula by replacing all instances of $(\alpha \Leftrightarrow \beta)$ with $((\neg \alpha \lor \beta) \land (\neg \beta \lor \alpha))$. (See Exercise 2.3)

Theorem 2.2. Let ρ_1, \ldots, ρ_n be predicate symbols and Δ be a formula. If Δ is positive relative to every ρ_i , then the parallel circumscription $CIRC[\Delta; \rho_1, \ldots, \rho_n]$ is equivalent to the conjunction of the basic circumscriptions $\bigwedge_{i=1}^n CIRC[\Delta; \rho_i]$. *Proof.* See the proof of Proposition 14 of Lifschitz (1994).

2.6.2 EXAMPLE: CIRCUMSCRIPTION OF HAPPENS

Let $\Delta = Happens(E1, T1) \wedge Happens(E2, T2)$. We compute $CIRC[\Delta; Happens]$ by rewriting Δ as the logically equivalent formula

$$(e = E1 \land t = T1) \lor (e = E2 \land t = T2) \Rightarrow Happens(e, t)$$

and then applying Theorem 2.1, which gives

$$(e = E1 \land t = T1) \lor (e = E2 \land t = T2) \Leftrightarrow Happens(e, t)$$

2.6.3 EXAMPLE: CIRCUMSCRIPTION OF INITIATES

Let $\Sigma = Initiates(E1(x), F1(x), t) \wedge Initiates(E2(x, y), F2(x, y), t)$. We compute $CIRC[\Sigma; Initiates]$ by rewriting Σ as

$$\exists x (e = E1(x) \land f = F1(x)) \lor \exists x, y (e = E2(x, y) \land f = F2(x, y)) \Rightarrow Initiates(e, f, t)$$

and then applying Theorem 2.1, which gives

$$\exists x (e = EI(x) \land f = FI(x)) \lor \exists x, y (e = E2(x, y) \land f = F2(x, y)) \Leftrightarrow Initiates(e, f, t)$$

Numerous examples of computing circumscription are given in the remainder of this book.

2.7 DOMAIN DESCRIPTIONS

We solve commonsense reasoning problems by creating an event calculus domain description. A *domain description* consists of the following:

- a collection of axioms describing the commonsense domain or domains of interest, called an axiomatization
- · observations of world properties at various times
- a narrative of known world events

In general, we should aim for elaboration-tolerant axiomatizations that can easily be extended to handle new scenarios or phenomena. John McCarthy defines a formalism as *elaboration tolerant* to the degree that it is easy to extend knowledge represented using the formalism. Elaboration-tolerant formalisms allow an axiomatization to be extended through the addition of new axioms rather than by performing surgery on existing axioms. Circumscription helps provide elaboration tolerance in the event calculus because it enables the incorporation of new event effects and occurrences by adding axioms. The types of axioms we may use to describe commonsense domains are summarized in Table 2.1 and described in detail in the rest of this book.

Observations consist of *HoldsAt* and *ReleasedAt* formulas.

Definition 2.7. If β is a fluent term and τ is a timepoint term, then $HoldsAt(\beta, \tau)$ and $ReleasedAt(\beta, \tau)$ are **observations**.

A narrative consists of event occurrence formulas and temporal ordering formulas that constrain their order.

Definition 2.8. If α is an event term and τ is a timepoint term, then $Happens(\alpha, \tau)$ is an *event occurrence formula*.

Table 2.1 Event Calculus Formulas Used for Commonsense Reasoning^a

Formula	Form	Defined in
Unique names axiom $[\Omega]$	$U[\phi_1,\ldots,\phi_n]$	Section 2.4.1
Observation $[\Gamma]$	(\neg) HoldsAt (β, τ) or	Section 2.7
	(\neg) ReleasedAt (β, τ)	Land the sta
Event occurrence	$Happens(\alpha, \tau)$	Section 2.7
formula $[\Delta_1]$	10 C	
Temporal ordering	$\tau_1 < \tau_2, \tau_1 \leq \tau_2, \tau_1 = \tau_2, \dots$	Section 2.7
formula $[\Delta_1]$		
Positive effect axiom $[\Sigma]$	$\gamma \Rightarrow Initiates(\alpha, \beta, \tau)$	Section 3.1
Negative effect axiom $[\Sigma]$	$\gamma \Rightarrow Terminates(\alpha, \beta, \tau)$	Section 3.1
Fluent precondition axiom $[\Sigma]$	$\gamma \Rightarrow \delta(\alpha, \beta, \tau)$	Section 3.3.1
Action precondition axiom $[\Psi]$	$Happens(\alpha, \tau) \Rightarrow \gamma$	Section 3.3.2
State constraint $[\Psi]$	$\gamma_1, \gamma_1 \Rightarrow \gamma_2, \text{ or } \gamma_1 \Leftrightarrow \gamma_2$	Section 3.4
Trigger axiom $[\Delta_2]$	$\gamma \Rightarrow Happens(\alpha, \tau)$	Section 4.1
Release axiom $[\Sigma]$	$\gamma \Rightarrow Releases(\alpha, \beta, \tau)$	Section 5.3
Effect constraint [Σ]	$\gamma \wedge \delta_1(\alpha, \beta_1, \tau) \Rightarrow \delta_2(\alpha, \beta_2, \tau)$	Section 6.4
Causal constraint $[\Delta_2]$	$\theta(\beta,\tau) \wedge$	Section 6.5
	$\pi_1(\beta_1,\tau) \wedge \cdots \wedge \pi_n(\beta_n,\tau) \Rightarrow$	
	$Happens(\alpha, \tau)$	
Trajectory axiom [Π]	$\gamma \Rightarrow Trajectory(\beta_1, \tau_1, \beta_2, \tau_2)$	Section 7.1
Antitrajectory axiom [Π]	$\gamma \Rightarrow$	Section 7.2
	AntiTrajectory $(\beta_1, \tau_1, \beta_2, \tau_2)$	Harry F.
Event occurrence	$Happens(\alpha_1, \tau) \wedge \gamma \Rightarrow$	Section 8.1.2
constraint $[\Psi]$	(\neg) Happens (α_2, τ)	
Positive cumulative	$\gamma \wedge (\neg)$ Happens $(\alpha_1, \tau) \wedge \cdots \wedge$	Section 8.2
effect axiom $[\Sigma]$	(\neg) Happens $(\alpha_{\Omega}, \tau) \Rightarrow$	
	Initiates (α, β, τ)	giant al.
Negative cumulative	$\gamma \wedge (\neg)$ Happens $(\alpha_1, \tau) \wedge \cdots \wedge$	Section 8.2
effect axiom $[\Sigma]$	(\neg) Happens $(\alpha_n, \tau) \Rightarrow$	
	Terminates (α, β, τ)	
Disjunctive event	$Happens(\alpha, \tau) \Rightarrow$	Section 9.2
axiom $[\Delta_2]$	$Happens(\alpha_1, \tau) \lor \cdots \lor$	
	$Happens(\alpha_n, \tau)$	
Cancellation axiom $[\Theta]$	$\gamma \Rightarrow Ab_i(\ldots, \tau)$	Section 12.3

 $^{{}^{8}\}alpha, \, \alpha_{1}, \, \ldots, \, \alpha_{n} = \text{event terms}; \, \beta, \, \beta_{1}, \, \ldots, \, \beta_{n} = \text{fluent terms}; \, \gamma, \, \gamma_{1}, \, \gamma_{2} = \text{conditions}; \, \delta, \, \delta_{1}, \, \delta_{2} = \text{Initiates or Terminates}; \, \pi_{1}, \, \ldots, \, \pi_{n} = \text{Initiated or Terminated}; \, \theta = \text{Stopped or Started}; \, \tau, \, \tau_{1}, \, \tau_{2} = \text{timepoint terms}; \, \phi_{1}, \, \ldots, \, \phi_{n} = \text{function symbols}.$

34

Definition 2.9. If τ_1 and τ_2 are timepoint terms, then $\tau_1 < \tau_2$, $\tau_1 \le \tau_2$, $\tau_1 = \tau_2$, $\tau_1 \ge \tau_2$, $\tau_1 > \tau_2$, and $\tau_1 \ne \tau_2$ are *timepoint comparisons*.

Definition 2.10. A *temporal ordering formula* is a conjunction of timepoint comparisons.

We now define a domain description.

Definition 2.11. An event calculus domain description is given by

 $CIRC[\Sigma; Initiates, Terminates, Releases] \land CIRC[\Delta_1 \land \Delta_2; Happens] \land CIRC[\Theta; Ab_1, \dots, Ab_n] \land \Omega \land \Psi \land \Pi \land \Gamma \land E \land CC$

where

- Σ is a conjunction of positive effect axioms, negative effect axioms, release axioms, effect constraints, positive cumulative effect axioms, and negative cumulative effect axioms.
- Δ₁ is a conjunction of event occurrence formulas and temporal ordering formulas (the narrative).
- Δ₂ is a conjunction of trigger axioms, causal constraints, and disjunctive event axioms.
- Θ is a conjunction of cancellation axioms containing Ab_1, \ldots, Ab_n .
- Ω is a conjunction of unique names axioms.
- Ψ is a conjunction of state constraints, action precondition axioms, and event occurrence constraints.
- Π is a conjunction of trajectory axioms and antitrajectory axioms.
- Γ is a conjunction of observations.
- E is a conjunction of axioms such as EC or DEC.
- CC is the conjunction of axioms to support causal constraints defined in Section 6.5.

The axiomatization consists of Σ , Δ_2 , Θ , Ω , Ψ , Π , E, and CC, the observations consist of Γ , and the narrative consists of Δ_1 . We write Δ to mean the conjunction of Δ_1 and Δ_2 .

Event calculus reasoning is nonmonotonic, because event calculus domain descriptions make use of circumscription.

2.7.1 EXAMPLE: SLEEP

Let us revisit the example in Section 1.4.2. We use an agent sort with the variable a. The event WakeUp(a) represents that agent a wakes up, the event FallAsleep(a) represents that agent a falls asleep, and the fluent Awake(a) represents that agent a is awake.

Our axiomatization consists of several axioms. We use a positive effect axiom to represent that, if an agent wakes up, then the agent will be awake:

$$Initiates(WakeUp(a), Awake(a), t)$$
 (2.10)

We use a negative effect axiom to represent that, if an agent falls asleep, then the agent will no longer be awake:

$$Terminates(FallAsleep(a), Awake(a), t)$$
 (2.11)

We have the following observations and narrative. At timepoint 0, Nathan is not awake and this fact is subject to the commonsense law of inertia:

$$\neg HoldsAt(Awake(Nathan), 0)$$
 (2.12)

$$\neg ReleasedAt(Awake(Nathan), 0)$$
 (2.13)

We have a narrative consisting of a single event occurrence. At timepoint 1, Nathan wakes up:

$$Happens(WakeUp(Nathan), 1)$$
 (2.14)

Given these axioms and the conjunction of axioms EC, we can show that Nathan will be awake at, say, timepoint 3. The Halmos symbol ■ is used to indicate the end of a proof.

Proposition 2.1. Let $\Sigma = (2.10) \wedge (2.11)$, $\Delta = (2.14)$, $\Omega = U[WakeUp, FallAsleep]$, and $\Gamma = (2.12) \wedge (2.13)$. Then we have

$$CIRC[\Sigma; Initiates, Terminates, Releases] \land CIRC[\Delta; Happens] \land \Omega \land \Gamma \land EC \vdash HoldsAt(Awake(Nathan), 3)$$

Proof. From $CIRC[\Sigma; Initiates, Terminates, Releases]$ and Theorems 2.1 and 2.2, we have

$$(Initiates(e,f,t) \Leftrightarrow \exists a \ (e = WakeUp(a) \land f = Awake(a))) \land$$

$$(Terminates(e,f,t) \Leftrightarrow \exists a \ (e = FallAsleep(a) \land f = Awake(a))) \land$$

$$\neg Releases(e,f,t)$$

$$(2.15)$$

From $CIRC[\Delta; Happens]$ and Theorem 2.1, we have

$$Happens(e, t) \Leftrightarrow (e = WakeUp(Nathan) \land t = 1)$$
 (2.16)

From (2.16) and EC3, we have $\neg StoppedIn(1, Awake(Nathan), 3)$. From (2.16) and EC13, we have $\neg ReleasedIn(1, Awake(Nathan), 3)$. From (2.16), (2.15), 1 < 3, $\neg StoppedIn(1, Awake(Nathan), 3)$, $\neg ReleasedIn(1, Awake(Nathan), 3)$, and EC14, we have HoldsAt(Awake(Nathan), 3).

We can also show that Nathan will be awake at timepoint 3 using the conjunction of axioms DEC.

Proposition 2.2. Let $\Sigma = (2.10) \wedge (2.11)$, $\Delta = (2.14)$, $\Omega = U[WakeUp, FallAsleep]$, and $\Gamma = (2.12) \wedge (2.13)$. Then we have

$$CIRC[\Sigma; Initiates, Terminates, Releases] \land CIRC[\Delta; Happens] \land \Omega \land \Gamma \land DEC \vdash HoldsAt(Awake(Nathan), 3).$$

Proof. From $CIRC[\Sigma; Initiates, Terminates, Releases]$ and Theorems 2.1 and 2.2, we have

$$(Initiates(e,f,t) \Leftrightarrow \exists a \ (e = WakeUp(a) \land f = Awake(a))) \land$$

$$(Terminates(e,f,t) \Leftrightarrow \exists a \ (e = FallAsleep(a) \land f = Awake(a))) \land$$

$$\neg Releases(e,f,t)$$

$$(2.17)$$

From $CIRC[\Delta; Happens]$ and Theorem 2.1, we have

$$(e = WakeUp(Nathan) \land t = 1) \Leftrightarrow Happens(e, t)$$
 (2.18)

Using DEC, we proceed one timepoint at a time. From (2.17), we have $\neg \exists e (Happens(e, 0) \land Releases(e, Awake(Nathan), 0))$. From this, (2.13), and DEC8, we have

$$\neg ReleasedAt(Awake(Nathan), 1)$$
 (2.19)

From (2.17), (2.18), and DEC9, we have

$$HoldsAt(Awake(Nathan), 2)$$
 (2.20)

From (2.17), we have $\neg \exists e (Happens(e, 1) \land Releases(e, Awake(Nathan), 1))$. From this, (2.19), and DEC8, we have

$$\neg ReleasedAt(Awake(Nathan), 2)$$
 (2.21)

From (2.18), we have $\neg \exists e (Happens(e, 2) \land Terminates(e, Awake(Nathan), 2))$. From this, (2.20), (2.21), and DEC5, we have HoldsAt(Awake(Nathan), 3).

2.7.2 INCONSISTENCY

Inconsistency can arise in a domain description in a number of ways. Here are some common ways in which inconsistency can arise using the EC and DEC axioms.

Simultaneously initiating and terminating a fluent produces inconsistency. For example, given

Initiates (E(o), F(o), t)Terminates (E(o), F(o), t)Happens (E(O1), 0)

we can show both HoldsAt(F(O1), 1) and $\neg HoldsAt(F(O1), 1)$.

Simultaneously releasing and initiating or terminating a fluent produces inconsistency. For example, from

Releases (E(o), F(o), t)Initiates (E(o), F(o), t)Happens (E(OI), 0)

we can show both ReleasedAt(F(O1), 1) and $\neg ReleasedAt(F(O1), 1)$.

Inconsistency can arise from the use of effect axioms and state constraints. For example, given

Initiates(E(o), F1(o), t)	(2.22)
$HoldsAt(F1(o), t) \Leftrightarrow$	HoldsAt(F2(o),t)	(2.23)
$\neg HoldsAt(F)$	(2(O1), 0)	(2.24)
$\neg ReleasedAt(F2(O1), 1)$		(2.25)
Happens (E	E(OI), 0)	(2.26)

we can show both $\neg HoldsAt(F2(O1), 1)$, from (2.24), (2.25), and other appropriate axioms, and HoldsAt(F2(O1), 1), from (2.26), (2.22), (2.23), and other appropriate axioms.

2.8 REASONING TYPES

Several types of reasoning may be performed using the event calculus, such as deduction, abduction, postdiction, and model finding. The Discrete Event Calculus Reasoner program discussed in Chapter 13, and answer set programming discussed in Chapter 15, can perform all these reasoning types. For the purposes of the definitions in this section, let Σ , Δ_1 , Δ_2 , Θ , Ω , Ψ , Π , Γ , E, and CC be formulas as defined in Section 2.7, Δ be a conjunction of Δ_1 and Δ_2 , and Γ' be a conjunction of observations.

2.8.1 DEDUCTION AND TEMPORAL PROJECTION

Deduction or temporal projection consists of determining the state that results from performing a sequence of actions. For example, given that a fan is set on a table and turned on, deduction or temporal projection determines that the fan is on the table and turning.

Definition 2.12. A *deduction* or *temporal projection problem* consists of determining whether it is the case that

$$CIRC[\Sigma; Initiates, Terminates, Releases] \land CIRC[\Delta; Happens] \land CIRC[\Theta; Ab_1, ..., Ab_n] \land \Omega \land \Psi \land \Pi \land \Gamma \land E \land CC \vdash \Gamma'$$

Propositions 2.1 and 2.2 are deduction problems. From the fact that Nathan woke up, we can deduce that afterward he was awake.

2.8.2 ABDUCTION AND PLANNING

Abduction consists of determining what events might lead from an initial state to a final state. Similarly, planning consist of generating a sequence of actions to bring about a final state, called a goal, starting from an initial state. Suppose that the initial state is that Nathan is in his bedroom on the second floor and that the goal or final state is that Nathan is outside his house. Abduction or planning will produce a sequence of actions in which Nathan walks out of his bedroom, walks downstairs, opens the front door, and walks outside.

Definition 2.13. Let $\Phi =$

```
CIRC[\Sigma; Initiates, Terminates, Releases] \land CIRC[\Delta_1 \land \Delta_2; Happens] \land CIRC[\Theta; Ab_1, \dots, Ab_n] \land \Omega \land \Psi \land \Pi \land \Gamma \land E \land CC
```

An *abduction* or *planning problem* consists of taking Σ , Δ_2 , Θ , Ω , Ψ , Π , Γ , Γ' (the goal), E, and CC as input and producing as output zero or more Δ_1 (called *plans* for Γ') such that Φ is consistent and $\Phi \vdash \Gamma'$.

2.8.3 EXAMPLE: SLEEP ABDUCTION

Given that Nathan was not awake and then he was awake, we can abduce that he woke up. Abduction can be performed using answer set programming. We create a file called sleep.pl containing the following:

```
initiated(F,T) :- happens(E,T), initiates(E,F,T).
terminated(F,T) :- happens(E,T), terminates(E,F,T).
holdsAt(F,T+1):- holdsAt(F,T), not terminated(F,T), time(T).
:- holdsAt(F,T+1), not holdsAt(F,T), not initiated(F,T), time(T).
holdsAt(F,T+1) :- happens(E,T), initiates(E,F,T).
:- holdsAt(F,T+1), happens(E,T), terminates(E,F,T).
\{holdsAt(F,T)\}: -fluent(F), time(T).
\{happens(E,T)\} := event(E), time(T).
time(0).
fluent(awake(nathan)).
event(wakeUp(nathan)).
event(fallAsleep(nathan)).
initiates(wakeUp(nathan),awake(nathan),T) :- time(T).
terminates(fallAsleep(nathan),awake(nathan),T) :- time(T).
:- holdsAt(awake(nathan).0).
holdsAt(awake(nathan).1).
We then run clingo -n 0 sleep.lp, which produces the following output:
clingo version 4.2.1
Reading from sleep.lp
Solving ...
Answer: 1
time(0) fluent(awake(nathan)) event(wakeUp(nathan))
event(fallAsleep(nathan)) holdsAt(awake(nathan),1)
initiates(wakeUp(nathan).awake(nathan).0)
initiated(awake(nathan),0) happens(wakeUp(nathan),0)
terminates(fallAsleep(nathan),awake(nathan),0)
SATISFIABLE
Models
         : 1
Calls
Time
         : 0.002s (Solving: 0.00s 1st Model: 0.00s Unsat: 0.00s)
CPU Time : 0.000s
```

The clingo option -n 0 is used to request all stable models. The result is one stable model in which happens (wakeUp(nathan), 0) is abduced.

2.8.4 POSTDICTION

Postdiction consists of determining the initial state given a sequence of events and a final state. For example, given that Nathan threw a ball and the ball was flying toward the wall, postdiction determines that Nathan was previously holding the ball.

```
Definition 2.14. Let \Phi =
```

```
CIRC[\Sigma; Initiates, Terminates, Releases] \land CIRC[\Delta; Happens] \land CIRC[\Theta; Ab_1, ..., Ab_n] \land \Omega \land \Psi \land \Pi \land \Gamma \land E \land CC
```

A postdiction problem consists of taking Σ , Δ , Θ , Ω , Ψ , Π , E, CC, and Γ' as input, and producing as output zero or more Γ such that Φ is consistent and $\Phi \vdash \Gamma'$.

For example, postdiction allows us to determine that Nathan was asleep before he woke up. We add the following action precondition axiom:

$$Happens(WakeUp(a), t) \Rightarrow \neg HoldsAt(Awake(a), t)$$
 (2.27)

We do not know whether Nathan was asleep at timepoint 1. We know that Nathan woke up at timepoint 1:

Happens(WakeUp(Nathan), 1)

From this and (2.27), we conclude that Nathan was asleep at timepoint 1:

 $\neg HoldsAt(Awake(Nathan), 1)$

2.8.5 MODEL FINDING

Model finding consists of generating models from states and events. For example, given that Nathan went to sleep and sleeping occurs at home or at a hotel, model finding produces models in which Nathan sleeps at home and models in which Nathan sleeps at a hotel.

Definition 2.15. A *model finding problem* consists of taking Σ , Δ , Θ , Ω , Ψ , Π , Γ , E, and CC as input, and producing as output zero or more structures \mathcal{M} such that

 $\mathcal{M} \models \mathit{CIRC}[\Sigma; \mathit{Initiates}, \mathit{Terminates}, \mathit{Releases}] \land \mathit{CIRC}[\Delta; \mathit{Happens}] \land \mathit{CIRC}[\Theta; \mathit{Ab}_1, \ldots, \mathit{Ab}_n] \land \Omega \land \Psi \land \Pi \land \Gamma \land E \land CC$

BIBLIOGRAPHIC NOTES

Event calculus basics and axioms

McCarthy (1963) defined a *fluent* as "a predicate or function whose argument is a situation." He borrowed the term from Newton (1670/1969, pp. 72 and 73), who used it to mean a time-varying quantity. See Guicciardini's (1999) description of Newton's fluents and fluxions. The running exclusive or (XOR) notation is from Hayes (1985, p. 72) and E. Davis (1990, p. 32). Running XOR is a special case of the AND-OR connective of Shapiro (1979, pp. 190 and 191). Bibliographic notes for first-order logic are provided in Appendix A.

The conjunction of axioms EC and associated definitions are taken from a paper by R. Miller and Shanahan (1999), which was later revised and expanded (R. Miller & Shanahan, 2002). The conjunction of axioms EC consists of axioms and definitions from the following sections of both versions of the paper:

- Section 2, which provides the basic classical logic axiomatization of the event calculus
- Section 3.2, which revises the axioms and definitions of Section 2 for a version
 of the event calculus in which initiating and terminating a fluent at the same
 time produces inconsistency

- · Section 3.5, which adds axioms to those of Section 2 to support gradual change
- Section 3.7, which revises the axioms and definitions of Section 2 for a version
 of the event calculus in which fluents may be released from the commonsense
 law of inertia

The conjunction of axioms DEC was introduced by Mueller (2004a). R. Miller and Shanahan (2002, p. 452) provide a list of the many formulations of the event calculus in forms of logic programming, in classical logic, in modal logic, and as action languages.

Figures 2.1 and 2.2 show the evolution of the classical logic event calculus. The forced separation version of the event calculus is the first version that largely

- Original logic programming version of the event calculus (Kowalski & Sergot, 1986)
- **2.** Simplified version of the event calculus (Kowalski, 1986, 1992); introduces *Happens*
- 3. Simplified version of the event calculus (Eshghi, 1988)
- 4. Simplified event calculus (Shanahan, 1989)
- **5.** Simplified event calculus (Shanahan, 1990, sec. 1)
 - (a) Continuous change (sec. 5)
- 6. Simplified event calculus (Shanahan, 1997b, sec. 13.1)
 - (a) Continuous change (sec. 13.3)
- **7.** Circumscriptive event calculus (Shanahan, 1995a, sec. 3; Shanahan, 1997b, sec. 14.3); first classical logic version of the event calculus
 - (a) State constraints and ramifications (Shanahan, 1995a, sec. 7; Shanahan, 1997b, sec. 15.1)
 - (b) Nondeterministic effects (Shanahan, 1995a, sec. 8; Shanahan, 1997b, sec. 15.2)
 - (c) Release from commonsense law of inertia (Shanahan, 1997b, sec. 15.3)
 - (d) Concurrent events (Shanahan, 1995a, sec. 9; Shanahan, 1997b, sec. 15.4)
 - (e) Continuous change (Shanahan, 1995a, sec 10; Shanahan, 1997b, sec. 15.5)
- **8.** Event calculus using forced separation (Shanahan, 1996, sec. 2); includes *Releases* but no *Initially*_N
 - (a) Continuous change (sec. 3)
- **9.** Event calculus using forced separation (R. Miller & Shanahan, 1996, sec. 3); includes *Releases*, *InitialisedTrue*, and *InitialisedFalse*
 - (a) Continuous change described using differential equations (sec. 3); treats continuously varying parameters and discontinuities
- 10. Event calculus using forced separation (Shanahan, 1997b, sec. 16.3)
 - (a) State constraints and ramifications (pp. 323-325)
 - (b) Continuous change (sec. 16.4)

FIGURE 2.1

- 1. Event calculus (Shanahan, 1998, 2004); slightly different set of axioms; equivalent to event calculus using forced separation with continuous change
- **2.** Event calculus (Shanahan, 1999b); makes extensions to the forced separation event calculus to deal with the ramification problem
 - (a) State constraints (sec. 2)
 - **(b)** Effect constraints (sec. 3)
 - (c) Causal constraints (sec. 4); adds *Initiated*, *Terminated*, *Started*, and *Stopped*
- **3.** Full event calculus (Shanahan, 1999a, sec. 3.1); forced separation version with three-argument *Happens* (R. Miller & Shanahan, 1994) to represent event occurrences with duration
 - (a) Causal constraints (Shanahan, 1999a, sec. 4.2)
 - **(b)** Concurrent events and continuous change (sec. 5); adds *Cancels*, *Cancelled*, and *Trajectory* predicates
- **4.** Classical logic event calculus (R. Miller & Shanahan, 1999); forced separation version with more variations
 - (a) Narrative information and planning (sec. 2.3)
 - **(b)** Nonnegative time (sec. 3.1)
 - (c) Initiating and terminating a fluent at the same time produces inconsistency (sec. 3.2)
 - (d) Action preconditions (sec. 3.3)
 - (e) Frame and nonframe fluents (sec. 3.4)
 - (f) Continuous change (sec. 3.5)
 - (g) Event occurrences with duration (sec. 3.6)
 - (h) Release from commonsense law of inertia (sec. 3.7)
 - (i) Mathematical modeling (sec. 3.8)
- 5. Discrete event calculus (Mueller, 2004a)
- **6.** Discrete event calculus with branching time (Mueller, 2007a)
- 7. Epistemic functional event calculus (R. Miller, Morgenstern, & Patkos, 2013)

FIGURE 2.2

Evolution of the classical logic event calculus (1998-2013).

resembles the version used in this book. It is called forced separation because the axioms of the event calculus are outside the scope of any circumscription, a technique that can be traced back to the filtered preferential entailment or filtering of Sandewall (1989b, 1994). Table 2.2 shows the evolution of the axiom that determines when a fluent is true.

Reification

McCarthy (1987) defines reification as "making objects out of sentences and other entities" (p. 1034). McCarthy (1979) introduces reification in order to reason about knowledge and belief in first-order logic. He introduces terms to represent concepts such as "'Mike's telephone number' in the sentence 'Pat knows Mike's

42

Table 2.2 Evolution of the HoldsAt axiom

Version	HoldsAt Axiom
Original event calculus	Holds(after(e u)) if Initiates(e u)
(Kowalski & Sergot, 1986)	The state of the s
Event calculus	HoldsAt(r n) if Happens(e) and
(Kowalski, 1986, 1992)	Initiates(e r) and e < n and
	not ∃e* [Happens(e*) and
	Terminates($e^* r$) and $e < e^*$ and $e^* < n$]
Event calculus	$holds(f, e2) \leftarrow initiates(e1, f),$
(Eshghi, 1988)	e1 < e2, $persists(f, e1, e3), e2 \le e3$
Simplified event calculus	holds-at(P, T) if
(Shanahan, 1989)	happens(E) and $E < T$ and
	initiates(E, P) and not clipped(E, P, T)
Simplified event calculus	holds-at(P, T2) if
(Shanahan, 1990, sec. 1)	happens(E) and
	time(E, T1) and $T1 < T2$ and
	initiates(E, P) and not clipped(T1, P, T2)
Simplified event calculus	$HoldsAt(f,t2) \leftarrow$
(Shanahan, 1997b, sec. 13.1)	Happens(a,t1) ∧
	Initiates $(a, f, t1) \wedge t1 < t2 \wedge$
	not Clipped(t1, f, t2)
Circumscriptive event calculus	$HoldsAt(p,t) \leftrightarrow$
(Shanahan, 1995a, sec. 3)	$\forall s [State(t,s) \land Holdsln(p,s)]$
Event calculus	$HoldsAt(f,t2) \leftarrow$
(Shanahan, 1996, sec. 2)	Happens(a,t1) ∧
	Initiates $(a, f, t1) \wedge t1 < t2 \wedge$
	$\neg Clipped(t1, f, t2)$
Full event calculus	$HoldsAt(f,t3) \leftarrow$
(Shanahan, 1999a, sec. 3.1)	Happens(a,t1,t2) ∧
	Initiates(a, f, t1) \wedge t2 < t3 \wedge
	$\neg Clipped(t1, f, t3)$
Discrete event calculus	$Happens(e,t) \land Initiates(e,f,t) \Rightarrow$
(Mueller, 2004a)	HoldsAt(f, t + 1)

telephone number'" (p. 129). He uses the convention that concept symbols start with an uppercase letter; thus, *Mike* represents the concept of Mike, *mike* represents Mike himself, *Telephone(Mike)* represents the concept of Mike's telephone number, *telephone(mike)* represents Mike's telephone number itself, *know(pat, Telephone(Mike))* represents that Pat knows Mike's telephone number, and *dial(pat, telephone(mike))* represents that Pat dials Mike's telephone number. The notion of reification was present in the original situation calculus of McCarthy and Hayes (1969). The reified notation *raining(x)(s)* and the nonreified notation

raining(x, s) are both given as ways of representing that the fluent raining(x) is true in situation s (p. 478). The action notation opens(sf, k) is used within an axiom schema (p. 480). Hayes (1971, p. 511) considers symbols such as MovE and CLIMB to represent functions that return actions. Kowalski (1979) introduces into the situation calculus the notation Holds(f, s) (p. 134), which represents that fluent f is true in situation f.

Lifschitz (1987a, pp. 48-50) introduces techniques for reification in the situation calculus. These techniques are incorporated into the event calculus by Shanahan (1995a, p. 257; 1997b, pp. 37, 38, and 58). Lifschitz uses a many-sorted logic with sorts for actions, fluents, situations, and truth values. He uses the predicate holds(f, s) (p. 39) to represent that fluent f is true in situation s. He introduces fluent function symbols to represent functions that return fluents, and action function symbols to represent functions that return actions. For example, $paint(Block_1, Blue)$ is an action term in which paint is an action function symbol (p. 48).

Following Reiter's (1980a) introduction of "axioms specifying that all constants are pairwise distinct" (p. 248), and a proposal of McCarthy (1986, pp. 96-97), Lifschitz (1987a, pp. 44, 50) introduces the U notation for defining unique names axioms. A system that assumes unique names axioms is said to use the unique names assumption (Genesereth & Nilsson, 1987, p. 120). Pirri and Reiter (1999) provide a rich formalization of the situation calculus. They use a many-sorted second-order logic (p. 326), action function symbols to represent functions that return actions (p. 327), and unique names axioms for action function symbols (p. 331). They use a nonreified notation for fluents (p. 327).

In addition to the situation calculus and the event calculus, several other logics have been proposed that use reified fluents or events. McDermott (1982) introduces a temporal logic for reasoning about action in which $(T \ s \ p)$ represents that fact p is true in state s (p. 108) and $(Occ \ sl \ s2 \ e)$ represents that event e occurs over the interval specified by sl and sl (p. 110). A fact such as $(ON \ A \ B)$ denotes the set of states in which l is on l, and an event such as $(MOVE \ A \ B)$ denotes the set of intervals over which l is moved to l Shoham (1987, pp. 96-99; 1988, pp. 43-46) introduces a logic in which l is moved to l Shoham (1987, pp. 96-99; 1988, pp. 43-46) introduces a logic in which l interval specified by l and l Bacchus, Tenenberg, and Koomen (1991, pp. 100-102) compare reified and nonreified temporal logics. Ma and Knight (2001) review the use of reification in several temporal logics.

Time intervals

Allen (1983) introduces a temporal representation based on time intervals. He defines a number of relations that may hold between intervals of time, such as *before*, *equal*, *meets*, *overlaps*, *during*, *starts*, and *finishes*. Allen (1984) introduces an interval-based temporal logic in which HOLDS(p,t) represents that property p is true during interval t (p. 128) and OCCUR(e,t) represents that event e occurs over interval t (pp. 132 and 133). The property p may contain logical connectives and quantifiers (p. 130).

In the event calculus, fluents are true at timepoints rather than time intervals. Following Shoham (1987, p. 94) and E. Davis (1990, p. 150), we may define a time interval as the set of timepoints that fall in the interval. Let the function Start(i) represent the start timepoint of interval i, the function End(i) represent the end timepoint of interval i, and the predicate In(t,i) represent that timepoint t falls in the interval i. We define In in terms of Start and End:

$$In(t,i) \Leftrightarrow Start(i) < t < End(i)$$

We may then represent that a fluent f is true over an interval i:

$$In(t,i) \Rightarrow HoldsAt(f,t)$$

E. Davis (1990, p. 153) shows that Allen's (1983) relations over intervals can be defined in terms of *Start* and *End*. For example:

$$Before(i_1, i_2) \Leftrightarrow End(i_1) < Start(i_2)$$

 $Equal(i_1, i_2) \Leftrightarrow (Start(i_1) = Start(i_2) \wedge End(i_1) = End(i_2))$
 $Meets(i_1, i_2) \Leftrightarrow End(i_1) = Start(i_2)$

Nonmonotonic reasoning

Minsky (1974, p. 75) criticized the monotonicity of logic, which led (Israel, 1985; Minsky, 1991b, p. 378) to the development of nonmonotonic reasoning methods (Bobrow, 1980). Minsky (1974) used the word *monotonicity* after a suggestion from Vaughan R. Pratt (McDermott & Doyle, 1980, p. 44). Previously, Hayes (1973) called this the "extension property" (p. 46), and Minsky (1961) noted that "in a mathematical domain a theorem, once proved, remains true when one proves other theorems" (p. 217). This property of logic was well known, as shown in Table 2.3. Pratt recalls the following:

Marvin Minsky (whose office on the 8th floor of 545 Tech Square was across the AI playroom from mine) ran into me as I was walking out of my office into the playroom and asked me whether logicians had a name for the notion that one rule of inference could turn off another, or something to that effect. I said I'd never

Table 2.3 Monotonicity of Logic

heard of such a thing, but that logical systems normally were monotonic in the sense that if you added an axiom or rule you could only get more theorems, so that the sort of system he was contemplating would be nonmonotonic. Neither of us had anything to add to this and that was the last I heard about any of that for a couple of years until I started seeing the phrase "nonmonotonic logic" in the literature (personal communication, June 9, 2005).

Minker (1993) provides an overview of nonmonotonic reasoning. Book-length treatments of nonmonotonic reasoning are provided by Gabbay, Hogger, and Robinson (1994), Antoniou (1997), and Brewka, Dix, and Konolige (1997). A collection of readings on nonmonotonic reasoning is provided by Ginsberg (1987). Nonmonotonic logics include default logic (Reiter, 1980b), the nonmonotonic logics of McDermott and Doyle (1980), and autoepistemic logic (R. C. Moore, 1985b). Earlier nonmonotonic reasoning methods include the THNOT of PLANNER (Hewitt, 1972), the Unless operator of Sandewall (1972), and negation as failure (K. L. Clark, 1978).

Circumscription

McCarthy (1977, pp. 1040 and 1041; 1980; 1984a; 1986) introduced the nonmonotonic reasoning method of circumscription. The definitive treatment of circumscription is provided by Lifschitz (1994). Reiter (1982) studies the relationship of circumscription and predicate completion. Methods for computing circumscription are described by Lifschitz (1985, 1994) and Genesereth and Nilsson (1987, pp. 132-152). Computational aspects of circumscription are explored by Kolaitis and Papadimitriou (1990). Algorithms for computing circumscription are provided by Gabbay and Ohlbach (1992) and Doherty, Łukaszewicz, and Szałas (1997). Not all circumscriptions reduce to formulas of first-order logic, Lifschitz (1985, p. 123) gives the example of using circumscription to assert that the binary relation denoted by a predicate is the transitive closure of the binary relation denoted by another predicate, which is not first-order expressible (Aho & Ullman, 1979, pp. 119 and 120; Nerode & Shore, 1997, p. 126). See also the discussions of M. Davis (1980), McCarthy (1980), and Genesereth and Nilsson (1987). Predicate completion was introduced by K. L. Clark (1978, pp. 303-305). Genesereth and Nilsson (1987) and Russell and Norvig (2009) explain how to compute predicate completion.

Formalizing domains

E. Davis (1999) provides a useful guide to formalizing domains in first-order logic. Elaboration tolerance is discussed by McCarthy (1998a) and Parmar (2003).

Writing proofs

Velleman (1994), Garnier and Taylor (1996), and Solow (2002) describe techniques for discovering and writing proofs. Reiter (2001, pp. 389-400) provides rules for finding proofs.

Reasoning types

Temporal projection is discussed by Wilensky (1983), Hanks and McDermott (1987), and Dean and Boddy (1988). Lifschitz (1989) discusses a number of different types of commonsense reasoning, such as "temporal projection" (p. 207) and "temporal explanation with unknown initial conditions" (p. 208), and provides a benchmark problem for each type of reasoning. Abduction is discussed by Charniak and McDermott (1985, chap. 8), Shanahan (1989; 1997b, chap. 17; 2000), Denecker, Missiaen, and Bruynooghe (1992), and Hobbs, Stickel, Appelt, and Martin (1993). Reiter (1996, p. 12) points out some drawbacks of abductive reasoning. Postdiction is discussed by E. Giunchiglia, Lee, Lifschitz, McCain, and Turner (2004, p. 65).

EXERCISES

- **2.1** List five models of the formula $P(A, B) \wedge P(B, C)$.
- **2.2** Suppose Awake(a) and Asleep(a) are functions. What conjunction of formulas does the expression U[Awake, Asleep] stand for?
- **2.3** Give some examples of formulas that are positive relative to a predicate Q and some that are not positive relative to Q.
- **2.4** Compute the circumscription of *R* in the conjunction of the following formulas:

$$P(x) \land Q(x) \Rightarrow R(x)$$

$$R(A)$$

$$R(B)$$

- 2.5 (Research Problem) Investigate the combination of the event calculus and the contexts of McCarthy (1987, 1993) and Guha (1992). Introduce a sort for contexts and a predicate ist(c,f) that represents that formula f is true in context c. See also the proposal of F. Giunchiglia and Ghidini (1998).
- **2.6** (Research Problem) Investigate how contexts could be used to facilitate the use of multiple representations in the event calculus.

PART

Commonsense Phenomena

Communiserise

The Effects of Events

Events change the state of the world. When an event occurs, some properties of the world that are false become true and some properties of the world that are true become false. This chapter is concerned with the representation of the effects of events on world properties. We discuss positive and negative effect axioms, commonly used effect axiom idioms, preconditions, and state constraints.

3.1 POSITIVE AND NEGATIVE EFFECT AXIOMS

In the event calculus, the effects of events are described by two predicates. The predicate $Initiates(\alpha, \beta, \tau)$ represents that, if an event α occurs at timepoint τ , then fluent β will be true after τ . The predicate $Terminates(\alpha, \beta, \tau)$ represents that, if an event α occurs at timepoint τ , then fluent β will be false after τ . We represent the effects of events using effect axioms.

The changes produced by an event may depend on the context in which the event occurs; an event may have one effect in one context and another effect in another context. Therefore, effect axioms contain conditions representing contexts.

Definition 3.1. If γ is a condition representing the context, α is an event term, β is a fluent term, and τ is a timepoint term, then

$$\gamma \Rightarrow Initiates(\alpha, \beta, \tau)$$

is a *positive effect axiom*. This represents that, if γ is true and α occurs at τ , then β will be true after τ .

Definition 3.2. If γ is a condition representing the context, α is an event term, β is a fluent term, and τ is a timepoint term, then

$$\gamma \Rightarrow Terminates(\alpha, \beta, \tau)$$

is a *negative effect axiom*. This represents that, if γ is true and α occurs at τ , then β will be false after τ .

Using the conjunction of axioms EC, a fluent is true (false) for times greater than the time of the initiating (terminating) event. Using the conjunction of axioms DEC, a fluent is true (false) starting one timepoint after the time of the initiating (terminating) event. For example, suppose we have *Initiates*(*Init*, *Fluent*, *t*), *Happens*(*Init*, 1),

Terminates (Term, Fluent, t), and Happens (Term, 4). Figure 3.1 shows when Fluent is true using the conjunction of axioms EC; Figure 3.2 shows when Fluent is true using DEC.

FIGURE 3.1

Truth value of a fluent in EC.

FIGURE 3.2

Truth value of a fluent in DEC.

3.1.1 EXAMPLE: TELEPHONE

We perform complex commonsense reasoning about the effects of events whenever we use a telephone. The behavior of a phone is highly context-sensitive. If we pick up an idle phone, we expect to get a dial tone. But if we pick up a phone that is ringing, we expect to be connected to the caller.

We can represent our knowledge about telephones using positive and negative effect axioms. If an agent picks up an idle phone, the phone will have a dial tone and will no longer be idle:

$$HoldsAt(Idle(p), t) \Rightarrow$$
 (3.1)
 $Initiates(PickUp(a, p), DialTone(p), t)$

$$HoldsAt(Idle(p), t) \Rightarrow$$
 (3.2)
 $Terminates(PickUp(a, p), Idle(p), t)$

After picking up a phone, an agent may decide not to place a call. If an agent sets down a phone with a dial tone, the phone will be idle and will no longer have a dial tone:

$$HoldsAt(DialTone(p), t) \Rightarrow$$
 (3.3)
 $Initiates(SetDown(a, p), Idle(p), t)$

$$HoldsAt(DialTone(p), t) \Rightarrow$$
 (3.4)
 $Terminates(SetDown(a, p), DialTone(p), t)$

When phone p_1 has a dial tone and an agent dials phone p_2 from p_1 , what happens depends on the state of p_2 . If p_2 is idle, then p_1 will be ringing p_2 , p_1 will no longer have a dial tone, and p_2 will no longer be idle:

$$HoldsAt(DialTone(p_1), t) \land HoldsAt(Idle(p_2), t) \Rightarrow$$
 (3.5)
 $Initiates(Dial(a, p_1, p_2), Ringing(p_1, p_2), t)$

$$HoldsAt(DialTone(p_1), t) \land HoldsAt(Idle(p_2), t) \Rightarrow$$
 (3.6)
 $Terminates(Dial(a, p_1, p_2), DialTone(p_1), t)$

$$HoldsAt(DialTone(p_1), t) \land HoldsAt(Idle(p_2), t) \Rightarrow$$
 (3.7)
 $Terminates(Dial(a, p_1, p_2), Idle(p_2), t)$

If p_2 is not idle, then p_1 will have a busy signal:

$$HoldsAt(DialTone(p_1), t) \land \neg HoldsAt(Idle(p_2), t) \Rightarrow$$
 (3.8)
 $Initiates(Dial(a, p_1, p_2), BusySignal(p_1), t)$

$$HoldsAt(DialTone(p_1), t) \land \neg HoldsAt(Idle(p_2), t) \Rightarrow$$
 (3.9)
 $Terminates(Dial(a, p_1, p_2), DialTone(p_1), t)$

If an agent sets down a phone with a busy signal, then the phone will be idle and will no longer have a busy signal:

$$HoldsAt(BusySignal(p), t) \Rightarrow$$
 (3.10)
 $Initiates(SetDown(a, p), Idle(p), t)$

$$HoldsAt(BusySignal(p), t) \Rightarrow$$
 (3.11)
 $Terminates(SetDown(a, p), BusySignal(p), t)$

A call may go unanswered. If phone p_1 is ringing phone p_2 and an agent sets down p_1 , then p_1 will be idle, p_2 will be idle, and p_1 will no longer be ringing p_2 :

$$HoldsAt(Ringing(p_1, p_2), t) \Rightarrow$$
 (3.12)
 $Initiates(SetDown(a, p_1), Idle(p_1), t)$

$$HoldsAt(Ringing(p_1, p_2), t) \Rightarrow$$
 (3.13)
 $Initiates(SetDown(a, p_1), Idle(p_2), t)$

$$HoldsAt(Ringing(p_1, p_2), t) \Rightarrow$$
 (3.14)
 $Terminates(SetDown(a, p_1), Ringing(p_1, p_2), t)$

A call may be answered. If phone p_1 is ringing phone p_2 and an agent picks up p_2 , then p_1 will be connected to p_2 and p_1 will no longer be ringing p_2 :

$$HoldsAt(Ringing(p_1, p_2), t) \Rightarrow$$
 (3.15)
 $Initiates(PickUp(a, p_2), Connected(p_1, p_2), t)$

$$HoldsAt(Ringing(p_1, p_2), t) \Rightarrow$$
 (3.16)
 $Terminates(PickUp(a, p_2), Ringing(p_1, p_2), t)$

A call may be completed. If phone p_1 is connected to phone p_2 and an agent sets down p_1 , then p_1 will be idle, p_2 will be disconnected, and p_1 will no longer be connected to p_2 :

$$HoldsAt(Connected(p_1, p_2), t) \Rightarrow$$
 (3.17)
 $Initiates(SetDown(a, p_1), Idle(p_1), t)$

$$HoldsAt(Connected(p_1, p_2), t) \Rightarrow$$
 (3.18)
 $Initiates(SetDown(a, p_1), Disconnected(p_2), t)$

$$HoldsAt(Connected(p_1, p_2), t) \Rightarrow$$
 (3.19)
 $Terminates(SetDown(a, p_1), Connected(p_1, p_2), t)$

Similarly, if phone p_1 is connected to phone p_2 and an agent sets down p_2 , then p_2 will be idle, p_1 will be disconnected, and p_1 will no longer be connected to p_2 :

$$HoldsAt(Connected(p_1, p_2), t) \Rightarrow$$
 (3.20)
 $Initiates(SetDown(a, p_2), Idle(p_2), t)$

$$HoldsAt(Connected(p_1, p_2), t) \Rightarrow$$
 (3.21)
 $Initiates(SetDown(a, p_2), Disconnected(p_1), t)$

$$HoldsAt(Connected(p_1, p_2), t) \Rightarrow$$
 (3.22)
 $Terminates(SetDown(a, p_2), Connected(p_1, p_2), t)$

If an agent sets down a phone that is disconnected, then the phone will be idle and the phone will no longer be disconnected:

$$HoldsAt(Disconnected(p), t) \Rightarrow$$
 (3.23)
 $Initiates(SetDown(a, p), Idle(p), t)$

$$HoldsAt(Disconnected(p), t) \Rightarrow$$
 (3.24)
 $Terminates(SetDown(a, p), Disconnected(p), t)$

Let us now use this axiomatization to solve a particular reasoning problem. We start by specifying some observations. At timepoint 0, all phones are idle, no phones have a dial tone or busy signal, no phones are ringing other phones, no phones are connected to other phones, and no phones are disconnected:

$$HoldsAt(Idle(p), 0)$$
 (3.25)
 $\neg HoldsAt(DialTone(p), 0)$ (3.26)
 $\neg HoldsAt(BusySignal(p), 0)$ (3.27)
 $\neg HoldsAt(Ringing(p_1, p_2), 0)$ (3.28)
 $\neg HoldsAt(Connected(p_1, p_2), 0)$ (3.29)

We specify that fluents are never released from the commonsense law of inertia:

 $\neg HoldsAt(Disconnected(p), 0)$

$$\neg ReleasedAt(f,t)$$
 (3.31)

(3.30)

We specify a narrative. One agent picks up the phone and dials another agent, and then the other agent answers:

$$Happens(PickUp(Agent1, Phone1), 0)$$
 (3.32)

We can then show that the two agents will be connected.

Proposition 3.1. Let Σ be the conjunction of (3.1) through (3.24). Let $\Delta = (3.32) \wedge (3.33) \wedge (3.34)$. Let $\Omega = U[PickUp, SetDown, Dial] \wedge U[Idle, DialTone, Ringing, BusySignal, Connected, Disconnected]. Let <math>\Gamma$ be the conjunction of (3.25) through (3.31). Then we have

$$CIRC[\Sigma; Initiates, Terminates, Releases] \land CIRC[\Delta; Happens] \land \\ \Omega \land \Gamma \land DEC \vdash HoldsAt(Connected(Phone 1, Phone 2), 3)$$

Proof. From $CIRC[\Sigma; Initiates, Terminates, Releases]$ and Theorems 2.1 and 2.2, we have

$$Initiates(e, f, t) \Leftrightarrow \tag{3.35}$$

$$\exists a, p \ (e = PickUp(a, p) \land f = DialTone(p) \land HoldsAt(Idle(p), t)) \lor$$

$$\exists a, p \ (e = SetDown(a, p) \land f = Idle(p) \land HoldsAt(DialTone(p), t)) \lor$$

$$\exists a, p_1, p_2 \ (e = Dial(a, p_1, p_2) \land$$

$$f = Ringing(p_1, p_2) \land$$

$$HoldsAt(DialTone(p_1), t) \land$$

$$HoldsAt(Idle(p_2), t)) \lor$$

$$\exists a, p_1, p_2 \ (e = Dial(a, p_1, p_2) \land$$

$$f = BusySignal(p_1) \land$$

$$HoldsAt(DialTone(p_1), t) \land$$

$$\neg HoldsAt(Idle(p_2), t)) \lor$$

$$\exists a, p \ (e = SetDown(a, p) \land f = Idle(p) \land HoldsAt(BusySignal(p), t)) \lor$$

$$\exists a, p_1, p_2 \ (e = SetDown(a, p_1) \land$$

$$f = Idle(p_1) \land$$

$$HoldsAt(Ringing(p_1, p_2), t)) \lor$$

$$\exists a, p_1, p_2 \ (e = SetDown(a, p_1) \land$$

$$f = Idle(p_2) \land$$

$$\begin{aligned} & HoldsAt(Ringing(p_1,p_2),t)) \vee \\ & \exists a, p_1, p_2 \ (e = PickUp(a,p_2) \land \\ & f = Connected(p_1,p_2) \land \\ & HoldsAt(Ringing(p_1,p_2),t)) \vee \\ & \exists a, p_1, p_2 \ (e = SetDown(a,p_1) \land \\ & f = Idle(p_1) \land \\ & HoldsAt(Connected(p_1,p_2),t)) \vee \\ & \exists a, p_1, p_2 \ (e = SetDown(a,p_1) \land \\ & f = Disconnected(p_2) \land \\ & HoldsAt(Connected(p_1,p_2),t)) \vee \\ & \exists a, p_1, p_2 \ (e = SetDown(a,p_2) \land \\ & f = Idle(p_2) \land \\ & HoldsAt(Connected(p_1,p_2),t)) \vee \\ & \exists a, p_1, p_2 \ (e = SetDown(a,p_2) \land \\ & f = Disconnected(p_1) \land \\ & HoldsAt(Connected(p_1,p_2),t)) \vee \\ & \exists a, p_1, p_2 \ (e = SetDown(a,p) \land f = Idle(p) \land HoldsAt(Disconnected(p),t)) \\ & Terminates(e,f,t) \Leftrightarrow (3.36) \\ & \exists a, p \ (e = PickUp(a,p) \land f = Idle(p) \land HoldsAt(DialTone(p),t)) \vee \\ & \exists a, p_1, p_2 \ (e = Dial(a,p_1,p_2) \land \\ & f = DialTone(p_1) \land \\ & HoldsAt(DialTone(p_1),t) \land \\ & HoldsAt(Idle(p_2),t)) \vee \\ & \exists a, p_1, p_2 \end{aligned}$$

(3.37)

$$(e = Dial(a, p_1, p_2) \land f = Idle(p_2) \land f = Dial(a, p_1, p_2) \land f = BusySignal(p) \land HoldsAt(BusySignal(p), t)) \lor \exists a, p (e = SetDown(a, p) \land f = BusySignal(p) \land HoldsAt(BusySignal(p), t)) \lor \exists a, p_1, p_2 (e = SetDown(a, p_1) \land f = Ringing(p_1, p_2) \land f = Connected(p_1, p_2) \land f = Disconnected(p) \land f = Disconnected(p) \land f = Disconnected(p) \land f = Disconnected(p, t) f = Ringing(p_1, t) f = Rin$$

From $CIRC[\Delta; Happens]$ and Theorem 2.1, we have

$$Happens(e,t) \Leftrightarrow$$

$$(e = PickUp(Agent1, Phone1) \land t = 0) \lor$$

$$(e = Dial(Agent1, Phone1, Phone2) \land t = 1) \lor$$

$$(e = PickUp(Agent2, Phone2) \land t = 2)$$

$$(3.38)$$

From (3.32) (which follows from (3.38)), (3.25), (3.1) (which follows from (3.35)), and DEC9, we have

$$HoldsAt(DialTone(Phone 1), 1)$$
 (3.39)

From (3.38) and (3.36), we have $\neg \exists e (Happens(e, 0) \land Terminates(e, Idle (Phone 2), 0))$. From this, (3.25), (3.31), and DEC5, we have

$$HoldsAt(Idle(Phone2), 1)$$
 (3.40)

From (3.33) (which follows from (3.38)), (3.39), (3.40), (3.5) (which follows from (3.35)), and DEC9, we have HoldsAt(Ringing(Phone1, Phone2), 2). From this, (3.34) (which follows from (3.38)), (3.15) (which follows from (3.35)), and DEC9, we have HoldsAt(Connected(Phone1, Phone2), 3).

3.2 EFFECT AXIOM IDIOMS

In this section, we present several commonly used idioms involving effect axioms.

Setting and resetting

One event sets a fluent; another event resets the fluent. If o is set, then o will be on, whereas, if o is reset, then o will no longer be on:

Flipping

An event flips the truth value of a fluent. If o is not on and o is flipped, then o will be on, but, if o is on and o is flipped, then o will no longer be on:

$$\neg HoldsAt(On(o), t) \Rightarrow Initiates(Flip(o), On(o), t)$$

$$HoldsAt(On(o), t) \Rightarrow Terminates(Flip(o), On(o), t)$$

Selection

An event selects from among a number of values. If the value is v_1 and the value v_2 is selected, then the value will be v_2 and will no longer be v_1 :

$$Initiates(Select(o, v_2), Value(o, v_2), t)$$

```
HoldsAt(Value(o, v_1), t) \land v_1 \neq v_2 \Rightarrow

Terminates(Select(o, v_2), Value(o, v_1), t)
```

We may wish to represent explicitly that a value is changed from one value to another:

```
Initiates(Change(o, v_1, v_2), Value(o, v_2), t)
```

```
HoldsAt(Value(o, v_1), t) \land v_1 \neq v_2 \Rightarrow

Terminates(Change(o, v_1, v_2), Value(o, v_1), t)
```

Functional modification

An event modifies a value by applying some function. If the value is v and the function F is applied, then the value will be F(v):

```
HoldsAt(Value(o, v), t) \Rightarrow

Initiates(ApplyF(o), Value(o, F(v)), t)
```

$$HoldsAt(Value(o, v), t) \land v \neq F(v) \Rightarrow$$

 $Terminates(ApplyF(o), Value(o, v), t)$

A common example is incrementing a value:

```
HoldsAt(Value(o, v), t) \Rightarrow Initiates(Increment(o), Value(o, v + 1), t)
HoldsAt(Value(o, v), t) \Rightarrow Terminates(Increment(o), Value(o, v), t)
```

Many-to-many mapping

In general, the mapping between events and fluents is many-to-many. One event may initiate (or terminate) many fluents:

```
Initiates (E(o), F1(o), t)
Initiates (E(o), F2(o), t)
```

Many events may initiate (or terminate) one fluent:

```
Initiates (E1(o), F(o), t)
Initiates (E2(o), F(o), t)
```

3.3 PRECONDITIONS

Consider the action of turning on a device. We might represent this as follows:

That is, if an agent turns on a device, then the device will be on. But there are many things that may prevent the device from going on. The device might be unplugged, it might be broken, its on-off switch might be broken, and so on. A condition that prevents an event from having its intended effects, or that prevents an event from occurring, is called a *qualification*. An event is said to be qualified whenever one or more of its qualifications are true. The problem of representing and reasoning about qualifications is known as the *qualification problem*.

A partial solution to the qualification problem is to use preconditions. (Other solutions are to use state constraints, which are described in Section 3.4, and default reasoning, which is discussed in Chapter 12.) In this section we describe two types of preconditions for events: fluent preconditions and action preconditions. Fluent preconditions allow us to represent qualifications that prevent events from having their intended effects; action preconditions allow us to represent qualifications that prevent events from occurring.

3.3.1 FLUENT PRECONDITIONS

A *fluent precondition* is a requirement that must be satisfied for the occurrence of an event to have an effect. An event whose fluent precondition is not satisfied may occur, but the event will not have the intended effect.

Definition 3.3. If γ is a condition, α is an event term, β is a fluent term, and τ is a timepoint term, then

$$\gamma \Rightarrow Initiates(\alpha, \beta, \tau)$$

and

$$\gamma \Rightarrow Terminates(\alpha, \beta, \tau)$$

are *fluent precondition axioms*. We say that γ is a fluent precondition of α . A fluent precondition axiom is the same thing as an effect axiom.

For example, if an agent turns on a device, then, provided the device is not broken, the device will be on:

$$\neg HoldsAt(Broken(d), t) \Rightarrow Initiates(TurnOn(a, d), On(d), t)$$

If a device is broken, then the event of turning on the device can occur, but it will not have the intended effect.

3.3.2 ACTION PRECONDITIONS

An action precondition is a requirement that must be satisfied for the occurrence of an event. An event whose action precondition is not satisfied cannot occur.

Definition 3.4. If γ is a condition, α is an event term, and τ is a timepoint term, then

$$Happens(\alpha, \tau) \Rightarrow \gamma$$

is an action precondition axiom. We say that γ is an action precondition of α .

By contraposition this is equivalent to $\neg \gamma \Rightarrow \neg Happens(\alpha, \tau)$. Thus, if an event occurs whose action precondition is not true, then inconsistency arises.

Action precondition axioms provide an elaboration-tolerant way of expressing qualifications. Whenever we wish to add a qualification, we may simply add an action precondition axiom. Fluent precondition axioms can also be made elaboration tolerant by using default reasoning, as discussed in Section 12.4.

3.3.3 EXAMPLE: WALKING THROUGH A DOOR

Suppose that in order for an agent to walk through a door, the agent must be near the door:

$$Happens(WalkThroughDoor(a,d),t) \Rightarrow HoldsAt(Near(a,d),t)$$
 (3.41)

Suppose further that Nathan is not near a door and walks through a door:

$$\neg HoldsAt(Near(Nathan, Door), 1)$$
 (3.42)

$$Happens(WalkThroughDoor(Nathan, Door), 1)$$
 (3.43)

We then get inconsistency.

Proposition 3.2. The conjunction of (3.41)–(3.43) is inconsistent.

Proof. From (3.43) and (3.41), we have HoldsAt(Near(Nathan, Door), 1), which contradicts (3.42).

3.4 STATE CONSTRAINTS

Some properties of the world follow other properties in a lawlike fashion. We represent relationships that hold among properties over all timepoints using state constraints.

Definition 3.5. If γ_1 and γ_2 are conditions, then γ_1 , $\gamma_1 \Rightarrow \gamma_2$, and $\gamma_1 \Leftrightarrow \gamma_2$ are *state constraints*.

Table 3.1 shows some typical state constraints involving one, two, and three or more fluents. In this section, we describe some sample uses of state constraints.

Irreflexive and antisymmetric relation

Suppose we have a fluent $On(o_1, o_2)$, which represents that an object o_1 is on top of an object o_2 . We can use state constraints to specify that On denotes an irreflexive and antisymmetric relation. That is, an object can never be on top of itself:

$$\neg HoldsAt(On(o, o), t)$$

and, if one object o_1 is on top of another object o_2 , then o_2 cannot also be on top of o_1 :

$$HoldsAt(On(o_1, o_2), t) \land o_1 \neq o_2 \Rightarrow \neg HoldsAt(On(o_2, o_1), t)$$

Functional and total relation

Consider a fluent At(o, l), which represents that object o is located at location l. We may specify that At denotes a functional and total relation. An object is in at most one location at a time:

$$HoldsAt(At(o, l_1), t) \wedge HoldsAt(At(o, l_2), t) \Rightarrow l_1 = l_2$$

and, at all times, every object has a location:

$$\exists l \, HoldsAt(At(o,l),t)$$

State constraints can be used to address the qualification problem, as demonstrated in the following example: Let Occupies(p, s) represent that a chess piece p occupies

Table 3.1 Typical State Constraints

State Constraint	Axiom
Reflexive relation	HoldsAt(R(a,a),t)
Irreflexive relation	$\neg HoldsAt(R(a,a),t)$
Symmetric relation	$HoldsAt(R(a,b),t) \Rightarrow HoldsAt(R(b,a),t)$
Antisymmetric relation	$HoldsAt(R(a,b),t) \land a \neq b \Rightarrow$
	$\neg HoldsAt(R(b,a),t)$
Transitive relation	$HoldsAt(R(a,b),t) \land HoldsAt(R(b,c),t) \Rightarrow$
	HoldsAt(R(a,c),t)
Intransitive relation	$HoldsAt(R(a,b),t) \land HoldsAt(R(b,c),t) \Rightarrow$
	$\neg HoldsAt(R(a,c),t)$
Trichotomous relation	$HoldsAt(R(a,b),t) \stackrel{.}{\lor} HoldsAt(R(b,a),t) \stackrel{.}{\lor} a = b$
Total relation	$\exists b \; HoldsAt(R(a,b),t)$
Functional relation	$HoldsAt(R(a,b),t) \wedge HoldsAt(R(a,c),t) \Rightarrow b = c$
Surjective relation	$\exists a \ HoldsAt(R(a,b),t)$
Injective relation	$HoldsAt(R(a,c),t) \land HoldsAt(R(b,c),t) \Rightarrow a = b$
Negation	$HoldsAt(R(a_1,,a_n),t) \Leftrightarrow$
	$\neg HoldsAt(S(a_1,,a_n),t)$
Converse	$HoldsAt(R(a,b),t) \Leftrightarrow HoldsAt(S(b,a),t)$
Composite	$HoldsAt(R(a,b),t) \land HoldsAt(S(b,c),t) \Leftrightarrow$
	HoldsAt(T(a,c),t)
Union	$HoldsAt(R(a_1,,a_n),t) \Leftrightarrow$
1	$HoldsAt(S_1(a_1,,a_n),t) \lor \cdots \lor$
	$HoldsAt(S_k(a_1,,a_n),t)$
Intersection	$HoldsAt(R(a_1,,a_n),t) \Leftrightarrow$
	$HoldsAt(S_1(a_1,,a_n),t) \wedge \cdots \wedge$
	$HoldsAt(S_k(a_1,,a_n),t)$
Exactly one	$HoldsAt(R_1(a_1,,a_n),t) \dot{\lor} \cdots \dot{\lor}$
	$HoldsAt(R_k(a_1,\ldots,a_n),t)$

a square s of a chessboard. We wish to represent that it is not possible to move a piece onto a square that is already occupied. We may do this by specifying that *Occupies* denotes an injective relation. That is, at most one piece occupies a square at a time:

$$HoldsAt(Occupies(p_1, s), t) \land HoldsAt(Occupies(p_2, s), t) \Rightarrow p_1 = p_2$$

A state constraint used to represent a qualification that prevents an event from occurring is called a *qualification constraint*. State constraints provide an elaboration-tolerant way of expressing qualifications because, whenever we wish to add a qualification, we may simply add a state constraint.

Negation

We may wish to specify that one fluent represents the negation of another fluent. An example is the fact that a device is off if and only if it is not on:

$$HoldsAt(Off(d), t) \Leftrightarrow \neg HoldsAt(On(d), t)$$

Intersection

A light is lit if and only if it is on and not broken:

$$HoldsAt(Lit(l), t) \Leftrightarrow HoldsAt(On(l), t) \land \neg HoldsAt(Broken(l), t)$$

Exactly one

At all times, a person is either lying, sitting, or standing:

$$HoldsAt(Lying(p),t) \dot{\lor}$$
 (3.44)
 $HoldsAt(Sitting(p),t) \dot{\lor}$
 $HoldsAt(Standing(p),t)$

3.4.1 EXAMPLE: TELEPHONE REVISITED

An important use of state constraints is to simplify the specification of initial conditions. We can use state constraints to tighten up the telephone axiomatization given in Section 3.1.1.

We add several axioms. A phone cannot be ringing itself:

$$\neg HoldsAt(Ringing(p,p),t)$$
 (3.45)

If phone p_1 is ringing phone p_2 , then p_2 cannot be ringing p_1 :

$$HoldsAt(Ringing(p_1, p_2), t) \land p_1 \neq p_2 \Rightarrow$$
 (3.46)
 $\neg HoldsAt(Ringing(p_2, p_1), t)$

A phone cannot be connected to itself:

$$\neg HoldsAt(Connected(p,p),t)$$
 (3.47)

If phone p_1 is connected to phone p_2 , then p_2 cannot be connected to p_1 :

$$HoldsAt(Connected(p_1, p_2), t) \land p_1 \neq p_2 \Rightarrow$$
 (3.48)
 $\neg HoldsAt(Connected(p_2, p_1), t)$

At any time, a phone either is idle, has a dial tone, has a busy signal, is ringing another phone, is being rung by another phone, is connected to another phone, or is disconnected:

$$HoldsAt(Idle(p),t) \dot{\vee}$$

$$HoldsAt(DialTone(p),t) \dot{\vee}$$

$$HoldsAt(BusySignal(p),t) \dot{\vee}$$

$$\exists p_1 HoldsAt(Ringing(p,p_1),t) \dot{\vee}$$

$$\exists p_1 HoldsAt(Ringing(p_1,p),t) \dot{\vee}$$

$$\exists p_1 HoldsAt(Connected(p,p_1),t) \dot{\vee}$$

$$\exists p_1 HoldsAt(Connected(p_1,p),t) \dot{\vee}$$

$$HoldsAt(Disconnected(p),t)$$

These state constraints simplify specification of initial conditions. For example, from HoldsAt(Idle(Phone1), 0), HoldsAt(Idle(Phone2), 0), (3.45), (3.46), (3.47), (3.48), and (3.49), we have all of the following:

```
¬HoldsAt(DialTone(Phone1), 0)
¬HoldsAt(BusySignal(Phone1), 0)
¬HoldsAt(Ringing(Phone1, Phone1), 0)
¬HoldsAt(Ringing(Phone1, Phone2), 0)
¬HoldsAt(Connected(Phone1, Phone2), 0)
¬HoldsAt(Disconnected(Phone1, Phone2), 0)
¬HoldsAt(Disconnected(Phone2), 0)
¬HoldsAt(BusySignal(Phone2), 0)
¬HoldsAt(Ringing(Phone2, Phone2), 0)
¬HoldsAt(Ringing(Phone2, Phone1), 0)
¬HoldsAt(Connected(Phone2, Phone1), 0)
¬HoldsAt(Connected(Phone2, Phone1), 0)
¬HoldsAt(Connected(Phone2, Phone1), 0)
```

Therefore, we no longer have to specify these initial conditions explicitly.

BIBLIOGRAPHIC NOTES

GPS

An early problem-solving program was GPS (Newell & Simon, 1961). GPS uses subgoaling to find a sequence of operators that transforms an object from an initial state into a goal state. The subgoal to transform an object a into an object b is achieved as follows:

- 1. If a and b are the same, return with success.
- **2.** Find a difference d between a and b.
- **3.** Invoke subgoal to reduce d between a and b, producing a'.
- **4.** Recursively invoke subgoal to transform a' into b.

The subgoal to reduce d between a and b is achieved as follows:

- 1. Select relevant operator (action) o.
- **2.** Invoke subgoal to apply o to a, producing a'.

The subgoal to apply o to a is achieved as follows:

- 1. If a is not of the required form c for the application of o, then
 - (a) Find a difference d between a and c.
 - **(b)** Invoke subgoal to reduce d between a and c, producing a'.
 - (c) Recursively invoke subgoal to apply o to a', producing a''.
- **2.** Otherwise, apply o to a, producing a'.

GPS evolved into the SOAR problem-solving and learning architecture (Rosenbloom, Laird, & Newell, 1993).

QA3

An early program for reasoning about action and change was QA3 (Green, 1969). The program uses a version of the situation calculus to represent knowledge and uses resolution theorem proving (Robinson, 1965) to solve planning problems such as McCarthy's (1963) monkey and bananas problem.

STRIPS

Another early program for reasoning about action and change was STRIPS (Fikes & Nilsson, 1971; Fikes, Hart, & Nilsson, 1972a, 1972b). STRIPS solves planning problems. It takes a set of operator descriptions, a goal formula, and an initial world model given by a set of formulas and produces a sequence of operators that transforms the initial world model into a model in which the goal is true. An operator description consists of a precondition, a delete list, and an add list. The precondition specifies the conditions under which the operator is applicable, the delete list specifies the formulas that are deleted by the operator, and the add list specifies the formulas that are added by the operator. STRIPS deals with the commonsense law of inertia by making the assumption that, when an operator is applied, any formulas not deleted or added by the operator stay the same. This is called the STRIPS assumption by Waldinger (1977, p. 120). Lifschitz (1987b) formalizes the semantics of STRIPS. A STRIPS operator description

```
Operator: o
Precondition: c
Delete list: d_1, \ldots, d_n
Add list: a_1, \ldots, a_n
is similar to the set of event calculus formulas
c \Rightarrow Terminates(o, d_1, t)
\vdots
c \Rightarrow Terminates(o, d_n, t)
c \Rightarrow Initiates(o, a_1, t)
\vdots
c \Rightarrow Initiates(o, a_n, t)
```

Inconsistency

In EC and DEC, simultaneously initiating and terminating a fluent produces inconsistency. This is also the case in most of the versions of the classical logic event calculus (Shanahan, 1996, 1997b, 1999a, 2004). But in the basic axiomatization of

the event calculus of R. Miller and Shanahan (1999, pp. 1-3; 2002, pp. 453-455) (not the particular version of R. Miller and Shanahan used in this book called EC), simultaneously initiating and terminating a fluent results in two classes of models: one in which the fluent is true and one in which the fluent is false. This can be used to represent nondeterminism. R. Miller and Shanahan (2002, pp. 459 and 460) give the following example:

Initiates(TossCoin, HeadsUp, t)
Terminates(TossCoin, HeadsUp, t)
Happens(TossCoin, 2)

(Nondeterminism can still be represented with EC and DEC using release axioms as discussed in Section 5.2, determining fluents as discussed in Section 9.1, or disjunctive event axioms as discussed in Section 9.2.)

Qualification problem

The qualification problem was first described by McCarthy and Hayes (1969, p. 489). They considered the problem of how to represent exceptions to statements about the effects of looking up and dialing a person's telephone number. The phrase "qualification problem" appears to have been first used in print by Hayes (1973, p. 56). He uses the example of a robot that concludes that it can drive to the airport and then notices a flat tire. McCarthy (1977, p. 1040) presents the qualification problem and discusses the countless ways a boat could be prevented from crossing a river in the missionaries and cannibals problem. The qualification problem is also discussed by McCarthy (1980, pp. 27 and 28; 1987, p. 1033) and Hayes (1971, pp. 515 and 516). Our definitions of qualifications, qualified events, and the qualification problem are from Kvarnström and Doherty (2000a). Ginsberg and Smith (1987a, 1988a) propose the use of state constraints for representing qualifications, and F. Lin and Reiter (1994, section 2) call these "qualification constraints."

Preconditions

The distinction between action preconditions and fluent preconditions is from R. Miller and Shanahan (2002, p. 464). Baral (1995) makes a similar distinction between an "executability condition of an action" and "preconditions of effects" (p. 2017). Our representation of an action precondition axiom is from Shanahan and Witkowski (2004). This representation must be used with caution when solving abduction or planning problems, as pointed out by R. Miller and Shanahan (2002, p. 465): If the initial situation is not completely specified, then Happens(event, time) becomes a plan for achieving the precondition.

State constraints

McCarthy and Hayes (1969, p. 478) give the following transitive law in the situation calculus:

 $\forall x. \forall y. \forall z. \forall s. in(x, y, s) \land in(y, z, s) \supset in(x, z, s)$

Green (1969) introduces a kind of axiom that represents "an implication that holds for a fixed state" (p. 78). State constraints (Genesereth & Nilsson, 1987, p. 267) are also called "domain constraints" (Ginsberg & Smith, 1987b, p. 237). E. Davis (1990) calls state constraints "state coherence axioms" (p. 193). Such constraints in the event calculus are discussed by Shanahan (1995a, pp. 255, 262; 1996, p. 685; 1997b, pp. 11, 39, 40, 275, 285, 286, 323, and 324; 1999a, pp. 417-419). Reiter (2001, pp. 401-406) discusses the treatment of state constraints in the situation calculus. Doherty, Gustafsson, Karlsson, and Kvarnström (1998, p. 16) discuss domain constraints in temporal action logics. Gustafsson and Doherty (1996) call state constraints that mention multiple timepoints "transition constraints" (p. 92). They give an example that in the event calculus is represented as

 $\neg HoldsAt(Alive(a), t) \Rightarrow \neg HoldsAt(Alive(a), t + 1)$

EXERCISES

- **3.1** Write an axiom to formalize that a person who eats is no longer hungry.
- 3.2 Write an axiom to formalize the following. If two agents are in the same room, the first agent is listening to the second agent, and the first agent tells the second agent a fact, then the second agent will know that fact.
- **3.3** Using the axiom written in Exercise 3.2, prove that, if Nathan and Ryan are in the same room, Ryan is listening to Nathan, and Nathan tells Ryan a particular fact, then Ryan will know that fact.
- **3.4** Formalize that if an agent is outside, it is cold outside, and the agent is not wearing a coat, then the agent is cold. Incorporate other weather conditions such as rain. Include axioms for putting on and taking off a coat.
- 3.5 Formalize the opening of a book to a particular page number and the closing of a book.
- **3.6** Formalize the formation and dissolution of interpersonal relationships such as friendship and marriage (Dyer, 1983; Schank & Abelson, 1977).
- 3.7 Simple axioms for waking up and falling asleep are given in Section 2.7.1. Create a more detailed formalization of the human sleep cycle. Incorporate getting out of bed, getting tired, lying in bed, and waiting to fall asleep.
- **3.8** Formalize lighting and putting out a fire.
- 3.9 State constraint (3.44) says that a person is either lying, sitting, or standing. Add appropriate event predicates, fluent predicates, and axioms to formalize lying down on something, sitting down on something, and standing up.
- **3.10** Write state constraints relating various expressions for time of day, such as daytime, nighttime, morning, afternoon, and evening.

- 66
- **3.11** Are there any bugs in the formalization of a telephone in Sections 3.1.1 and 3.4.1? Consider the following scenarios:
 - Two agents dial one another simultaneously.
 - One agent dials another agent at the same instant that the other agent picks up the phone.
- **3.12** Prove Proposition 3.1 using the conjunction of axioms EC instead of the conjunction of axioms DEC.

The Triggering of Events

So far, we have addressed that when an event occurs, a fluent changes its truth value. What about the opposite? That is, when a fluent changes its truth value, an event occurs; more generally, when a particular condition becomes true, an event occurs. We call such an event a *triggered event*. An example of a triggered event is a ball bouncing off of a wall when it reaches the wall. This chapter addresses the triggering of events in response to conditions; we also discuss triggered fluents.

4.1 TRIGGER AXIOMS

We specify when a triggered event occurs using a trigger axiom.

Definition 4.1. If γ is a condition, α is an event term, and τ is a timepoint term, then

$$\gamma \Rightarrow Happens(\alpha, \tau)$$

is a trigger axiom.

4.1.1 EXAMPLE: ALARM CLOCK

Whenever we use an alarm clock, we perform commonsense reasoning about triggered events. The alarm going off is a triggered event, and we can formalize the operation of an alarm clock using trigger axioms.

We start with some effect axioms. If a clock's alarm time is t_1 and an agent sets the clock's alarm time to t_2 , then the clock's alarm time will be t_2 and will no longer be t_1 :

$$HoldsAt(AlarmTime(c, t_1), t) \land t_1 \neq t_2 \Rightarrow$$
 (4.1)
 $Initiates(SetAlarmTime(a, c, t_2), AlarmTime(c, t_2), t)$

$$HoldsAt(AlarmTime(c, t_1), t) \land t_1 \neq t_2 \Rightarrow$$
 (4.2)
 $Terminates(SetAlarmTime(a, c, t_2), AlarmTime(c, t_1), t)$

If an agent turns on a clock's alarm, then it will be on:

$$Initiates(TurnOnAlarm(a, c), AlarmOn(c), t)$$
(4.3)

68

If an agent turns off a clock's alarm, then it will no longer be on:

$$Terminates(TurnOffAlarm(a, c), AlarmOn(c), t)$$
 (4.4)

If an alarm starts beeping, then it will be beeping:

$$Initiates(StartBeeping(c), Beeping(c), t)$$
 (4.5)

If an agent turns off a clock's alarm, then the clock will no longer be beeping:

$$Terminates(TurnOffAlarm(a, c), Beeping(c), t)$$
 (4.6)

We have a state constraint that says that a clock has a unique alarm time at any given time:

$$HoldsAt(AlarmTime(c, t_1), t) \land HoldsAt(AlarmTime(c, t_2), t) \Rightarrow t_1 = t_2$$
 (4.7)

Now we use a trigger axiom. If a clock's alarm time is the present moment and the alarm is on, then the clock starts beeping:

$$HoldsAt(AlarmTime(c, t), t) \land HoldsAt(AlarmOn(c), t) \Rightarrow$$
 (4.8)
 $Happens(StartBeeping(c), t)$

Let us use the following observations and narrative. At timepoint 0, the alarm is not on, the alarm is not beeping, and the alarm time is set to 10:

$$\neg HoldsAt(AlarmOn(Clock), 0)$$
 (4.9)

$$\neg HoldsAt(Beeping(Clock), 0)$$
 (4.10)

$$HoldsAt(AlarmTime(Clock, 10), 0)$$
 (4.11)

$$\neg ReleasedAt(f,t)$$
 (4.12)

At timepoint 0, Nathan sets the alarm clock for timepoint 2; and at timepoint 1, he turns on the alarm:

$$Happens(SetAlarmTime(Nathan, Clock, 2), 0)$$
 (4.13)

$$Happens(TurnOnAlarm(Nathan, Clock), 1)$$
 (4.14)

We can then show that the alarm clock will be beeping at timepoint 3.

Proposition 4.1. Let $\Sigma = (4.1) \land (4.2) \land (4.3) \land (4.4) \land (4.5) \land (4.6), \Delta = (4.8) \land (4.13) \land (4.14), \Omega = U[SetAlarmTime, TurnOnAlarm, TurnOffAlarm, StartBeeping] <math>\land U[AlarmTime, AlarmOn, Beeping], \Psi = (4.7), and \Gamma = (4.9) \land (4.10) \land (4.11) \land (4.12).$ Then we have

$$CIRC[\Sigma; Initiates, Terminates, Releases] \land CIRC[\Delta; Happens] \land \Omega \land \Psi \land \Gamma \land DEC \vdash HoldsAt(Beeping(Clock), 3)$$

Proof. From $CIRC[\Sigma; Initiates, Terminates, Releases]$ and Theorems 2.1 and 2.2, we have

$$Initiates(e, f, t) \Leftrightarrow$$
 (4.15)

$$\exists a, c, t_1, t_2 (e = SetAlarmTime(a, c, t_2)) \land$$

$$f = AlarmTime(c, t_2) \land$$

$$HoldsAt(AlarmTime(c,t_{1}),t) \wedge t_{1} \neq t_{2}) \vee \\ \exists a,c \ (e = TurnOnAlarm(a,c) \wedge f = AlarmOn(c)) \vee \\ \exists c \ (e = StartBeeping(c) \wedge f = Beeping(c)) \\ Terminates(e,f,t) \Leftrightarrow \qquad (4.16) \\ \exists a,c,t_{1},t_{2} \ (e = SetAlarmTime(a,c,t_{2}) \wedge \\ f = AlarmTime(c,t_{1}) \wedge \\ HoldsAt(AlarmTime(c,t_{1}),t) \wedge \\ t_{1} \neq t_{2}) \vee \\ \exists a,c \ (e = TurnOffAlarm(a,c) \wedge f = AlarmOn(c)) \vee \\ \exists a,c \ (e = TurnOffAlarm(a,c) \wedge f = Beeping(c)) \\ \neg Releases(e,f,t) \qquad (4.17)$$

From $CIRC[\Delta; Happens]$ and Theorem 2.1, we have

$$Happens(e, t) \Leftrightarrow \tag{4.18}$$

$$\exists c \ (e = StartBeeping(c) \land HoldsAt(AlarmTime(c, t), t) \land$$

 $HoldsAt(AlarmOn(c), t)) \lor$ $(e = SetAlarmTime(Nathan, Clock, 2) \land t = 0) \lor$ $(e = TurnOnAlarm(Nathan, Clock) \land t = 1)$

From (4.13) (which follows from (4.18)), (4.11), $10 \neq 2$, (4.1) (which follows from (4.15)), and DEC9, we have

$$HoldsAt(AlarmTime(Clock, 2), 1)$$
 (4.19)

From (4.18) and (4.16), we have $\neg \exists e (Happens(e, 1) \land Terminates(e, AlarmTime (Clock, 2), 1))$. From this, (4.19), (4.12), and DEC5, we have

$$HoldsAt(AlarmTime(Clock, 2), 2)$$
 (4.20)

From (4.14) (which follows from (4.18)), (4.3) (which follows from (4.15)), and DEC9, we have

$$HoldsAt(AlarmOn(Clock), 2)$$
 (4.21)

From (4.20), (4.21), and (4.8) (which follows from (4.18)), we have *Happens* (*StartBeeping*(*Clock*), 2). From this, (4.5) (which follows from (4.15)), and DEC9, we have *HoldsAt*(*Beeping*(*Clock*), 3).

4.2 PREVENTING REPEATED TRIGGERING

As long as the condition of a trigger axiom is true, an event is triggered. We must take steps to ensure that events are not repeatedly triggered. In the example in Section 4.1.1, the trigger axiom (4.8) does not repeatedly trigger because the condition is true only at a single instant, when the alarm timepoint equals the current timepoint. In most other cases, we will require a method to prevent repeated triggering.

This may be accomplished using trigger axioms and effect axioms of the form

$$\neg HoldsAt(\beta, \tau) \land \gamma \Rightarrow Happens(\alpha, \tau)$$

$$Initiates(\alpha, \beta, \tau)$$

or

$$HoldsAt(\beta, \tau) \land \gamma \Rightarrow Happens(\alpha, \tau)$$

 $Terminates(\alpha, \beta, \tau).$

4.2.1 EXAMPLE: BANK ACCOUNT SERVICE FEE

An example in which we prevent the repeated triggering of events in this way is the charging of service fees. We formalize a bank account that charges a monthly service fee if the balance falls below a minimum amount at any time during the month.

First, we describe the basic operation of the account using effect axioms. If the balance of account a_1 is greater than or equal to some amount and that amount is transferred from a_1 to account a_2 , then the balance of a_2 increases by that amount and the balance of a_1 decreases by that amount:

 $x_3 > 0 \land x_1 \ge x_3 \Rightarrow$

HoldsAt(Balance(
$$a_1, x_1$$
), t) \land (4.22)
HoldsAt(Balance(a_2, x_2), t) \land
 $x_3 > 0 \land x_1 \ge x_3 \Rightarrow$
Initiates(Transfer(a_1, a_2, x_3), Balance($a_2, x_2 + x_3$), t)
HoldsAt(Balance(a_1, x_1), t) \land (4.23)
HoldsAt(Balance(a_2, x_2), t) \land
 $x_3 > 0 \land x_1 \ge x_3 \Rightarrow$
Terminates(Transfer(a_1, a_2, x_3), Balance(a_2, x_2), t)
HoldsAt(Balance(a_1, x_1), t) \land (4.24)
HoldsAt(Balance(a_2, x_2), t) \land

Initiates(Transfer(
$$a_1, a_2, x_3$$
), Balance($a_1, x_1 - x_3$), t)
HoldsAt(Balance(a_1, x_1), t) \land (4.25)
HoldsAt(Balance(a_2, x_2), t) \land

$$x_3 > 0 \land x_1 \ge x_3 \Rightarrow$$

Terminates(Transfer(a_1, a_2, x_3), Balance(a_1, x_1), t)

We have a state constraint that says that an account has a unique balance at any given time:

$$HoldsAt(Balance(a, x_1), t) \land HoldsAt(Balance(a, x_2), t) \Rightarrow$$
 (4.26)
 $x_1 = x_2$

We also have a trigger axiom that says that if the balance in an account falls below the minimum balance and a service fee has not yet been charged to the account, then a service fee is charged to the account:

$$HoldsAt(Balance(a, x), t) \land \qquad (4.27)$$

$$x < MinimumBalance(a) \land$$

$$\neg HoldsAt(ServiceFeeCharged(a), t) \Rightarrow$$

$$Happens(ChargeServiceFee(a), t)$$

When a service fee is charged to an account, a note is made of this fact so that the account is not repeatedly charged:

$$Initiates(Charge Service Fee(a), Service Fee Charged(a), t)$$
 (4.28)

This is reset once each month:

$$EndOfMonth(t) \Rightarrow Happens(MonthlyReset(a), t) \tag{4.29}$$

$$Forming tes(MonthlyReset(a), ServiceFee(Charned(a), t) \tag{4.20}$$

$$Terminates(MonthlyReset(a), ServiceFeeCharged(a), t)$$
 (4.30)

If a service fee is charged to an account, then the balance of the account decreases by the amount of the service fee:

$$HoldsAt(Balance(a, x), t) \Rightarrow$$
 (4.31)
 $Initiates(ChargeServiceFee(a), Balance(a, x - ServiceFee(a)), t)$

$$HoldsAt(Balance(a, x), t) \Rightarrow$$
 (4.32)
 $Terminates(ChargeServiceFee(a), Balance(a, x), t)$

Let us use the following observations and narrative about two bank accounts. Initially, a service fee has not been charged to the first account, the balance in both accounts is 1000, the minimum balance of the first account is 500, and the service fee of the first account is 5:

$$\neg HoldsAt(ServiceFeeCharged(Account1), 0) \qquad (4.33) \\ HoldsAt(Balance(Account1, 1000), 0) \qquad (4.34) \\ HoldsAt(Balance(Account2, 1000), 0) \qquad (4.35) \\ MinimumBalance(Account1) = 500 \qquad (4.36) \\ ServiceFee(Account1) = 5 \qquad (4.37) \\ \neg ReleasedAt(f, t) \qquad (4.38)$$

Two transfers are made from the first account to the second account. A transfer of 200 is made and then a transfer of 400 is made:

72

We can show that, after these transfers, the balance in the first account will be 395. **Proposition 4.2.** Let $\Sigma = (4.22) \wedge (4.23) \wedge (4.24) \wedge (4.25) \wedge (4.28) \wedge (4.30) \wedge (4.31) \wedge (4.32)$, $\Delta = (4.27) \wedge (4.29) \wedge (4.39) \wedge (4.40)$, $\Omega = U[Transfer, Charge ServiceFee, MonthlyReset] \wedge U[Balance, ServiceFeeCharged]$, $\Psi = (4.26)$, and $\Gamma = (4.33) \wedge (4.34) \wedge (4.35) \wedge (4.36) \wedge (4.37) \wedge (4.38)$. Then we have

 $CIRC[\Sigma; Initiates, Terminates, Releases] \land CIRC[\Delta; Happens] \land \\ \Omega \land \Psi \land \Gamma \land DEC \vdash HoldsAt(Balance(Account1, 395), 3)$

Proof. From $CIRC[\Sigma; Initiates, Terminates, Releases]$ and Theorems 2.1 and 2.2, we have

Initiates (e, f, t)
$$\Leftrightarrow$$
 (4.41)
$$\exists a_1, a_2, x_1, x_2, x_3 \ (e = Transfer(a_1, a_2, x_3) \land f = Balance(a_2, x_2 + x_3) \land HoldsAt(Balance(a_1, x_1), t) \land HoldsAt(Balance(a_2, x_2), t) \land x_3 > 0 \land x_1 \geq x_3) \lor \\
\exists a_1, a_2, x_1, x_2, x_3 \ (e = Transfer(a_1, a_2, x_3) \land f = Balance(a_1, x_1 - x_3) \land HoldsAt(Balance(a_1, x_1), t) \land HoldsAt(Balance(a_2, x_2), t) \land x_3 > 0 \land x_1 \geq x_3) \lor \\
\exists a (e = ChargeServiceFee(a) \land f = ServiceFeeCharged(a)) \lor \\
\exists a, x \ (e = ChargeServiceFee(a) \land f = ServiceFeeCharged(a)) \lor \\
\exists a_1, a_2, x_1, x_2, x_3 \ (e = Transfer(a_1, a_2, x_3) \land f = Balance(a_2, x_2) \land HoldsAt(Balance(a_1, x_1), t) \land HoldsAt(Balance(a_1, x_1), t) \land HoldsAt(Balance(a_2, x_2), t) \land x_3 > 0 \land x_1 \geq x_3) \lor \\
\exists a_1, a_2, x_1, x_2, x_3 \ (e = Transfer(a_1, a_2, x_3) \land f = Balance(a_1, x_1) \land HoldsAt(Balance(a_1, x_1), t) \land HoldsAt(Balance(a_1, x_1), t) \land HoldsAt(Balance(a_1, x_1), t) \land HoldsAt(Balance(a_1, x_2), t) \land x_3 > 0 \land x_1 \geq x_3) \lor \\
\exists a \ (e = MonthlyReset(a) \land f = ServiceFeeCharged(a)) \lor \exists a \ (e = MonthlyReset(a) \land f = ServiceFeeCharged(a)) \lor \exists a \ (e = MonthlyReset(a) \land f = ServiceFeeCharged(a)) \lor \exists a \ (e = MonthlyReset(a) \land f = ServiceFeeCharged(a)) \lor \exists a \ (e = MonthlyReset(a) \land f = ServiceFeeCharged(a)) \lor \exists a \ (e = MonthlyReset(a) \land f = ServiceFeeCharged(a)) \lor \exists a \ (e = MonthlyReset(a) \land f = ServiceFeeCharged(a)) \lor \exists a \ (e = MonthlyReset(a) \land f = ServiceFeeCharged(a)) \lor \exists a \ (e = MonthlyReset(a) \land f = ServiceFeeCharged(a)) \lor \exists a \ (e = MonthlyReset(a) \land f = ServiceFeeCharged(a)) \lor \exists a \ (e = MonthlyReset(a) \land f = ServiceFeeCharged(a)) \lor \exists a \ (e = MonthlyReset(a) \land f = ServiceFeeCharged(a)) \lor \exists a \ (e = MonthlyReset(a) \land f = ServiceFeeCharged(a)) \lor \exists a \ (e = MonthlyReset(a) \land f = ServiceFeeCharged(a)) \lor \exists a \ (e = MonthlyReset(a) \land f = ServiceFeeCharged(a)) \lor \exists a \ (e = MonthlyReset(a) \land f = ServiceFeeCharged(a)) \lor \exists a \ (e = MonthlyReset(a) \land f = ServiceFeeCharged(a)) \lor \exists a \ (e = MonthlyReset(a) \land f = ServiceFeeCharged(a)) \lor a \ (e = MonthlyReset(a) \land f = ServiceFeeCharged(a)) \lor a \ (e =$$

$$\exists a, x (e = ChargeServiceFee(a) \land$$

 $f = Balance(a, x) \land$

HoldsAt(Balance(a, x), t))

$$\neg Releases(e, f, t)$$
 (4.43)

From $CIRC[\Delta; Happens]$ and Theorem 2.1, we have

$$Happens(e,t) \Leftrightarrow$$
 (4.44)

 $\exists a, x (e = ChargeServiceFee(a) \land$

 $HoldsAt(Balance(a, x), t) \land$

 $x < MinimumBalance(a) \land$

 $\neg HoldsAt(ServiceFeeCharged(a), t)) \lor$

 $\exists a (e = MonthlyReset(a) \land EndOfMonth(t)) \lor$

 $(e = Transfer(Account1, Account2, 200) \land t = 0) \lor$

 $(e = Transfer(Account1, Account2, 400) \land t = 1)$

From (4.39) (which follows from (4.44)), (4.34), (4.35), 200 > 0, $1000 \ge 200$, (4.24) (which follows from (4.41)), and DEC9, we have

$$HoldsAt(Balance(Account1, 800), 1)$$
 (4.45)

From (4.39) (which follows from (4.44)), (4.34), (4.35), 200 > 0, $1000 \ge 200$, (4.22) (which follows from (4.41)), and DEC9, we have

$$HoldsAt(Balance(Account2, 1200), 1)$$
 (4.46)

From (4.26), (4.34), (4.36), $\neg (1000 < 500)$, and (4.44), we have $\neg Happens(Charge ServiceFee(Account 1), 0)$. From this, (4.44), and (4.41), we have $\neg \exists e (Happens(e, 0) \land Initiates(e, ServiceFeeCharged(Account 1), 0))$. From this, (4.33), (4.38), and DEC6, we have

$$\neg HoldsAt(ServiceFeeCharged(Account1), 1)$$
 (4.47)

From (4.40) (which follows from (4.44)), (4.45), (4.46), 400 > 0, $800 \ge 400$, (4.24) (which follows from (4.41)), and DEC9, we have

$$HoldsAt(Balance(Account1, 400), 2)$$
 (4.48)

From (4.26), (4.45), (4.36), \neg (800 < 500), and (4.44), we have \neg Happens(Charge ServiceFee(Account1), 1). From this, (4.44), and (4.41), we have \neg ∃e (Happens(e, 1) \land Initiates(e, ServiceFeeCharged(Account1), 1)). From this, (4.47), (4.38), and DEC6, we have

$\neg HoldsAt(ServiceFeeCharged(Account1), 2)$

From this, (4.48), (4.36), 400 < 500, and (4.27) (which follows from (4.44)), we have Happens(ChargeServiceFee(Account1), 2). From this, (4.48), (4.37), (4.31) (which follows from (4.41)), and DEC9, we have HoldsAt(Balance(Account1, 395), 3).

4.3 TRIGGERED FLUENTS

74

So far, we have discussed how a trigger axiom is used to represent that a certain event occurs when a certain condition becomes true. What if we would like to represent that a fluent becomes true (or false) when a condition becomes true? This cannot be represented directly in the event calculus. Instead, we must introduce an event that is triggered by the condition and that initiates or terminates the fluent.

Thus, we represent that the condition γ initiates a fluent β as follows:

 $\gamma \Rightarrow Happens(\alpha, \tau)$ $Initiates(\alpha, \beta, t)$

We represent that the condition γ terminates a fluent β as follows:

 $\gamma \Rightarrow Happens(\alpha, \tau)$ Terminates(α, β, t)

BIBLIOGRAPHIC NOTES

Shanahan (1990) introduced an early form of the trigger axiom into a simplified version of the original event calculus (Kowalski & Sergot, 1986). Shanahan (1995a, pp. 268-272; 1997b, pp. 305-313) uses a predicate *Triggers*(*s*, *e*) to represent that an event *e* occurs in state *s*. Trigger axioms in the form used in this book were introduced by Shanahan (1996, p. 685) and are discussed in detail by Shanahan (1997b, pp. 258-265, 325-329). The method for representing triggered fluents is from Morgenstern (2001, p. 353).

Proposals for incorporating triggered events into the situation calculus have been made by Pinto (1994), R. Miller (1996), and Reiter (1996). See the discussion in the Bibliographic notes of Chapter 16. Pinto (1998a) uses triggered events in the situation calculus to represent the starting and stopping of current in an electrical circuit.

Tran and Baral (2004b) incorporate triggered events into an action language inspired by \mathcal{A} (Gelfond & Lifschitz, 1993), implement the language as an answer set program (Baral, 2003), and apply triggered events to the modeling of molecular interactions in cells. The triggering rule (Tran & Baral, 2004b, p. 555)

$$g_1, \ldots, g_m$$
 n_triggers b

represents that action b normally occurs when conditions g_1, \ldots, g_m are true. The inhibition rule (p. 555)

$$h_1,\ldots,h_l$$
 inhibits c

represents that action c does not occur when conditions h_1, \ldots, h_l are true.

Triggered events are represented in action language C+E. Giunchiglia, Lee, Lifschitz, McCain, and Turner (2004) using action dynamic laws of the form (p. 70)

caused F if G

where F is an action and G is a condition. C+ is discussed in Section 16.3.1.

EXERCISES

- **4.1** Add a snooze alarm to the alarm clock axiomatization in Section 4.1.1. If, when the alarm is beeping, an agent presses the snooze button, then the alarm stops beeping and starts beeping again after nine timepoints.
- **4.2** Use the extended alarm clock axiomatization in Exercise 4.1 to prove that, if a particular alarm clock is set, the clock starts beeping at the appropriate time, and an agent hits the snooze button, then the alarm stops beeping after that time and is beeping 10 timepoints later.
- **4.3** Rework the axiomatization in Section 4.2.1 so that a monthly fee is charged at the end of each month rather than immediately.
- **4.4** Formalize the operation of a mousetrap. Prove that a mouse entering the trap is caught.
- **4.5** Formalize a price notification service for traders of financial instruments. When the price of a financial instrument falls below or rises above a certain level, the service informs the trader. Prove that, if the trader requests notification of when stock XYZ falls below 100, then when the stock falls below that level the service informs the trader.
- **4.6** Formalize that you introduce yourself when meeting someone for the first time.

282 0000

- (1) A der son ezer den fortige utagn glock axie, in ere mer in Seenan Adellag.

 What the classest beginning an agent provide a concrete name, then regulation

 stops beginnered statis beginning against the compounts.
- 4.2 Use the expended characteristics, actions again on Exercise 1. To prove their it is proven their it is proportion of application of applications of the characteristic state. Such as the open provention that is considered to the characteristic state.
 (or classification for the characteristic large.)
- 13 Recent the acceptant of in Section 2.3, so that a recently to is charged at the polyrice of the acceptant transformed at the contract of the contract of
 - 4.4 Formatics the operation of a mouse itso, if swelther a collect entertainment is to a release.
 - 4. Formalis a groce de incered son se, per ruces or mentrich manning or officer. Ny harest properties of the control distribution of the control of the c
 - A de l'immandre man y au anno martin de la sentre de comprime y mai communitation de de la communitation de de La communitation de la communitation de la sentre de communitation de la communitation de la communitation de

The Commonsense Law of Inertia

A quality of the commonsense world is that objects tend to stay in the same state unless they are affected by events. A book sitting on a table remains on the table unless it is picked up, a light stays on until it is turned off, and a falling object continues to fall until it hits something. This is known as the commonsense law of inertia. This chapter discusses the representation of the commonsense law of inertia in the event calculus. We retrace the development of the DEC axioms, and we discuss the enforcement of the commonsense law of inertia and the release of fluents from inertia.

5.1 REPRESENTATION OF THE COMMONSENSE LAW OF INERTIA

How should we represent the commonsense law of inertia? Let us consider a version of the event calculus with integer time, using the example of turning on a light. We first represent the effects of events; we represent that, if a light is turned on, then the light will be on at the next timepoint:

$$Happens(TurnOn(l), t) \Rightarrow HoldsAt(On(l), t+1)$$
 (5.1)

Suppose two lights are off at timepoint 0, and the second light is turned on at timepoint 0:

$\neg HoldsAt(On(Light1), 0)$	(5.2)
$\neg HoldsAt(On(Light2), 0)$	(5.3)
Happens(TurnOn(Light2), 0)	(5.4)
$Light2 \neq Light1$	(5.5)

We can show that the second light will be on at timepoint 1.

Proposition 5.1. If $\Sigma = (5.1)$, $\Delta = (5.4)$, $\Omega = (5.5)$, and $\Gamma = (5.2) \wedge (5.3)$, then $\Sigma \wedge \Delta \wedge \Omega \wedge \Gamma \vdash HoldsAt(On(Light2), 1)$.

Proof. From (5.1) and (5.4), we have HoldsAt(On(Light2), 1).

5.1.1 FRAME PROBLEM

What can we say about the first light? We would like to reason that, because we were not told that the first light was turned on, it will still be off: $\neg HoldsAt(On(Light1), 1)$. Sadly, this does not follow from the domain description $\Sigma \wedge \Delta \wedge \Omega \wedge \Gamma$. The trouble

is that we have represented which fluents change truth value when an event occurs but we have not represented which fluents do not change truth value. The problem of representing and reasoning about which fluents do not change when an event occurs is known as the *frame problem*. Several types of axioms have been proposed for specifying when fluents do not change truth value.

5.1.2 CLASSICAL FRAME AXIOMS

A classical frame axiom represents that a given fluent does not change when a given event occurs. For example, we represent that, if light l is off and a different light is turned on, then l will still be off:

$$\neg HoldsAt(On(l_1), t) \land$$

$$Happens(TurnOn(l_2), t) \land$$

$$l_1 \neq l_2 \Rightarrow$$

$$\neg HoldsAt(On(l_1), t+1)$$

$$(5.6)$$

We can then show that after the second light is turned on, the first light is off.

Proposition 5.2. If $\Sigma = (5.1)$, $\Delta = (5.4)$, $\Omega = (5.5)$, $\Gamma = (5.2) \land (5.3)$, and CFA = (5.6), then $\Sigma \land \Delta \land \Omega \land \Gamma \land CFA \vdash \neg HoldsAt(On(Light1), 1)$.

Proof. From (5.2), (5.4), (5.5), and (5.6), we have
$$\neg HoldsAt(On(Light1), 1)$$
.

Unfortunately, classical frame axioms are unable to cope with several events occurring at one timepoint. For instance, if we are also given that the first light is turned on at timepoint 0:

$$Happens(TurnOn(Light1), 0)$$
 (5.7)

then inconsistency results.

Proposition 5.3. *If* $\Sigma = (5.1)$, $\Delta = (5.4) \wedge (5.7)$, $\Omega = (5.5)$, $\Gamma = (5.2) \wedge (5.3)$, and *CFA* = (5.6), then $\Sigma \wedge \Delta \wedge \Omega \wedge \Gamma \wedge CFA$ is inconsistent. *Proof.* From (5.2), (5.4), (5.5), and (5.6), we have

$$\neg HoldsAt(On(Light1), 1)$$
 (5.8)

From (5.1) and (5.7), we have HoldsAt(On(Light1), 1), which contradicts (5.8). Notice also that, if we remove (5.4), then we are unable to conclude $\neg HoldsAt(On(Light1), 1)$. Classical frame axioms were developed for use within the situation calculus, which is discussed in Section 16.1. They are only useful in the event calculus if exactly one event occurs at each timepoint.

5.1.3 EXPLANATION CLOSURE AXIOMS

Another type of axiom, an *explanation closure axiom*, represents that a given fluent does not change unless certain events occur. For example, we represent that, if a light is off and the light is not turned on, then the light will still be off:

$$\neg HoldsAt(On(l), t) \land$$

$$\neg Happens(TurnOn(l), t) \Rightarrow$$

$$\neg HoldsAt(On(l), t + 1)$$
(5.9)

If we had

$$\neg Happens(TurnOn(LightI), 0)$$

then we could show $\neg HoldsAt(On(Light1), 1)$ from (5.2) and (5.9). But this does not yet follow from the domain description. An additional mechanism is required to limit events to those that are known to have occurred.

5.1.4 MINIMIZING EVENT OCCURRENCES

We use the mechanism of circumscription described in Section 2.6 to minimize event occurrences, by minimizing the extension of the *Happens* predicate. This gives us the desired result. If the first and second lights are initially off and the second light is turned on, then the first light will still be off:

Proposition 5.4. Let $\Sigma = (5.1)$, $\Delta = (5.4)$, $\Omega = (5.5)$, $\Gamma = (5.2) \land (5.3)$, and ECA = (5.9). Then we have $\Sigma \land CIRC[\Delta; Happens] \land \Omega \land \Gamma \land ECA \vdash \neg HoldsAt$ (On(Light1), 1).

Proof. From $CIRC[\Delta; Happens]$ and Theorem 2.1, we have

$$Happens(e, t) \Leftrightarrow (e = TurnOn(Light2) \land t = 0)$$

From this and (5.5), we have $\neg Happens(TurnOn(Light1), 0)$. From this, (5.2), and (5.9), we have $\neg HoldsAt(On(Light1), 1)$.

5.1.5 INTRODUCTION OF INITIATES PREDICATE

So far, this method requires us to enumerate all explanation closure axioms for the domain such as (5.9). We can avoid this by introducing the predicate Initiates(e, f, t), which represents that, if event e occurs at timepoint t, then fluent f will be true at t+1:

$$Happens(e,t) \wedge Initiates(e,f,t) \Rightarrow$$
 (5.10)
 $HoldsAt(f,t+1)$

We can then generalize the explanation closure axiom (5.9) into:

$$\neg HoldsAt(f,t) \land \tag{5.11}$$

$$\neg \exists e \ (Happens(e,t) \land Initiates(e,f,t)) \Rightarrow$$

$$\neg HoldsAt(f,t+1)$$

Now suppose that instead of (5.1), we have

Initiates(TurnOn(l), On(l), t)

In order to show $\neg HoldsAt(On(Light1), 1)$ from $\neg HoldsAt(On(Light1), 0)$, we must show

$$\neg \exists e (Happens(e, 0) \land Initiates(e, On(Light1), 0))$$

From the circumscription of *Happens* in (5.4), we have

$$Happens(e, 0) \Leftrightarrow e = TurnOn(Light2)$$

Thus we require:

 \neg Initiates(TurnOn(Light2), On(Light1), 0)

But this does not yet follow from the domain description. We require a method to limit the effects of events to those that are known.

5.1.6 MINIMIZING EVENT EFFECTS

Again we use circumscription, this time to minimize the effects of events, by minimizing the extension of *Initiates*. We can again show, this time using *Initiates*, that after turning on the second light, the first light will still be off:

Proposition 5.5. Let $\Sigma = (5.12)$, $\Delta = (5.4)$, $\Omega = (5.5)$, $\Gamma = (5.2) \land (5.3)$, and $DI = (5.10) \land (5.11)$. Then we have $CIRC[\Sigma; Initiates] \land CIRC[\Delta; Happens] \land \Omega \land \Gamma \land D1 \vdash \neg HoldsAt(On(LightI), 1)$.

Proof. From $CIRC[\Sigma; Initiates]$ and Theorem 2.1, we have

$$Initiates(e, f, t) \Leftrightarrow \exists l \ (e = TurnOn(l) \land f = On(l))$$
 (5.12)

From $CIRC[\Delta; Happens]$ and Theorem 2.1, we have

$$Happens(e, t) \Leftrightarrow (e = TurnOn(Light2) \land t = 0)$$
 (5.13)

From (5.12) and (5.5), we have

 \neg Initiates(TurnOn(Light2), On(Light1), 0)

From this and (5.13), we have

 $\neg \exists e (Happens(e, 0) \land Initiates(e, On(Light1), 0))$

From this, (5.2), and (5.11), we have $\neg HoldsAt(On(Light1), 1)$.

These are the beginnings of DEC. The axiom (5.11) is similar to DEC6, and (5.10) is the same as DEC9.

5.1.7 INTRODUCTION OF TERMINATES PREDICATE

Along similar lines, we introduce the predicate Terminates(e, f, t), which represents that, if event e occurs at timepoint t, then fluent f will be false at t + 1. We have an axiom similar to DEC5 and one that is the same as DEC10:

$$HoldsAt(f,t) \land \qquad (5.14)$$

$$\neg \exists e (Happens(e,t) \land Terminates(e,f,t)) \Rightarrow \\ HoldsAt(f,t+1)$$

$$Happens(e,t) \land Terminates(e,f,t) \Rightarrow$$
 (5.15)
 $\neg HoldsAt(f,t+1)$

5.1.8 DISCUSSION

The effects of events are enforced by (5.10) and (5.15), whereas the commonsense law of inertia is enforced by (5.11) and (5.14). In the conjunction of axioms EC, the

effects of events are enforced by EC14 and EC15, whereas the commonsense law of inertia is enforced by EC9, EC10, EC14, and EC15. For instance, EC14 specifies that a fluent f that is initiated by an event that occurs at timepoint t_1 is true at timepoint $t_2 > t_1$ provided that $\neg StoppedIn(t_1, f, t_2)$, which by EC3 is equivalent to

$$\neg \exists e, t (Happens(e, t) \land t_1 < t < t_2 \land Terminates(e, f, t))$$

Notice that EC14 and EC15 enforce both the effects of events and the commonsense law of inertia. EC14 and EC15 enforce the commonsense law of inertia after a fluent has been initiated or terminated by an occurring event, whereas EC9 and EC10 enforce the commonsense law of inertia in all cases. If, for example, the truth value of a fluent is known at timepoint t, then EC9 and EC10 can be used to determine the truth value of the fluent after timepoint t.

Some redundancy exists between, say, EC9 and EC14, because after a fluent is initiated by an occurring event, both EC9 and EC14 specify that the fluent is true until it is terminated by an occurring event. This redundancy is not present in the conjunction of axioms DEC.

5.2 REPRESENTING RELEASE FROM THE COMMONSENSE LAW OF INERTIA

We may not always wish the commonsense law of inertia to be in force. In this section, we describe how fluents can be released from the commonsense law of inertia and then, at a later time, can again be made subject to this law.

5.2.1 EXAMPLE: YALE SHOOTING SCENARIO

We start by considering the example of shooting a turkey. If a gun is loaded at timepoint 1 and used to shoot a turkey at timepoint 3, then the gun will fire and the turkey will no longer be alive. This simple example assumes that the shooter does not miss. In this case, the fact that the gun is loaded is subject to the commonsense law of inertia

This example is due to Steve Hanks and Drew McDermott. If an agent loads a gun, then the gun will be loaded:

$$Initiates(Load(a, g), Loaded(g), t)$$
 (5.16)

If a gun is loaded and agent a_1 shoots the gun at agent a_2 , then a_2 will no longer be alive:

$$HoldsAt(Loaded(g), t) \Rightarrow$$
 (5.17)
 $Terminates(Shoot(a_1, a_2, g), Alive(a_2), t)$

If a gun is loaded and an agent shoots the gun, then the gun will no longer be loaded:

$$HoldsAt(Loaded(g), t) \Rightarrow$$
 (5.18)
 $Terminates(Shoot(a_1, a_2, g), Loaded(g), t)$

Consider the following observations and narrative. Initially, the turkey is alive and the gun is not loaded:

$$HoldsAt(Alive(Turkey), 0)$$
 (5.19)
 $\neg HoldsAt(Loaded(Gun), 0)$ (5.20)

Nathan loads the gun at timepoint 0, waits at timepoint 1, and shoots the turkey at timepoint 2:

$$Happens(Load(Nathan, Gun), 0)$$
 (5.21)

$$Happens(Wait(Nathan), 1)$$
 (5.22)

$$Happens(Shoot(Nathan, Turkey, Gun), 2)$$
 (5.23)

We can then show that the turkey will no longer be alive at timepoint 3.

Proposition 5.6. Let $\Sigma = (5.16) \land (5.17) \land (5.18)$, $\Delta = (5.21) \land (5.22) \land (5.23)$, $\Omega = U[Load, Wait, Shoot] \land U[Loaded, Alive]$, and $\Gamma = (5.19) \land (5.20)$, and $D2 = (5.10) \land (5.11) \land (5.14) \land (5.15)$. Then we have

$$CIRC[\Sigma; Initiates, Terminates, Releases] \land CIRC[\Delta; Happens] \land \\ \Omega \land \Gamma \land D2 \vdash \neg HoldsAt(Alive(Turkey), 3)$$

Proof. See Exercise 5.3.

5.2.2 RELEASING FROM INERTIA

By contrast, consider a gun that is loaded at timepoint 1 and whose chamber is spun at timepoint 2. If the trigger is pulled at timepoint 3, then the gun may or may not fire (the chamber may still be spinning). We may model this by specifying that, after the gun's chamber is spun, the gun's readiness to shoot is released from the commonsense law of inertia. Then, at any given timepoint after the gun's readiness to shoot is released, the gun may or may not be loaded.

This models a chamber that continues to spin, so that at any given timepoint after the chamber is spun, the gun may or may not be ready to shoot, independently of whether it is ready to shoot at other timepoints. Thus, if the domain of the timepoint sort is the integers and the gun's readiness to shoot is released for n timepoints, then there are 2^n classes of models. (We might instead wish to model a chamber that spins only for an instant. For a way of doing this, see Section 9.1.1.)

We now introduce the *Releases* and *ReleasedAt* predicates. Releases(e, f, t) represents that, if event e occurs at timepoint t, then fluent f will be released from the commonsense law of inertia at t+1. ReleasedAt(f, t) represents that fluent f is released from the commonsense law of inertia at timepoint t. Thus, we have

$$Happens(e,t) \land Releases(e,f,t) \Rightarrow ReleasedAt(f,t+1)$$
 (5.24)

This is DEC11. We can use *Releases* and *ReleasedAt* to represent our uncertainty about whether a given fluent is true or false at a given timepoint.

We incorporate *ReleasedAt* into (5.14) and (5.11), which gives us the following revised generalized explanation closure axioms:

$$HoldsAt(f,t) \land \neg ReleasedAt(f,t) \land$$
 (5.25)
 $\neg \exists e (Happens(e,t) \land Terminates(e,f,t)) \Rightarrow$ $HoldsAt(f,t+1)$

$$\neg HoldsAt(f,t) \land \neg ReleasedAt(f,t) \land$$

$$\neg \exists e (Happens(e,t) \land Initiates(e,f,t)) \Rightarrow$$

$$\neg HoldsAt(f,t+1)$$
(5.26)

(5.25) is DEC5 and (5.26) is DEC6.

Thus at any given timepoint a fluent either is, or is not, subject to the commonsense law of inertia. When a fluent is subject to the commonsense law of inertia, its truth value will be the same as its previous value, unless the fluent is true and it is terminated by an occurring event or the fluent is false and it is initiated by an occurring event. When a fluent is released from the commonsense law of inertia, its truth value may or may not be the same as it was previously. That is, its truth value may fluctuate.

5.2.3 RESTORING INERTIA

We have so far specified how a fluent becomes released from the commonsense law of inertia. We must also specify how a fluent is again made subject to this law. Although we could add an *Unreleases* predicate, it is convenient to allow *Inititates* and *Terminates* to serve this role because, when a fluent is made subject to the commonsense law of inertia, its truth value is usually also specified.

We have an axiom stating that, if a fluent is initiated or terminated by an event that occurs at timepoint t, then the fluent will no longer be released from the commonsense law of inertia at t + 1:

$$Happens(e,t) \land (Initiates(e,f,t) \lor Terminates(e,f,t)) \Rightarrow$$
 (5.27)
 $\neg ReleasedAt(f,t+1)$

This is DEC12.

5.2.4 EXPLANATION CLOSURE AXIOMS FOR RELEASEDAT

So far, we have specified when *ReleasedAt* changes truth value, using (5.24) and (5.27). We have not specified when this predicate does not change truth value. We therefore add the following two generalized explanation closure axioms for *ReleasedAt*:

$$ReleasedAt(f,t) \land \qquad (5.28)$$

$$\neg \exists e \ (Happens(e,t) \land (Initiates(e,f,t) \lor Terminates(e,f,t))) \Rightarrow \qquad ReleasedAt(f,t+1)$$

$$\neg ReleasedAt(f,t) \land (5.29)$$

$$\neg \exists e (Happens(e,t) \land Releases(e,f,t)) \Rightarrow$$

$$\neg ReleasedAt(f,t+1)$$

(5.28) is DEC7 and (5.29) is DEC8.

5.2.5 EXAMPLE: RUSSIAN TURKEY SCENARIO

This example is due to Erik Sandewall. We modify the example in Section 5.2.1 as follows. If a gun is loaded and an agent spins the gun, then the gun's readiness to shoot will no longer be subject to the commonsense law of inertia:

$$HoldsAt(Loaded(g), t) \Rightarrow Releases(Spin(a, g), Loaded(g), t)$$
 (5.30)

Instead of waiting at timepoint 1, Nathan spins the gun:

$$Happens(Spin(Nathan, Gun), 1)$$
 (5.31)

Notice that given axioms (5.15), (5.27), and (5.29), axiom (5.18) ensures that, after a loaded gun is fired, the gun is no longer loaded and *Loaded(Gun)* is no longer released from the commonsense law of inertia.

The fluent term *Alive(Turkey)* is subject to the commonsense law of inertia at all times:

$$\neg ReleasedAt(Alive(Turkey), t)$$
 (5.32)

Only initially is *Loaded(Gun)* subject to the commonsense law of inertia:

$$\neg ReleasedAt(Loaded(Gun), 0)$$
 (5.33)

We can then show that there are two possible outcomes: (1) If the gun is loaded at timepoint 2, then the turkey will no longer be alive at timepoint 3, and (2) if the gun is not loaded at timepoint 2, then the turkey will still be alive at timepoint 3.

Proposition 5.7. Let $\Sigma = (5.16) \land (5.17) \land (5.18) \land (5.30), \Delta = (5.21) \land (5.31) \land (5.23), \ \Omega = U[Load, Spin, Shoot] \land U[Loaded, Alive], \ and \ \Gamma = (5.19) \land (5.20) \land (5.32) \land (5.33), \ and \ D3 = (5.10) \land (5.15) \land (5.24) \land (5.25) \land (5.26) \land (5.27) \land (5.28) \land (5.29). \ Then we have$

$$CIRC[\Sigma; Initiates, Terminates, Releases] \land (5.34)$$

$$CIRC[\Delta; Happens] \land \Omega \land \Gamma \land D3 \land HoldsAt(Loaded(Gun), 2)$$

$$\vdash \neg HoldsAt(Alive(Turkey), 3)$$

as well as

$$CIRC[\Sigma; Initiates, Terminates, Releases] \land (5.35)$$

$$CIRC[\Delta; Happens] \land \Omega \land \Gamma \land D3 \land \neg HoldsAt(Loaded(Gun), 2)$$

 $\vdash HoldsAt(Alive(Turkey), 3)$

Proof. See Exercise 5.4.

In the Russian turkey scenario, release from the commonsense law of inertia is used to model nondeterminism. Nondeterminism is discussed further in Chapter 9. Release from the commonsense law of inertia is also useful for representing indirect effects (discussed in Chapter 6) and continuous change (discussed in Chapter 7).

5.3 RELEASE AXIOMS

A fluent is released from the commonsense law of inertia as follows.

Definition 5.1. If γ is a condition, α is an event term, β is a fluent term, and τ is a timepoint term, then

$$\gamma \Rightarrow Releases(\alpha, \beta, \tau)$$

is a *release axiom*. This represents that, if γ is true and α occurs at τ , then β will be released from the commonsense law of inertia after τ .

A fluent is again made subject to the commonsense law of inertia as follows. We represent that, if γ is true and α occurs at τ , then β will no longer be released from the commonsense law of inertia after τ using a positive or negative effect axiom:

$$\gamma \Rightarrow Initiates(\alpha, \beta, \tau)$$

 $\gamma \Rightarrow Terminates(\alpha, \beta, \tau)$

In the *Inititates* case, the fluent will become true and not released; in the *Terminates* case, the fluent will become false and not released.

In EC, a fluent is released for times greater than the time of the releasing event and is not released for times greater than the time of the initiating or terminating event. In DEC, a fluent is released starting one timepoint after the time of the releasing event and is not released starting one timepoint after the time of the initiating or terminating event. For example, suppose we have *Releases(Rel, Fluent, t)*, *Happens(Rel, 1)*, *Initiates(Init, Fluent, t)*, and *Happens(Init, 4)*. Figure 5.1 shows when *Fluent* is released using the conjunction of axioms EC; Figure 5.2 shows when *Fluent* is released using DEC.

FIGURE 5.1

Released fluent in EC.

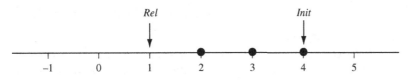

FIGURE 5.2

Released fluent in DEC.

BIBLIOGRAPHIC NOTES

Frame problem

The frame problem was first described by McCarthy and Hayes (1969, p. 487). According to Shanahan (1997b), "McCarthy relates that he was reading a book on geometry at the time he coined the term 'frame problem,' and that he thought of the frame problem as analogous to that of choosing a co-ordinate frame" (p. 25). Hayes (1971) defines a frame as "a classification of statements into groups which are independent in the sense that an action may alter members of one group without affecting any of the other groups" (p. 497). See also the discussions of McCarthy (1977, p. 1040) and Lifschitz (1990b, p. 366). An introduction to the frame problem is provided by Shanahan (2002), and a book-length treatment is provided by Shanahan (1997b). Earlier book-length discussions are provided by Brown (1987), Pylyshyn (1987), and Ford and Pylyshyn (1996).

Frame axioms

Frame axioms were introduced by McCarthy and Hayes (1969, pp. 484 and 485). Hayes (1971) was apparently the first to call them "'frame' axioms" (p. 514). We use the term *classical frame axiom* from Kautz and Selman (1996, p. 1197) to distinguish the frame axioms of McCarthy and Hayes from explanation closure axioms. Classical frame axioms were originally written in the situation calculus. Using Reiter's notation, a sample classical frame axiom is:

$$on(d_2, s) \wedge d_1 \neq d_2 \supset on(d_2, do(turn_off(d_1), s))$$

Using Shanahan's notation, the same axiom is written as:

```
Holds(On(d_2), s) \land d_1 \neq d_2 \rightarrow Holds(On(d_2), Result(TurnOff(d_1), s))
```

To handle e events and f fluents, on the order of $2 \cdot e \cdot f$ classical frame axioms are required (Reiter, 2001, p. 22).

Kowalski (1974, 1979, pp. 133-146) introduces a way of combining classical frame axioms that relies on representing that fluent $F(x_1, \ldots, x_n)$ is true in situation σ as $Holds(F(x_1, \ldots, x_n), \sigma)$ rather than $F(x_1, \ldots, x_n, \sigma)$. See the discussions of Nilsson (1980, pp. 311-315) and Shanahan (1997b, pp. 231-241). Using Shanahan's notation, suppose we have the effect axiom:

```
\neg Holds(On(d), Result(TurnOff(d), s))
```

We can then use a single frame axiom:

$$Holds(f, s) \land f \neq On(d) \rightarrow Holds(f, Result(TurnOff(d), s))$$

instead of several frame axioms:

```
Holds(On(d_2), s) \land d_1 \neq d_2 \rightarrow Holds(On(d_2), Result(TurnOff(d_1), s))

Holds(Broken(d_1), s) \rightarrow Holds(Broken(d_1), Result(TurnOff(d_1), s))
```

Explanation closure axioms were first proposed by Haas (1987), who called them "domain-specific frame axioms" (p. 343). They were further developed and named

"explanation-closure" axioms by Schubert (1990, p. 25). E. Davis (1990) proposed similar axioms for "framing primitive events by fluents" (p. 206). Using Reiter's situation calculus notation, a sample explanation closure axiom is:

$$on(d, s) \land \neg on(d, do(a, s)) \supset a = turn_off(d)$$

which corresponds to the single effect axiom:

$$\neg on(d, do(turn_off(d), s))$$

Pednault (1989) proposed two constraints to facilitate the generation of classical frame axioms: (1) separate effect axioms must be written for each fluent, and (2) the effects of actions must be completely specified by the effect axioms.

Synthesizing the proposals of Haas, Schubert, E. Davis, and Pednault, Reiter (1991; 2001, pp. 28-32) provided a method for automatically constructing explanation closure axioms given a set of effect axioms. To handle f fluents, on the order of $2 \cdot f$ explanation closure axioms are required (Reiter, 2001, p. 27). Explanation closure axioms were first used in the event calculus by Shanahan and Witkowski (2004). Axioms DEC5, DEC6, DEC7, and DEC8, which resemble explanation closure axioms extended to allow fluents to be released from the commonsense law of inertia, were introduced by Mueller (2004a). Our review of classical frame axioms and explanation closure axioms is loosely based on that of Ernst, Millstein, and Weld (1997, pp. 1170 and 1171). The form of explanation closure axiom we give,

$$HoldsAt(F, t) \land \neg Happens(E_1, t) \land \cdots \land \neg Happens(E_n, t) \Rightarrow HoldsAt(F, t + 1)$$

is logically equivalent to the form usually given:

$$HoldsAt(F, t) \land \neg HoldsAt(F, t + 1) \Rightarrow$$

 $Happens(E_1, t) \lor \cdots \lor Happens(E_n, t)$

Shanahan (1996, pp. 684 and 685, 1997b, pp. 315-330) introduced the forced separation version of the event calculus in which *Inititates*, *Terminates*, and *Releases* are circumscribed separately from *Happens* and the observation (*HoldsAt*) formulas and event calculus axioms are outside the scope of any circumscription. The technique of forced separation derives from the following previous proposals: (1) the filtered preferential entailment or filtering of Sandewall (1989b, 1994, pp. 213-215, 242, and 243), in which minimization is applied to effect axioms ("action laws") but not to observation formulas, which in turn derives from the preferential entailment of (Shoham 1988, p. 76); (2) the proposal of Crawford and Etherington (1992) to separate the description of the system from the observations; (3) the extension of Sandewall's techniques by Doherty and Łukaszewicz (1994) and Doherty (1994), in which circumscription is applied to schedule statements involving the Occlude predicate but not to observation statements or to the nochange axiom, as discussed in Section 16.2.1; (4) the method of Kartha and Lifschitz (1995), in which circumscription is applied to effect axioms and state constraints but not to observation formulas (Shanahan, 1997b, pp. 315-318); and (5) the method of F. Lin (1995), in which the Caused predicate is minimized using circumscription or predicate completion.

88

E. Davis (1990) discusses the need for axioms of "nonoccurrence of extraneous events" (p. 208) when using explanation closure axioms. The rationale for the use of circumscription over less powerful methods is given by Shanahan (1998):

We could use negation-as-failure (or rather, say, predicate completion). Using circumscription does allow for the addition of, for example, disjunctive facts, however. Predicate completion is only defined for a certain class of theories. Event [sic] though this class encompasses most of what we're interested in, there doesn't seem any point in ruling out exceptions. (p. 329)

Commonsense law of inertia

The phrase *commonsense law of inertia* was originated by John McCarthy (personal communication, May 18, 2005; Lifschitz, 1987c, p. 186). The phrase appears to have been first used in print by Lifschitz (1987a, p. 45; 1987c, p. 186). Hanks and McDermott (1987) mention the "inertia of the world" (p. 395) and attribute the phrase "inertial property of facts" (p. 394) to John McCarthy. Fluents subject to the commonsense law of inertia are sometimes called "frame fluents" (Lifschitz, 1990b, p. 370; R. Miller & Shanahan, 2002, p. 471) or are said to be "in the frame" (Lifschitz, 1990b, p. 369; R. Miller & Shanahan, 2002, p. 474) or to "belong to the frame" (R. Miller & Shanahan, 1996, p. 67).

Yale shooting scenario

The Yale shooting scenario was introduced by Hanks and McDermott (1985; 1986; 1987, pp. 387-390), who use the scenario to point out problems with McCarthy's (1984a, 1986) initial attempt at solving the frame problem using circumscription. The scenario and the various treatments of it are discussed at length by Shanahan (1997b). The scenario is also discussed by Reiter (2001, pp. 43-46) and Sandewall (1994, pp. 151 and 152, 197-201). Sun (1995, p. 589) points out that most solutions incorrectly predict that a person who is not shot will be alive forever. This problem could be avoided in a probabilistic treatment—see Section 17.3. The Russian turkey scenario was introduced by Sandewall (1991, 1994, pp. 155 and 156) and is discussed by Kartha and Lifschitz (1994, p. 344) and Shanahan (1997b, pp. 299-301).

Release from inertia

Release from the commonsense law of inertia and the *Releases* predicate were introduced into the event calculus by Shanahan (1997b, pp. 299-301), drawing on the occlusion or **X** predicate of Sandewall (1989b, sec. 6; 1994, chap. 11) and the **releases** construct of Kartha and Lifschitz (1994, p. 344). The *ReleasedAt* predicate was incorporated into the event calculus by R. Miller and Shanahan (1999, pp. 17-19, 2002, pp. 471-474). The *ReleasedAt* predicate is similar to the occlusion or **X** predicate of Sandewall. A precursor to *ReleasedAt* is the *Frame* predicate of Lifschitz (1990b, p. 370), which we may relate to *ReleasedAt* via the axiom

 $Frame(f) \Leftrightarrow \forall t \neg ReleasedAt(f, t)$

Based on McCarthy's (1984a, 1986, 1987) earlier proposals, Lifschitz (1990b, p. 370) proposes the following axiom for the situation calculus:

$$Frame(f) \land \neg Ab(f, a, s) \supset Holds(f, Result(a, s)) \equiv Holds(f, s)$$

which is an ancestor of the following axioms for the event calculus (R. Miller & Shanahan, 2002, p. 466):

$$HoldsAt(f, t_2) \leftarrow [HoldsAt(f, t_1) \land t_1 < t_2 \\ \land Frame(f) \land \neg Clipped(t_1, f, t_2)] \\ \neg HoldsAt(f, t_2) \leftarrow [\neg HoldsAt(f, t_1) \land t_1 < t_2 \\ \land Frame(f) \land \neg Declipped(t_1, f, t_2)]$$

EXERCISES

- 5.1 List three everyday scenarios in which the commonsense law of inertia is not in force.
- **5.2** Sketch out event calculus representations of the scenarios you listed in Exercise 5.1.
- **5.3** Prove Proposition 5.6.
- **5.4** Prove Proposition 5.7.
- **5.5** (Research Problem) Pursue the proposal of Lifschitz (1990b, p. 372) to have several frames in which the commonsense law of inertia holds.

TVD in ACCE () this is a discount point of Care). The EVI Fire EVI Transition is a local transition of the EVI and other community are the many and the second of the EVI Transition of the EvI Transi

i same the Aller and the whole the second of the control of

which we incompatible trace and exactes for the event abrebig (IC willer as Ships on Tubility (IC willer as

Halleshiff of Holleshiff of the State of the

PAPEROISES

- A List the story is an engage of the military and some sound self. List
 - 5. C. Skef in our event usleador regionglia. Leas et de social et yet inner in contract de social et de la contract de la c
 - diameter part system & to
 - Table to the Pay of the
- 3.5. * (1830) and the first form form the proposition to estimate the profit of the contract of the second to the contract of the second to th

Indirect Effects of Events

Suppose that a book is sitting on a table in a living room and an agent is in the living room. Normally, when the agent walks out of the room, the book remains in the living room; but, if the agent picks up the book and walks out of the living room, then the book is no longer in the living room. That is, an indirect effect or ramification of the agent walking out of the living room is that the book the agent is holding changes location. The problem of representing and reasoning about the indirect effects of events is known as the *ramification problem*. This chapter presents several methods for representing indirect effects and dealing with the ramification problem in the event calculus. We discuss the use of effect axioms, primitive and derived fluents, release axioms and state constraints, effect constraints, causal constraints, and trigger axioms.

6.1 EFFECT AXIOMS

One way of representing indirect effects is to represent them the same way that direct effects are represented, namely, using positive and negative effect axioms.

6.1.1 EXAMPLE: CARRYING A BOOK

An agent picks up a book; the book then moves along with the agent. We start with the following spatial theory. If an agent walks from room r_1 to room r_2 , then the agent will be in r_2 and will no longer be in r_1 :

$$Initiates(Walk(a, r_1, r_2), InRoom(a, r_2), t)$$
 (6.1)

$$r_1 \neq r_2 \Rightarrow Terminates(Walk(a, r_1, r_2), InRoom(a, r_1), t)$$
 (6.2)

An object is in one room at a time:

$$HoldsAt(InRoom(o, r_1), t) \land HoldsAt(InRoom(o, r_2), t) \Rightarrow$$

$$r_1 = r_2$$
(6.3)

If an agent is in the same room as an object and the agent picks up the object, then the agent will be holding the object:

$$HoldsAt(InRoom(a, r), t) \land HoldsAt(InRoom(o, r), t) \Rightarrow$$
 (6.4)
 $Initiates(PickUp(a, o), Holding(a, o), t)$

If an agent is holding an object and the agent lets go of the object, then the agent will no longer be holding the object:

$$HoldsAt(Holding(a, o), t) \Rightarrow$$
 (6.5)
 $Terminates(LetGoOf(a, o), Holding(a, o), t)$

We then represent the indirect effects of walking while holding an object using positive and negative effect axioms. If an agent is holding an object and the agent walks from room r_1 to room r_2 , then the object will be in r_2 and will no longer be in r_1 :

$$HoldsAt(Holding(a, o), t) \Rightarrow$$
 (6.6)
 $Initiates(Walk(a, r_1, r_2), InRoom(o, r_2), t)$

$$HoldsAt(Holding(a, o), t) \land r_1 \neq r_2 \Rightarrow$$
 (6.7)
 $Terminates(Walk(a, r_1, r_2), InRoom(o, r_1), t)$

Now consider the following observations and narrative. Nathan and the book start out in the living room:

$$\neg ReleasedAt(f,t)$$
 (6.8)

$$HoldsAt(InRoom(Nathan, LivingRoom), 0)$$
 (6.9)

$$HoldsAt(InRoom(Book, LivingRoom), 0)$$
 (6.10)

Nathan picks up the book and walks into the kitchen:

$$Happens(PickUp(Nathan, Book), 0)$$
 (6.11)

$$Happens(Walk(Nathan, LivingRoom, Kitchen), 1)$$
 (6.12)

We also have

$$LivingRoom \neq Kitchen$$
 (6.13)

We can then show that the book will be in the kitchen.

Proposition 6.1. Let $\Sigma = (6.1) \land (6.2) \land (6.4) \land (6.5) \land (6.6) \land (6.7), \Delta = (6.11) \land (6.12), \Omega = U[Walk, PickUp, LetGoOf] \land U[InRoom, Holding] \land (6.13), \Psi = (6.3), and <math>\Gamma = (6.8) \land (6.9) \land (6.10)$. Then we have

$$CIRC[\Sigma; Initiates, Terminates, Releases] \land CIRC[\Delta; Happens] \land \Omega \land \Psi \land \Gamma \land EC \vdash HoldsAt(InRoom(Book, Kitchen), 2)$$

Proof. From $CIRC[\Sigma; Initiates, Terminates, Releases]$ and Theorems 2.1 and 2.2, we have

$$Initiates(e, f, t) \Leftrightarrow \qquad (6.14)$$

$$\exists a, r_1, r_2 \ (e = Walk(a, r_1, r_2) \land f = InRoom(a, r_2)) \lor$$
 $\exists a, o, r \ (e = PickUp(a, o) \land f = Holding(a, o) \land f = HoldsAt(InRoom(a, r), t) \land f = HoldsAt(InRoom(a, r), t) \lor f = InRoom(a, r_2) \lor f = InR$

(6.22)

From (6.12) (which follows from (6.17)), (6.20), (6.6) (which follows from (6.14)), 1 < 2, (6.21), (6.22), and EC14, we have HoldsAt(InRoom(Book, Kitchen), 2), as required.

 $\neg ReleasedIn(1, InRoom(Book, Kitchen), 2)$

From (6.16) and EC13, we have

6.1.2 DISCUSSION

The advantage of the method of using effect axioms to represent indirect effects is its simplicity. The disadvantage of this method is that more axioms may be required than with other methods. For example, suppose we add *Run* as another way of getting from one room to another:

```
Initiates(Run(a, r_1, r_2), InRoom(a, r_2), t)
r_1 \neq r_2 \Rightarrow Terminates(Run(a, r_1, r_2), InRoom(a, r_1), t)
```

Previously we represented the indirect effects of walking while holding an object. Now we must represent the indirect effects of running while holding an object as well:

```
HoldsAt(Holding(a, o), t) \Rightarrow
Initiates(Run(a, r_1, r_2), InRoom(o, r_2), t)
HoldsAt(Holding(a, o), t) \Rightarrow
Terminates(Run(a, r_1, r_2), InRoom(o, r_1), t)
```

The indirect effects of changing rooms do not come for free.

6.2 PRIMITIVE AND DERIVED FLUENTS

Another way of dealing with the ramification problem is to divide fluents into two categories: primitive fluents, or fluents directly affected by events, and derived fluents, or fluents indirectly affected by events. The truth value of a primitive fluent is determined by effect axioms, whereas the truth value of a derived fluent is determined by state constraints. The derived fluent is released from the commonsense law of inertia at all times, so its truth value is permitted to vary and is determined by state constraints.

6.2.1 EXAMPLE: DEVICE

We start with some positive and negative effect axioms. If an agent switches on a device, then the device will be switched on:

$$Initiates(SwitchOn(a,d), SwitchedOn(d), t)$$
(6.23)

If an agent switches off a device, then the device will no longer be switched on:

$$Terminates(SwitchOff(a, d), SwitchedOn(d), t)$$
 (6.24)

If an agent plugs in a device, then the device will be plugged in:

$$Initiates(PlugIn(a,d), PluggedIn(d), t)$$
(6.25)

If an agent unplugs a device, then the device will no longer be plugged in:

$$Terminates(Unplug(a, d), PluggedIn(d), t)$$
 (6.26)

We use a state constraint to represent the fact that a device is on whenever the device is switched on and the device is plugged in:

$$HoldsAt(On(d), t) \Leftrightarrow$$
 (6.27)
 $HoldsAt(SwitchedOn(d), t) \wedge HoldsAt(PluggedIn(d), t)$

The order in which the device is switched on and plugged in does not matter. The device will be on once it is both switched on and plugged in.

Unlike the use of effect axioms for representing indirect effects, when we add other events that initiate or terminate *SwitchedOn*, we do not have to add any further axioms. The state constraint (6.27) represents an indirect effect of *SwitchedOn*, no matter how *SwitchedOn* is initiated or terminated. The same is true for *Plugged In*.

Consider the following observations and narrative. Initially, the device is neither switched on nor plugged in:

ReleasedAt(
$$On(d), t$$
)(6.28) $\neg ReleasedAt(SwitchedOn(d), t)$ (6.29) $\neg ReleasedAt(PluggedIn(d), t)$ (6.30) $\neg HoldsAt(SwitchedOn(Device1), 0)$ (6.31) $\neg HoldsAt(PluggedIn(Device1), 0)$ (6.32)

Then Nathan switches on and plugs in the device:

We can show that the device will then be on.

Proposition 6.2. Let $\Sigma = (6.23) \land (6.24) \land (6.25) \land (6.26)$, $\Delta = (6.33) \land (6.34)$, $\Omega = U[SwitchOn, PlugIn] \land U[SwitchedOn, PluggedIn, On], <math>\Psi = (6.27)$, and $\Gamma = (6.28) \land (6.29) \land (6.30) \land (6.31) \land (6.32)$. Then we have

$$CIRC[\Sigma; Initiates, Terminates, Releases] \land CIRC[\Delta; Happens] \land \Omega \land \Psi \land \Gamma \land EC \vdash HoldsAt(On(Device1), 2)$$

Proof. From $CIRC[\Sigma; Initiates, Terminates, Releases]$ and Theorems 2.1 and 2.2, we have

Initiates(e, f, t)
$$\Leftrightarrow$$
 (6.35)
 $\exists a, d \ (e = SwitchOn(a, d) \land f = SwitchedOn(d)) \lor$
 $\exists a, d \ (e = PlugIn(a, d) \land f = PluggedIn(d))$
Terminates(e, f, t) \Leftrightarrow (6.36)
 $\exists a, d \ (e = SwitchOff(a, d) \land f = SwitchedOn(d)) \lor$
 $\exists a, d \ (e = Unplug(a, d) \land f = PluggedIn(d))$

(6.37)

 $\neg Releases(e, f, t)$ From $CIRC[\Delta; Happens]$ and Theorem 2.1, we have

$$Happens(e, t) \Leftrightarrow$$
 (6.38)
 $(e = SwitchOn(Nathan, Device1) \land t = 0) \lor$
 $(e = PlugIn(Nathan, Device1) \land t = 1)$

From (6.38), (6.36), and EC3, we have

$$\neg StoppedIn(0, SwitchedOn(Device1), 2)$$
 (6.39)

From (6.37) and EC13, we have

$$\neg ReleasedIn(0, SwitchedOn(Device1), 2)$$
 (6.40)

From (6.33) (which follows from (6.38)), (6.23) (which follows from (6.35)), 0 < 2, (6.39), (6.40), and EC14, we have

$$HoldsAt(SwitchedOn(Device1), 2)$$
 (6.41)

From (6.38) and EC3, we have

$$\neg StoppedIn(1, PluggedIn(Device1), 2)$$
 (6.42)

From (6.37) and EC13, we have

$$\neg ReleasedIn(1, PluggedIn(Device1), 2)$$
 (6.43)

From (6.34) (which follows from (6.38)), (6.25) (which follows from (6.35)), 1 < 2, (6.42), (6.43), and EC14, we have

$$HoldsAt(PluggedIn(Device1), 2)$$
 (6.44)

From
$$(6.41)$$
, (6.44) , and (6.27) , we have $HoldsAt(On(Device1), 2)$.

6.3 RELEASE AXIOMS AND STATE CONSTRAINTS

Another method of dealing with the ramification problem involves temporarily releasing a fluent from the commonsense law of inertia. First, we release the fluent, and we make the fluent subject to a state constraint while it is released. Later, we make the fluent subject to the commonsense law of inertia again.

6.3.1 EXAMPLE: CARRYING A BOOK REVISITED

An agent picks up a book. While the agent is holding the book, its location is not subject to the commonsense law of inertia. Instead, its location varies with the location of the agent holding it.

We modify the example in Section 6.1.1 to use release axioms and state constraints instead of effect axioms. If an agent picks up an object, then the room of the object will be released from the commonsense law of inertia:

$$Releases(PickUp(a, o), InRoom(o, r), t)$$
 (6.45)

Whenever an agent is holding an object, if the agent is in one room, then the object is also in that room:

$$HoldsAt(Holding(a, o), t) \land$$
 (6.46)
 $HoldsAt(InRoom(a, r), t) \Rightarrow$
 $HoldsAt(InRoom(o, r), t)$

If an agent is in a room and the agent lets go of an object, then the object will be in the room, and the fact that the object is in that room will no longer be released from the commonsense law of inertia:

$$HoldsAt(InRoom(a, r), t) \Rightarrow$$
 (6.47)
 $Initiates(LetGoOf(a, o), InRoom(o, r), t)$

Unlike with the use of effect axioms for representing indirect effects, if we add running as another way of moving from room to room, we do not have to add any further axioms. The state constraint (6.46) represents an indirect effect of an agent's location, no matter how the agent's location is changed.

Suppose we have the following observations and narrative. At first, Nathan and the book are in the living room:

$$\neg ReleasedAt(f,t)$$
 (6.48)

$$HoldsAt(InRoom(Nathan, LivingRoom), 0)$$
 (6.49)

$$HoldsAt(InRoom(Book, LivingRoom), 0)$$
 (6.50)

Then Nathan picks up the book and walks into the kitchen:

$$Happens(PickUp(Nathan, Book), 0)$$
 (6.51)

$$Happens(Walk(Nathan, LivingRoom, Kitchen), 1)$$
 (6.52)

We also have the fact that the living room and the kitchen are not the same room:

$$LivingRoom \neq Kitchen$$
 (6.53)

We can show that the book will end up in the kitchen.

Proposition 6.3. If $\Sigma = (6.1) \land (6.2) \land (6.4) \land (6.5) \land (6.45) \land (6.47), \Delta = (6.51) \land (6.52), \quad \Omega = U[Walk, PickUp, LetGoOf] \land U[InRoom, Holding] \land (6.53), \quad \Psi = (6.3) \land (6.46), \text{ and } \Gamma = (6.48) \land (6.49) \land (6.50), \text{ then}$

$$CIRC[\Sigma; Initiates, Terminates, Releases] \land CIRC[\Delta; Happens] \land \Omega \land \Psi \land \Gamma \land EC \vdash HoldsAt(InRoom(Book, Kitchen), 2).$$

Proof. From $CIRC[\Sigma; Initiates, Terminates, Releases]$ and Theorems 2.1 and 2.2, we have

$$Initiates(e, f, t) \Leftrightarrow (6.54)$$

$$\exists a, r_1, r_2 (e = Walk(a, r_1, r_2) \land f = InRoom(a, r_2)) \lor$$

$$\exists a, o, r (e = PickUp(a, o) \land$$

$$f = Holding(a, o) \land$$

$$HoldsAt(InRoom(a, r), t) \land$$

$$HoldsAt(InRoom(o, r), t)) \lor$$

$$\exists a, o, r (e = LetGoOf(a, o) \land f = InRoom(o, r) \land HoldsAt(InRoom(a, r), t))$$

$$Terminates(e, f, t) \Leftrightarrow (6.55)$$

$$\exists a, r_1, r_2 (e = Walk(a, r_1, r_2) \land f = InRoom(a, r_1) \land r_1 \neq r_2) \lor (6.56)$$

$$\exists a, o (e = LetGoOf(a, o) \land f = Holding(a, o) \land f = InRoom(o, r))$$

$$(6.56)$$

From $CIRC[\Delta; Happens]$ and Theorem 2.1, we have

$$Happens(e, t) \Leftrightarrow$$
 (6.57)
 $(e = PickUp(Nathan, Book) \land t = 0) \lor$
 $(e = Walk(Nathan, LivingRoom, Kitchen) \land t = 1)$

From (6.57), (6.55), and EC3, we have

$$\neg StoppedIn(0, Holding(Nathan, Book), 2)$$
 (6.58)

From (6.56) and EC13, we have

$$\neg ReleasedIn(0, Holding(Nathan, Book), 2)$$
 (6.59)

From (6.51) (which follows from (6.57)), (6.49), (6.50), (6.4) (which follows from (6.54)), (6.58), (6.59), and EC14, we have

$$HoldsAt(Holding(Nathan, Book), 2)$$
 (6.60)

From (6.57) and EC3, we have

$$\neg StoppedIn(1, InRoom(Nathan, Kitchen), 2)$$
 (6.61)

From (6.57) and EC13, we have

$$\neg Released(1, InRoom(Nathan, Kitchen), 2)$$
 (6.62)

From (6.52) (which follows from (6.57)), (6.1) (which follows from (6.54)), 1 < 2, (6.61), (6.62), and EC14, we have HoldsAt(InRoom(Nathan, Kitchen), 2). From this, (6.60), and (6.46), we have HoldsAt(InRoom(Book, Kitchen), 2).

6.4 EFFECT CONSTRAINTS

Another way of representing indirect effects is to use universally quantified formulas involving *Initiates* and *Terminates*.

Definition 6.1. If γ is a condition, δ_1 and δ_2 are *Initiates* or *Terminates*, α is an event term, β_1 and β_2 are fluent terms, and τ is a timepoint term, then

$$(\gamma \wedge \delta_1(\alpha, \beta_1, \tau)) \Rightarrow \delta_2(\alpha, \beta_2, \tau)$$

is an effect constraint.

6.4.1 EXAMPLE: CARRYING A BOOK REVISITED

Consider again the example in Section 6.1.1. We may represent the indirect effects of walking from one room to another using effect constraints:

$$HoldsAt(Holding(a, o), t) \land$$
 (6.63)
 $Initiates(e, InRoom(a, r), t) \Rightarrow$
 $Initiates(e, InRoom(o, r), t)$

$$HoldsAt(Holding(a, o), t) \land$$
 (6.64)
 $Terminates(e, InRoom(a, r), t) \Rightarrow$
 $Terminates(e, InRoom(o, r), t)$

Unfortunately, we cannot use predicate completion and Theorems 2.1 and 2.2 to compute $CIRC[(6.1) \land (6.2) \land (6.4) \land (6.5) \land (6.63) \land (6.64); Initiates, Terminates, Releases], because Initiates is contained in the antecedent of (6.63) and Terminates is contained in the antecedent of (6.64). (This can be handled by answer set programming—see Section 15.3.4.) Instead we simply use (6.63) and (6.64) to derive the effect axioms in Section 6.1.1 that represent the indirect effects. From (6.63) and$

$$Initiates(Walk(a, r_1, r_2), InRoom(a, r_2), t)$$

we have

$$HoldsAt(Holding(a, o), t) \Rightarrow$$

 $Initiates(Walk(a, r_1, r_2), InRoom(o, r_2), t)$

which is (6.6). From (6.64) and

$$r_1 \neq r_2 \Rightarrow Terminates(Walk(a, r_1, r_2), InRoom(a, r_1), t)$$

we have

$$HoldsAt(Holding(a, o), t) \land r_1 \neq r_2 \Rightarrow$$

 $Terminates(Walk(a, r_1, r_2), InRoom(o, r_1), t)$

which is (6.7).

6.5 CAUSAL CONSTRAINTS

Michael Thielscher devised the electronic circuit shown in Figure 6.1 in order to point out problems with solutions to the ramification problem based on dividing fluents

FIGURE 6.1

Thielscher's circuit (Thielscher, 1996, p. 19).

into primitive and derived fluents, as discussed in Section 6.2. The circuit consists of a battery (B), three switches (S1, S2, and S3), a relay (R), and a light (L). A switch can be open or closed, the relay can be activated or not activated, and the light can be lit or not lit. Relay R is activated whenever S1 and S3 are closed. Light L is lit whenever S1 and S2 are closed. Relay R is connected to switch S2, so that when R is activated, S2 is opened.

One behavior of this circuit is as follows. Suppose that initially S1 is open, S2 and S3 are closed, R is not activated, and L is not lit. If we close S1, then R will be activated and S2 will be opened. Because S2 is open, the result will be that light L is not lit.

Now suppose we try to model this behavior using primitive and derived fluents. We use primitive fluents for S1 and S3:

initiates(Close(SI), Closea(SI), t)	(0.03)
Terminates(Open(SI), Closed(SI), t)	(6.66)

$$Initiates(Close(S3), Closed(S3), t)$$

$$(6.67)$$

$$Terminates(Open(S3), Closed(S3), t)$$
 (6.68)

We use derived fluents for R and L:

$$HoldsAt(Activated(R), t) \Leftrightarrow$$
 (6.69)
 $HoldsAt(Closed(S1), t) \wedge HoldsAt(Closed(S3), t)$

$$HoldsAt(Lit(L), t) \Leftrightarrow$$
 (6.70)
 $HoldsAt(Closed(SI), t) \land HoldsAt(Closed(S2), t)$

It is not clear what to use for S2, which appears to be both primitive and derived. On the one hand, S2 can be manually opened and closed:

$$Initiates(Close(S2), Closed(S2), t)$$
 (6.71)

$$Terminates(Open(S2), Closed(S2), t)$$
 (6.72)

On the other hand, S2 is open whenever R is activated:

$$\neg HoldsAt(Closed(S2), t) \Leftrightarrow HoldsAt(Activated(R), t)$$
 (6.73)

Unfortunately, if we use all three axioms (6.71), (6.72), and (6.73), then we get inconsistency. To see this, consider the following observations and narrative:

$$\neg HoldsAt(Closed(SI), 0)$$
 (6.74)

$$HoldsAt(Closed(S2), 0)$$
 (6.75)

$$HoldsAt(Closed(S3), 0)$$
 (6.76)

$$\neg HoldsAt(Activated(R), 0)$$
 (6.77)

$$\neg HoldsAt(Lit(L), 0)$$
 (6.78)

$$\neg ReleasedAt(f,t)$$
 (6.79)

$$Happens(Close(S1), 0)$$
 (6.80)

Proposition 6.4. Let $\Sigma = (6.65) \land (6.66) \land (6.67) \land (6.68) \land (6.71) \land (6.72)$, $\Delta = (6.80)$, $\Omega = U[Close, Open, Activate, Light] \land U[Closed, Activated, Lit]$, and $\Psi = (6.69) \land (6.70) \land (6.73)$, and $\Gamma = (6.74) \land (6.75) \land (6.76) \land (6.77) \land (6.78)$ $\land (6.79)$. Then $CIRC[\Sigma; Initiates, Terminates, Releases] \land CIRC[\Delta; Happens] \land \Omega \land \Psi \land \Gamma \land DEC$ is inconsistent.

Proof. From $CIRC[\Sigma; Initiates, Terminates, Releases]$ and Theorems 2.1 and 2.2, we have

Initiates(e, f, t)
$$\Leftrightarrow$$
 (6.81)
(e = Close(S1) \wedge f = Closed(S1)) \vee

$$(e = Close(S2) \land f = Closed(S2)) \lor$$

$$(e = Close(S3) \land f = Closed(S3))$$

$$Terminates(e, f, t) \Leftrightarrow$$

$$(e = Open(S1) \land f = Closed(S1)) \lor$$

$$(e = Open(S2) \land f = Closed(S2)) \lor$$

$$(e = Open(S3) \land f = Closed(S3))$$

$$\neg Releases(e, f, t).$$

$$(6.83)$$

From $CIRC[\Delta; Happens]$ and Theorem 2.1, we have

$$Happens(e, t) \Leftrightarrow$$
 (6.84)
 $(e = Close(SI) \land t = 0)$

From (6.80) (which follows from (6.84)), (6.65) (which follows from (6.81)), and DEC9, we have HoldsAt(Closed(S1), 1). From this, (6.76), and (6.69), we have HoldsAt(Activated(R), 1). From this and (6.73), we have

$$\neg HoldsAt(Closed(S2), 1)$$
 (6.85)

Yet, from (6.84) and (6.82), we have $\neg \exists e (Happens(e, 0) \land Terminates(e, Closed(S2), 0))$. From this, (6.75), (6.79), and DEC5, we have HoldsAt (Closed(S2), 1), which contradicts (6.85).

Thus, it does not work for S2 to be both a primitive and derived fluent.

In order to deal with this circuit, or any commonsense reasoning problem in which indirect effects interact with one another instantaneously, Murray Shanahan enhances the event calculus as follows. First, he adds the following four predicates.

Started(f, t): Fluent f is true at timepoint t, or f is initiated by an event that occurs at t. We say that f is started at t.

Stopped(f, t): Fluent f is false at timepoint t, or f is terminated by an event that occurs at t. We say that f is stopped at t.

Initiated (f, t): Fluent f is started at timepoint t, and f is not terminated by any event that occurs at t.

Terminated(f, t): Fluent f is stopped at timepoint t, and f is not initiated by any event that occurs at t.

Second, he adds the following axioms.

Axiom CC1.

$$Started(f,t) \Leftrightarrow HoldsAt(f,t) \vee \exists e (Happens(e,t) \wedge Initiates(e,f,t))$$

Axiom CC2.

$$Stopped(f,t) \Leftrightarrow \neg HoldsAt(f,t) \lor \exists e (Happens(e,t) \land Terminates(e,f,t))$$

Axiom CC3.

$$Initiated(f,t) \Leftrightarrow Started(f,t) \land \neg \exists e (Happens(e,t) \land Terminates(e,f,t))$$

Axiom CC4.

$$Terminated(f, t) \Leftrightarrow Stopped(f, t) \land \neg \exists e (Happens(e, t) \land Initiates(e, f, t))$$

We use CC to mean the conjunction of axioms CC1 through CC4. Third, Shanahan introduces a new type of axiom called a causal constraint.

Definition 6.2. If α is an event term, β and β_1, \ldots, β_n are fluent terms, θ is *Stopped* or *Started*, π_1, \ldots, π_n are *Initiated* or *Terminated*, and τ is a timepoint term, then

$$\theta(\beta,\tau) \wedge \pi_1(\beta_1,\tau) \wedge \cdots \wedge \pi_n(\beta_n,\tau) \Rightarrow Happens(\alpha,\tau)$$

is a causal constraint.

6.5.1 EXAMPLE: THIELSCHER'S CIRCUIT

We now show how causal constraints can be used to deal properly with Thielscher's circuit. Our axiomatization of the circuit is the same as Shanahan's, except that we use events such as Close(SI) instead of CloseI, use fluents such as Closed(SI) instead of SwitchI, and have axioms for opening and closing all switches.

We use the observations and narrative just discussed, and we have the following effect axioms:

$$Initiates(Close(s), Closed(s), t)$$
(6.86)

$$Terminates(Open(s), Closed(s), t)$$
(6.87)

$$Initiates(Activate(r), Activated(r), t)$$
(6.88)

$$Initiates(Light(l), Lit(l), t)$$
(6.89)

We have the following causal constraints:

$$Stopped(Lit(L), t) \land \qquad (6.90)$$

$$Initiated(Closed(SI), t) \land$$

$$Initiated(Closed(S2), t) \Rightarrow$$

$$Happens(Light(L), t)$$

$$Started(Closed(S2), t) \land$$
 (6.91)
 $Initiated(Activated(R), t) \Rightarrow$
 $Happens(Open(S2), t)$

$$Stopped(Activated(R), t) \land \qquad (6.92)$$

$$Initiated(Closed(S1), t) \land$$

$$Initiated(Closed(S3), t) \Rightarrow$$

$$Happens(Activate(R), t)$$

Given this axiomatization we can show that after switch S1 is closed, light L will not be lit.

Proposition 6.5. Let $\Sigma = (6.86) \land (6.87) \land (6.88) \land (6.89), \Delta = (6.80) \land (6.90) \land (6.91) \land (6.92), \quad \Omega = U[Close, Open, Activate, Light] \land U[Closed, Activated, Lit], and <math>\Gamma = (6.74) \land (6.75) \land (6.76) \land (6.77) \land (6.78) \land (6.79)$. Then we have

$$CIRC[\Sigma; Initiates, Terminates, Releases] \land CIRC[\Delta; Happens] \land$$

$$\Omega \wedge \Gamma \wedge DEC \wedge CC \vdash \neg HoldsAt(Lit(L), 1)$$

Proof. From $CIRC[\Sigma; Initiates, Terminates, Releases]$ and Theorems 2.1 and 2.2, we have

Initiates(e, f, t)
$$\Leftrightarrow$$
 (6.93)

$$\exists s \ (e = Close(s) \land f = Closed(s)) \lor$$

$$\exists r \ (e = Activate(r) \land f = Activated(r)) \lor$$

$$\exists l \ (e = Light(l) \land f = Lit(l))$$

Terminates
$$(e, f, t) \Leftrightarrow$$
 (6.94)

$$\exists s \ (e = Open(s) \land f = Closed(s))$$

$$\neg Releases(e, f, t)$$
 (6.95)

From $CIRC[\Delta; Happens]$ and Theorem 2.1, we have

$$Happens(e,t) \Leftrightarrow \qquad (6.96)$$

$$(e = Close(SI) \land t = 0) \lor$$

$$(e = Light(L) \land$$

$$Stopped(Lit(L),t) \land$$

$$Initiated(Closed(SI),t) \land$$

$$Initiated(Closed(S2),t)) \lor$$

$$(e = Open(S2) \land$$

$$Started(Closed(S2),t) \land$$

$$Initiated(Activated(R),t)) \lor$$

$$(e = Activate(R) \land$$

$$Stopped(Activated(R),t) \land$$

$$Initiated(Closed(SI),t) \land$$

$$Initiated(Closed(S3),t)$$

From (6.77) and CC2, we have

$$Stopped(Activated(R), 0)$$
 (6.97)

From (6.80) (which follows from (6.96)), and (6.86) (which follows from (6.93)), we have $\exists e \ (Happens(e, 0) \land Initiates(e, Closed(SI), 0))$. From this and CC1, we have

$$Started(Closed(S1), 0)$$
 (6.98)

From (6.94) and (6.96), we have $\neg \exists e (Happens(e, 0) \land Terminates(e, Closed(S1), 0))$. From this, (6.98), and CC3, we have

$$Initiated(Closed(S1), 0)$$
 (6.99)

From (6.76) and CC1, we have

$$Started(Closed(S3), 0)$$
 (6.100)

From (6.94) and (6.96), we have $\neg \exists e (Happens(e, 0) \land Terminates(e, Closed(S3), 0))$. From this, (6.100), and CC3, we have Initiated(Closed(S3), 0). From this, (6.97), (6.99), and (6.92) (which follows from (6.96)), we have Happens(Activate(R), 0). From this and (6.88) (which follows from (6.93)), we have $\exists e (Happens(e, 0) \land Initiates(e, Activated(R), 0))$. From this and CC1, we have

$$Started(Activated(R), 0)$$
 (6.101)

From (6.94), we have $\neg \exists e (Happens(e, 0) \land Terminates(e, Activated(R), 0))$. From this, (6.101), and CC3, we have

$$Initiated(Activated(R), 0)$$
 (6.102)

From (6.75) and CC1, we have Started(Closed(S2), 0). From this, (6.102), and (6.91) (which follows from (6.96)), we have Happens(Open(S2), 0). From this and (6.87) (which follows from (6.94)), we have $\exists e (Happens(e, 0) \land Terminates(e, Closed(S2), 0))$. From this and CC3, we have $\neg Initiated(Closed(S2), 0)$.

From this and (6.96), we have $\neg Happens(Light(L), 0)$. From this and (6.93), we have $\neg \exists e \ (Happens(e, 0) \land Initiates(e, Lit(L), 0))$. From this, (6.78), (6.79), and DEC6, we have $\neg HoldsAt(Lit(L), 1)$.

6.6 TRIGGER AXIOMS

There is a further option for representing indirect effects. If the indirect effects are delayed and not instantaneous, then we can represent them using the trigger axioms described in Section 4.1. We can in fact use trigger axioms to represent the behavior of Thielscher's circuit (Figure 6.1). In this case, with the conjunction of axioms DEC the light will light up for two timepoints before going out again; with the conjunction of axioms EC the light will light up for an instant and then go out.

6.6.1 EXAMPLE: THIELSCHER'S CIRCUIT WITH DELAYS

Instead of causal constraints, we use the following trigger axioms:

We add the following effect axiom to those already given:

$$Terminates(Unlight(l), Lit(l), t)$$
 (6.107)

Given the observations and narrative, we can show that the light is lit at timepoint 2 and is not lit at timepoint 4.

Proposition 6.6. Let $\Sigma = (6.86) \land (6.87) \land (6.88) \land (6.89) \land (6.107)$, $\Delta = (6.80) \land (6.103) \land (6.104) \land (6.105) \land (6.106)$, $\Omega = U[Close, Open, Activate, Light] \land U[Closed, Activated, Lit]$, and $\Gamma = (6.74) \land (6.75) \land (6.76) \land (6.77) \land (6.78) \land (6.79)$. Then we have

$$CIRC[\Sigma; Initiates, Terminates, Releases] \land CIRC[\Delta; Happens] \land \\ \Omega \land \Gamma \land DEC \vdash HoldsAt(Lit(L), 2) \land \neg HoldsAt(Lit(L), 4)$$

Proof. From $CIRC[\Sigma; Initiates, Terminates, Releases]$ and Theorems 2.1 and 2.2, we have

Initiates(e, f, t)
$$\Leftrightarrow$$
 (6.108)

$$\exists s (e = Close(s) \land f = Closed(s)) \lor$$

$$\exists r (e = Activate(r) \land f = Activated(r)) \lor$$

$$\exists l (e = Light(l) \land f = Lit(l))$$

Terminates
$$(e, f, t) \Leftrightarrow$$

$$\exists s \ (e = Open(s) \land f = Closed(s)) \lor$$

$$\exists l \ (e = Unlight(l) \land Lit(l))$$
(6.109)

$$\neg Releases(e, f, t)$$
 (6.110)

From $CIRC[\Delta; Happens]$ and Theorem 2.1, we have

$$Happens(e,t) \Leftrightarrow \qquad (6.111)$$

$$(e = Close(SI) \land t = 0) \lor (e = Light(L) \land \neg HoldsAt(Lit(L),t) \land \land HoldsAt(Closed(SI),t) \land \land HoldsAt(Closed(S2),t)) \lor (e = Unlight(L) \land HoldsAt(Lit(L),t) \land (\neg HoldsAt(Closed(SI),t) \lor \neg HoldsAt(Closed(S2),t))) \lor (e = Open(S2) \land HoldsAt(Closed(S2),t) \land HoldsAt(Activated(R),t)) \lor (e = Activate(R), \land \land \neg HoldsAt(Activated(R),t) \land HoldsAt(Closed(SI),t) \land HoldsAt(Closed(SI),t) \land HoldsAt(Closed(SI),t) \land HoldsAt(Closed(SI),t) \land HoldsAt(Closed(SI),t))$$

First we show that the light goes on. From (6.80) (which follows from (6.111)), (6.86) (which follows from (6.108)), and DEC9 we have

$$HoldsAt(Closed(SI), 1)$$
 (6.112)

From (6.77) and (6.111), we have $\neg Happens(Open(S2), 0)$. From this and (6.109), we have $\neg \exists e \ (Happens(e, 0) \land Terminates(e, Closed(S2), 0))$. From this, (6.75), (6.79), and DEC5, we have

$$HoldsAt(Closed(S2), 1)$$
 (6.113)

From (6.74), (6.111), and (6.108), we have $\neg \exists e (Happens(e, 0) \land Initiates(e, Lit(L), 0))$. From this, (6.78), (6.79), and DEC6, we have $\neg HoldsAt(Lit(L), 1)$. From this, (6.112), (6.113), and (6.103) (which follows from (6.111)), we have Happens(Light(L), 1). From this, (6.89) (which follows from (6.108)), and DEC9, we have

$$HoldsAt(Lit(L), 2)$$
 (6.114)

Second we show that the light goes off again. From (6.74) and (6.111), we have $\neg Happens(Activate(R), 0)$. From this and (6.108), we have $\neg \exists e \ (Happens(e, 0) \land Initiates(e, Activated(R), 0))$. From this, (6.77), (6.79), and DEC6, we have

$$\neg HoldsAt(Activated(R), 1)$$
 (6.115)

From (6.111) and (6.109), we have $\neg \exists e$ (Happens(e, 0) \land Terminates(e, Closed (S3), 0)). From this, (6.76), (6.79), and DEC5, we have HoldsAt (Closed(S3), 1). From this, (6.115), (6.112), and (6.106) (which follows from (6.111)), we have Happens(Activate(R), 1). From this, (6.88) (which follows from (6.108)), and DEC9, we have

$$HoldsAt(Activated(R), 2)$$
 (6.116)

From (6.115) and (6.111), we have $\neg Happens(Open(S2), 1)$. From this and (6.109), we have $\neg \exists e (Happens(e, 1) \land Terminates(e, Closed(S2), 1))$. From this, (6.113), (6.79), and DEC5, we have

$$HoldsAt(Closed(S2), 2)$$
 (6.117)

From this, (6.116), and (6.105) (which follows from (6.111)), we have Happens(Open(S2), 2). From this, (6.87) (which follows from (6.109)), and DEC10, we have

$$\neg HoldsAt(Closed(S2), 3)$$
 (6.118)

From (6.111) and (6.109), we have $\neg \exists e$ ($Happens(e, 1) \land Terminates(e, Closed(SI), 1)$). From this, (6.112), (6.79), and DEC5, we have HoldsAt (Closed(SI), 2). From this, (6.117), and (6.111), we have $\neg Happens(Unlight(L), 2)$. From this and (6.109), we have $\neg \exists e$ ($Happens(e, 2) \land Terminates(e, Lit(L), 2)$). From this, (6.114), (6.79), and DEC5, we have HoldsAt (Lit(L), 3). From this, (6.118), and (6.104) (which follows from (6.111)), we have Happens(Unlight(L), 3). From this, (6.107) (which follows from (6.109)), and DEC10, we have $\neg HoldsAt(Lit(L), 4)$.

6.6.2 EXAMPLE: SHANAHAN'S CIRCUIT WITH DELAYS

Shanahan showed that if the circuit is modified to that shown in Figure 6.2, then an axiomatization of the circuit using causal constraints as in Section 6.5 produces inconsistency. We can properly represent the behavior of this circuit using trigger axioms. The circuit implements a buzzer that is turned on and off with S1; we ignore the light in this discussion. A moment after S1 is closed, relay R is activated. A moment after R is activated, S2 is open. A moment after S2 is open, R is not activated. A moment after relay R is not activated, S2 is closed. A moment after S2 is closed,

FIGURE 6.2

Shanahan's circuit (Shanahan, 1996b, p. 145).

R is activated again. The cycle repeats. In a real circuit, the result of a relay quickly and repeatedly activating and deactivating is a buzzing sound.

We have the following trigger axioms:

$$\neg HoldsAt(Lit(L), t) \land \qquad (6.119)$$

$$HoldsAt(Closed(S1), t) \land \qquad (6.119)$$

$$HoldsAt(Closed(S2), t) \Rightarrow \qquad \qquad Happens(Light(L), t)$$

$$HoldsAt(Lit(L), t) \land \qquad (6.120)$$

$$(\neg HoldsAt(Closed(S1), t) \lor \neg HoldsAt(Closed(S2), t)) \Rightarrow \qquad \qquad Happens(Unlight(L), t)$$

$$HoldsAt(Closed(S2), t) \land \qquad (6.121)$$

$$HoldsAt(Activated(R), t) \Rightarrow \qquad \qquad Happens(Open(S2), t)$$

$$\neg HoldsAt(Activated(R), t) \land \qquad (6.122)$$

$$HoldsAt(Closed(S1), t) \land \qquad \qquad (6.122)$$

$$HoldsAt(Closed(S3), t) \Rightarrow \qquad \qquad Happens(Activate(R), t)$$

$$HoldsAt(Activated(R), t) \land$$
 (6.123)
 $(\neg HoldsAt(Closed(S1), t) \lor$
 $\neg HoldsAt(Closed(S2), t) \lor$
 $\neg HoldsAt(Closed(S3), t)) \Rightarrow$
 $Happens(Deactivate(R), t)$

We add the following effect axiom to those already given:

$$Terminates(Deactivate(r), Activated(r), t)$$
 (6.124)

We use the observations and narrative as detailed before.

With the conjunction of axioms EC, the circuit buzzes with infinite frequency, whereas with the conjunction of axioms DEC, it buzzes with finite frequency. Using DEC, we can show that R activates at timepoint 1, S2 opens at timepoint 2, and R deactivates at timepoint 3.

Proposition 6.7. Let $\Sigma = (6.86) \land (6.87) \land (6.88) \land (6.89) \land (6.107) \land (6.124)$, $\Delta = (6.80) \land (6.119) \land (6.120) \land (6.121) \land (6.122) \land (6.123)$, $\Omega = U[Close, Open, Activate, Deactivate, Light, Unlight] \land U[Closed, Activated, Lit], and Γ = (6.74) \land (6.75) \land (6.76) \land (6.77) \land (6.78) \land (6.79)$. Then we have

$$CIRC[\Sigma; Initiates, Terminates, Releases] \land CIRC[\Delta; Happens] \land \\ \Omega \land \Gamma \land DEC \vdash Happens(Activate(R), 1) \land \\ HoldsAt(Activated(R), 2) \land \\ Happens(Open(S2), 2) \land \\ \neg HoldsAt(Closed(S2), 3) \land \\ Happens(Deactivate(R), 3) \land \\ \neg HoldsAt(Activated(R), 3)$$

Proof. From $CIRC[\Sigma; Initiates, Terminates, Releases]$ and Theorems 2.1 and 2.2, we have

Initiates(e, f, t)
$$\Leftrightarrow$$
 (6.125)
 $\exists s (e = Close(s) \land f = Closed(s)) \lor$
 $\exists r (e = Activate(r) \land f = Activated(r)) \lor$
 $\exists l (e = Light(l) \land f = Lit(l))$

Terminates(e, f, t)
$$\Leftrightarrow$$
 (6.126)
 $\exists s \ (e = Open(s) \land f = Closed(s)) \lor$
 $\exists l \ (e = Unlight(l) \land Lit(l)) \lor$
 $\exists r \ (e = Deactivate(r) \land f = Activated(r))$

$$\neg Releases(e, f, t)$$
 (6.127)

From $CIRC[\Delta; Happens]$ and Theorem 2.1, we have

$$Happens(e,t) \Leftrightarrow (6.128)$$

$$(e = Close(SI) \land t = 0) \lor$$

$$(e = Light(L) \land$$

$$\neg HoldsAt(Lit(L),t) \land$$

 $HoldsAt(Closed(S1), t) \land$ $HoldsAt(Closed(S2), t)) \lor$ $(e = Unlight(L) \land$ $HoldsAt(Lit(L),t) \wedge$ $(\neg HoldsAt(Closed(S1), t) \lor$ $\neg HoldsAt(Closed(S2),t))) \lor$ $(e = Open(S2) \land$ $HoldsAt(Closed(S2), t) \land$ $HoldsAt(Activated(R), t)) \lor$ $(e = Activate(R) \land$ $\neg HoldsAt(Activated(R), t) \land$ $HoldsAt(Closed(S1), t) \land$ $HoldsAt(Closed(S2), t) \land$ $HoldsAt(Closed(S3), t)) \lor$ $(e = Deactivate(R) \land$ $HoldsAt(Activated(R), t) \land$ $(\neg HoldsAt(Closed(SI), t) \lor$ $\neg HoldsAt(Closed(S2), t) \lor$ $\neg HoldsAt(Closed(S3), t)))$

From (6.80) (which follows from (6.128)), (6.86) (which follows from (6.125)), and DEC9, we have

$$HoldsAt(Closed(SI), 1)$$
 (6.129)

From (6.74) and (6.128), we have $\neg Happens(Activate(R), 0)$. From this and (6.125), we have $\neg \exists e (Happens(e, 0) \land Initiates(e, Activated(R), 0))$. From this, (6.77), (6.79), and DEC6, we have

$$\neg HoldsAt(Activated(R), 1)$$
 (6.130)

From (6.126), (6.128), and (6.77), we have $\neg \exists e (Happens(e, 0) \land Terminates (e, Closed(S2), 0))$. From this, (6.75), (6.79), and DEC5, we have

$$HoldsAt(Closed(S2), 1)$$
 (6.131)

From (6.128) and (6.126), we have $\neg \exists e (Happens(e, 0) \land Terminates (e, Closed (S3), 0))$. From this, (6.76), (6.79), and DEC5, we have

$$HoldsAt(Closed(S3), 1)$$
 (6.132)

From this, (6.130), (6.129), (6.131), and (6.122) (which follows from (6.128)), we have

Happens(Activate(R), 1)

From this, (6.88) (which follows from (6.125)), and DEC9, we have

$$HoldsAt(Activated(R), 2)$$
 (6.133)

From (6.130) and (6.128), we have $\neg Happens(Open(S2), 1)$. From this and (6.126), we have $\neg \exists e(Happens(e, 1) \land Terminates(e, Closed(S2), 1))$. From this, (6.131), (6.79), and DEC5, we have

(6.134)

From this, (6.133), and (6.121) (which follows from (6.128)), we have

Happens(Open(S2), 2)

From this, (6.87) (which follows from (6.126)), and DEC10, we have

$$\neg HoldsAt(Closed(S2), 3)$$
 (6.135)

From (6.126) and (6.128), we have $\neg \exists e (Happens(e, 1) \land Terminates (e, Closed (S1), 1))$. From this, (6.129), (6.79), and DEC5, we have

$$HoldsAt(Closed(S1), 2)$$
 (6.136)

From (6.126) and (6.128), we have $\neg \exists e (Happens(e, 1) \land Terminates (e, Closed (S3), 1))$. From this, (6.132), (6.79), and DEC5, we have HoldsAt(Closed(S3), 2). From this, (6.126), (6.128), (6.136), and (6.134), we have $\neg \exists e (Happens(e, 2) \land Terminates(Activated(R), 2))$. From this, (6.133), (6.79), and DEC5, we have HoldsAt(Activated(R), 3). From this, (6.135), and (6.123) (which follows from (6.128)), we have

Happens(Deactivate(R), 3)

From this, (6.124) (which follows from (6.126)), and DEC10, we have $\neg HoldsAt(Activated(R), 3)$.

Delayed indirect effects such as the results of dropping an object may be represented using trajectory and antitrajectory axioms, which are described in Chapter 7.

BIBLIOGRAPHIC NOTES

Ramification problem

Minsky (1961) noted something similar to the frame and ramification problems:

One problem that has been a great nuisance to us arises in connection with non-mathematical problems in which actions affect the state of some subject domain. ... One must then deduce all the consequences of an action in so far as it affects propositions that one is planning to use. (p. 217)

Green (1969, p. 98) mentions a problem with representing the effects of pushing an object that accidentally hits and moves other objects. Waldinger (1977, pp. 124-129) discusses the difficulty of representing "actions with indirect side effects" (p. 125) using the add lists and delete lists of STRIPS (Fikes & Nilsson, 1971). He gives the examples of pushing a row of boxes to the right by pushing the leftmost box and moving each component of a complex object by moving the object.

Finger (1987) considers ramifications in the context of automating the design of such things as electronic circuits, computer programs, and robot plans. The task is to

find a design (similar to a plan) D that achieves a goal specification G given a world model W. He defines a *ramification* as a formula N such that $W \models (D \land G) \supset N$ (p. 9) and provides the example that consuming fuel is a ramification of driving an automobile (p. 69). He presents methods for finding ramifications (pp. 92-126) and using them to (1) eliminate inconsistent goals if a ramification is known to be impossible, (2) reduce the search space by providing additional constraints, and (3) provide additional heuristics (pp. 70-71). He defines the *ramification problem* as the problem of having to anticipate and deal with an unbounded set of consequences of a design (p. 16).

Taking their inspiration from Finger, Ginsberg and Smith (1987b, 1988b) define the *ramification problem* as the problem representing all the consequences of an action. They propose an approach to the ramification problem based on state constraints and possible worlds. A *possible world* is defined as a set of logical formulas. The consequences of an action performed in a world S are determined by finding the nearest possible worlds to S in which the direct effects of the action hold. They consider what a household robot would have to reason about and formalize a room in a house with a television set, plant, two ventilation ducts, and other objects. A state constraint represents that the room is stuffy if and only if both ventilation ducts are blocked. When a plant is blocking one duct and a television set is moved on top of the other duct, two nearest possible worlds result: one in which both ducts are blocked and the room is stuffy, and another in which the plant is no longer blocking a duct, the television set is blocking a duct, and the room is not stuffy.

Haas (1987) uses the example of a robot carrying a box and encodes the location of the box (*InRoom*) using a state constraint. Schubert (1990) uses the robot example and encodes "implicit effects" (p. 32) within both state constraints (his axiom A8, p. 33) and explanation closure axioms (his axiom A20, p. 35). The robot examples derive from the robot world model of Fikes and Nilsson (1971) and Fikes, Hart, and Nilsson (1972a) and from the blocks world (Winston, 1970; Winograd, 1972; Sacerdoti, 1977).

In the formulation of the situation calculus of Reiter (1991, 2001) and Pirri and Reiter (1999), a successor state axiom for a fluent specifies the truth value of the fluent in the successor situation $do(\alpha, \sigma)$ that results from performing action α in situation σ . Thus, a successor axiom for a fluent completely specifies how actions affect the fluent. Reiter (1991; 2001, pp. 23-35) presents a method for automatically compiling effect axioms into successor state axioms in order to solve the frame problem. F. Lin and Reiter (1994, sec. 5) and Reiter (2001, pp. 401-402) propose a method for dealing with state constraints in the situation calculus. The method involves making the effects implied by state constraints explicit. Additional effect axioms are derived from state constraints, and then effect axioms are compiled into successor state axioms as usual. They use an example of painting blocks. The action paint(b,c) represents painting block b color c. An effect axiom states that the color of block b in the situation do(paint(b,c),s) is c. A state constraint says that a block

has a unique color in a situation. Their method arrives at the indirect effect that a block is no longer red after it is painted yellow. Note that we would not treat this as an indirect effect but would rather simply have the two (direct) effect axioms as follows:

```
Initiates(Paint(b, c), Color(b, c), t)

HoldsAt(Color(b, c<sub>1</sub>), t) \land c<sub>1</sub> \neq c<sub>2</sub> \Rightarrow

Terminates(Paint(b, c<sub>2</sub>), Color(b, c<sub>1</sub>), t)
```

Similarly, Baral (2003, pp. 233-238) considers the indirect effects resulting from the constraint that an object can be at one location at a time.

Effect axioms

Kakas and Miller (1997a, p. 6) point out that, if effect axioms alone are used to represent indirect effects, then incompletely specified initial situations can lead to unintended models. Suppose that the observations and narrative in the example in Section 6.1 are empty. Then, there are models of the domain description in which the following formulas are true:

HoldsAt(Holding(Nathan, Book), 0) HoldsAt(InRoom(Nathan, Kitchen), 0) HoldsAt(InRoom(Book, LivingRoom), 0)

Primitive and derived fluents

The distinction between primitive and derived fluents goes back to STRIPS (Fikes & Nilsson, 1971), which had the notions of a "primitive clause" and a "derived clause" (p. 198). Fahlman (1974, pp. 18-20) distinguishes "primary data" and "secondary data." Kowalski (1979) classifies relations into "primitive" and "derived" (p. 137) in his version of the situation calculus. Lifschitz (1987a) distinguishes "primitive fluents" (p. 45) and fluents "defined in terms of primitive fluents" (p. 44). He writes a state constraint that defines *clear* in terms of the primitive fluent *at* (p. 50):

$$holds(clear l, s) \equiv \forall b \neg holds(at(b, l), s)$$

Lifschitz (1990b) makes a similar distinction between "frame fluents" and "arbitrary fluents" (p. 370). Shanahan (1999b) discusses the division of fluents into "primitive" and "derived" (p. 141) in the event calculus. State constraints for representing ramifications were introduced into the classical logic event calculus by Shanahan (1995a, pp. 262-264; 1997b, pp. 323-325). The reasons for using state constraints to encode indirect effects rather than effect axioms include "[avoiding] duplication of the same information on the consequent side of several action laws" (Sandewall, 1996, p. 99) and "[ensuring] a modular representation and ... dramatically [shortening] an axiomatisation" (Shanahan, 1999b, p. 141). Shanahan (1997b, pp. 123-124) calculates that the number of effect axioms needed to replace a state constraint

$$HoldsAt(\beta_1, t) \land \cdots \land HoldsAt(\beta_n, t) \Rightarrow HoldsAt(\beta, t)$$

is on the order of $\sum_{i=1}^{n} m_i$, where m_i is the number of effect axioms for β_i . Baral (2003) argues for the use of constraints rather than effect axioms to represent ramifications and uses the example of having to add separate effect axioms for the indirect effects of every type of transportation: " $drive_to(Y)$, $fly_to(Y)$, $take_a_train_to(Y)$, $take_a_bus_to(Y)$ " (p. 233).

Walking turkey scenario

Baker (1991, pp. 19-21) first described the walking turkey scenario due to Matthew L. Ginsberg: When a turkey that is walking is shot, it is no longer walking. F. Lin (1995) treats the ramification problem in the situation calculus by introducing a predicate Caused(p, v, s), which represents that fluent p is caused to have truth value v in situation v. (A similar proposal is made by McCain and Turner, 1995.) The walking turkey scenario is treated as follows. The direct effect of shooting is specified by the effect axiom (F. Lin, 1995, p. 1989).

```
Caused(dead, true, do(shoot, s))
```

The indirect effect of shooting on walking is specified by the "causal rule" (p. 1990):

$$dead(s) \supset Caused(walking, false, s)$$

The following successor state axiom for *dead* follows from the predicate completion (K. L. Clark, 1978, pp. 303-305) of *Caused* in the conjunction of effect axioms and causal rules (simplified from Lin, 1995, p. 1990):

```
walking(do(a, s)) \equiv
walking(s) \land \neg dead(s) \land a \neq shoot
```

Thus, the following indirect effect of shoot is derived (simplified from p. 1990):

```
\negwalking(do(shoot, s))
```

Gustafsson and Doherty (1996) treat indirect effects in the features and fluents framework, which is discussed in Section 16.2. They handle the walking turkey scenario using the "causal constraint" (we would handle this using an effect constraint) (p. 93)

$$\forall t[t] \neg alive \gg \neg walking$$

which gets translated into (p. 93)

```
\forall t[(\neg Holds(t, alive) \rightarrow \neg Holds(t, walking)) \land (Holds(t-1, alive) \land \neg Holds(t, alive) \rightarrow Occlude(t, walking))]
```

The event calculus analog of Gustafsson and Doherty's treatment of the walking turkey scenario is:

```
Terminates(Shoot(a,b),Alive(b),t)
Releases(Shoot(a,b),Walking(b),t)
\neg HoldsAt(Alive(a),t) \Rightarrow \neg HoldsAt(Walking(a),t).
```

Effect constraints

Shanahan (1997b, pp. 286-288, 324-325; 1999b, pp. 141-142) devised the effect constraint as a simple way of handling the walking turkey scenario in the event calculus. We need only add the effect constraint:

 $Terminates(e, Alive(a), t) \Rightarrow Terminates(e, Walking(a), t)$

Fluent calculus

Thielscher (1996, 1997) proposes the following method to deal with indirect effects in the fluent calculus. We are given a set of direct effect descriptions, causal relationships, and state constraints. A causal relationship is an expression such as (Thielscher, 1997, p. 323)

sw1 causes light if sw2

The successor state resulting from performing an action α in a state of the world is computed as follows. The direct effects of α are first computed, giving the first intermediate state. Zero or more additional intermediate states are obtained by repeatedly applying causal relationships to intermediate states. Any intermediate state satisfying the state constraints is a successor state. Thus, causal relationships are permitted to interact with one another before a successor state is obtained. A successor state is not guaranteed to exist, and there may be several successor states. Thielscher also proposes a method for automatically compiling state constraints into causal relationships.

Causal constraints

The circuit in Figure 6.1 is taken from Thielscher (1996, p. 19). This circuit is a slight modification of the circuit of Thielscher (1995), which in turn was inspired by Lifschitz's (1990b, pp. 371-372) circuit consisting of two switches and a light. Thielscher's circuit, which is handled by the methods he proposed, led to the introduction of causal constraints into the event calculus by Shanahan (1999b). The event calculus axioms for causal constraints and the axiomatization of Thielscher's circuit are from Shanahan (1999b). Our proof of Proposition 6.5 is based on that of Shanahan (1999b, pp. 143-144). The modified version of Thielscher's circuit (Figure 6.2) is taken from Shanahan (1999b, p. 145), who proves that a formalization of the circuit using causal constraints results in inconsistency. Shanahan (1999b, p. 146) suggests that this circuit could be more properly modeled by taking delays into account.

EXERCISES

6.1 Suppose that in the example in Section 6.5.1, (6.90) is replaced by the state constraint

 $HoldsAt(Lit(L), t) \Leftrightarrow HoldsAt(Closed(S1), t) \land HoldsAt(Closed(S2), t)$

Does the axiomatization still yield the conclusion that the light is off?

- **6.2** Suppose that in the example in Section 6.5.1, *Initiated* is replaced by *Started* in (6.90), (6.91), and (6.92). Does the axiomatization yield the conclusion that the light is off?
- 6.3 Formalize the circuit of Figure 6.1 using effect axioms, effect constraints, and state constraints instead of causal constraints. Discuss the advantages and disadvantages of this axiomatization as compared to that using causal constraints.
- 6.4 Formalize the following example from Denecker, Dupré, and Belleghem (1998, pp. 4-5): An electronic counter is connected to an input line. The value of the counter is initially zero. The value of the input line is initially false. The value of the input line may fluctuate arbitrarily between false and true. The counter counts how many times the input line changes from false to true. That is, whenever the value of the input line changes from false to true, the value of the counter is incremented by one.
- **6.5** (Research Problem) Automate the translation of circuit diagrams into event calculus axiomatizations.

Continuous Change

Discrete change is change that is limited to a countable, usually finite, set of timepoints. We represent discrete change in the event calculus using effect axioms. In a number of commonsense domains ranging from the physical to the mental, we find continuous change. A function f(t) is continuous at a point t_0 if and only if for every $\epsilon > 0$, there is a $\delta > 0$ such that $|t - t_0| < \delta$ implies $|f(t) - f(t_0)| < \epsilon$. A function is continuous on an interval if and only if it is continuous at all points of the interval. Examples of continuous change include the change in the height of a falling object, the location of a projectile, the water level of a filling bathtub, the volume of a balloon in the process of inflation, the frequency of a siren, the hunger level of an animal, and the anger level of a person. In the discrete event calculus, time is limited to the integers; there we speak of gradual change. In this chapter, we discuss the representation of continuous change and gradual change in the event calculus. We retrace the development of *Trajectory*. We discuss the use of trajectory and antitrajectory axioms.

TRAJECTORY AXIOMS

How should we represent continuous change? Let us consider the changing height of a falling object without air resistance.

7.1.1 EXAMPLE: FALLING OBJECT

An object O1 is at rest at height H prior to timepoint T_1 , starts to fall at timepoint T_1 , and hits the ground at timepoint $T_2 = T_1 + \sqrt{2H/G}$, where G is the acceleration due to gravity (9.8 m/s^2) :

$$t \le T_1 \Rightarrow HoldsAt(Height(O1, H), t)$$
 (7.1)

$$t \leq T_1 \Rightarrow HoldsAt(Height(O1, H), t)$$

$$t > T_1 \land t \leq T_2 \Rightarrow HoldsAt(Height(O1, H - \frac{1}{2}G(t - T_1)^2), t)$$

$$t > T_2 \Rightarrow HoldsAt(Height(O1, 0), t)$$

$$(7.1)$$

$$(7.2)$$

$$t > T_2 \Rightarrow HoldsAt(Height(O1, 0), t)$$
 (7.3)

We have a state constraint that says that an object has a unique height at any given time:

$$HoldsAt(Height(o, h_1), t) \land HoldsAt(Height(o, h_2), t) \Rightarrow$$
 (7.4)
$$h_1 = h_2$$

The height of O1 is released from the commonsense law of inertia:

$$ReleasedAt(Height(O1, h), t)$$
 (7.5)

From this axiomatization, we can determine the height of O1 at any timepoint. For instance, if $(T_1 + 2) \le T_2$, then the height of O1 at timepoint $T_1 + 2$ is H - 2G.

Proposition 7.1. If $(T_1 + 2) \le T_2$, $\Psi = (7.4)$, and $\Gamma = (7.1) \land (7.2) \land (7.3) \land (7.5)$, then $\Psi \land \Gamma \vdash HoldsAt(Height(O1, H - 2G), T_1 + 2)$.

Proof. From
$$(T_1 + 2) > T_1$$
, $(T_1 + 2) \le T_2$, and (7.2) , we have $HoldsAt(Height(O1, H - \frac{1}{2}G((T_1 + 2) - T_1)^2), T_1 + 2)$ or $HoldsAt(Height(O1, H - 2G), T_1 + 2)$.

Although this axiomatization describes a falling object, it fails to capture our commonsense knowledge about falling objects. Namely, when an object is dropped, it starts to fall; when an object hits the ground, it stops falling. Therefore, we integrate events into our representation of continuous change. One event will set in motion an episode of continuous change, whereas another event will stop the episode. We use fluents to represent episodes of continuous change.

7.1.2 EXAMPLE: FALLING OBJECT WITH EVENTS

We model a falling object using events. We have an episode of no change (the object at rest above the ground), followed by an episode of continuous change (falling), followed by another episode of no change (the object hits the ground).

We use the following axiomatization. If an agent drops an object, then the object will be falling, and the height of the object will be released from the commonsense law of inertia:

$$Initiates(Drop(a, o), Falling(o), t)$$
(7.6)

$$Releases(Drop(a, o), Height(o, h), t)$$
 (7.7)

In EC and DEC, events are instantaneous. Notice that we are using the fluent *Falling* here as a way of representing an event with duration or a process. (We present a modification of EC for events with duration in Appendix C.)

We describe the motion of the object from the moment it is dropped until it stops falling as follows:

$$HoldsAt(Height(o, h), t_1) \wedge \tag{7.8}$$

$$Happens(Drop(a, o), t_1) \wedge 0 < t_2 \wedge$$

$$\neg StoppedIn(t_1, Falling(o), t_1 + t_2) \Rightarrow$$

$$HoldsAt(Height(o, h - \frac{1}{2}Gt_2^2), t_1 + t_2)$$

If an object hits the ground, then the object will no longer be falling:

$$Terminates(HitGround(o), Falling(o), t)$$
 (7.9)

A falling object hits the ground when its height becomes zero:

$$HoldsAt(Falling(o), t) \land$$
 (7.10)
 $HoldsAt(Height(o, 0), t) \Rightarrow$
 $Happens(HitGround(o), t)$

If an object hits the ground and the height of the object is h, then the height of the object will no longer be released from the commonsense law of inertia and the height of the object will be h:

$$HoldsAt(Height(o, h), t) \Rightarrow$$
 (7.11)

Initiates(HitGround(o), Height(o, h), t)

An object has a unique height:

$$HoldsAt(Height(o, h_1), t) \land HoldsAt(Height(o, h_2), t) \Rightarrow$$
 (7.12)
 $h_1 = h_2$

At timepoint 0, Nathan drops an apple whose height is G/2:

$$\neg HoldsAt(Falling(Apple), 0)$$
 (7.13)

$$HoldsAt(Height(Apple, G/2), 0)$$
 (7.14)

$$Happens(Drop(Nathan, Apple), 0)$$
 (7.15)

We can show that the apple will hit the ground at timepoint 1 and that its height at timepoint 2 will be zero.

Proposition 7.2. Let $\Sigma = (7.6) \wedge (7.7) \wedge (7.9) \wedge (7.11)$, $\Delta = (7.10) \wedge (7.15)$, $\Omega = U[Drop, HitGround] \wedge U[Falling, Height]$, $\Psi = (7.12)$, $\Pi = (7.8)$, and $\Gamma = (7.13) \wedge (7.14)$. Then we have

$$CIRC[\Sigma; Initiates, Terminates, Releases] \land CIRC[\Delta; Happens] \land$$

$$\Omega \wedge \Psi \wedge \Pi \wedge \Gamma \wedge EC$$

 $\vdash HoldsAt(Height(Apple, 0), 1) \land$

 $Happens(HitGround(Apple), 1) \land$

HoldsAt(Height(Apple, 0), 2)

Proof. From $CIRC[\Sigma; Initiates, Terminates, Releases]$ and Theorems 2.1 and 2.2, we have

$$Initiates(e, f, t) \Leftrightarrow \tag{7.16}$$

 $\exists a, o (e = Drop(a, o) \land f = Falling(o)) \lor$

 $\exists o, h (e = HitGround(o) \land$

 $f = Height(o, h) \land$

HoldsAt(Height(o, h), t))

$$Terminates(e, f, t) \Leftrightarrow$$
 (7.17)

 $\exists o (e = HitGround(o) \land f = Falling(o))$

$$Releases(e, f, t) \Leftrightarrow$$
 (7.18)

 $\exists a, o, h (e = Drop(a, o) \land f = Height(o, h))$

From $CIRC[\Delta; Happens]$ and Theorem 2.1, we have

$$Happens(e,t) \Leftrightarrow (7.19)$$

$$\exists o \ (e = HitGround(o) \land HoldsAt(Falling(o),t) \land HoldsAt(Height(o,0),t)) \lor (e = Drop(Nathan, Apple) \land t = 0)$$

We can show

$$\neg \exists t (0 < t < 1 \land Happens(HitGround(Apple), t))$$
 (7.20)

To see this, suppose, to the contrary, that

$$\exists t (0 < t < 1 \land Happens(HitGround(Apple), t))$$

Let $Happens(HitGround(Apple), \tau)$ be the first such event. That is, we have

$$0 < \tau < 1 \tag{7.21}$$

$$Happens(HitGround(Apple), \tau)$$
 (7.22)

$$\neg \exists \tau' (0 < \tau' < \tau \land Happens(HitGround(Apple), \tau'))$$
 (7.23)

From (7.22) and (7.19), we have

$$HoldsAt(Height(Apple, 0), \tau)$$
 (7.24)

From (7.17), (7.23), and EC3, we have $\neg StoppedIn(0, Falling(Apple), \tau)$. From this, (7.14), (7.15) (which follows from (7.19)), $0 < \tau$ (which follows from (7.21)), and (7.8), we have

$$HoldsAt(Height(Apple, \frac{1}{2}G(1-\tau^2)), \tau)$$

From this, (7.21), and (7.12), we have $\neg HoldsAt(Height(Apple, 0), \tau)$, which contradicts (7.24).

From (7.17), (7.20), and EC3, we have

$$\neg StoppedIn(0, Falling(Apple), 1)$$
 (7.25)

From this, (7.14), (7.15) (which follows from (7.19)), 0 < 1, and (7.8), we have

$$HoldsAt(Height(Apple, 0), 1)$$
 (7.26)

From (7.18), we have

$$\neg ReleasedIn(0, Falling(Apple), 1)$$

From this, (7.15) (which follows from (7.19)), (7.6) (which follows from (7.16)), 0 < 1, (7.25), and EC14, we have HoldsAt(Falling(Apple), 1). From this, (7.26), and (7.10) (which follows from (7.19)), we have

$$Happens(HitGround(Apple), 1)$$
 (7.27)

From (7.17) and EC3, we have

$$\neg StoppedIn(1, Height(Apple, 0), 2)$$
 (7.28)

From (7.18), (7.19), and EC13, we have $\neg ReleasedIn(1, Height(Apple, 0), 2)$. From this, (7.27), (7.26), (7.11) (which follows from (7.16)), 1 < 2, (7.28), and EC14, we have HoldsAt(Height(Apple, 0), 2).

7.1.3 INTRODUCTION OF TRAJECTORY PREDICATE

We introduce the predicate $Trajectory(\beta_1, \tau_1, \beta_2, \tau_2)$, which allows us to express (7.8) more compactly.

Definition 7.1. If γ is a condition, β_1 and β_2 are fluent terms, and τ_1 and τ_2 are timepoint terms, then

$$\gamma \Rightarrow Trajectory(\beta_1, \tau_1, \beta_2, \tau_2)$$

is a *trajectory axiom*. This represents that, if γ is true, fluent β_1 is initiated by an event that occurs at timepoint τ_1 , and $\tau_2 > 0$, then fluent β_2 will be true at timepoint $\tau_1 + \tau_2$.

Thus, instead of (7.8) we may simply write:

$$HoldsAt(Height(o,h),t_1) \Rightarrow \tag{7.29}$$

$$Trajectory(Falling(o),t_1,Height(o,h-\frac{1}{2}Gt_2^2),t_2)$$

Using the *Trajectory* predicate, we show that the apple hits the ground at timepoint 1 and that it has zero height at timepoint 2.

Proposition 7.3. Let $\Sigma = (7.6) \wedge (7.7) \wedge (7.9) \wedge (7.11)$, $\Delta = (7.10) \wedge (7.15)$, $\Omega = U[Drop, HitGround] \wedge U[Falling, Height]$, $\Psi = (7.12)$, $\Pi = (7.29)$, and $\Gamma = (7.13) \wedge (7.14)$. Then we have

 $CIRC[\Sigma; Initiates, Terminates, Releases] \land CIRC[\Delta; Happens] \land$ $\Omega \land \Psi \land \Pi \land \Gamma \land EC$

 $\vdash HoldsAt(Height(Apple, 0), 1) \land \\$

 $Happens(HitGround(Apple), 1) \land$

HoldsAt(Height(Apple, 0), 2)

Proof. The proof is identical to that of Proposition 7.2, except that (7.8) is replaced by the conjunction of (7.29), (7.6) (which follows from (7.16)), and EC5.

7.2 ANTITRAJECTORY AXIOMS

The AntiTrajectory predicate is analogous to the Trajectory predicate, except that it is brought into play when a fluent is terminated rather than initiated by an occurring event.

Definition 7.2. If γ is a condition, β_1 and β_2 are fluent terms, and τ_1 and τ_2 are timepoint terms, then

$$\gamma \Rightarrow AntiTrajectory(\beta_1, \tau_1, \beta_2, \tau_2)$$

is an antitrajectory axiom. This represents that if γ is true, fluent β_1 is terminated by an event that occurs at timepoint τ_1 , and $\tau_2 > 0$, then fluent β_2 will be true at timepoint $\tau_1 + \tau_2$.

7.2.1 EXAMPLE: HOT AIR BALLOON

This example and the trajectory and antitrajectory axioms are due to Rob Miller and Murray Shanahan. We have two effect axioms. If an agent turns on the heater of a hot air balloon, then the heater will be on:

$$Initiates(TurnOnHeater(a,b), HeaterOn(b), t)$$
 (7.30)

If an agent turns off the heater of a hot air balloon, then the heater will no longer be on:

$$Terminates(TurnOffHeater(a, b), HeaterOn(b), t)$$
 (7.31)

We have a state constraint:

$$HoldsAt(Height(b, h_1), t) \land$$
 (7.32)
 $HoldsAt(Height(b, h_2), t) \Rightarrow$ $h_1 = h_2$

We have the following trajectory and antitrajectory axioms:

$$HoldsAt(Height(b,h),t_1) \Rightarrow$$
 (7.33)
 $Trajectory(HeaterOn(b),t_1,Height(b,h+V\cdot t_2),t_2)$

$$HoldsAt(Height(b,h),t_1) \Rightarrow$$
 (7.34)
 $AntiTrajectory(HeaterOn(b),t_1,Height(b,h-V\cdot t_2),t_2)$

where V is the velocity of the balloon.

We have the following observations and narrative. The balloon starts out at height 0:

$$HoldsAt(Height(Balloon, 0), 0)$$
 (7.35)

The height of a balloon is always released from the commonsense law of inertia:

$$ReleasedAt(Height(b,h),t)$$
 (7.36)

At timepoint 0 the heater is turned on, and at timepoint 2 the heater is turned off:

$$Happens(TurnOffHeater(Nathan, Balloon), 2)$$
 (7.38)

We can show that the height of the balloon is 2V at timepoint 2 and is V at timepoint 3.

Proposition 7.4. Let $\Sigma = (7.30) \land (7.31), \ \Delta = (7.37) \land (7.38), \ \Omega = U[TurnOn]$ Heater, TurnOffHeater] \wedge U[HeaterOn, Height], $\Psi = (7.32)$, $\Pi = (7.33) \wedge (7.34)$, and $\Gamma = (7.35) \wedge (7.36)$. Then we have

$$CIRC[\Sigma; Initiates, Terminates, Releases] \land CIRC[\Delta; Happens] \land \\ \Omega \land \Psi \land \Pi \land \Gamma \land EC$$

$$\vdash$$
 HoldsAt(Height(Balloon, 2V), 2) \land HoldsAt(Height(Balloon, V), 3)

Proof. From $CIRC[\Sigma; Initiates, Terminates, Releases]$ and Theorems 2.1 and 2.2, we have

$$Initiates(e, f, t) \Leftrightarrow \tag{7.39}$$

 $\exists a, b \ (e = TurnOnHeater(a, b) \land HeaterOn(b))$

$$Terminates(e, f, t) \Leftrightarrow$$
 (7.40)

 $\exists a, b \ (e = TurnOffHeater(a, b) \land HeaterOn(b))$

$$\neg Releases(e, f, t)$$
 (7.41)

From $CIRC[\Delta; Happens]$ and Theorem 2.1, we have

$$Happens(e,t) \Leftrightarrow$$
 (7.42)

 $(e = TurnOnHeater(Nathan, Balloon) \land t = 0) \land (e = TurnOffHeater(Nathan, Balloon) \land t = 2)$

From (7.42) and EC3, we have $\neg StoppedIn(0, HeaterOn(Balloon), 2)$. From this, (7.37) (which follows from (7.42)), (7.30) (which follows from (7.39)), 0 < 2, (7.35), (7.33), and EC5, we have

$$HoldsAt(Height(Balloon, 2V), 2)$$
 (7.43)

From (7.42) and EC4, we have $\neg StartedIn(2, HeaterOff(Balloon), 3)$. From this, (7.38) (which follows from (7.42)), (7.31) (which follows from (7.40)), 0 < 1, (7.43), (7.34), and EC6, we have HoldsAt(Height(Balloon, V), 3).

7.3 USING ANTITRAJECTORY INSTEAD OF RELEASES

We may sometimes use AntiTrajectory to replace Releases.

7.3.1 EXAMPLE: FALLING OBJECT WITH ANTITRAJECTORY

Consider again the example of the falling object. First, we state that the height of an object is always released from the commonsense law of inertia:

$$ReleasedAt(Height(o,h),t)$$
 (7.44)

Then, we replace (7.7) and (7.11) with

$$HoldsAt(Height(o, h), t_1) \Rightarrow$$
 (7.45)
 $AntiTrajectory(Falling(o), t_1, Height(o, h), t_2)$

That is, when an object stops falling, its height stays constant.

We can show that the apple hits the ground at timepoint 1, and has a height of zero at timepoint 2.

Proposition 7.5. Let $\Sigma = (7.6) \wedge (7.9)$, $\Delta = (7.10) \wedge (7.15)$, $\Omega = U[Drop, HitGround] \wedge U[Falling, Height]$, $\Psi = (7.12)$, $\Pi = (7.29) \wedge (7.45)$, and $\Gamma = (7.13) \wedge (7.14) \wedge (7.44)$. Then we have

 $CIRC[\Sigma; Initiates, Terminates, Releases] \land CIRC[\Delta; Happens] \land \\ \Omega \land \Psi \land \Pi \land \Gamma \land EC \\ \vdash HoldsAt(Height(Apple, 0), 1) \land \\ Happens(HitGround(Apple), 1) \land \\ HoldsAt(Height(Apple, 0), 2)$

Proof. From $CIRC[\Sigma; Initiates, Terminates, Releases]$ and Theorems 2.1 and 2.2, we have

Initiates(e,f,t)
$$\Leftrightarrow$$
 (7.46)
 $\exists a, o \ (e = Drop(a, o) \land f = Falling(o))$

Terminates(e, f, t)
$$\Leftrightarrow$$
 (7.47)
 $\exists o (e = HitGround(o) \land f = Falling(o))$

$$\neg Releases(e, f, t)$$
 (7.48)

From $CIRC[\Delta; Happens]$ and Theorem 2.1, we have

$$Happens(e,t) \Leftrightarrow (7.49)$$

$$\exists o \ (e = HitGround(o) \land HoldsAt(Falling(o), t) \land HoldsAt(Height(o, 0), t)) \lor (e = Drop(Nathan, Apple) \land t = 0)$$

We can show

$$\neg \exists t (0 < t < 1 \land Happens(HitGround(Apple), t))$$
 (7.50)

Suppose for contradiction that

$$\exists t (0 < t < 1 \land Happens(HitGround(Apple), t))$$

Let $Happens(HitGround(Apple), \tau)$ be the first such event. Thus we have

$$0 < \tau < 1 \tag{7.51}$$

$$Happens(HitGround(Apple), \tau).$$
 (7.52)

$$\neg \exists \tau' (0 < \tau' < \tau \land Happens(HitGround(Apple), \tau'))$$
 (7.53)

From (7.52) and (7.49), we have

$$HoldsAt(Height(Apple, 0), \tau)$$
 (7.54)

From (7.47), (7.53), and EC3, we have $\neg StoppedIn(0, Falling(Apple), \tau)$. From this, (7.15) (which follows from (7.49)), (7.6) (which follows from (7.46)), $0 < \tau$ (which follows from 7.51), (7.14), (7.29), and EC5, we have

$$HoldsAt(Height(Apple, \frac{1}{2}G(1-\tau^2)), \tau)$$

From this, (7.51), and (7.12), we have $\neg HoldsAt(Height(Apple, 0), \tau)$, which contradicts (7.54).

From (7.47), (7.50), and EC3, we have

$$\neg StoppedIn(0, Falling(Apple), 1)$$
 (7.55)

From this, (7.15) (which follows from (7.49)), (7.6) (which follows from (7.46)), 0 < 1, (7.14), (7.29), and EC5, we have

$$HoldsAt(Height(Apple, 0), 1)$$
 (7.56)

From (7.48), we have

 $\neg ReleasedIn(0, Falling(Apple), 1)$

From this, (7.55), (7.15) (which follows from (7.49)), (7.6) (which follows from (7.46)), 0 < 1, and EC14, we have HoldsAt(Falling(Apple), 1). From this, (7.56), and (7.10) (which follows from (7.49)), we have

$$Happens(HitGround(Apple), 1)$$
 (7.57)

From (7.46), (7.49), and EC4, we have $\neg StartedIn(1, Falling(Apple), 2)$. From this, (7.57), (7.9) (which follows from (7.47)), 0 < 1, (7.56), (7.45), and EC6, we have HoldsAt(Height(Apple, 0), 2).

BIBLIOGRAPHIC NOTES

Hendrix (1973) extends the language of STRIPS (Fikes & Nilsson, 1971) to deal with "continuous, gradual change" (Hendrix, 1973, p. 146). A process such as filling a bucket is subject to "continuance conditions" (p. 161), or conditions necessary for the process to continue. Filling a bucket has the continuance conditions that the tap must be turned on, the bucket must be facing up, and the amount of water in the bucket must be less than its capacity. When any such condition is violated, the filling process is interrupted. Proposals for integrating continuous change into the situation calculus have been made by Gelfond, Lifschitz, and Rabinov (1991), Pinto (1994), and R. Miller and Shanahan (1994). See the discussion in the Bibliographic notes of Chapter 16. Proposals have been made for other formalisms for reasoning about action and change (Herrmann & Thielscher, 1996; McDermott, 1982; Sandewall, 1989a; Van Belleghem, Denecker, & De Schreye, 1994). The area of qualitative reasoning, discussed in Section 17.1, deals with continuous change. Shanahan (1995a) introduced the classical logic event calculus, which included the *Trajectory* predicate (p. 268). This predicate was previously introduced by Shanahan (1990) into a simplified version of the original event calculus (Kowalski & Sergot, 1986).

The example of a falling object has been used by McCarthy (1963), McCarthy and Hayes (1969, p. 479), and Shanahan (1990, p. 598). The method for showing ¬StoppedIn(0, Falling(Apple), 1) in the proofs of Propositions 7.2, 7.3,

7.5, and 10.2 is taken from Shanahan (1997b, pp. 328-329; 2004, p. 161). Reiter (2001, pp. 149-150) discusses the use of fluents to represent processes or actions with duration. The *AntiTrajectory* predicate was introduced by R. Miller and Shanahan (1999, pp. 13-15; 2002, pp. 466-470). The hot air balloon example is from R. Miller and Shanahan (1999, p. 14; 2002, p. 468). Shanahan (1990) shows how multiple flows into a vessel can be handled. Van Belleghem, Denecker, and De Schreye (1994) show how to handle multiple simultaneous (and possibly continuously changing) influences on a quantity. R. Miller and Shanahan (1996) treat continuously changing parameters in the event calculus using differential equations. We have discussed trajectories in the context of continuous change. But as R. Miller and Shanahan (2002, p. 468) note, trajectories are not required to be continuous. They give the example of using a trajectory axiom to model a blinking light.

EXERCISES

- 7.1 Formalize an expanding balloon.
- 7.2 Formalize the following. A person's level of hunger gradually increases. When a person's hunger level rises above a certain threshold, the person starts to eat. When a person finishes eating, the person's hunger level is lowered and starts to increase again.
- **7.3** Extend the formalization of the falling object in Section 7.1.2 so that (1) an object *P* is initially resting on a high object *Q*; (2) when *P* is pushed, *P* is no longer on *Q* and *P* starts falling; and (3) after *P* hits the ground, *P* rests on the ground.
- 7.4 Extend the formalization of the hot air balloon in Section 7.2.1 to deal with what happens when the balloon hits the ground.
- 7.5 Formalize a puck bouncing off a wall in the game of air hockey. Assume there is no friction. Assume there is a horizontal wall at y = 0 and a puck. If the y coordinate of a moving puck is 0, then the puck will bounce off the wall.
- 7.6 Extend the formalization of air hockey so that an agent may hit the puck with a mallet.
- 7.7 Formalize a rocket with constant thrust. When the thrust is on, it moves upward with an acceleration of T G, where T is the acceleration due to the thrust. When the thrust is off, it falls with an acceleration of G.
- **7.8** Formalize snow falling from the sky. When it is snowing, snowflakes fall. Model the falling of individual snowflakes.

Concurrent Events

The event calculus allows several events to occur at the same time, because we may have event occurrences $Happens(\alpha_1, \tau_1)$ and $Happens(\alpha_2, \tau_2)$ such that $\alpha_1 \neq \alpha_2$ and $\tau_1 = \tau_2$. In this case, we say that the event occurrences are concurrent or simultaneous. In this chapter, we first consider some concurrent event occurrences that we might want to prohibit and methods for prohibiting them. Then, we discuss concurrent event occurrences that have cumulative and canceling effects and how to handle them.

8.1 RESTRICTING CONCURRENCY

The commonsense world places certain restrictions on what events can occur simultaneously. This section presents two methods for representing these restrictions in the event calculus: (1) state constraints and (2) event occurrence constraints.

8.1.1 STATE CONSTRAINTS

The first method of restricting concurrency is to use state constraints. This method relies on the fact that, if the effects of two events are inconsistent with a state constraint, then those events cannot occur concurrently. Consider an agent that can walk from one room to another. We have the effect axioms:

$$Initiates(Walk(a, r_1, r_2), InRoom(a, r_2), t)$$

 $r_1 \neq r_2 \Rightarrow Terminates(Walk(a, r_1, r_2), InRoom(a, r_1), t)$

Now, a commonsense fact is that an agent cannot walk into one room at the same time that the agent walks into some other room. This can be represented using a state constraint that says that an agent can be in one room at a time:

$$HoldsAt(InRoom(a, r_1), t) \land$$
 (8.1)
 $HoldsAt(InRoom(a, r_2), t) \Rightarrow$
 $r_1 = r_2$

Given these axioms, we cannot, say, have both Nathan walking into the kitchen at timepoint 0:

Happens (Walk (Nathan, Hallway, Kitchen), 0)

128

and Nathan walking into the living room at timepoint 0:

Happens(Walk(Nathan, Hallway, LivingRoom), 0)

If we did, we would get inconsistency. We could show

 $HoldsAt(InRoom(Nathan, Kitchen), 1) \land$

HoldsAt(InRoom(Nathan, LivingRoom), 1)

which contradicts (8.1).

Similarly, the fact that two agents cannot simultaneously pick up the same object can be represented using a state constraint that says that an object can be held by one agent at a time:

$$HoldsAt(Holding(a_1, o), t) \land HoldsAt(Holding(a_2, o), t) \Rightarrow a_1 = a_2$$

8.1.2 EVENT OCCURRENCE CONSTRAINTS

The second method of restricting concurrency is to use *event occurrence constraints*, or formulas involving two or more atoms of the form $Happens(\alpha, \tau)$, where α is an event term and τ is a timepoint term. We now describe several common idioms.

Totally ordered plans

When solving abduction or planning problems, we may wish to insist that the plan be a *totally ordered plan*, or simple sequence of event occurrences. We can do this with an event occurrence constraint that says that at most one event can occur at a time:

$$Happens(e_1,t) \wedge Happens(e_2,t) \Rightarrow e_1 = e_2$$

Different conflicting actions of two agents

It may be desirable to restrict concurrency for different but conflicting actions of two agents. Consider the following effect axioms dealing with moving a jar and putting a penny in a jar:

$$Initiates(Move(a, j, l_1, l_2), At(j, l_2), t)$$

$$l_1 \neq l_2 \Rightarrow Terminates(Move(a, j, l_1, l_2), At(j, l_1), t)$$

$$HoldsAt(At(p,l),t) \land HoldsAt(At(j,l),t) \Rightarrow$$

 $Initiates(PutIn(a,p,j,l),In(p,j),t)$

We may wish to state that an agent cannot place a penny in a jar at the same time that another agent moves the jar, even though this is permitted by these axioms. We can do this by adding the axiom

$$Happens(Move(a_1, j, l_1, l_2), t) \land a_1 \neq a_2 \Rightarrow \neg Happens(PutIn(a_2, p, j, l_1), t)$$

Similar conflicting actions of two agents

It is sometimes desirable to restrict concurrency for similar actions of two agents. Suppose we have an effect axiom that says that, if a piece of food is not eaten and an agent eats the piece of food, then the piece of food will be eaten:

```
\neg HoldsAt(Eaten(p), t) \Rightarrow
Initiates(Eat(a, p), Eaten(p), t)
```

Nothing will prevent two agents from simultaneously eating the same piece of food. To prevent this, we may add the axiom

```
Happens(Eat(a_1, p), t) \land a_1 \neq a_2 \Rightarrow \neg Happens(Eat(a_2, p), t)
```

Different conflicting actions of one agent

We may wish to restrict concurrency for different but conflicting actions within a single agent. An agent may not be able to pat the agent's head and rub the agent's stomach at the same time:

```
Happens(PatHead(a), t) \Rightarrow \neg Happens(RubStomach(a), t)
```

Similar conflicting actions of one agent

We may also wish to restrict concurrency for similar actions within a single agent. Even if an agent can be holding several objects at the same time, the agent may not be able to pick up two objects simultaneously:

```
Happens(PickUp(a, o_1), t) \land Happens(PickUp(a, o_2), t) \Rightarrow o_1 = o_2
```

8.1.3 DISCUSSION

In order to recognize situations that might require restrictions on concurrency, we look for actions that use, consume, or provide the same resource at the same time.

Notice that EC and DEC disallow concurrent event occurrences with contradictory effects. If a fluent is simultaneously initiated and terminated by an occurring event, we get inconsistency. Consider the effect axioms

```
Initiates(Break(a, d), Broken(d), t)
Terminates(Fix(a, d), Broken(d), t)
```

and the event occurrence formulas

```
Happens(Break(Nathan, TV), 1)
Happens(Fix(Nathan, TV), 1)
```

From these we have both HoldsAt(Broken(TV), 2) and $\neg HoldsAt(Broken(TV), 2)$.

8.2 CUMULATIVE AND CANCELING EFFECTS

When several events occur at the same time, the effects of those events might differ from what the effects would have been had the events occurred at different times. Specifically, two or more concurrent events can produce new, additional effects.

In this case, we say that the effects of the events are cumulative. Further, one event can cancel the normal effects of another event.

We represent cumulative effects using modified effect axioms.

Definition 8.1. If γ is a condition, α and $\alpha_1, \ldots, \alpha_n$ are event terms, β is a fluent term, and τ is a timepoint term, then

$$\gamma \wedge (\neg) Happens(\alpha_1, \tau) \wedge \cdots \wedge (\neg) Happens(\alpha_n, \tau) \Rightarrow Initiates(\alpha, \beta, \tau)$$

is a *positive cumulative effect axiom*. This represents that, if γ is true and α and $\alpha_1, \ldots, \alpha_n$ all occur at τ , then β will be true after τ .

Definition 8.2. If γ is a condition, α and $\alpha_1, \ldots, \alpha_n$ are event terms, β is a fluent term, and τ is a timepoint term, then

$$\gamma \wedge (\neg) Happens(\alpha_1, \tau) \wedge \cdots \wedge (\neg) Happens(\alpha_n, \tau) \Rightarrow Terminates(\alpha, \beta, \tau)$$

is a *negative cumulative effect axiom*. This represents that if γ is true and α and $\alpha_1, \ldots, \alpha_n$ all occur at τ , then β will be false after τ .

We represent that one event cancels the effect of another event as follows. Suppose that a positive effect axiom represents that, if γ is true, then α_1 initiates a fluent β :

$$\gamma \Rightarrow Initiates(\alpha_1, \beta, \tau)$$

In order to represent that α_2 cancels the effect β of α_1 , we rewrite this axiom as:

$$\gamma \land \neg Happens(\alpha_2, \tau) \Rightarrow Initiates(\alpha_1, \beta, \tau)$$

We treat negative effect axioms in a similar fashion.

8.2.1 EXAMPLE: CAMERA WITH FLASH

Consider a camera with a flash unit. If a camera's shutter is released at the same instant that its flash is triggered, then we have the cumulative effect that a properly exposed picture is taken:

$$Happens(TriggerFlash(c), t) \Rightarrow$$
 (8.2)

Initiates(ReleaseShutter(c), ProperlyExposedPicture(t), t)

If a camera's shutter is released and its flash is not triggered at the same instant, then an improperly exposed picture is taken:

$$\neg Happens(TriggerFlash(c), t) \Rightarrow$$
 (8.3)

Initiates(ReleaseShutter(c), ImproperlyExposedPicture(t), t)

The shutter is released at timepoints 0 and 1, but only at timepoint 1 is the flash triggered:

$$\neg ReleasedAt(f,t)$$
 (8.4)

$$Happens(ReleaseShutter(Camera), 0)$$
 (8.5)

$$Happens(TriggerFlash(Camera), 1)$$
 (8.6)

$$Happens(ReleaseShutter(Camera), 1)$$
 (8.7)

We can show that an improperly exposed picture is taken at timepoint 0 and that a properly exposed picture is taken at timepoint 1.

Proposition 8.1. Let $\Sigma = (8.2) \wedge (8.3)$, $\Delta = (8.5) \wedge (8.6) \wedge (8.7)$, $\Omega = U[Trigger\ Flash,\ ReleaseShutter] \wedge U[ProperlyExposedPicture,\ ImproperlyExposedPicture], and <math>\Gamma = (8.4)$. Then we have

 $CIRC[\Sigma; Initiates, Terminates, Releases] \land CIRC[\Delta; Happens] \land$

 $\Omega \wedge \Gamma \wedge DEC$

 $\vdash HoldsAt(ImproperlyExposedPicture(0), 1) \ \land \\$

HoldsAt(ProperlyExposedPicture(1), 2)

Proof. From $CIRC[\Sigma; Initiates, Terminates, Releases]$ and Theorems 2.1 and 2.2, we have

Initiates(e,f,t)
$$\Leftrightarrow$$
 (8.8)
 $\exists c \ (e = ReleaseShutter(c) \land$
 $f = ProperlyExposedPicture(t) \land$
 $Happens(TriggerFlash(c),t)) \lor$
 $\exists c \ (e = ReleaseShutter(c) \land$
 $f = ImproperlyExposedPicture(t) \land$
 $\neg Happens(TriggerFlash(c),t))$

$$\neg Terminates(e, f, t)$$
 (8.9)

$$\neg Releases(e, f, t)$$
 (8.10)

From $CIRC[\Delta; Happens]$ and Theorem 2.1, we have

$$Happens(e,t) \Leftrightarrow$$
 (8.11)
 $(e = ReleaseShutter(Camera) \land t = 0) \lor$
 $(e = TriggerFlash(Camera) \land t = 1) \lor$
 $(e = ReleaseShutter(Camera) \land t = 1)$

From (8.11), we have $\neg Happens(TriggerFlash(Camera), 0)$. From this, (8.5) (which follows from (8.11)), (8.3) (which follows from (8.8)), and DEC9, we have HoldsAt(ImproperlyExposedPicture(0), 1). From (8.6) and (8.7) (which both follow from (8.11)), (8.2) (which follows from (8.8)), and DEC9, we have HoldsAt(ProperlyExposedPicture(1), 2).

8.2.2 EXAMPLE: MOVING ROBOT

Another example is that of a simple robot. At any time, the robot has a unique location in two-dimensional space:

$$HoldsAt(Location(r, x_1, y_1), t) \land$$
 (8.12)

132

$$HoldsAt(Location(r, x_2, y_2), t) \Rightarrow x_1 = x_2 \land y_1 = y_2$$

And at any time, a robot has a unique direction given by an angle in radians measured counterclockwise from the x axis:

$$HoldsAt(Direction(r, d_1), t) \land$$
 (8.13)
 $HoldsAt(Direction(r, d_2), t) \Rightarrow$
 $d_1 = d_2$

A robot has a left wheel and a right wheel. The wheels can be moved separately or at the same time. Moving the left wheel cancels the effect of moving the right wheel, and moving the right wheel cancels the effect of moving the left wheel. Thus, if a robot moves only its left wheel, then the robot will rotate clockwise by $\pi/180$ radians (1 degree):

$$\neg Happens(MoveRightWheel(r), t) \land \qquad (8.14)$$

$$HoldsAt(Direction(r, d), t) \Rightarrow$$

$$Initiates(MoveLeftWheel(r), Direction(r, d - \pi/180), t)$$

$$\neg Happens(MoveRightWheel(r), t) \land$$

$$HoldsAt(Direction(r, d), t) \Rightarrow$$

$$Terminates(MoveLeftWheel(r), Direction(r, d), t)$$

$$(8.15)$$

If a robot moves its only right wheel, then the robot will rotate counterclockwise by $\pi/180$ radians:

$$\neg Happens(MoveLeftWheel(r), t) \land \qquad (8.16)$$

$$HoldsAt(Direction(r, d), t) \Rightarrow$$

$$Initiates(MoveRightWheel(r), Direction(r, d + \pi/180), t)$$

$$\neg Happens(MoveLeftWheel(r), t) \land \qquad (8.17)$$

$$HoldsAt(Direction(r, d), t) \Rightarrow$$

$$Terminates(MoveRightWheel(r), Direction(r, d), t)$$

Moving the left and right wheels simultaneously has a cumulative effect. Namely, if a robot moves its left and right wheels at the same time, then the robot will move forward by one unit:

$$Happens(MoveLeftWheel(r), t) \land \tag{8.18}$$

$$HoldsAt(Location(r, x, y), t) \land$$

$$HoldsAt(Direction(r, d), t) \Rightarrow$$

$$Initiates(MoveRightWheel(r), Location(r, x + Cos(d), y + Sin(d)), t)$$

$$Happens(MoveLeftWheel(r), t) \land \qquad (8.19)$$

$$HoldsAt(Location(r, x, y), t) \Rightarrow$$

$$Terminates(MoveRightWheel(r), Location(r, x, y), t)$$

Consider the following observations and narrative. The robot is initially at location (0,0), and its direction is 0 (facing right):

$$\neg ReleasedAt(f,t)$$
 (8.20)

$$HoldsAt(Location(Robot, 0, 0), 0)$$
 (8.21)

$$HoldsAt(Direction(Robot, 0), 0)$$
 (8.22)

At timepoint 0, the robot moves its right wheel; at timepoint 1, the robot moves both its left and right wheels:

$$Happens(MoveRightWheel(Robot), 0)$$
 (8.23)

$$Happens(MoveLeftWheel(Robot), 1)$$
 (8.24)

$$Happens(MoveRightWheel(Robot), 1)$$
 (8.25)

We can show that at timepoint 2, the robot will be at location $\langle Cos(\pi/180), Sin(\pi/180) \rangle$.

Proposition 8.2. Let $\Sigma = (8.14) \land (8.15) \land (8.16) \land (8.17) \land (8.18) \land (8.19),$ $\Delta = (8.23) \land (8.24) \land (8.25),$ $\Omega = U[MoveLeftWheel, MoveRightWheel] \land U[Direction, Location], <math>\Psi = (8.12) \land (8.13), and \Gamma = (8.20) \land (8.21) \land (8.22). Then we have$

$$CIRC[\Sigma; Initiates, Terminates, Releases] \land CIRC[\Delta; Happens] \land$$

$$\Omega \wedge \Psi \wedge \Gamma \wedge DEC$$

$$\vdash$$
 HoldsAt(*Location*(*Robot*, *Cos*(π /180), *Sin*(π /180)), 2)

Proof. From $CIRC[\Sigma; Initiates, Terminates, Releases]$ and Theorems 2.1 and 2.2, we have

Initiates(e,f,t)
$$\Leftrightarrow$$
 (8.26)
$$\exists r,d \ (e = MoveLeftWheel(r) \land f = Direction(r,d-\pi/180) \land \\ \neg Happens(MoveRightWheel(r),t) \land \\ HoldsAt(Direction(r,d),t)) \lor \\ \exists r,d \ (e = MoveRightWheel(r) \land f = Direction(r,d+\pi/180) \land \\ \neg Happens(MoveLeftWheel(r),t) \land \\ HoldsAt(Direction(r,d),t)) \lor \\ \exists r,x,y,d \ (e = MoveRightWheel(r) \land f = Location(r,x+Cos(d),y+Sin(d)) \land \\ Happens(MoveLeftWheel(r),t) \land \\ HoldsAt(Location(r,x,y),t) \land \\ HoldsAt(Direction(r,d),t)) \\ Terminates(e,f,t) \Leftrightarrow (8.27)$$

134

From $CIRC[\Delta; Happens]$ and Theorem 2.1, we have

$$Happens(e, t) \Leftrightarrow$$
 (8.29)
 $(e = MoveRightWheel(Robot) \land t = 0) \lor$
 $(e = MoveLeftWheel(Robot) \land t = 1) \lor$
 $(e = MoveRightWheel(Robot) \land t = 1)$

From (8.29), we have $\neg Happens(MoveLeftWheel(Robot), 0)$. From this, (8.23) (which follows from (8.29)), (8.22), (8.16) (which follows from (8.26)), and DEC9, we have

$$HoldsAt(Direction(Robot, \pi/180), 1)$$
 (8.30)

From (8.29) and (8.27), we have $\neg \exists e$ ($Happens(e, 0) \land Terminates(e, Location (Robot, 0, 0), 0)$). From this, (8.21), (8.20), and DEC5, we have HoldsAt (Location (Robot, 0, 0), 1). From this, (8.24) and (8.25) (which both follow from (8.29)), (8.30), (8.18) (which follows from (8.26)), and DEC9, we have $HoldsAt(Location(Robot, Cos (\pi/180), Sin(\pi/180)), 2$).

BIBLIOGRAPHIC NOTES

Our discussion of restricting concurrency draws on the notions of "exclusive and shared resources" of Pinto (1994, p. 59), the "complete exclusion" and "conflict exclusion" of Ernst, Millstein, and Weld (1997, p. 1171), and the "interference" and "competing needs" of Blum and Furst (1997, p. 286). The technique of preventing more than one event from occurring at a time is used in the event calculus by Shanahan and Witkowski (2004). The example of putting a penny in a jar is based on the example of loading cargo into a rocket of Veloso (1989).

Pinto (1994, pp. 57-66) introduces a function + that maps two actions a_1 and a_2 into the action of performing a_1 and a_2 simultaneously. He discusses the "precondition interaction problem," which is that, in a given situation it may be possible to perform a_1 and it may be possible to perform a_2 , yet it may not be possible to perform $a_1 + a_2$. He uses the example of an agent that can paint wall A or paint wall B but cannot paint both walls A and B simultaneously. He proposes a predicate $precInt(a_1, a_2)$, which represents that the preconditions of a_1 interact with the preconditions of a_2 , and the axiom (p. 59):

$$Poss(a_1 + a_2, s) \equiv Poss(a_1, s) \land Poss(a_2, s) \land \neg precInt(a_1, a_2)$$

The predicate Poss(a, s) represents that it is possible to perform action a in situation s. Pinto proposes that $precInt(a_1, a_2)$ could be determined on the basis of which resources are required to perform a_1 and a_2 and whether the use of those resources must be exclusive or can be shared. For example, a brush, wall, paint canister, and light are required to paint a wall. The use of the brush, wall, and paint canister must be exclusive, but the use of the light can be shared.

Pinto (1994) also discusses the "effect interaction problem," which is that concurrent actions may have cumulative and canceling effects, called "synergy" and "cancellation" (p. 60). He proposes to deal with this problem by breaking effects into "primary" and "secondary" effects (p. 61). Primary effects are the effects that must always occur when an action is performed; secondary effects are the effects that are subject to synergy and cancellation. He represents primary effects using effect axioms and secondary effects using state constraints. He treats the soup bowl scenario by using state constraints that determine when the bowl of soup is lifted or spilled. The analog in the event calculus consists of two effect axioms and two state constraints:

Initiates(LiftLeft, LiftedLeft, t) Initiates(LiftRight, LiftedRight, t) $HoldsAt(Lifted, t) \Leftrightarrow HoldsAt(LiftedLeft, t) \land HoldsAt(LiftedRight, t)$ $HoldsAt(Spilled, t) \Leftrightarrow HoldsAt(LiftedLeft, t) \dot{\lor} HoldsAt(LiftedRight, t)$

Reiter (1996) presents a variation on Pinto's (1994) approach. Reiter adds a sort called "concurrent" (p. 3) for sets of actions, redefines do as a function from sets of actions and situations to situations, and discusses successor state axioms that take concurrency into account. See also the review of Reiter (2001, chap. 7). Baral and Gelfond (1997) extend action language \mathcal{A} for concurrent actions.

Following the work in the situation calculus, Shanahan (1995a, pp. 265-268; 1997b, pp. 301-304) introduces a method for handling concurrent events with cumulative and canceling effects into the event calculus. The notation $e_1 \& e_2$ (also $e_1 + e_2$) represents a compound event that consists of e_1 and e_2 . The predicate Cancels(e_1, e_2) represents that, if e_1 occurs concurrently with e_2 , then e_1 cancels the effects of e_2 . Shanahan extends the circumscriptive event calculus for concurrent events and shows that it can handle a problem involving a shopping cart. If the cart is pushed, then it moves forward; if it is pulled, then it moves backward. But if it is pushed and pulled at the same time, then it spins around. Shanahan (1999a, pp. 424-426) incorporates concurrent events into the forced separation version of the event calculus. In this case, the predicate is $Cancels(e_1, e_2, f)$, which represents that e_1 cancels the effect of e_2 on fluent f. Finally, R. Miller and Shanahan (1999, pp. 7-8; 2002, pp. 460-461) show that concurrent events with cumulative and canceling effects can be represented using effect axioms with Happens preconditions, which we call cumulative effect axioms. R. Miller and Shanahan (1999, p. 8; 2002, pp. 460-461) show how to handle the soup bowl scenario using their approach. Shanahan (1996) uses the example of a robot but not to demonstrate concurrent events with cumulative and canceling effects. R. Miller and Shanahan (1996) treat the case of a robot that can vary its bearing continuously as it moves.

EXERCISES

- 8.1 Write an algorithm that takes an axiomatization (list of axioms) as input and produces suggestions for possible event occurrence constraints as output. The idea is that these constraints are examined by a person, who decides whether they should be added to the axiomatization. The algorithm should work by looking for events that initiate or terminate fluents that are the preconditions of other events. Specifically, whenever it is the case that
 - Initiates (α_1, β, τ) , and $\neg HoldsAt(\beta, \tau)$ is an action or fluent precondition of α_2 , or
 - Terminates (α_1, β, τ) , and $HoldsAt(\beta, \tau)$ is an action or fluent precondition of α_2 ,

(where α_1 and α_2 are event terms, β is a fluent term, and τ is a timepoint term), the algorithm should produce as output an axiom that states that α_1 and α_2 cannot occur simultaneously.

8.2 Extend the algorithm in Exercise 8.1 to suggest event occurrence constraints for similar actions of one or two agents.

- **8.3** Formalize the mixing of two colors of paint together as follows. If yellow paint is placed on a palette, the result is yellow. If blue paint is placed on a palette, the result is blue. But if yellow and blue paint are placed on a palette, the result is green.
- **8.4** Formalize the ripping of a piece of paper as follows. If the paper is pulled left, it moves left. If it is pulled right, it moves right. But if it is simultaneously pulled left and right, it rips. Discuss what a more detailed axiomatization of ripping a paper would look like.
- **8.5** Formalize the clapping of hands.

- Weiter it aswelled a treeteg of third to secretarise, a gaptim out considered. Also the locality systems and it weiter of the countries of a policy of a policy of a secretarial system. They were bounded a compacted by a swellow to the good and bear an equivalent
- 3.4 1. renalize the implies of appear in papear as inflowed fits a renoul is justice left.
 if energy take it is a purpodrished definer as replicionally in the simulation and a renal renal configuration.
 Fruit is easiered as in a renal configuration.
 The renal definition is renally to the late.
 - Section of the safety and other and appeals of

Nondeterministic Effects of Events

An event has *nondeterministic effects* if the event can have two or more alternative effects. For example, flipping a coin has two alternative effects: the coin may land with heads showing, or it may land with tails showing. We represent nondeterministic effects of events in the event calculus by allowing event occurrences to give rise to several classes of models. In this chapter, we describe two ways of representing nondeterministic effects in the event calculus: determining fluents and disjunctive event axioms. These techniques enable the representation of uncertainty about the effects of events.

9.1 DETERMINING FLUENTS

One way of representing nondeterministic effects is to use determining fluents. A *determining fluent* is a fluent that (1) is released from the commonsense law of inertia so that its truth value is permitted to vary arbitrarily from timepoint to timepoint and (2) is used in the condition of one or more effect axioms in order to determine the effects of events on other fluents.

Suppose that DF is a fluent that is released from the commonsense law of inertia:

ReleasedAt(DF, t)

Then, this fluent may be used to determine whether the effect of E is F1:

 $HoldsAt(DF, t) \Rightarrow Initiates(E, F1, t)$

or whether the effect of E is F2:

 $\neg HoldsAt(DF, \tau) \Rightarrow Initiates(E, F2, t)$

9.1.1 EXAMPLE: ROULETTE WHEEL

We consider the example of spinning a roulette wheel that can land on the numbers 1, 2, or 3. We use a determining fluent *WheelNumberDeterminer*. We make the wheel an argument of this fluent so that at any given timepoint different wheels may land on different numbers. This fluent is released from the commonsense law of inertia:

$$ReleasedAt(WheelNumberDeterminer(w, n), t)$$
 (9.1)

For any given wheel, this fluent specifies one of the numbers 1, 2, or 3 at any given timepoint:

$$HoldsAt(WheelNumberDeterminer(w, n), t) \Rightarrow$$
 (9.2)
 $n = 1 \lor n = 2 \lor n = 3$

And for any given wheel, this fluent specifies a unique number at any given timepoint:

$$HoldsAt(WheelNumberDeterminer(w, n_1), t) \land$$
 (9.3)
 $HoldsAt(WheelNumberDeterminer(w, n_2), t) \Rightarrow$ $n_1 = n_2$

We have several effect axioms. If the determining fluent specifies a particular number for a wheel and a dealer spins the wheel, then the wheel will be on that number:

$$HoldsAt(WheelNumberDeterminer(w, n), t) \Rightarrow$$
 (9.4)
 $Initiates(Spin(d, w), WheelNumber(w, n), t)$

If a wheel is on one number, the determining fluent specifies another number for the wheel, the first number is different from the second number, and a dealer spins the wheel, then the wheel will no longer be on the first number:

$$HoldsAt(WheelNumber(w, n_1), t) \land$$

$$HoldsAt(WheelNumberDeterminer(w, n_2), t) \land$$

$$n_1 \neq n_2 \Rightarrow$$

$$Terminates(Spin(d, w), WheelNumber(w, n_1), t)$$

$$(9.5)$$

If a dealer resets a wheel, then the wheel is no longer on any number:

$$Terminates(Reset(d, w), WheelNumber(w, n), t)$$
 (9.6)

We have a state constraint that says that the wheel is on at most one number at a time:

$$HoldsAt(WheelNumber(w, n_1), t) \land$$
 (9.7)
 $HoldsAt(WheelNumber(w, n_2), t) \Rightarrow$ $n_1 = n_2$

Suppose that a wheel that is not on any number is spun:

$$\neg HoldsAt(WheelNumber(Wheel, n), 0)$$

$$\neg ReleasedAt(WheelNumber(Wheel, n), t)$$

$$(9.8)$$

$$\neg ReleasedAt(WheelNumber(Wheel, n), t)$$
 (9.9)

$$Happens(Spin(Dealer, Wheel), 0)$$
 (9.10)

We can show that the wheel will be on one of the numbers 1, 2, or 3 and that, if it lands on a given number, it will still be on that number one timepoint later.

Proposition 9.1. Let $\Sigma = (9.4) \land (9.5) \land (9.6)$, $\Delta = (9.10)$, $\Omega = U[Spin, Reset] \land U[WheelNumberDeterminer, WheelNumber], <math>\Psi = (9.2) \land (9.3) \land (9.7)$, and $\Gamma = (9.1) \land (9.8) \land (9.9)$. Then we have

$$CIRC[\Sigma; Initiates, Terminates, Releases] \land CIRC[\Delta; Happens] \land$$

 $\Omega \land \Psi \land \Gamma \land EC \vdash (HoldsAt(WheelNumber(Wheel, 1), 1) \lor$
 $HoldsAt(WheelNumber(Wheel, 2), 1) \lor$

$$HoldsAt(WheelNumber(Wheel, 3), 1)) \land (HoldsAt(WheelNumber(Wheel, k), 1) \Rightarrow HoldsAt(WheelNumber(Wheel, k), 2))$$

Proof. From $CIRC[\Sigma; Initiates, Terminates, Releases]$ and Theorems 2.1 and 2.2, we have

Initiates(e,f,t)
$$\Leftrightarrow$$
 (9.11)
$$\exists d, w, n \ (e = Spin(d, w) \land f = WheelNumber(w, n) \land holdsAt(WheelNumberDeterminer(w, n), t))$$

$$Terminates(e,f,t) \Leftrightarrow (9.12)$$

$$\exists d, w, n_1, n_2 \ (e = Spin(d, w) \land f = WheelNumber(w, n_1) \land holdsAt(WheelNumber(w, n_1), t) \land holdsAt(WheelNumberDeterminer(w, n_2), t) \land n_1 \neq n_2) \lor$$

$$\exists d, w, n \ (e = Reset(d, w) \land f = WheelNumber(w, n))$$

$$\neg Releases(e, f, t) (9.13)$$

From $CIRC[\Delta; Happens]$ and Theorem 2.1, we have

$$Happens(e, t) \Leftrightarrow (e = Spin(Dealer, Wheel) \land t = 0)$$
 (9.14)

First, we show

 $HoldsAt(WheelNumber(Wheel, 1), 1) \lor HoldsAt(WheelNumber(Wheel, 2), 1) \lor HoldsAt(WheelNumber(Wheel, 3), 1)$

We consider three cases, which, from (9.2) and (9.3), are exhaustive.

Case 1: HoldsAt(WheelNumberDeterminer(Wheel, 1), 0).

From this, (9.10) (which follows from (9.14)), (9.4) (which follows from (9.11)), 0 < 1, $\neg StoppedIn(0, WheelNumber(Wheel, 1), 1)$ (which follows from (9.14) and EC3), $\neg ReleasedIn(0, WheelNumber(Wheel, 1), 1)$ (which follows from (9.14) and EC13), and EC14, we have HoldsAt(WheelNumber(Wheel, 1), 1).

 $Case\ 2: Holds At (Wheel Number Determiner (Wheel, 2), 0).$

By a similar argument, we have HoldsAt(WheelNumber(Wheel, 2), 1).

Case 3: *HoldsAt(WheelNumberDeterminer(Wheel*, 3), 0).

By a similar argument, we have HoldsAt(WheelNumber(Wheel, 3), 1). Second, we show

 $HoldsAt(WheelNumber(Wheel, k), 1) \Rightarrow HoldsAt(WheelNumber(Wheel, k), 2)$

Let κ be an arbitrary integer. We must show

 $HoldsAt(WheelNumber(Wheel, \kappa), 1) \Rightarrow HoldsAt(WheelNumber(Wheel, \kappa), 2)$

Suppose $HoldsAt(WheelNumber(Wheel, \kappa), 1)$. From this, 1 < 2, PersistsBetween $(1, WheelNumber(Wheel, \kappa), 2)$ (which follows from (9.9) and EC7), $\neg Clipped$ $(1, WheelNumber(Wheel, \kappa), 2)$ (which follows from (9.14) and EC1), and EC9, we have $HoldsAt(WheelNumber(Wheel, \kappa), 2)$, as required.

9.2 DISJUNCTIVE EVENT AXIOMS

Another way of representing nondeterministic effects is to use disjunctive event axioms.

Definition 9.1. If α and $\alpha_1, \ldots, \alpha_n$ are event terms and τ is a timepoint term, then

$$Happens(\alpha, \tau) \Rightarrow$$

 $Happens(\alpha_1, \tau) \lor \cdots \lor Happens(\alpha_n, \tau)$

is a disjunctive event axiom.

9.2.1 EXAMPLE: RUNNING AND DRIVING

We start with a disjunctive event axiom that says that, if an agent goes to a location, then the agent runs or drives to that location:

$$Happens(Go(a, l), t) \Rightarrow$$
 (9.15)
 $Happens(Run(a, l), t) \lor$

We have an effect axiom that says that, if an agent runs to a location, then the agent will be tired:

Happens(Drive(a, l), t)

$$Initiates(Run(a, l), Tired(a), t)$$
 (9.16)

Suppose we are told that Nathan was initially not tired and went to the bookstore:

$$\neg ReleasedAt(f,t)$$
 (9.17)

$$\neg HoldsAt(Tired(Nathan), 0)$$
 (9.18)

$$Happens(Go(Nathan, Bookstore), 0)$$
 (9.19)

The event *Go(Nathan, Bookstore)* has a nondeterministic effect: Nathan may or may not be tired afterward. Now suppose we are told that Nathan was tired afterward:

$$HoldsAt(Tired(Nathan), 1)$$
 (9.20)

We can then show that Nathan must have run to the bookstore.

We cannot use predicate completion and Theorem 2.1 to compute

$$CIRC[(9.15) \land (9.19); Happens]$$
 (9.21)

(This can be handled by answer set programming—see Section 15.3.3.) Instead we replace (9.21) with

$$(Happens(e,t) \Leftrightarrow (9.22)$$

$$(e = Go(Nathan, Bookstore) \land t = 0) \land$$

$$(e = Run(Nathan, Bookstore) \land t = 0)) \lor$$

$$(Happens(e,t) \Leftrightarrow$$

$$(e = Go(Nathan, Bookstore) \land t = 0) \land$$

$$(e = Drive(Nathan, Bookstore) \land t = 0))$$

Proposition 9.2. Let $\Sigma = (9.16)$, $\Delta = (9.22)$, $\Omega = U[Go, Run, Drive]$, and $\Gamma = (9.17) \wedge (9.18) \wedge (9.20)$. Then we have

$$CIRC[\Sigma; Initiates, Terminates, Releases] \land \Delta \land \Omega \land \Gamma \land EC$$

 $\vdash Happens(Run(Nathan, Bookstore), 0)$

Proof. Suppose, to the contrary, that

$$\neg Happens(Run(Nathan, Bookstore), 0)$$
 (9.23)

From $CIRC[\Sigma; Initiates, Terminates, Releases]$ and Theorems 2.1 and 2.2, we have

$$Initiates(e, f, t) \Leftrightarrow \exists a, l \ (e = Run(a, l) \land Tired(a))$$
 (9.24)

$$\neg Terminates(e, f, t)$$
 (9.25)

$$\neg Releases(e, f, t)$$
 (9.26)

From (9.17) and EC7, we have

$$PersistsBetween(0, Tired(Nathan), 1)$$
 (9.27)

From (9.24), (9.22), (9.23), and EC2, we have $\neg Declipped(0, Tired (Nathan), 1))$. From this, (9.18), 0 < 1, (9.27), and EC10, we have $\neg HoldsAt(Tired(Nathan), 1)$, which contradicts (9.20). Therefore, we have Happens(Run(Nathan, Bookstore), 0), as required.

BIBLIOGRAPHIC NOTES

The method of determining fluents was introduced by Shanahan (1997b, pp. 294-297, 301; 1999a, pp. 419-420). The roulette wheel example is similar to other examples of nondeterminism such as flipping a coin (Kartha, 1994, pp. 386-387; Shanahan, 1999a, p. 419) and Raymond Reiter's scenario of throwing an object onto a chessboard (Baral, 1995, p. 2018; Elkan, 1996, p. 63; Kartha & Lifschitz, 1994, p. 344; F. Lin, 1996, p. 671; Shanahan, 1995a, pp. 264-265; 1997b, pp. 290-298; 1999a, pp. 419-420). Disjunctive event axioms were introduced by Shanahan (1997b, pp. 297-298, 342-345, 359-361). Our formalization of the example of running and driving using

disjunctive event axioms is based on Shanahan's (1997b, pp. 359-361) formalization of Kartha's (1994, pp. 382-383) bus ride scenario.

EXERCISES

- 9.1 Formalize that a lightbulb burns out at a random time.
- 9.2 Formalize the operation of buttons and lights used in game shows. There are two contestants. Each contestant has a button and a light. The light goes on for the first contestant to push the button. If both contestants press their button at the same instant, the tie is broken at random and only one light goes on.
- **9.3** Extend the formalization in Exercise 9.2 for *n* contestants.
- **9.4** Formalize that a balloon may or may not pop when it comes into contact with a pin.
- **9.5** List three everyday scenarios involving nondeterminism, and sketch out event calculus representations of them.

PART

Commonsense Domains

Commonsense Domains

Space

Many instances of commonsense reasoning involve space. In this chapter, we present two event calculus axiomatizations of space: relational space and metric space. We describe how these axiomatizations can be used to solve some sample problems. A closely related issue that we consider is object identity: Two objects observed at different times and locations in space may or may not be the same object.

10.1 RELATIONAL SPACE

In the commonsense world, objects stand in various spatial relations to other objects. For example, a pencil is in a jar, a person is in a room, a person is holding a book, a glass is on a table, or a person is wearing a shirt. A *relational space* consists of a set of objects and a binary relation on the set. In this section we present a representation of a relational space in the event calculus. (Other representations of relational space are discussed in Sections 6.1.1, 6.3.1, and 6.4.1.)

10.1.1 BASIC REPRESENTATION

We start with a basic representation of relational space, which serves as a prototype for more elaborate representations. The representation consists of:

- an object sort, with variables o, o_1, o_2, \dots
- an agent sort, which is a subsort of the object sort, with variables a, a_1, a_2, \ldots
- a fluent $IN(o_1, o_2)$, which represents an abstract spatial relation between object o_1 and object o_2
- an event $MOVE(a, o_1, o_2, o_3)$, which represents the action of agent a adding the abstract spatial relation between object o_1 and object o_3 , and dropping the abstract spatial relation between object o_1 and object o_2

IN represents an irreflexive, antisymmetric, intransitive, and functional relation. **Axiom RS1.**

 $\neg HoldsAt(IN(o,o),t)$

Axiom RS2.

 $HoldsAt(IN(o_1, o_2), t) \Rightarrow \neg HoldsAt(IN(o_2, o_1), t)$

Axiom RS3.

$$HoldsAt(IN(o_1, o_2), t) \land HoldsAt(IN(o_2, o_3), t) \Rightarrow$$

 $\neg HoldsAt(IN(o_1, o_3), t)$

Axiom RS4.

$$HoldsAt(IN(o, o_1), t) \wedge HoldsAt(IN(o, o_2), t) \Rightarrow o_1 = o_2$$

MOVE initiates and terminates IN.

Axiom RS5.

$$Initiates(MOVE(a, o_1, o_2, o_3), IN(o_1, o_3), t)$$

Axiom RS6.

$$Terminates(MOVE(a, o_1, o_2, o_3), IN(o_1, o_2), t)$$

10.1.2 EXTENDED REPRESENTATION

We now extend the basic representation to deal with agents and physical objects within rooms. We add the following subsorts of the object sort:

- a physical object sort, with variables p, p_1, p_2, \ldots
- a room sort, with variables r, r_1, r_2, \ldots

As shown in Table 10.1, we use IN to represent different spatial relationships between objects, depending on the sorts of the arguments of IN, and MOVE to represent different spatial actions, depending on the sorts of the arguments to MOVE. For example, $IN(p_1, p_2)$ represents that physical object p_1 is in or inside physical object p_2 , whereas IN(p, a) represents that agent a is holding physical object p.

Table 10.1 Meaning of IN and MOVE^a

Fluent or Event	Meaning
$IN(p_1,p_2)$	p_1 is in p_2
IN(a,r)	a is in r
IN(p,r)	p is in r
IN(p,a)	a is holding p
$MOVE(a, p_1, r, p_2)$	a (in r) puts p_1 (in r) into p_2
$MOVE(a, p_1, p_2, r)$	a (in r) removes p_1 from p_2 into r
$MOVE(a, a, r_1, r_2)$	a goes from r_1 to r_2
MOVE(a, p, r, a)	a (in r) picks up p
MOVE(a, p, a, r)	a (in r) sets down p into r

^aa is an agent; p, p₁, and p₂ are physical objects;

r, r_1 , and r_2 are rooms.

The fluent IN(o, r) represents that object o is directly in room r. We introduce a fluent INROOM(o, r), which represents that object o is indirectly in room r. **Axiom RS7.**

$$HoldsAt(IN(o, r), t) \Rightarrow HoldsAt(INROOM(o, r), t)$$

Axiom RS8.

$$HoldsAt(IN(o_1, o_2), t) \land HoldsAt(INROOM(o_2, r), t) \Rightarrow$$

 $HoldsAt(INROOM(o_1, r), t)$

An object can be indirectly in at most one room at a time.

Axiom RS9.

$$HoldsAt(INROOM(o, r_1), t) \land HoldsAt(INROOM(o, r_2), t) \Rightarrow r_1 = r_2$$

We then replace the general RS5 and RS6 with the more specific RS10 through RS19, which follow.

In order for an agent to put physical object p_1 into physical object p_2 , the agent and p_1 must be directly in the same room and p_2 must be indirectly in that room. **Axiom RS10.**

$$HoldsAt(IN(a,r),t) \land \\ HoldsAt(IN(p_1,r),t) \land \\ HoldsAt(INROOM(p_2,r),t) \Rightarrow \\ Initiates(MOVE(a,p_1,r,p_2),IN(p_1,p_2),t)$$

Axiom RS11.

$$HoldsAt(IN(a,r),t) \land \\ HoldsAt(IN(p_1,r),t) \land \\ HoldsAt(INROOM(p_2,r),t) \Rightarrow \\ Terminates(MOVE(a,p_1,r,p_2),IN(p_1,r),t)$$

In order for an agent to remove physical object p_1 from physical object p_2 and put p_1 in a room, the agent must be directly in that room.

Axiom RS12.

$$HoldsAt(IN(a,r),t) \Rightarrow$$

 $Initiates(MOVE(a,p_1,p_2,r),IN(p_1,r),t)$

Axiom RS13.

$$HoldsAt(IN(a,r),t) \Rightarrow$$

 $Terminates(MOVE(a,p_1,p_2,r),IN(p_1,p_2),t)$

In order for an agent to go from room r_1 to room r_2 , the agent must be directly in r_1 . **Axiom RS14.**

$$HoldsAt(IN(a,r_1),t) \Rightarrow$$

 $Initiates(MOVE(a,a,r_1,r_2),IN(a,r_2),t)$

Axiom RS15.

 $HoldsAt(IN(a, r_1), t) \Rightarrow$ $Terminates(MOVE(a, a, r_1, r_2), IN(a, r_1), t)$

In order for an agent to pick up a physical object, the agent and the physical object must be directly in the same room.

Axiom RS16.

 $HoldsAt(IN(a,r),t) \land \\ HoldsAt(IN(p,r),t) \Rightarrow \\ Initiates(MOVE(a,p,r,a),IN(p,a),t)$

Axiom RS17.

 $HoldsAt(IN(a,r),t) \land HoldsAt(IN(p,r),t) \Rightarrow$ Terminates(MOVE(a,p,r,a),IN(p,r),t)

In order for an agent to set down a physical object into a room, the agent must be holding the physical object, and the agent must be directly in the room. **Axiom RS18.**

 $HoldsAt(IN(p,a),t) \land HoldsAt(IN(a,r),t) \Rightarrow Initiates(MOVE(a,p,a,r),IN(p,r),t)$

Axiom RS19.

 $HoldsAt(IN(p,a),t) \land \\ HoldsAt(IN(a,r),t) \Rightarrow \\ Terminates(MOVE(a,p,a,r),IN(p,a),t)$

10.1.3 EXAMPLE: MOVING A NEWSPAPER AND A BOX

Lisa, a newspaper, and a box are in the living room. She puts the newspaper in the box, picks up the box, and walks into the kitchen:

HoldsAt(IN(Lisa, LivingRoom), 0)	(10.1)
HoldsAt(IN(Newspaper, LivingRoom), 0)	(10.2)
HoldsAt(IN(Box, LivingRoom), 0)	(10.3)
Happens(MOVE(Lisa, Newspaper, LivingRoom, Box), 0)	(10.4)
Happens (MOVE (Lisa, Box, Living Room, Lisa), 1)	(10.5)
Happens (MOVE (Lisa, Lisa, Living Room, Kitchen), 2)	(10.6)
Lisa then sets down the box and walks back into the living room:	

The fluent *INROOM* is always released from the commonsense law of inertia, and *IN* is never released from this law:

$$ReleasedAt(INROOM(o_1, o_2), t)$$
 (10.9)

$$\neg ReleasedAt(IN(o_1, o_2), t)$$
 (10.10)

We can show that Lisa will be in the living room, but the newspaper and box will be in the kitchen.

Proposition 10.1. Let Σ be the conjunction of RS10 through RS19. Let Δ be the conjunction of (10.4), (10.5), (10.6), (10.7), and (10.8). Let Ω be U[IN, INROOM]. Let Ψ be the conjunction of RS1 through RS4, and RS7 through RS9. Let Γ be the conjunction of (10.1), (10.2), (10.3), (10.9), and (10.10). Then we have

$$CIRC[\Sigma; Initiates, Terminates, Releases] \land CIRC[\Delta; Happens] \land$$

$$\Omega \wedge \Psi \wedge \Gamma \wedge EC$$

$$\vdash HoldsAt(IN(Lisa, LivingRoom), 5) \land$$

$$HoldsAt(IN(Box, Kitchen), 5) \land$$

Proof. From $CIRC[\Sigma; Initiates, Terminates, Releases]$ and Theorems 2.1 and 2.2, we have

$$Initiates(e,f,t) \Leftrightarrow \qquad (10.11)$$

$$\exists a, p_1, p_2, r \ (e = MOVE(a, p_1, r, p_2) \ \land f = IN(p_1, p_2) \ \land HoldsAt(IN(a, r), t) \ \land HoldsAt(IN(p_1, r), t) \ \land HoldsAt(INROOM(p_2, r), t)) \ \lor \\
\exists a, p_1, p_2, r \ (e = MOVE(a, p_1, p_2, r) \ \land f = IN(p_1, r), \ \land HoldsAt(IN(a, r), t)) \ \lor \\
\exists a, r_1, r_2 \ (e = MOVE(a, a, r_1, r_2) \ \land f = IN(a, r_2) \ \land HoldsAt(IN(a, r_1), t)) \ \lor \\
\exists a, p, r \ (e = MOVE(a, p, r, a) \ \land f = IN(p, a) \ \land HoldsAt(IN(a, r), t) \ \lor \\
\exists a, p, r \ (e = MOVE(a, p, a, r) \ \land f = IN(p, r) \ \land HoldsAt(IN(p, a), t) \ \land HoldsAt(IN(p, a), t))$$

$$Terminates(e,f,t) \Leftrightarrow (10.12)$$

$$\exists a, p_1, p_2, r (e = MOVE(a, p_1, r, p_2) \land f = IN(p_1, r) \land holdsAt(IN(a, r), t) \land holdsAt(IN(p_1, r), t) \land holdsAt(INROOM(p_2, r), t)) \lor \\
\exists a, p_1, p_2, r (e = MOVE(a, p_1, p_2, r) \land f = IN(p_1, p_2) \land holdsAt(IN(a, r), t)) \lor \\
\exists a, r_1, r_2 (e = MOVE(a, a, r_1, r_2) \land f = IN(a, r_1) \land holdsAt(IN(a, r_1), t)) \lor \\
\exists a, p, r (e = MOVE(a, p, r, a) \land f = IN(p, r) \land holdsAt(IN(a, r), t) \land holdsAt(IN(p, r), t)) \lor \\
\exists a, p, r (e = MOVE(a, p, a, r) \land holdsAt(IN(p, a), t) \land holdsAt(IN(a, r), t))$$

$$\neg Releases(e, f, t)$$
 (10.13)

From $CIRC[\Delta; Happens]$ and Theorem 2.1, we have

$$Happens(e, t) \Leftrightarrow (10.14)$$
 $(e = MOVE(Lisa, Newspaper, LivingRoom, Box) \land t = 0) \lor$
 $(e = MOVE(Lisa, Box, LivingRoom, Lisa) \land t = 1) \lor$
 $(e = MOVE(Lisa, Lisa, LivingRoom, Kitchen) \land t = 2) \lor$
 $(e = MOVE(Lisa, Box, Lisa, Kitchen) \land t = 3) \lor$
 $(e = MOVE(Lisa, Lisa, Kitchen, LivingRoom) \land t = 4)$

From (10.1), 0 < 2, PersistsBetween(0, IN(Lisa, LivingRoom), 2) (which follows from (10.10) and EC7), $\neg Clipped(0, IN(Lisa, LivingRoom), 2)$ (which follows from (10.12), (10.14), and EC1), and EC9, we have

$$HoldsAt(IN(Lisa, LivingRoom), 2)$$
 (10.15)

From (10.6) (which follows from (10.14)), (10.15), RS14 (which follows from (10.11)), 2 < 4, $\neg StoppedIn(2, IN(Lisa, Kitchen), 4)$ (which follows from (10.12), (10.14), and EC3), $\neg ReleasedIn(2, IN(Lisa, Kitchen), 4)$ (which follows from (10.13) and EC13), and EC14, we have HoldsAt(IN(Lisa, Kitchen), 4). From this,

(10.8) (which follows from (10.14)), RS14 (which follows from (10.11)), 4 < 5, $\neg StoppedIn(4, IN(Lisa, LivingRoom), 5)$ (which follows from (10.14) and EC3), $\neg ReleasedIn(4, IN(Lisa, LivingRoom), 5)$ (which follows from (10.13) and EC13), and EC14, we have HoldsAt(IN(Lisa, LivingRoom), 5).

From (10.1), 0 < 1, PersistsBetween(0, IN(Lisa, LivingRoom), 1) (which follows from (10.10) and EC7), $\neg Clipped(0, IN(Lisa, LivingRoom), 1)$ (which follows from (10.12), (10.14), and EC1), and EC9, we have

$$HoldsAt(IN(Lisa, LivingRoom), 1)$$
 (10.16)

From (10.3), 0 < 1, PersistsBetween(0, IN(Box, LivingRoom), 1) (which follows from (10.10) and EC7), $\neg Clipped(0, IN(Box, LivingRoom), 1)$ (which follows from (10.12), (10.14), and EC1), and EC9, we have

$$HoldsAt(IN(Box, LivingRoom), 1)$$
 (10.17)

From (10.6) (which follows from (10.14)), (10.15), RS14 (which follows from (10.11)), 2 < 3, $\neg StoppedIn(2, IN(Lisa, Kitchen), 3)$ (which follows from (10.14) and EC3), $\neg ReleasedIn(2, IN(Lisa, Kitchen), 3)$ (which follows from (10.13) and EC13), and EC14, we have

$$HoldsAt(IN(Lisa, Kitchen), 3)$$
 (10.18)

From (10.5) (which follows from (10.14)), (10.16), (10.17), RS16, 1 < 3, $\neg StoppedIn(1, IN(Box, Lisa), 3)$ (which follows from (10.12), (10.14), and EC3), $\neg ReleasedIn(1, IN(Box, Lisa), 3)$ (which follows from (10.13) and EC13), and EC14, we have HoldsAt(IN(Box, Lisa), 3). From this, (10.7) (which follows from (10.14)), (10.18), RS18 (which follows from (10.11)), 3 < 5, $\neg StoppedIn(3, IN(Box, Kitchen), 5)$ (which follows from (10.12), (10.14), and EC3), $\neg ReleasedIn(3, IN(Box, Kitchen), 5)$ (which follows from (10.13) and EC13), and EC14, we have

$$HoldsAt(IN(Box, Kitchen), 5)$$
 (10.19)

From (10.3) and RS7, we have HoldsAt(INROOM(Box, LivingRoom), 0). From this, (10.4) (which follows from (10.14)), (10.1), (10.2), RS10, 0 < 5, $\neg StoppedIn(0, IN(Newspaper, Box), 5)$ (which follows from (10.12), (10.14), and EC3), $\neg ReleasedIn(0, IN(Newspaper, Box), 5)$ (which follows from (10.13) and EC13), and EC14, we have

$$HoldsAt(IN(Newspaper, Box), 5)$$
 (10.20)

From (10.19) and RS7, we have HoldsAt(INROOM(Box, Kitchen), 5). From this, (10.20), and RS8, we have HoldsAt(INROOM(Newspaper, Kitchen), 5).

10.2 METRIC SPACE

Definition 10.1. A *metric space* is a set M of objects called *points* and a function d (the distance function or metric) from $M \times M$ to the set of real numbers such that, for every $x, y, z \in M$,

- d(x, y) > 0
- d(x, y) = 0 if and only if x = y
- d(x, y) = d(y, x)
- $d(x, z) \le d(x, y) + d(y, z)$ (known as the *triangle inequality*)

The commonsense world involves objects located at specific points in a metric space and objects that trace specific paths over time in that space. For example, when an apple located eight feet above the ground starts to fall, it follows a particular path toward the ground. In this section, we present a representation of metric space in the event calculus. (Another representation of metric space is discussed in Section 8.2.2.)

We start with a basic representation as we did for relational space:

- an object sort, with variables o, o_1, o_2, \dots
- a real number sort, with variables $x, x_1, x_2, \ldots; y, y_1, y_2, \ldots;$ and z, z_1, z_2, \ldots
- a representation for points in three-dimensional space consisting of triples of real numbers \(\lambda x, y, z \rangle\)
- a fluent AT(o, x, y, z), which represents that object o is located at point $\langle x, y, z \rangle$
- a function $D(x_1, y_1, z_1, x_2, y_2, z_2)$, which represents the distance between the points $\langle x_1, y_1, z_1 \rangle$ and $\langle x_2, y_2, z_2 \rangle$

We may wish to require an object to be located at one point at a time via the following axiom.

Axiom MS1.

$$HoldsAt(AT(o, x_1, y_1, z_1), t) \land HoldsAt(AT(o, x_2, y_2, z_2), t) \Rightarrow x_1 = x_2 \land y_1 = y_2 \land z_1 = z_2$$

We specify the *DIST* function.

Axiom MS2.

$$DIST(x_1, y_1, z_1, x_2, y_2, z_2) = \sqrt{(x_1 - x_2)^2 + (y_1 - y_2)^2 + (z_1 - z_2)^2}$$

We can then extend this basic representation with motion and collisions.

10.2.1 EXAMPLE: TWO BASEBALLS COLLIDING

Nathan and Ryan each throw a baseball into the air. A moment later, the baseballs collide.

We treat this example using both relational and metric space. We start with some effect axioms. If an agent is holding an object and the agent throws the object into the air with a velocity vector $\langle v_x, v_y, v_z \rangle$, where the z axis represents up, then the object will be flying with that velocity vector:

$$HoldsAt(IN(o, a), t) \Rightarrow$$

$$Initiates(Throw(a, o, v_x, v_y, v_z), Flying(o, v_x, v_y, v_z), t)$$

$$(10.21)$$

If an agent is holding an object and the agent throws the object into the air, then the agent will no longer be holding the object:

$$HoldsAt(IN(o,a),t) \Rightarrow (10.22)$$

$$Terminates(Throw(a, o, v_x, v_y, v_z), IN(o, a), t)$$

If an object is thrown into the air, then its location and velocity will no longer be subject to the commonsense law of inertia:

$$HoldsAt(IN(o,a),t) \Rightarrow$$
 (10.23)

 $Releases(Throw(a, o, v_x, v_y, v_z), AT(o, x, y, z), t)$

$$HoldsAt(IN(o,a),t) \Rightarrow$$
 (10.24)

Releases (Throw $(a, o, v_{x1}, v_{v1}, v_{z1})$, Velocity $(o, v_{x2}, v_{v2}, v_{z2})$, t)

We specify the location and velocity of the flying object using the following trajectory axioms:

$$HoldsAt(AT(o, x_0, y_0, z_0), t) \land$$

$$x_1 = x_0 + v_x t_2 \land$$

$$y_1 = y_0 + v_y t_2 \land$$

$$z_1 = z_0 + v_z t_2 - \frac{1}{2}Gt_2^2 \Rightarrow$$

$$Trajectory(Flying(o, v_x, v_y, v_z), t_1, AT(o, x_1, y_1, z_1), t_2)$$

$$(10.25)$$

$$v_{z2} = v_{z1} - Gt_2 \Rightarrow \tag{10.26}$$

 $Trajectory(Flying(o, v_x, v_y, v_{z1}), t_1, Velocity(o, v_x, v_y, v_{z2}), t_2)$

We have state constraints that say that at any given moment an object has a unique velocity and is flying with a unique velocity:

$$HoldsAt(Velocity(o, v_{x1}, v_{y1}, v_{z1}), t) \wedge$$

$$HoldsAt(Velocity(o, v_{x2}, v_{y2}, v_{z2}), t) \Rightarrow$$

$$v_{x1} = v_{x2} \wedge v_{y1} = v_{y2} \wedge v_{z1} = v_{z2}$$

$$HoldsAt(Flying(o, v_{x1}, v_{y1}, v_{z1}), t) \wedge$$

$$HoldsAt(Flying(o, v_{x2}, v_{y2}, v_{z2}), t) \Rightarrow$$

$$v_{x1} = v_{x2} \wedge v_{y1} = v_{y2} \wedge v_{z1} = v_{z2}$$

$$(10.28)$$

We use a trigger axiom to represent that an elastic collision occurs when two flying objects are at the same location:

$$o_{1} \neq o_{2} \wedge$$

$$HoldsAt(Flying(o_{1}, v_{1x}, v_{1y}, v_{1z}), t) \wedge$$

$$HoldsAt(Flying(o_{2}, v_{2x}, v_{2y}, v_{2z}), t) \wedge$$

$$HoldsAt(AT(o_{1}, x, y, z), t) \wedge$$

$$HoldsAt(AT(o_{2}, x, y, z), t) \Rightarrow$$

$$Happens(Collide(o_{1}, o_{2}), t)$$

$$(10.29)$$

We use effect axioms to represent that, when object o_1 elastically collides with object o_2 , object o_1 assumes the velocity of o_2 :

$$HoldsAt(Velocity(o_1, v_{1x}, v_{1y}, v_{1z}), t) \land$$

$$HoldsAt(Velocity(o_2, v_{2x}, v_{2y}, v_{2z}), t) \Rightarrow$$

$$Initiates(Collide(o_1, o_2), Flying(o_1, v_{2x}, v_{2y}, v_{2z}), t)$$

$$(10.30)$$

$$HoldsAt(Velocity(o_1, v_x, v_y, v_z), t) \Rightarrow$$

$$Terminates(Collide(o_1, o_2), Flying(o_1, v_x, v_y, v_z), t)$$

$$(10.31)$$

That is, two elastically colliding objects exchange their velocities. We assume the objects are points of equal mass.

Let us use the following observations and narrative. Initially, one baseball is at rest at location (0, 0, G/2), and another baseball is at rest at location (1, 0, G/2):

$$\neg ReleasedAt(f,t)$$
 (10.32)
 $HoldsAt(AT(Baseball1,0,0,G/2),0)$ (10.33)
 $HoldsAt(Velocity(Baseball1,0,0,0),0)$ (10.34)
 $HoldsAt(AT(Baseball2,1,0,G/2),0)$ (10.35)
 $HoldsAt(Velocity(Baseball2,0,0,0),0)$ (10.36)

Nathan is holding the first baseball, and Ryan is holding the second baseball:

$$HoldsAt(IN(Baseball1, Nathan), 0)$$
 (10.37)

$$HoldsAt(IN(Baseball2, Ryan), 0)$$
 (10.38)

Nathan and Ryan throw the baseballs toward one another. Nathan throws the first baseball with velocity (1,0,0), and Ryan throws the second baseball with velocity (-1,0,0):

$$Happens(Throw(Nathan, Baseball 1, 1, 0, 0), 0)$$
 (10.39)

$$Happens(Throw(Ryan, Baseball2, -1, 0, 0), 0)$$
 (10.40)

We also have the fact that the two baseballs are not the same object:

$$Baseball1 \neq Baseball2$$
 (10.41)

We can then show that the baseballs will collide. In order to show this, we must assume that the two baseballs are the only objects in the metric space:

$$HoldsAt(AT(o, x, y, z), t) \Rightarrow (o = Baseball1 \lor o = Baseball2)$$
 (10.42)

Without this assumption, either of the baseballs might first collide with some other object.

We start with a lemma that states that, if object o_1 collides with object o_2 , then o_2 collides with o_1 :

Lemma 10.1. If $\Gamma = (10.29)$, then we have

$$CIRC[\Gamma; Happens] \land Happens(Collide(o_1, o_2), t) \Rightarrow$$

 $Happens(Collide(o_2, o_1), t)$

Proof. Let ω_1 and ω_2 be arbitrary objects, and τ be an arbitrary timepoint. We must show

$$CIRC[\Gamma; Happens] \land Happens(Collide(\omega_1, \omega_2), \tau) \Rightarrow$$

$$Happens(Collide(\omega_2, \omega_1), \tau)$$

Suppose the following:

$$CIRC[\Gamma; Happens]$$
 (10.43)

$$Happens(Collide(\omega_1, \omega_2), \tau)$$
 (10.44)

From (10.43) and Theorem 2.1, we have

$$Happens(Collide(o_1, o_2), t) \Leftrightarrow$$
 (10.45)

$$\exists v_{1x}, v_{1y}, v_{1z}, v_{2x}, v_{2y}, v_{2z}, x, y, z$$

$$(o_1 \neq o_2 \land$$

 $HoldsAt(Flying(o_1, v_{1x}, v_{1y}, v_{1z}), t) \land$

 $HoldsAt(Flying(o_2, v_{2x}, v_{2y}, v_{2z}), t) \land$

 $HoldsAt(AT(o_1, x, y, z), t) \land$

 $HoldsAt(AT(o_2, x, y, z), t))$

From this and (10.44), we have:

$$\omega_1 \neq \omega_2$$
. (10.46)

$$HoldsAt(Flying(\omega_1, VIX, VIY, VIZ), \tau)$$
 (10.47)

$$HoldsAt(Flying(\omega_2, V2X, V2Y, V2Z), \tau)$$
 (10.48)

$$HoldsAt(AT(\omega_1, X, Y, Z), \tau)$$
 (10.49)

$$HoldsAt(AT(\omega_2, X, Y, Z), \tau)$$
 (10.50)

for some V1X, V1Y, V1Z, V2X, V2Y, V2Z, X, Y, and Z. From (10.46), (10.47), (10.48), (10.49), (10.50), and (10.45), we have $Happens(Collide(\omega_2, \omega_1), \tau)$, as required.

Now we show that the baseballs collide.

Proposition 10.2. Let Σ be the conjunction of (10.21), (10.22), (10.23), (10.24), (10.30), and (10.31). Let Δ be the conjunction of (10.29), (10.39), and (10.40). Let Ω be U[IN, AT, Flying, Velocity] \wedge U[Throw, Collide] \wedge (10.41). Let Ψ be the conjunction of RS1 through RS4, MS1, (10.27), (10.28), and (10.42). Let Π be the conjunction of (10.25) and (10.26). Let Γ be the conjunction of (10.32), (10.33), (10.34), (10.35), (10.36), (10.37), and (10.38). Then we have

$$\mathit{CIRC}[\Sigma; \mathit{Initiates}, \mathit{Terminates}, \mathit{Releases}] \land \mathit{CIRC}[\Delta; \mathit{Happens}] \land$$

$$\Omega \wedge \Psi \wedge \Pi \wedge \Gamma \wedge EC$$

 \vdash *Happens*(*Collide*(*Baseball1*, *Baseball2*), 0.5)

Proof. From $CIRC[\Sigma; Initiates, Terminates, Releases]$ and Theorems 2.1 and 2.2, we have

Initiates(e, f, t)
$$\Leftrightarrow$$
 (10.51)
 $\exists a, o, v_x, v_y, v_z \ (e = Throw(a, o, v_x, v_y, v_z) \land f = Flying(o, v_x, v_y, v_z) \land$

To see this, suppose to the contrary that

$$\exists o, t (0 < t < 0.5 \land Happens(Collide(Baseball1, o), t))$$

Let $Happens(Collide(Baseball1, \omega), \tau)$ be the first such event. That is, we have

$$0 < \tau < 0.5$$
 (10.56)

$$Happens(Collide(Baseball1, \omega), \tau)$$
 (10.57)

$$\neg \exists \omega', \tau' (0 < \tau' < \tau \land Happens(Collide(Baseball1, \omega'), \tau'))$$
 (10.58)

From (10.57) and (10.54), we have

$$Baseball1 \neq \omega$$
 (10.59)

$$HoldsAt(AT(Baseball1, X1, Y1, Z1), \tau)$$
 (10.60)

$$HoldsAt(AT(\omega, XI, YI, ZI), \tau)$$
 (10.61)

for some X1, Y1, and Z1. From (10.59), (10.60), (10.61), and (10.42), we have $\omega = Baseball2$. From (10.52), (10.58), and EC3, we have $\neg StoppedIn(0, Flying(Baseball1, 1,0,0), \tau)$. From this, (10.39) (which follows from (10.54)), (10.37), (10.21) (which follows from (10.51)), $0 < \tau$ (which follows from (10.56)), (10.33), (10.25), and EC5, we have $HoldsAt(AT(Baseball1, \tau, 0, \frac{1}{2}G(1 - \tau^2)), \tau)$. From this, (10.60), (10.61), and $\omega = Baseball2$, we have

$$HoldsAt(AT(Baseball2,\tau,0,\frac{1}{2}G(1-\tau^2)),\tau)$$
 (10.62)

From (10.58), we have

$$\neg \exists \tau' (0 < \tau' < \tau \land Happens(Collide(Baseball1, Baseball2), \tau'))$$
 (10.63)

From (10.54), we have CIRC[(10.29); Happens]. From this, (10.63), and Lemma 10.1, we have

$$\neg \exists \tau' (0 < \tau' < \tau \land Happens(Collide(Baseball2, Baseball1), \tau'))$$

From this, (10.52), and EC3, we have $\neg StoppedIn(0, Flying(Baseball2, -1, 0, 0), \tau)$. From this, (10.40) (which follows from (10.54)), (10.38), (10.21) (which follows from (10.51)), $0 < \tau$ (which follows from (10.56)), (10.35), (10.25), and EC5, we have $HoldsAt(AT(Baseball2, 1 - \tau, 0, \frac{1}{2}G(1 - \tau^2)), \tau)$. From this, (10.56), and MS1, we have $\neg HoldsAt(AT(Baseball2, \tau, 0, \frac{1}{2}G(1 - \tau^2)), \tau)$, which contradicts (10.62). From (10.52), (10.55), and EC3, we have

$$\neg StoppedIn(0, Flying(Baseball1, 1, 0, 0), 0.5)$$
 (10.64)

From this, (10.39) (which follows from (10.54)), (10.37), (10.21) (which follows from (10.51)), 0 < 0.5, (10.33), (10.25), and EC5, we have

$$HoldsAt(AT(Baseball1, 0.5, 0, \frac{3}{8}G), 0.5)$$
 (10.65)

From (10.53) and EC13, we have $\neg ReleasedIn(0, Flying(Baseball1, 1, 0, 0), 0.5)$. From this, (10.39) (which follows from (10.54)), (10.37), (10.21) (which follows from (10.51)), 0 < 0.5, (10.64), and EC14, we have

$$HoldsAt(Flying(Baseball1, 1, 0, 0), 0.5)$$
 (10.66)

Using similar arguments we can show

$$HoldsAt(AT(Baseball2, 0.5, 0, \frac{3}{8}G), 0.5)$$
 (10.67)
 $HoldsAt(Flying(Baseball2, -1, 0, 0), 0.5)$ (10.68)

$$HoldsAt(Flying(Baseball2, -1, 0, 0), 0.5)$$

$$(10.68)$$

From (10.41), (10.66), (10.68), (10.65), (10.67), and (10.29) (which follows from (10.54)), we have Happens (Collide (Baseball 1, Baseball 2), 0.5).

10.3 OBJECT IDENTITY

We can express object identity in first-order logic using the atom $o_1 = o_2$, which represents that o_1 and o_2 are the same object. The commonsense world of space and time places certain restrictions on object identity, which we can reason about using the event calculus. In this section, we consider the problem of observing the locations of two objects over time and determining whether the two objects must be the same, may be the same, or must be different.

We use the following spatial theory. The predicate $Adjacent(l_1, l_2)$ represents that location l_1 is adjacent to location l_2 . The event $Move(o, l_1, l_2)$ represents that object o moves from location l_1 to location l_2 . The fluent At(o, l) represents that object o is located at location l. An object is at exactly one location at a time:

$$HoldsAt(At(o, l_1), t) \land HoldsAt(At(o, l_2), t) \Rightarrow l_1 = l_2$$
 (10.69)

$$\exists l \, HoldsAt(At(o,l),t)$$
 (10.70)

Two objects cannot occupy the same location at the same time:

$$HoldsAt(At(o_1, l), t) \wedge HoldsAt(At(o_2, l), t) \Rightarrow o_1 = o_2$$
 (10.71)

The *Adjacent* predicate is symmetric:

$$Adjacent(l_1, l_2) \Leftrightarrow Adjacent(l_2, l_1)$$
 (10.72)

If an object is at location l_1 , which is adjacent to location l_2 , and the object moves from l_1 to l_2 , then the object will be at l_2 and will no longer be at l_1 :

$$HoldsAt(At(o, l_1), t) \land Adjacent(l_1, l_2) \Rightarrow$$
 (10.73)

 $Initiates(Move(o, l_1, l_2), At(o, l_2), t)$

$$HoldsAt(At(o, l_1), t) \land Adjacent(l_1, l_2) \Rightarrow$$
 (10.74)

 $Terminates(Move(o, l_1, l_2), At(o, l_1), t)$

10.3.1 EXAMPLE: ONE SCREEN

Consider the following scenario involving three locations: The location LI is to the left of L2, which is to the left of L3:

$$Adjacent(l_1, l_2) \Leftrightarrow (10.75)$$

$$(l_1 = L1 \land l_2 = L2) \lor$$

(10.83)

$$(l_1 = L2 \land l_2 = L1) \lor$$

$$(l_1 = L2 \land l_2 = L3) \lor$$

$$(l_1 = L3 \land l_2 = L2)$$

Our view of location L2 is blocked by a screen.

Suppose we observe the following: At timepoint 0, we observe an object, let us call it OI, at LI and nothing at L3. At timepoint 1, we observe no objects at L1 or L3. At timepoint 2, we observe an object, let us call it O2, at L3 and nothing at L1. We observe nothing about L2 because it is blocked by a screen.

Thus, we have the following observations:

$$HoldsAt(At(O1,L1),0)$$
 (10.76)

 $\neg HoldsAt(At(o,L3),0)$
 (10.77)

 $\neg HoldsAt(At(o,L1),1)$
 (10.78)

 $\neg HoldsAt(At(o,L3),1)$
 (10.79)

 $HoldsAt(At(O2,L3),2)$
 (10.80)

 $\neg HoldsAt(At(o,L1),2)$
 (10.81)

 $\neg ReleasedAt(f,t)$
 (10.82)

We can then show that O1 and O2 must be the same object.

Proposition 10.3. Let $\Sigma = (10.73) \wedge (10.74)$, $\Psi = (10.69) \wedge (10.70) \wedge (10.71) \wedge (10.72)$, and $\Gamma = (10.75) \wedge (10.76) \wedge (10.77) \wedge (10.78) \wedge (10.79) \wedge (10.80) \wedge (10.81) \wedge (10.82)$. Suppose

 $CIRC[\Sigma; Initiates, Terminates, Releases] \land \Psi \land \Gamma \land DEC$

Then O1 = O2.

Proof. From $CIRC[\Sigma; Initiates, Terminates, Releases]$ and Theorems 2.1 and 2.2, we have

 $Initiates(e, f, t) \Leftrightarrow$

$$\exists o, l_1, l_2 (e = Move(o, l_1, l_2) \land f = At(o, l_2) \land HoldsAt(At(o, l_1), t) \land Adjacent(l_1, l_2))$$

$$Terminates(e, f, t) \Leftrightarrow \qquad (10.84)$$

$$\exists o, l_1, l_2 (e = Move(o, l_1, l_2) \land f = At(o, l_1) \land HoldsAt(At(o, l_1), t) \land Adjacent(l_1, l_2))$$

$$\neg Releases(e, f, t) \qquad (10.85)$$

From (10.80) and the contrapositive of DEC6, we have

$$HoldsAt(At(O2, L3), 1) \lor$$

$$ReleasedAt(At(O2,L3),2) \lor$$

$$\exists e (Happens(e, 1) \land Initiates(e, At(O2, L3), 1))$$

From this, (10.79), and (10.82), we have

$$\exists e (Happens(e, 1) \land Initiates(e, At(O2, L3), 1))$$

From this, (10.83), and (10.75), we have

$$HoldsAt(At(O2, L2), 1)$$

$$(10.86)$$

From (10.78), we have $\neg HoldsAt(At(O1,L1), 1)$. From this and the contrapositive of DEC5, we have

$$\neg HoldsAt(At(O1,L1),0) \lor$$

$$ReleasedAt(At(O1,L1),1) \lor$$

$$\exists e (Happens(e, 0) \land Terminates(e, At(O1, L1), 0))$$

From this, (10.76), and (10.82), we have

$$\exists e (Happens(e, 0) \land Terminates(e, At(O1, L1), 0))$$

From this, (10.84), and (10.75), we have Happens(Move(O1, L1, L2), 0). From this, (10.76), (10.75), (10.83), and DEC9, we have

From this, (10.86), and (10.71), we have
$$O1 = O2$$
.

10.3.2 EXAMPLE: TWO SCREENS

Now consider the following scenario involving five locations: The location L1 is to the left of L2, which is to the left of L3, which is to the left of L3, which is to the left of L5:

$$Adjacent(l_{1}, l_{2}) \Leftrightarrow (10.87)$$

$$(l_{1} = L1 \land l_{2} = L2) \lor$$

$$(l_{1} = L2 \land l_{2} = L1) \lor$$

$$(l_{1} = L2 \land l_{2} = L3) \lor$$

$$(l_{1} = L3 \land l_{2} = L2) \lor$$

$$(l_{1} = L3 \land l_{2} = L4) \lor$$

$$(l_{1} = L4 \land l_{2} = L3) \lor$$

$$(l_{1} = L4 \land l_{2} = L5) \lor$$

$$(l_{1} = L5 \land l_{2} = L4)$$

Locations L2 and L4 are blocked by screens.

This time we observe the following. At timepoint 0, we observe O1 at L1 and nothing at L5. At timepoint 4, we observe O2 at L5 and nothing at L1. We never observe an object at L3, and we never observe anything about L2 or L4.

Thus, we have the following observations:

HoldsAt(At(O1,L1),0)	(10.88)
$\neg HoldsAt(At(o, L5), 0)$	(10.89)
HoldsAt(At(O2,L5),4)	(10.90)
$\neg HoldsAt(At(o, L1), 4)$	(10.91)
$\neg HoldsAt(At(o, L3), t)$	(10.92)
$\neg ReleasedAt(f,t)$	(10.93)

In this case, we can show that *O1* and *O2* cannot be the same object. (See Exercise 10.5.)

BIBLIOGRAPHIC NOTES

Hayes (1985) describes the following ontology for liquids. Liquids can be lazy or energetic. Lazy liquids can be still or moving. Rain is a lazy moving liquid, and a splash is an energetic liquid. Liquids can be bulk or divided. Bulk and divided liquids can be supported by a two-dimensional object, supported by a three-dimensional object, or unsupported. A mist is a lazy, still, divided, unsupported liquid. A river is a lazy, moving, bulk liquid supported by a three-dimensional object.

E. Davis (1990, pp. 241-310) reviews a number of spatial representations including geometric entities, occupancy arrays, constructive solid geometry, boundary representations, topological route maps, and configuration spaces. E. Davis (1995) describes a formal language for describing objects in two-dimensional space. The language provides the following entities: real number, point, length, angle, direction, area, vector, frame of reference, interval, arc, region, directed curve, scale mapping, and collection of regions. Partial and inexact information can be expressed in the language. For example, the language can be used to represent a circle whose diameter is between 1 and 2 inches, with a triangular hole somewhere inside it.

Randell, Cui, and Cohn (1992) introduce what has become known as the *region* connection calculus (RCC), a logic for spatial reasoning. RCC is based on a single predicate C(x, y), which represents that region x connects with region y. A number of predicates can be defined in terms of C to represent that one region is disconnected from another region, one region is a part of another region, one region overlaps another region, and so forth. Cohn, Bennett, Gooday, and Gotts (1997) provide an introduction to RCC.

Kuipers (2000) describes the *spatial semantic hierarchy*, a collection of interacting representations of large-scale space. Representations are classified along two dimensions: (1) qualitative and quantitative, and (2) sensory, control, causal, topological, and metrical. In this hierarchy, our representation of relational space is

classified as qualitative and topological, whereas our representation of metric space is classified as quantitative and metrical. Kuipers discusses several implementations of the spatial semantic hierarchy within real and virtual robots. Remolina and Kuipers (2004) define a theory of topological maps using many-sorted logic and circumscription. Topological and metric spaces are discussed by Marsden (1974).

Our axiomatizations of space use techniques developed in previous event calculus axiomatizations of space (Morgenstern, 2001; Shanahan, 2004, 1996). Our representation of metric space in the event calculus is based on that of Shanahan (1996), which is adapted from his previous situation calculus representation (Shanahan, 1995b). Shanahan (1995b, 1996) uses the predicate Occupies(o, r) to represent that object o occupies region r, where a region is a set of points in two-dimensional space. Shanahan (1996) represents a robot that can rotate, move in the direction it is facing, and stop moving when it bumps into an object.

Morgenstern (2001) develops spatial representations in the event calculus for reasoning about cracking an egg and pouring its contents into a bowl. She uses the fluent shape(o) = r to represent that object o occupies region r, the fluent At(o, l) to represent that object o is at location l, and the event Move(o, l) to represent that object o moves to location l. Objects and locations are related by the Above fluent. Morgenstern represents object parts, object sets, eggs, eggshells, egg insides, packages, open and closed containers, solid and liquid phases, material, falling, pouring, leaking, breaking, and cracking. Shanahan (2004) provides representations in the event calculus for reasoning about egg cracking, including representations of parts and wholes of objects. Synge (1960, pp. 94-96) provides equations for the velocities of two objects after collision. The object identity examples involving one and two screens are taken from Cassimatis (2002).

EXERCISES

- 10.1 Add doors to the formalization in Section 10.1. Modify Axioms RS14 and RS15 so that, in order for an agent to go from one room to another, the two rooms must have a door in common.
- 10.2 Extend the formalization in Section 10.1 to represent that one physical object is on another physical object. Because in and on are different spatial relations, one spatial relation IN is no longer sufficient. Use IN₁ to represent in and IN₂ to represent on. Write state constraints across IN₁ and IN₂. For example, an object cannot be both in and on another object.
- **10.3** Extend the formalization in Section 10.1 to represent that one physical object is a part of another physical object. Use *IN*₃ to represent "is a part of."
- 10.4 Extend the formalization in Section 10.1 to represent that an agent is wearing one or more items of clothing.
- **10.5** In the object identity example in Section 10.3.2, prove that *O1* and *O2* cannot be the same object.

- 10.6 Create an event calculus formalization of the grid-based space used in ThoughtTreasure (Mueller, 1998). There are many grids, each consisting of a rectangular array of cells. For any given grid, a given object is located at a unique cell (row, column) in that grid at a time. (An object may be in several grids at a time.) If an agent walks from one cell in a grid to another cell in that grid, then the agent will be at that other cell. In order for an agent to walk from one cell to another, the two cells must be adjacent.
- **10.7** Formalize riding in a car. Include getting into the car, getting out of the car, and driving from one location to another along a street.

- 10.6 Curille an every called a correct allocate the place beast space of the filles of books of space of the filles are properly as a first and the correct of the filles of the fill
- definition that makes the pair of the area on the source two cases to a subscaping of factors and goald gifting the source of the source of the factors of the source of t
- 1917 Francis e Francisco de Sea. Inflance genires ser the songermagnes states and a and driving ser manifest scanlagers, and to survive as the states.

The Mental States of Agents 1

Many instances of commonsense reasoning involve the mental states of agents. An *agent* is an entity that performs purposeful actions in the world in which it exists. Examples of agents are people, animals, organizations, robots, and computer programs. In order to represent and reason about agent behavior—in particular, to interpret an agent's actions and make predictions about an agent's future actions—we must model the mental states of agents. In this chapter, we address agent behavior, which requires the modeling of beliefs, goals, and plans. We discuss the modeling of emotions. We describe the epistemic functional event calculus for reasoning about knowledge and action.

11.1 BELIEFS, GOALS, AND PLANS

Agent behavior can be reactive or goal-driven.

11.1.1 REACTIVE BEHAVIOR

Consider the following example of commonsense reasoning:

Ryan is driving along when a squirrel leaps out in front of the car. What will Ryan do? He will slam on the brakes.

Here we are reasoning about the *reactive behavior* of an agent, in which an agent immediately performs an action in response to the situation the agent encounters. We may represent reactive behavior in the event calculus using trigger axioms, which are of the form

 $\gamma \Rightarrow Happens(\alpha, \tau)$

where γ is a condition, α is an event term, and τ is a timepoint term.

11.1.2 GOAL-DRIVEN BEHAVIOR

Whereas some agent behavior is reactive, much behavior is goal-driven.

Ryan has not eaten for a while. He gets hungry. He walks into the kitchen. The refrigerator is empty. He goes to a sandwich shop across the street. He eats a sandwich.

168

Here Ryan initiates a goal to eat some food in response to his hunger. He forms a plan to eat some food in the kitchen. We use these notions of goals and plans to interpret Ryan's actions and predict his future actions. We understand that Ryan walks into the kitchen because of his goal to eat. We understand that his plan involves taking some food out of the refrigerator. He is acting on his belief that there is food in the refrigerator. When he learns the refrigerator is empty, we expect him to revise his plan and go somewhere else.

Intuitively, a *belief* of an agent is a property considered by the agent to be true or false. A *goal* of an agent is a property that the agent desires to be true. An agent's *plan* for a goal consists of actions that the agent intends to perform in order to achieve the goal. An agent activates certain goals in certain situations. An agent's goals tend to persist until they are achieved. When an agent has a goal, the agent activates a plan for achieving the goal. When a plan is active, an agent tries to execute the plan. If a plan fails, an agent activates an alternative plan. When a goal succeeds, whether intentionally or accidentally, the goal and plan are dropped.

11.1.3 FORMALIZATION

We now formalize these notions. We represent a plan as a list of actions. We introduce a list sort and terms of the form

$$[\tau_1, \dots, \tau_n] \tag{11.1}$$

where τ_1, \ldots, τ_n are terms. Several functions can be applied to a list: The *Head* of (11.1) is τ_1 , its *Tail* is $[\tau_2, \ldots, \tau_n]$, and its *Length* is *n*. An axiomatization of lists is provided in Section A.6.2.

We then use the following sorts:

- an agent sort, with variables a, a_1, a_2, \ldots
- a belief sort, which is a subsort of the fluent sort, with variables b, b_1, b_2, \ldots
- a goal sort, which is a subsort of the fluent sort, with variables g, g_1, g_2, \dots
- a plan sort, which is a subsort of the list sort, with variables p, p_1, p_2, \dots

In the event calculus, it is natural to represent persistent goals and plans as fluents subject to the commonsense law of inertia. We represent beliefs, goals, and plans using the following fluents:

Believe(a, b): Agent a has belief b; that is, a believes that b is true.

Goal(a, g): Agent a has an active goal g.

Plan(a, g, p): Agent a has an active plan p for an active goal g.

We may thus write, for example, HoldsAt(Believe(Agent, At(Agent, Kitchen)), 0). Beliefs, goals, and plans may be added (activated) and dropped (deactivated). **Axiom A1.**

Initiates(AddBelief(a,b), Believe(a,b), t)

Axiom A2.

Terminates(DropBelief(a, b), Believe(a, b), t)

Axiom A3.

Initiates(AddGoal(a, g), Goal(a, g), t)

Axiom A4.

Terminates(DropGoal(a, g), Goal(a, g), t)

Axiom A5.

Initiates(AddPlan(a, g, p), Plan(a, g, p), t)

Axiom A6.

Terminates(DropPlan(a, g, p), Plan(a, g, p), t)

Plans are activated for goals as follows. If an agent has a goal, the agent does not believe the goal is true, and no plans are yet active for the goal, then the agent selects and activates a plan for the goal.

Axiom A7.

 $HoldsAt(Goal(a,g),t) \land$ $\neg HoldsAt(Believe(a,g),t) \land$ $SelectedPlan(a,g,p,t) \land$ $\neg \exists p_1 HoldsAt(Plan(a,g,p_1),t) \Rightarrow$ Happens(AddPlan(a,g,p),t)

We use SelectedPlan(a, g, p, t) to mean that at time t, plan p is the plan selected by agent a for goal g. For a particular domain or problem, we must supply a definition for SelectedPlan(a, g, p, t). This predicate represents the agent's planning knowledge, which is assumed to be fixed over time. If we wish to allow an agent to learn or modify its planning knowledge over time, then we must use a fluent instead of a predicate.

Plans are executed and managed as follows. At each timepoint, provided that the agent believes the plan to be sound and the agent does not believe the goal to be true, the agent executes the next action of the plan, and the plan is updated to consist of the remaining actions. Note that Axioms A9 and A10 together update the plan: Axiom A9 drops the current list of planned actions at the same time that Axiom A10 adds a new list of planned actions that is the tail of the current list (provided that the tail is not empty and the other conditions are met).

Axiom A8.

 $HoldsAt(Plan(a,g,p),t) \land$ $\neg HoldsAt(Believe(a,g),t) \land$ $SoundPlan(a,g,p,t) \Rightarrow$ Happens(Head(p),t)

Axiom A9.

 $HoldsAt(Plan(a, g, p), t) \Rightarrow Happens(DropPlan(a, g, p), t)$

Axiom A10.

 $HoldsAt(Plan(a,g,p),t) \land$ $Length(p) > 1 \land$ $\neg HoldsAt(Believe(a,g),t) \land$ $SoundPlan(a,g,p,t) \Rightarrow$ Happens(AddPlan(a,g,Tail(p)),t)

We use SoundPlan(a, g, p, t) to mean that at time t, agent a believes that p is a sound plan for achieving goal g. Notice what happens if the agent believes the plan to be unsound or believes the goal to be true: The plan is dropped. If the goal is false, then a new plan for the goal is activated by Axiom A7. For a particular domain or problem, we must supply a definition for SoundPlan(a, g, p, t).

This formalization does not deal with multiple active goals, which lead to multiple active plans, which lead to the concurrent execution of plan actions, which may lead to inconsistency (see Exercise 11.7).

Goal success is treated as follows. If an agent has an active goal and the agent believes that the goal is true, then the agent drops the goal.

Axiom A11.

$$HoldsAt(Goal(a, g), t) \land HoldsAt(Believe(a, g), t) \Rightarrow$$

 $Happens(DropGoal(a, g), t)$

In order to reason about an agent in a particular domain or problem using Axioms A1 through A11, we must supply the following:

- Event calculus axioms: These represent the domain.
- Belief revision axioms: These specify how an agent's beliefs are updated in response to events and are typically of the form:

$$\gamma \Rightarrow Initiates(\alpha, Believe(a, \beta), \tau)$$

and

$$\gamma \Rightarrow Terminates(\alpha, Believe(a, \beta), \tau)$$

where γ is a condition, α is an event term, β is a fluent term, a is an agent term, and τ is a timepoint term.

• Goal activation axioms: These are typically of the form

$$\gamma \Rightarrow Happens(AddGoal(a, \beta), \tau)$$

where γ is a condition, a is an agent term, β is a fluent term, and τ is a timepoint term.

• *Planning axioms*: These supply definitions for SelectedPlan(a, g, p, t) and SoundPlan(a, g, p, t).

11.1.4 EXAMPLE: HUNGRY CAT SCENARIO

This example is due to Michael Winikoff, Lin Padgham, James Harland, and John Thangarajah.

A cat is sitting on the floor. He is hungry and would love to eat a cookie sitting on a nearby table. He plans to jump onto a nearby chair and, from the chair, onto the table. But after the cat jumps onto the chair, someone moves the chair away from the table. The cat then modifies his plan. He plans to jump onto a nearby shelf and then onto the table. When he jumps onto the shelf, he notices a cupcake lying there, so he gobbles it up immediately and is satiated.

We start by providing the event calculus axioms for the domain. We use a simple spatial theory. If an agent is on surface s_1 , it is possible to jump from s_1 to surface s_2 , and the agent jumps from s_1 to s_2 , then the agent will be on s_2 :

$$HoldsAt(On(a, s_1), t) \land HoldsAt(CanJump(s_1, s_2), t) \Rightarrow$$
 (11.2)
 $Initiates(Jump(a, s_1, s_2), On(a, s_2), t)$

In this case, the agent will no longer be on surface s_1 :

$$HoldsAt(On(a, s_1), t) \land HoldsAt(CanJump(s_1, s_2), t) \Rightarrow$$
 (11.3)
 $Terminates(Jump(a, s_1, s_2), On(a, s_1), t)$

If surface s_1 is moved from surface s_2 to surface s_3 , then it will be possible to jump from s_1 to s_3 :

$$Initiates(Move(s_1, s_2, s_3), CanJump(s_1, s_3), t)$$

$$(11.4)$$

In this case, it will no longer be possible to jump from surface s_1 to surface s_2 :

$$Terminates(Move(s_1, s_2, s_3), CanJump(s_1, s_2), t)$$
(11.5)

We use a simple theory of eating. If an agent is on a surface, some food is on the surface, and the agent eats the food, then the agent will be satiated:

$$HoldsAt(On(a,s),t) \wedge HoldsAt(On(f,s),t) \Rightarrow$$
 (11.6)
 $Initiates(Eat(a,f), Satiated(a),t)$

If an agent eats food that is on a surface, then the food will no longer be on the surface:

$$HoldsAt(On(a,s),t) \wedge HoldsAt(On(f,s),t) \Rightarrow$$
 (11.7)
 $Terminates(Eat(a,f),On(f,s),t)$

We provide axioms for belief revision:

$$HoldsAt(Believe(a, On(a, s_1)), t) \land$$
 (11.8)
 $HoldsAt(Believe(a, CanJump(s_1, s_2)), t) \Rightarrow$
 $Initiates(Jump(a, s_1, s_2), Believe(a, On(a, s_2)), t)$

$$HoldsAt(Believe(a, On(a, s_1)), t) \land$$

$$HoldsAt(Believe(a, CanJump(s_1, s_2)), t) \Rightarrow$$

$$Terminates(Jump(a, s_1, s_2), Believe(a, On(a, s_1)), t)$$

$$(11.9)$$

$$Initiates(Move(s_1, s_2, s_3), Believe(a, CanJump(s_1, s_3)), t)$$
(11.10)

$$Terminates(Move(s_1, s_2, s_3), Believe(a, CanJump(s_1, s_2)), t)$$
 (11.11)

$$HoldsAt(Believe(a, On(a, s)), t) \land$$
 (11.12)
 $HoldsAt(Believe(a, On(f, s)), t) \Rightarrow$
 $Initiates(Eat(a, f), Believe(a, Satiated(a)), t)$

$$HoldsAt(Believe(a, On(a, s)), t) \land$$
 (11.13)
 $HoldsAt(Believe(a, On(f, s)), t) \Rightarrow$
 $Terminates(Eat(a, f), Believe(a, On(f, s)), t)$

We provide planning axioms. We give a definition for SelectedPlan(a, g, p, t) that enables the agent to plan trips consisting of one and two jumps in order to obtain food:

$$SelectedPlan(a,g,p,t) \Leftrightarrow \qquad (11.14)$$

$$\exists s_1, s_2, f (HoldsAt(Believe(a,On(a,s_1)),t) \land \\ HoldsAt(Believe(a,CanJump(s_1,s_2)),t) \land \\ HoldsAt(Believe(a,On(f,s_2)),t) \land \\ g = Satiated(a) \land \\ p = [Jump(a,s_1,s_2),Eat(a,f)]) \lor \\ \exists s_1, s_2, s_3, f (HoldsAt(Believe(a,On(a,s_1)),t) \land \\ HoldsAt(Believe(a,CanJump(s_1,s_2)),t) \land \\ HoldsAt(Believe(a,CanJump(s_2,s_3)),t) \land \\ HoldsAt(Believe(a,On(f,s_3)),t) \land \\ g = Satiated(a) \land \\ p = [Jump(a,s_1,s_2),Wait(a),Jump(a,s_2,s_3),Eat(a,f)])$$

We give a definition for SoundPlan(a, g, p, t) that deals with the plans selected by (11.14). An agent's plan is sound if and only if for every jumping action in the plan, the agent believes it is possible to jump from the source surface to the destination surface:

$$SoundPlan(a, g, p, t) \Leftrightarrow$$

$$\forall s_1, s_2 (Jump(a, s_1, s_2) \in p \Rightarrow$$

$$HoldsAt(Believe(a, CanJump(s_1, s_2)), t))$$

$$(11.15)$$

In addition to the goal-driven behavior, the agent also has a reactive behavior. If the agent is not satiated, the agent is on a surface, and some food is on the surface, then the agent will eat the food:

$$\neg HoldsAt(Satiated(a), t) \land$$

$$HoldsAt(On(a, s), t) \land$$

$$HoldsAt(On(f, s), t) \Rightarrow$$

$$Happens(Eat(a, f), t)$$

$$(11.16)$$

We specify some observations. The cat has the goal of being satiated, and no plans are active:

$$\neg ReleasedAt(f,t)$$
 (11.17)

$$HoldsAt(Goal(a, g), 0) \Leftrightarrow$$
 (11.18)
 $a = Cat \land g = Satiated(Cat)$

$$\neg HoldsAt(Plan(a, g, p), 0)$$
 (11.19)

The cat is on the floor, food is on the table and the shelf, and it is possible to jump from the floor to the chair, from the chair to the table, and from the shelf to the table:

$$HoldsAt(On(o, s), 0) \Leftrightarrow$$
 (11.20)
 $(o = Cat \land s = Floor) \lor$
 $(o = Food1 \land s = Table) \lor$
 $(o = Food2 \land s = Shelf)$

$$HoldsAt(CanJump(s_1, s_2), 0) \Leftrightarrow$$
 (11.21)
 $(s_1 = Floor \land s_2 = Chair) \lor$
 $(s_1 = Chair \land s_2 = Table) \lor$
 $(s_1 = Shelf \land s_2 = Table)$

The cat believes the cat is on the floor, believes food is on the table, does not believe food is on the shelf, and believes it is possible to jump from the floor to the chair, from the chair to the table, and from the shelf to the table:

$$HoldsAt(Believe(a, On(o, s)), 0) \Leftrightarrow$$
 (11.22)
 $(a = Cat \land o = Cat \land s = Floor) \lor$
 $(a = Cat \land o = Foodl \land s = Table)$

$$HoldsAt(Believe(a, CanJump(s_1, s_2)), 0) \Leftrightarrow$$
 (11.23)
 $(a = Cat \land s_1 = Floor \land s_2 = Chair) \lor$
 $(a = Cat \land s_1 = Chair \land s_2 = Table) \lor$
 $(a = Cat \land s_1 = Shelf \land s_2 = Table)$

The cat does not believe the cat is satiated:

$$\neg HoldsAt(Believe(Cat, Satiated(Cat)), 0)$$
 (11.24)

The narrative consists of someone moving the chair at timepoint 2:

$$Happens(Move(Chair, Table, Shelf), 2)$$
 (11.25)

We can show that the cat will eat the food on the shelf.

Proposition 11.1. Let Σ be the conjunction of A1 through A6, (11.2), (11.3), (11.4), (11.5), (11.6), (11.7), (11.8), (11.9), (11.10), (11.11), (11.12), and (11.13). Let Δ be the conjunction of A7 through A11, (11.16), and (11.25). Let $\Omega = U[AddBelief, DropBelief, AddGoal, DropGoal, AddPlan, DropPlan, Jump, Move, Eat] <math>\wedge U[Believe, Goal, Plan, On, CanJump, Satiated]$. Let Γ be the conjunction of L1 through L8 (the axiomatization of lists of Section A.6.2), (11.14), (11.15), (11.17), (11.18), (11.19), (11.20), (11.21), (11.22), (11.23), and (11.24). Then we have

 $CIRC[\Sigma; Initiates, Terminates, Releases] \land CIRC[\Delta; Happens] \land$ $\Omega \land \Gamma \land DEC \vdash Happens(Eat(Cat, Food2), 6)$

Proof. From $CIRC[\Sigma; Initiates, Terminates, Releases]$ and Theorems 2.2, and 2.1, we have

```
Initiates(e, f, t) \Leftrightarrow
                                                                                                  (11.26)
\exists a, b \ (e = AddBelief(a, b) \land f = Believe(a, b)) \lor
\exists a, g (e = AddGoal(a, g) \land f = Goal(a, g)) \lor
\exists a, g, p (e = AddPlan(a, g, p) \land f = Plan(a, g, p)) \lor
\exists a, s_1, s_2 (e = Jump(a, s_1, s_2) \land
f = On(a, s_2) \wedge
HoldsAt(On(a, s_1), t) \land
HoldsAt(CanJump(s_1, s_2), t)) \lor
\exists s_1, s_2, s_3 \ (e = Move(s_1, s_2, s_3) \land f = CanJump(s_1, s_3)) \lor
\exists a, f, s (e = Eat(a, f) \land
f = Satiated(a) \land
HoldsAt(On(a, s), t) \land
HoldsAt(On(f,s),t)) \lor
\exists a, s_1, s_2 (e = Jump(a, s_1, s_2) \land
f = Believe(a, On(a, s_2)) \land
HoldsAt(Believe(a, On(a, s_1)), t) \land
HoldsAt(Believe(a, CanJump(s_1, s_2)), t)) \lor
\exists a, s_1, s_2, s_3 \ (e = Move(s_1, s_2, s_3) \land f = Believe(a, CanJump(s_1, s_3))) \lor
\exists a, f (e = Eat(a, f) \land
f = Believe(a, Satiated(a)) \land
HoldsAt(Believe(a, On(a, s)), t) \land
HoldsAt(Believe(a, On(f, s)), t))
Terminates(e, f, t) \Leftrightarrow
                                                                                                  (11.27)
\exists a, b \ (e = DropBelief(a, b) \land f = Believe(a, b)) \lor
\exists a, g (e = DropGoal(a, g) \land f = Goal(a, g)) \lor
\exists a, g, p \ (e = DropPlan(a, g, p) \land f = Plan(a, g, p)) \lor
\exists a, s_1, s_2
(e = Jump(a, s_1, s_2) \land
f = On(a, s_1) \wedge
HoldsAt(On(a, s_1), t) \land
HoldsAt(CanJump(s_1, s_2), t)) \lor
\exists s_1, s_2, s_3 \ (e = Move(s_1, s_2, s_3) \land f = CanJump(s_1, s_2)) \lor
\exists a, f, s
(e = Eat(a, f) \land
f = On(f,s) \wedge
```

```
HoldsAt(On(a, s), t) \land
             HoldsAt(On(f,s),t)) \vee
             \exists a, s_1, s_2 (e = Jump(a, s_1, s_2) \land
            f = Believe(a, On(a, s_1)) \land
             HoldsAt(Believe(a, On(a, s_1)), t) \land
            HoldsAt(Believe(a, CanJump(s_1, s_2)), t)) \lor
             \exists a, s_1, s_2, s_3 \ (e = Move(s_1, s_2, s_3) \land f = Believe(a, CanJump(s_1, s_2))) \lor
             \exists a, f, s (e = Eat(a, f) \land
            f = Believe(a, On(f, s)) \land
            HoldsAt(Believe(a, On(a, s)), t) \land
            HoldsAt(Believe(a, On(f, s)), t))
             \neg Releases(e, f, t)
                                                                                                        (11.28)
From CIRC[\Delta; Happens] and Theorem 2.1, we have
                   Happens(e,t) \Leftrightarrow
                                                                                                        (11.29)
                   \exists a, g, p (e = AddPlan(a, g, p) \land
                   \neg HoldsAt(Believe(a,g),t) \land
                   HoldsAt(Goal(a, g), t) \land
                   SelectedPlan(a, g, p, t) \land
                   \neg \exists p_1 HoldsAt(Plan(a, g, p_1), t)) \lor
                   \exists a, g, p (e = Head(p) \land
                   HoldsAt(Plan(a, g, p), t) \land
                   \neg HoldsAt(Believe(a,g),t) \land
                   SoundPlan(a, g, p, t)) \lor
                   \exists a, g, p \ (e = DropPlan(a, g, p) \land HoldsAt(Plan(a, g, p), t)) \lor
                   \exists a, g, p \ (e = AddPlan(a, g, Tail(p)) \land
                   HoldsAt(Plan(a, g, p), t) \land
                   Length(p) > 1 \land
                   \neg HoldsAt(Believe(a, g), t) \land
                   SoundPlan(a, g, p, t)) \lor
                   \exists a, g (e = DropGoal(a, g) \land
                   HoldsAt(Goal(a, g), t) \land
                   HoldsAt(Believe(a, g), t)) \lor
                   \exists a, f, s (e = Eat(a, f) \land
                   \neg HoldsAt(Satiated(a), t) \land
                   HoldsAt(On(a, s), t) \wedge
                   HoldsAt(On(f,s),t)) \vee
                   (e = Move(Chair, Table, Shelf) \land t = 2)
```

We proceed one timepoint at a time, starting with timepoint 0. We start by determining what events occur at timepoint 0.

Timepoint 0: Events Let $P_1 = [Jump(Cat, Floor, Chair), Wait(Cat), Jump (Cat, Chair, Table), Eat(Cat, Food1)]. Using (11.29), we proceed to show that one event occurs:$

$$Happens(e, 0) \Leftrightarrow$$
 (11.30)
 $e = AddPlan(Cat, Satiated(Cat), P_1)$

From (11.19), we have

$$\neg \exists e, a, g, p \ (e = Head(p) \land$$

$$H_{a} H_{a} A_{b} P_{b} P_{a} (a, g, p) \bigcirc A$$

$$(11.31)$$

 $HoldsAt(Plan(a, g, p), 0) \land$

 $\neg HoldsAt(Believe(a,g),0) \land$

SoundPlan(a,g,p,0))

$$\neg \exists e, a, g, p \ (e = DropPlan(a, g, p) \land HoldsAt(Plan(a, g, p), 0)) \tag{11.32}$$

$$\neg \exists e, a, g, p \ (e = AddPlan(a, g, Tail(p)) \land \qquad (11.33)$$

 $HoldsAt(Plan(a, g, p), 0) \land$

 $Length(p) > 1 \land$

 $\neg HoldsAt(Believe(a, g), 0) \land$

SoundPlan(a, g, p, 0))

From (11.18) and (11.24), we have

$$\neg \exists e, a, g \ (e = DropGoal(a, g) \land \tag{11.34}$$

 $HoldsAt(Goal(a, g), 0) \land$

HoldsAt(Believe(a,g),0))

From (11.20), we have

$$\neg \exists e, a, f, s (e = Eat(a, f) \land \tag{11.35}$$

 $\neg HoldsAt(Satiated(a), 0) \land$

 $HoldsAt(On(a, s), 0) \land$

HoldsAt(On(f,s),0))

From (11.22), (11.23), and (11.14), we have

$$SelectedPlan(a, g, p, 0) \Leftrightarrow a = Cat \land g = Satiated(Cat) \land p = P_1$$

From this, (11.18), (11.19), (11.24), (11.31), (11.32), (11.33), (11.34), (11.35), and (11.29), we have (11.30).

Next we determine the values of relevant fluents at timepoint 1.

Timepoint 1: Fluents From (11.30) and (11.27), we have

 $\neg \exists e, o, s \, (Happens(e, 0) \land Terminates(e, On(o, s), 0))$

From this, (11.20), (11.17), and DEC5, we have

$$HoldsAt(On(Cat, Floor), 1)$$
 (11.36)

$$HoldsAt(On(Food1, Table), 1)$$
 (11.37)

$$HoldsAt(On(Food2, Shelf), 1)$$
 (11.38)

From (11.30) and (11.26), we have

$$\neg \exists e, o, s (Happens(e, 0) \land Initiates(e, On(o, s), 0))$$

From this, (11.20), (11.17), and DEC6, we have

$$\neg (o = Cat \land s = Floor) \land$$

$$\neg (o = Food1 \land s = Table) \land$$

$$\neg (o = Food2 \land s = Shelf) \Rightarrow$$

$$\neg HoldsAt(On(o, s), 1)$$
(11.39)

From (11.30) and (11.26), we have

$$\neg \exists e (Happens(e, 0) \land Initiates(e, Believe(Cat, Satiated(Cat)), 0))$$

From this, (11.24), (11.17), and DEC6, we have

$$\neg HoldsAt(Believe(Cat, Satiated(Cat)), 1)$$
 (11.40)

From (11.30) and (11.27), we have

$$\neg \exists e, a, s_1, s_2 \ (Happens(e, 0) \land Terminates(e, Believe(a, CanJump(s_1, s_2)), 0))$$

From this, (11.23), (11.17), and DEC5, we have

$$HoldsAt(Believe(Cat, CanJump(Floor, Chair)), 1)$$
 (11.41)

$$HoldsAt(Believe(Cat, CanJump(Chair, Table)), 1)$$
 (11.42)

$$HoldsAt(Believe(Cat, CanJump(Shelf, Table)), 1)$$
 (11.43)

From (11.30), A5 (which follows from (11.26)), and DEC9, we have

$$HoldsAt(Plan(Cat, Satiated(Cat), P_1), 1)$$
 (11.44)

We proceed to show the following:

$$a \neq Cat \lor g \neq Satiated(Cat) \lor p \neq P_1 \Rightarrow$$
 (11.45)
 $\neg HoldsAt(Plan(a, g, p), 1)$

Let α be an arbitrary agent, γ be an arbitrary fluent, and π be an arbitrary list. We must show

$$\alpha \neq Cat \lor \gamma \neq Satiated(Cat) \lor \pi \neq P_1 \Rightarrow \neg HoldsAt(Plan(\alpha, \gamma, \pi), 1)$$

Suppose $\alpha \neq Cat \lor \gamma \neq Satiated(Cat) \lor \pi \neq P_1$. From this, (11.30), and (11.26), we have

$$\neg \exists e (Happens(e, 0) \land Initiates(e, Plan(\alpha, \gamma, \pi), 0))$$

From this, (11.17), (11.19), and DEC6, we have $\neg HoldsAt(Plan(\alpha, \gamma, \pi), 1)$ as required.

From (11.30) and (11.27), we have

$$\neg \exists e (Happens(e, 0) \land Terminates(e, Goal(Cat, Satiated(Cat)), 0))$$

From this, (11.18), (11.17), and DEC5, we have

$$HoldsAt(Goal(Cat, Satiated(Cat)), 1)$$
 (11.46)

We proceed to show

$$a \neq Cat \lor g \neq Satiated(Cat) \Rightarrow \neg HoldsAt(Goal(a, g), 1)$$
 (11.47)

Let α be an arbitrary agent and γ be an arbitrary fluent. We must show

$$\alpha \neq Cat \lor \gamma \neq Satiated(Cat) \Rightarrow \neg HoldsAt(Goal(\alpha, \gamma), 1)$$

Suppose $\alpha \neq Cat \lor \gamma \neq Satisted(Cat)$. From (11.30) and (11.26), we have

$$\neg \exists e (Happens(e, 0) \land Initiates(e, Goal(\alpha, \gamma), 0))$$

From this, (11.18), $\alpha \neq Cat \lor \gamma \neq Satiated(Cat)$, (11.17), and DEC6, we have $\neg HoldsAt(Goal(\alpha, \gamma), 1)$ as required.

Timepoint 1: Events Using (11.29), we proceed to show

$$Happens(e, 1) \Leftrightarrow$$
 (11.48)
 $e = Jump(Cat, Floor, Chair) \lor$
 $e = DropPlan(Cat, Satiated(Cat), P_1) \lor$
 $e = AddPlan(Cat, Satiated(Cat), Tail(P_1))$

From (11.46), (11.47), and (11.44), we have

$$\neg \exists a, g, p \ (e = AddPlan(a, g, p) \land$$

$$\neg HoldsAt(Believe(a, g), 1) \land$$

$$HoldsAt(Goal(a, g), 1) \land$$

$$SelectedPlan(a, g, p, 1) \land$$

$$\neg \exists p_1 \ HoldsAt(Plan(a, g, p_1), 1))$$

$$(11.49)$$

From (11.40) and (11.47), we have

$$\neg \exists e, a, g \ (e = DropGoal(a, g) \land$$

$$HoldsAt(Goal(a, g), 1) \land$$

$$HoldsAt(Believe(a, g), 1))$$
(11.50)

From (11.36), (11.37), (11.38), and (11.39), we have

$$\neg \exists e, a, f, s (e = Eat(a, f) \land$$

$$\neg HoldsAt(Satiated(a), 1) \land$$

$$HoldsAt(On(a, s), 1) \land$$

$$HoldsAt(On(f, s), 1))$$

$$(11.51)$$

From (11.41), (11.42), (11.43), (11.15), L5, and L6, we have

$$SoundPlan(Cat, Satiated(Cat), P_1, 1)$$

From this, (11.49), (11.50), (11.51), (11.45), (11.44), (11.40), (11.29), L1, L3, and L4, we have (11.48).

Timepoint 2: Fluents Using similar arguments we can show

$$HoldsAt(On(o, s), 2) \Leftrightarrow$$
 (11.52)
 $(o = Cat \land s = Chair) \lor$

$$(o = Food2 \land s = Shelf)$$

$$HoldsAt(Believe(a, CanJump(s_1, s_2)), 1) \Leftrightarrow \qquad (11.53)$$

$$(a = Cat \land s_1 = Floor \land s_2 = Chair) \lor \qquad (a = Cat \land s_1 = Shelf \land s_2 = Table) \lor \qquad (a = Cat \land s_1 = Shelf \land s_2 = Table)$$

$$\neg HoldsAt(Believe(Cat, Satiated(Cat)), 2) \qquad (11.54)$$

$$HoldsAt(Plan(Cat, Satiated(Cat)), 2) \qquad (11.55)$$

$$a \neq Cat \lor g \neq Satiated(Cat) \lor p \neq Tail(P_1), 2) \qquad (11.55)$$

$$a \neq Cat \lor g \neq Satiated(Cat), 2 \Rightarrow HoldsAt(Gal(Cat, Satiated(Cat)), 2) \qquad (11.57)$$

$$a \neq Cat \lor g \neq Satiated(Cat), 3 \Rightarrow HoldsAt(Goal(a, g, p), 2) \qquad (11.57)$$

$$a \neq Cat \lor g \neq Satiated(Cat), 3 \Rightarrow HoldsAt(Goal(a, g), 2) \qquad (11.58)$$

$$Timepoint 2: Events We proceed to show$$

$$Happens(e, 2) \Leftrightarrow \qquad (11.59)$$

$$e = Move(Chair, Table, Shelf) \lor \qquad e \Rightarrow Move(Chair, Table, Shelf) \lor \qquad e \Rightarrow Move(Chair, Table, Shelf) \lor \qquad e \Rightarrow Move(Cat, Satiated(Cat), Tail(P_1)) \lor \qquad e \Rightarrow AddPlan(Cat, Satiated(Cat), Tail(Tail(P_1)))$$

$$From (11.57), (11.58), and (11.55), we have$$

$$\neg \exists a, g, p (e \Rightarrow AddPlan(a, g, p) \land \qquad (11.60)$$

$$\neg HoldsAt(Believe(a, g), 2) \land \qquad SelectedPlan(a, g, p, 2) \land \qquad \neg \exists p_1 HoldsAt(Plan(a, g, p_1), 2))$$

$$From (11.54) \text{ and } (11.58), \text{ we have}$$

$$\neg \exists e, a, g (e \Rightarrow DropGoal(a, g) \land \qquad (11.61)$$

$$HoldsAt(Goal(a, g), 2) \land \qquad HoldsAt(Goal(a, g), 2) \land \qquad HoldsAt(On(a, s), 2) \land \qquad HoldsAt(On(f, s), 2))$$

 $(o = Food1 \land s = Table) \lor$

180

From (11.53), (11.15), L5, and L6, we have

 $SoundPlan(Cat, Satiated(Cat), Tail(P_1), 2)$

From this, (11.60), (11.61), (11.62), (11.56), (11.55), (11.54), (11.29), L1, L2, L3, and L4, we have (11.59).

Timepoint 3: Fluents Using similar arguments we can show

$$HoldsAt(On(o, s), 3) \Leftrightarrow$$
 (11.63)
 $(o = Cat \land s = Chair) \lor$
 $(o = Food1 \land s = Table) \lor$
 $(o = Food2 \land s = Shelf)$

$$HoldsAt(Believe(a, CanJump(s_1, s_2)), 3) \Leftrightarrow$$
 (11.64)
 $(a = Cat \land s_1 = Floor \land s_2 = Chair) \lor$
 $(a = Cat \land s_1 = Chair \land s_2 = Shelf) \lor$
 $(a = Cat \land s_1 = Shelf \land s_2 = Table)$

$$\neg HoldsAt(Believe(Cat, Satiated(Cat)), 3)$$
 (11.65)

$$HoldsAt(Plan(Cat, Satiated(Cat), Tail(Tail(P_1))), 3)$$
 (11.66)

$$a \neq Cat \lor g \neq Satiated(Cat) \lor p \neq Tail(Tail(P_1)) \Rightarrow$$
 (11.67)
 $\neg HoldsAt(Plan(a, g, p), 3)$

$$HoldsAt(Goal(Cat, Satiated(Cat)), 3)$$
 (11.68)

$$a \neq Cat \lor g \neq Satiated(Cat) \Rightarrow \neg HoldsAt(Goal(a, g), 3)$$
 (11.69)

Timepoint 3: Events At timepoint 3, the cat no longer believes that the plan is sound. So the cat does not act on the plan, and the plan is dropped. We proceed to show

$$Happens(e,3) \Leftrightarrow (11.70)$$

 $e = DropPlan(Cat, Satiated(Cat), Tail(Tail(P_1)))$

From (11.68), (11.69), and (11.66), we have

$$\neg\exists a, g, p \ (e = AddPlan(a, g, p) \land$$

$$\neg HoldsAt(Believe(a, g), 3) \land$$

$$HoldsAt(Goal(a, g), 3) \land$$

$$SelectedPlan(a, g, p, 3) \land$$

$$\neg\exists p_1 \ HoldsAt(Plan(a, g, p_1), 3))$$

$$(11.71)$$

From (11.64), (11.15), L5, and L6, we have

 $\neg SoundPlan(Cat, Satiated(Cat), Tail(Tail(P_1)), 3)$

From this, (11.66), and (11.67), we have

$$\neg \exists e, a, g, p \ (e = Head(p) \land$$

$$HoldsAt(Plan(a, g, p), 3) \land$$

$$\neg HoldsAt(Believe(a, g), 3) \land$$

$$SoundPlan(a, g, p, 3))$$
(11.72)

$$\neg \exists e, a, g, p \ (e = AddPlan(a, g, Tail(p)) \land$$

$$HoldsAt(Plan(a, g, p), 3) \land$$

$$Length(p) > 1 \land$$

$$\neg HoldsAt(Believe(a, g), 3) \land$$

$$SoundPlan(a, g, p, 3))$$

$$(11.73)$$

From (11.65) and (11.69), we have

$$\neg \exists e, a, g \ (e = DropGoal(a, g) \land$$

$$HoldsAt(Goal(a, g), 3) \land$$

$$HoldsAt(Believe(a, g), 3))$$

$$(11.74)$$

From (11.63), we have

$$\neg\exists e, a, f, s (e = Eat(a, f) \land$$

$$\neg HoldsAt(Satiated(a), 3) \land$$

$$HoldsAt(On(a, s), 3) \land$$

$$HoldsAt(On(f, s), 3))$$
(11.75)

From (11.71), (11.72), (11.73), (11.74), (11.75), (11.67), (11.66), and (11.29), we have (11.70).

Timepoint 4: Fluents Using similar arguments we can show

$$HoldsAt(On(o, s), 4) \Leftrightarrow$$
 (11.76)
 $(o = Cat \land s = Chair) \lor$
 $(o = Food1 \land s = Table) \lor$
 $(o = Food2 \land s = Shelf)$

$$HoldsAt(Believe(a, On(o, s)), 4) \Leftrightarrow$$
 (11.77)
 $(a = Cat \land o = Cat \land s = Chair) \lor$
 $(a = Cat \land o = Food1 \land s = Table)$

$$HoldsAt(Believe(a, CanJump(s_1, s_2)), 4) \Leftrightarrow$$

$$(a = Cat \land s_1 = Floor \land s_2 = Chair) \lor$$

$$(a = Cat \land s_1 = Chair \land s_2 = Shelf) \lor$$

$$(a = Cat \land s_1 = Shelf \land s_2 = Table)$$
(11.78)

$$\neg HoldsAt(Believe(Cat, Satiated(Cat)), 4)$$
 (11.79)

$$\neg HoldsAt(Plan(a, g, p), 4)$$
 (11.80)

$$HoldsAt(Goal(Cat, Satiated(Cat)), 4)$$
 (11.81)

$$a \neq Cat \lor g \neq Satiated(Cat) \Rightarrow \neg HoldsAt(Goal(a, g), 4)$$
 (11.82)

Timepoint 4: Events Because no plans are active at timepoint 4, a new plan is activated. Let $P_2 = [Jump(Cat, Chair, Shelf), Wait(Cat), Jump(Cat, Shelf, Table), Eat(Cat, Food1)]. We proceed to show$

$$Happens(e, 4) \Leftrightarrow$$
 (11.83)
 $e = AddPlan(Cat, Satiated(Cat), P_2)$

From (11.80), we have

$$\neg \exists e, a, g, p \ (e = Head(p) \land$$

$$HoldsAt(Plan(a, g, p), 4) \land$$

$$\neg HoldsAt(Believe(a, g), 4) \land$$

$$SoundPlan(a, g, p, 4))$$

$$(11.84)$$

$$\neg \exists e, a, g, p \ (e = DropPlan(a, g, p) \land HoldsAt(Plan(a, g, p), 4))$$
 (11.85)

$$\neg \exists e, a, g, p \ (e = AddPlan(a, g, Tail(p)) \land$$

$$HoldsAt(Plan(a, g, p), 4) \land$$

$$Length(p) > 1 \land$$

$$\neg HoldsAt(Believe(a, g), 4) \land$$

$$SoundPlan(a, g, p, 4))$$

$$(11.86)$$

From (11.81), (11.82), and (11.79), we have

$$\neg \exists e, a, g \ (e = DropGoal(a, g) \land$$

$$HoldsAt(Goal(a, g), 4) \land$$

$$HoldsAt(Believe(a, g), 4))$$

$$(11.87)$$

From (11.76), we have

$$\neg\exists e, a, f, s \ (e = Eat(a, f) \land$$

$$\neg HoldsAt(Satiated(a), 4) \land$$

$$HoldsAt(On(a, s), 4) \land$$

$$HoldsAt(On(f, s), 4))$$

$$(11.88)$$

From (11.77), (11.78), and (11.14), we have

$$SelectedPlan(a, g, p, 4) \Leftrightarrow a = Cat \land g = Satiated(Cat) \land p = P_2$$

From this, (11.81), (11.82), (11.80), (11.79), (11.84), (11.85), (11.86), (11.87), (11.88), and (11.29), we have (11.83).

(11.95)

Timepoint 5: Fluents Using similar arguments we can show

$$HoldsAt(On(o, s), 5) \Leftrightarrow$$
 (11.89)
 $(o = Cat \land s = Chair) \lor$
 $(o = Food1 \land s = Table) \lor$
 $(o = Food2 \land s = Shelf)$

$$HoldsAt(Believe(a, CanJump(s_1, s_2)), 5) \Leftrightarrow$$
 (11.90)
 $(a = Cat \land s_1 = Floor \land s_2 = Chair) \lor$
 $(a = Cat \land s_1 = Chair \land s_2 = Shelf) \lor$
 $(a = Cat \land s_1 = Shelf \land s_2 = Table)$
 $\neg HoldsAt(Believe(Cat, Satiated(Cat)), 5)$ (11.91)
 $HoldsAt(Plan(Cat, Satiated(Cat), P_2), 5)$ (11.92)

$$a \neq Cat \lor g \neq Satiated(Cat) \lor p \neq P_2 \Rightarrow$$
 (11.93)
 $\neg HoldsAt(Plan(a, g, p), 5)$

$$HoldsAt(Goal(Cat, Satiated(Cat)), 5)$$
 (11.94)
 $a \neq Cat \lor g \neq Satiated(Cat) \Rightarrow \neg HoldsAt(Goal(a, g), 4)$ (11.95)

Timepoint 5: Events The new plan is acted on. We proceed to show

$$Happens(e, 5) \Leftrightarrow$$
 (11.96)
 $e = Jump(Cat, Chair, Shelf) \lor$
 $e = DropPlan(Cat, Satiated(Cat), P_2) \lor$
 $e = AddPlan(Cat, Satiated(Cat), Tail(P_2))$

From (11.94), (11.95), and (11.92), we have

$$\neg\exists a, g, p \ (e = AddPlan(a, g, p) \land$$

$$\neg HoldsAt(Believe(a, g), 5) \land$$

$$HoldsAt(Goal(a, g), 5) \land$$

$$SelectedPlan(a, g, p, 5) \land$$

$$\neg\exists p_1 \ HoldsAt(Plan(a, g, p_1), 5))$$

$$(11.97)$$

From (11.91) and (11.95), we have

$$\neg \exists e, a, g (e = DropGoal(a, g) \land$$

$$HoldsAt(Goal(a, g), 5) \land$$

$$HoldsAt(Believe(a, g), 5))$$
(11.98)

From (11.89), we have

$$\neg \exists e, a, f, s (e = Eat(a, f) \land$$

$$\neg HoldsAt(Satiated(a), 5) \land$$

$$HoldsAt(On(a, s), 5) \land$$

$$HoldsAt(On(f, s), 5))$$
(11.99)

From (11.90), (11.15), L5, and L6, we have

 $SoundPlan(Cat, Satiated(Cat), P_2, 5)$

From this, (11.97), (11.98), (11.99), (11.93), (11.92), (11.91), (11.29), L1, L3, and L4, we have (11.96).

Timepoint 6: Fluents Using similar arguments we can show

$$HoldsAt(On(o, s), 6) \Leftrightarrow$$
 (11.100)
 $(o = Cat \land s = Shelf) \lor$
 $(o = Food1 \land s = Table) \lor$
 $(o = Food2 \land s = Shelf)$

 $\neg HoldsAt(Believe(Cat, Satiated(Cat)), 6)$ (11.101)

Timepoint 6: Events From (11.101), (11.100), (11.16) (which follows from (11.29)), we have Happens(Eat(Cat, Food2), 6) as required. (At timepoint 7, the cat is satiated, the plan is not further acted upon, and the goal to be satiated is dropped.)

11.2 EMOTIONS

We use the theory of human emotions and emotional reactions to events proposed by Andrew Ortony, Gerald L. Clore, and Allan Collins.

11.2.1 EMOTION THEORY

The emotion theory specifies several emotion classes, each consisting of several emotions or emotional reactions. For each emotion, *eliciting conditions* determine under what circumstances the emotion is elicited.

Well-being emotions are reactions to desirable or undesirable events. For example, if a desirable event occurs, then a *joy* emotion is elicited, whereas if an undesirable event occurs, then a *distress* emotion is elicited.

Fortunes-of-others emotions are reactions to events involving others. They vary according to whether they are desirable or undesirable for the self and whether they are believed to be desirable or undesirable for the other person. For example, if an event occurs that is undesirable for the self and desirable for the other person, then a resentment emotion is elicited.

Prospect-based emotions are reactions to events that are likely to occur but have not yet occurred and reactions to anticipated events that occur or fail to occur. They vary according to whether they are desirable or undesirable and whether they have not yet occurred, they have occurred, or they have failed to occur. For example, if a desirable event is likely to occur, then a hope emotion is elicited; if an undesirable event has failed to occur, then the relief emotion is elicited. Attribution emotions are reactions to actions performed by the self or others of which the self approves or disapproves. For example, if the self performs an

action approved by the self, then the *pride* emotion is elicited; if another person performs an action approved by the self, then the *appreciation* emotion is elicited.

Compound emotions are combinations of well-being and attribution emotions. For example, gratitude is a combination of joy and appreciation.

Attraction emotions are positive and negative reactions to objects. For example, a person likes or dislikes various objects.

11.2.2 FORMALIZATION

We now formalize in the event calculus (parts of) the theory of Ortony, Clore, and Collins. We have the following sorts:

- a belief sort, with variables b, b_1, b_2, \ldots
- · an event sort, which is a subsort of the belief sort
- a negated event sort, which is also a subsort of the belief sort
- a fluent sort, with variables f, f_1, f_2, \dots
- an object sort, with variables o, o_1, o_2, \dots
- an agent sort, which is a subsort of the object sort, with variables a, a_1, a_2, \ldots
- a real number sort, with variables x, x_1, x_2, \dots
- an event sort, with variables e, e_1, e_2, \dots

We also introduce a function symbol *Not*, which denotes a function that maps events to their negations.

We start with the following fluents that represent factors used to specify the eliciting conditions of emotions.

Believe(a, b): If b is an event term, then agent a believes that b has occurred. If b is a negated event term Not(e), then agent a believes that e has not occurred. Desirability(a_1, a_2, e, x): Agent a_1 believes that the desirability of event e to agent a_2 is x, where $-1 \le x \le 1$. Agents a_1 and a_2 may be the same. Praiseworthiness(a_1, a_2, e, x): Agent a_1 believes that the praiseworthiness of an action e performed by agent a_2 is x, where $-1 \le x \le 1$. Agents a_1 and a_2 may be the same.

Anticipate(a, e, x): Agent a anticipates that event e will occur with likelihood x, where $0 \le x \le 1$.

We have the following fluents for well-being emotions:

Joy(a, e): Agent a is joyful about event e. Distress(a, e): Agent a is distressed about event e.

We have the following fluents for fortunes-of-others emotions:

 $HappyFor(a_1, a_2, e)$: Agent a_1 is happy for agent a_2 regarding event e. $SorryFor(a_1, a_2, e)$: Agent a_1 is sorry for agent a_2 regarding event e.

186

Resentment (a_1, a_2, e) : Agent a_1 is resentful of agent a_2 regarding event e. Gloating (a_1, a_2, e) : Agent a_1 gloats toward agent a_2 regarding event e.

We have the following fluents for prospect-based emotions:

Hope(a, e): Agent a is hopeful about an anticipated event e.

Fear(a, e): Agent a is fearful about an anticipated event e.

Satisfaction(a, e): Agent a is satisfied that event e occurred.

Disappointment(a, e): Agent a is disappointed that event e did not occur.

Relief(a, e): Agent a is relieved that event e did not occur.

Fears Confirmed (a, e): The fears of a are confirmed by the occurrence of event e.

We have the following fluents for attribution emotions:

Pride(a, e): Agent a is proud of performing action e.

SelfReproach(a, e): Agent a feels self-reproach for performing action e.

Appreciation (a_1, a_2, e) : Agent a_1 is appreciative of agent a_2 for performing action e.

 $Reproach(a_1, a_2, e)$: Agent a_1 is reproachful of agent a_2 for performing action e.

We have the following fluents for compound emotions:

 $Gratitude(a_1, a_2, e)$: Agent a_1 is grateful toward agent a_2 regarding event e.

Anger (a_1, a_2, e) : Agent a_1 is angry at agent a_2 regarding event e.

Gratification(a, e): Agent a is gratified about event e.

Remorse(a, e): Agent a is remorseful about event e.

We have the following fluents for attraction emotions:

Like(a, o): Agent a likes object o.

Dislike(a, o): Agent a dislikes object o.

We now present a number of axioms, starting with those for adding and dropping these fluents.

Axiom E1.

Initiates(AddBelief(a, b), Believe(a, b), t)

Axiom E2.

Terminates(DropBelief(a, b), Believe(a, b), t)

Axiom E3.

 $Initiates(AddDesirability(a_1, a_2, e, x), Desirability(a_1, a_2, e, x), t)$

Axiom E4.

Terminates($DropDesirability(a_1, a_2, e, x)$, $Desirability(a_1, a_2, e, x)$, t)

Axiom E5.

Initiates (AddPraiseworthiness (a_1, a_2, e, x) , Praiseworthiness (a_1, a_2, e, x) , t)

```
Axiom E6.
       Terminates (Drop Praiseworthiness (a_1, a_2, e, x), Praiseworthiness (a_1, a_2, e, x), t)
Axiom E7.
                    Initiates(AddAnticipate(a, e, x), Anticipate(a, e, x), t)
Axiom E8.
                  Terminates(DropAnticipate(a, e, x), Anticipate(a, e, x), t)
Axiom E9.
                              Initiates(AddJoy(a, e), Joy(a, e), t)
Axiom E10.
                            Terminates(DropJoy(a, e), Joy(a, e), t)
Axiom E11.
                         Initiates(AddDistress(a, e), Distress(a, e), t)
Axiom E12.
                       Terminates(Drop Distress(a, e), Distress(a, e), t)
Axiom E13.
                  Initiates (AddHappyFor (a_1, a_2, e), HappyFor (a_1, a_2, e), t)
Axiom E14.
                Terminates(DropHappyFor(a_1, a_2, e), HappyFor(a_1, a_2, e), t)
Axiom E15.
                   Initiates(AddSorryFor(a_1, a_2, e), SorryFor(a_1, a_2, e), t)
Axiom E16.
                 Terminates(DropSorryFor(a_1, a_2, e), SorryFor(a_1, a_2, e), t)
Axiom E17.
                 Initiates(AddResentment(a_1, a_2, e), Resentment(a_1, a_2, e), t)
Axiom E18.
               Terminates (DropResentment(a_1, a_2, e), Resentment(a_1, a_2, e), t)
Axiom E19.
                   Initiates(AddGloating(a_1, a_2, e), Gloating(a_1, a_2, e), t)
Axiom E20.
                  Terminates (Drop Gloating(a_1, a_2, e), Gloating(a_1, a_2, e), t)
Axiom E21.
                            Initiates(AddHope(a, e), Hope(a, e), t)
Axiom E22.
                          Terminates(DropHope(a, e), Hope(a, e), t)
```

```
Axiom E23.
                           Initiates(AddFear(a, e), Fear(a, e), t)
Axiom E24.
                         Terminates(DropFear(a, e), Fear(a, e), t)
Axiom E25.
                    Initiates(AddSatisfaction(a, e), Satisfaction(a, e), t)
Axiom E26.
                  Terminates(Drop Satisfaction(a, e), Satisfaction(a, e), t)
Axiom E27.
                Initiates(AddDisappointment(a, e), Disappointment(a, e), t)
Axiom E28.
              Terminates(DropDisappointment(a, e), Disappointment(a, e), t)
Axiom E29.
                          Initiates(AddRelief(a, e), Relief(a, e), t)
Axiom E30.
                        Terminates(DropRelief(a, e), Relief(a, e), t)
Axiom E31.
                Initiates(AddFearsConfirmed(a, e), FearsConfirmed(a, e), t)
Axiom E32.
              Terminates(DropFearsConfirmed(a, e), FearsConfirmed(a, e), t)
Axiom E33.
                          Initiates(AddPride(a, e), Pride(a, e), t)
Axiom E34.
                        Terminates(DropPride(a, e), Pride(a, e), t)
Axiom E35.
                   {\it Initiates}(Add Self Reproach(a,e), Self Reproach(a,e), t)
Axiom E36.
                 Terminates(DropSelfReproach(a,e), SelfReproach(a,e), t) \\
Axiom E37.
               Initiates(AddAppreciation(a_1, a_2, e), Appreciation(a_1, a_2, e), t)
Axiom E38.
             Terminates(DropAppreciation(a_1, a_2, e), Appreciation(a_1, a_2, e), t)
Axiom E39.
                  Initiates(AddReproach(a_1, a_2, e), Reproach(a_1, a_2, e), t)
```

Axiom E40.

 $Terminates(DropReproach(a_1, a_2, e), Reproach(a_1, a_2, e), t)$

Axiom E41.

 $Initiates(AddGratitude(a_1, a_2, e), Gratitude(a_1, a_2, e), t)$

Axiom E42.

 $Terminates(DropGratitude(a_1, a_2, e), Gratitude(a_1, a_2, e), t)$

Axiom E43.

 $Initiates(AddAnger(a_1, a_2, e), Anger(a_1, a_2, e), t)$

Axiom E44.

 $Terminates(DropAnger(a_1, a_2, e), Anger(a_1, a_2, e), t)$

Axiom E45.

Initiates(AddGratification(a, e), Gratification(a, e), t)

Axiom E46.

Terminates(DropGratification(a, e), Gratification(a, e), t)

Axiom E47.

Initiates(AddRemorse(a, e), Remorse(a, e), t)

Axiom E48.

Terminates(DropRemorse(a, e), Remorse(a, e), t)

Axiom E49.

Initiates(AddLike(a, o), Like(a, o), t)

Axiom E50.

Terminates(DropLike(a, o), Like(a, o), t)

Axiom E51.

Initiates(AddDislike(a, o), Dislike(a, o), t)

Axiom E52.

Terminates(DropDislike(a, o), Dislike(a, o), t)

We continue with state constraints on desirability, praiseworthiness, and anticipation.

Axiom E53.

 $HoldsAt(Desirability(a_1, a_2, e, x_1), t) \land HoldsAt(Desirability(a_1, a_2, e, x_2), t) \Rightarrow$

 $x_1 = x_2$

Axiom E54.

 $HoldsAt(Desirability(a_1, a_2, e, x), t) \Rightarrow -1 \leq x \leq 1$

Axiom E55.

 $HoldsAt(Praiseworthiness(a_1, a_2, e, x_1), t) \land HoldsAt(Praiseworthiness(a_1, a_2, e, x_2), t) \Rightarrow$

 $x_1 = x_2$

Axiom E56.

 $HoldsAt(Praiseworthiness(a_1, a_2, e, x), t) \Rightarrow -1 \leq x \leq 1$

Axiom E57.

 $HoldsAt(Anticipate(a, e, x_1), t) \land HoldsAt(Anticipate(a, e, x_2), t) \Rightarrow x_1 = x_2$

Axiom E58.

 $HoldsAt(Anticipate(a, e, x), t) \Rightarrow 0 \le x \le 1$

We now present axioms for eliciting emotions.

Axiom E59.

 $\neg HoldsAt(Joy(a,e),t) \land$ $HoldsAt(Desirability(a,a,e,x),t) \land x > 0 \land$ $HoldsAt(Believe(a,e),t) \Rightarrow$ Happens(AddJoy(a,e),t)

Axiom E60.

 $\neg HoldsAt(Distress(a,e),t) \land \\ HoldsAt(Desirability(a,a,e,x),t) \land x < 0 \land \\ HoldsAt(Believe(a,e),t) \Rightarrow \\ Happens(AddDistress(a,e),t)$

Axiom E61.

 $\neg HoldsAt(HappyFor(a_1,a_2,e),t) \land \\ HoldsAt(Desirability(a_1,a_2,e,x_1),t) \land x_1 > 0 \land \\ HoldsAt(Desirability(a_1,a_1,e,x_2),t) \land x_2 > 0 \land \\ HoldsAt(Like(a_1,a_2),t) \land \\ HoldsAt(Believe(a_1,e),t) \land \\ a_1 \neq a_2 \Rightarrow \\ Happens(AddHappyFor(a_1,a_2,e),t)$

Axiom E62.

 $\neg HoldsAt(SorryFor(a_1,a_2,e),t) \land \\ HoldsAt(Desirability(a_1,a_2,e,x_1),t) \land x_1 < 0 \land \\ HoldsAt(Desirability(a_1,a_1,e,x_2),t) \land x_2 < 0 \land \\ HoldsAt(Like(a_1,a_2),t) \land \\ HoldsAt(Believe(a_1,e),t) \land \\ \end{matrix}$

$$a_1 \neq a_2 \Rightarrow$$

 $Happens(AddSorryFor(a_1, a_2, e), t)$

Axiom E63.

 $\neg HoldsAt(Resentment(a_1,a_2,e),t) \land \\ HoldsAt(Desirability(a_1,a_2,e,x_1),t) \land x_1 > 0 \land \\ HoldsAt(Desirability(a_1,a_1,e,x_2),t) \land x_2 < 0 \land \\ HoldsAt(Dislike(a_1,a_2),t) \land \\ HoldsAt(Believe(a_1,e),t) \land \\ a_1 \neq a_2 \Rightarrow \\ Happens(AddResentment(a_1,a_2,e),t)$

Axiom E64.

 $\neg HoldsAt(Gloating(a_1,a_2,e),t) \land \\ HoldsAt(Desirability(a_1,a_2,e,x_1),t) \land x_1 < 0 \land \\ HoldsAt(Desirability(a_1,a_1,e,x_2),t) \land x_2 > 0 \land \\ HoldsAt(Dislike(a_1,a_2),t) \land \\ HoldsAt(Believe(a_1,e),t) \land \\ a_1 \neq a_2 \Rightarrow \\ Happens(AddGloating(a_1,a_2,e),t)$

Axiom E65.

 $\neg HoldsAt(Hope(a,e),t) \land$ $HoldsAt(Desirability(a,a,e,x_1),t) \land x_1 > 0 \land$ $HoldsAt(Anticipate(a,e,x_2),t) \land x_2 > 0 \land$ $a_1 \neq a_2 \Rightarrow$ Happens(AddHope(a,e),t)

Axiom E66.

 $\neg HoldsAt(Fear(a,e),t) \land$ $HoldsAt(Desirability(a,a,e,x_1),t) \land x_1 < 0 \land$ $HoldsAt(Anticipate(a,e,x_2),t) \land x_2 > 0 \Rightarrow$ Happens(AddFear(a,e),t)

Axiom E67.

 $\neg HoldsAt(Satisfaction(a,e),t) \land$ $HoldsAt(Desirability(a,a,e,x_1),t) \land x_1 > 0 \land$ $HoldsAt(Anticipate(a,e,x_2),t) \land x_2 > 0 \land$ $HoldsAt(Believe(a,e),t) \Rightarrow$ Happens(AddSatisfaction(a,e),t)

Axiom E68.

 $\neg HoldsAt(Disappointment(a, e), t) \land HoldsAt(Desirability(a, a, e, x_1), t) \land x_1 > 0 \land$

 $HoldsAt(Anticipate(a, e, x_2), t) \land x_2 > 0 \land HoldsAt(Believe(a, \neg e), t) \Rightarrow Happens(AddDisappointment(a, e), t)$

Axiom E69.

 $\neg HoldsAt(Relief(a,e),t) \land$ $HoldsAt(Desirability(a,a,e,x_1),t) \land x_1 < 0 \land$ $HoldsAt(Anticipate(a,e,x_2),t) \land x_2 > 0 \land$ $HoldsAt(Believe(a,\neg e),t) \Rightarrow$ Happens(AddRelief(a,e),t)

Axiom E70.

 $\neg HoldsAt(FearsConfirmed(a, e), t) \land HoldsAt(Desirability(a, a, e, x_1), t) \land x_1 < 0 \land HoldsAt(Anticipate(a, e, x_2), t) \land x_2 > 0 \land HoldsAt(Believe(a, e), t) \Rightarrow Happens(AddFearsConfirmed(a, e), t)$

Axiom E71.

 $\neg HoldsAt(Pride(a,e),t) \land \\ HoldsAt(Praiseworthiness(a,a,e,x),t) \land x > 0 \land \\ HoldsAt(Believe(a,e),t) \Rightarrow \\ Happens(AddPride(a,e),t)$

Axiom E72.

 $\neg HoldsAt(SelfReproach(a,e),t) \land \\ HoldsAt(Praiseworthiness(a,a,e,x),t) \land x < 0 \land \\ HoldsAt(Believe(a,e),t) \Rightarrow \\ Happens(AddSelfReproach(a,e),t)$

Axiom E73.

 $\neg HoldsAt(Appreciation(a_1,a_2,e),t) \land$ $HoldsAt(Praiseworthiness(a_1,a_2,e,x),t) \land x > 0 \land$ $HoldsAt(Believe(a_1,e),t) \land a_1 \neq a_2 \Rightarrow$ $Happens(AddAppreciation(a_1,a_2,e),t)$

Axiom E74.

 $\neg HoldsAt(Reproach(a_1, a_2, e), t) \land$ $HoldsAt(Praiseworthiness(a_1, a_2, e, x), t) \land x < 0 \land$ $HoldsAt(Believe(a_1, e), t) \land a_1 \neq a_2 \Rightarrow$ $Happens(AddReproach(a_1, a_2, e), t)$

We specify compound emotions using state constraints.

Axiom E75.

 $HoldsAt(Gratitude(a_1, a_2, e), t) \Leftrightarrow HoldsAt(Joy(a_1, e), t) \land HoldsAt(Appreciation(a_1, a_2, e), t)$

Axiom E76.

 $HoldsAt(Anger(a_1, a_2, e), t) \Leftrightarrow HoldsAt(Distress(a_1, e), t) \land HoldsAt(Reproach(a_1, a_2, e), t)$

Axiom E77.

 $HoldsAt(Gratification(a, e), t) \Leftrightarrow HoldsAt(Joy(a, e), t) \land HoldsAt(Pride(a, e), t)$

Axiom E78.

 $HoldsAt(Remorse(a, e), t) \Leftrightarrow HoldsAt(Distress(a, e), t) \land HoldsAt(SelfReproach(a, e), t)$

11.2.3 EXAMPLE: LOTTERY

If we are told that Lisa likes Kate, who just won the lottery, we should infer that Kate will be happy and Lisa will be happy for Kate. We assume that when any agent wins the lottery, all agents are aware of it:

$$Initiates(WinLottery(a_1), Believe(a_2, WinLottery(a_1)), t)$$
 (11.102)

We have the following observations and narrative. Initially, Kate is not joyful about any events, and Lisa is not happy for Kate regarding any events:

$\neg ReleasedAt(f,t)$	(11.103)
$\neg HoldsAt(Joy(Kate, e), 0)$	(11.104)
$\neg HoldsAt(HappyFor(Lisa, Kate, e), 0)$	(11.105)

Kate and Lisa do not believe any events have occurred:

$\neg HoldsAt(Believe(Kate, e), 0)$	(11.106)
$\neg HoldsAt(Believe(Lisa, e), 0)$	(11.107)

Lisa likes Kate, Kate believes that her winning the lottery is highly desirable to herself, Lisa believes that Kate winning the lottery is highly desirable to Kate, and Lisa believes that Kate winning the lottery is highly desirable to Lisa:

HoldsAt(Like(Lisa, Kate), t)	(11.108)
HoldsAt(Desirability(Kate, Kate, WinLottery(Kate), 1), t)	(11.109)
HoldsAt(Desirability(Lisa, Kate, WinLottery(Kate), 1), t)	(11.110)

HoldsAt(Desirability(Lisa, Lisa, WinLottery(Kate), 1), t) (11.111)

Kate wins the lottery:

$$Happens(WinLottery(Kate), 0)$$
 (11.112)

We can show that Kate will be happy, and Lisa will be happy for Kate.

Proposition 11.2. Let Σ be the conjunction of E9, E13, and (11.102). Let Δ be the conjunction of E59, E61, and (11.112). Let Ω be U[AddJoy, AddHappyFor, WinLottery] \wedge U[Joy, HappyFor, Believe, Desirability, Like]. Let Ψ be the conjunction of E53 and E54. Let Γ be the conjunction of (11.103), (11.104), (11.105), (11.106), (11.107), (11.108), (11.109), (11.110), and (11.111). Then we have

 $CIRC[\Sigma; Initiates, Terminates, Releases] \land CIRC[\Delta; Happens] \land$ $\Omega \land \Psi \land \Gamma \land DEC \vdash HoldsAt(Joy(Kate, WinLottery(Kate)), 2) \land$ HoldsAt(HappyFor(Lisa, Kate, WinLottery(Kate)), 2)

Proof. From $CIRC[\Sigma; Initiates, Terminates, Releases]$ and Theorems 2.2, and 2.1, we have

Initiates(e, f, t)
$$\Leftrightarrow$$
 (11.113)
 $\exists a, e_1 \ (e = AddJoy(a, e_1) \land f = Joy(a, e_1)) \lor$
 $\exists a_1, a_2, e_1 \ (e = AddHappyFor(a_1, a_2, e_1) \land f = HappyFor(a_1, a_2, e_1)) \lor$
 $\exists a_1, a_2 \ (e = WinLottery(a_1) \land f = Believe(a_2, WinLottery(a_1)))$
 $\neg Terminates(e, f, t)$ (11.114)

$$\neg Releases(e, f, t)$$
 (11.115)

From $CIRC[\Delta; Happens]$ and Theorem 2.1, we have

$$\begin{aligned} & \text{Happens}(e,t) \Leftrightarrow & (11.116) \\ & \exists a,e_1,x \, (e = AddJoy(a,e_1) \land \\ & \neg \textit{HoldsAt}(\textit{Joy}(a,e_1),t) \land \\ & \textit{HoldsAt}(\textit{Desirability}(a,a,e_1,x),t) \land \\ & x > 0 \land \\ & \textit{HoldsAt}(\textit{Believe}(a,e_1),t)) \lor \\ & \exists a_1,a_2,e_1,x_1,x_2 \, (e = AddHappyFor(a_1,a_2,e_1) \land \\ & \neg \textit{HoldsAt}(\textit{HappyFor}(a_1,a_2,e_1),t) \land \\ & \textit{HoldsAt}(\textit{Desirability}(a_1,a_2,e_1,x_1),t) \land \\ & x_1 > 0 \land \\ & \textit{HoldsAt}(\textit{Desirability}(a_1,a_1,e_1,x_2),t) \land \\ & x_2 > 0 \land \\ & \textit{HoldsAt}(\textit{Believe}(a_1,e_1),t) \land \\ & a_1 \neq a_2) \lor \\ & (e = \textit{WinLottery}(\textit{Kate}) \land t = 0) \end{aligned}$$

From (11.112) (which follows from (11.116)), (11.102) (which follows from (11.113)), and DEC9, we have the following:

$$HoldsAt(Believe(Kate, WinLottery(Kate)), 1)$$
 (11.117)

$$HoldsAt(Believe(Lisa, WinLottery(Kate)), 1)$$
 (11.118)

From (11.113), (11.116), and (11.106), we have $\neg \exists e (Happens(e, 0) \land Initiates(e, Joy(Kate, e_1), 0))$. From this, (11.104), (11.103), and DEC6, we have $\neg HoldsAt(Joy(Kate, e), 1)$. From this, (11.109), 1 > 0, (11.117), and E59 (which follows from (11.116)), we have

$$Happens(AddJoy(Kate, WinLottery(Kate)), 1)$$
 (11.119)

From (11.113), (11.116), and (11.107), we have $\neg \exists e (Happens(e, 0) \land Initiates(e, HappyFor(Lisa, Kate, e_1), 0))$. From this, (11.105), (11.103), and DEC6, we have $\neg HoldsAt(HappyFor(Lisa, Kate, e), 1)$. From this, (11.110), (11.111), (11.108), (11.118), $Lisa \neq Kate$, and E61 (which follows from (11.116)), we have

$$Happens(AddHappyFor(Lisa, Kate, WinLottery(Kate)), 1)$$
 (11.120)

From (11.119), E9 (which follows from (11.113)), and DEC9, we have HoldsAt(Joy(Kate, WinLottery(Kate)), 2). From (11.120), E13 (which follows from (11.113)), and DEC9, we have $HoldsAt(HappyFor\ (Lisa, Kate, WinLottery\ (Kate)), 2)$.

11.3 THE EPISTEMIC FUNCTIONAL EVENT CALCULUS

Jiefei Ma, Rob Miller, Leora Morgenstern, and Theodore Patkos introduced the *epistemic functional event calculus* (EFEC), an extension of the event calculus for reasoning about knowledge and action. Like the traditional event calculus, it supports reasoning about triggered events, concurrent events with cumulative and canceling effects, and nondeterministic effects of events. In addition, it supports reasoning about an agent's knowledge about past, present, and future fluent values and event occurrences.

The following shopping outlet scenario was used as a benchmark problem for the development of EFEC:

After a customer purchases an item at a computer terminal, the customer picks up the item at the correct merchandise counter, which is indicated on a display. Prizes are handed out at one of the counters after an item is successfully picked up. If the customer tries to collect the item from the wrong counter, the customer's purchase is canceled.

EFEC allows us to represent that the customer's knowledge determines where the customer picks up the item. The customer acquires this knowledge through a *sensing action*.

196

Reasoning using EFEC can be performed using answer set programming. Rule sets for EFEC along with examples including the shopping outlet scenario are available for download (Ma, Miller, Morgenstern, & Patkos, 2013b).

EFEC is built using the *functional event calculus* (FEC), which extends the event calculus with non-truth-valued fluents. We first describe FEC, and then we proceed to a discussion of EFEC.

11.3.1 FEC BASICS

FEC uses the event, fluent, and timepoint sorts of the event calculus as well as a value sort, with variables v, v_1 , v_2 ,

The predicates and functions of FEC are as follows:

Happens(e, t): Event e happens or occurs at timepoint t.

ValueOf(f, t) = v: (Similar to HoldsAt.) The value of fluent f at timepoint t is v. CausesValue(e, f, v, t): (Similar to Initiates and Terminates.) If event e occurs at timepoint t, then the value of fluent f is v after t.

PossVal(f, v): The value v is a possible value of fluent f.

11.3.2 FEC AXIOMATIZATION

FEC consists of the following axioms and definitions.

Definition FEC1.

$$ValueCaused(f, v, t) \stackrel{\text{def}}{=} \exists e (Happens(e, t) \land CausesValue(e, f, v, t))$$

Definition FEC2.

$$Other Val Caused Between (f, v_1, t_1, t_2) \stackrel{\text{def}}{=} \\ \exists t, v \ (Value Caused (f, v, t) \land t_1 \leq t < t_2 \land v \neq v_1)$$

Axiom FEC3.

$$(ValueOf(f, t_1) = v \lor ValueCaused(f, v, t_1)) \land t_1 < t_2 \land \neg OtherValCausedBetween(f, v, t_1, t_2) \Rightarrow ValueOf(f, t_2) = v$$

Axiom FEC4.

$$t_1 < t_2 \land OtherValCausedBetween(f, v, t_1, t_2) \land$$

 $\neg \exists t (t_1 \le t < t_2 \land ValueCaused(f, v, t)) \Rightarrow$
 $ValueOf(f, t_2) \ne v$

Axiom FEC5.

$$ValueOf(f,t) = v \Rightarrow PossVal(f,v)$$

11.3.3 EFEC BASICS

EFEC defines knowledge using a *possible worlds* approach, in which an agent is defined to know a fact if and only if the fact is true in all worlds the agent considers possible. EFEC adds a collection of parallel timelines or *worlds* to the single timeline of the traditional event calculus. Each world is composed of a set of *instants*. In EFEC, the timepoint sort is no longer a subset of the real number sort, but rather an arbitrary sort.

EFEC adds the following to FEC:

- a world sort, with variables w, w_1 , w_2 , ...
- an instant sort, with variables i, i_1, i_2, \ldots
- a function \(\lambda w, i \rangle \), which represents the timepoint corresponding to world \(w \) and instant \(i \)
- a predicate $i_1 < i_2$, which represents that instant i_1 precedes instant i_2
- a predicate $t_1 < t_2$, which represents that timepoint t_1 precedes timepoint t_2
- an event Sense(f), which represents that the agent senses the value of fluent f
- a constant W_a , which represents the actual world

EFEC also introduces a fluent K(w), which represents the accessibility of world w. The expression $ValueOf(K(w_2), \langle w_1, i \rangle) = True$ represents that world w_2 is accessible from world w_1 at instant i.

11.3.4 EFEC AXIOMATIZATION

EFEC consists of the following axioms.

Axiom EFEC1.

$$\forall t \,\exists w, i \, (t = \langle w, i \rangle)$$

Axiom EFEC2.

$$\langle w_1, i_1 \rangle = \langle w_2, i_2 \rangle \Leftrightarrow w_1 = w_2 \wedge i_1 = i_2$$

Axiom EFEC3.

$$\langle w_1, i_1 \rangle < \langle w_2, i_2 \rangle \Leftrightarrow w_1 = w_2 \wedge i_1 \prec i_2$$

 \leq , >, and \geq are abbreviations defined appropriately in terms of < and =.

Axiom EFEC4.

$$PossVal(K(w), v) \Leftrightarrow v = True \lor v = False$$

Axiom EFEC5.

$$ValueOf(K(w), \langle w, i \rangle) = True$$

Axiom EFEC6.

$$ValueOf(K(w_2), \langle w_1, i \rangle) = True \Rightarrow ValueOf(K(w_1), \langle w_2, i \rangle) = True$$

Axiom EFEC7.

$$ValueOf(K(w_2), \langle w_1, i \rangle) = True \land ValueOf(K(w_3), \langle w_2, i \rangle) = True \Rightarrow ValueOf(K(w_3), \langle w_1, i \rangle) = True$$

Axiom EFEC8. If the agent senses a fluent f in world w_1 at instant i and the value of f in w_1 at i is different from the value of f in a world w_2 at i, then the value of $K(w_2)$ is false in w_1 after i. That is, w_2 is not accessible from w_1 after i.

$$ValueOf(f, \langle w_1, i \rangle) \neq ValueOf(f, \langle w_2, i \rangle) \Rightarrow$$

 $CausesValue(Sense(f), K(w_2), False, \langle w_1, i \rangle)$

Axiom EFEC9. The agent knows in world w_1 at instant i_1 that the value of fluent f is not value v at instant i_2 if and only if, for every world w_2 accessible from w_1 at i_1 , the value of f in w_2 at i_2 is not v.

$$KnowsValueIsNot(\langle w_{1},i_{1}\rangle,f,i_{2},v)\Leftrightarrow \\ \forall w_{2} (f\neq K(w_{2})\wedge \\ (ValueOf(K(w_{2}),\langle w_{1},i_{1}\rangle)=True\Rightarrow ValueOf(f,\langle w_{2},i_{2}\rangle)\neq v))$$

Axiom EFEC10. The agent knows in world w at instant i_1 that the value of fluent f is value v_1 at instant i_2 if and only if, for every other possible value v_2 of f, the agent knows in w at i_1 that the value of f is not v_2 at i_2 .

$$\begin{aligned} &\textit{KnowsValueIs}(\langle w, i_1 \rangle, f, i_2, v_1) \Leftrightarrow \\ \forall v_2 \left(\textit{PossVal}(f, v_2) \land v_2 \neq v_1 \Rightarrow \textit{KnowsValueIsNot}(\langle w, i_1 \rangle, f, i_2, v_2) \right) \end{aligned}$$

Axiom EFEC11.

$$KnowsValue(t, f, i) \Leftrightarrow \exists v \ KnowsValueIs(t, f, i, v)$$

Axiom EFEC12. The agent knows in world w_1 at instant i_1 that event e happens at instant i_2 if and only if, for every world w_2 accessible from w_1 at i_1 , event e happens in w_2 at i_2 .

$$KnowsHappens(\langle w_1, i_1 \rangle, e, i_2) \Leftrightarrow \\ \forall w_2 \left(ValueOf(K(w_2), \langle w_1, i_1 \rangle) = True \Rightarrow Happens(e, \langle w_2, i_2 \rangle) \right)$$

Axiom EFEC13. The agent knows in world w_1 at instant i_1 that event e does not happen at instant i_2 if and only if, for every world w_2 accessible from w_1 at i_1 , event e does not happen in w_2 at i_2 .

$$KnowsNotHappens(\langle w_1, i_1 \rangle, e, i_2) \Leftrightarrow \\ \forall w_2 \left(ValueOf(K(w_2), \langle w_1, i_1 \rangle) = True \Rightarrow \neg Happens(e, \langle w_2, i_2 \rangle) \right)$$

Axiom EFEC14.

$$\textit{KnowsIfHappens}(t,e,i) \Leftrightarrow \\ \textit{KnowsHappens}(t,e,i) \lor \textit{KnowsNotHappens}(t,e,i)$$

The following axioms support representation of unconditional events, events conditional on knowledge, and triggered events.

Axiom EFEC15.

 $Perform(e, i) \Rightarrow Happens(e, \langle w, i \rangle)$

Axiom EFEC16.

 $PerformIfValueKnownIs(e, f, v, i) \Rightarrow$ $(Happens(e, \langle w, i \rangle) \Leftrightarrow KnowsValueIs(\langle w, i \rangle, f, i, v))$

Axiom EFEC17.

 $Triggered(e,t) \Rightarrow Happens(e,t)$

Further axioms are required to ensure that sufficient accessible worlds exist to represent lack of knowledge in the initial instant and after nondeterministic event occurrences.

BIBLIOGRAPHIC NOTES

Beliefs and knowledge

Formal models of beliefs and knowledge are provided by R. C. Moore (1980, 1985a), Morgenstern (1988), E. Davis (1990, pp. 351-393), and Scherl and Levesque (2003). Possible worlds semantics is discussed by Hintikka (1962) and Kripke (1963). Fagin, Halpern, Moses, and Vardi (1995) provide a book-length treatment of reasoning about knowledge. Joseph Halpern, John McCarthy, and Heinrich Wansing debate the merits of modal logic versus first-order logic for representing mental states (J. Y. Halpern, 1999, 2000; McCarthy, 1997, 1999, 2000; Wansing, 1998). McCarthy (1998b) discusses giving robots knowledge of their own mental states. Elgot-Drapkin and Perlis (1990) and Elgot-Drapkin, Kraus, Miller, Nirkhe, and Perlis (1999) describe a logic called active logic for modeling the step-by-step reasoning processes of agents. Bratman (1987) treats the notions of beliefs, desires, and intentions. The epistemic functional event calculus (EFEC) was introduced by R. Miller, Morgenstern, and Patkos (2013) and Ma, Miller, Morgenstern, and Patkos (2013a).

Our axiomatization of beliefs in the event calculus is a simplified version of the one of Lévy and Quantz (1998). They develop a variant of the event calculus called the situated event calculus, which adds a situation argument to the event calculus predicates. They provide belief axioms such as

$$Initiates(adopt(p, s_f), believes(p, f, t_f), t_b, s_b) \leftarrow Holds_at(f, t_f, s_f)$$

which represents that, if a person p adopts a situation s_f at timepoint t_b in situation s_b , and fluent f is true at timepoint t_f in situation s_f , then after t_b in s_b person p will believe that f is true at timepoint t_f .

Reactive behavior

Our representation of reactive behavior is similar to the stimulus-response rules of behaviorism (Watson, 1924). Brooks (1990) provides a language for reactive behaviors that compiles into code to be run on an architecture for controlling mobile robots (Brooks, 1985).

Goals and plans

Our event calculus axiomatization of goal-driven behavior is loosely based on agent control mechanisms such as those of Simon (1967); Fikes, Hart, and Nilsson (1972b); Wilensky (1983); Genesereth and Nilsson (1987, pp. 325-327); Bratman, Israel, and Pollack (1988); Mueller (1990); Rao and Georgeff (1992); Shoham (1993); Beaudoin (1994); Wooldridge (2000); and Winikoff, Padgham, Harland, and Thangarajah (2002). The hungry cat scenario is taken from Winikoff et al. (2002).

The persistence of plans and goals was pointed out by Lewin (1926/1951) and G. A. Miller, Galanter, and Pribram (1960). The study of planning is a large area within the field of artificial intelligence (Fikes & Nilsson, 1971; Ghallab, Nau, & Traverso, 2004; Newell & Simon, 1972; Sacerdoti, 1974, 1977; Wilensky, 1983) A collection of readings on planning is provided by Allen, Hendler, and Tate (1990). Logical formalizations of goals and plans as mental states are provided by Morgenstern (1988), Cohen and Levesque (1990), and E. Davis (1990, pp. 413-430).

Commonsense psychology

A number of researchers have analyzed the notions of the mental states and the events people use to model themselves and others. These notions are variously known as commonsense psychology, folk psychology, and theory of mind. Heider (1958) treats interpersonal relations and notions of perception, action, desire, pleasure, and sentiment. He provides relations such as "p SIMILAR TO o INDUCES p LIKES o, OR p TENDS TO LIKE A SIMILAR o" (p. 184).

Schank and Abelson (1977) provide a taxonomy of human goals and plans for achieving those goals. They classify goals according to whether they are to be repeatedly satisfied (s-hunger, s-sex, s-sleep), are pursued for enjoyment (e-travel, e-entertainment, e-competition), are to be achieved (a-good-job, a-possessions, a-social-relationships), are states to be preserved (p-health, p-job, p-possessions, p-social-relationship), involve imminent threats (c-health, c-fire, c-storm), or are instrumental to other goals (i-prep, d-know, d-prox, d-cont). They describe named plans and planboxes for achieving goals. For instance, a named plan use(food) for the goal of satisfying hunger (s-hunger) consists of knowing (d-know) the location of some food, being near (d-prox) the food, having physical control (d-cont) over the food, and eating the food.

Smedslund (1997) provides a system of commonsense psychological propositions (45 definitions and 56 axioms). The propositions are broken up into the following categories: persons, acting, wanting, believing, feeling, interpersonal processes, intrapersonal processes, and personal change. Sample axioms are "P wants X, if, and only if, other things equal, P prefers X to not-X" (p. 29) and "P is happy, if, and only if, and to the extent that, P believes that at least one of P's wants is being, or is going to be, fulfilled" (p. 51). A. S. Gordon (2004) provides pre-formal representations of 372 strategies from 10 planning domains.

Emotions

Dyer (1983, pp. 103-139) presents a model of human emotions for story understanding. The representation of an emotion consists of a sign (positive or negative), story

character experiencing the emotion, goal situation giving rise to the emotion, character toward whom the emotion is directed, strength, and expectation (expected or unexpected). A number of emotions can be represented using this scheme. Gratitude, for example, is represented as a positive emotion directed toward a character that caused a goal success for the character experiencing the emotion. Hope is represented as a positive emotion associated with an active goal that is expected to succeed.

Mueller (1990, pp. 53-56) extends Dyer's representation to model the influence of emotions on daydreaming and the influence of daydreaming on emotions. For example, an emotion of interest associated with an active goal initiates a stream of thought involving various scenarios for achieving the goal. If success of the goal is imagined, then an emotion of hope is initiated. Certain emotions are associated with certain personal goals. For example, embarrassment is defined as a negative emotion that results from a failed social esteem goal.

We formalize in the event calculus the model of emotions of Ortony, Clore, and Collins (1988). Our formalization is loosely based on the situation calculus formalization of O'Rorke and Ortony (1994). Some differences are as follows. O'Rorke and Ortony (p. 296) define emotional reactions using state constraints such as

$$joy(P, F, S) \leftarrow wants(P, F, S) \wedge holds(F, S)$$

rather than using trigger axioms and effect axioms. They represent that emotional reactions result directly from the fact that a fluent is true rather than from the fact that an agent believes that an event has occurred. They do not use real-valued functions for desirability, praiseworthiness, and anticipation, as suggested by Ortony, Clore, and Collins (1988, pp. 181-190).

Sanders (1989) presents a formalization of emotions using an extended version of Shoham's (1988) temporal logic. She treats emotions involving obligation, permission, and prohibition, namely, the emotions of anger, gratitude, approval, disapproval, shame, and guilt. For example, an axiom states that x is grateful to y if and only if (1) x believes that y performed an action a, (2) x wanted y to perform a, (3) x believes that a benefits x, and (4) x believes that y performed a without expecting anything in return. As in our axiomatization, the emotions of an agent arise from the beliefs of the agent. Unlike in our axiomatization, Sanders defines emotions using state constraints rather than trigger axioms and effect axioms.

EXERCISES

- **11.1** Formalize the reactive behavior of a driver. If a driver sees a squirrel in front of the car, then the driver will slam on the brakes.
- 11.2 If we remove the reactive behavior Axiom (11.16), then when the cat jumps onto the shelf the cat sticks to his original plan, jumping from the shelf to the table, ignoring the cookie on the shelf. Prove that if this axiom is removed, then the cat eats the food on the table.

- 202
- 11.3 Suppose that we remove Axiom (11.16), but we modify the axiomatization so that the agent drops plans that are nonoptimal. A plan is nonoptimal if a shorter plan exists. Provide appropriate modifications to Axioms A1–A11 so that nonoptimal plans are dropped. Note that when a nonoptimal plan is dropped, a new plan should be activated by Axiom A7. Modify other axioms as needed. Prove that the cat eats the food on the shelf.
- **11.4** Discuss the advantages and disadvantages of reactive rules versus rules that look for nonoptimal plans.
- 11.5 Extend the formalization in Section 11.2 so that (1) each emotion has an associated strength, (2) the strength is set appropriately based on desirability, praiseworthiness, and the likelihood of the anticipated event, (3) the strength of an emotion decays over time, and (4) an emotion is dropped when its strength drops below a certain threshold.
- 11.6 Formalize the operation of mental defense mechanisms (Freud, 1936/1946; Suppes & Warren, 1975). Use trigger axioms and determining fluents to apply transformations to the beliefs of an agent at each timepoint.
- 11.7 (Research problem) Extend the formalization in Section 11.1 to deal with multiple active goals and plans. Add priorities to active goals and a mechanism to select which active goal to work on at any moment.
- 11.8 (Research problem) McCarthy (1990) discusses a news story about a furniture salesman who is robbed. Formalize the knowledge necessary to represent and reason about this story.
- 11.9 (Research problem) Formalize processes of human daydreaming (Mueller, 1990) in the event calculus. Daydreaming consists of recalling past experiences, imagining alternative versions of past experiences, and imagining possible future experiences.

PART

Default Reasoning

Default Reasoning

Commonsense reasoning requires default reasoning. As we engage in commonsense reasoning, we make certain assumptions so that we can proceed. If we later gain more information, then we may have to revise those assumptions. For example, if we are told that Nathan went to sleep, we might assume that he went to sleep in his home. If we are told that he cooked breakfast, we might imagine him in his kitchen. If we later learn that he was actually at a hotel, our understanding of these events will have to be modified.

We have so far considered two special cases of default reasoning: assuming that unexpected events do not occur and assuming that events do not have unexpected effects. In this chapter, we consider default reasoning in general. We discuss atemporal default reasoning and then temporal default reasoning. We describe a general method for default reasoning about time based on the circumscription of abnormality predicates and how this method can be used to address the qualification problem. We then discuss the representation of default events and properties.

12.1 ATEMPORAL DEFAULT REASONING

We start by introducing default reasoning with some examples that do not involve time. Consider the following formula:

$$Apple(x) \Rightarrow Red(x)$$

This states that apples are always red. If we wish to represent that apples are sometimes red, we may use a formula such as the following:

$$Apple(x) \land \neg Ab_1(x) \Rightarrow Red(x)$$
 (12.1)

The predicate $Ab_1(x)$ is called an *abnormality predicate*. It represents that x is abnormal in a way that prevents us from concluding that it is red given that it is an apple. Thus, (12.1) states that all apples that are not abnormal in fashion 1 are red. How do we specify when an apple is abnormal in fashion 1?

One possibility is that we could specify the necessary and sufficient conditions. We could represent that an apple is abnormal in fashion 1 if and only if it is a Granny Smith apple or it is rotten:

$$Ab_1(x) \Leftrightarrow GrannySmith(x) \vee Rotten(x)$$
 (12.2)

206

But what about other conditions that might make an apple abnormal in fashion 1? If we wished to add other conditions, then we would have to modify (12.2):

$$Ab_1(x) \Leftrightarrow$$
 (12.3)
 $GrannySmith(x) \lor Rotten(x) \lor NewtownPippin(x)$

An alternative is to use the following approach, which is more elaboration tolerant. We start by specifying some sufficient conditions for an apple being abnormal in fashion 1:

$$GrannySmith(x) \Rightarrow Ab_1(x)$$

$$Rotten(x) \Rightarrow Ab_1(x)$$
(12.4)
(12.5)

$$NewtownPippin(x) \Rightarrow Ab_1(x)$$
 (12.6)

Then we circumscribe Ab_1 in formulas (12.4) to (12.6). Let Θ be the conjunction of (12.4), (12.5), and (12.6). By Theorem 2.1, $CIRC[\Theta; Ab_1]$ is equivalent to (12.3). This circumscription allows us to jump to the conclusion that the necessary and sufficient conditions are specified by (12.3), given that the sufficient conditions are specified by Θ .

Now suppose that a particular apple A is not a Granny Smith apple, not rotten, and not a Newtown Pippin apple:

Apple(A) $\neg GrannySmith(A)$ $\neg Rotten(A)$ $\neg NewtownPippin(A)$

We can conclude from (12.3) that A is not abnormal in fashion 1:

$$\neg Ab_1(A)$$

From this and (12.1), we can conclude that A is red:

We jump to the conclusion that A is red given that it is not a Granny Smith apple, not rotten, and not a Newtown Pippin apple.

12.2 TEMPORAL DEFAULT REASONING

Now we introduce time. In fact, previous chapters have already discussed a form of default reasoning about time. The event calculus assumes by default that (1) unexpected events do not occur and (2) events have no unexpected effects.

12.2.1 EVENT OCCURRENCES

Although it is abnormal for an event to occur at any given timepoint, events sometimes do occur. We specify what events are known to occur in the conjunction Δ of a domain description, which is described in Section 2.7. We write event calculus formulas containing the predicate Happens(e, t), which represents that timepoint t is abnormal

with respect to event e. We then use circumscription to minimize the extension of *Happens* in the conjunction Δ , which minimizes event occurrences.

12.2.2 EVENT EFFECTS

It is also abnormal for an event to have any given effect. We specify the known effects of events in the conjunction Σ of a domain description. We write event calculus formulas containing the abnormality predicates *Initiates*, *Terminates*, and *Releases*. We then circumscribe these predicates in the conjunction Σ in order to minimize event effects.

12.2.3 USING MINIMIZED EVENTS AND EFFECTS

Having minimized *Happens*, *Initiates*, *Terminates*, and *Releases*, we then write formulas containing these predicates that are outside the scope of the circumscription of these predicates. An example is axiom DEC5 of the discrete event calculus:

$$HoldsAt(f,t) \land \neg ReleasedAt(f,t+1) \land \neg \exists e (Happens(e,t) \land Terminates(e,f,t)) \Rightarrow HoldsAt(f,t+1)$$

This axiom states that a fluent f that is true at timepoint t is also true at t+1, unless f is released from the commonsense law of inertia at t+1 or there is an event e that occurs at t and terminates f at t.

12.3 DEFAULT REASONING METHOD

We now present the following general method for default reasoning about time based on the method just discussed:

- 1. We specify a set of abnormality predicates. Typically we use predicate symbols of the form Ab_i , where i is a positive integer.
- 2. We use the abnormality predicates within various event calculus formulas such as effect axioms. (Table 2.1 provides a list of types of event calculus formulas.)
- **3.** We form a conjunction Θ of cancellation axioms. If γ is a condition, ρ is an abnormality predicate symbol of arity $n+1, \tau_1, \ldots, \tau_n$ are terms, and τ is a timepoint term, then

$$\gamma \Rightarrow \rho(\tau_1, \ldots, \tau_n, \tau)$$

is a *cancellation axiom* for ρ .

4. We compute the circumscription of the abnormality predicates in the conjunction of cancellation axioms Θ.

This method requires that we add the following clause to the definition of a condition in Section 2.5: If ρ is an abnormality predicate symbol of arity $n + 1, \tau_1, \ldots, \tau_n$ are terms, and τ is a timepoint term, then $\rho(\tau_1, \ldots, \tau_n, \tau)$ is a condition.

The domain description is

 $CIRC[\Sigma; Initiates, Terminates, Releases] \land CIRC[\Delta_1 \land \Delta_2; Happens] \land$

$$CIRC[\Theta; \rho_1, \ldots, \rho_n] \wedge \Omega \wedge \Psi \wedge \Pi \wedge \Gamma \wedge E \wedge CC$$

where ρ_1, \ldots, ρ_n are the abnormality predicate symbols, Θ is a conjunction of cancellation axioms containing ρ_1, \ldots, ρ_n , and $\Sigma, \Delta_1, \Delta_2, \Omega, \Psi, \Pi, \Gamma, E$, and CC are as defined in Section 2.7.

12.4 DEFAULTS AND THE QUALIFICATION PROBLEM

Default reasoning can be used to address the qualification problem (introduced in Section 3.3). Default reasoning provides a more elaboration-tolerant way of specifying qualifications that prevent events from having their intended effects.

First, we add abnormality predicates to effect axioms, which are the same as fluent precondition axioms. We write effect axioms of the form

$$\gamma \wedge \neg \rho(\tau_1, \dots, \tau_n, \tau) \Rightarrow Initiates(\alpha, \beta, \tau)$$

or

$$\gamma \wedge \neg \rho(\tau_1, \dots, \tau_n, \tau) \Rightarrow Terminates(\alpha, \beta, \tau)$$

where γ is a condition, ρ is an abnormality predicate symbol of arity n+1, τ_1, \ldots, τ_n are terms, τ is a timepoint term, α is an event term, and β is a fluent term. Second, whenever we wish to add a qualification, we add a cancellation axiom for ρ .

Default reasoning can also be used to represent qualifications that prevent events from occurring. But action precondition axioms (discussed in Section 3.3.2) already provide an elaboration tolerant way of expressing such qualifications.

12.4.1 EXAMPLE: DEVICE REVISITED

Consider the example of turning on a device. We introduce the abnormality predicate $Ab_1(d, t)$, which represents that device d is abnormal in some way at timepoint t. We use this predicate in an effect axiom. If a device is not Ab_1 and an agent turns on the device, then the device will be on:

$$\neg Ab_1(d,t) \Rightarrow Initiates(TurnOn(a,d),On(d),t)$$
 (12.7)

We add cancellation axioms that represent qualifications. A device is Ab_1 if its switch is broken:

$$HoldsAt(BrokenSwitch(d), t) \Rightarrow Ab_1(d, t)$$
 (12.8)

A device is Ab_1 if it is not plugged in:

$$\neg HoldsAt(PluggedIn(d), t) \Rightarrow Ab_1(d, t)$$
 (12.9)

A particular antique device never works:

$$Ab_1(AntiqueDevice1, t)$$
 (12.10)

Now consider the following observations and narrative in which the device is initially off and then the device is turned on:

$$\neg HoldsAt(On(Device1), 0)$$
 (12.11)

$$\neg ReleasedAt(f,t)$$
 (12.12)

$$Happens(TurnOn(Nathan, Device1), 0)$$
 (12.13)

Suppose that the device's switch is not broken, the device is plugged in, and the device is not the antique device:

$$\neg HoldsAt(BrokenSwitch(Device1), 0)$$
 (12.14)

$$HoldsAt(PluggedIn(Device1), 0)$$
 (12.15)

$$Device1 \neq AntiqueDevice1$$
 (12.16)

We can then show that the device will be on at timepoint 1.

Proposition 12.1. Let $\Sigma = (12.7)$, $\Delta = (12.13)$, $\Theta = (12.8) \wedge (12.9) \wedge (12.10)$, $\Omega = (12.16) \wedge U[On, BrokenSwitch, PluggedIn]$, and $\Gamma = (12.11) \wedge (12.12) \wedge (12.14) \wedge (12.15)$. Then we have

$$CIRC[\Sigma; Initiates, Terminates, Releases] \land CIRC[\Delta; Happens] \land CIRC[\Theta; Ab_1] \land \Omega \land \Gamma \land DEC \\ \vdash HoldsAt(On(Device1), 1)$$

Proof. From $CIRC[\Sigma; Initiates, Terminates, Releases]$ and Theorems 2.1 and 2.2, we have

Initiates
$$(e, f, t) \Leftrightarrow$$
 (12.17)
 $\exists a, d \ (e = TurnOn(a, d) \land f = On(d) \land \neg Ab_1(d, t))$

$$\neg Terminates(e, f, t)$$
 (12.18)

$$\neg Releases(e, f, t)$$
 (12.19)

From $CIRC[\Delta; Happens]$ and Theorem 2.1, we have

$$Happens(e, t) \Leftrightarrow (e = TurnOn(Nathan, Device1) \land t = 0)$$
 (12.20)

From $CIRC[\Theta; Ab_1]$ and Theorem 2.1, we have

$$Ab_1(d,t) \Leftrightarrow$$
 (12.21)
 $HoldsAt(BrokenSwitch(d),t) \lor$
 $\neg HoldsAt(PluggedIn(d),t) \lor$
 $d = AntiqueDevice1$

From this, (12.14), (12.15), and (12.16), we have $\neg Ab_1(Device1, 0)$. From this, (12.13) (which follows from (12.20)), (12.7) (which follows from (12.17)), and DEC9, we have HoldsAt(On(Device1), 1).

12.4.2 EXAMPLE: BROKEN DEVICE

Suppose that instead of (12.14), (12.15), and (12.16), we have the fact that the device's switch is broken:

$$HoldsAt(BrokenSwitch(Device1), 0)$$
 (12.22)

We can then show that the device will *not* be on at timepoint 1.

Proposition 12.2. Let $\Sigma = (12.7)$, $\Delta = (12.13)$, $\Theta = (12.8) \land (12.9) \land (12.10)$, $\Omega = U[On, BrokenSwitch, PluggedIn]$, and $\Gamma = (12.11) \land (12.12) \land (12.22)$. Then we have

 $CIRC[\Sigma; Initiates, Terminates, Releases] \land CIRC[\Delta; Happens] \land CIRC[\Theta; Ab_1] \land \Omega \land \Gamma \land DEC \\ \vdash \neg HoldsAt(On(Device1), 1)$

Proof. From $CIRC[\Sigma; Initiates, Terminates, Releases]$ and Theorems 2.1 and 2.2, we have (12.17), (12.18), and (12.19). From $CIRC[\Delta; Happens]$ and Theorem 2.1, we have (12.20). From $CIRC[\Theta; Ab_1]$ and Theorem 2.1, we have (12.21). From (12.21) and (12.22), we have $Ab_1(Device1, 0)$. From this and (12.17), we have $\neg \exists e (Happens(e, 0) \land Initiates(e, On(Device1), 0))$. From this, (12.11), (12.12), and DEC6, we have $\neg HoldsAt(On(Device1), 1)$.

12.4.3 STRONG AND WEAK QUALIFICATIONS

Patrick Doherty and Jonas Kvarnström proposed a distinction between strong and weak qualifications. If an event is *strongly qualified*, then it will not have its intended effects; if an event is *weakly qualified*, then it may or may not have its intended effects. A weakly qualified event results in two classes of models: one in which the event has its intended effects and one in which the event does not. Thus, weakly qualified events have nondeterministic effects. Weak qualifications can be represented using determining fluents (introduced in Section 9.1). A determining fluent is introduced for each weak qualification.

12.4.4 EXAMPLE: ERRATIC DEVICE

Let us extend our device example to erratic devices. If a device is erratic, then when it is turned on, it may or may not go on. We introduce the determining fluent DeterminingFluent(d). We add a cancellation axiom that states that if a device is erratic and the determining fluent is true, then the device is Ab_1 :

$$HoldsAt(Erratic(d), t) \land$$
 (12.23)
 $HoldsAt(DeterminingFluent(d), t) \Rightarrow$
 $Ab_1(d, t)$

Now suppose that the device's switch is not broken, the device is plugged in, the device is erratic, and Nathan turns on the device at timepoint 0. We can show that if *DeterminingFluent(Device1)* is false at timepoint 0, then the device will be on at timepoint 1. But if *DeterminingFluent(Device1)* is true at timepoint 0, then the

device will not be on at timepoint 1. We use the following observations. The device is erratic:

$$HoldsAt(Erratic(Device1), 0)$$
 (12.24)

The determining fluent is always released from the commonsense law of inertia, and *On, BrokenSwitch, PluggedIn*, and *Erratic* are never released from this law:

$$ReleasedAt(DeterminingFluent(d), t)$$
 (12.25)

$$\neg ReleasedAt(On(d), t)$$
 (12.26)

$$\neg ReleasedAt(BrokenSwitch(d), t)$$
 (12.27)

$$\neg ReleasedAt(PluggedIn(d), t)$$
 (12.28)

$$\neg ReleasedAt(Erratic(d), t)$$
 (12.29)

Proposition 12.3. Let $\Sigma = (12.7)$, $\Delta = (12.13)$, $\Theta = (12.8) \wedge (12.9) \wedge (12.23)$, $\Omega = U[On, BrokenSwitch, PluggedIn, Erratic, DeterminingFluent], and <math>\Gamma = (12.11) \wedge (12.14) \wedge (12.15) \wedge (12.24) \wedge (12.25) \wedge (12.26) \wedge (12.27) \wedge (12.28) \wedge (12.29)$. Then we have

$$CIRC[\Sigma; Initiates, Terminates, Releases] \land CIRC[\Delta; Happens] \land CIRC[\Theta; Ab_1] \land \Omega \land \Gamma \land DEC$$

 $\vdash (\neg HoldsAt(DeterminingFluent(Device1), 0) \Rightarrow$

 $HoldsAt(On(Device1), 1)) \land$

 $(HoldsAt(DeterminingFluent(Device1), 0) \Rightarrow$

 $\neg HoldsAt(On(Device1), 1))$

Proof. See Exercise 12.1.

12.5 DEFAULT EVENTS AND PROPERTIES

Default reasoning can be used to represent events that occur by default, as well as properties that are true or false by default.

12.5.1 DEFAULT EVENTS

A default event is represented by an axiom of the form

$$\gamma \wedge \neg \rho(\tau_1, \ldots, \tau_n, \tau) \Rightarrow Happens(\alpha, \tau)$$

where γ is a condition, ρ is an abnormality predicate symbol of arity n+1, τ_1, \ldots, τ_n are terms, τ is a timepoint term, and α is an event term.

We may specify that normally a watch beeps every 3600 timepoints, starting at timepoint 0:

Remainder
$$(t, 3600) = 0 \land \neg Ab_1(w, t) \Rightarrow$$

 $Happens(Beep(w), t)$

Using the alarm clock axiomatization in Section 4.1.1, we may rewrite the trigger axiom (4.8) as follows:

 $HoldsAt(AlarmTime(c,t),t) \land HoldsAt(AlarmOn(c),t) \land \neg Ab_1(c,t) \Rightarrow Happens(StartBeeping(c),t)$

This states that normally a clock starts beeping when its alarm time is the current time.

12.5.2 DEFAULT PROPERTIES

A default property such as a typical color or location is represented by a formula of the form

$$\neg \rho(\tau_1, \ldots, \tau_n, \tau) \Rightarrow HoldsAt(\beta, \tau)$$

where ρ is an abnormality predicate symbol of arity $n+1, \tau_1, \ldots, \tau_n$ are terms, τ is a timepoint term, and β is a fluent term.

Suppose we have an apple sort with variable a. We represent the typical color of apples as follows:

$$\neg Ab_1(a,t) \Rightarrow HoldsAt(Red(a),t)$$

We add cancellation axioms representing when apples are not red:

 $HoldsAt(GrannySmith(a), t) \Rightarrow Ab_1(a, t)$ $HoldsAt(Rotten(a), t) \Rightarrow Ab_1(a, t)$ $HoldsAt(NewtownPippin(a), t) \Rightarrow Ab_1(a, t)$

Suppose we have a living room sort with variable l and a television sort with variable v. We represent the typical location of a television as follows:

$$\neg Ab_1(l,t) \Rightarrow \exists v HoldsAt(InRoom(v,l),t)$$

BIBLIOGRAPHIC NOTES

Frames and inheritance networks

Minsky (1974) proposed a knowledge structure called *frames* for representing typical situations. The slots of a frame have default assignments that "can be easily displaced by new items that fit better the current situation" (p. 2). A number of framelike knowledge representation languages with defaults have been developed (Bobrow & Winograd, 1977; Charniak, Riesbeck, & McDermott, 1980, chap. 15; Roberts & Goldstein, 1977). Frames are reviewed by Brachman and Levesque (2004, chap. 8). Work on semantic networks (Ceccato, 1966; Quillian, 1968; Winston, 1970) and frames led to the development of inheritance networks (Fahlman, 1979; Horty, Thomason, & Touretzky, 1990; Stein, 1992),

which can be used for default reasoning; inheritance networks are reviewed by Brachman and Levesque (2004, chap. 10).

Benchmark problems

Three benchmark problems were important in the development of logic-based methods for default reasoning: the Tweety example, the Nixon diamond, and the Yale shooting scenario. Reiter (1978, p. 215; 1980b, pp. 82-83) introduced the Tweety example, which can be traced back to work on semantic networks (A. M. Collins & Quillian, 1969). The example is as follows. All birds fly except for penguins, which do not fly. If we are told that Tweety is a bird, then we should conclude that Tweety flies. But if we are told that Tweety is a penguin, then we should retract the conclusion that Tweety flies and conclude that Tweety does not fly. Reiter (1980b) introduced default logic to deal with examples of default reasoning such as this. Lifschitz (1999) discusses the success of default logic.

The Nixon diamond, introduced by Reiter and Criscuolo (1981, p. 274), is an example of conflicting defaults. The example is as follows. Quakers are typically pacifists, and Republicans are typically not pacifists. If we are told that John is both a Quaker and a Republican, what shall we conclude? The Yale shooting scenario is discussed in Section 5.2.1.

Logic-based methods for default reasoning are reviewed by Brachman and Levesque (2004) and Russell and Norvig (2009). See also the discussion of non-monotonic reasoning methods in the Bibliographic notes of Chapter 2.

Methods based on circumscription

McCarthy (1977) proposed circumscription as a "candidate for solving the qualification problem" (p. 1040). McCarthy (1980, pp. 36-37) introduced the method of circumscription of abnormality for default reasoning using a predicate called *prevents*. McCarthy (1984a, 1986, 1987) and Grosof (1984) further developed the method and introduced the *ab* predicate. Levesque (1981, chap. 6) proposed a similar method involving *prototypical predicates*, or the negations of abnormality predicates. The prototypical predicate $\nabla \rho$: i(x) represents that x is prototypical with respect to the *i*th default property of ρ . For example, we can write the following:

$$\nabla Apple : 1(x) \Rightarrow Red(x)$$

 $GrannySmith(x) \Rightarrow \neg \nabla Apple : 1(x)$

The analogous formulas using abnormality predicates are:

$$Apple(x) \land \neg Ab_1(x) \Rightarrow Red(x)$$
$$GrannySmith(x) \Rightarrow Ab_1(x)$$

Defaults are applied by a function $\Delta Ext(m)$, which extends a knowledge base m with formulas such as

$$Apple(x) \land \neg K \neg \nabla Apple : 1(x) \Rightarrow \nabla Apple : 1(x)$$

which states that if x is an apple and it is not known that x is not prototypical with respect to the first default property of apples, then x is prototypical with respect to this property.

The method of default reasoning used in this chapter is one of a number of proposed methods based on circumscription, which are summarized in Table 12.1. For each method, the table lists the techniques used in the method, an example of a

Table 12.1 Default Reasoning Methods Based on Circumscription^a

Method	Example	CIRC	Result
(A)	$\Phi = 0.000 \text{ max for the } 0.000$	$CIRC[\Phi; Ab; Q] \vdash$	Q(B)
var	$(P(x) \land \neg Ab(x) \Rightarrow Q(x)) \land$	$Ab(x) \Leftrightarrow x = A$	an abo
(Lifschitz, 1994;	$\neg Q(A) \land P(A) \land P(B) \land$	e copport na liber	100
McCarthy, 1986)	$A \neq B$	Andrew Congression	
(B)	Φ=	CIRC[Φ; Ab; Q] ⊢	Q(B)
cancellation +	$(P(x) \land \neg Ab(x) \Rightarrow Q(x)) \land$	$Ab(x) \Leftrightarrow x = A$	
var	$Ab(A) \wedge P(A) \wedge P(B) \wedge$	Kingglip lang i , c	45 a.
(Lifschitz, 1994;	$A \neq B$	with u.t. u. Marketine	4
McCarthy, 1986)	Landa Santa Carlo Santa Car	art 1984 Yes	100
(C)	$\Phi =$	$CIRC[\Phi; Ab_1; Q] \land$	
conjunction +	$(P(x) \land \neg Ab_1(x) \Rightarrow Q(x)) \land$	$CIRC[\Phi; Ab_2; Q] \vdash$	
var	$(R(x) \land \neg Ab_2(x) \Rightarrow \neg Q(x)) \land$	$(Ab_1(x) \Leftrightarrow P(x) \land$	1
(Lifschitz, 1994;	$P(A) \wedge R(A)$	$R(x) \wedge \neg Ab_2(x)) \wedge$	
McCarthy, 1986)	all lets of the straightful for	$(Ab_2(x) \Leftrightarrow P(x) \land$	4.00
	atta a contract regardates se	$R(x) \wedge \neg Ab_1(x)$	1,004
(D)	Φ =	$CIRC[\Phi; Ab_1; Q] \land$	Q(B)
cancellation +	$(P(x) \land \neg Ab_1(x) \Rightarrow Q(x)) \land$	$CIRC[\Phi; Ab_2; Q] \vdash$	$\neg Q(A)$
conjunction +	$(R(x) \land \neg Ab_2(x) \Rightarrow \neg Q(x)) \land$	$(Ab_1(x) \Leftrightarrow R(x)) \land$	
var	$(R(x) \Rightarrow P(x)) \land R(A) \land$	$\neg Ab_2(x)$	
(Lifschitz, 1994;	$P(B) \land \neg R(B) \land A \neq B \land$		
McCarthy, 1986)	$(R(x) \Rightarrow Ab_1(x))$		a the fire
(E)	Φ =	$CIRC[\Phi; Ab_1; Q] \land$	Q(B)
conjunction +	$(P(x) \land \neg Ab_1(x) \Rightarrow Q(x)) \land$	$CIRC[\Phi; Ab_2; Q, Ab_1]$	$\neg Q(A)$
priorities +	$(R(x) \land \neg Ab_2(x) \Rightarrow \neg Q(x)) \land$	$\vdash (Ab_1(x) \Leftrightarrow R(x)) \land$	
var	$(R(x) \Rightarrow P(x)) \land R(A) \land$	$\neg Ab_2(x)$	
(Lifschitz, 1994;	$P(B) \land \neg R(B) \land A \neq B$	8	
McCarthy, 1986)	1000 000 0 000	9433, 20 H	
(F)	$\Phi_1 = (P(x) \Rightarrow Ab_1(x)) \land$	$CIRC[\Phi_1;Ab_1,Ab_2] \land$	T(A)
cancellation +	$(Q(x) \Rightarrow Ab_2(x))$	$CIRC[\Phi_2; Ab_3] \land$	
conjunction +	$\Phi_2 = (R(x) \Rightarrow Ab_3(x))$	Ф3 Н	
filtering +	$\Phi_3 =$	$(Ab_1(x) \Leftrightarrow P(x)) \land$	
parallel =	$(S(x) \land \neg Ab_1(x) \Rightarrow T(x)) \land$	$(Ab_2(x) \Leftrightarrow Q(x)) \land$	10°5 pa
forced separation	$(U(x) \land \neg Ab_2(x) \Rightarrow V(x)) \land$	$(Ab_3(x) \Leftrightarrow R(x))$	100
(Shanahan, 1997b)	$(W(x) \land \neg Ab_3(x) \Rightarrow Y(x)) \land$	1. 10. 10. 10. 10. 10. 10. 10. 10. 10. 1	
less hand of own a	$S(A) \wedge \neg P(A)$	rance of Marin	late a some

^acancellation = cancellation of inheritance axioms; conjunction = conjunction of circumscriptions; parallel = parallel circumscription; var = circumscription with varied constants.

domain theory, the circumscriptions of the domain theory, and the results entailed by the circumscriptions. Methods (A) and (B) address default reasoning problems such as the Tweety example. Methods (C), (D), and (E) address problems of conflicting defaults such as the Nixon diamond. Method (F) was developed to deal with problems involving action and change such as the Yale shooting scenario.

Methods (A) through (E) use circumscription with varied constants (Lifschitz, 1994, sec. 2.3). In basic circumscription (defined in Section A.7), the extension of a predicate is minimized without allowing the extensions of other predicates to vary. The extensions of other predicates are fixed. In *circumscription with varied constants*, the extension of one predicate is minimized while allowing the extensions of certain other predicates to vary. If Γ is a formula containing the predicate symbols $\rho, \psi_1, \ldots, \psi_n$, then the circumscription of ρ in Γ with ψ_1, \ldots, ψ_n varied, written $CIRC[\Gamma; \rho; \psi_1, \ldots, \psi_n]$, is the formula of second-order logic

$$\Gamma \wedge \neg \exists \phi, \nu_1, \ldots, \nu_n (\Gamma(\phi, \nu_1, \ldots, \nu_n) \wedge \phi < \rho)$$

where ϕ and ν_1, \ldots, ν_n are distinct predicate variables with the same arities and argument sorts as ρ and ψ_1, \ldots, ψ_n , respectively, and $\Gamma(\phi, \nu_1, \ldots, \nu_n)$ is the formula obtained from Γ by replacing each occurrence of ρ with ϕ and each occurrence of ψ_i with ν_i for each $i \in \{1, \ldots, n\}$.

Methods (C) through (F) use conjunctions of circumscriptions. Method (C) adopts the skeptical stance that, because the defaults about Q(A) conflict, neither Q(A) nor $\neg Q(A)$ should be concluded.

Methods (B), (D), and (F) use cancellation of inheritance axioms (Genesereth & Nilsson, 1987, p. 129; Lifschitz, 1994, sec. 4.1; McCarthy, 1986, p. 93), which are called cancellation axioms in this chapter. Antoniou (1997, pp. 158-159) and Brewka, Dix, and Konolige (1997, pp. 18-19) criticize the use of cancellation of inheritance axioms on elaboration tolerance grounds. Consider the example given for (D). Notice that whenever we add an axiom $\rho_1(x) \land \neg \rho_2(x) \Rightarrow \neg Q(x)$ to the domain theory, where ρ_1 is a predicate symbol and ρ_2 is an abnormality predicate symbol, we must also remember to add a cancellation of inheritance axiom $\rho_1(x) \Rightarrow Ab_1(x)$. But also notice that this is not the only possible order of elaboration of the domain theory. After writing the axiom $P(x) \land \neg Ab_1(x) \Rightarrow Q(x)$, we might then think of a situation in which this default does not apply. We would then write a cancellation axiom $\rho_1(x) \Rightarrow Ab_1(x)$. Having canceled the default, we would then proceed to write an axiom describing what the new default is in this situation: $\rho_1(x) \land \neg \rho_2(x) \Rightarrow \neg Q(x)$.

Antoniou (1997) and Brewka, Dix, and Konolige (1997) advocate replacing cancellation of inheritance axioms with prioritized circumscription. Method (E) replaces the cancellation of inheritance axiom in method (D) with the use of priorities on abnormality predicate symbols. The abnormality predicate symbol Ab_2 is given a higher priority than Ab_1 by allowing Ab_1 to vary in the circumscription of Ab_2 . This method can be generalized. For example, we may specify that Ab_3 has a higher priority than Ab_2 , which has a higher priority than Ab_1 , as follows:

Method	Example	CIRC	Result
(B') cancellation + filtering	$\Phi_1 = Ab(A)$ $\Phi_2 =$ $(P(x) \land \neg Ab(x) \Rightarrow Q(x)) \land$ $P(A) \land P(B) \land A \neq B$	$CIRC[\Phi_1; Ab] \land \Phi_2 \vdash Ab(x) \Leftrightarrow x = A$	Q(B)
(D') cancellation + conjunction + filtering	$\Phi_{1} = (R(x) \Rightarrow Ab_{1}(x))$ $\Phi_{2} = (\bot \Rightarrow Ab_{2}(x))$ $\Phi_{3} = (P(x) \land \neg Ab_{1}(x) \Rightarrow Q(x)) \land (R(x) \land \neg Ab_{2}(x) \Rightarrow \neg Q(x)) \land (R(x) \Rightarrow P(x)) \land R(A) \land P(B) \land \neg R(B) \land A \neq B$	$CIRC[\Phi_1;Ab_1] \land CIRC[\Phi_2;Ab_2] \land \Phi_3 \vdash (Ab_1(x) \Leftrightarrow R(x)) \land \neg Ab_2(x)$	Q(B) ¬Q(A)

Table 12.2 Default Reasoning Using Basic Circumscription and Filtering

 $CIRC[\Phi; Ab_1; Q] \land CIRC[\Phi; Ab_2; Q, Ab_1] \land CIRC[\Phi; Ab_3; Q, Ab_1, Ab_2]$

Etherington (1988, p. 47) criticizes the use of priorities on the grounds that it is difficult to determine what the priorities should be.

Method (F) incorporates the technique of filtering (Doherty, 1994; Doherty & Łukaszewicz, 1994; Sandewall, 1989b, 1994), in which the domain theory is partitioned and only some parts of the partition are circumscribed. Filtering is related to the process of delimited completion (Genesereth & Nilsson, 1987, p. 132). Method (F), which is used in this chapter, is called forced separation in Shanahan (1996, 1997b). In forced separation, a domain theory is partitioned into formulas Φ_1, \ldots, Φ_n , disjoint sets of predicates are circumscribed in Φ_i for each $i \in \{1, \ldots, n-1\}$, and Φ_n is not circumscribed. The combination of cancellation, conjunction, and filtering from method (F) can be used to solve problems addressed by methods (B) and (D), as shown in Table 12.2.

Our treatment of the qualification problem is patterned after that of E. Giunchiglia, Lee, Lifschitz, McCain, and Turner (2004, pp. 67-68). Doherty and Kvarnström (1997) propose the distinction between strong and weak qualifications. See also the discussion of Thielscher (2001, pp. 27-29). Williams (1997) describes a framework for modeling revision of beliefs.

EXERCISES

- 12.1 Prove Proposition 12.3.
- **12.2** Formalize the slippery block scenario described by Thielscher (2001, p. 27). A surface is a block or a table. Normally when a block is moved from one

- surface to another, the block ends up on the second surface. If the block is slippery, however, then the block may (or may not) end up on the table rather than the second surface.
- 12.3 Formalize Lifschitz's (2003) problem of choosing a place for dinner. Each night, Peter eats at either the Chinese restaurant or the Italian restaurant. On Mondays, the Italian restaurant is closed. Peter prefers not to eat at the same restaurant two nights in a row. Use the formalization to determine where Peter eats on Sundays.
- 12.4 Formalize the Russian airplane hijack scenario elaborated by Kvarnström and Doherty (2000a) based on a suggestion from Lifschitz (1997). Boris, Dimiter, and Erik are at their respective homes getting ready for a business trip. Dimiter gets drunk. Erik grabs a comb. They each stop off at the office on their way to the airport. While at the office, Boris picks up a gun. They each try to board a plane, which then flies to Stockholm. Normally, if a person is at the airport, then the person can board the plane. However, people carrying guns are not permitted to board the plane, and drunk people may or may not be permitted to board the plane. The problem is then to show that Erik and the comb will be in Stockholm, Boris will still be at the airport, and Dimiter may or may not be at Stockholm.
- 12.5 (Research problem) In Section 11.2, we introduce the predicates Like(a, o) and Dislike(a, o). Formalize the default rules given by Heider (1958, chap. 7) regarding the ways people tend to evaluate or feel about people or things.

2) Topicidade it designed by order officers property of our commencer against From ordering manage fine (our main solvens). A commencer is a contract of wind symposium.

- 4.4 Founday 1 of clere's 1 to the endown of all offices, placetic sames for fit and agent and for fit angles. For the endown for the endown of the endown
- 2 * Form that the Russian supplies fitted a countries had not used by New stricts that

 13 more per 000 epices of the supplies fitted from the estimate of the Bare. The second for the fitted fitted to the supplies of the s
- (5) An Alexandre and maintended season in the control of the co

PART

Programs and Applications

The Discrete Event Calculus Reasoner

This chapter describes the Discrete Event Calculus Reasoner, which uses satisfiability (SAT) to solve event calculus problems. The program can be used to perform automated deduction, abduction, postdiction, and model finding. We discuss the architecture of the program and the encoding of SAT problems. We present some simple examples of how the program is used and then present a more complicated example. We discuss the language used to describe commonsense reasoning problems to the program. The Discrete Event Calculus Reasoner can be downloaded from decreasoner.sourceforge.net.

13.1 DISCRETE EVENT CALCULUS REASONER ARCHITECTURE

The architecture of the Discrete Event Calculus Reasoner is shown in Figure 13.1. The program works as follows:

- 1. A domain description is provided as input to the program.
- **2.** The main program sends the domain description to the SAT encoder.
- 3. The SAT encoder encodes the domain description as a SAT problem.
- **4.** The SAT encoder sends the SAT problem back to the main program.
- **5.** The main program sends the SAT problem to the SAT solver. The SAT problem is expressed in the standard DIMACS format used by SAT solvers.
- **6.** A complete SAT solver is run in order to find all models. The Discrete Event Calculus Reasoner uses the Relsat SAT solver. If Relsat does not find any models, then the Walksat solver is run in order to find near-miss models.
- 7. The SAT solver sends models back to the main program.
- **8.** The main program decodes the models from the SAT solver and produces them as output.

13.2 ENCODING SATISFIABILITY PROBLEMS

In order to encode the domain description as a SAT problem, the domain of every sort is limited to a finite set. The timepoint sort is restricted to the integers $\{0, \ldots, n\}$

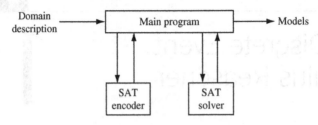

FIGURE 13.1

Discrete Event Calculus Reasoner architecture.

for some $n \geq 0$. An existential quantification $\exists \nu \ \Phi(\nu)$ is replaced by $\bigvee_i \Phi(\nu_i)$, and a universal quantification $\forall \nu \ \Phi(\nu)$ is replaced by $\bigwedge_i \Phi(\nu_i)$, where ν_i are the constants of the sort of ν . The unique names assumption is used.

SAT solving is facilitated by DEC. (The efficient solution of event calculus problems using SAT was the original motivation for the development of DEC.) DEC uses integers for timepoints, unlike EC, which uses real numbers. DEC replaces triply quantified time in many of the EC axioms with doubly quantified time, resulting in smaller SAT encodings.

13.3 SIMPLE EXAMPLES

In this section we present some simple examples of how the Discrete Event Calculus Reasoner is used to perform various types of reasoning.

13.3.1 DEDUCTION

The first example is a deduction problem. We create an input file containing the following domain description:

```
sort agent
fluent Awake(agent)
event WakeUp(agent)
[agent.time] Initiates(WakeUp(agent).Awake(agent),time).
agent James
!HoldsAt(Awake(James),0).
Delta: Happens(WakeUp(James),0).
completion Delta Happens
range time 0 1
```

We define sorts and predicates. We define an agent sort, a fluent *Awake*, and an event *WakeUp*. The fluent and the event both take a single argument that is an agent. Next, we provide an axiom stating that, if an agent wakes up, then that agent will be awake. The symbols [and] indicate universal quantification. Next we specify the observations and narrative. We define a constant *James* whose sort is agent. We specify that James is not awake at timepoint 0 and that he wakes up at timepoint 0. The symbol! indicates negation. For deduction we specify completion of the *Happens* predicate in the formulas labeled Delta. Finally, we specify the range of the time sort. There are two timepoints: 0 and 1.

When we run the program on this input, it produces the following output:

```
model 1:
0
Happens(WakeUp(James), 0).
1
+Awake(James).
```

For each model, the fluents that are true at timepoint 0 are shown, followed by differences in the truth values of fluents from one timepoint to the next. Fluents that become true are preceded by + (plus sign), and fluents that become false are preceded by - (minus sign). There is one model, and HoldsAt(Awake(James), 1) is true in that model. Thus, the domain description entails that James is awake at timepoint 1.

An alternative output format is available that shows the truth values of all fluents at all timepoints. This format is obtained by adding the following line to the input file:

```
option timediff off
```

The program then produces the following output:

```
model 1:
0
!HoldsAt(Awake(James), 0).
!ReleasedAt(Awake(James), 0).
Happens(WakeUp(James), 0).
1
!Happens(WakeUp(James), 1).
!ReleasedAt(Awake(James), 1).
HoldsAt(Awake(James), 1).
```

13.3.2 ABDUCTION

We can turn the deduction problem into an abduction or planning problem by making several changes. First, we specify a *goal* for James to be awake at timepoint 1. Second, we no longer specify that James wakes up because this is the *plan* we would like the program to find. Third, we do not specify completion of the *Happens* predicate. Our new domain description is as follows:

```
sort agent
fluent Awake(agent)
event WakeUp(agent)
[agent, time] Initiates(WakeUp(agent), Awake(agent), time).
agent James
!HoldsAt(Awake(James).0).
HoldsAt(Awake(James),1).
range time 0 1
```

When we run this input through the program, we get a single model in which James wakes up:

```
model 1:
0
Happens (WakeUp (James), 0).
+Awake(James).
```

13.3.3 POSTDICTION

Next, we turn the deduction problem into a postdiction problem. First, we add an action precondition axiom stating that, in order for an agent to wake up, the agent must not be awake. Second, we remove the fact that James is not awake at timepoint 0 because this is the fact we would like the program to find. This gives us the following domain description:

```
sort agent
fluent Awake(agent)
event WakeUp(agent)
[agent, time] Initiates(WakeUp(agent), Awake(agent), time).
[agent.time]
Happens(WakeUp(agent), time) -> !HoldsAt(Awake(agent), time).
agent James
Delta: Happens(WakeUp(James),0).
HoldsAt(Awake(James).1).
completion Delta Happens
range time 0 1
```

From this, the program produces a single model in which James is not awake at timepoint 0:

```
model 1:
0
Happens(WakeUp(James), 0).
1
+Awake(James).
```

13.3.4 MODEL FINDING

We can turn the postdiction problem into a model-finding problem by removing the observations, narrative, and completion of *Happens* in Delta:

```
fluent Awake(agent)
event WakeUp(agent)

[agent.time] Initiates(WakeUp(agent), Awake(agent), time).

[agent.time] Happens(WakeUp(agent), time) -> !HoldsAt(Awake(agent), time).

agent James

range time 0 1
```

We then get three models:

```
model 1:
0
Happens(WakeUp(James), 0).
1
+Awake(James).
-
model 2:
0
1
-
model 3:
0
Awake(James).
1
```

That is, James is either awake or not awake at timepoint 0. If he is not awake at timepoint 0, then he may wake up (model 1) or may not wake up (model 2). If he

is awake at timepoint 0 (model 3), then he cannot wake up at timepoint 0. (Event occurrences are disallowed at the final timepoint, which is 1 in this case.)

13.4 EXAMPLE: TELEPHONE

In this section, we run the telephone example in Section 3.1.1 through the Discrete Event Calculus Reasoner. The domain description is as follows:

```
sort agent
sort phone
agent Agent1, Agent2
phone Phone1. Phone2
fluent Ringing(phone, phone)
fluent DialTone(phone)
fluent BusySignal(phone)
fluent Idle(phone)
fluent Connected(phone, phone)
fluent Disconnected(phone)
event PickUp(agent,phone)
event SetDown(agent,phone)
event Dial(agent, phone, phone)
[agent.phone.time]
HoldsAt(Idle(phone).time) ->
Initiates(PickUp(agent,phone),DialTone(phone),time).
[agent,phone,time]
HoldsAt(Idle(phone),time) ->
Terminates(PickUp(agent,phone),Idle(phone),time).
[agent,phone,time]
HoldsAt(DialTone(phone),time) ->
Initiates(SetDown(agent,phone),Idle(phone),time).
[agent,phone,time]
HoldsAt(DialTone(phone), time) ->
Terminates(SetDown(agent.phone), DialTone(phone), time).
[agent,phone1,phone2,time]
HoldsAt(DialTone(phonel), time) &
HoldsAt(Idle(phone2), time) ->
Initiates(Dial(agent,phone1,phone2),Ringing(phone1,phone2),time).
```

```
[agent,phone1,phone2,time]
HoldsAt(DialTone(phone1),time) &
HoldsAt(Idle(phone2),time) ->
Terminates(Dial(agent,phone1,phone2),DialTone(phone1),time).
[agent.phone1.phone2.time]
HoldsAt(DialTone(phonel).time) &
HoldsAt(Idle(phone2).time) ->
Terminates(Dial(agent,phone1,phone2),Idle(phone2),time).
[agent.phone1.phone2.time]
HoldsAt(DialTone(phone1), time) &
!HoldsAt(Idle(phone2).time) ->
Initiates(Dial(agent,phone1,phone2),BusySignal(phone1),time).
[agent,phone1,phone2,time]
HoldsAt(DialTone(phonel),time) &
!HoldsAt(Idle(phone2).time) ->
Terminates(Dial(agent,phone1,phone2),DialTone(phone1),time).
[agent.phone,time]
HoldsAt(BusySignal(phone).time) ->
Initiates(SetDown(agent,phone), Idle(phone), time).
[agent,phone,time]
HoldsAt(BusySignal(phone),time) ->
Terminates(SetDown(agent,phone),BusySignal(phone),time).
[agent,phone1,phone2,time]
HoldsAt(Ringing(phonel.phone2).time) ->
Initiates(SetDown(agent,phonel),Idle(phonel),time).
[agent.phone1,phone2,time]
HoldsAt(Ringing(phone1,phone2),time) ->
Initiates(SetDown(agent,phone1),Idle(phone2),time).
[agent,phone1,phone2,time]
HoldsAt(Ringing(phone1,phone2),time) ->
Terminates(SetDown(agent,phone1),Ringing(phone1,phone2),time).
[agent,phone1,phone2,time]
HoldsAt(Ringing(phone1,phone2),time) ->
Initiates(PickUp(agent,phone2),Connected(phone1,phone2),time).
[agent,phone1,phone2,time]
HoldsAt(Ringing(phonel.phone2).time) ->
Terminates(PickUp(agent,phone2),Ringing(phone1,phone2),time).
```

```
[agent.phone1.phone2.time]
HoldsAt(Connected(phone1,phone2).time) ->
Initiates(SetDown(agent,phonel),Idle(phonel),time).
[agent,phone1,phone2,time]
HoldsAt(Connected(phone1,phone2),time) ->
Initiates(SetDown(agent,phone1),Disconnected(phone2),time).
[agent,phone1,phone2,time]
HoldsAt(Connected(phone1,phone2),time)->
Terminates(SetDown(agent,phone1),Connected(phone1,phone2),time).
[agent,phone1,phone2,time]
HoldsAt(Connected(phone1,phone2),time)->
Initiates(SetDown(agent,phone2),Idle(phone2),time).
[agent,phone1,phone2,time]
HoldsAt(Connected(phone1,phone2),time)->
Initiates(SetDown(agent,phone2),Disconnected(phone1),time).
[agent,phone1,phone2,time]
HoldsAt(Connected(phone1,phone2),time)->
Terminates(SetDown(agent,phone2),Connected(phone1,phone2),time).
[agent,phone,time]
HoldsAt(Disconnected(phone), time) ->
Initiates(SetDown(agent,phone),Idle(phone),time).
[agent.phone.time]
HoldsAt(Disconnected(phone), time) ->
Terminates(SetDown(agent,phone),Disconnected(phone),time).
Delta: Happens(PickUp(Agent1, Phone1), 0).
Delta: Happens(Dial(Agent1, Phone1, Phone2), 1).
Delta: Happens(PickUp(Agent2, Phone2), 2).
[phone] HoldsAt(Idle(phone).0).
[phone] !HoldsAt(DialTone(phone).0).
[phone] !HoldsAt(BusySignal(phone),0).
[phone1,phone2] !HoldsAt(Ringing(phone1,phone2),0).
[phone1,phone2] !HoldsAt(Connected(phone1,phone2),0).
[phone] !HoldsAt(Disconnected(phone),0).
completion Delta Happens
range time 0 3
```

The output is as follows:

```
model 1:
0
Idle(Phone1).
Idle(Phone2).
Happens(PickUp(Agent1, Phone1), 0).
1
-Idle(Phone1).
+DialTone(Phone1).
Happens(Dial(Agent1, Phone1, Phone2), 1).
2
-DialTone(Phone1).
-Idle(Phone2).
+Ringing(Phone1, Phone2).
Happens(PickUp(Agent2, Phone2), 2).
3
-Ringing(Phone1, Phone2).
+Connected(Phone1, Phone2).
```

13.5 DISCRETE EVENT CALCULUS REASONER LANGUAGE

Domain descriptions are described using the Discrete Event Calculus Reasoner language. A domain description consists of zero or more formulas, and zero or more statements. The syntax for formulas, which is based on that of the Bliksem theorem prover, is shown in Figure 13.2. The meanings of the symbols used in formulas are shown in Table 13.1. As in this book, predicate symbols, function symbols, and nonnumeric constants start with an uppercase letter and variables start with a lowercase letter. The sort of a variable is determined by removing trailing digits from

```
Term ::= Constant | Variable | FunctionSymbol(Term,...,Term) |
Term + Term | Term - Term | Term * Term | Term / Term |
Term % Term | - Term | (Term)

Atom ::= PredicateSymbol(Term,...,Term) | Term < Term |
Term <= Term | Term = Term | Term >= Term |
Term > Term | Term != Term

Formula ::= Atom | ! Formula | Formula & Formula |
Formula | Formula | Formula -> Formula |
Formula <-> Formula | (Variable,..., Variable) Formula |
[Variable,..., Variable] Formula | (Formula)
```

FIGURE 13.2

Discrete Event Calculus Reasoner formula syntax.

Table 13.1 Discrete Event Calculus Reasoner Formula Symbols

Symbol	Meaning	Symbol	Meaning
+	Addition	!=	Not equal to
	Subtraction, negation	!	Logical negation
*	Multiplication	&	Conjunction (AND, ∧)
/	Division	11	Disjunction (OR, V)
%	Remainder	->	Implication
<	Less than	<->	Bi-implication
<=	Less than or equal to	{ }	Existential quantifier (3)
=	Equal to	[]	Universal quantifier (∀)
>=	Greater than or equal to	()	Grouping
>	Greater than	, .	Separator

Table 13.2 Discrete Event Calculus Reasoner Statements

Statement	Meaning
sort Sort,, Sort	Define sorts
function FunctionSymbol(Sort,, Sort): Sort	Define function
predicate PredicateSymbol(Sort,,Sort)	Define predicate
event EventSymbol(Sort,, Sort)	Define event
fluent FluentSymbol(Sort,, Sort)	Define fluent
noninertial FluentSymbol,, FluentSymbol	Define noninertial fluents
Sort Constant	Define constant
completion Label PredicateSymbol	Specify completion
load Filename	Load file
option OptionName OptionValue	Specify option
range Sort Integer Integer	Specify range

the variable. For example, the sort of the variable time1 is time. Some Discrete Event Calculus Reasoner statements are shown in Table 13.2. A *noninertial fluent* is one that is released from the commonsense law of inertia at all timepoints.

BIBLIOGRAPHIC NOTES

The Discrete Event Calculus Reasoner was introduced by Mueller (2004a, 2004b). DIMACS format is specified by DIMACS (1993). The Relsat SAT solver is discussed by Bayardo Jr. and Schrag (1997), and Walksat is discussed by Selman, Kautz, and Cohen (1993). The technique of restricting the event calculus to a finite universe to enable SAT solving was introduced by Shanahan and Witkowski (2004). The restriction of first-order logic to a finite universe is discussed by Kautz and Selman (1992) and Jackson (2000). To produce a compact conjunctive normal form, the

Discrete Event Calculus Reasoner uses the technique of renaming subformulas, which is described by Plaisted and Greenbaum (1986) and E. Giunchiglia and Sebastiani (1999). The Bliksem theorem prover is described by de Nivelle (1999).

EXERCISES

- **13.1** Formalize and run the Tweety example in the Bibliographic notes of Chapter 12 in the Discrete Event Calculus Reasoner.
- **13.2** Using the Discrete Event Calculus Reasoner, formalize and run Shanahan's (1997b) kitchen sink scenario, which is described in Chapter 1.
- **13.3** Formalize the WALK x-schema of Narayanan (1997), and use the Discrete Event Calculus Reasoner to perform temporal projection for a scenario involving walking.
- **13.4** (Research problem) Formalize scuba diving, and use the Discrete Event Calculus Reasoner to understand scuba-diving incident reports. See Section 14.2 for a discussion of the use of the event calculus in natural language understanding.
- 13.5 (Research problem) The Discrete Event Calculus Reasoner currently produces models as output. Extend the Discrete Event Calculus Reasoner and a SAT solver to produce proofs for deduction problems using the techniques discussed by McMillan and Amla (2003, sec. 2).

Selven i se grann ancia, ar anter ante som to essett anti-fical education i comann essential de tago i servici superindros transferencia de todos de formación el man a como esta como en como esta como esta como en como esta como esta como esta como esta como esta como esta como

EXEMINENT

- Shakanin padhe sininthian to rest from an action of the fill of th
- The Allert Mark Control of the Contr
- e de la companya del companya de la companya del companya de la co
- ed all described and the second of the secon

Applications

The availability of techniques for commonsense reasoning presents an enormous opportunity in that there are many areas that have only begun to be explored that can benefit from the use of commonsense reasoning. Commonsense reasoning provides two important benefits to computer applications:

- Commonsense reasoning can be used to give applications a greater degree of
 understanding about the human world. Users can be freed from having to state
 everything explicitly because commonsense reasoning can be used to infer what
 is obvious to a person.
- Commonsense reasoning can be used to give computer programs more flexibility. An application can adapt to an unexpected real-world problem by reasoning about it in order to come up with a solution.

In this chapter, we describe several applications that have been built using commonsense reasoning in the event calculus, in business systems, natural language understanding, and vision.

14.1 BUSINESS SYSTEMS

An important area of application of the event calculus is business systems. In this section, we review two areas in which the event calculus has been applied: payment protocols and workflow modeling.

14.1.1 PAYMENT PROTOCOLS

Pinar Yolum and Munindar P. Singh have used the event calculus to incorporate commonsense knowledge and reasoning about *commitments* into electronic payment systems. Using Shanahan's (2000) event calculus planner, they have implemented a mechanism that enables customer and merchant applications to (1) keep track of their commitments, (2) determine what actions are currently possible, and (3) plan actions to achieve goals.

Instead of describing a payment protocol as a finite state machine (FSM), as is traditionally done, the commitments inherent in the protocol are extracted and described using the event calculus. Applications that implement the protocol can then

234

use the event calculus description to reason about their commitments. This makes the applications more flexible than those based on FSMs. An FSM describes only which actions are currently possible, not why they are possible. By using commonsense reasoning to reason about commitments, applications can generate their own plans for achieving their goals and cope with unanticipated situations.

NetBill protocol

The mechanism is implemented for the NetBill protocol, which is used for the online purchase of digital products. This protocol works as follows:

- 1. A customer requests a price quote for a product from a merchant.
- 2. The merchant provides a price quote to the customer.
- 3. The customer sends a purchase request to the merchant.
- 4. The merchant delivers the product, in an encrypted form, to the customer.
- 5. The customer sends an electronic payment order (EPO) to the merchant.
- 6. The merchant sends the EPO to the NetBill server.
- The NetBill server debits the customer's account and credits the merchant's account.
- 8. The NetBill server sends a receipt to the merchant.
- The merchant sends the receipt and a decryption key for the product to the customer.
- 10. The customer decrypts the product.

Commitments are created at various points in this protocol. When the merchant provides a price quote, the merchant makes a commitment to deliver the product if the customer sends a purchase request. When the customer sends a purchase request, the customer makes a commitment to pay for the product if it is delivered.

Suppose that a customer has not yet purchased a certain product the merchant application wishes to sell. The merchant application can reason that it is possible to send an unsolicited price quote to the customer. There is nothing in the protocol that prohibits this, and it might lead to a sale. Similarly, a customer application can reason that it is possible to send a purchase request without having first received a price quote. In this case, the customer makes a commitment to pay if the product is delivered, which the merchant has not promised to do.

Formalization

We now describe part of the event calculus formalization of these notions. We start with the representation of commitments. We use the following fluents to represent commitments:

 $C(a_1, a_2, f)$: Agent a_1 is committed to agent a_2 to bring about fluent f. This is called a *base-level commitment*.

 $CC(a_1, a_2, c, f)$: If fluent c is true, then agent a_1 is committed to a_2 to bring about fluent f. This is called a *conditional commitment*.

We have effect axioms for creating and discharging base-level and conditional commitments:

$$Initiates(CreateC(a_1, a_2, f), C(a_1, a_2, f), t)$$

$$(14.1)$$

$$Initiates(CreateCC(a_1, a_2, c, f), CC(a_1, a_2, c, f), t)$$

$$(14.2)$$

Terminates (Discharge
$$C(a_1, a_2, f), C(a_1, a_2, f), t$$
) (14.3)

$$Terminates(DischargeCC(a_1, a_2, c, f), CC(a_1, a_2, c, f), t)$$
 (14.4)

We have a trigger axiom that, states that, if a_1 is committed to a_2 to bring about f and f is true, then the commitment is discharged:

$$HoldsAt(C(a_1, a_2, f), t) \land HoldsAt(f, t) \Rightarrow$$
 (14.5)
 $Happens(DischargeC(a_1, a_2, f), t)$

We also have trigger axioms stating that, if a_1 has a conditional commitment to a_2 to bring about f if c is true and c is true, then a base-level commitment of a_1 to a_2 to bring about f is created and the conditional commitment is discharged:

$$HoldsAt(CC(a_1, a_2, c, f), t) \land HoldsAt(c, t) \Rightarrow$$

$$Happens(CreateC(a_1, a_2, f), t)$$
(14.6)

$$HoldsAt(CC(a_1, a_2, c, f), t) \land HoldsAt(c, t) \Rightarrow$$
 (14.7)
 $Happens(DischargeCC(a_1, a_2, c, f), t)$

Next we represent part of the NetBill protocol and associated commitments. We use the following events:

RequestQuote(c, m, p): Customer c sends merchant m a request for a price quote for product p.

SendQuote(m, c, p, a): Merchant m sends customer c a quote of amount a for product p.

RequestPurchase(c, m, p, a): Customer c sends merchant m a request to purchase product p for amount a.

Deliver(m, c, p): Merchant m delivers product p to customer c.

SendEPO(c, m, a): Customer c sends merchant m an EPO for amount a.

We use the following fluents:

QuoteRequested(c, m, p): Customer c has sent merchant m a request for a price quote for product p.

QuoteSent(m, c, p, a): Merchant m has sent customer c a quote of amount a for product p.

PurchaseRequested(c, m, p, a): Customer c has sent merchant m a request to purchase product p for amount a.

Delivered(m, c, p): Merchant m has delivered product p to customer c.

EPOSent(c, m, a): Customer c has sent merchant m an EPO for amount a.

Effect axioms relate these events and fluents:

Initiates(RequestQuote(c, m, p), QuoteRequested(c, m, p), t)	
Initiates(SendQuote(m,c,p,a),QuoteSent(m,c,p,a),t)	(14.9)
$\label{linitiates} Initiates(Request Purchase(c, m, p, a), Purchase Requested(c, m, p, a), t)$	(14.10)
Initiates(Deliver(m, c, p), Delivered(m, c, p), t)	(14.11)
Initiates(SendEPO(c, m, a), EPOSent(c, m, a), t)	(14.12)

We now use effect axioms to describe the effects of NetBill events on commitments. If the merchant sends the customer a price quote for a product, then the merchant will have a conditional commitment to deliver the product if the customer promises to pay the quoted price for the product:

Initiates(SendQuote(
$$m, c, p, a$$
), (14.13)
 $CC(m, c, PurchaseRequested(c, m, p, a), Delivered(m, c, p)), t)$

If the merchant has yet not delivered a given product to the customer and the customer sends a purchase request for the product to the merchant, then the customer will have a conditional commitment to pay for the product if the merchant delivers it:

$$\neg HoldsAt(Delivered(m, c, p), t) \Rightarrow$$

$$Initiates(RequestPurchase(c, m, p, a),$$

$$CC(c, m, Delivered(m, c, p), EPOSent(c, m, a)), t)$$

$$(14.14)$$

Scenario

Let us now consider a specific scenario. Suppose that a particular customer has not yet purchased anything from a particular music store:

$\neg HoldsAt(PurchaseRequested(Jen, MusicStore, p, a), 0)$	(14.15)	
$\neg HoldsAt(Delivered(MusicStore, Jen, p), 0)$	(14.16)	
$\neg HoldsAt(EPOSent(Jen, MusicStore, a), 0)$	(14.17)	

Further suppose that the music store has the goal to sell the customer a particular CD:

$$\exists t (HoldsAt(Delivered(MusicStore, Jen, BritneyCD), t) \land (14.18)$$

 $HoldsAt(EPOSent(Jen, MusicStore, 14.99), t))$

We can then show that there are several ways this goal can be achieved (see Exercises 14.1–14.3). The music store can start by sending an unsolicited price quote:

Happens (SendQuote (MusicStore, Jen, BritneyCD, 14.99), 1)		
Happens (RequestPurchase (Jen, MusicStore, BritneyCD, 14.99), 2)	(14.20)	
Happens(Deliver(MusicStore, Jen, BritneyCD), 3)	(14.21)	
${\it Happens} (Send EPO (Jen, Music Store, 14.99), 4)$		
ner can start by sending an unsolicited purchase request:		

The customer can start by sending an unsolicited purchase request

$$Happens(SendEPO(Jen, MusicStore, 14.99), 3)$$
 (14.25)

The music store can even start by delivering the product:

$$Happens(Deliver(MusicStore, Jen, BritneyCD), 1)$$
 (14.26)

$$Happens(SendEPO(Jen, MusicStore, 14.99), 2)$$
 (14.27)

Thus, the event calculus provides the music store with several possible ways a sale could occur. The music store could perform additional commonsense reasoning to determine which course of action is best.

14.1.2 WORKFLOW MODELING

A method for using the event calculus to specify, simulate, and execute workflows has been defined by Nihan Kesim Cicekli and Yakup Yildirim. A workflow consists of a set of business activities and dependencies among the activities. For example, the workflow in a newspaper might consist of (1) a set of activities w_1, \ldots, w_n in which reporters write stories; (2) a set of activities e_1, \ldots, e_n in which editors edit stories written by reporters, where for each $i \in \{1, \ldots, n\}$, e_i depends on w_i ; and (3) a pagination activity p in which the stories are put into place on pages, which depends on all the activities e_1, \ldots, e_n .

The Workflow Management Coalition defines several types of dependencies that can be part of a workflow.

In a *sequence*, one activity follows another activity; this is the case for e_i and w_i , just described.

In an *AND-split*, several activities follow one activity, and these activities are performed in parallel.

In an *AND-join*, an activity starts after several other activities have all ended; this is the case for *p*.

In an *XOR-split*, one of several activities follows an activity, depending on what condition is true.

In an *XOR-join*, an activity starts after any of several other activities have ended. In an *iteration*, one or more activities are repeatedly performed while a condition is true.

The basic method for modeling workflows in the event calculus is as follows. We use DEC. The fluent Active(a) represents that activity a is active, and the fluent Completed(a) represents that activity a is completed. The event Start(a) represents that activity a starts, and the event End(a) represents that activity a ends. Effect axioms state that, if an activity starts, then it will be active and no longer completed, and, if an activity ends, then it will be completed and no longer active:

Initiates(Start(a), Active(a), t)
Terminates(Start(a), Completed(a), t)
Initiates(End(a), Completed(a), t)
Terminates(End(a), Active(a), t)

Dependencies are represented using trigger axioms that start activities in appropriate situations. The following trigger axiom represents a sequence in which activity A is followed by activity B.

```
\neg HoldsAt(Active(B), t) \land \\ \neg HoldsAt(Completed(A), t-1) \land \\ HoldsAt(Completed(A), t) \Rightarrow \\ Happens(Start(B), t)
```

The following trigger axioms represent an AND-split in which C1–C3 follow B.

```
\neg HoldsAt(Active(C1),t) \land \\ \neg HoldsAt(Completed(B),t-1) \land \\ HoldsAt(Completed(B),t) \Rightarrow \\ Happens(Start(C1),t) \\ \neg HoldsAt(Active(C2),t) \land
```

```
\neg HoldsAt(Active(C2), t) \land \\ \neg HoldsAt(Completed(B), t - 1) \land \\ HoldsAt(Completed(B), t) \Rightarrow \\ Happens(Start(C2), t)
```

```
\neg HoldsAt(Active(C3), t) \land \\ \neg HoldsAt(Completed(B), t-1) \land \\ HoldsAt(Completed(B), t) \Rightarrow \\ Happens(Start(C3), t)
```

The following trigger axiom represents an AND-join in which D starts after C1–C3 end.

```
\neg HoldsAt(Active(D), t) \land \\ ((\neg HoldsAt(Completed(CI), t-1) \land HoldsAt(Completed(CI), t)) \lor \\ (\neg HoldsAt(Completed(C2), t-1) \land HoldsAt(Completed(C2), t)) \lor \\ (\neg HoldsAt(Completed(C3), t-1) \land HoldsAt(Completed(C3), t))) \land \\ HoldsAt(Completed(C1), t) \land \\ HoldsAt(Completed(C2), t) \land \\ HoldsAt(Completed(C3), t) \Rightarrow \\ Happens(Start(D), t)
```

The following trigger axioms represent an XOR-split in which E1 follows D if E1C is true, in which E2 follows D if E2C is true, and in which E3 follows D if E3C is true.

```
\neg HoldsAt(Active(EI), t) \land \\ \neg HoldsAt(Completed(D), t-1) \land \\ HoldsAt(Completed(D), t) \land \\
```

```
Happens(Start(E1), t)
\neg HoldsAt(Active(E2), t) \land \\ \neg HoldsAt(Completed(D), t-1) \land \\ HoldsAt(Completed(D), t) \land \\ HoldsAt(E2C, t) \Rightarrow \\ Happens(Start(E2), t)
\neg HoldsAt(Active(E3), t) \land
```

 $HoldsAt(E1C, t) \Rightarrow$

 $\neg HoldsAt(Active(E3), t) \land \\ \neg HoldsAt(Completed(D), t - 1) \land \\ HoldsAt(Completed(D), t) \land \\ HoldsAt(E3C, t) \Rightarrow \\ Happens(Start(E3), t)$

The following trigger axioms represent an XOR-join in which F starts after E1, E2, or E3 ends.

```
\neg HoldsAt(Active(F),t) \land \\ ((\neg HoldsAt(Completed(EI),t-1) \land HoldsAt(Completed(EI),t)) \lor \\ (\neg HoldsAt(Completed(E2),t-1) \land HoldsAt(Completed(E2),t)) \lor \\ (\neg HoldsAt(Completed(E3),t-1) \land HoldsAt(Completed(E3),t))) \Rightarrow \\ Happens(Start(F),t)
```

The following trigger axioms represent an iteration in which activity F is repeatedly performed while a condition FC is true. When FC is false, activity G is performed.

```
\neg HoldsAt(Active(F), t) \land \\ \neg HoldsAt(Completed(F), t-1) \land \\ HoldsAt(Completed(F), t) \land \\ HoldsAt(FC, t) \Rightarrow \\ Happens(Start(F), t). \\ \neg HoldsAt(Active(G), t) \land \\ \neg HoldsAt(Completed(F), t-1) \land \\ HoldsAt(Completed(F), t) \Rightarrow \\ \neg HoldsAt(FC, t) \Rightarrow \\
```

Once a workflow is modeled using the event calculus, temporal projection can be used to simulate the workflow. The model can also be used by a workflow manager in a workflow management system to manage the execution of a workflow by the workflow participants. The event calculus enables the past, present, and possible future states of a workflow to be queried at any point in the simulation or execution of the workflow.

Happens(Start(G), t)

14.2 NATURAL LANGUAGE UNDERSTANDING

Understanding natural language text or speech involves building representations of the meaning of that text or speech. The event calculus can be used to perform commonsense reasoning in order to build representations of meaning, and formulas of the event calculus can be used to represent meaning.

For example, we can use a semantic parser to convert the English sentence *Nathan* wakes up into the event calculus formula

Happens(WakeUp(Nathan), 0)

Then, suppose we have the following representations of commonsense knowledge:

 $Initiates(WakeUp(a), Awake(a), t) \\ Happens(WakeUp(a), t) \Rightarrow \neg HoldsAt(Awake(a), t)$

We can reason using the event calculus in order to build the following representation of the sentence's meaning:

¬HoldsAt(Awake(Nathan), 0)
Happens(WakeUp(Nathan), 0)
HoldsAt(Awake(Nathan), 1)

In general, the event calculus can be used in a natural language understanding system as follows:

- 1. The set of domains to be understood by the system is determined.
- 2. Commonsense knowledge about the domains is represented using the event calculus.
- 3. For each natural language input:
 - (a) The input is parsed by syntactic and/or semantic parsers into predicate-argument structure representations, which resemble event calculus *Happens* and *HoldsAt* formulas.
 - **(b)** The predicate-argument structure representations are converted into event calculus *Happens* and *HoldsAt* formulas.
 - (c) The event calculus formulas are fed to an event calculus reasoning program, which uses the commonsense knowledge to produce additional event calculus formulas, or inferences.
 - (d) The inferences are produced as output.

The output can be used for various purposes, including dialog management, information retrieval, question answering, summarization, updating a database, and user modeling.

14.2.1 STORY UNDERSTANDING

The event calculus can be used to address the problem of *story understanding*, which consists of taking a story as input, understanding it, and then answering questions

about it. Commonsense reasoning can be used to fill in details not explicitly stated in the input story. The Discrete Event Calculus Reasoner program can be used to build detailed models of a story, which represent the events that occur and the properties that are true or false at various times.

For example, the children's story by Raymond Briggs (1999, pp. 4–8) begins as follows:

Hooray! It is snowing! James gets dressed. He runs outside. He makes a pile of snow. He makes it bigger and bigger. He puts a big snowball on top.

Given a domain description representing this text consisting of (1) a basic axiomatization of space and intentions, (2) observations of the initial state, and (3) a narrative of events, the Discrete Event Calculus Reasoner produces the following model.¹ The first input event is that it starts snowing outside James's house at timepoint 0:

```
0
Happens(StartSnowing(JamesOutside),0).
```

From this input event, it is inferred that it is snowing outside James's house at timepoint 1:

```
1
+Snowing(JamesOutside).
```

The next input event is that James wakes up:

```
Happens(WakeUp(James), 1).
```

It is inferred that he is no longer asleep and is awake:

```
2
-Asleep(James).
+Awake(James).
```

Next, it is inferred that James becomes happy:

```
Happens (BecomeHappy (James), 2).
```

A trigger axiom states that if an agent is awake, likes snow, and is in a room that looks out onto a location where it is snowing, then the agent will become happy. It is also inferred that James intends to play outside his house:

```
Happens(IntendToPlay(James, JamesOutside), 2).
```

A trigger axiom activates an intention for an agent to play when the agent has an unsatisfied need for play, likes snow, is awake, and is in a room that looks out onto an outside area where it is snowing. From these events, it is inferred that James is no longer calm, is happy, and intends to play outside his house:

¹This model is taken from Section 4 of a paper by Mueller (2003) published by the Association for Computational Linguistics.

```
3
-Calm(James).
+Happy(James).
+IntentionToPlay(James, JamesOutside).
```

The next input events are that James cries for joy and gets up from his bed:

```
Happens(CryForJoy(James), 3).
4
Happens(RiseFrom(James, JamesBed), 4).
```

It is inferred that James is no longer lying on his bed, is no longer lying down, and is standing up:

```
5
-LyingOn(James, JamesBed).
-Lying(James).
+Standing(James).
```

Next, we have the input event that James gets dressed, from which it is inferred that he is dressed:

```
Happens(GetDressed(James), 5).
6
+Dressed(James).
```

The next input event is that James walks through the door of his bedroom, from which it is inferred that he is no longer in his bedroom, is in the hallway, and is near the staircase.

```
Happens(WalkThroughDoor12(James, JamesDoor2F1), 6).
7
-At(James, JamesBedroom2F1).
+At(James, JamesHallway2F1).
+NearPortal(James, JamesStaircase1To2).
```

We have the input event that James walks down the staircase, from which it is inferred that he is no longer in the hallway, is no longer near the door of his bedroom, is in the foyer, and is near the front door and the kitchen door:

```
Happens(WalkDownStaircase(James, JamesStaircase1To2), 7).
8
-At(James, JamesHallway2F1).
-NearPortal(James, JamesDoor2F1).
+At(James, JamesFoyer1F1).
+NearPortal(James, JamesFrontDoor1F1).
+NearPortal(James, JamesKitchenDoor1F1).
```

The next input event is that James unlocks the front door, from which it is inferred that the front door is unlocked:

```
Happens(DoorUnlock(James, JamesFrontDoor1Fl), 8).
9
+DoorUnlocked(JamesFrontDoor1Fl).
```

The input is provided that James opens the front door, and it is inferred that the door is open:

```
Happens(DoorOpen(James, JamesFrontDoor1F1), 9).
10
+DoorIsOpen(JamesFrontDoor1F1).
```

The input is then provided that James walks through the front door, from which it is inferred that he is no longer in the foyer, is no longer near the kitchen door or the staircase, and is outside:

```
Happens(WalkThroughDoor21(James, JamesFrontDoor1Fl), 10).

11
-At(James, JamesFoyer1Fl).
-NearPortal(James, JamesKitchenDoor1Fl).
-NearPortal(James, JamesStaircase1To2).
+At(James, JamesOutside).
```

The input is provided that James plays at timepoint 11:

```
+ActOnIntentionToPlay(James, JamesOutside). Happens(Play(James, JamesOutside), 11).
```

It is inferred that the need to play is satisfied:

```
12
-ActOnIntentionToPlay(James, JamesOutside).
-IntentionToPlay(James, JamesOutside).
+SatiatedFromPlay(James).
```

It is provided as input that James picks up some snow, rolls it into a ball, and lets go of it:

```
Happens(HoldSome(James, Snowball1, Snow1), 12).
13
+Holding(James, Snowball1).
Happens(RollAlong(James, Snowball1, Snow1), 13).
14
-Diameter(Snowball1, 1).
+Diameter(Snowball1, 2).
Happens(LetGoOf(James, Snowball1), 14).
15
-Holding(James, Snowball1).
```

James does the same to make another snowball:

```
Happens(HoldSome(James, Snowball2, Snow1), 15).
```

```
244
```

```
+Holding(James, Snowball2).
Happens(RollAlong(James, Snowball2, Snow1), 16).
17
-Diameter(Snowball2, 1).
+Diameter(Snowball2, 2).
```

Finally, we have the input event that James places the second snowball on top of the first:

```
Happens(PlaceOn(James, Snowball2, Snowball1), 17).
18
-Holding(James, Snowball2).
+On(Snowball2, Snowball1).
```

14.3 VISION

Murray Shanahan and David Randell use the event calculus to implement the higher-level vision component of Ludwig, an upper-torso humanoid robot. Ludwig has two arms, each with three degrees of freedom, and a stereo camera hooked up to a head with two degrees of freedom (pan and tilt). The low-level vision component uses off-the-shelf edge detection software to map raw images from the camera into a list of edges. The list of edges is fed to the higher-level vision component, which is responsible for recognizing shapes. This component is implemented using the event calculus in Prolog.

The higher-level vision component consists of three layers. The first layer generates hypotheses about what regions are in view, based on the input list of edges. The second layer generates hypotheses about what aspects are in view, based on what regions are in view. The *aspects* of a shape are the various ways it can appear when viewed from different angles; for example, a wedge viewed from above appears to be a rectangle, but a wedge viewed from the side appears to be a triangle. The third layer generates hypotheses about what shapes are in view, based on the aspects that are in view over time.

We present here a simplified version of Ludwig's third layer. The predicate $Arc(s, a_1, a_2)$ represents that, by gradually changing the orientation of a shape s with respect to the camera, it is possible for the appearance of s to change from aspect a_1 to aspect a_2 . For example, the appearance of a wedge can change from a rectangle to a rectangle plus an adjacent triangle, but it cannot change immediately from a rectangle to a triangle—it must first appear as a rectangle plus an adjacent triangle. The predicate Shape(o, s) represents that object o has shape s. The fluent Aspect(o, a) represents that the appearance of object o changes from aspect a_1 to aspect a_2 .

We start with state constraints that say that an object has unique shape and aspect:

```
Shape(o, s_1) \land Shape(o, s_2) \Rightarrow s_1 = s_2

HoldsAt(Aspect(o, a_1), t) \land HoldsAt(Aspect(o, a_2), t) \Rightarrow a_1 = a_2
```

We have effect axioms that state that if the aspect of an object is a_1 , the shape of the object is s, it is possible for the appearance of s to change from aspect a_1 to aspect a_2 , and the object changes from a_1 to a_2 , then the aspect of the object will be a_2 and will no longer be a_1 :

```
HoldsAt(Aspect(o,a_1),t) \land Shape(o,s) \land (Arc(s,a_1,a_2) \lor Arc(s,a_2,a_1)) \Rightarrow Initiates(Change(o,a_1,a_2),Aspect(o,a_2),t) 
HoldsAt(Aspect(o,a_1),t) \land Shape(o,s) \land
```

Now, suppose we have the following visual knowledge about two shapes *Shape1* and *Shape2*:

 $(Arc(s, a_1, a_2) \lor Arc(s, a_2, a_1)) \Rightarrow$ Terminates(Change(o, a₁, a₂), Aspect(o, a₁), t)

```
Arc(Shape1, a_1, a_2) \Leftrightarrow
(a_1 = Aspect1 \land a_2 = Aspect2)
Arc(Shape2, a_1, a_2) \Leftrightarrow
((a_1 = Aspect1 \land a_2 = Aspect3) \lor
(a_1 = Aspect3 \land a_2 = Aspect2))
```

Further, suppose we observe at timepoint 0 that *Object1* has *Aspect1* and at timepoint 1 that *Object1* has *Aspect2*:

```
HoldsAt(Aspect(Object1, Aspect1), 0)
HoldsAt(Aspect(Object1, Aspect2), 1)
```

We can then show that the shape of *Object1* must be *Shape1* and not *Shape2*:

Note that this inference depends crucially on the sequence of images over time rather than on a single image. These sorts of inferences are supported by the ability of the event calculus to reason about time.

BIBLIOGRAPHIC NOTES

Lenat and Guha (1991b) and Lieberman, Liu, Singh, and Barry (2004) argue for the use of commonsense reasoning in applications and present numerous examples. The payment protocol application of the classical logic event calculus is from Yolum and Singh (2004); our formalization is adapted from theirs. NetBill is described by Sirbu and Tygar (1995). The workflow modeling application is from Cicekli and Yildirim (2000). They use a logic programming version of the event calculus; the axioms we present are adapted to the classical logic event calculus. Terminology relating

to workflows is defined by the Workflow Management Coalition (1999). Others have used the event calculus for workflow modeling; Wilk (2004) discusses the use of the classical logic event calculus in a hospital workflow management system.

Textbooks on natural language processing are by Allen (1995), Manning and Schütze (1999), and Jurafsky and Martin (2009). Deep natural language understanding systems are discussed by Ram and Moorman (1999). Commonsense reasoning is used by a number of deep natural language and discourse understanding systems (Charniak, 1972; Dahlgren, McDowell, & Stabler, 1989; Dyer, 1983; Hobbs, Stickel, Appelt, & Martin, 1993; Mueller, 1998; J. D. Moore, 1995; Norvig, 1989; Schank & Abelson, 1977; Schank, Kass, & Riesbeck, 1994). Halpin, Moore, and Robertson (2004) use a simplified event calculus to represent event occurrences in stories. van Lambalgen and Hamm (2005) use the classical logic event calculus to represent the semantics of tense and aspect in natural language. Predicate-argument structure representations are used in the Proposition Bank (Palmer, Gildea, & Kingsbury, 2005) annotated corpus. A modern syntactic parser is that of M. Collins (1999, 2003). Some semantic parsers are those of Alshawi (1992), Beale, Nirenburg, and Mahesh (1995), Blackburn and Bos (2005), Gildea and Jurafsky (2002), McCord, Murdock, and Boguraev (2012), and Punyakanok, Roth, and Yih (2008).

The problem of story understanding and systems for story understanding are reviewed by Domeshek, Jones, and Ram (1999), Mueller (2002), and Mani (2013). The use of the Discrete Event Calculus Reasoner for modeling children's stories is discussed by Mueller (2003). This program has also been used to model stories involving scripts, such as eating in a restaurant and kidnapping (Mueller, 2004c, 2007b). Nelson and Mateas (2008) use the Discrete Event Calculus Reasoner for executing and reasoning about game designs.

The use of the event calculus for robot perception is discussed by Shanahan (1999c, 2005). The Ludwig robot is discussed by Shanahan and Randell (2004) and Shanahan (2005, pp. 116–125). The axioms we present are simplified versions of axioms in the third layer of Ludwig's vision system. Koenderink and van Doorn (1979) discuss the notion of an aspect of an object and the representation of the shape of an object as a connected graph whose nodes represent aspects and whose links represent visual events.

EXERCISES

- **14.1** In the scenario in Section 14.1.1, prove that the sequence of events starting with *SendQuote* achieves the goal of selling the customer the CD.
- **14.2** In the scenario in Section 14.1.1, prove that the sequence of events starting with *RequestPurchase* achieves the goal of selling the customer the CD.
- **14.3** In the scenario in Section 14.1.1, prove that the sequence of events starting with *Deliver* achieves the goal of selling the customer the CD.

- **14.4** (Research problem) Use the event calculus to model the semantics of your favorite programming language.
- **14.5** (Research problem) Use the event calculus to build an automated advisor for your favorite computer program.
- **14.6** (Research problem) Use the event calculus to model the operation of a stock exchange.

- a vita a mena a satria dan manangan menasa. Sa a tabah pata benjada dalam sa vita sa vita sa vita sa vita sa v Tabah sa manangan bandan sa manangan sa vita s
 - · Sty Leading Competition of the style of the style
- The Property William based on the State of Calles of Court of the Calles of Calles of

Commonsense Reasoning Using Answer Set Programming

15

Answer set programming is an approach to knowledge representation and reasoning. Knowledge is represented as *answer set programs*, and reasoning is performed by *answer set solvers*. Answer set programming enables default reasoning, which is required in commonsense reasoning. It supports event calculus reasoning and handles some types of event calculus formulas whose circumscription cannot be computed using predicate completion, including effect constraints, disjunctive event axioms, and definitions of compound events.

In this chapter, we discuss the use of answer set programming for commonsense reasoning. We first describe the syntax and semantics of answer set programs. We then present the theory and practice of answer set programming for event calculus reasoning. Finally, we discuss two useful tools for answer set programming: the F2LP program and the $\mathcal E$ language. Resources for this chapter are available at decreasoner.sourceforge.net/csr/ecasp/.

15.1 ANSWER SET PROGRAMMING

The syntax of answer set programs derives from the Prolog language. We use the syntax of the ASP-Core-2 standard. The semantics of answer set programs is defined by the *stable model semantics* introduced by Michael Gelfond and Vladimir Lifschitz.

An answer set program consists of a set of rules of the form

$$\alpha : \beta$$
.

which represents that α , the *head* of the rule, is true if β , the *body* of the rule, is true. Here is an answer set program:

The first rule

p.

is called a *fact*. It has an empty body and is written without the :- (if) connective. The symbol, indicates conjunction (\land). The token not refers to *negation as failure* and is different from classical negation (\neg). The expression not $\ q$ represents that $\ q$ is not found to be true.

We can perform automated reasoning on this program by placing it in a file example. Ip and running the answer set grounder and solver clingo on the file.

```
$ clingo -n 0 example.lp
clingo version 4.2.1
Reading from example.lp
Solving...
Answer: 1
p r
SATISFIABLE

Models : 1
Calls : 1
Time : 0.001s
CPU Time : 0.000s
$
```

The command-line option -n 0 requests all stable models. Models refers to stable models, which are also called *answer sets*. The program has one Answer or stable model in which p and r are true.

If we add the following to the program:

```
s.
q:-s.
then clingo produces
Answer: 1
ps q
```

Notice that r is no longer found to be true, because q is found to be true.

We can also write rules with disjunction in the head:

```
r | q :- p.
```

(The DLV answer set grounder and solver uses v instead of |.) Given this rule and

р.

clingo produces two stable models:

```
Answer: 1
p r
Answer: 2
p q
```

A rule with an empty head is called a *constraint*. If we run clingo on the previous program and the constraint

```
:- r.
```

then we only get one stable model

```
Answer: 1 p q
```

The clingo program is a combination of the answer set grounder gringo and the answer set solver clasp. A grounder converts an answer set program containing variables into an equivalent program not containing any variables. It operates by replacing variables with ground terms. For example, if we ground

```
p(a,b).

q(X,Y):-p(X,Y).

we get

p(a,b).

q(a,a):-p(a,a).

q(a,b):-p(a,b).

q(b,a):-p(b,a).

q(b,b):-p(b,b).
```

15.1.1 SYNTAX OF ANSWER SET PROGRAMS

The *syntax* of answer set programs is defined as follows.

Definition 15.1. A *signature* σ consists of the following disjoint sets:

- A set of *constants*.
- For every $n \in \{1, 2, 3, ...\}$, a set of *n*-ary *function symbols*.
- For every $n \in \{0, 1, 2, ...\}$, a set of *n*-ary *predicate symbols*.

Given a signature σ and a set of *variables* disjoint from the signature, we define answer set programs as follows.

Definition 15.2. A *term* is defined inductively as follows:

- · A constant is a term.
- A variable is a term.
- If τ_1 and τ_2 are terms, then τ , $\tau_1 + \tau_2$, $\tau_1 \tau_2$, $\tau_1 * \tau_2$, and τ_1 / τ_2 are terms. The symbols +, -, *, and / are the *arithmetic symbols*.
- If ϕ is an *n*-ary function symbol and τ_1, \ldots, τ_n are terms, then $\phi(\tau_1, \ldots, \tau_n)$ is a term.
- Nothing else is a term.

Definition 15.3. A *ground term* is a term containing no variables and no arithmetic symbols.

Definition 15.4. An *atom* is defined inductively as follows:

- If ρ is an *n*-ary predicate symbol and τ_1, \ldots, τ_n are terms, then $\rho(\tau_1, \ldots, \tau_n)$ is an atom.
- If ρ is a 0-ary predicate symbol, then ρ is an atom.
- If τ_1 and τ_2 are terms, then $\tau_1 < \tau_2$, $\tau_1 <= \tau_2$, $\tau_1 = \tau_2$, $\tau_1 != \tau_2$, $\tau_1 > \tau_2$, and $\tau_1 >= \tau_2$ are atoms. The symbols <, <=, =, !=, >, and >= are the *comparative predicates*.
- Nothing else is an atom.

Definition 15.5. A *ground atom* is an atom containing no variables, no arithmetic symbols, and no comparative predicates.

Definition 15.6. A rule is

$$\alpha_1 \mid \ldots \mid \alpha_k := \beta_1, \ldots, \beta_m, \text{ not } \gamma_1, \ldots, \text{ not } \gamma_n.$$

where $\alpha_1, \ldots, \alpha_k, \beta_1, \ldots, \beta_m, \gamma_1, \ldots, \gamma_n$ are atoms. $\alpha_1 \mid \ldots \mid \alpha_k$ is the **head** of the rule, and β_1, \ldots, β_m , not γ_1, \ldots , not γ_n is its **body**.

Definition 15.7. A *fact* is a rule whose body is empty (m = 0 and n = 0).

Definition 15.8. A *constraint* is a rule whose head is empty (k = 0).

Definition 15.9. A *ground rule* is a rule containing no variables, no arithmetic symbols, and no comparative predicates.

Definition 15.10. A *logic program*, answer set program, or program is a set of rules. **Definition 15.11.** A traditional rule is a rule whose head contains a single atom (k = 1).

Definition 15.12. A *traditional program* is a set of traditional rules.

Definition 15.13. A *ground program* is a program containing no variables, no arithmetic symbols, and no comparative predicates.

Answer set programming languages, such as those of lparse, gringo, and DLV, and the standard ASP-Core-2, further specify the following:

- Constants are integers or start with a lowercase letter.
- Variables start with an uppercase letter.
- · Function symbols start with a lowercase letter.
- · Predicate symbols start with a lowercase letter.

15.1.2 SEMANTICS OF ANSWER SET PROGRAMS

The stable models semantics of ground programs is defined as follows.

Definition 15.14. An *interpretation I* is a set of ground atoms. If α is a ground atom, then $\alpha \in I$ represents that α is true, whereas $\alpha \notin I$ represents that α is false.

Definition 15.15. An interpretation *I satisfies* a rule

$$\alpha_1 \mid \ldots \mid \alpha_k : -\beta_1, \ldots, \beta_m$$
, not γ_1, \ldots , not γ_n .

if and only if

$$\{\alpha_1, \ldots, \alpha_k\} \cap I \neq \emptyset \text{ or } \{\beta_1, \ldots, \beta_m\} \not\subseteq I \text{ or } \{\gamma_1, \ldots, \gamma_n\} \cap I \neq \emptyset$$

That is, a rule is satisfied by an interpretation if and only if the head of the rule is satisfied by the interpretation if the body of the rule is satisfied by the interpretation.

Definition 15.16. An interpretation I is a **model** of a program Π if and only if I satisfies r for every $r \in \Pi$.

Definition 15.17. The *reduct* of a program Π relative to an interpretation I, written Π^I is the set of all rules

$$\alpha_1 \mid \ldots \mid \alpha_k : \beta_1, \ldots, \beta_m$$

such that

$$\alpha_1 \mid \ldots \mid \alpha_k : \beta_1, \ldots, \beta_m, \text{ not } \gamma_1, \ldots, \text{ not } \gamma_n.$$

is an element of Π , and $\{\gamma_1, \ldots, \gamma_n\} \cap I = \emptyset$.

Definition 15.18. An interpretation I is a *stable model* of a program Π if and only if I is a minimal model of Π^I relative to set inclusion.

15.1.3 STABLE MODELS: EXAMPLE 1

Let Π be the following program:

```
holdsAt(awake,2) :- holdsAt(awake,1), not happens(fallAsleep,1).
holdsAt(awake.1).
```

This program has three models:

```
{happens(fallAsleep,1), holdsAt(awake,1)}
{happens(fallAsleep,1), holdsAt(awake,1), holdsAt(awake,2)}
{holdsAt(awake,1), holdsAt(awake,2)}
```

We can show that $I = \{ \text{holdsAt(awake,1)}, \text{holdsAt(awake,2)} \}$ is a stable model of Π . The reduct Π^I is

$$holdsAt(awake,2) :- holdsAt(awake,1).$$
 (15.1)
 $holdsAt(awake,1).$ (15.2)

I satisfies (15.1) and (15.2). Therefore I is a model of the reduct Π^{I} . We can show that I is minimal by considering all its subsets.

- 1. {holdsAt(awake, 2)} satisfies (15.1), but does not satisfy (15.2).
- **2.** {holdsAt(awake, 1)} satisfies (15.2), but does not satisfy (15.1).
- **3.** \varnothing satisfies (15.1), but does not satisfy (15.2).

Therefore I is a minimal model of Π^{I} , and I is a stable model of Π .

The output of clingo on this program is

```
Answer: 1
holdsAt(awake,1) holdsAt(awake,2)
```

The program Π has one stable model.

15.1.4 STABLE MODELS: EXAMPLE 2

Suppose we add happens (fallAsleep, 1) to the previous program Π :

```
holdsAt(awake,2) :- holdsAt(awake,1), not happens(fallAsleep,1).
holdsAt(awake,1).
happens(fallAsleep,1).
```

The program now has two models:

```
{happens(fallAsleep,1), holdsAt(awake,1)}
{happens(fallAsleep,1), holdsAt(awake,1), holdsAt(awake,2)}
```

We can show that $I = \{\text{happens(fallAsleep,1)}, \text{holdsAt(awake,1)}\}$, which lacks holdsAt(awake,2), is a stable model. The reduct Π^I is

I is a model of the reduct Π^I because I satisfies (15.3) and (15.4). We can also show that I is minimal.

- 1. {holdsAt(awake, 1)} satisfies (15.3), but does not satisfy (15.4).
- 2. {happens(fallAsleep, 1)} satisfies (15.4), but does not satisfy (15.3).
- **3.** \emptyset does not satisfy (15.3) or (15.4).

Therefore I is a stable model of Π .

The output of clingo on this program is

```
Answer: 1
holdsAt(awake,1) happens(fallAsleep,1)
```

15.1.5 STABLE MODELS: EXAMPLE 3

Here is an example of an interpretation that is a model but is not a stable model. Consider the following program Π :

This program has two models:

Although $I = \{a, b\}$ is a model of Π , it is not a stable model of Π . The reduct Π^I is

I satisfies (15.5) and (15.6), but I is not minimal because \emptyset , which is a subset of I, also satisfies (15.5) and (15.6). $I = \emptyset$ is a stable model of Π .

15.1.6 CHOICE RULES

Ilkka Niemelä, Patrik Simons, and Timo Soininen introduce several extensions to answer set programming, including the *choice rule*.

Definition 15.19. A choice rule is

$$\{\alpha_1; \ldots; \alpha_k\} := \beta_1, \ldots, \beta_m, \text{ not } \gamma_1, \ldots, \text{ not } \gamma_n.$$

where $\alpha_1, \ldots, \alpha_k, \beta_1, \ldots, \beta_m, \gamma_1, \ldots, \gamma_n$ are atoms.

This specifies that, if the body is satisfied, then any subset of the atoms in the head can be true. For example, given the program

```
p. {q;r} :- p.
```

```
clingo produces
```

```
Answer: 1
p
Answer: 2
p q
Answer: 3
p r
Answer: 4
p r q
```

A choice rule of the form

```
\{\alpha_1; \ldots; \alpha_k\} := \beta_1, \ldots, \beta_m, \text{ not } \gamma_1, \ldots, \text{ not } \gamma_n.
```

can be translated into the following traditional rules:

$$eta':=eta_1,\ldots,eta_m$$
, not γ_1,\ldots , not γ_n . $lpha_1:=eta'$, not $\overline{lpha_1}$. $lpha_k:=eta'$, not $\overline{lpha_k}$. $\overline{lpha_1}:=\operatorname{not}lpha_1$. $lpha_k:=\operatorname{not}lpha_k$.

where β' is a new atom that represents that the body of the choice rule is true, and $\overline{\alpha_1}, \dots, \overline{\alpha_k}$ are new atoms that represent the negation of $\alpha_1, \dots, \alpha_k$ respectively. This is one way of describing the semantics of choice rules. Answer set solvers implement choice rules in more efficient ways.

The choice rule $\{\alpha\}$ is useful for exempting an atom α from stability checking. This is used in event calculus reasoning to exempt *HoldsAt* and *Happens* from minimization:

```
{holdsAt(F,T)} :- fluent(F), time(T).
{releasedAt(F,T)} :- fluent(F), time(T).
```

15.2 EVENT CALCULUS IN ANSWER SET PROGRAMMING: THEORY

We present the theory behind event calculus reasoning in answer set programming. We discuss an alternative definition of stable models in terms of the operator SM and its relation to the traditional definition. We specify the conditions under which SM is equivalent to circumscription. We show that these conditions are satisfied by event calculus domain descriptions, enabling SM to be used instead of circumscription for event calculus reasoning. Finally, we discuss the EC2ASP translation of event calculus problems into logic programs and the correctness of the translation.

15.2.1 SM

Paolo Ferraris, Joohyung Lee, and Vladimir Lifschitz introduce an alternative definition of stable model in terms of the *SM* operator, whose definition is similar to that of circumscription. This definition of stable model is more general than the definition of Section 15.1.2 in several ways:

- *SM* applies to first-order formulas, which may be syntactically more complex than answer set programming rules.
- *SM* addresses non-Herbrand models. (Herbrand structures and models are defined in Appendix A.3.3.)
- SM allows us to specify which predicates are subject to stability checking. The
 predicates that are subject to stability checking are referred to as intensional
 predicates.

The intensional predicates specify the predicates we would like to characterize based on nonintensional predicates. In the event calculus, we would like to characterize intensional predicates such as *Initiates* and *Terminates* by a conjunction of formulas that contain nonintensional predicates such as *HoldsAt* and *ReleasedAt*.

The stable models of a first-order formula Γ relative to a list of intensional predicates ρ_1, \ldots, ρ_n are defined as the models of $SM[\Gamma; \rho_1, \ldots, \rho_n]$, which is a second-order formula defined in Section A.8.

15.2.2 RELATION BETWEEN SM AND STABLE MODELS

Consider the following sentence:

$$\forall x \left(\neg P(x) \Rightarrow Q(x) \right) \tag{15.7}$$

SM[(15.7); P, Q] is

$$\forall x (\neg P(x) \land Q(x))$$

Now consider the following logic program:

$$g(X) := not p(X).$$
 (15.8)

If we introduce at least one constant, then the Herbrand models of SM[(15.7); P, Q] are identical to the stable models of (15.8). In general, we can characterize the relationship between SM and the stable models of Section 15.1.2 as follows.

Definition 15.20. If r is a rule of the form

$$\alpha_1 \mid \ldots \mid \alpha_k := \beta_1, \ldots, \beta_m, \text{ not } \gamma_1, \ldots, \text{ not } \gamma_n.$$

then the FOL-representation of r, written FOL[r], is the first-order formula

$$\forall \nu_1, \ldots, \nu_p (\beta_1 \wedge \ldots \wedge \beta_m \wedge \neg \gamma_1 \wedge \ldots \wedge \neg \gamma_n \Rightarrow \alpha_1 \vee \ldots \vee \alpha_k)$$

where v_1, \ldots, v_p are all the variables in r.

Definition 15.21. If Π is a logic program, then the *FOL-representation* of Π , written $FOL[\Pi]$, is the conjunction of the FOL-representations of the rules of Π .

For example, if Π is the logic program

$$q(a)$$
.
 $p(X) := q(X)$, not $r(X)$.

then $FOL[\Pi]$ is the first-order formula

$$q(a) \land \forall X (q(X) \land \neg r(X) \Rightarrow p(X))$$
 (15.9)

To simplify the discussion in this chapter, we violate the case conventions for firstorder logic described in Section 2.1.5. In (15.9), X is a variable, a is a constant, and p, q, and r are predicate symbols.

Definition 15.22. Let σ be a signature, and let \mathcal{S} be a Herbrand structure of σ . Then \overline{S} is defined as the set of all $\rho(a_1, \ldots, a_n)$ such that $n \in \{0, 1, 2, \ldots\}, \rho$ is an *n*-ary predicate symbol of σ , and $\langle a_1, \ldots, a_n \rangle \in \rho^{\mathcal{S}}$.

Theorem 15.1. Let σ be a signature containing at least one constant and a finite number of predicate symbols ρ_1, \ldots, ρ_n . Let Π be a traditional logic program of σ , and let S be a Herbrand structure of σ . Then

$$\overline{S}$$
 is a stable model of Π

if and only if

$$S$$
 is a model of $SM[FOL[\Pi]; \rho_1, \ldots, \rho_n]$

Proof. See the proof of Theorem 1 of Ferraris, Lee, and Lifschitz (2011).

15.2.3 RELATION BETWEEN SM AND CIRCUMSCRIPTION

In this section, we characterize the conditions under which SM and CIRC produce the same results. It is important to note that the definitions and results related to SM assume that the logical connectives are limited to \bot (false), \land , \lor , and \Rightarrow . Other logical connectives are considered to be abbreviations:

- $\begin{array}{ccc} \bullet & \top \stackrel{def}{\equiv} \bot \Rightarrow \bot \\ \bullet & \neg \Gamma \stackrel{def}{\equiv} \Gamma \Rightarrow \bot \\ \bullet & \Gamma_1 \Leftrightarrow \Gamma_2 \stackrel{def}{\equiv} (\Gamma_1 \Rightarrow \Gamma_2) \wedge (\Gamma_2 \Rightarrow \Gamma_1) \end{array}$

Definition 15.23. An occurrence of a symbol \circ in a formula Γ is *strictly positive* if and only if the occurrence of \circ is not in the antecedent of an implication.

For example, in the sentence

$$(\forall x\,(Q(x)\Rightarrow P(x)))\wedge(\forall x\,(P(x)\Rightarrow R(x)))$$

the first occurrence of the predicate symbol P is strictly positive and the second one is not. In the sentence

$$((P(A) \lor P(B)) \land (\forall x (P(x) \lor Q(x) \Rightarrow R(x)))$$

the first occurrence of the symbol \vee is strictly positive and the second one is not.

Definition 15.24. A formula Γ is *canonical* relative to predicate symbols ρ_1, \ldots, ρ_n if and only if, for every ρ_i ,

- 1. no occurrence of ρ_i in Γ is in the antecedents of more than one implication, and
- **2.** for every occurrence of ρ_i in Γ , if the occurrence is in the scope of a strictly positive occurrence of \exists or \vee in Γ , then the occurrence is strictly positive in Γ .

Here are several examples. The effect axiom

$$\forall a, t ((P(a) \Rightarrow Q(a)) \Rightarrow Initiates(E(a), F(a), t))$$

is canonical relative to Initiates but not relative to P, because the occurrence of P is in the antecedents of two implications. Similarly,

$$\forall a, t (\neg P(a) \Rightarrow Initiates(E(a), F(a), t))$$

is not canonical relative to P, because $\neg P(a)$ is an abbreviation for $P(a) \Rightarrow \bot$, and P occurs in the antecedents of two implications:

$$\forall a, t ((P(a) \Rightarrow \bot) \Rightarrow Initiates(E(a), F(a), t))$$

The sentence

$$\forall x (P(x) \lor (Q(x) \Rightarrow R(x)))$$

is not canonical relative to Q because the occurrence of Q is not strictly positive in the scope of the strictly positive occurrence of \vee .

The conjunction of two effect axioms

$$\forall a, e, t \ (HoldsAt(F(a), t) \land Initiates(e, G(a), t) \Rightarrow Initiates(e, H(a), t)) \land \\ \forall a, e, t \ (HoldsAt(J(a), t) \land Initiates(e, K(a), t) \Rightarrow Initiates(e, L(a), t))$$

is canonical relative to *Initiates* because every occurrence of *Initiates* satisfies the conditions of Definition 15.24.

We can now state a precise relationship between SM and CIRC. It turns out that, for canonical formulas, they are logically equivalent.

Theorem 15.2. If formula Γ is canonical relative to predicate symbols ρ_1, \ldots, ρ_n , then

$$SM[\Gamma; \rho_1, \ldots, \rho_n] \Leftrightarrow CIRC[\Gamma; \rho_1, \ldots, \rho_n]$$

Proof. See the proof of Theorem 1 of Lee and Palla (2012).

15.2.4 USE OF SM FOR EVENT CALCULUS REASONING

The circumscribed formulas in an event calculus domain description have the following properties:

- Σ is canonical relative to *Initiates*, *Terminates*, *Releases*.
- Δ is canonical relative to *Happens*.
- Θ is canonical relative to Ab_1, \ldots, Ab_n .

We can therefore use SM instead of CIRC for reasoning in the event calculus.

Theorem 15.3. Let

$$D_C = CIRC[\Sigma; Initiates, Terminates, Releases] \land$$

$$CIRC[\Delta; Happens] \land$$

$$CIRC[\Theta; Ab_1, ..., Ab_n] \land \Xi$$

be an event calculus domain description as specified in Definition 2.11, with $\Xi = \Omega \wedge \Psi \wedge \Pi \wedge \Gamma \wedge E \wedge CC$. Let

$$D_S = SM[\Sigma; Initiates, Terminates, Releases] \land \\ SM[\Delta; Happens] \land \\ SM[\Theta; Ab_1, \dots, Ab_n] \land \Xi$$

Then $D_C \Leftrightarrow D_S$.

Proof. This follows from Theorem 15.2.

So far, we have shown that *SM* can be used for event calculus reasoning. But *SM* operates on formulas and not logic programs. We next discuss the translation of an event calculus domain description into an equivalent logic program.

15.2.5 EC2ASP

Joohyung Lee and Ravi Palla define a translation *EC2ASP* for turning an event calculus domain description into a logic program. Let

$$D = CIRC[\Sigma; Initiates, Terminates, Releases] \land$$

$$CIRC[\Delta; Happens] \land$$

$$CIRC[\Theta; Ab_1, \dots, Ab_n] \land \Xi$$

be an event calculus domain description. The EC2ASP translation of D into a logic program, written

 $EC2ASP[\Sigma; \Delta; \Theta; \Xi; Initiates, Terminates, Releases, Happens, Ab_1, ..., Ab_n]$ is computed as follows (Lee & Palla, 2012).

EC2ASP: Step 1

We construct formula Ξ' from Ξ as follows. First, we rewrite all definitional axioms of the form

$$\forall v (\rho(v) \Leftrightarrow \Gamma)$$

as

$$\forall \nu (\Gamma \urcorner \Rightarrow \rho(\nu))$$

where $\Gamma^{\neg \neg}$ is obtained from Γ by prepending $\neg \neg$ (double negation) to all occurrences of the intensional predicates *Initiates*, *Terminates*, *Releases*, *Happens*, Ab_1, \ldots, Ab_n . Second, we prepend $\neg \neg$ to all strictly positive occurrences of the intensional predicates in the remaining axioms of Ξ .

For example, CC1, which is

 $Started(f,t) \Leftrightarrow HoldsAt(f,t) \vee \exists e (Happens(e,t) \wedge Initiates(e,f,t))$

is rewritten as

$$HoldsAt(f,t) \lor \exists e (\neg \neg Happens(e,t) \land \neg \neg Initiates(e,f,t)) \Rightarrow Started(f,t)$$

Prepending double negation is necessary to eliminate unwanted cycles in the predicate dependency graph. For example, CC1 has an edge in the predicate dependency graph from *Started* to *Happens*, and a causal constraint may have an edge from *Happens* to *Started*. Because of the minimality condition in the definition of a stable model (Definition 15.18), *Started* and *Happens* atoms would be eliminated, giving an incorrect result. See the example of Section 15.1.5.

EC2ASP: Step 2

We eliminate quantifiers from $\Sigma \wedge \Delta \wedge \Theta \wedge \Xi'$ using the method given in Section 5.2 of the paper by Lee and Palla (2012).

EC2ASP: Step 3

We convert the resulting quantifier-free formula into a logic program using a set of transformations defined by Cabalar, Pearce, and Valverde (2005).

EC2ASP: Step 4

We add choice rules to the resulting program for all nonintensional predicates.

15.2.6 CORRECTNESS OF EC2ASP

We have the following correctness result for the EC2ASP translation.

Definition 15.25. Let Γ_1 and Γ_2 be formulas of signature ρ , and let σ be a subsignature of ρ . We say that Γ_1 is σ -equivalent to Γ_2 , written $\Gamma_1 \Leftrightarrow_{\sigma} \Gamma_2$ if and only if the class of models of Γ_1 restricted to σ is identical to the class of models of Γ_2 restricted to σ .

Theorem 15.4. Let

$$D_C = CIRC[\Sigma; Initiates, Terminates, Releases] \land CIRC[\Delta; Happens] \land CIRC[\Theta; Ab_1, ..., Ab_n] \land \Xi$$

be an event calculus domain description of signature σ that contains a finite number of predicate symbols. Let

$$D_S = SM[FOL[EC2ASP[\Sigma; \Delta; \Theta; \Xi; Initiates, Terminates, Releases, Happens, Ab_1, ..., Ab_n]]]$$

Then $D_C \Leftrightarrow_{\sigma} D_S$.

Proof. See the Proof of Theorem 8 of Lee and Palla (2012).

15.3 EVENT CALCULUS IN ANSWER SET PROGRAMMING: PRACTICE

We now discuss how to solve event calculus reasoning problems using answer set programming. We discuss how to write a domain description and how to run a solver on the domain description.

15.3.1 WRITING THE DOMAIN DESCRIPTION

Expressing event calculus domain descriptions as answer set programs is similar to expressing these domain descriptions in first-order logic. The main difference is that the syntax of answer set programs is more restrictive. What can be expressed as a single first-order formula may require several rules. For example, the formula

$$(P(x) \lor Q(x)) \land R(x) \Rightarrow S(x)$$

must be expressed as two rules:

```
s(X) := p(X), r(X).

s(X) := q(X), r(X).
```

The formula

$$(\neg \exists y \ P(x, y)) \land Q(x) \Rightarrow R(x)$$

must also be expressed as two rules:

```
p1(X) := p(X,Y).

r(X) := q(X), \text{ not } p1(X).
```

where p1 is a new predicate symbol.

Here are some examples of how event calculus formulas are expressed as answer set programming rules. (A complete list of the various types of event calculus formulas is given in Section 2.7.)

We use predicate symbols to represent that an entity is of a particular sort and declare entities using these symbols:

```
object(leaf).
```

We declare events and fluents in terms of these entities:

```
fluent(height(0,H)) :- object(0), height(H).
fluent(falling(0)) :- object(0).
event(startFalling(0)) :- object(0).
event(hitsGround(0)) :- object(0).
```

We specify the effects of events:

```
\label{eq:continuous} \begin{split} & \text{initiates}(\text{startFalling}(0),\text{falling}(0),\text{T}) :- \text{ object}(0), \text{ time}(\text{T}). \\ & \text{releases}(\text{startFalling}(0),\text{height}(0,\text{H}),\text{T}) :- \text{ object}(0), \text{ height}(\text{H}), \\ & \text{time}(\text{T}). \\ & \text{initiates}(\text{hitsGround}(0),\text{height}(0,\text{H}),\text{T}) :- \text{ holdsAt}(\text{height}(0,\text{H}),\text{T}), \\ & \text{object}(0), \end{split}
```

```
\label{eq:height(H), time(T).} $$ \operatorname{terminates(hitsGround(0),falling(0),T)} :- \operatorname{object(0), time(T).} $$
```

We specify trajectories:

```
 \begin{array}{lll} trajectory(falling(0),T,height(0,H2),X):- \\ holdsAt(height(0,H1),T), & H2=H1-X*X, & object(0), & height(H1), \\ offset(X), & time(T). \end{array}
```

We specify triggered events:

```
happens(hitsGround(0),T) :-
holdsAt(falling(0),T), holdsAt(height(0,0),T), object(0),
time(T).
```

We specify state constraints:

```
:- H1!=H2, holdsAt(height(0,H1),T), holdsAt(height(0,H2),T), object(0), height(H1), height(H2), time(T).
```

We specify initial conditions and event occurrences:

```
:- holdsAt(falling(leaf),0).
holdsAt(height(leaf,9),0).
happens(startFalling(leaf),0).
```

If the reasoning type is abduction or planning, then we exempt happens from stability checking:

```
\{happens(E,T)\} :- event(E), time(T), T<maxtime.
```

We may also wish to specify that fluents are not released at timepoint 0:

```
:- releasedAt(F,0), fluent(F).
```

15.3.2 RUNNING THE SOLVER

We select an answer set grounder and solver such as clingo. We place the domain description in a file such as file.lp. We also need the rules for the event calculus. The DEC rules (dec.lp) are provided in Figure 15.1, and the CC rules (cc.lp) are provided in Figure 15.2. The clingo program supports double negation as failure such as not not p(X). In lparse, this can be represented as {not p(X)}0. We then run clingo:

```
clingo -c maxtime=3 -n O file.lp dec.lp | format-output 3
```

The format-output program developed by Kim (2009) converts the output of answer set solvers into the more readable format produced by the Discrete Event Calculus Reasoner. The fluents that are true at timepoint 0 are shown, followed by differences in the truth values of fluents from one timepoint to the next. Fluents that become true are preceded by + (plus sign), and fluents that become false are preceded by - (minus sign).

```
time(0..maxtime).
\{holdsAt(F,T)\} :- fluent(F), time(T).
\{releasedAt(F,T)\}: fluent(F), time(T).
stoppedIn(T1,F,T2) :- happens(E,T), T1<T, T<T2,
  terminates(E,F,T), event(E), fluent(F), time(T).
  time(T1), time(T2).
startedIn(T1,F,T2) :- happens(E,T), T1<T, T<T2.
  initiates(E,F,T), event(E), fluent(F), time(T),
  time(T1), time(T2).
holdsAt(F2,T1+T2): - happens(E,T1), initiates(E,F1.T1), O<T2.
  trajectory(F1,T1,F2,T2), not stoppedIn(T1,F1,T1+T2),
  event(E), fluent(F1), fluent(F2), time(T1), time(T2).
  T1+T2<maxtime.
holdsAt(F2,T1+T2):- happens(E,T1), terminates(E,F1,T1), 0<T2,
  antiTrajectory(F1,T1,F2,T2), not startedIn(T1,F1,T1+T2),
  event(E), fluent(F1), fluent(F2), time(T1), time(T2),
  T1+T2<maxtime.
initiated1(F,T): - happens(E,T), initiates(E,F,T), event(E),
  fluent(F), time(T).
terminated1(F,T) :- happens(E,T), terminates(E,F,T), event(E).
  fluent(F), time(T).
released1(F,T) :- happens(E,T), releases(E,F,T), event(E),
  fluent(F), time(T).
holdsAt(F,T+1):- holdsAt(F,T), not releasedAt(F,T+1),
  not terminated1(F,T), fluent(F), time(T), T<maxtime.
:- holdsAt(F,T+1), not holdsAt(F,T), not releasedAt(F,T+1),
  not initiated1(F,T), fluent(F), time(T), T<maxtime.
releasedAt(F,T+1) := releasedAt(F,T), not initiated1(F,T).
  not terminated1(F,T), fluent(F), time(T). T<maxtime.
:- releasedAt(F,T+1), not releasedAt(F,T), not released1(F,T),
  fluent(F), time(T), T<maxtime.
holdsAt(F,T+1) :- happens(E,T), initiates(E,F,T), event(E),
  fluent(F), time(T), T<maxtime.
:- holdsAt(F,T+1), happens(E,T), terminates(E,F,T), event(E),
  fluent(F), time(T), T < maxtime.
releasedAt(F,T+1) :- happens(E,T), releases(E,F,T), event(E).
  fluent(F), time(T), T < maxtime.
:- releasedAt(F,T+1), happens(E,T), initiates(E,F,T),
  event(E), fluent(F), time(T), T<maxtime.
:- releasedAt(F,T+1), happens(E,T), terminates(E,F,T),
  event(E), fluent(F), time(T), T<maxtime.
```

FIGURE 15.1

```
started(F,T) :- holdsAt(F,T).
started(F,T) :- not not happens(E,T), not not initiates(E,F,T),
    event(E), fluent(F), time(T).
stopped(F,T) :- not holdsAt(F,T), fluent(F), time(T).
stopped(F,T) :- not not happens(E,T), not not terminates(E,F,T),
    event(E), fluent(F), time(T).
initiated(F,T) :- started(F,T), not terminated1(F,T).
terminated(F,T) :- stopped(F,T), not initiated1(F,T).
```

FIGURE 15.2

CC rules for event calculus reasoning (cc.1p)

15.3.3 EXAMPLE: RUNNING AND DRIVING

The circumscription of the running and driving example in Section 9.2.1 can be handled in answer set programming. We specify entities, fluents, and events:

```
agent(nathan).
location(bookstore).

fluent(tired(A)) :- agent(A).

event(go(A,L)) :- agent(A), location(L).
event(run(A,L)) :- agent(A), location(L).
event(drive(A,L)) :- agent(A), location(L).
```

We write a disjunctive event axiom that specifies that, if an agent goes to a location, then the agent runs or drives to that location:

```
happens(run(A,L),T) | happens(drive(A,L),T) :- happens(go(A,L),T).
```

We write an effect axiom that says that, if an agent runs to a location, then the agent will be tired:

```
initiates(run(A,L),tired(A),T) :- agent(A), location(L), time(T).
```

Now we specify that Nathan was initially not tired and went to the bookstore:

```
:- holdsAt(tired(nathan),0).
happens(go(nathan,bookstore),0).
```

Finally, we specify that Nathan was tired afterward:

```
holdsAt(tired(nathan),1).
```

We specify that fluents are not released at timepoint 0:

```
:- releasedAt(F.O), fluent(F).
```

We then run clingo as follows:

```
clingo -c maxtime=1 -n 0 dec.lp rundrive.lp | format-output 1
```

It is correctly inferred that Nathan ran to the bookstore:

```
Answer: 1
0
happens(run(nathan,bookstore),0)
happens(go(nathan,bookstore),0)
1
+tired(nathan)
```

15.3.4 EXAMPLE: CARRYING A BOOK

The circumscription of the example of carrying a book in Section 6.4.1 can be handled in answer set programming. We specify entities, fluents, and events:

```
agent(nathan).
object(book).
object(A) :- agent(A).
room(livingRoom).
room(kitchen).

event(letGoOf(A,O)) :- agent(A), object(O).
event(pickUp(A,O)) :- agent(A), object(O).
event(walk(A,R1,R2)) :- agent(A), room(R1), room(R2).
fluent(inRoom(O,R)) :- object(O), room(R).
fluent(holding(A,O)) :- agent(A), object(O).
```

We use effect axioms to represent that, if an agent walks from room r_1 to room r_2 , then the agent will be in r_2 and will no longer be in r_1 :

```
initiates(walk(A,R1,R2),inRoom(A,R2),T) :- agent(A), room(R1),
    room(R2), time(T).

terminates(walk(A,R1,R2),inRoom(A,R1),T) :- R1!=R2, agent(A),
    room(R1), room(R2), time(T).
```

We specify that an object is in one room at a time:

```
:- R1!=R2, holdsAt(inRoom(0,R1),T), holdsAt(inRoom(0,R2),T), object(0), room(R1), room(R2), time(T).
```

We specify that, if an agent is in the same room as an object and the agent picks up the object, then the agent will be holding the object:

```
initiates(pickUp(A,0),holding(A,0),T) :- holdsAt(inRoom(A,R),T), holdsAt(inRoom(0,R),T), agent(A), object(0), room(R), time(T).
```

Further, if an agent is holding an object and the agent lets go of the object, then the agent will no longer be holding the object:

```
terminates(letGoOf(A,0),holding(A,0),T) :- holdsAt(holding(A,0),T), agent(A), object(0), time(T).
```

We use effect constraints to represent the indirect effects of walking from one room to another:

```
initiates(E,inRoom(0,R),T) :- initiates(E,inRoom(A,R),T),
  holdsAt(holding(A,0), T).

terminates(E,inRoom(0,R),T) :- terminates(E,inRoom(A,R),T),
  holdsAt(holding(A,0), T).
```

Now we specify that Nathan and the book start out in the living room. Nathan picks up the book and walks into the kitchen. He lets go of the book and walks into the living room.

```
:- holdsAt(holding(A,A),T), agent(A).
happens(pickUp(nathan,book),0).
happens(walk(nathan,livingRoom,kitchen),1).
happens(letGoOf(nathan,book),2).
happens(walk(nathan,kitchen,livingRoom),3).
We specify that fluents are not released at timepoint 0:
:- releasedAt(F,0), fluent(F).
Finally, we run clingo as follows:
```

clingo -c maxtime=4 -n O dec.lp book.lp | format-output 4

holdsAt(inRoom(nathan,livingRoom),0).
holdsAt(inRoom(book,livingRoom),0).
:- holdsAt(holding(nathan,book),0).

It is correctly inferred that, at the end, the book is in the kitchen and Nathan is in the living room:

```
Answer: 1
happens(pickUp(nathan,book),0)
inRoom(book,livingRoom)
inRoom(nathan,livingRoom)
1
+holding(nathan.book)
inRoom(book,livingRoom)
inRoom(nathan, livingRoom)
happens(walk(nathan, livingRoom, kitchen), 1)
-inRoom(book,livingRoom)
-inRoom(nathan,livingRoom)
+inRoom(book,kitchen)
+inRoom(nathan,kitchen)
holding(nathan,book)
happens(letGoOf(nathan,book).2)
3
```

```
-holding(nathan,book)
inRoom(nathan,kitchen)
inRoom(book,kitchen)
happens(walk(nathan,kitchen,livingRoom),3)
4
-inRoom(nathan,kitchen)
+inRoom(book,kitchen)
inRoom(book,kitchen)
```

15.4 F2LP

The F2LP program, which was developed by Joohyung Lee and Ravi Palla, is a useful tool for answer set programming. It automates the translation of first-order formulas under the stable models semantics into answer set programs. The logical symbols supported by F2LP are shown in Table 15.1. Answer set program rules may also be provided in the input to F2LP; these are written to output unchanged.

15.5 E

The $\mathcal E$ action language, which was developed by Antonis Kakas and Rob Miller, can be used as a high-level language for answer set programming. We define $\mathcal E$ and describe how an $\mathcal E$ domain description can be translated into an answer set program. **Definition 15.26.** An $\mathcal E$ signature σ consists of disjoint sets of fluents, events, and timepoints.

For the purposes of our translation of \mathcal{E} into answer set programs, we assume that fluents and events are answer set program atoms, and we assume that timepoints are answer set program terms. We define an \mathcal{E} statement and the translation of a statement into an answer set program rule as follows.

Table	15.1	Symbols	Supported	by	F2LP
CONTRACTOR STREET, STR	rathshirt west to the			concuration	•

Name	F2LP	First-order logic
Conjunction	&	^
Disjunction		V
Implication	->	⇒
Implication	<-	3
Default negation	not	
Classical negation	-	_
True	true	Т
False	false	1
Universal quantification	![X,Y,Z]:	$\forall x, y, z$
Existential quantification	?[X,Y,Z]:	$\exists x, y, z$

Definition 15.27. If β is a fluent and τ is a timepoint, then

 β holds-at au

is a statement. It is translated into the rule

 $holdsAt(\beta, \tau)$.

Definition 15.28. If β is a fluent and τ is a timepoint, then

 $-\beta$ holds-at τ

is a statement. It is translated into the rule

:- holdsAt(β , τ).

Definition 15.29. If α is an event and τ is a timepoint, then

lpha happens-at au

is a statement. It is translated into the rule

happens (α, τ) .

Definition 15.30. If α is an event, β is a fluent, $\gamma_1, \ldots, \gamma_n$ are fluents, and π is initiates or terminates, then

 $\alpha \pi \beta$ when $(-)\gamma_1, \ldots, (-)\gamma_n$

is a statement. It is translated into the rule

 $\pi(\alpha, \beta, \tau) := (\text{not}) \text{ holdsAt}(\gamma_1, \tau), \dots, (\text{not}) \text{ holdsAt}(\gamma_n, \tau).$

where τ is a new variable.

BIBLIOGRAPHIC NOTES

The stable models semantics for logic programming was introduced by Gelfond and Lifschitz (1988). Book-length treatments of answer set programming are by Baral (2003), Gebser, Kaminski, Kaufmann, and Schaub (2013), and Gelfond and Kahl (2014). Answer set programming is also discussed by Gelfond (2008).

Prolog is discussed by Clocksin and Mellish (2003). ASP-Core-2 is specified by Calimeri et al. (2012). The <code>lparse</code> program is described by Syrjänen (2000). The <code>gringo</code>, <code>clasp</code>, and <code>clingo</code> programs are described by Gebser, Kaminski, Ostrowski, Schaub, and Thiele (2009), Gebser, Ostrowski, Kaminski, Kaufmann, and Schaub (2010), and Gebser, Kaminski, Kaufmann, and Schaub (2013). The <code>DLV</code> program is described by Bihlmeyer, Faber, Ielpa, Lio, and Pfeifer (2014).

Gelfond and Lifschitz (1991) extend answer set programming with classical negation. Niemelä, Simons, and Soininen (1999) introduce the choice rule. The translation of choice rules into traditional rules is from Janhunen and Niemelä (2011).

SM was defined by Ferraris, Lee, and Lifschitz (2007, 2011). Lee and Palla (2012), Palla (2012), and Kim, Lee, and Palla (2009) developed the theory behind solving event calculus reasoning problems using answer set programming. They define the

translation *EC2ASP* and prove its correctness. The FOL-representation of a logic program is defined by Lee, Lifschitz, and Palla (2008). Predicate dependency graphs are described by Lee and Palla (2012) and Palla (2012). Double negation as failure in logic programs is discussed by Lifschitz, Tang, and Turner (1999).

The F2LP program is described by Lee and Palla (2009). The $\mathcal E$ action language is described by Kakas and Miller (1997a, 1997b). Dimopoulos, Kakas, and Michael (2004) provide a translation of $\mathcal E$ domain descriptions into answer set programs without the use of the holdsAt, happens, initiates, and terminates predicate symbols. For example, f holds-at t is translated into f(t) rather than holdsAt(f,t). The $\mathcal E$ language has been further developed into $\mathcal M$ odular- $\mathcal E$ (Kakas, Michael, & Miller, 2005, 2011), which addresses the ramification and qualification problems.

EXERCISES

15.1 Let Π be the following program:

```
p.
r :- p, not q.
s :- t, not r.
```

Show that $I = \{p, r\}$ is a stable model of Π .

15.2 Let Π be the following program:

```
p | q :- r.
r :- not t.
t | u :- v.
v.
```

Show that $I = \{p, r, u, v\}$ is a stable model of Π .

15.3 Write a program to convert \mathcal{E} domain descriptions into answer set programs using the translation described in Section 15.5.

end of modifications of MCF 201 exceptions at favoring but MCF, and arriver in the coneffect of discount from each 6800 rates from a factor of the desired and each of the coneffect of a larger of the factor of the factor of the factor of the factor of the content of the factor of the facto

s yeugen a amag for the first post of the first had been for the magen of mergon of the entropy of the first of the first of the entropy of the first of the entropy of the

II a fine fine a fire triple to helt a new

त्रका प्रमुख का विशेषक वर्त । इ.से.

PART

Logical and Nonlogical Methods

bus la igo. Isoigelse/ abodte/

Logics for Commonsense Reasoning

Why the event calculus? How does the event calculus stack up against other logical formalisms for commonsense reasoning? There are many such formalisms. In this chapter, we review four important families—the situation calculus, the features and fluents framework, action languages, and the fluent calculus—discussing their relationship to the event calculus.

16.1 THE SITUATION CALCULUS

The main difference between the situation calculus and the event calculus is that the situation calculus uses branching time, whereas the traditional event calculus uses linear time. In the event calculus, there is a single time line on which events occur, and all events are considered to be actual events. In the situation calculus, time is represented by a tree, and each event may give rise to a different possible future; therefore, events are considered to be hypothetical events. A point in time is represented by a situation. In this section, we use a standard version of the situation calculus described by Raymond Reiter. Notational variants of the situation calculus are shown in Table 16.1.

16.1.1 RELATIONAL AND FUNCTIONAL FLUENTS

The truth value of a relational fluent is represented by

$$(\neg)F(x_1,\ldots,x_n,\sigma)$$

which represents that fluent $F(x_1, ..., x_n)$ is true (false) in situation σ . The value of a functional fluent is represented by

$$f(x_1,\ldots,x_n,\sigma)=v$$

which represents that fluent $f(x_1, \ldots, x_n)$ has value ν in situation σ .

16.1.2 **ACTIONS**

The performance of an action is represented by

$$\sigma' = do(\alpha, \sigma)$$

Source	Fluent	Successor
McCarthy and Hayes (1969)	$F(x_1,\ldots,x_n,\sigma)$	$result(\pi,\alpha,\sigma)$
McCarthy (1980)	$F(x_1,\ldots,x_n,\sigma)$	$result(\alpha, \sigma)$
Russell and Norvig (2009)	$F(x_1,\ldots,x_n,\sigma)$	$Result(\alpha, \sigma)$
Hayes (1973)	$F(x_1,\ldots,x_n,\sigma)$	$R(\alpha, \sigma)$
Hayes (1971), Reiter (2001),	$F(x_1,\ldots,x_n,\sigma)$	$do(\alpha, \sigma)$
and Brachman and Levesque (2004)		
Green (1969) and Winston (1984)	$F(x_1,\ldots,x_n,\sigma)$	$A(x_1,\ldots,x_n,\sigma)$
Kowalski (1979)	$Holds(\phi, \sigma)$	$result(\alpha, \sigma)$
Shanahan (1997b)	$Holds(\phi, \sigma)$	Result(α, σ)
E. Davis (1990)	$true_in(\sigma, \phi)$	$result(\sigma, \alpha)$
	$value_in(\sigma, \phi)$	A Section 18
Charniak and McDermott (1985)	$(T \sigma \phi)$	result σ (do π α)
Genesereth and Nilsson (1987)	$T(\phi,\sigma)$	$Do(\alpha, \sigma)$

Table 16.1 Situation calculus notational variants^a

which represents that situation σ' is the successor situation that results from performing action α in situation σ . There is an initial situation, called S_0 .

16.1.3 ACTION EFFECTS

An effect axiom of the form

$$R(x_1,\ldots,x_n,\sigma)\supset (\neg)F(x_1,\ldots,x_n,do(\alpha,\sigma))$$

represents that under the conditions given by $R(x_1, \ldots, x_n, \sigma)$, fluent $F(x_1, \ldots, x_n)$ is true (false) in the situation that results from performing action α in situation σ .

The effect axioms for each fluent $F(x_1, \ldots, x_n)$ are compiled into a single successor state axiom as follows. The conditions under which an action α initiates the fluent are collected into a single formula $\gamma_F^+(x_1, \ldots, x_n, \alpha, \sigma)$, and the conditions under which α terminates the fluent are collected into a single formula $\gamma_F^-(x_1, \ldots, x_n, \alpha, \sigma)$. The *successor state axiom* is then as follows:

$$F(x_1,\ldots,x_n,do(\alpha,\sigma)) \equiv \gamma_F^+(x_1,\ldots,x_n,\alpha,\sigma) \vee (F(x_1,\ldots,x_n,\sigma) \wedge \neg \gamma_F^-(x_1,\ldots,x_n,\alpha,\sigma))$$

This states that a fluent is true in the situation that results from performing an action α in situation σ if and only if (1) α initiates the fluent or (2) the fluent is true in σ and α does not terminate the fluent. (Notice the resemblance of $\gamma_F^+(x_1,\ldots,x_n,\alpha,\sigma)$ to $Initiates(\alpha,F(x_1,\ldots,x_n),\sigma)$ in the event calculus and of $\gamma_F^-(x_1,\ldots,x_n,\alpha,\sigma)$ to $Terminates(\alpha,F(x_1,\ldots,x_n),\sigma)$.)

 $[^]a\alpha$, action; π , person; σ , situation; ϕ , fluent; A, action predicate; F, fluent predicate; x_1, \ldots, x_n , action and fluent arguments.

16.1.4 ACTION PRECONDITIONS

An action precondition axiom of the form

$$Poss(A(x_1,...,x_n),\sigma) \equiv P(x_1,...,x_n,\sigma)$$

represents that it is possible to perform the action $A(x_1, \ldots, x_n)$ in situation σ if and only if $P(x_1, \ldots, x_n, \sigma)$ is true. A situation is executable if and only if all the actions leading to that situation are possible to perform. Nonexecutable situations are those resulting from one or more impossible actions.

16.1.5 EQUIVALENCE OF THE SITUATION CALCULUS AND THE EVENT CALCULUS

Robert Kowalski and Fariba Sadri have proved the equivalence of a version of the situation calculus similar to that of Reiter and a version of the event calculus. Their version of the situation calculus assumes that no fluents are true in the initial situation and includes terms representing transitions from one situation to another. Their version of the event calculus differs from the one described in this book as follows:

- It supports branching time.
- It does not support concurrent events.
- It does not support release from the commonsense law of inertia.
- It does not support continuous change.
- It has an initial situation, and no fluents are true in the initial situation.
- It includes terms representing transitions from one situation to another.

Their version supports a distinction between actual and hypothetical situations, but this is not required for the equivalence proof. Their version of the event calculus does not support continuous time, which is also the case for the discrete event calculus. An equivalence result between the situation calculus and a branching time version of the discrete event calculus is presented in Appendix D.

16.1.6 DISCUSSION

Like the event calculus, the situation calculus supports context-sensitive effects of events, indirect effects, preconditions of actions, and the commonsense law of inertia.

The situation calculus can be used to represent and reason about hypothetical events and situations, which cannot be done in the event calculus unless it is extended to support branching time, as proposed by Kowalski and Sadri.

The situation calculus supports functional fluents, which are not supported by the event calculus. Nonetheless, a functional fluent may be represented in the event calculus by (1) using a relational fluent, (2) adding an extra argument to the relational fluent, and (3) adding state constraints ensuring that the relational fluent is functional. For example, if we wish to represent a functional fluent F(x) = y, we instead use a

relational fluent F(x, y) and the following state constraints:

$$HoldsAt(F(x, y_1), t) \land HoldsAt(F(x, y_2), t) \Rightarrow y_1 = y_2$$

 $\exists y \, HoldsAt(F(x, y), t)$

The basic situation calculus does not support continuous change because of the discrete nature of the tree of situations. The basic situation calculus also does not support triggered events because many hypothetical events are possible in any given situation. Nondeterminism is also not supported in the basic situation calculus. A number of extensions to the situation calculus have been proposed to address these phenomena.

The basic situation calculus does not support the representation of actual situations and actual events. Two methods for extending the situation calculus to support these have been proposed:

- Situations are designated as actual using a predicate actual(s), and actions are
 designated as actually occurring in a situation using a predicate occurs(a, s).
 Time may also be added, and a function start(s) may be used to represent the
 start time of a situation.
- A time line is added to the situation calculus, times are associated with actual situations using a function State(t), and actions are designated as actually occurring at a time using a predicate Happens(a, t).

Concurrent events cannot normally be represented in the situation calculus, because each transition from situation to situation represents a single event. Extensions have been proposed in which sets of concurrent events can be associated with transitions.

16.2 THE FEATURES AND FLUENTS FRAMEWORK

The features and fluents framework was developed by Erik Sandewall. The framework includes a specialized logic called discrete fluent logic and a methodology for assessing the range of applicability of logics. Discrete fluent logic (DFL) was recast in many-sorted first-order logic with equality by Patrick Doherty and Witold Łukaszewicz. This work gave rise to a class of logics called temporal action logics (TAL) developed by Doherty, Joakim Gustafsson, Lars Karlsson, and Jonas Kvarnström. TAL uses the pointwise minimization of occlusion with nochange premises (PMON) entailment method, which is one of the entailment methods defined in the features and fluents framework.

16.2.1 TEMPORAL ACTION LOGICS

TAL has many similarities with the event calculus. Like the event calculus, and unlike the situation calculus, TAL uses linear time. (In general, the features and fluents framework supports both linear and branching time.) Like the event calculus, TAL uses circumscription to enforce the commonsense law of inertia. TAL has a predicate, Occlude(t, f), similar to the event calculus predicate ReleasedAt(f, t),

which represents that a fluent f is released from the commonsense law of inertia at timepoint t. The event calculus inherited this construct from the features and fluents framework. TAL uses discrete time, like the discrete event calculus. Whereas the discrete event calculus uses the integers $\{\ldots, -2, -1, 0, 1, 2, \ldots\}$ for representing time, TAL uses the non-negative integers $\{0, 1, 2, \ldots\}$. The relation between the event calculus and TAL is explored in Appendix E.

TAL consists of two languages: a narrative description language, $\mathcal{L}(ND)$, and a fluent logic language, $\mathcal{L}(FL)$. Commonsense reasoning problems are described using $\mathcal{L}(ND)$, which is a specialized language. Descriptions in $\mathcal{L}(ND)$ are then translated into $\mathcal{L}(FL)$, which is a many-sorted first-order language. We now describe how things are represented in $\mathcal{L}(ND)$ and translated into $\mathcal{L}(FL)$.

Observation statements

The $\mathcal{L}(ND)$ expression

$$[\tau] f(\omega_1, \ldots, \omega_n) = v$$

represents that fluent $f(\omega_1, \dots, \omega_n)$ has the value v at timepoint $\tau \cdot f$ is called a feature hence the name features and fluents. (We call f a fluent symbol.)

If f has a Boolean domain, then the $\mathcal{L}(FL)$ translation of $[\tau] f(\omega_1, \dots, \omega_n) = T$ is the observation statement

$$Holds(\tau, f(\omega_1, \ldots, \omega_n))$$

and the translation of $[\tau] f(\omega_1, \dots, \omega_n) = F$ is the observation statement

$$\neg Holds(\tau, f(\omega_1, \ldots, \omega_n))$$

If f has a non-Boolean domain, then the $\mathcal{L}(FL)$ translation of $[\tau] f(\omega_1, \dots, \omega_n) = v$ is the observation statement

$$Holds(\tau, f(\omega_1, \ldots, \omega_n, v))$$

Axioms in $\mathcal{L}(FL)$ ensure that f is functional:

$$Holds(\tau, f(\omega_1, \dots, \omega_n, v_1)) \wedge Holds(\tau, f(\omega_1, \dots, \omega_n, v_2)) \rightarrow v_1 = v_2$$
 (16.1)

$$\exists v \, Holds(\tau, f(\omega_1, \dots, \omega_n, v))$$
 (16.2)

Action occurrences and effects

Action occurrences and the effects of actions are represented as follows. The $\mathcal{L}(ND)$ action occurrence statement

$$[\tau_1, \tau_2] a(\omega_1, \ldots, \omega_n)$$

represents that action $a(\omega_1, \ldots, \omega_n)$ occurs between timepoints τ_1 and τ_2 . The $\mathcal{L}(ND)$ action law schema

$$[\tau_1, \tau_2] \alpha \rightsquigarrow ([\tau_1] \gamma \rightarrow [\tau_1, \tau_2] \phi := \nu)$$

represents that if action α occurs between τ_1 and τ_2 and condition γ is true at τ_1 , then the value of fluent ϕ will be ν starting at τ_2 . The value of ϕ is unchanged at τ_1 and is permitted to vary at timepoints $\tau_1 + 1$ to $\tau_2 - 1$.

If $\tau_2 = \tau_1 + 1$, then the action is called a single-step action. In this case, the meaning is the same as in the discrete event calculus:

- TAL $[\tau, \tau + 1] \alpha$ is the same as DEC Happens (α, τ)
- TAL $[\tau, \tau + 1] \alpha \sim ([\tau] \gamma \rightarrow [\tau, \tau + 1] \phi := T)$ is the same as DEC $Initiates(\alpha, \phi, \tau)$
- TAL $[\tau, \tau + 1] \alpha \rightsquigarrow ([\tau] \gamma \rightarrow [\tau, \tau + 1] \phi := F)$ is the same as DEC *Terminates* (α, ϕ, τ)

Action occurrences statements and action law schemata are translated into $\mathcal{L}(FL)$ schedule statements as follows. For each action occurrence statement $[\tau_1, \tau_2]$ $a(\omega_1, \ldots, \omega_n)$ and corresponding action law schema $[t_1, t_2]$ $a(x_1, \ldots, x_n) \rightarrow \Delta$, we form a $\mathcal{L}(ND)$ reassignment formula $[\tau_1, \tau_2]$ Δ' , where Δ' is Δ with τ_1 substituted for t_1 , t_2 substituted for t_2 , t_2 substituted for t_3 , and so on. For example, from

and

278

$$[t_1, t_2]$$
 Wake $Up(a) \rightsquigarrow awake(a) := T$

we form the reassignment formula

$$[1,2] awake(Nathan) := T (16.3)$$

We then translate the reassignment formula into $\mathcal{L}(FL)$. The translation of a reassignment formula $[\tau_1, \tau_2] f(\omega_1, \dots, \omega_n) := v$ is the schedule statement

$$Holds(\tau_2, f(\omega_1, \dots, \omega_n, v)) \land \\ \forall t, d \ (t_1 < t \le t_2 \rightarrow Occlude(t, f(\omega_1, \dots, \omega_n, d)))$$

For example, the translation of (16.3) is

$$Holds(2, awake(Nathan)) \land Occlude(2, awake(Nathan))$$

The predicate Occlude(t, f) represents that the truth value of fluent f may change between timepoints t-1 and t, which is the same as ReleasedAt(f, t) in the event calculus. This constraint is enforced by the following nochange axiom of $\mathcal{L}(FL)$, which states that if a fluent f is not occluded at timepoint t+1, then the truth value of f does not change from timepoint t to t+1:

$$\neg Occlude(t+1,f) \to Holds(t,f) \equiv Holds(t+1,f)$$
 (16.4)

This is equivalent to the conjunction of the axioms

$$Holds(t,f) \land \neg Occlude(t+1,f) \rightarrow Holds(t+1,f)$$
 (16.5)

and

$$\neg Holds(t,f) \land \neg Occlude(t+1,f) \rightarrow \neg Holds(t+1,f)$$
 (16.6)

These axioms resemble axioms of the discrete event calculus. Axiom (16.5) resembles DEC5:

$$(HoldsAt(f,t) \land \neg ReleasedAt(f,t+1) \land \neg \exists e (Happens(e,t) \land Terminates(e,f,t))) \Rightarrow HoldsAt(f,t+1)$$

Axiom (16.6) resembles DEC6:

$$(\neg HoldsAt(f,t) \land \neg ReleasedAt(f,t+1) \land \neg \exists e (Happens(e,t) \land Initiates(e,f,t))) \Rightarrow \neg HoldsAt(f,t+1)$$

Scenario descriptions

A TAL scenario description is given by

$$CIRC[\Sigma; Occlude] \land \Psi \land \Gamma \land TAL$$

where Σ is a conjunction of schedule statements derived from action occurrence statements and action law schemata; Ψ is a conjunction of domain constraints, or state constraints; Γ is a conjunction of observation statements; and TAL is a conjunction of foundational axioms and the nochange axiom (16.4). We use a notation that highlights the similarity of TAL scenario descriptions and event calculus domain descriptions, which are defined in Section 2.7. The TAL notation for Σ is Γ_{SCD} , Ψ is Γ_{DOMC} , Γ is Γ_{OBS} , and TAL = $\Gamma_{FA} \wedge \Gamma_{NCG}$, where $\Gamma_{NCG} = (16.4)$. The scenario description may entail various formulas, such as Holds formulas, as in the event calculus.

Discussion

Like the event calculus, TAL supports actions with duration, the commonsense law of inertia, dynamic release from the commonsense law of inertia, concurrent events, context-sensitive effects, indirect effects, and nondeterministic effects.

Unlike the event calculus, TAL supports functional fluents. As described in Section 16.1, functional fluents can be represented in the event calculus using relational fluents and state constraints. These state constraints are similar to the $\mathcal{L}(FL)$ axioms (16.1) and (16.2). TAL supports a type of fluent called a *durational fluent*, which is a fluent whose value is always a default value except when the fluent is occluded.

Several features of the event calculus are not supported by TAL: continuous change, continuous time, time less than zero, and triggered events (because action occurrence statements have no provision for conditions). Event occurrences are represented explicitly in the event calculus using Happens; in TAL, event occurrences are represented explicitly in $\mathcal{L}(ND)$ but not in $\mathcal{L}(FL)$. (In some versions of TAL, a predicate Occurs is introduced.)

16.3 ACTION LANGUAGES

Instead of using the general-purpose language of predicate logic for reasoning about action, specialized action languages can be developed. The original action languages were STRIPS and ADL; a number of action languages, such as \mathcal{A} , \mathcal{AR}_0 , \mathcal{A}_C , \mathcal{B} , \mathcal{C} , $\mathcal{C}+$, \mathcal{BC} , and \mathcal{E} , have since been developed.

The simple action language A was introduced by Michael Gelfond and Vladimir Lifschitz. In A, action effects are represented using expressions of the form

a causes
$$f$$
 if f_1, \ldots, f_n

where a is an action, and f, f_1, \ldots, f_n are (possibly negated) fluents. \mathcal{AR}_0 extends \mathcal{A} for indirect effects and nondeterminism. \mathcal{AC} extends \mathcal{A} for concurrent actions. \mathcal{B} extends \mathcal{A} for indirect effects. \mathcal{C} is based on a causal theory of actions. $\mathcal{C}+$ is an extension of \mathcal{C} . \mathcal{BC} extends \mathcal{B} with features from \mathcal{C} such as static causal laws. \mathcal{E} is similar to the event calculus, and a mapping between the event calculus and \mathcal{E} has been described. The \mathcal{E} language is discussed in Section 15.5. In this section, we discuss action language $\mathcal{C}+$.

16.3.1 C+

The C+ action language was developed by Enrico Giunchiglia, Joohyung Lee, Vladimir Lifschitz, Norman McCain, and Hudson Turner. Like the event calculus and TAL, C+ uses linear time. Like the discrete event calculus, C+ uses discrete time. Unlike the event calculus, the situation calculus, and TAL, which are based on the first-order and sometimes second-order logic, C+ is based on propositional logic. C+ uses concepts like reduct that are similar to those used in answer set programming.

Reasoning problems in $\mathcal{C}+$ can be transformed into SAT problems, as can reasoning problems of the discrete event calculus. The SAT-based approach used in the discrete event calculus derives from the SAT-based approach used in $\mathcal{C}+$.

Syntax of C+

We start with a *signature*, which consists of a set of constants, and a domain dom(c) associated with each constant c. The domain of a Boolean constant is $\{\mathbf{t}, \mathbf{f}\}$. If c is a constant and $v \in dom(c)$, then c = v is a C + atom. A C + formula is defined as follows:

- · An atom is a formula.
- The symbols \perp (false) and \top (true) are formulas (zero-place connectives).
- If f_1 is a formula, and f_2 is a formula, then $\neg f_1, f_1 \land f_2$, and $f_1 \lor f_2$ are formulas.
- If c is a Boolean constant, then $c = \mathbf{t}$ is abbreviated c and $c = \mathbf{f}$ is abbreviated $\neg c$.

The set of fluents and the set of actions are disjoint subsets of the set of constants. Fluents are further divided into simple fluents and statically determined fluents. A *fluent formula* is a formula whose constants are fluents, and an *action formula* is a formula whose constants are actions.

Although C+ is based on propositional logic, a first-order notation is often used. We may define a set of constants $p(x_1, \ldots, x_n)$, where x_1, \ldots, x_n are taken from finite sets. For example, we may represent the location of an object using the set of constants InRoom(x), where $x \in \{Nathan, Book\}$.

A C+ causal law is an expression of the form

caused f if g after h

or

caused f if g

where f, g, and h are formulas. A number of abbreviations for causal laws are defined.

• The effects of actions are represented using expressions of the form

a causes f if c

where a is an action formula, and f and c are fluent formulas. This is an abbreviation for **caused** f **if** \top **after** $a \wedge c$. The formula f cannot contain statically determined fluents. The condition c enables context-sensitive effects of actions to be represented.

• If f is a simple fluent, then the expression

inertial f

specifies that f is subject to the commonsense law of inertia at all times. This is an abbreviation for **caused** f = v **if** f = v **after** f = v, for each $v \in dom(f)$.

Action preconditions are represented using expressions of the form

nonexecutable a if c

where a is an action formula, and c is a fluent formula. This stands for **caused** \bot **if** \top **after** $a \land c$.

· Triggered actions are represented using causal laws of the form

caused a if c

where a is an action formula, and c is a fluent formula.

• If a is an action, then the expression

exogenous a

specifies that a may or may not occur at each timepoint. This stands for **caused** a = v if a = v, for each $v \in dom(a)$. If **exogenous** a is not specified, then in order for a to occur it must be caused to occur.

• State constraints are represented using expressions of the form

constraint c

where c is a fluent formula. This stands for caused \perp if $\neg c$.

 $\mathcal{C}+$ treats indirect effects in an elegant way. They are represented using causal laws of the form

caused f if g

where f and g are fluent formulas. Such a causal law represents that f is an indirect effect of any actions that bring about g. For example, we may represent that if an

282

agent is holding an object, and the agent is in a room, then the object will also be in that room:

```
caused InRoom(o) = r if Holding(a) = o \land InRoom(a) = r
```

The closest analog to this in the event calculus is the pair of effect constraints:

 $HoldsAt(Holding(a, o), t) \land Initiates(e, InRoom(a, r), t) \Rightarrow Initiates(e, InRoom(o, r), t) \land HoldsAt(InRoom(a, r), t) \land Initiates(e, Holding(a, o), t) \Rightarrow Initiates(e, InRoom(o, r), t)$

But these formulas do not allow for the possibility that Holding(a) = o or InRoom(a) = r may be the result of interacting concurrent events.

We have so far described the syntax of $\mathcal{C}+$. The semantics of a $\mathcal{C}+$ theory is given by a translation into a causal theory. We first define the syntax and semantics of causal theories, and then specify the translation of a $\mathcal{C}+$ theory into a causal theory.

Syntax of causal theories

We have a signature, as in C+. Causal theory atoms and formulas are as in C+. A *causal rule* is an expression of the form

$$f_1 \Leftarrow f_2$$

where f_1 and f_2 are causal theory formulas. This represents that f_1 has a cause if f_2 is true. f_1 is called the head of the causal rule, and f_2 is called the body of the causal rule. A *causal theory* consists of a set of causal rules.

Semantics of causal theories

An interpretation I for a signature is a mapping from each constant c of the signature to an element of dom(c). We define what it means for a formula ψ to be true in an interpretation I, written $I \models \psi$, as follows:

- If c is a constant and $v \in dom(c)$, then $I \models c = v$ if and only if I(c) = v.
- It is not the case that $I \models \bot$.
- It is the case that $I \models \top$.
- If α is a formula, then $I \models \neg \alpha$ if and only if it is not the case that $I \models \alpha$.
- If α and β are formulas, then $I \models \alpha \land \beta$ if and only if $I \models \alpha$ and $I \models \beta$.
- If α and β are formulas, then $I \models \alpha \vee \beta$ if and only if $I \models \alpha$ or $I \models \beta$.

An interpretation I is a *model* of a set of formulas Φ , written $I \models \Phi$, if and only if $I \models \psi$ for every $\psi \in \Phi$.

The *reduct* of a causal theory T relative to an interpretation I, written reduct(T, I), is the set of every head of a causal rule $r \in T$ such that the body of r is true in I. An interpretation I is a *model* of a causal theory T, written $I \models T$, if and only if I is the unique model of the set of formulas reduct(T, I). That is, there must be exactly one model of reduct(T, I), and that model must equal I. A causal theory T entails a formula ψ , written $T \models \psi$, if and only if, for every I such that $I \models T$, we have $I \models \psi$.

Reduction to propositional logic

A causal theory T is *definite* if and only if (1) the head of every causal rule in T is an atom or \bot and (2) no atom is the head of an infinite number of causal rules of T. If a causal theory is definite, its semantics may be restated in terms of a reduction to propositional logic.

From a causal theory, we form a conjunction of propositional formulas, called the completion of the causal theory, as follows: First, for each atom a, we add to the conjunction

$$a \equiv g_1 \vee \cdots \vee g_m$$

where $m \ge 0$ and g_1, \ldots, g_m are the bodies of the causal rules in which a appears as the head. Second, for each causal rule of the form $\bot \Leftarrow f$, we add to the conjunction

$$\neg f$$

Third, we add to the conjunction

$$\left(\bigvee_{v} c = v\right) \wedge \left(\bigwedge_{v_1, v_2} v_1 = v_2 \vee \neg (c = v_1 \wedge c = v_2)\right)$$

for all constants c, where v, v_1 , and v_2 range over dom(c), so that each constant equals exactly one value.

Translation from C+ to causal theories

We define the length-N translation of a C+ theory into a causal theory, where N is a positive integer. A C+ theory can be viewed as representing a *transition system*, or a directed graph whose nodes represent states, and whose links represent actions or sets of concurrently executed actions. There is a one-to-one correspondence between the models of the length-N translation of a C+ theory and the paths of length N through the transition system represented by the theory.

We define a set of *timepoints* $\{0, 1, 2, ..., N\}$. The set of constants in the causal theory is the set of all pairs t:c, where t is a timepoint, and c is a constant in the C+ theory. (For simplicity, our discussion ignores the fact that actions do not occur at timepoint N.) The domain associated with each t:c in the causal theory is the domain associated with c in the C+ theory. The *translation* of a C+ formula f at timepoint t, written t:f, is a causal theory formula obtained by substituting t:c for every constant c in f.

If f is a fluent, $v \in dom(f)$, and t is a timepoint, then t : f = v represents that f has the value v at t.

If a is a Boolean action and t is a timepoint, then t: a represents that a occurs at t.

In order to expose the meanings of the C+ expressions already mentioned, we specify here the translation of each expression separately. The translation may be defined more simply in terms of just the two causal laws **caused** f **if** g **after** h and **caused** f **if** g.

• A C+ expression representing the effects of actions

is translated into a set of causal rules

$$t+1: f \Leftarrow (t:a) \land (t:c)$$

for each $t \in \{0, 1, 2, \dots, N-1\}$.

A C+ expression of the form

inertial f

is translated into a set of causal rules

$$t+1: f = v \Leftarrow (t+1: f = v) \land (t: f = v)$$

for each $v \in dom(f)$ and $t \in \{0, 1, 2, ..., N - 1\}$.

• We also add causal rules stating that the initial values of simple fluents are arbitrary. For each simple fluent f and $v \in dom(f)$ in the C+ theory, we add

$$0: f = v \Leftarrow 0: f = v \tag{16.7}$$

For a statically determined fluent, (16.7) is not added. The value of a statically determined fluent at a timepoint t is strictly determined by the values of other fluents and actions at t. Statically determined fluent constants can be used for default reasoning.

A C+ precondition

nonexecutable a if c

is translated into a set of causal rules

$$\perp \Leftarrow (t:a) \land (t:c)$$

for each $t \in \{0, 1, 2, ..., N\}$

• A C+ expression representing a triggered action

caused a if c

is translated into a set of causal rules

$$t:a \Leftarrow t:c$$

for each $t \in \{0, 1, 2, ..., N\}$.

A C+ expression of the form

exogenous a

is translated into a set of causal rules

$$t: a = v \Leftarrow t: a = v$$

for each $v \in dom(a)$ and $t \in \{0, 1, 2, ..., N\}$.

A C+ state constraint

constraint c

is translated into a set of causal rules

$$\perp \Leftarrow \neg t : c$$

for each
$$t \in \{0, 1, 2, ..., N\}$$
.

• A C+ expression representing an indirect effect

caused
$$f$$
 if g

is translated into a set of causal rules

$$t: f \Leftarrow t: g$$

for each $t \in \{0, 1, 2, ..., N\}$.

Discussion

 $\mathcal{C}+$ supports many of the same features as the event calculus. Like the event calculus, it supports the commonsense law of inertia, concurrent events with cumulative and canceling effects, context-sensitive effects, indirect effects, nondeterministic effects (via **may cause**), preconditions, state constraints, and triggered events. Unlike the event calculus, $\mathcal{C}+$ does not support continuous change or continuous time.

16.4 THE FLUENT CALCULUS

The fluent calculus was developed by Michael Thielscher, Steffen Hölldobler, and Josef Schneeberger. The fluent calculus adds the notion of states to the notions of actions, fluents, and situations of the situation calculus.

16.4.1 **STATES**

A state represents a set of fluents and is defined inductively as follows:

- Ø is a state.
- If f is a fluent, then f is a state.
- If z_1 and z_2 are states, then $z_1 \circ z_2$ is a state.
- Nothing else is a state.

The function \circ is associative and commutative. The expression Holds(f, z) represents that fluent f is true in state z and is defined as follows:

$$Holds(f, z) \stackrel{\text{def}}{\equiv} \exists z' (z = f \circ z')$$

Situations and states are related as follows. The function State(s) represents the state associated with situation s. The expression Holds(f, s) represents that fluent f is true in situation s and is defined as:

$$Holds(f, s) \stackrel{\mathsf{def}}{=} Holds(f, State(s))$$

As in the situation calculus, Do(a, s) represents the situation that results from performing action a in situation s and the initial situation is called S_0 .

16.4.2 PLUS AND MINUS MACROS

The macros + (plus sign) and - (minus sign) are used to specify the addition and removal of fluents from states:

$$z_1 - \varnothing = z_2 \stackrel{\text{def}}{=} z_2 = z_1$$

$$z_1 - f = z_2 \stackrel{\text{def}}{=} (z_2 = z_1 \lor z_2 \circ f = z_1) \land \neg Holds(f, z_2)$$

$$z_1 - (f_1 \circ f_2 \circ \dots \circ f_n) = z_2 \stackrel{\text{def}}{=} \exists z (z_1 - f_1 = z \land z - (f_2 \circ \dots \circ f_n) = z_2)$$

$$z_2 = (z_1 - \vartheta^-) + \vartheta^+ \stackrel{\text{def}}{=} \exists z (z_1 - \vartheta^- = z \land z_2 = z \circ \vartheta^+)$$

The states ϑ^- and ϑ^+ represent sets of fluents.

16.4.3 STATE UPDATE AXIOMS

The effects of each action a are represented using state update axioms for a, which are of the form:

$$Poss(a, s) \wedge \Delta(s) \supset State(Do(a, s)) = (State(s) - \vartheta^{-}) + \vartheta^{+}$$

where Poss(a, s) represents that a is possible in situation s, $\Delta(s)$ is a formula containing s, the state ϑ^- represents the set of fluents terminated by a under the conditions $\Delta(s)$, and the state ϑ^+ represents the set of fluents initiated by a under the conditions $\Delta(s)$. Notice that for a given action a, if we wish to be able to determine the effects of a in all cases for which Poss(a, s) is true, then the conditions $\Delta(s)$ of the state update axioms for a must exhaust all those cases. For example, the following state update axiom for the action WakeUp(p) states that, if a person wakes up, then the person will no longer be asleep and the person will be awake:

$$State(Do(WakeUp(p), s)) = (State(s) - Asleep(p)) + Awake(p)$$

16.4.4 NONDETERMINISTIC EFFECTS

The effect of flipping a coin is represented using the following state update axiom:

$$State(Do(Flip, s)) = State(s) + Heads \lor State(Do(Flip, s)) = State(s) - Heads$$

16.4.5 CONCURRENT ACTIONS

The fluent calculus deals with concurrent actions with cumulative or canceling effects by introducing concurrent actions. A *concurrent action* represents a set of actions and is defined inductively as follows:

- The empty action ϵ is a concurrent action.
- If a is an action, then a is a concurrent action.
- If c_1 and c_2 are concurrent actions, then $c_1 \circ c_2$ is a concurrent action.
- Nothing else is a concurrent action.

The function \circ on concurrent actions is associative and commutative. The expression $HoldsIn(c_1, c_2)$ represents that c_1 is contained in c_2 , and is defined as follows:

$$HoldsIn(c_1, c_2) \stackrel{\text{def}}{\equiv} \exists c' (c_2 = c_1 \circ c')$$

The effects of concurrent actions are then specified using state update axioms. For example, the following state update axioms represent that in order for a door to open, it must be pushed at the same time that its latch is turned.

$$Poss(Turn \circ c, s) \land \neg HoldsIn(Push, c) \supset State(Do(Turn \circ c, s)) = State(Do(c, s))$$

$$Poss(Push \circ c, s) \land \neg HoldsIn(Turn, c) \supset State(Do(Push \circ c, s)) = State(Do(c, s))$$

$$Poss(Turn \circ Push \circ c, s) \supset$$

 $State(Do(Turn \circ Push \circ c, s)) = State(Do(c, s)) + Open$

This is represented in the event calculus as follows:

$$Happens(Turn, t) \Rightarrow Initiates(Push, Open, t)$$

(The representation of cumulative and canceling effects in the event calculus is discussed in Section 8.2.)

16.4.6 DISCUSSION

Like the event calculus, the fluent calculus supports the commonsense law of inertia, concurrent events with cumulative and canceling effects, context-sensitive effects, indirect effects, nondeterministic effects, and preconditions. Methods have also been proposed for handling continuous change and triggered events in the fluent calculus. The treatment of indirect effects in the fluent calculus is described in the Bibliographic notes of Chapter 6.

16.5 DISCUSSION AND SUMMARY

Many of the best features of logics for commonsense reasoning have been incorporated into the classical logic event calculus. Yet the event calculus retains a certain simplicity compared to other logics. Figure 16.1 outlines the relationships between the logics and indicates some of the origins of features of the event calculus.

The situation calculus came first and has had a major influence on all the logics. The notion of fluents, use of frame axioms, use of reification, and distinction between primitive and derived fluents are all from the situation calculus. The treatment of concurrent events with cumulative or canceling effects was first perfected in the situation calculus and then integrated into the event calculus.

The classical logic event calculus derives from the original logic programming version of the event calculus, which introduced events, event occurrences, and fluents

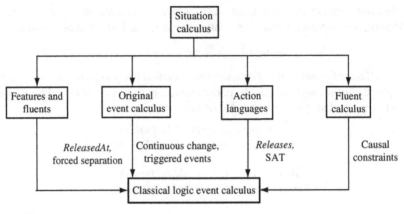

FIGURE 16.1

Logics for commonsense reasoning.

that are initiated and terminated. The treatment of continuous change and triggered events in the classical logic event calculus derives from work performed in the original event calculus.

The features and fluents framework has had several influences on the classical logic event calculus. The *ReleasedAt* predicate of the classical logic event calculus derives from the occlusion construct of features and fluents. The technique of forced separation, in which event calculus axioms are outside the scope of any circumscription, derives from the filtered preferential entailment or filtering of features and fluents.

Several features of the classical logic event calculus derive from action languages. The *Releases* predicate of the event calculus is taken from action languages. The use of SAT solvers to solve event calculus reasoning problems was inspired by the use of SAT solvers in action languages.

Work on the instantaneous propagation of interacting indirect effects was first performed in the fluent calculus. This work led to the introduction of causal constraints into the classical logic event calculus.

Logics for commonsense reasoning can model time as branching or linear and as discrete or continuous. Table 16.2 shows which logics use which models of time.

Table 16.2 Models of Time Used by Logics

	Branching Time	Linear Time
Discrete time Continuous time	Situation calculus Fluent calculus Branching discrete event calculus	TAL C+ Discrete event calculus Event calculus

BIBLIOGRAPHIC NOTES

The situation calculus

The version of the situation calculus we describe is that of Reiter (2001). Based on previous proposals (F. Lin & Reiter, 1994; Pinto, 1998b; Reiter, 1993), Pirri and Reiter (1999, p. 328) and Reiter (2001, p. 50) provide the following four foundational axioms for the situation calculus:

$$do(a_1, s_1) = do(a_2, s_2) \supset a_1 = a_2 \land s_1 = s_2$$
(16.8)

$$(\forall P).P(S_0) \land (\forall a, s)[P(s) \supset P(do(a, s))] \supset (\forall s)P(s) \tag{16.9}$$

$$\neg (s \sqsubset S_0) \tag{16.10}$$

$$s \sqsubset do(a, s') \equiv s = s' \lor s \sqsubset s' \tag{16.11}$$

Axiom (D.36) is a formula of second-order logic, an induction axiom, which allows us to prove general properties of situations and limits the set of situations to the smallest set S such that (1) $S_0 \in S$ and (2) $s \in S$ and a is an action implies $do(a, s) \in S$ (Reiter, 1993). Axiom (D.38) defines the ordering relation \square on situations.

Axioms (D.35) and (D.37) restrict the graph of situations to a tree; that is, these axioms identify a situation with the sequence of actions that led to it. The original situation calculus of McCarthy and Hayes (1969) does not contain this restriction. They define a situation as "the complete state of the universe at an instant of time" (p. 477). Shanahan (1997b, p. 43) calls (D.35) and (D.37) the axioms of arboreality. He provides the following alternative, called the situation-state axiom, which identifies a situation with the fluents that are true in it:

$$s1 = s2 \leftrightarrow \forall f [Holds(f, s1) \leftrightarrow Holds(f, s2)]$$

Thielscher (1999b) takes a third approach: He identifies a situation with a sequence of actions and adds a separate notion of state. He introduces a function *State* that maps a situation to a state, as discussed in Section 16.4.

The equivalence of versions of the situation calculus and the event calculus was proved by Kowalski and Sadri (1997), based on their previous work (Kowalski & Sadri, 1994). Gelfond, Lifschitz, and Rabinov (1991) discuss some of the apparent limitations of the situation calculus and outline ways of overcoming them. In order to deal with indirect effects in the situation calculus, they may be represented explicitly as effect axioms (F. Lin & Reiter, 1994, sec. 5; Reiter, 2001, pp. 401-402). Other methods are discussed in the Bibliographic notes of Chapter 6.

Continuous change

Gelfond, Lifschitz, and Rabinov (1991, pp. 170-171) sketch a method for handling continuous change in the situation calculus. They introduce a function *Time* that maps situations to real numbers. Situations have the cardinality of the real numbers. Changing quantities are represented using fluents. Building on previous work (Pinto & Reiter, 1993), Pinto (1994, chap. 6) presents a way of representing continuous change and triggered events in the situation calculus. He argues (pp. 3, 67) against the

290

approach of Gelfond et al. involving a continuum of situations. Instead, he proposes to represent episodes of continuous change within single situations. He introduces the function start(s), which represents the start time of a situation s, and end(s, a), which represents the end time of a situation s if action a is performed in s (p. 29), where a time is a non-negative real number.

Pinto and Reiter (1993) use a predicate start(s,t), which represents that t is the start time of s. Instead of representing continuous change using fluents, Pinto (1994) introduces the notion of a continuous parameter (p. 68). He then uses holds(p = f, s) to represent that in situation s, the value of parameter p is given by function of time f. Thus, starting at time start(s), the value of p at time t equals f(t). Actions initiate and terminate episodes of continuous change. An effect axiom of the form

$$Poss(a, s) \supset holds(p \doteq f, do(a, s))$$

represents that, if a is performed in s, it initiates an episode of continuous change within the situation do(a, s) in which p is described by f.

Actual situations and events

Pinto and Reiter (1993) and Pinto (1994, sec. 4.2) add actual situations and actual events to the situation calculus. The predicate actual(s) represents that s is an actual situation. The initial situation is actual. Every actual situation has at most one successor situation that is actual. The predecessor situation of an actual situation is actual. The predicate actual(s) represents that action a actually occurs in situation a and is defined by (p. 29):

$$occurs(a, s) \equiv actual(do(a, s))$$

Thus, actions occur along a single time line, as in the event calculus. If occurs(a, s), then a occurs at time start(do(a, s)). That is, an action a performed in situation s is considered to occur at the start time of the successor situation do(a, s).

Natural actions

Pinto (1994, p. 68) introduces the notion of a *natural action*, or action that is not performed by an agent but rather occurs as a result of physical laws, such as a falling ball hitting the floor. The predicate $\Pi_t(a, s, t)$ represents that natural action a is possible at time t in situation s. A natural action a is possible in a situation s—that is, Poss(a, s)—if and only if a is possible at end(s, a) in s and no other action is possible at a time greater than pstart(s) and less than or equal to pend(s, a) in s. Only one natural action is possible in each situation (p. 75). Thus, a sequence of possible natural actions uses linear time rather than branching time (p. 85). If a natural action a is possible in a situation s and a non-natural action does not occur before end(s, a), then a must occur in s (p. 75). For example, the natural action s fall occurs in situation s, which gives rise to successor situation s. This action initiates an episode of continuous change within s in which the height of the falling object is given by an equation of free-fall motion. A natural action s

 S_2 , which gives rise to successor situation S_3 . This is reminiscent of the operation of *Trajectory* in the event calculus.

Reiter (1996) presents some variations on Pinto's proposal. The last argument of every action predicate symbol is a time, which is a real number. The function time(a) represents the time of the action a. The predicate $\Pi_t(a, s, t)$ is dispensed with because the time of a is embedded in a and whether a natural action is possible at a time is represented directly using Poss.

Narrative time line

R. Miller and Shanahan (1994) introduce a narrative time line consisting of the non-negative real numbers into the situation calculus. The predicate Happens(a, t) represents that action a actually occurs at time t. The function State(t) represents the actual situation at time t. If an action a occurs at time t_1 , $State(t_1) = s_1$, and no other actions occur between t_1 and $t_2 > t_1$, then $State(t_2) = do(a, s_1)$. Thus, times greater than the time of occurrence of an action correspond to the successor situation given that action. All times before the first action occurs correspond to the initial situation S_0 .

Continuous change and triggered events

Using the approach of R. Miller and Shanahan (1994), and building on work by Baker (1991), R. Miller (1996) proposes a way of representing continuous change and triggered events in the situation calculus. He introduces valuations and continuously varying parameters. A *valuation* is a function from a parameter to a real number. The predicate Triggers(v, s, a) represents that action a is triggered given valuation v and situation s. For example, we may represent that, if a sink is filling, then the water will overflow when its height reaches a certain level:

$$Triggers(v, s, a) \leftrightarrow v(Height) = H \land Holds(Filling, s) \land a = Overflow$$

An action occurs if and only if it is performed or it is triggered.

Release from inertia

A proposal for permanently releasing a fluent from the commonsense law of inertia in the situation calculus is provided by Lifschitz (1990b, p. 370). He introduces the predicate Frame(f), which represents that fluent f is always subject to the law; $\neg Frame(f)$ represents that f is always released from the law.

Concurrent events

Ways of dealing with concurrent events in the situation calculus are discussed in the Bibliographic notes of Chapter 8.

Nondeterminism

F. Lin (1996) treats nondeterminism in the situation calculus. Mateus, Pacheco, and Pinto (2002) present a probabilistic version of the situation calculus. See also the Bibliographic notes of Chapter 9.

Knowledge machine

The Knowledge Machine (KM) system (P. Clark & Porter, 2004) contains a situation mechanism (P. Clark & Porter, 2000) that implements a version of the situation calculus. KM allows us to specify whether each fluent should or should not be subject to the commonsense law of inertia. A fluent subject to this law persists from a situation to a successor situation, provided that it is consistent for it to persist. The effects of actions are represented in KM using preconditions, add lists, and delete lists, along the lines of STRIPS (Fikes & Nilsson, 1971). The KM situation mechanism performs temporal projection. It does not perform abduction or postdiction, and it does not support nondeterminism, continuous change, or actions with duration.

The features and fluents framework

The features and fluents framework was introduced by Sandewall (1989a, 1989b, 1991, 1994). The framework has many facets. Sandewall (1994) formalizes a semantics for worlds inhabited by agents, called inhabited dynamical systems (IDS). He defines the syntax and semantics of several varieties of a logic called DFL. This logic is used to define *chronicles*, which specify a set of objects, the effects of events, event occurrences, and observed states. (Chronicles are similar to event calculus domain descriptions, discussed in Section 2.7.)

Assessment of logics

Sandewall presents the following systematic methodology for assessing logics for reasoning about action and change (p. 65). First, we formally define a set of chronicle classes. For example, Sandewall defines a chronicle class Ksp - IAd. Chronicles of this class involve accurate knowledge (K), complete knowledge of the initial state (s), pure prediction (p), context-free inertia and integer time (I), alternative effects of events (A), and deterministic change (d). Benchmark commonsense reasoning problems in Ksp - IAd include the Yale shooting scenario (Hanks & McDermott, 1987, pp. 387-390), the Stockholm delivery scenario (Sandewall, 1994, pp. 31-33), and the ferryboat connection scenario (Sandewall, 1994, pp. 154-155).

Second, for each chronicle class, we formally define the set of intended models for any chronicle of the class. Specifically, we define a model set function *Mod* from chronicles to sets of intended IDS models (p. 182), and a coercion function Ci from sets of IDS models to sets of DFL models (p. 185).

Third, we define *entailment methods*, or functions from chronicles to sets of DFL models (p. 195). Sandewall defines a number of such methods, including prototypical global minimization, original chronological minimization (OCM), prototypical chronological minimization (PCM), chronological minimization of occlusion and change (CMOC), chronological assignment and minimization of occlusion and change (CAMOC), global minimization of occlusion with nochange premises (GMON), and PMON premises (PMON, the basis of TAL).

Finally, we prove that one or more entailment methods are correctly applicable (p. 201) to one or more chronicle classes. An entailment method is *correctly applicable* to a chronicle class if and only if, for every chronicle c of the class, the

set of intended DFL models Ci(Mod(c)) equals the set of DFL models produced by applying the entailment method to c.

Sandewall focuses on the K-IA set of chronicle classes (pp. 159-168). He assesses the applicability of 12 entailment methods relative to the classes (pp. 201-211, 228-230, 244-252). The CAMOC and PMON entailment methods are found to be correctly applicable to K-IA. Sandewall (1996) assesses methods for dealing with indirect effects of events. Brandano (2001) makes some progress on assessing the event calculus using Sandewall's methodology.

Temporal action logics

Doherty and Łukaszewicz (1994) and Doherty (1994) recast features and fluents in first-order logic. TAL was previously called PMON; the most complete description of TAL (PMON) is provided by Doherty (1996) and a later treatment of TAL is provided by Doherty, Gustafsson, Karlsson, and Kvarnström (1998). Our description is a composite of Doherty (1996) and Doherty, Gustafsson, Karlsson, and Kvarnström (1998). Indirect effects may be represented in TAL using domain constraints or using the causal constraints introduced by Gustafsson and Doherty (1996). Karlsson, Gustafsson, and Doherty (1998) treat delayed effects of events in TAL. Karlsson and Gustafsson (1997) present TAL-C, an extension of TAL that supports concurrent events with cumulative and canceling effects. Kvarnström (2001) presents the VITAL program, a tool for performing commonsense reasoning using TAL. VITAL works by using "constraint propagation to find all possible models for a given narrative" (p. 41). TAL is used by the TALplanner planning system (Kvarnström, 2005; Kvarnström & Doherty, 2000b).

Action languages

Pednault (1989) introduced ADL, an action description language with a syntax similar to that of STRIPS (Fikes & Nilsson, 1971). Gelfond and Lifschitz (1993) introduced action language A, Kartha and Lifschitz (1994) introduced AR_0 , Baral and Gelfond (1997) introduced A_C , Gelfond and Lifschitz (1998) introduced B, and Kakas and Miller (1997a, 1997b) introduced action language E. R. Miller and Shanahan (2002) describe a mapping between \mathcal{E} and the classical logic event calculus. Vladimir Lifschitz and Erik Sandewall have debated the merits of action languages versus classical logic (Lifschitz, 1997a, 1997b; Sandewall, 1997). E. Giunchiglia and Lifschitz (1998) introduced action language C, based on the language of causal theories of McCain and Turner (1997). E. Giunchiglia, Lee, Lifschitz, McCain, and Turner (2004) introduced action language C+. Geffner (1990) introduced the distinction between what is true and what has a cause. E. Giunchiglia, Lee, Lifschitz, McCain, and Turner (2004, pp. 88, 89, 98) show that a causal theory in which all constants are Boolean can be translated into a theory of Reiter's (1980b) default logic. The causal calculator (CCALC) (E. Giunchiglia, Lee, Lifschitz, McCain, & Turner, 2004; McCain, 1997) uses satisfiability to solve reasoning problems expressed in the CCALC language, which is similar to C+. Lee, Lifschitz, and Yang (2013) introduced BC.

The fluent calculus

The fluent calculus was introduced and developed by Hölldobler and Schneeberger (1990), Hölldobler and Thielscher (1995), Bornscheuer and Thielscher (1996), and Thielscher (1995, 1996, 1997, 1999b). Thielscher (1999b, 2000) treats nondeterministic effects in the fluent calculus. The state update axiom for flipping a coin is based on Thielscher (1999b, p. 290). Thielscher (2000) discusses concurrent events in the fluent calculus. The state update axioms for opening a door are from Thielscher (1999c). The door latch scenario is due to Allen (1991). Thielscher (1995, 1996, 1999b, 2000) discusses indirect effects in the fluent calculus. Thielscher (1999a, 2000) treats continuous change in the fluent calculus.

Inferential frame problem

Thielscher (1999b) discusses how fluent calculus state update axioms solve the inferential frame problem of the situation calculus. The problem is to reduce the computational cost of determining the truth values of fluents in the successor situation Do(a, s) that results from performing action a in situation s. In the situation calculus, we must apply the successor state axiom for each fluent of interest. In the fluent calculus, we may reason about the truth values of fluents in the successor situation simply by applying a single-state update axiom for the action a. This reasoning is possible even in the presence of partial information about the truth values of fluents. Thielscher (2005b) presents the FLUX program for performing commonsense reasoning using the fluent calculus.

Cyc

A system that uses logic for commonsense reasoning is Cyc (Lenat, 1995; Lenat & Guha, 1990). Under development since 1983, Cyc is a large commonsense knowledge base, inference engine, and natural language processing system. Knowledge is represented in Cyc using CycL, whose syntax is based on the syntax of first-order logic and Lisp (Cycorp, 2014c, chap. 2). The inference engine (Cycorp, 2014a, 2014b, 2014d) uses the resolution principle (Robinson, 1965) and heuristic search (Pearl, 1984). It uses negation as failure to implement the unique names assumption (McCarthy, 1986; Reiter, 1980a) and minimization of abnormalities for default reasoning (McCarthy, 1984a). Cyc also has specialized inference procedures to deal with reflexivity, symmetry, transitivity, dates, lists, numbers, sets, strings, and inheritance (Cycorp, 2014c, chap. 11).

Cyc has two basic ways of representing time-varying properties. In the first representation, an element e of the collection SomethingExisting is divided into elements of SomethingExisting that represent e at different slices of time (Cycorp, 2002). These objects are called *temporal subabstractions* of e (Lenat & Guha, 1990, pp. 211-213). For example, the following formula represents that Nathan2007 is a temporal subabstraction of the person Nathan:

(subAbstrac Nathan Nathan2007)

Temporal subabstractions can be divided into further temporal subabstractions:

```
(subAbstrac Nathan2007 Nathan20070304)
(subAbstrac Nathan2007 Nathan20070305)
(subAbstrac Nathan2007 Nathan20070306)
```

Assertions are made about temporal subabstractions. The following formula states that Nathan was a scientist on March 4, 2007:

```
(occupationOf Nathan20070304 scientist)
```

The second representation uses the Temporal Thing collection, which has Time Interval, TimePoint, and Something Existing as specializations (Cycorp, 2002). A formula of the form (holds In t f) represents that formula f is true at all moments of temporal thing t. For example, the previous assertion can be represented as follows:

```
(holdsIn
(DayFn 4 (MonthFn March (YearFn 2007)))
(occupationOf Nathan scientist))
```

Assertions involving temporal subabstractions and those involving holdsIn are related by several axioms (Guha & Lenat, 1990b).

Cyc represents event occurrences using instances of the Event collection, which is a specialization of the Situation-Temporal collection (Cycorp, 2014c, sec. 8.1). Attributes of event instances are represented using various predicates. The time of occurrence of an event may be represented in a variety of ways:

```
\begin{array}{l} ({\tt dateOfEvent}\,e\,d) \\ ({\tt startingDate}\,e\,d) \\ ({\tt endingDate}\,e\,d) \\ ({\tt endingDate}\,e\,d) \\ ({\tt contiguousAfter}\,e_1\,e_2) \\ ({\tt endsAfterEndingOf}\,e_1\,e_2) \\ ({\tt overlapsStart}\,e_1\,e_2) \\ ({\tt startsAfterStartingOf}\,e_1\,e_2) \\ ({\tt temporallyFinishedBy}\,e_1\,e_2) \\ ({\tt temporallyIntersects}\,e_1\,e_2) \\ \vdots \\ \end{array}
```

where e, e_1 , and e_2 are event instances, and d is a date. The expression (subEvents e_1 e_2) represents that event e_2 is a part of event e_1 . The expression (event0ccursAt e l) represents that l is the location of event e. The Action collection is a specialization of the Event collection. The expression (performedBy e a) represents that a is the agent of action e.

The representation of event occurrences in Cyc is based on the proposal of Davidson (1967/2001) to represent event occurrences as objects and to represent the meanings of action sentences using predicates that take those objects as arguments. Under this proposal, the sentence "I flew my spaceship to the Morning Star" (p. 114) is represented as (p. 119)

```
(\exists x)(Flew(I, my spaceship, x)& To(the Morning Star, x))
```

Cyc does not have a standard representation for the preconditions and effects of events but, rather, uses a variety of predicates (Parmar, 2001). Cyc cannot simulate

296

the occurrence of events (Parmar, 2001), although previous versions of Cyc had the following rudimentary mechanism for temporal projection (Guha & Lenat, 1990a, pp. 46 and 47; Guha & Lenat, 1990b). Associated with each formula is an *interval of persistence* that specifies how long the formula is expected to remain true. A frame axiom states that if (1) a formula is proved true at timepoint t_0 without using this frame axiom, (2) the formula's interval of persistence is i, (3) $t_0 < t_1 < t_0 + i$, and (4) the formula is not abnormal with respect to this frame axiom at timepoint t_1 , then the formula is true at t_1 . Guha (1990) describes a way of handling the Yale shooting scenario in Cyc.

OpenCyc (Cycorp, 2002b) includes an implementation of a hierarchical task network planner (Ghallab, Nau, & Traverso, 2004, chap. 11). The planner supports preconditions, context-sensitive effects, and compound events. It does not support concurrent events with cumulative and canceling effects, continuous change, indirect effects, nondeterministic effects, release from the commonsense law of inertia, or triggered events. Cyc is discussed further in Section 19.1.1.

Other formalisms

Other logical formalisms for commonsense reasoning include McDermott's (1982) temporal logic, motivated action theory (Stein & Morgenstern, 1994), and \mathcal{LAP}_{\sim} (Castilho, Gasquet, & Herzig, 1999), which is based on dynamic logic (Harel, 1984; Pratt, 1976).

EXERCISES

- **16.1** (Research Problem) Write a program that translates event calculus domain descriptions into the input language of CCALC (E. Giunchiglia, Lee, Lifschitz, McCain, & Turner, 2004; McCain, 1997).
- **16.2** (Research Problem) Write a program that translates event calculus domain descriptions into the input language of VITAL (Kvarnström, 2001).

Nonlogical Methods for Commonsense Reasoning

This book uses the event calculus for commonsense reasoning, which is based on predicate logic. Why logic? What about other approaches to commonsense reasoning? In this chapter, we review several other important approaches to commonsense reasoning: qualitative reasoning, analogical processing, probabilistic reasoning, and the society of mind. We assess their strengths and weaknesses and discuss their relationships to the event calculus.

17.1 QUALITATIVE REASONING

Qualitative reasoning is concerned with explaining and predicting the behavior of physical systems. The task is to take as input a description of a physical system and an initial state and produce as output the possible behaviors of the system given the initial state. Some examples of physical systems modeled using this approach include a water pressure regulator, two tanks connected by a pipe, heat flow between two objects, boiling water in a pot, and a block connected to a spring. Several schemes for qualitative reasoning have been developed. In this section, we describe qualitative simulation (QSIM) which is representative.

17.1.1 QSIM

In QSIM, a physical system is described by a qualitative differential equation (QDE), which corresponds to an infinite set of ordinary differential equations. A QDE consists of a set of variables and a set of constraints on those variables. Possible constraints are x + y = z, xy = z, x = -y, $y = \frac{dx}{dt}$, $M^+(x, y)$, and $M^-(x, y)$, where x, y, and z are variables. The constraint $M^+(x, y)$ means that x is monotonically increasing with y, and $M^-(x, y)$ means that x is monotonically decreasing with y. Each variable is associated with landmark values $l_1 < \cdots < l_n$. A qualitative value of a variable consists of a landmark value l_i or interval (l_i, l_{i+1}) and a direction, which is increasing, steady, or decreasing. A state assigns a qualitative value to each variable.

Given a QDE and an initial state, the QSIM algorithm produces a *behavior tree*, or tree of states. The QSIM algorithm operates by repeatedly taking a state and generating successor states that satisfy the constraints. QSIM also allows a physical system to be described by multiple QDEs and transitions between the QDEs. For

example, a bouncing ball can be modeled using one QDE for motion through the air and another QDE for bouncing.

Qualitative reasoning can be used for commonsense reasoning about physical systems. But general commonsense reasoning requires reasoning about both continuous and discrete change. Qualitative reasoning is largely concerned with continuous change and is not concerned with discrete events and associated commonsense phenomena such as context-sensitive, indirect, and nondeterministic effects of events. The commonsense law of inertia is not represented (or even needed) in qualitative reasoning because the behaviors of the system are determined by the QDE.

It has been shown how qualitative descriptions of systems can be expressed in first-order logic and how system behaviors can be predicted using deduction. Some work has been performed on incorporating QSIM into the event calculus; see Exercises 17.2 and 17.3.

17.2 ANALOGICAL PROCESSING

A person who encounters a novel situation may not already have the commonsense knowledge necessary to reason about that situation. In such a case, the person might be able to reason about the novel situation by analogy to a familiar situation. For example, consider the case of sand being poured into a kitchen sink with the stopper in place. By analogy to the case of water, we can predict that the sand level will increase and that the sand will eventually spill onto the floor.

Some researchers have proposed that analogical processing can be used for commonsense reasoning and, moreover, that commonsense reasoning often involves analogical processing. In this section, we examine a particularly well-developed mechanism for analogical processing, the structure-mapping engine.

17.2.1 STRUCTURE-MAPPING ENGINE

The structure-mapping engine (SME) takes as input a base domain and a target domain and produces as output zero or more global mappings from the base domain to the target domain. A domain consists of a set of labeled ordered trees, or rooted trees such that (1) each node has an associated label and (2) the children of each node are ordered. Leaf nodes represent objects such as Beaker and Coffee. Nonleaf nodes represent functions such as Pressure and Temperature, attributes such as Liquid and Red, and relations such as Causes, Implies, and GreaterThan. The children of a nonleaf node represent the arguments of the function, attribute, or relation. A function node has one or more children, an attribute node has one child, and a relation node has two or more children.

Global mappings

A global mapping consists of (1) a one-to-one mapping M from nodes of the base domain to nodes of the target domain satisfying certain constraints, (2) candidate

inferences in the target domain, and (3) a score. The mapping M satisfies the following constraints:

- *M* maps object nodes to object nodes, function nodes to function nodes, attribute nodes to attribute nodes, and relation nodes to relation nodes.
- If *M* maps a base function or attribute node *b* to a target node, then *b* is not a root node. That is, function and attribute nodes are not mapped unless they are part of a larger structure.
- If M maps a base attribute or relation node b to a target node t, then b and t have
 the same label. Note that this constraint does not apply to object and function
 nodes.
- If M maps a function, attribute, or relation node b to a target node t, then M maps each child of b to a child of t.

Generating candidate inferences

In order to generate candidate inferences in the target domain, we start by forming the set C_b of all trees B of the base domain such that M maps any nonleaf node of B to a target node. That is, we form the set C_b of base domain trees having one or more mapped function, attribute, or relation nodes. These are the base domain trees involved in the analogy. Then, the target domain candidate inferences C_t consist of the base domain trees C_b with their object and function nodes relabeled using the terminology of the target domain. Specifically, for each object and function node b of C_b , we do the following: If b maps b to a target node b, then we relabel b with the label of b; otherwise, if b does not map b to any target node, then we relabel b with a new unique label.

The *score* is an estimate of the quality of the mapping M. A higher score is assigned to the extent that larger trees are mapped, base nodes are mapped to target nodes with the same label, and children of a base node are mapped to children of a target node in the right order.

Example

SME handles over 40 examples, one of which involves an analogy between water flow and heat flow. The base domain, water flow, is represented as follows:

Causes(GreaterThan(Pressure(Beaker), Pressure(Vial))
Flow(Beaker, Vial, Water, Pipe))
GreaterThan(Diameter(Beaker), Diameter(Vial))
Liquid(Water)
FlatTop(Water)

The target domain, heat flow, is represented as follows:

GreaterThan(Temperature(Coffee), Temperature(IceCube))
Flow(Coffee, IceCube, Heat, Bar)
Liquid(Coffee)
FlatTop(Coffee)

Given these base and target domains, SME produces three global mappings. The global mapping with the highest score (=5.99) includes the following mapping M:

> Beaker → Coffee Vial → IceCube Water → Heat $Pipe \mapsto Bar$ $Pressure(Beaker) \mapsto Temperature(Coffee)$ $Pressure(Vial) \mapsto Temperature(IceCube)$ $GreaterThan(Pressure(Beaker), Pressure(Vial)) \mapsto$

GreaterThan(Temperature(Coffee), Temperature(IceCube)) $Flow(Beaker, Vial, Water, Pipe) \mapsto$

Flow(Coffee, IceCube, Heat, Bar)

This global mapping includes the following candidate inference:

Causes(GreaterThan(Temperature(Coffee), Temperature(IceCube)), Flow(Coffee, IceCube, Heat, Bar))

Discussion

SME is not intended to be a complete method for commonsense reasoning. Although SME can find potential analogies and generate candidate inferences, it does not address the crucial problem of how to evaluate and possibly repair the inferences. It is assumed that other commonsense knowledge and commonsense reasoning mechanisms will be used to perform these tasks. An interesting line of research would be to integrate SME and the event calculus; see Exercise 17.4.

17.3 PROBABILISTIC REASONING

Some researchers have proposed the use of probability theory for commonsense reasoning. By using probability measures or other measures of uncertainty, we can quantify not only our uncertainty about a particular scenario but also our uncertainty about our knowledge of how the world works. We can quantify the degree to which we are certain about our formalization of a domain, such as how sure we are that a given action has given preconditions or effects. Using probabilistic reasoning, we can quantify our uncertainty about various sorts of commonsense conclusions derived from information that is given.

17.3.1 PROBABILITY AND ACTION

Let us consider how probability theory can be used to reason about a simple action, turning on a faucet. In order to reason about properties over time, we introduce a random variable for each relevant property and timepoint or time interval. We represent the fact that the faucet is running at time 0 as a Boolean random variable R_0 and the fact that the faucet is running at time 1 as a Boolean random variable R_1 .

In order to reason about events that occur in time, we introduce a random variable for each relevant event and timepoint or time interval. We represent the event of turning on the faucet at time 0 as a Boolean random variable T_0 .

Then we represent our knowledge of this domain. We do not specify a full joint distribution. Instead, we assume that for every time t and random variable v at time t:

- v is directly influenced by zero or more random variables V at time t-1.
- the random variable v and the random variables at all times less than or equal to
 t − 2 are conditionally independent given the random variables V.

In order to represent the effects of events, we specify the conditional probabilities of properties at time t given the properties and events at time t - 1. We consider the influence of R_0 and T_0 on R_1 . We specify that, if a faucet that is not running is turned on, it will be running with high probability:

$$P(R_1|\neg R_0, T_0) = 0.98 \tag{17.1}$$

(Here we deal only with the times 0 and 1. In a formulation with n times, we would write $P(R_t|\neg R_{t-1}, T_{t-1}) = 0.98$ for each $t \in \{1, 2, ..., n-1\}$.) If a faucet that is already running is turned on, it will be running with high probability:

$$P(R_1|R_0, T_0) = 0.99$$

Furthermore, we represent what happens when events do not occur. That is, we represent instances of the commonsense law of inertia. A faucet that is not running and is not turned on will not suddenly start running:

$$P(R_1|\neg R_0, \neg T_0) = 0.01 \tag{17.2}$$

A faucet that is running and is not turned on will continue to run:

$$P(R_1|R_0, \neg T_0) = 0.95$$

We can then perform temporal projection, abduction, and postdiction. For temporal projection, we may ask whether the faucet is running at time 1 given that it is not running at time 0 and is turned on at time 0. We see immediately from (17.1) that this is very likely.

For abduction, we may ask whether the faucet is turned on at time 0 given that it is not running at time 0 and is running at time 1. We must determine

$$P(T_0|\neg R_0,R_1)$$

From the definition of conditional probability, we have

$$P(T_0|\neg R_0, R_1) = \frac{P(R_1, \neg R_0, T_0)}{P(\neg R_0, R_1)}$$
(17.3)

Using the chain rule, we have

$$P(R_1, \neg R_0, T_0) = P(R_1|\neg R_0, T_0)P(\neg R_0|T_0)P(T_0)$$

From this and (17.1), we have

$$P(R_1, \neg R_0, T_0) = 0.98 \cdot P(\neg R_0 | T_0) P(T_0)$$
(17.4)

At this point we cannot proceed without further information. We first make an assumption regarding the independence of R_0 and T_0 :

$$P(R_0|T_0) = P(R_0) (17.5)$$

(In a more detailed model, we might not wish to make such an assumption. For example, an agent may be unlikely to turn on a faucet that is already running.) We must also specify prior probabilities for the faucet running at time 0 and the faucet being turned on at time 0:

$$P(R_0) = 0.5 (17.6)$$

$$P(T_0) = 0.1 (17.7)$$

From (17.4), (17.5), (17.6), and (17.7), we have

$$P(R_1, \neg R_0, T_0) = 0.98 \cdot 0.5 \cdot 0.1 = 0.049$$
 (17.8)

From the product rule, we have

$$P(\neg R_0, R_1) = P(R_1 | \neg R_0) P(\neg R_0)$$
(17.9)

By expanding the possible cases for T_0 , we have

$$P(R_1|\neg R_0) = P(R_1|\neg R_0, \neg T_0)P(\neg T_0|\neg R_0) + P(R_1|\neg R_0, T_0)P(T_0|\neg R_0)$$

From this, (17.2), (17.5), (17.7), and (17.1), we have

$$P(R_1|\neg R_0) = 0.01 \cdot 0.9 + 0.98 \cdot 0.1 = 0.107$$

From this, (17.9) and (17.6), we have

$$P(\neg R_0, R_1) = 0.107 \cdot 0.5 = 0.0535$$

From this, (17.3), and (17.8), we have

$$P(T_0|\neg R_0, R_1) = \frac{0.049}{0.0535} = 0.9159$$

Thus, it is likely that the faucet is turned on at time 0.

For postdiction, we may calculate the probability that the faucet is not running at time 0 given that it is turned on at time 0 and is running at time 1:

$$P(\neg R_0|T_0,R_1) = 0.4975$$

This calculation is performed in a fashion similar to the calculation for abduction.

This is a simple example involving just three random variables. It is apparent that using these techniques to perform commonsense reasoning on larger examples will be cumbersome.

17.3.2 BAYESIAN NETWORKS

A more convenient way of performing these calculations is to use Bayesian networks. A *Bayesian network* is a directed acyclic graph in which each node represents a random variable, and a directed link from node n_1 to node n_2 represents that n_1 directly influences n_2 . Each node n_1 is associated with a conditional probability table

that specifies the conditional probability for every value of n given every combination of values of every node that directly influences n or the prior probability of n if no nodes directly influence n.

Still, even using Bayesian networks, we must introduce a node for every property and event at every timepoint or time interval and specify the conditional probability table for every node. There are many probabilities to specify. In our faucet example, we had to specify probabilities for each instance of the commonsense law of inertia, because probability theory does not supply us with any general mechanism for representing this law.

17.4 SOCIETY OF MIND

Marvin Minsky developed the *society of mind* theory of human cognition, which proposes that the flexibility of human intelligence arises from the use of many different techniques, not simply one technique such as analogy, connectionism, logic, or probability. This theory starts with the following notions.

The mind consists of a vast collection of interacting simple processes, called agents, critics, or resources.

The agents use many different types of representations and many different methods of reasoning in order to exploit the advantages of each representation and reasoning method and to avoid their disadvantages.

Representations in different agents are connected to one another. These connections facilitate the simultaneous use of representations and switching between representations whenever difficulties are encountered with one of the representations.

The agents are concerned with various realms; examples include the aesthetic, physical, possessional, psychological, spatial, temporal, and topological realms. One or more agents may be concerned with any given realm.

Some agents are concerned with *reflection* or monitoring and influencing other agents. For example, reflective agents can notice other agents getting into loops and help them break out of those loops.

Minsky proposes various constructs that can be used to build up a society of mind.

A *frame* consists of slots and default values for the slots used to capture expectations about a frequently encountered class of situations. When a frame is applied to a situation, the default values may be used as is or they may be modified to match the situation.

A *frame-array* is a collection of frames that share one or more slots. The frames represent a class of situations from different perspectives, or they represent related classes of situations. The shared slots enable switching from one frame to another to facilitate shifting perspectives or situations.

A *transframe* is a type of frame that has slots for an origin, action, and destination and is used to represent the effects of actions. Transframes may be chained together by matching the destination of each transframe with the origin of the next transframe to predict the results of a sequence of actions.

A *K-line* is a memory structure that records what agents were used to solve a problem. The K-line is used to activate those agents when solving similar problems in the future.

A *paranome* is a mapping among alternative representations of a situation used by two or more agents. When one of the agents updates its representation, the paranome allows the other agents to update their representations appropriately.

Other constructs proposed by Minsky include censors, level-bands, micronemes, picture-frames, polynemes, pronomes, proto-specialists, and suppressors.

There are two ways of viewing the relationship between the society of mind and the event calculus:

- The event calculus could be viewed as one effective method for performing commonsense reasoning within a larger society of mind.
- Constructs from the society of mind could themselves be integrated into the event calculus—see Exercise 17.6.

In this section, we review three commonsense reasoning systems inspired by the society of mind: ThoughtTreasure, Polyscheme, and EM-ONE. All three systems involve collections of interacting agents. ThoughtTreasure and Polyscheme use multiple representation and reasoning methods. Polyscheme and EM-ONE use reflection.

17.4.1 THOUGHTTREASURE

The ThoughtTreasure commonsense reasoning and story understanding architecture/ system uses multiple representation and reasoning mechanisms, including finite automata, grids, path planning, logical formulas, theorem proving, and scripts. Reasoning is performed by a collection of agents that communicate over a shared data structure.

Commonsense domains

ThoughtTreasure represents and reasons about objects, time-varying properties, events, time, space, and goals. Time is represented using timepoints and time intervals. If t_1 and t_2 are timepoints, e is an event, and p is a property, then

$$@t_1:t_2|e$$

represents that e occurs from t_1 to t_2 , and

$$@t_1:t_2|p$$

represents that p is true from t_1 to t_2 . Space is represented by a network of *grids* (occupancy arrays). A physical object occupies one or more cells of a grid over a given time interval.

Reasoning types

ThoughtTreasure performs two types of reasoning: simulation and understanding. In simulation, the system takes as input a state of the world in which a character has

an active goal and produces as output the events and time-varying properties that follow from that state of the world. The system handles several benchmark problems involving simulation: moving a penny from one jar to another, traveling from Paris to New York, and watching television. In the television scenario, the system is told that a character Jim is located in a particular apartment grid containing various objects such as appliances and furniture. The system then produces a sequence of events in which Jim walks from his initial location in the grid to the television and turns it on.

In understanding, the system takes natural language text as input and parses the text into properties and events. Given these observations, the system produces as output zero or more models that tally with those observations. Each model consists of the input properties and events augmented with properties and events filled in by the system. Several benchmark problems involving understanding are handled: going to sleep, stepping outside a grocery store, and taking a shower. In the shower scenario, the system is told that Jim woke up and poured shampoo on his hair. The system produces a model in which Jim gets out of bed, walks to the shower, turns it on, picks up the shampoo, and pours it on his hair.

Discussion

ThoughtTreasure has no general mechanism to deal with the commonsense law of inertia. The burden falls on each agent to update representations appropriately. For example, if Jim is known to be at one location starting at time 0:

```
@0:na|[at-grid Jim AptGrid <gridsubspace 20 78>]
```

and the grid-walk agent simulates Jim walking to another location from time 2 to time 3:

```
@2:3|[grid-walk AptGrid 20 78 16 82]
```

then that agent updates the representations to reflect that Jim was at the first location from time 0 to time 3 and at the second location starting at time 3:

```
@0:3|[at-grid Jim AptGrid <gridsubspace 20 78>]
@3:inf|[at-grid Jim AptGrid <gridsubspace 16 82>]
```

Thus, knowledge of the effects of events is represented procedurally within agents. Similarly, knowledge about context-sensitive effects and preconditions of actions are represented procedurally within agents. For example, the agent that simulates a television represents that the television will not go on unless it is plugged in.

ThoughtTreasure does not have a general mechanism to deal with the indirect effects of events. Just as for the commonsense law of inertia, individual agents are responsible for performing the appropriate updates. For example, when the gridwalk agent simulates a character walking from one grid location to another, the agent moves not only the character but also all objects held by the character and all objects inside those objects.

ThoughtTreasure does not address continuous change, nondeterministic effects, or release from the commonsense law of inertia. Although ThoughtTreasure is able

to represent concurrent events, it does not address concurrent events with cumulative and canceling effects.

ThoughtTreasure is effective at simulation, but less effective at understanding. Both simulation and understanding are performed by agents. Although it is relatively easy to write agents for simulation, it is more difficult to write agents for understanding. Agents must be written to coordinate with one another in order to agree on an interpretation of the input.

ThoughtTreasure does not have a general mechanism for dealing with the problem of agent coordination. This problem is taken up in Polyscheme.

Agent coordination is not an issue in the event calculus because it does not use agents. Instead of representing knowledge procedurally within agents, the approach in the event calculus is to represent knowledge declaratively as logical formulas and to use off-the-shelf procedures for reasoning. The declarative approach allows us to use the best available search techniques, as integrated into off-the-shelf solvers. A procedural knowledge representation requires the procedures to deal with knowledge representation as well as search—a tall order.

17.4.2 POLYSCHEME

The Polyscheme cognitive architecture/system uses multiple representation and reasoning techniques, including scripts, transframes, hash tables, constraint graph propagation, rules, and single-layer neural networks. Reasoning is performed by a collection of communicating specialists: perception, attribute, physics, causal, temporal, identity hypothesis, identity, place, path, and reflective specialists. Each specialist uses its own techniques for representing and reasoning about the effects of events, context-sensitive effects of events, event preconditions, triggered events, and other commonsense phenomena.

Commonsense domains

Polyscheme represents and reasons about objects, object identity, time-varying properties, events, time, and space. Although specialists may use their own representations internally, specialists communicate using logical propositions. A proposition consists of a predicate, arguments, time interval, and world. Worlds, which are similar to the situations of the situation calculus, are used for hypothetical reasoning. Space is represented as a three-dimensional grid. Thus, for example, the proposition

```
at(x, p1-1-1, t1, R)
```

says that object x is at grid location p1-1-1 over time interval t1 in world R.

Reasoning types

The Polyscheme system performs both temporal projection and explanation. It handles the following temporal projection benchmark problems involving gravity:

A block starts to fall in back of a screen. Infer that the block must have fallen and hit the floor.

If you are then told that another block was in back of the screen, infer that the first block must have fallen and hit the second block.

Polyscheme handles the following explanation benchmark problems involving object identity:

A dry mouse walks behind a screen where there is known to be a puddle of water, and then a dry mouse emerges. Infer that the first and second mouse are not the same mouse.

A red ball rolls behind a screen, and then a red ball rolls out. Infer that the first and second ball are the same ball.

A ball rolls behind one screen, and then a ball rolls out of another screen that is separated from the first screen. Infer that the first and second ball are not the same ball.

A wood ball and a salt ball roll behind a screen. Then a ball rolls out, moves into a puddle of water, and does not melt. Infer that the ball that rolled out was the wooden ball.

(We show how the event calculus can be used to solve similar problems of object identity in Section 10.3.)

Focus mechanism

The coordination of the activities of specialists is accomplished in Polyscheme via a focus mechanism. At any moment, all specialists focus on a single proposition. A focus consists of a proposition and a focus mode, which is PERCEIVE, ASSERT, DENY, WONDER, FIND, ELABORATE, or IMAGINE. An attraction consists of a focus and charge. Polyscheme conducts a search for a solution to a commonsense reasoning problem using the following algorithm:

- 1. The specialists issue attractions.
- 2. The current focus is set to be the focus of the most highly charged attraction.
- **3.** The specialists concentrate on the current focus:
 - (a) Each specialist informs the reflective specialist whether it considers the truth value of the proposition to be true, false, or unknown.
 - (b) The reflective specialist determines whether the specialists agree or disagree.
 - (c) If the specialists disagree, then the reflective specialist issues attractions designed to move the specialists toward agreement. For example, the reflective specialist may issue an attraction to try to perceive the truth value of the proposition in the external environment or to imagine the consequences of the proposition being false.
- **4.** Go to step 1.

By setting the charges appropriately, various algorithms such as depth-first search, breadth-first search, stochastic simulation, and truth maintenance can be implemented or approximated. In contrast to systems that switch representation techniques only

when a difficulty is encountered, Polyscheme is able to make use of all representation techniques implemented by specialists at every step of the search.

Discussion

Polyscheme does not have a general way of dealing with the commonsense law of inertia. The burden is placed on the individual specialists to make the appropriate inferences. Polyscheme does not address continuous change, indirect effects, or nondeterministic effects. Polyscheme can represent concurrent events, but does not deal with concurrent events with cumulative and canceling effects.

Polyscheme improves on ThoughtTreasure by providing a focus mechanism to coordinate the activities of the specialists. An important problem in need of further research is how to set the attractions and charges in such a way as to avoid classical problems of search such as combinatorial explosion of alternatives, getting stuck at local maxima, and oscillation.

17.4.3 EM-ONE

The EM-ONE architecture/system for reflective commonsense thinking has its roots in the multilayer cognitive architectures of Marvin Minsky and Aaron Sloman. EM-ONE consists of a set of critics and a library of narratives or cases. Critics observe, diagnose, and repair problems both in the external world and in the internal mental world of the system. *Narratives* are representations of stories in a simulated world that serve as a source of commonsense knowledge for use by the critics.

Critics

A critic consists of a condition pattern, a narrative pattern, and an action. When a critic is invoked, its patterns are evaluated. If the condition pattern matches the current conditions and the narrative pattern matches a narrative, then the critic is engaged and its action is performed. Four types of critics are implemented in EM-ONE: reactive critics, deliberative critics, reflective critics, and metacritics.

Reactive critics propose and execute actions in the world in response to world conditions. For instance, one reactive critic in EM-ONE executes an immediate turn toward a person who has just called for help.

Deliberative critics reason about a situation before taking action. The critics conduct a heuristic search through a space of hypothetical worlds. Some deliberative critics in EM-ONE evaluate hypothetical worlds, and others generate new ones. Examples of critics that evaluate worlds are those that look for unachieved goals or unexpected consequences of actions. Examples of critics that generate new worlds are those that consult narratives in order to infer the effects of an event, infer a plan that a character might select in order to achieve a goal, or infer that a character might execute the next step of a plan.

Reflective critics reason about and modify the mental processes of the system. They consult *traces* of mental activity, which are records of the critics that are invoked or engaged, and the facts that critics assert or retract. One reflective critic

in EM-ONE is engaged when an action fails to produce the intended effect and the examination of the trace reveals that a narrative containing a precondition for that action was not consulted. The reflective critic then modifies the critic that failed to consult the narrative so that it will take this narrative into account in the future.

Metacritics are used to manage reactive, deliberative, and reflective critics. They implement Minsky's *critic-selector model*, in which a critic (1) notices a particular type of problem and (2) initiates an appropriate way of thinking about that type of problem.

Metacritics play a key role in the top-level control loop of EM-ONE, which is as follows:

- 1. Observations of the world are accepted.
- 2. Metacritics are invoked.
- 3. Some metacritics become engaged, which may lead to the invocation of reactive, deliberative, and reflective critics.
- **4.** Some invoked critics become engaged, and those critics may invoke other critics, which may become engaged, and so on.
- 5. Actions are executed in the world.
- 6. Go to step 1.

Commonsense domains

EM-ONE represents entities such as physical objects, characters, events, properties, and relations. Its narrative library represents knowledge about the commonsense domains of space, time, and the mental and social worlds. For example, one narrative says that the character named Pink attached a stick to a board, which caused the stick to be attached to the board. Another narrative says that Pink wants the stick to be visible, which implies that Pink believes that Pink wants the stick to be visible. Facts are represented in EM-ONE using a frame-based knowledge representation language.

Reasoning types

The deliberative critics of EM-ONE perform forms of temporal projection and planning. The reflective critics perform reflective reasoning. EM-ONE handles a benchmark problem that engages all types of critics. The benchmark problem involves two characters named Green and Pink in a simulated world. The world contains a table with only two legs. The problem is for Green to attach a third leg to the table. Green, as modeled by EM-ONE, attempts to attach a third leg to the table, but this fails because there is not enough space between the table and the ground. Green then asks Pink for help. Pink, also modeled by EM-ONE, mistakenly believes that Green wants to disassemble the table and starts removing a leg from the table. Green realizes that Pink has misunderstood its goal and informs Pink of its goal. Pink lifts up the table for Green, and Green successfully attaches the third leg to the table.

Discussion

EM-ONE represents and reasons about event effects and preconditions. It does not have general mechanisms for dealing with the commonsense law of inertia or indirect effects. EM-ONE performs a novel type of reasoning, reflection, which is not addressed in this book.

BIBLIOGRAPHIC NOTES

Qualitative reasoning

Qualitative reasoning was introduced by de Kleer (1975). de Kleer and Brown (1984) introduce component models for qualitative reasoning, Forbus (1984) introduces qualitative process (QP) theory, and Kuipers (1986) introduces QSIM. Kuipers (1994) discusses QSIM in detail. A collection of readings on qualitative reasoning is provided by Weld and de Kleer (1990). Sandewall (1989a) shows how to reason about physical systems using differential equations and logic. E. Davis (1990, pp. 312-320) formalizes in first-order logic a component model of a scale, and E. Davis (1992) formalizes in first-order logic a QP theory of heating a can of water.

Analogical processing

Gentner (1983) introduces the structure-mapping theory of analogy. Falkenhainer, Forbus, and Gentner (1989) describe the structure-mapping engine (SME). Holyoak and Thagard (1989) describe another algorithm, the analogical constraint mapping engine, that incorporates constraints for semantic similarity and pragmatic centrality, in addition to structural constraints similar to those used by SME. Gentner, Holyoak, and Kokinov (2001) discuss structure-mapping and a number of other proposals for analogical thinking. We give a condensed formalization of SME that does not capture all the details of the implementation. For example, SME allows different mapping constraints to be defined by the user. The example analogy between water flow and heat flow is from Falkenhainer, Forbus, and Gentner (1989). Labeled ordered trees are discussed by Aho, Hopcroft, and Ullman (1983).

Case-based reasoning

Case-based reasoning (CBR) (Kolodner, 1993) is similar to analogical processing. In CBR, a problem (target) is solved using the following steps: (1) a *case*, or past experience (base), similar to the current problem is retrieved; (2) the case is used to propose a solution; (3) the solution is evaluated; and (4) problems with the solution are repaired. Because CBR relies on a single case or a small number of cases (Kolodner, 1993, p. 14), CBR may have difficulty with problems whose solution requires the combination of many cases. The evaluation and repair steps are difficult challenges for CBR systems (Leake, 1996, pp. 11-12, 22-27), which is similar to the situation in analogical processing. Evaluation and repair are usually performed through rule-based reasoning, although some have proposed that CBR itself can be used for evaluation and repair (Kolodner, 1993, pp. 7, 461, and 462; Leake, 1995; Sycara,

1988). It is recognized that CBR is best used in advisory systems where human users perform evaluation and repair (Leake, 1996, pp. 11, 23).

What is missing from both analogical processing and CBR is a way of performing reasoning from first principles, or reasoning based on general knowledge, as described in this book. Along these lines, Forbus and Gentner (1997) and Forbus (2001, pp. 36-40) have proposed that human commonsense reasoning can be explained as a tight combination of analogical processing and first-principles qualitative reasoning. They propose that reasoning from first principles is gradually learned through generalization of many situations understood through analogical processing. They suggest that reasoning from first principles extends, rather than replaces, analogical processing.

The combination of analogical processing and qualitative reasoning has been implemented in the PHINEAS program (Falkenhainer, 1988). This program takes observations of a new domain as input and learns about the domain using SME to find an analogy to a previously known domain, using the analogy to generate hypotheses about the new domain, using qualitative reasoning to generate predictions, comparing those predictions against the observations, and revising its hypotheses if necessary.

Probabilistic reasoning

Books on probabilistic reasoning and reasoning about uncertainty are by Pearl (1988b) and J. Y. Halpern (2003). Russell and Norvig (2009) review probability theory, reasoning about uncertainty, probabilistic reasoning, and probabilistic reasoning over time. Hanks and Madigan (2005) review methods for probabilistic temporal reasoning. Our treatment of turning on a faucet is based on the treatments of the Yale shooting scenario of Pearl (1988a; 1988b, pp. 509-516) and Hanks and Madigan (2005).

Bayesian networks are discussed by Pearl (1988b), J. Y. Halpern (2003), and Russell and Norvig (2009). Kushmerick, Hanks, and Weld (1995) present a framework for probabilistic planning. Baral, Tran, and Tuan (2002) introduce PAL, a probabilistic action language based on action language \mathcal{A} . Tran and Baral (2004a) show how to represent the probabilistic causal models of Pearl (2000) in PAL.

Society of mind

Minsky developed the society of mind approach (Minsky & Papert, 1972, pp. 92-99; Minsky, 1974, 1977, 1980, 1982, 1986, 1991a, 1994, 2006), which uses communicating agents and societies of agents, diverse formalisms and representations, and reflection. Singh (2004) reviews the society of mind approach and work inspired by it. McCarthy et al. (2002), Minsky, Singh, and Sloman (2004), Singh and Minsky (2004), and Singh, Minsky, and Eslick (2004) propose society-of-mind-like architectures for human-level intelligence. ThoughtTreasure is described by Mueller (1998). Polyscheme is described by Cassimatis (2002), Cassimatis, Trafton, Bugajska, and Schultz (2004), and Cassimatis (2006). Search is discussed by Pearl (1984), Russell and Norvig (2009), and Hoos and Stützle (2005). EM-ONE is described by Singh (2005). An architecture for reflective thinking is described by Morgan (2013). Sloman

(2001) discusses the H-Cogaff three-layer architecture, and Minsky (2006) discusses the Model Six six-level architecture. Minsky (2006) discusses the critic-selector model. Other systems based on the society of mind approach include those of Riecken (1994), Singh (1998), and Hearn (2001).

Connectionism and neural networks

There are several other approaches related to commonsense reasoning. In the connectionist or neural network approach (McClelland, Rumelhart, & PDP Research Group, 1986; Rumelhart, McClelland, & PDP Research Group, 1986), a problem is represented as the activation levels of nodes in a network of nodes and directional links, and a solution is produced by the propagation of activation in the network. Representations in neural networks may be local or distributed. In a *local representation*, a concept is represented by a single node. In a *distributed representation*, a concept is represented as the pattern of activation across many nodes.

Sun (1994) presents a connectionist architecture for commonsense reasoning. The architecture consists of two connected neural networks: a network that uses local representations for rule application and a second network that uses distributed representations for similarity matching. The architecture is able to handle examples that combine rule-based and similarity-based reasoning. For example, the system is able to reason that geese may quack because ducks quack and geese and ducks are similar (pp. 23, 82-84). The architecture does not deal with events and time (Sun, 1996, p. 198).

Narayanan (1997) presents a model of representation and reasoning inspired by high-level motor control. He introduces a procedural representation called x-schemas, similar to Petri nets (Reisig, 1985), that can be used to represent and reason about motion words such as *walk*, *run*, *stumble*, and *fall*. Narayanan (1997, sec. 4.1) shows how x-schemas can be encoded as connectionist networks. He provides (sec. 3.7.1) an algorithm for temporal projection using x-schemas and suggests (sec. 3.8.2) that postdiction could be performed using the results of Portinale (1994).

EXERCISES

- 17.1 Write event calculus formulas to formalize the definition of a table used by the EM-ONE system (Singh, 2005): a table consists of "four sticks attached to a board" (p. 36).
- 17.2 (Research Problem) Continue the work of R. Miller and Shanahan (1996) on incorporating QSIM (Kuipers, 1994) into the event calculus.
- 17.3 (Research Problem) Jordan (2004) describes a system that tutors students in introductory physics. The system presents a problem to the student, who enters an answer and an explanation. The system uses abductive reasoning to build a proof for the student's answer and explanation. The proof exposes problems in the student's understanding, such as the *impetus misconception*,

- or the notion that a force must be continually applied to an object in order for it to move. Investigate how the event calculus, extended using the techniques of R. Miller and Shanahan (1996), could be used to diagnose common misconceptions of introductory physics students.
- 17.4 (Research Problem) Investigate ways of integrating SME (Falkenhainer, Forbus, & Gentner, 1989) and the event calculus. One idea is as follows: Given event calculus axioms describing a base domain and a target domain, SME could be used to find mappings from the base domain axioms to the target domain axioms and suggest additional target domain axioms.
- **17.5** (Research Problem) Develop techniques for probabilistic reasoning further with respect to various commonsense phenomena and benchmark problems.
- **17.6** (Research Problem) Investigate how constructs from the society of mind (Minsky, 1986), such as frame-arrays and paranomes, could be integrated into the event calculus.

- The state of the second of the great second interview of the second of t
- n i likus godi. Aktori je 17. stoletaj ted entjare 1988. gedent (1 tagredje ji) sen sio 1992. 199 Pre ular sa slicitir komunica i useja satrija postakanaga (2 tagredje) ka spojeke slige.
- The Aleks of the Aleks is proven a graphical from the following the analysis of the Aleks of the

Commonsense Reasoning Using Unstructured Information

Structured information is the information that computers can easily understand and reason with, such as algebraic expressions, logical formulas, frames, and database tables. Unstructured information is the information that is not represented in such a form and is difficult for computers to understand. Examples of unstructured information include natural language text, audio, images, and video. Because unstructured information is so easy for humans to create, it is abundant—much of the world's data is unstructured. Given that there is so much unstructured information available, the question arises of how we might be able to use it for automated commonsense reasoning.

In this chapter, we discuss the use of unstructured information, specifically natural language text, for commonsense reasoning. First, we describe attempts to use natural language as a programming language. We then review several restricted versions of English for reasoning, including reasoning in the event calculus. Then, we discuss automated reasoning directly using natural language. Next, we describe the Watson system for natural language question answering and the WatsonPaths system built on top of Watson, which use unstructured information as a source of knowledge for reasoning. Finally, we compare the various natural language reasoning systems and methods.

18.1 NATURAL LANGUAGE AS A PROGRAMMING LANGUAGE

In the 1960s, Jean Sammet, Mark Halpern, and others proposed to use natural language as a programming language. In the 1970s, several researchers started to build automatic programming systems that take a natural language specification of a problem as input and produce a computer program as output. We discuss two representative systems, SAFE and OWL.

18.1.1 **SAFE**

In the mid-1970s, Robert Balzer, Neil Goldman, and David Wile developed SAFE, a system that handles three texts taken from specification manuals. SAFE was a research system developed to demonstrate the feasibility of automatic programming.

The goal was to take a specification and automatically turn it into an executable computer program, eliminating the need for manual computer programming.

SAFE operates as follows:

```
Input: bracketed natural language specification → resolve imprecisions in input → Output: executable computer program
```

An example of an imprecision is provided by the following bracketed input sentence:

```
((THE MESSAGE) (IS DISTRIBUTED) TO (EACH ((ASSIGNED)) OFFICE))
```

Because offices can be assigned to both messages and keys, (EACH ((ASSIGNED)) OFFICE) is ambiguous. But earlier in the specification, messages were assigned for distribution, and distribution requires a message and an office. SAFE infers that a message is distributed to every office assigned to the message, and it produces the following code as output:

```
(FOR ALL (offices assigned TO message FOR ANYTHING)
  (distribute-process#2 message office))
```

18.1.2 OWL

Also in the mid-1970s, Peter Szolovits, Lowell B. Hawkinson, and William A. Martin developed a knowledge representation language based on English called OWL (which is different from the later web ontology language OWL). In OWL, "check sensitivity due to thyroid function" is represented as

```
(CHECK (SENSITIVITY (DUE (TO THYROID-FUNCTION))))
```

The SAFE program previously described is used to convert a specification into a computer program, which can then be run. In contrast, OWL directly executes specifications stored in the knowledge base. The OWL interpreter operates as follows:

```
Input: bracketed English description of desired procedure \longrightarrow match input to method in knowledge base \longrightarrow recursively invoke interpreter for unsatisfied preconditions \longrightarrow execute method and create execution trace
```

OWL also generates English explanations of methods in the knowledge base and execution traces.

18.2 REASONING WITH RESTRICTED NATURAL LANGUAGE

The attempts to use natural language for programming ran into difficulty because natural language is very complex. One response to the complexity of natural language

is to simplify or restrict it. Several researchers have introduced restricted versions of English and procedures for reasoning using them. We review some representative examples.

18.2.1 MONTAGOVIAN SYNTAX

In the late 1980s, David A. McAllester and Robert Givan introduced Montagovian syntax, inspired by Richard Montague's logical approach to natural language syntax and semantics. Montagovian syntax is both a restricted form of English and an alternative syntax for first-order logic.

Here are some sample expressions using this syntax:

```
(every police-officer (owns (some car)))
(every (child-of (some bird)) (friend-of (every bird-watcher)))
```

The meaning of these expressions is similar to their meaning in English. The symbols police-officer, car, bird, and bird-watcher are *class symbols*, which denote sets. The symbols owns, child-of, and friend-of are *binary relation symbols*, which denote binary relations.

Montagovian syntax is defined as follows:

Definition 18.1. A *class expression* is defined inductively as follows:

- A constant is a class expression.
- A class symbol is a class expression.
- A variable is a class expression.
- If ρ is a binary relation symbol and σ is a class expression, then $(\rho \text{ (some } \sigma))$ and $(\rho \text{ (every } \sigma))$ are class expressions.
- If ν is a variable and α is a formula, then $(\lambda \nu \alpha)$ is a class expression.
- Nothing else is a class expression.

Definition 18.2. An *atomic formula* is (some σ_1 σ_2) or (every σ_1 σ_2), where σ_1 and σ_2 are class expressions.

Definition 18.3. A *formula* is defined inductively as follows:

- An atomic formula is a formula.
- If α is a formula, then $\neg \alpha$ is a formula.
- If α and β are formulas, then $\alpha \wedge \beta$ and $\alpha \vee \beta$ are formulas.
- Nothing else is a formula.

Definition 18.4. A *literal* is an atomic formula or the negation of an atomic formula. Constants and variables denote singleton sets. We use several abbreviations:

- If τ is a constant or variable and σ is a class expression, then the atomic formulas (some $\tau \sigma$) and (every $\tau \sigma$) are equivalent, and we use ($\tau \sigma$) as an abbreviation for either atomic formula.
- If τ is a constant or variable and ρ is a binary relation, then the class expressions $(\rho \text{ (some } \tau))$ and $(\rho \text{ (every } \tau))$ are equivalent, and we use $(\rho \tau)$ as an abbreviation for either class expression.

• If σ is a class expression, then we use $\exists \sigma$ as an abbreviation for the atomic formula (some σ σ).

An example of the use of λ is $(\lambda \times (\forall \lambda))$, which denotes the set of all things bought by Yhazi. This is an abbreviation of $(\lambda \times (\forall \lambda))$.

We reason with Montagovian syntax using inference rules such as the following:

$$\frac{(\text{every } \sigma_1 \ \sigma_2) \quad (\text{every } \sigma_2 \ \sigma_3)}{(\text{every } \sigma_1 \ \sigma_3)}$$
(18.1)

$$\frac{(\text{every } \sigma_1 \ \sigma_3) \quad (\text{every } \sigma_1 \ \sigma_4) \quad \exists \sigma_1}{(\text{some } \sigma_3 \ \sigma_4)}$$
(18.2)

Thus, from

(every vermouth wine)
(every wine alcoholic-beverage)
(every vermouth before-dinner-drink)
∃vermouth

we can infer

(some alcoholic-beverage before-dinner-drink)

Namely, from (every vermouth wine), (every wine alcoholic-beverage), and (18.1), we infer (every vermouth alcoholic-beverage). From this, (every vermouth before-dinner-drink), \exists vermouth, and (18.2), we infer (some alcoholic-beverage before-dinner-drink).

McAllester and Givan define a polynomial time decision procedure for the satisfiability of a set Σ of literals, provided that Σ satisfies the following properties:

- the literals in Σ do not contain λ
- for every class expression σ that occurs in Σ , we can determine from Σ whether σ denotes the empty set

The decision procedure makes use of inference rules (18.1), (18.2), and others.

The use of Montagovian syntax for reasoning can be summarized as follows:

Input: Montagovian syntax literals satisfying properties \longrightarrow polynomial time decision procedure for satisfiability \longrightarrow Output: yes or no

18.2.2 ATTEMPTO CONTROLLED ENGLISH

In the late 1990s, Norbert E. Fuchs, Uta Schwertel, and Rolf Schwitter introduced Attempto Controlled English (ACE), a restricted form of English designed to support

the creation of precise technical specifications. The vocabulary of ACE consists of predefined function words and user-defined words. An ACE sentence is of the form

```
subject + verb + complements + adjuncts
```

Complex sentences can be created using modifiers, coordination of sentences and phrases, subordinate clauses, prepositional phrases, quantification, and negation.

Examples of ACE sentences are the following:

```
The new user enters an initial PIN.
The user enters a digit or a letter.
A customer of the bank gives the card to the teller.
John does not enter a valid code in the morning.
```

Using the Prolog language, ACE parses an input text and converts it into a representation called a discourse representation structure. ACE uses a set of interpretation principles to resolve ambiguity. For example, a pronoun always refers to the most recent noun phrase that agrees in number and gender, and a prepositional phrase always modifies the verb. If the user is not satisfied with the interpretation of a sentence, the user must rephrase it.

The Attempto reasoner can be used to prove that one ACE text logically follows from another ACE text. The reasoner operates by converting discourse representation structures into first-order logic and then invoking a first-order logic theorem prover. The operation of ACE can be summarized as follows:

```
Input: ACE texts \longrightarrow parse and translate into discourse representation structures \longrightarrow convert to first-order logic \longrightarrow invoke first-order theorem prover \longrightarrow Output: summary of results
```

18.2.3 PENG LIGHT AND THE EVENT CALCULUS

Rolf Schwitter describes how the PENG Light controlled natural language, which is similar to ACE, can be used to specify and reason with event calculus domain descriptions. The PENG Light language is designed so that it can be translated unambiguously into formal representation structures.

Here are examples of effect axioms expressed in PENG Light:

```
If an agent walks into a room then the agent will be in the room. If a device is running and an agent turns off the device then the device will no longer be running.
```

Here is an example of a narrative and observations expressed in PENG Light:

```
The dishwasher is running.
Mason walks into the kitchen.
Mason turns off the dishwasher.
```

PENG Light is used for event calculus reasoning as follows:

Input: PENG Light event calculus domain description → parse and translate into discourse representation structures → translate into Prolog rules and facts → reason using Prolog

The following Prolog rule is used to infer an event calculus event occurrence from a discourse representation structure event:

```
happens(E, T) :- event(E, Type), theta(E, time, S), timex(S, T).
```

18.3 REASONING DIRECTLY WITH NATURAL LANGUAGE

Most attempts at performing automated reasoning using natural language involve first converting natural language into a formal representation (such as through parsing). Another possibility is to reason directly using natural language without performing this conversion. In 2002, Push Singh introduced a prototype of such a system, called REFORMULATOR. This system applies *reformulation rules* to sets of English sentences to infer new English sentences. An example of a reformulation rule is as follows:

```
If the agent ?V ?NP, then ?NP will be ?AdjP The agent ?V ?NP \rightarrow ?NP is ?AdjP
```

NP is a noun phrase, V is a verb, and AdjP is an adjective phrase. Then, given the sentences

```
If the agent pushes the door, then the door will be open. The agent pushes the door.
```

The system applies the reformulation rule to infer the new sentence

```
The door is open.
```

REFORMULATOR operates as follows:

```
Input: English sentences, reformulation rules \longrightarrow repeatedly apply reformulation rules \longrightarrow Output: inferences
```

So far, we have discussed several systems that work with tightly controlled forms of natural language. SAFE, OWL, ACE, and PENG Light focus on the creation and execution of specifications. Montagovian syntax, ACE, PENG Light, and REFORMULATOR focus on reasoning. Watson differs from all these systems because it works with arbitrary, unrestricted natural language text.

18.4 WATSON

The Watson question answering system, developed by a team at IBM Research led by David Ferrucci, uses a large corpus of natural language text to provide precise answers to input questions. Unlike a search engine, which requires the user to locate the answer to a given question in a document, Watson picks out and returns the exact answer. We discuss Watson and WatsonPaths, which enables reasoning using Watson.

18.4.1 WATSON ARCHITECTURE

Watson is built using the Unstructured Information Management Architecture (UIMA), which allows us to define *pipelines*, each of which consists of a sequence of *components* and possibly other pipelines. Watson consists of many components that work together to process an input question.

Watson's high performance results from the use of multiple components operating over unstructured information and the merging and ranking of the results of these components using machine learning. If one component is unable to handle a particular input correctly, there is often another component that is able to. Components are also able to check the work of other components, which leads to better performance than could be achieved if all the components worked independently. Using multiple components also allows many people to develop the system together. To extend Watson to perform better on a certain class of problem, we can add a component designed to improve the system's performance on that class of problem.

A UIMA component has an initialize method that is invoked once when an instance of the component class is first created and a process method that is invoked when needed to process a new item.

UIMA components take their input from and write their output to a shared data structure called a *common analysis structure* (CAS). A CAS consists of text along with *annotations* of text spans. An annotation consists of a begin index, end index, entity type, covered text, and arbitrary properties and values.

The Watson architecture is a pipeline architecture in which processing proceeds in a single direction from one component to the next. There is also, however, a high degree of fan-out, so that one component may feed its output to a number of components each of which may in turn feed its output to a number of components. Watson is CPU-intensive and data-intensive. UIMA allows Watson to be scaled out across as many machines as necessary to achieve the desired throughput and response time.

A high-level view of the operation of Watson is as follows:

```
Input: question →
analyze question →
search for documents/passages and look up answers →
generate candidates →
search for supporting passages →
```

score passages and answers \longrightarrow merge equivalent answers \longrightarrow calculate final scores for answers \longrightarrow *Output*: answers with scores

18.4.2 QUESTION ANALYSIS

The first step in processing an input question is *question analysis*. This consists of parsing the question, identifying entities and relation instances in the question, resolving coreferences in the question, and identifying key elements of the question. Given the question

```
What disease causes right upper quadrant pain? question analysis identifies several key elements.
```

The question's *lexical answer type* (LAT) is disease. The LAT specifies the desired type of an answer to the question. It is later used by the type coercion components. LATs with modifiers, such as heart condition and skeletal finding, are also identified.

The question's *focus* is What disease. The focus is the part of the question that is to be replaced by the answer. If we replace the focus with the correct answer, then the result should be a true statement.

```
Cholecystitis causes right upper quadrant pain.
```

The focus is later used by context-dependent answer scoring components. The focus is identified by looking for patterns such as a noun phrase starting with an interrogative determiner (what or which). The basic algorithm for detecting the LAT is to use the headword of the focus.

The *question class* is FACTOID: DiseaseGivenFinding. The question class can modify which components are used to process the question and which machine learning models are used.

Watson uses the English Slot Grammar (ESG) parser and other recognizers and transformations to generate a dependency parse tree and predicate argument structure. ESG produces the following output for the example question:

```
.---- ndet what1(1) det
.----- subj(n) disease1(2) noun
o----- top cause1(3,2,203,u) verb
'----- obj(n) right upper quadrant pain(203) noun
| .- adjpre right3(4) qual
| .--- nadj upper1(5,7) adj
| .--- nnoun quadrant1(6) noun
'----- chsl(n) pain1(7,u) noun
```

The top-level node of the dependency parse tree is cause. The subject of cause is what disease, and the object of cause is right upper quadrant pain.

This example was parsed using a *chunk lexicon* for the medical domain based on the Unified Medical Language System (UMLS) (United States National Library of Medicine, 2014). ESG provides an analysis of the structure of the chunk right upper quadrant pain.

Relation extraction identifies the following relation instances in the example question:

```
causes(disease : focus, right upper quadrant pain)
findingOf(right upper quadrant pain, disease : focus)
```

A relation instance consists of a *relation name* such as causes and findingOf and one or more *arguments* such as disease and right upper quadrant pain.

18.4.3 PRIMARY SEARCH

After question analysis, the next step in the Watson pipeline is *primary search*. The goal of this step is to locate content relevant to answering the question. This involves converting a question into search engine queries and issuing these queries to search engines. Searches are performed both to retrieve *documents* and to retrieve *passages* consisting of one or more sentences. Search engines produce ranked lists of documents or passages and associated scores in response to a query.

To increase diversity, Watson uses two search engines: Indri (Lemur Project, 2014) and Lucene (Apache, 2014). Using both Indri and Lucene improves performance over using either search engine alone. Indri's existing passage retrieval capability is used. A two-phase mechanism for passage retrieval is implemented using Lucene: First, documents are retrieved using Lucene. Second, sentences are extracted from the documents and ranked using query-independent features such as sentence length and query-dependent features such as the degree of match between the sentence and the query.

Search queries are constructed from content words and phrases in the question. Words that are arguments of relation instances involving the focus are weighted higher. The following Indri queries are generated for the example question:

```
#combine(disease causes right upper quadrant pain)
#combine[passage20:6](disease causes right upper quadrant pain)
```

These queries retrieve documents and passages containing one or more of the search words; the more words that are found in a retrieved document or passage, the higher its score. The notation passage20:6 specifies that Indri should evaluate dynamically generated passages of length 20 words created every six words. Watson extends the beginning and the end of each retrieved passage to sentence boundaries.

Searches are issued against a corpus of documents for the given application of Watson. For competing on the Jeopardy! television game show, the corpus includes Wikipedia (Wikimedia Foundation, 2014a), dictionaries, literary works, and news stories. For the Watson Medical Engine, the corpus includes medical textbooks, dictionaries, guidelines, and journal articles.

18.4.4 ANSWER LOOKUP

In addition to performing text searches, Watson performs *answer lookup*, which consists of looking up potential answers in structured resources. The structured resources for Jeopardy! include DBpedia (2014) and IMDb (2014). The structured resources for the Watson Medical Engine include UMLS and IBM's Structured Knowledge Base for Medical (SKB).

18.4.5 SKB

SKB provides informativeness scores for signs, symptoms, and laboratory tests relative to diseases. For example, given

```
findingOf(right upper quadrant pain, disease : focus)
```

the SKB answer lookup component retrieves all diseases associated with right upper quadrant pain and the corresponding informativeness scores.

SKB's informativeness scores are based on the *pointwise mutual information* between two medical concepts, which is calculated using the equation

$$pmi(c_1, c_2) = \log_2 \frac{P(c_1, c_2)}{P(c_1)P(c_2)}$$

where $P(c_1, c_2)$ is the probability that c_1 and c_2 co-occur, $P(c_1)$ is the probability of c_1 , and $P(c_2)$ is the probability of c_2 . These probabilities are estimated from a corpus of medical texts.

18.4.6 CANDIDATE GENERATION

Once search and answer lookup have been performed, candidate generation is performed, which consists of generating candidate answers along with their scores to be used by downstream components. Several methods are used to identify likely answer candidates in a document. For documents and passages, entities identified by entity recognizers and hyperlink anchor text are generated as candidates. For documents, the titles of the documents are generated as candidates. Answers produced by answer lookup are also generated as candidates along with scores. For example, candidate generation produces candidates such as the following:

cholecystitis 0.812 (from document) gallstones 0.724 (from passage) cholelithiasis 0.714 (from passage) acute pancreatitis 0.697 (from SKB answer lookup)

18.4.7 SUPPORTING EVIDENCE RETRIEVAL

Once candidate answers have been generated, *supporting evidence retrieval* is performed. For each candidate answer, a new query is constructed from the candidate

answer and the question. Watson uses the Indri search engine for supporting evidence retrieval. For the candidate cholecystitis, an Indri query such as the following is generated:

#combine[passage20:6](cholecystitis disease causes right upper quadrant pain)

For each candidate answer and passage retrieved for the answer, a number of *context-dependent answer scorers* are run. Each such scorer produces a score that measures the degree to which the passage provides evidence that the candidate is the correct answer to the question. Each passage is analyzed similarly to how questions are analyzed. The passage is parsed, entities and relation instances are identified, and coreferences are resolved. The search is run against a corpus, which can be the same as the corpus used in primary search or a different corpus.

Supporting evidence retrieval improves system performance. By adding the candidate answer to the search query, it retrieves relevant passages that might have been missed by primary search. For example, primary search might retrieve the passage

Abdominal pain, nausea, and vomiting are symptoms of cholecystitis.

and generate the candidate <code>cholecystitis</code>. The trouble is that this passage does not match the question well—only the words <code>pain</code> and <code>cholecystitis</code> are contained in the question and candidate—so the passage does not receive a very high score from the answer scorers. But supporting evidence retrieval might return the following passage:

Cholecystitis causes RUQ tenderness.

This passage does match the question well, taking into account that RUQ is an abbreviation for right upper quadrant. This passage receives a high score from the answer scorers with respect to the correct answer cholecystitis.

18.4.8 TERM MATCHING

A *term* is a word or *phrase*, which is a sequence of words. Terms are identified by the ESG parser and other recognizers. Answer scorers depend on *term matchers*, which compute a measure of the degree of match between two terms called the *term match score*. Watson may be configured with different term matchers depending on the application. Different answer scorers may also use different term matchers. Watson contains a variety of term matchers, including the following:

- The *text equality term matcher* returns 1.0 if the term strings are equal ignoring case and 0.0 otherwise.
- The chunk headword term matcher returns 0.64 if the headwords of the chunk terms are equal ignoring case and 0.0 otherwise. Chunks are identified by the ESG parser using a chunk lexicon. The headword of the chunk right upper quadrant pain is pain.

- The *whitespace term matcher* returns 0.1 if any word in one term equals any word in the other term ignoring case and 0.0 otherwise.
- The WordNet synonym term matcher returns 1.0 if the terms are synonyms according to WordNet and 0.0 otherwise.

The scores from multiple term matchers may be combined by taking the maximum or using functions learned with machine learning techniques.

18.4.9 TERM WEIGHTING

Less frequent terms like appendicitis are more informative than frequent terms like the. Therefore, some answer scorers multiply term match scores by the *inverse document frequency* (idf), which is computed from a large corpus using the equation

$$idf(t) = \log_2 \frac{N}{c(t) + 1}$$

where c(t) is the number of documents that contain term t and N is the total number of documents in the large corpus.

The *idf-weighted term match score* of a question term and a passage term is the product of (1) the idf of the question term and (2) the term match score of the question term and the passage term.

18.4.10 ANSWER SCORING

Scorers are broken down into *context-dependent answer scorers* and *context-independent answer scorers*. As previously described, context-dependent answer scorers produce a score for a candidate in the context of a given passage. Context-independent answer scorers do not involve passages. They simply score the degree to which a candidate is the correct answer to the question using other resources such as structured resources.

Context-dependent answer scoring

A context-dependent answer scorer might be fed the following:

Candidate: cholecystitis

Question: What disease causes right upper quadrant pain?

Focus: What disease

Passage: Cholecystitis may cause right upper quadrant pain.

The scorer's job is to produce a score of how well the passage supports the answer to the question. Watson contains a number of context-dependent answer scorers. We discuss four of them: the passage term match scorer, the textual alignment candidate scorer, the skip-bigram scorer, and the logical form answer candidate scorer.

Passage term match scorer

The passage term match scorer computes how well the terms in the question match the terms in the passage without regard to the order of terms. It uses the following algorithm:

- 1. For each question term in the question, compute a *question term score* equal to the maximum of the idf-weighted term match scores between the question term and all the passage terms in the passage.
- 2. Return the sum of the question term scores.

Textual alignment candidate scorer

The textual alignment candidate scorer (TACS) computes how well the question matches the passage, taking into account the order of terms. TACS uses the algorithm of Smith and Waterman (1981), which has been used for nucleotide and protein sequence matching, to find local alignments between the question and the passage. Idf weighting is used, and high credit is given for matching the focus in the question with the candidate answer in the passage.

Syntactic-semantic graph

The next two answer scorers make use of a *syntactic-semantic graph* of the question and the passage. The syntactic portion of the graph for a text consists of a predicate-argument structure representation abstracted from the ESG parse of the text. The semantic portion of the graph for a text consists of the relation instances extracted from the text by relation extraction.

Skip-bigram scorer

A *skip-bigram* is defined to be a pair of terms that are either (1) directly connected to each other in the syntactic-semantic graph or (2) both directly connected to a third common node in the graph. The *skip-bigram scorer* computes how well the skip-bigrams in the question graph match the skip-bigrams in the passage graph. The focus in the question graph is assumed to be an exact match for the candidate answer in the passage graph. Idf weighting is not used in the skip-bigram scorer because it was found to hurt performance.

Logical form answer candidate scorer

The *logical form answer candidate scorer* (LFACS) computes how well the question matches the passage based on how well their syntactic-semantic graphs match, subject to the constraint that the focus in the question graph must correspond to the candidate answer in the passage graph. The LFACS algorithm, which is similar to the structure-mapping algorithm described in Section 17.2, is as follows:

- 1. Align the question graph to the passage graph, to the degree possible.
- 2. For each question term in the question graph, compute a *question term score* equal to the product of (a) the *structural match score* of the question term and (b) the idf-weighted term match score of the question term and the corresponding passage term in the passage graph.
- 3. Return the sum of the question term scores.

The structural match score of a question term is computed as follows:

- For each path from the question term to the focus in the question graph, compute a path score equal to the product of all (a) idf-weighted term match scores and (b) edge match scores between the terms and edges along the path in the question graph and the corresponding terms and edges in the passage graph.
- 2. Return the maximum of the path scores.

Edge match scores are similar to term match scores. If two edges have the same relation name, their edge match score is 1.0.

Context-independent answer scoring

A context-independent answer scorer takes a question and a candidate answer (along with all the associated annotations in the CAS) and returns a score of how well the candidate answer answers the question.

Type coercion

An important set of context-independent answer scorers are the *type coercion* components. These take the question's LAT and candidate answer as input and produce a measure of the degree to which the candidate answer is an instance of the LAT. Type coercion components use structured resources such as WordNet, YAGO (Max Planck Institute for Computer Science, 2014), and UMLS.

18.4.11 FINAL MERGING AND RANKING

After supporting evidence retrieval and answer scoring, final merging and ranking are performed. A final score is computed using machine learning techniques for each candidate answer. The candidate answers are then sorted by decreasing score and produced as output. The details of final merging and ranking are as follows.

Feature merging

Watson components such as candidate generation and answer scorers generate *features*, which consist of a name and a numeric value. At various points in processing, multiple values of a feature need to be combined into a single number. For example, context-dependent answer scorers such as LFACS produce a score for each candidate answer and passage retrieved for that answer. As part of final merging and ranking, these scores are combined into a single LFACS score for each candidate answer. This is done using a *feature merging* process that combines feature values using a particular function such as maximum or sum assigned to each feature name.

The function maximum was found to work best for LFACS feature merging. Therefore, if LFACS produces the following scores for passages retrieved for the candidate answer cholecystitis

Cholecystitis	is associated with RUQ pain.	0.798
Cholecystitis	may cause right upper quadrant pain.	0.821
Abdominal pair	n is a symptom of cholecystitis.	0.677

then the maximum score 0.821 is used as the single LFACS score for the candidate answer cholecystitis.

Standardized features

For every feature produced by the candidate generators and answer scorers, a *standardized* version of that feature is computed for use in machine learning. For each question and every candidate answer, the standardized version of each feature is computed using the equation

$$x_i' = \frac{x_i - \mu_i}{\sigma_i}$$

where μ_i and σ_i are the mean and standard deviation, respectively, of the values of x_i for all the candidate answers to the question.

Logistic regression models

Watson uses machine learning techniques to estimate binary logistic regression models for classifying whether candidate answers are incorrect (0) or correct (1). A score between 0.0 and 1.0 for a candidate answer with feature values x_1, \ldots, x_n is computed using the logistic function

$$score = \frac{1}{1 + e^{-(\beta_0 + \sum_{i=1}^n \beta_i x_i)}}$$
 (18.3)

where β_0 is the *intercept* and β_1, \ldots, β_n are the *feature weights*. Together, β_0 and β_1, \ldots, β_n are the *model*.

A model is *trained* by finding the values of β_0, \ldots, β_n that provide the best fit between the scores computed using (18.3) and the correct scores as given by an *answer key*. A model is *applied* by using (18.3) to compute scores.

To train Watson's models, we must supply representative questions along with correct answer strings or regular expressions for each question. The more questions the better. *Training questions* are used for training, and *test questions* are used for testing trained models.

Machine learning phases

In Watson, models are trained and applied in several *phases*. When Watson is run on training questions, the models are trained and applied in each phase. Once the models are trained and Watson is run on test questions or on new, live questions, the models are only applied in each phase.

- 1. In the *hitlist normalization phase*, for each question, candidate answers whose strings are equal are merged using feature merging, standardized feature values are computed, and the *hitlist normalization model* is (trained and) applied.
- 2. In the *base phase*, the top 100 answers from the hitlist normalization phase are retained, the standardized features are recomputed, and the *base model* is (trained and) applied.

3. In the *answer merging phase*, equivalent answers like gallstones and cholelithiasis are merged using feature merging, the standardized features are recomputed, and the *answer merging model* is (trained and) applied to produce a final score for each candidate answer.

Synonym and inflection dictionaries and pattern-based methods are used to detect equivalent candidate answers. When several candidate answers are detected to be equivalent, the string of the one with the highest score is used as the string of the merged candidate answer.

Watson can also use different models for different question classes.

18.4.12 WATSONPATHS

WatsonPaths is a reasoning system built on top of Watson. Like Watson, it is implemented using UIMA. Consider the following question:

```
What is the treatment for jaundice and right upper quadrant pain aggravated by fatty foods?
```

Answering this question requires two steps: First, we must determine the patient's disease. Second, we must determine the treatment for that disease. WatsonPaths answers this *top-level question* by asking Watson multiple *subquestions*. First, it asks the following subquestions:

```
What disease causes jaundice?
What disease causes right upper quadrant pain aggravated by
fatty foods?
```

Then, given the diseases returned in response to these subquestions, WatsonPaths asks further subquestions:

```
What is the treatment for cholecystitis? What is the treatment for gallstones?
```

WatsonPaths uses the following algorithm:

- 1. Identify important *factors* in the top-level question and add them to the *assertion graph*, which consists of nodes and links. Each node and link has an associated *score*. In our example, WatsonPaths adds nodes with score 1.0 for the factors jaundice and right upper quadrant pain aggravated by fatty foods.
- 2. Use *question asking strategies* to ask Watson subquestions based on nodes in the graph whose score is above a threshold.
- 3. In response to answers to these subquestions, add nodes and links to the graph. Links in a WatsonPaths assertion graph include indicates, causes, associatedWith, affects, contains, and matches. In our example, WatsonPaths adds a causes link from cholecystitis to jaundice and a

causes link from cholecystitis to right upper quadrant pain aggravated by fatty foods.

- **4.** Use Bayesian inference to recalculate the scores associated with nodes and links in the graph as it is updated. This is done by the *belief engine*.
- If a stopping condition is reached, exit with a set of conclusions along with scores for those conclusions.
- 6. Go to step 2.

We summarize the operation of WatsonPaths as follows:

```
Input: top-level question → identify important factors in the question → add the factors to the graph → repeatedly ask subquestions and update graph and scores → Output: conclusions and scores
```

The interface to WatsonPaths allows the user to explore the assertion graph and drill down into the evidence for each node and link in the graph, including the evidence for answers returned by Watson. WatsonPaths also allows the user to teach WatsonPaths and Watson to improve the performance of both systems on various subtasks of the top-level question answering task.

18.4.13 WATSONPATHS FOR COMMONSENSE REASONING

Watson serves as a dynamic medical knowledge base to support medical reasoning in WatsonPaths. It answers questions such as What disease causes right upper quadrant pain? Similarly, Watson can serve as a dynamic commonsense knowledge base to support commonsense reasoning. It can be trained to answer questions about commonsense knowledge such as object properties, event effects, preconditions, and goals:

```
What is the color of the sky?
What is a pen used for?
What is the effect of eating a large meal?
What is a precondition of eating dinner?
What is the goal of drinking alcohol?
What goal is initiated by being hungry?
```

We can also use it for story understanding. Roger Schank and Robert Abelson introduced the example

```
Willa was hungry.
She took out the Michelin Guide.
```

The MICRO PAM program generates an explanation of this story using structured information. This can be reimplemented in WatsonPaths using unstructured information. We supply WatsonPaths with the following subquestion generation strategies:

Source Type	Target Type	Question	MICRO PAM Link	Direction
State	Goal	What goal is initiated by state?	initiate	Forward
Goal	Plan	What is a plan for goal?	planFor	Forward
Plan	Goal	What is a subgoal of plan?	subgoal	Forward
Event	Goal	What is the goal of event?	instantiation	Backward

Given the above story, WatsonPaths asks forward and backward questions to an instance of Watson previously trained on questions of these types. The result is a WatsonPaths assertion graph containing the following nodes and links:

```
state: Willa was hungry. →
initiate (What goal is initiated by Willa was hungry?) →
goal: satisfy hunger →
planFor (What is a plan for satisfy hunger?) →
plan: eat at a restaurant →
subgoal (What is a subgoal of eat at a restaurant?) →
goal: find a good restaurant →
instantiation (What is the goal of She took out the Michelin Guide?) →
event: She took out the Michelin Guide.
```

18.4.14 THE ADAPTWATSON METHODOLOGY

The key to developing a successful Watson application is applying the AdaptWatson methodology, an empirical method for developing artificial intelligence applications. This methodology provides an efficient way of driving up the performance of an intelligent application to meet performance objectives. This methodology consists of the following steps:

- Acquire a large amount of natural language content about the application domain.
- 2. Acquire training and test data using human annotators or crowdsourcing.
- 3. Generate ideas for components.
- **4.** Implement the components or use state-of-the-art components where available.
- **5.** Perform component-level tests and drive up the performance of the components.
- **6.** Use machine learning to learn which components work and how to weight their contribution.
- 7. Evaluate the end-to-end impact of adding the components to the system.

- **8.** Perform *accuracy analysis* to identify problem areas and generate ideas for improving the components or acquiring additional content.
- **9.** Perform *headroom analysis* to estimate the maximum end-to-end impact of successfully implementing the improvements or adding the content.
- **10.** If the headroom of the proposed improvement or content acquisition is significant, implement the improvement or acquire the content.
- 11. Iterate on the above until performance objectives are met.
- Recurse on the above. Use the same methodology to develop subcomponents as needed.

18.5 COMPARISON

Systems and methods for reasoning using natural language are compared in Table 18.1. All the systems support chaining in some form. SAFE, OWL, and Montagovian syntax required bracketed input and do not accept free-form English. ACE and PENG Light add a parser so that input does not need to be bracketed, but they restrict input to expressions of a controlled language. REFORMULATOR does not require bracketed input, but can only reason with natural language expressions that are matched by reformulation rules. Watson and WatsonPaths work with arbitrary natural language text, and they are able to exploit the redundancy in large natural language corpora.

BIBLIOGRAPHIC NOTES

Automatic programming

Sammet (1966) proposed to use natural language as a programming language. M. Halpern (1966) makes a strong case for the use of natural language as a programming language and points out the advantages of exploiting the redundancy in natural language. Automatic programming is discussed by Balzer (1985). SAFE is discussed by Balzer, Goldman, and Wile (1978). OWL is discussed by Szolovits,

Table 18.1	Natural	Language	Reasoning	Systems and
Methodsa				

	SAFE	OWL	MS	AP	R	W
Can perform chaining Accepts nonbracketed text	✓	✓	\	√ ✓	1	V
Accepts unrestricted text Exploits redundancy	1 1					1

^aMS, Montagovian syntax; R, REFORMULATOR; W, Watson/WatsonPaths; AP, Attempto Controlled English and PENG Light.

Hawkinson, and Martin (1977). Swartout (1977) provides examples of OWL methods and describes OWL's explanation generator.

Reasoning with natural language

Montague (1970) wrote, "There is in my opinion no important theoretical difference between natural languages and the artificial languages of logicians" (p. 373). He introduced what is now called Montague grammar in a series of papers; they are reprinted in a book by Thomason (1974). A introductory book on Montague grammar is by Dowty, Wall, and Peters (1981). Montagovian syntax is described by McAllester and Givan (1989, 1992). There have been many proposals for logics that are closer to natural language than classical predicate logic (Iwańska & Shapiro, 2000). Some examples are the proposals of Lakoff (1970), Suppes (1979), Hobbs (1985), Hoeksema (1986), van Benthem (1987), Schubert and Hwang (1989), Purdy (1991), Sánchez Valencia (1991), Ali and Shapiro (1993), and MacCartney and Manning (2008). Books on formal semantics of natural language are by Portner (2005) and Blackburn and Bos (2005). Attempto Controlled English is described by Fuchs, Schwertel, and Schwitter (1999). The Attempto reasoner is discussed by Fuchs and Schwertel (2002). Discourse representation structures are described by Kamp and Reyle (1993). The use of PENG Light for specifying event calculus domain descriptions is described by Schwitter (2011). P. Clark, Harrison, Jenkins, Thompson, and Wojcik (2005) also use restricted English for specifying the effects of events. Kuhn (2014) provides a comprehensive survey and classification of 100 controlled natural languages based on English. Singh (2002) describes REFORMULATOR. See also the discussions of Liu and Singh (2004a) and Singh, Barry, and Liu (2004).

Watson

Early question answering systems include Baseball (Green, Jr., Wolf, Chomsky, & Laughery, 1961), LUNAR (Woods, 1973), and QUALM (Lehnert, 1978). Book-length treatments of question answering systems are by Maybury (2004) and Strzalkowski and Harabagiu (2008). An introduction to Watson is provided by Ferrucci (2012). UIMA is described by Ferrucci and Lally (2004). Scaling up Watson is discussed by Epstein et al. (2012). Watson's question analysis is described by Lally et al. (2012). The ESG parser is described by McCord (2006a, 2006b, 2010). Watson's parsing, predicate argument structure generation, and relation extraction are described by McCord, Murdock, and Boguraev (2012). Watson's primary search, answer lookup, and candidate generation are described by Chu-Carroll et al. (2012). SKB is discussed by Ferrucci, Levas, Bagchi, Gondek, and Mueller (2013). Supporting evidence retrieval and answer scoring are described by Murdock, Fan, Lally, Shima, and Boguraev (2012). LFACS is described by Murdock (2011) and Murdock, Fan, Lally, Shima, and Boguraev (2012). The structuremapping algorithm is described by Falkenhainer, Forbus, and Gentner (1989). Pointwise mutual information and inverse document frequency are discussed by Manning and Schütze (1999). Watson's type coercion components are described by Murdock, Kalyanpur, et al. (2012). Watson's final merging and ranking is described by Gondek et al. (2012). The Watson Medical Engine is described by Ferrucci, Levas, Bagchi, Gondek, and Mueller (2013). WatsonPaths is discussed by Lally et al. (2014). The Willa example was introduced by Schank and Abelson (1977, p. 71). The code for MICRO PAM, a simplified version of PAM (Wilensky, 1978, 1983), and the Willa example are given by Schank and Riesbeck (1981). The AdaptWatson methodology is described by Ferrucci and Brown (2012). Empirical methods for artificial intelligence are discussed by Cohen (1995).

EXERCISES

- **18.1** Write a program that takes bracketed natural language specifications as input and produces programs as output.
- **18.2** Define a controlled language for event calculus domain descriptions. Write a program that converts a domain description written using the controlled language into an answer set program.
- **18.3** Write a program that takes English sentences and reformulation rules as input and produces inferred English sentences as output.

by Condek dimit (2017), he William Stradelid managistes, his or Ecological (2018), and the end of the Cological (2018), and the end of the Cological (2018), and the end of the

23770014

- e tege a como septimente, materiale node sono estado en energado e en Maria. Anoque en entre estado en entre estado en entre entre en
- The rest of the result of the second process of the second process of the result of th
- person services. The model for consequence this strending is a significant registry in a 27 to 6 to The consequence of the person of the consequence of the consequen

Knowledge Acquisition

Anowledge () Tell

Acquisition of Commonsense Knowledge 19

How do we acquire the knowledge necessary for commonsense reasoning? In this chapter, we discuss systems and methods for acquiring this knowledge. First, we discuss the manual acquisition of commonsense knowledge in Cyc, WordNet, and ThoughtTreasure. We then describe systems for crowdsourcing commonsense knowledge, including Open Mind Common Sense (OMCS) and LEARNER. Next, we review games for acquiring commonsense knowledge, including Verbosity and Common Consensus. We then present methods for mining relation instances and implicit knowledge from natural language text. Next, we describe how to perform reasoning in the event calculus using knowledge acquired through crowdsourcing. After that, we compare the systems and methods for acquiring commonsense knowledge. Finally, we review estimates of the size of human commonsense knowledge.

19.1 MANUAL ACQUISITION OF COMMONSENSE KNOWLEDGE

One method for acquiring commonsense knowledge is to enter the knowledge by hand. We discuss several systems for which this is the primary method.

19.1.1 CYC

Douglas B. Lenat started development of the Cyc commonsense knowledge base and reasoning system in 1983. The Cyc representation language, CycL, was originally based on frames (lists of slot name-value pairs), and knowledge acquisition was performed using a frame editor. Starting in 1989, Cyc began to shift away from frames, and CycL evolved into a language based on first-order logic, with extensions for default reasoning and reification. In 1990, *contexts*, also known as *microtheories*, were added to Cyc. Contexts provide a way of keeping alternative and possibly conflicting axiomatizations separate. For example, we can keep our axiomatizations of relational space and metric space in two different contexts. A context consists of a context name and a set of CycL sentences. Contexts are also organized into a hierarchy. As of 2014, Cyc contains over 500,000 terms and about 7,000,000 assertions (Cycorp, 2014e).

Knowledge acquisition

In Cyc, acquisition of commonsense knowledge is performed by *ontological engineers* or knowledge engineers who assert CycL sentences into contexts using a graphical user interface. For example, the engineer enters

```
#$FoodMt
```

into the microtheory dialog box and the sentence

```
(#$implies (#$isa ?x #$RedApple)
(#$colorOf ?x #$Red))
```

into the sentence dialog box and clicks Assert Formula. A variant of CycL called knowledge entry text (KE text) can also be used for entry:

```
In Mt: FoodMt
F: (implies (isa ?x RedApple) (colorOf ?x Red))
```

Text files containing CycL sentences can also be loaded into Cyc.

Rapid Knowledge Formation tools

In 1999, the Rapid Knowledge Formation (RKF) program was started by the Defense Advanced Research Projects Agency (DARPA). Its goal was to develop technologies allowing subject matter experts to enter knowledge directly into knowledge bases instead of requiring knowledge engineers to enter knowledge. A set of acquisition tools were developed for Cyc as part of this project. Tools are provided for

- identifying microtheories relevant to a topic
- listing the similarities and differences between two concepts
- deciding where to place a new concept in the hierarchy
- finding concepts related to a concept
- suggesting relations between two concepts
- · defining a concept using a natural language phrase
- defining a fact using a natural language sentence
- defining a concept by modifying the definition of a similar concept
- · defining IF-THEN rules
- defining a script, its participants, its events, and the ordering of its events

Feedback to the ontological engineer is provided by *knowledge entry facilitation* (KE facilitation) rules. Four types of feedback are provided: requirements, strong suggestions, weak suggestions, and neighbor suggestions. For example:

- Requirement: An arity must be defined for a relation.
- Strong suggestion: A state change event type should have a type defined for the
 object of the state change.
- Weak suggestion: A duration should be defined for an event type.
- Neighbor suggestion: Something that is true of one concept may also be true of a similar concept.

Several other acquisition tools have been developed for Cyc. The Factivore tool allows entry of facts such as properties of objects. The Predicate Populator allows entry of relations between concepts, such as the ingredients of a salad. The Abductive Sentence Suggestor uses machine learning on facts stored in the knowledge base to suggest new rules. Cyc also runs machine learning at night to identify inconsistencies and possible omissions in the knowledge base.

19.1.2 WORDNET

George A. Miller started development of the WordNet lexical database in 1985. WordNet contains words, phrases, and *synsets* (synonym sets), which are sets of words and phrases with the same meaning. It contains two types of relations useful for commonsense reasoning: *lexical relations* between words/phrases and *semantic relations* between synsets. Examples of lexical relations are antonym and participle. Examples of semantic relations are hyponym/hypernym (IS-A), member, part, and cause. WordNet 3.0 contains 117,659 synsets and 220 cause relations between verb synsets such as the following:

```
cause|affect,impress,move,strike|feel,experience
cause|encourage|hope
cause|enrage|rage
cause|feed.give|eat
cause|give|have,have_got,hold
cause|incite,instigate,set_off,stir_up|act,move
cause|keep_up|stay_up,sit_up
cause|lay,put_down,repose|lie
cause|open.open_up|open.open_up
cause|remind|remember,retrieve,recall,call_back,call_up,recollect,think
cause|resonate,come_across|understand
cause|resuscitate,revive|come_to,revive,resuscitate
cause|strengthen,beef_up,fortify|strengthen
```

In WordNet, acquisition is performed by lexicographers who enter data into plain text files called *lexicographer files*. Each line of a lexicographer file defines a synset. Relations are defined using short character sequences such as ! (antonym), \le (participle), @ (hypernym), #m (member), #p (part), and > (cause).

Here is an example of a synset definition:

```
{ canine, [ dog, cat1,! ] pooch, domestic_dog, canid,@ }
```

This specifies a synset consisting of the words canine, dog, and pooch, and the phrase domestic dog. If a word or phrase occurs in more than one synset in a file, it is followed by a number that serves to uniquely identify the occurrence. The notation [dog, cat1,!] defines an antonym relation between the word dog in this synset and the word cat in another synset in the same file where it appears as cat1 in that

synset's definition. The notation canid,@ defines a hypernym relation between this synset and another synset that contains the word canid.

Feedback to the lexicographer is provided when WordNet's grind program is run to convert the lexicographer files into a WordNet database. Error messages are produced when syntax errors are detected and when a reference to a word or phrase in a relation specification cannot be resolved.

Elaboration of entered data consists of filling in inverse relations. For example, if the synset containing canid is a hypernym of the synset containing dog, then the synset containing dog is a hyponym of the synset containing canid.

19.1.3 THOUGHTTREASURE

The ThoughtTreasure commonsense knowledge base and architecture for natural language processing was begun in 1993. It contains both declarative and procedural knowledge. Its declarative knowledge includes English and French words, phrases, and inflections; verb argument structure; names; concepts; relations among concepts including IS-A and part; facts; scripts; and spatial grids. Its procedural knowledge consists of a collection of agents for textual entity recognition, planning, model finding, question answering, and question asking. ThoughtTreasure 0.00022 contains 27,093 concepts and 51,305 assertions (Mueller, 2000). The contents of ThoughtTreasure 0.00022, including linguistic knowledge, were converted to CycL for loading into OpenCyc. This dump consists of 72,554 constants and 547,651 assertions.

Acquisition of declarative knowledge

In ThoughtTreasure, acquisition of declarative knowledge is performed by knowledge engineers who enter knowledge into plain text files using a concise format. The format is designed to speed knowledge entry and enable the presentation of lots of related knowledge on the screen during entry. Here is an example using the format:

```
=concept//
==action//
==action-open//open.Véz/ouvrir.Véy/
|r1=grasper|r2=physical-object|leadto2=state-open|
==state//
==state-open//open.Az/ouvert.Ay/
|r1=physical-object|
```

Indentation is used to express hierarchy. This text defines the concept concept; action, which is a concept; action-open, which is an action; state, which is a concept; and state-open, which is a state. This also specifies words for expressing the concepts action-open and state-open. The concept action-open is expressed in English by *open*. The *feature character* z indicates English. This is a verb (V), and it takes a direct object (é). This concept can also be expressed as ouvrir in French (y). The feature character A indicates an adjective. Words and

phrases are specified using their citation forms, such as the infinitive for a verb and the singular form for a noun. An inflection dictionary maps citation forms such as *open* to inflections:

```
open.Az/
open.Vz/
open.f/
open.p1S/opens.p3S/open.pP/
opened.i/opened.d/opening.e/
```

Several types of feedback on declarative knowledge are provided. When the knowledge is loaded into ThoughtTreasure, messages are produced when syntax errors are detected and when a concept is defined multiple times. ThoughtTreasure also provides several tools to mine the knowledge base for patterns and potential problems, such as phrase derivation patterns, suffixes that identify the gender of French nouns, and lexical entries ambiguous as to part of speech.

The example text also specifies that the type of the first argument of action-open is grasper, the type of the second argument of action-open is physical-object, and the effect of this action is state-open. The notation

```
leadto2=state-open
```

inside the definition for action-open is an abbreviation for

```
[leadto2 action-open state-open]
```

which in turn is an abbreviation for

```
[leadto [action-open ?x ?y] [state-open ?y]]
```

Acquisition of procedural knowledge

In ThoughtTreasure, acquisition of procedural knowledge is performed by programmers who write code in the C language. For example, the following code defines the TVSetOff planning agent, which turns off a television set:

```
WAIT_TS(cx, sg, ts, (Dur)10, STFAILURE);
    return;
}
failure:
    TOSTATE(cx, sg, STFAILURE);
}
```

A planning agent is a finite state machine. In state STBEGIN, the DbRetrievePart function is used to retrieve the power switch of the television set. The SG function is used to initiate a subgoal for the power switch to be off (which is achieved by another planning agent). If the subgoal succeeds, then the agent transitions to state 1. Otherwise, the agent transitions to state STFAILURE, and the agent terminates with failure. In state 1, the WAIT_PTN function is used to wait until the television set is off, upon which the agent transitions to state STSUCCESS and the agent terminates with success. The WAIT_TS function is used to wait for 10 s, after which the agent transitions to state STFAILURE and the agent terminates with failure. The programmer tests procedural knowledge by integrating it into the system and testing the system on existing or new test cases.

19.2 CROWDSOURCING COMMONSENSE KNOWLEDGE

Manual entry of commonsense knowledge tends to be a slow process, and it tends to require specialists. An alternative is to design crowdsourcing systems that allow many nonspecialists to enter commonsense knowledge quickly.

19.2.1 OPEN MIND COMMON SENSE

The OMCS project to acquire commonsense knowledge from volunteer contributors over the Internet was started in 1999 by Push Singh. Users sign up for an account and then log in to enter knowledge into the OMCS knowledge base. In 2002, OMCS contained 456,195 facts (Singh et al., 2002). In 2014, OMCS contains about 1.1 million facts (Catherine Havasi, personal communication, June 11, 2014).

Acquisition of commonsense knowledge is performed using a collection of *elicitation activities*, each with its own entry screen. Some of the activities require knowledge to be entered into templates, and other activities allow entry of free-form text.

Template-based activities

Template-based activities display a template with zero or more blanks filled in and ask the user to fill in the remaining blanks. Examples of templates are the following:

Free-form activities

Free-form activities allow the user to enter arbitrary sentences. One free-form activity asks the user to supply a story given a title. For example, in response to the title Playing Hockey, a user entered the following story:

```
I grabbed my ice skates and hockey stick.
I walked over to the ice rink.
I saw that the hockey game had already started.
```

Another free-form activity presents a story and asks the user to enter knowledge useful for understanding the story. For example, a user was presented with the following:

```
Frank and Will are friends. Frank punched Will.
```

In response, the user entered the following:

```
Frank got upset.
Frank may not like Will anymore.
Will is probably hurt.
Frank could get in trouble for hurting Will.
```

Generation of plausible facts

A mechanism was designed and implemented by Thomas Lin to allow OMCS to suggest new plausible facts when a user enters a fact (but an interface to it was not deployed on the OMCS web site). Plausible facts are generated using a collection of analogical inference rules such as the following:

```
?NP1 ?V1 ?NP2
?NP3 ?V1 ?NP4
?NP3 ?V2 ?NP4
→
?NP1 ?V2 ?NP2
```

NP is a noun phrase and V is a verb (possibly including auxiliary verbs). These can be recognized using part-of-speech taggers and syntactic parsers. For example, suppose the user enters

```
A mother can have a baby.
```

and the following facts were previously entered:

```
A child can have a goldfish.
A child can feed a goldfish.
```

Rule 19.1 then generates the following plausible fact:

```
A mother can feed a baby.
```

A more complex analogical inference rule is the following:

```
?NP1 ?V1 ?NP2 (19.2)
?NP2 ?V2 ?NP3
?NP1 ?V3 ?NP3
```

```
?NP4 ?V1 ?NP5
?NP5 ?V2 ?NP6
→
?NP4 ?V3 ?NP6
```

The score for a plausible fact generated from the consequent of a rule is computed based on the number of distinct matches of the antecedent of the rule against facts in the knowledge base. A plausible fact that is generated more ways gets a higher score.

Extracting structured knowledge

Patterns were used to convert commonsense knowledge expressed as free-form text in OMCS's knowledge base into a more structured representation. For example, using the pattern

```
The effect of ?NP1 is ?NP2
```

facts such as the following were extracted:

```
(The effect of (buying a hamburger) is (having less money))
(The effect of (celebrating) is (being happy))
(The effect of (chatting with friends) is (a cozy feeling))
(The effect of (creating art) is (pleasure))
(The effect of (eating) is (feeling full))
(The effect of (giving a gift) is (to make someone happy))
(The effect of (going on strike) is (to harm management))
(The effect of (hurting someone else) is (pain))
(The effect of (mailing a letter) is (communicating with someone))
```

19.2.2 LEARNER

The LEARNER system for acquiring commonsense knowledge from volunteer contributors was begun in 2001 by Timothy Chklovski. It uses analogy to drive the acquisition of single-sentence facts such as cats eat mice. The user selects a concept such as cat or newspaper, the user enters several facts about the concept, and then the system asks follow-up questions about the concept. For example, for newspaper, Learner may ask:

```
newspapers contain information?
all newspapers have pages?
newspapers are for reading?
newspapers can contain recipes?
```

The user then answers each question with either Yes, No, Some/Sometimes, Matter of opinion, or Nonsensical question.

For a natural language sentence to be accepted by LEARNER, (1) the parser must be able to parse it, (2) it must not be an imperative sentence, (3) it must not use the past tense or a past perfect or present perfect construction, (4) it must not start with a pronoun, demonstrative determiner, or possessive determiner, and (5) it must not contain conjunctions.

Facts acquired by Learner are automatically classified into the following categories: ISA, QUALIFIED-ISA, DEFINITION, ACTION, QUALIFIED-ACTION, ACTION-ON, PROPERTY, COMPARATIVE, FUNCTION, MADE-OF, PART-OF, REQUIRES, and POSSIBLE STATE. Learner accepts simple facts about actions such as qualified actions (kangaroos jump very high) and requirements (writing requires literacy). But Learner does not address knowledge about scripts, goals, and the effects of events (Chklovski, 2003b, p. 37).

Learner was used to elaborate a subset of the OMCS knowledge base. The OMCS facts accepted by Learner were used as the initial knowledge base, which was then grown by contributors who entered new facts and responded to follow-up questions posed by Learner. A total of 31,620 new facts were acquired, starting from an initial set of 53,447 accepted OMCS facts (Chklovski, 2003b, p. 129).

Generation of follow-up questions

In Learner, follow-up questions are generated based on previously entered facts as follows:

- Other concepts in the knowledge base similar to the selected concept are identified. The similarity of two concepts is computed based on how many facts they share, giving greater weight to concepts sharing properties that are more rare. For example, for the selected concept newspaper, the similar concept book is identified.
- 2. Follow-up questions are generated from facts about a similar concept that involve properties not already asserted about the selected concept. The similar concept in these facts is replaced by the selected concept. For example, if the property of containing information is not already asserted about newspaper, then book in

books contain information is replaced by newspaper, which yields the follow-up question newspapers contain information?

Natural language resources are used to inflect words properly.

Representation of sentences

Learner represents sentences as atoms of the form

property(concept) = truth-value

The sentence cats eat mice is converted into both

cat-eat(mouse)=1

and

eat-mouse(cat)=1

Natural language resources are used to convert an inflected word into its base form. Learner also deals with negation. For example, cats do not fly is converted into

$$fly(cat)=0$$

Computing similarity

The similarity of two concepts is computed in Learner as follows. We first define FreqWt, the weight of a property, as follows:

$$FreqWt(p) = \begin{cases} 2 & \text{if } \mathcal{C}(p) = \emptyset \\ 1 + 1/\log_2(|\mathcal{C}(p)| + 1) & \text{otherwise} \end{cases}$$

where C(p) is the set of all concepts for which p is true in the knowledge base ($\{c \mid p(c) = 1\}$). FreqWt gives a higher weight to properties that are more rarely true in the knowledge base. We then define Wt, the weight assigned to two truth values of a predicate, as follows:

$$Wt(tv_1, tv_2, p) = \begin{cases} FreqWt(p) & \text{if } tv_1 = tv_2 = 1\\ -1.5 & \text{if } tv_1 \neq tv_2\\ 0 & \text{if } tv_1 = tv_2 = 0 \end{cases}$$

We then compute the similarity of concepts c and c' as follows:

$$Sim(c, c') = \sum_{p \in P} Wt(p(c), p(c'), p)$$

where P is the set of all properties in the knowledge base and p(c) is the truth value of c in the knowledge base.

19.2.3 OPEN MIND COMMONS AND CONCEPTNET

The Open Mind Commons interface for knowledge acquisition was begun in 2006 by Robert Speer. The user navigates to a concept, and then the user is asked to evaluate existing facts involving the concept, evaluate plausible facts about the concept generated by analogy, and enter new facts about the concept by filling in templates.

For example, when the user navigates to orchestra, the user is asked several things. First, the user is asked to evaluate the following existing facts:

```
You are likely to find a flute in an orchestra.
You are likely to find a snare drum in an orchestra.
An orchestra plays music.
Orchestra is related to music group.
```

Second, the user is asked to evaluate the following new, plausible facts:

```
You are likely to find a trumpet in an orchestra. You are likely to find a harmonica in an orchestra.
```

Third, the user is asked to fill in the following templates:

```
You are likely to find _____ in an orchestra. An orchestra is _____.
```

Open Mind Commons replaces the previous interface to OMCS as well as its back-end database. Open Mind Commons adds knowledge directly to the ConceptNet commonsense knowledge base developed by Hugo Liu, Catherine Havasi, Robert Speer, Jason B. Alonso, and colleagues. ConceptNet was originally populated by extracting (*relation*, *concept*, *concept*) triples from the OMCS knowledge base. Each ConceptNet record consists of the following fields:

- Relation
- Concept1
- Concept2
- Value: positive for true and negative for false, with a higher magnitude corresponding to a higher degree of validation by sources
- Sources
- Surface text: original natural language sentence

The relations in ConceptNet include IsA, UsedFor, HasA, CapableOf, Desires, CreatedBy, PartOf, Causes, HasFirstSubevent, AtLocation, HasProperty, LocatedNear, DefinedAs, SymbolOf, ReceivesAction, HasPrerequisite, MotivatedByGoal, CausesDesire, MadeOf, HasSubevent, and HasLastSubevent.

ConceptNet 5 contains 36,963 records with a relation of Causes, which represents the effects of events. The following patterns are used to extract Causes records from OMCS:

```
The effect of ?XP1 is that ?S2
The effect of ?XP1 is ?NP2
The consequence of ?XP1 is that ?XP2
The consequence of ?XP1 is ?XP2
Something that might happen as a consequence of ?XP1 is that ?XP2
Something that might happen as a consequence of ?XP1 is ?XP2
?AdvP ?NP1 causes you to ?VP2
?AdvP ?NP1 causes ?NP2
```

NP is a noun phrase, VP is a verb phrase, AdvP is an adverb phrase, S is a sentence, and XP is an NP, VP, or S.

ConceptNet 5 includes knowledge from other projects including DBpedia, Wiktionary (Wikimedia Foundation, 2014b), and WordNet.

19.2.4 ANALOGYSPACE

Open Mind Commons uses a technique called AnalogySpace, developed by Robert Speer, Catherine Havasi, and Henry Lieberman, to generate plausible facts to be evaluated by contributors. AnalogySpace is inspired by the method of latent semantic analysis (LSA) used in information retrieval. Like LSA, Analogy space uses the technique of singular value decomposition. AnalogySpace uses the *property(concept)* representation of LEARNER.

Knowledge base

We define an AnalogySpace knowledge base as a set KB of atoms of the form

$$property(concept) = value$$

such that, if $p(c) = v_1 \in KB$ and $p(c) = v_2 \in KB$, then $v_1 = v_2$. That is, p(c) can only have one value in KB. As in ConceptNet, positive values indicate true and negative values indicate false.

We convert ConceptNet into an initial knowledge base KB_0 by forming the set of atoms

for every $\langle relation, concept1, concept2, value \rangle$ in ConceptNet. We then form a set $\{c_1, \ldots, c_m\}$ of all concepts in KB_0 and a set $\{p_1, \ldots, p_n\}$ of all properties in KB_0 . We then convert KB_0 into an m-by-n real matrix A whose (i,j)th element is

$$\left\{ \begin{array}{l} \nu \ \ \text{if} \ (p_j(c_i) = v) \in KB_0 \\ 0 \ \ \text{otherwise} \end{array} \right.$$

Singular value decomposition

We define singular value decomposition as follows.

Definition 19.1. If A is an m-by-n real matrix, then a singular value decomposition of A is a factorization $A = U \Sigma V^T$, where

- $U = [u_1, \ldots, u_m]$ is an orthogonal m-by-m real matrix
- $V = [v_1, ..., v_n]$ is an orthogonal *n*-by-*n* real matrix
- $\Sigma = diag(\sigma_1, \ldots, \sigma_p)$ is an *m*-by-*n* real matrix, where $\sigma_1 \ge \ldots \ge \sigma_p \ge 0$ and $p = \min(m, n)$

The following theorem guarantees that such a decomposition exists.

Theorem 19.1. If A is a real m-by-n matrix, then a singular value decomposition of A exists.

Proof. See Theorem 2.5.2 of Golub and Van Loan (1996) or Theorem 4.1.1 of Watkins (2010).

The rank of A is the number of nonzero values in $\{\sigma_1, \ldots, \sigma_p\}$.

Truncated singular value decomposition

We define truncated singular value decomposition as follows.

Definition 19.2. If $U\Sigma V^T$ is a singular value decomposition of a real matrix A and k < rank(A), then

$$A_k = \sum_{i=1}^k \sigma_i u_i v_i^T$$

is a k-truncated singular value decomposition of A.

Truncated singular value decomposition gives the closest approximation of a given rank to a given matrix.

Theorem 19.2. If A is a real matrix, k < rank(A), and A_k is a k-truncated singular value decomposition of A, then

$$\min_{rank(B)=k} ||A - B||_2 = ||A - A_k||_2$$

Proof. See Theorem 2.5.3 of Golub and Van Loan (1996) or Theorem 4.2.15 of Watkins (2010).

Generation of plausible facts

We generate plausible facts as follows. Given A, we compute its k-truncated singular value decomposition A_k , with k < rank(A). For a large knowledge base, AnalogySpace typically uses k = 150. We convert A_k into a plausible knowledge base KB_1 by forming the set of atoms

$$\{p_j(c_i) = (A_k)_{ij}\}$$

The plausible facts are then defined as the first N atoms p(c) = v in KB_1 , sorted in descending order by v, such that p(c) is not in the original knowledge base KB_0 .

Example: flat similarity

Like LEARNER, AnalogySpace can generate plausible facts based on a notion of *flat similarity*, namely, the degree to which two concepts share properties. Suppose we have atoms that represent that flutes and oboes are woodwinds, bass guitars and electric pianos are electric instruments, flutes are in orchestras, and bass guitars are in jazz bands.

```
IsA-woodwind(flute)=1
IsA-woodwind(oboe)=1
IsA-electric_instrument(bass_guitar)=1
IsA-electric_instrument(electric_piano)=1
AtLocation-orchestra(flute)=1
AtLocation-jazz_band(bass_guitar)=1
```

Flutes and oboes are similar because they share the property of being a woodwind. Bass guitars and electric pianos are similar because they share the property of being an electric instrument. Given these atoms, AnalogySpace with k=2 produces the following plausible facts:

```
AtLocation-orchestra(oboe)=0.4472
AtLocation-jazz_band(electric_piano)=0.4472
```

Because flutes and oboes are similar, and flutes are in orchestras, it is plausible that oboes are also in orchestras. Similarly, because bass guitars and electric pianos are similar, and bass guitars are in jazz bands, it is plausible that electric pianos are also in jazz bands.

Example: deep similarity

Unlike LEARNER, however, AnalogySpace can generate plausible facts based on a notion of *deep similarity*, namely, the degree to which two concepts share properties

that themselves are similar. Suppose we have atoms that represent that violins are classical instruments and in orchestras, and that electric guitars are twentieth century instruments and in jazz bands:

```
IsA-classical_instrument(violin)=1
AtLocation-orchestra(violin)=1
IsA-20th_century_instrument(electric_guitar)=1
AtLocation-jazz_band(electric_guitar)=1
```

Being a classical instrument and being in an orchestra are similar properties, because these are both properties of violins. Similarly, being a twentieth century instrument and being in a jazz band are similar properties, because these are both properties of electric guitars. Now suppose we also have atoms that represent that flutes are in orchestras, bass guitars are in jazz bands, oboes are classical instruments, and electric pianos are twentieth century instruments:

```
AtLocation-orchestra(flute)=1
AtLocation-jazz_band(bass_guitar)=1
IsA-classical_instrument(oboe)=1
IsA-20th_century_instrument(electric_piano)=1
```

Given these atoms, AnalogySpace with k = 2 produces the following plausible facts:

```
AtLocation-orchestra(oboe)=0.5
AtLocation-jazz_band(electric_piano)=0.5
```

Flutes and oboes do not share any properties. But, because flutes and oboes share the properties of being in an orchestra and being a classical instrument, which are similar properties, and flutes are in orchestras, it is plausible that oboes are in orchestras. Similarly, bass guitars and electric pianos do not share any properties. But, because bass guitars and electric pianos share the properties of being in a jazz band and being a twentieth century instrument, which are similar properties, and bass guitars are in jazz bands, it is plausible that electric pianos are in jazz bands.

19.3 GAMES FOR ACQUISITION OF COMMONSENSE KNOWLEDGE

Related to crowdsourcing efforts like OMCS is the idea of using games to motivate people to contribute commonsense knowledge. We review several representative systems.

19.3.1 **ANIMAL**

An early example of a multiuser game for acquiring knowledge was the ANIMAL program written by Nathan Teichholtz in 1973. The program stores knowledge acquired from multiple users in a common data file ANIMAL.GME. The user thinks of an animal and the computer tries to guess the name of the animal by asking yesno questions. When the computer guesses incorrectly, the computer asks the user

to provide a yes-no question that distinguishes the animal guessed by the computer from the animal the user was thinking of. As games are played, the program grows a knowledge base about properties of animals (or any other category, after changing ANIMAL to that category in the program).

19.3.2 GAME FOR INTERACTIVE OPEN MIND IMPROVEMENT

In 2002, David Garcia, Catherine Havasi, and Katherine Todd implemented the Game for Interactive Open Mind Improvement (GIOMI), a game for rating facts in the OMCS knowledge base. The user selects a topic, the user is presented with facts about that topic from OMCS, and then the user is asked to rate them as good or bad. Users receive points for each rating, and the number of points per rating increases during a session.

19.3.3 VERBOSITY

In 2006, Luis von Ahn, Mihir Kedia, and Manuel Blum introduced Verbosity, a game for acquiring commonsense knowledge. A user logs in and is paired with another randomly selected logged-in user. One user is assigned the role of *narrator*, whereas the other user becomes the *guesser*. A concept such as book is presented to the narrator but not the guesser. The narrator's goal is to get the guesser to type the name of the concept. The narrator can provide hints to the guesser by filling in templates such as the following:

is	a kind of	
is	used for	
is	typically near/in/on	
	the opposite of	
	related to	

The guesses are provided to the narrator, and the narrator can tell the guesser whether a guess is or is not getting closer to the right answer. 212,090 facts from Verbosity were added to ConceptNet (Speer, Havasi, & Surana, 2010, p. 107).

19.3.4 COMMON CONSENSUS

In 2006, Henry Lieberman, Dustin A. Smith, and Alea Teeters introduced Common Consensus, a game for acquiring commonsense knowledge about goals. The system selects a goal such as watch television from the knowledge base. It then asks the user a question using one of the following templates designed to elicit particular types of goal-related knowledge:

- Supergoal: Why would you want to goal?
- Subgoal: What is something you can do if you wanted to goal?
- Similar goal: What is another goal similar to goal?
- Duration: About how long would it take to goal?

- Instrument: What are some things you would use to goal?
- Location: Where are some places you would goal?

The user types in multiple answers (except for Duration questions) and receives points for each answer equal to the number of other users who gave that answer or a similar answer.

19.4 MINING COMMONSENSE KNOWLEDGE

Instead of having specialists or nonspecialists contribute commonsense knowledge, another approach is to extract, learn, or mine commonsense knowledge from large natural language text corpora.

19.4.1 MINING RELATION INSTANCES FROM TEXT

In 1992, Marti A. Hearst proposed to mine relation instances from large text corpora and described several pattern-based rules for extracting likely instances of the hyponym or IS-A relation from text. They include the following:

```
?NPO (such as|including|especially) ?NP1 ?NP2 ...

> ISA(?NP1, ?NPO)
ISA(?NP2, ?NPO)
:

such ?NPO as ?NP1 ?NP2 ...

> ISA(?NP1, ?NPO)
ISA(?NP2, ?NPO)
:

?NP1 ?NP2 ... (or|and) other ?NPO

> ISA(?NP1, ?NPO)
ISA(?NP2, ?NPO)
ISA(?NP2, ?NPO)
:
```

For example, given

```
\dots sudden dyspnea, syncope, and other findings including orthopnea and hypoxemia \dots
```

these patterns allow us to extract

```
IS-A(sudden dyspnea, finding)
IS-A(syncope, finding)
IS-A(orthopnea, finding)
IS-A(hypoxemia, finding)
```

Hearst also presented the following method for learning new patterns for extracting instances of a given relation:

- 1. Start with a list of known instances of the relation.
- Search a corpus for sentences containing both arguments of any of the known instances of the relation.
- 3. Generalize the retrieved sentences to form pattern-based rules.

For example, starting with the instances

```
IS-A(syncope, finding)
IS-A(hypoxemia, finding)
```

we retrieve the sentences

```
Syncope is a relatively common finding. Hypoxemia was the only significant finding.
```

We generalize these sentences into the following rule:

```
?NP1 (was|is) (a|the) ADV ADJ ?NPO

→
ISA(?NP1, ?NPO)
```

19.4.2 MINING IMPLICIT KNOWLEDGE FROM TEXT

In 2002, Lenhart K. Schubert started developing the KNEXT system for extracting commonsense knowledge implicit in natural language sentences. The system takes parsed English sentences in Penn Treebank format as input and produces English sentences, called *factoids*, and logical forms as output.

For example, given the parse

KNEXT produces the factoids

```
A GRANDFATHER MAY CREATE A PAINTING.
A MALE MAY HAVE A GRANDFATHER.
A PAINTING CAN BE BEAUTIFUL.
```

and the logical forms

```
(:I (:Q THE GRANDFATHER.N) CREATE.V (:Q A{N} PAINTING.N))
(:I (:Q DET MALE*.N) HAVE.V (:Q DET GRANDFATHER.N))
(:I (:Q DET PAINTING.N) BEAUTIFUL.A)
```

Using Charniak's (2000) parser, KNEXT extracted 67,632,550 unique factoids from weblogs and 53,945,110 unique factoids from Wikipedia (J. M. Gordon, Van Durme, & Schubert, 2010, p. 10). The number of unique factoids continued to grow as more text was processed.

Logical forms

The language for logical forms is a simplified version of *episodic logic*, a logic that resembles natural language. An expression of the form

$$(: I \ a_1 \ p \ a_2 \dots)$$

represents the application of predicate p to arguments a_1, a_2, \ldots The expression

represents quantification, where q is a quantifier and p is a predicate.

Extracting logical forms

KNEXT extracts logical forms from a parse tree by recursively applying an ordered list of 80 pattern-based rules to the tree. A pattern-based rule is of the form

$$tree-pattern \rightarrow logical-form-template$$

An example is the following:

$$((* \sim NP \ VP) \ (NP) \ (* \sim VP) \ (VP) \ (*))$$
 \rightarrow
 $(:I \ 2 \ 4)$

The pattern (* $^{\sim}$ NP VP) matches zero or more subtrees not of type NP or VP, and the pattern (NP) matches a subtree of type NP. Whenever a rule's tree pattern matches a node of the tree, the rule's logical form template is instantiated and returned. Instantiating the logical form template involves replacing each (1-origin) index i by an abstracted version of the extracted logical form corresponding to the ith element of the tree pattern. Abstracting a logical form involves removing modifiers and generalizing entities to types.

Sharpening quantifiers

Jonathan Gordon and Lenhart Schubert developed a rule-based method for sharpening the quantifiers in logical forms produced by KNEXT such as DET into stronger quantifiers such as some, many, and all-or-most. The method takes logical forms as input and produces episodic logic sentences as output. For example, given

```
(:I (:Q DET MALE*.N) HAVE.V (:Q DET GRANDFATHER.N))
the method produces
```

```
(many-or-some x: [x male.n]
  (some e:
          (some y: [y person.n]
          [[x (have-as grandfather.n) y] ** e])))
```

Given an input logical form (: I $a_1 p a_2 ...$), a stronger quantifier is selected based on the strength of the association between a_1 and $p a_2 ...$ as measured by pointwise mutual information—see Section 18.4.5.

1.5 million sharpened sentences have been produced (Schubert, Gordon, Stratos, & Rubinoff, 2011).

Extracting the effects of events

Gordon and Schubert developed a method for extracting entailment rules from parsed English sentences, including rules for the effects of events. The method is based on identifying expectation violations. For example, the sentence

```
Matt turned on the light, but it didn't light up. can be abstracted into the inference rule
```

```
If a person turns on a light, then it may light up.
```

The first implementation of this method used TGrep2 patterns to identify candidate sentences for abstracting into inference rules. The TGrep2 patterns were later converted into TTT transductions that identify candidate sentences and transform them into initial logical forms.

19.5 EVENT CALCULUS REASONING OVER ACQUIRED COMMONSENSE KNOWLEDGE

Here is an example of how we can reason using the event calculus over commonsense knowledge acquired through crowdsourcing. We start with 396,018 facts from the OMCS knowledge base. We look through the knowledge base and notice that the effects of events are represented various ways. Some examples are the following:

```
If before you go to a restaurant the situation is you are hungry, then afterwards the situation is likely to be you are full

The effect of attending a rock concert is ringing ears
```

```
In the event "Billy is a soccer player. Billy scored a goal.", something that changed was Billy feels happy
```

Unlike the other examples, the first example includes both a fluent that becomes false after the event (hungry) and a fluent that becomes true after the event (full). Let us extract all facts of this type using the following regular expression:

```
If before you (.*) the situation is (.*) then afterwards the situation is likely to be (.*)
```

Sometimes acting in a play causes the audience to laugh.

This yields 215 facts. We assume that the first group matched with (.*) contains an event and that the second and third groups contain fluents.

We then analyze the syntax of events and fluents extracted using the previous regular expression. The top three syntactic patterns for events are as follows:

verb noun	106/215	49%
verb preposition noun	26/215	12%
verb	15/215	7%

The top three syntactic patterns for fluents are as follows:

adjective	114/430	27%
noun	31/430	7%
you are/were adjective	23/430	5%

We then take the 215 facts and convert the ones whose extracted events and fluents match these syntactic patterns into event calculus effect axioms. This yields 41 *Initiates* axioms and 41 *Terminates* axioms. Examples are as follows:

```
% If before you sleep the situation is tired, then afterwards
the situation
% is likely to be rested
initiates(sleep(A),rested(A),T) :- holdsAt(tired(A),T).
terminates(sleep(A),tired(A),T) :- agent(A), time(T).

% If before you eat vegetables the situation is hungry, then
afterwards
% the situation is likely to be full
initiates(eatVegetables(A),full(A),T) :- holdsAt(hungry(A),T).
terminates(eatVegetables(A),hungry(A),T) :- agent(A), time(T).
```

We can then reason using these extracted axioms using answer set programming. For example, we specify that John starts out tired and hungry. He sleeps and then eats vegetables.

```
agent(john).
holdsAt(tired(john),0).
holdsAt(hungry(john),0).
happens(sleep(john),1).
happens(eatVegetables(john),2).
:- releasedAt(F,0), fluent(F).
```

We then run clingo on this example along with the extracted axioms and the DEC rules. It is correctly inferred that (1) after sleeping, John is rested and no longer tired and (2) after eating vegetables, John is full and no longer hungry:

```
Answer: 1
0
hungry(john)
tired(john)
1
tired(john)
hungry(john)
happens(sleep(john),1)
```

```
2
-tired(john)
+rested(john)
hungry(john)
happens(eatVegetables(john),2)
3
-hungry(john)
+full(john)
rested(john)
```

19.6 COMPARISON OF ACQUISITION METHODS

Systems and methods for acquisition of commonsense knowledge are compared in Table 19.1. The earlier systems tend to rely on specialists for knowledge entry, whereas the later crowdsourcing systems acquire knowledge from nonspecialists. Cyc and many of the crowdsourcing systems provide feedback during knowledge entry. Many years after Cyc was first introduced, it still stacks up very well against the newer systems.

Although many of the systems acquire the effects of events, of the systems reviewed only Cyc and ThoughtTreasure clearly represent the arguments of an event, the arguments of the effects of the event, and how the arguments in the event map to the arguments of the effects of the event. For example, although OMCS contains facts from which argument information could conceivably be extracted such as

If before you serve customers the situation is the customers are waiting, then afterwards the situation is likely to be the customers are happy

it also contains many facts that do not contain this information such as

The effect of hurting someone else is pain

Table	19.1	Commonsense	Knowledge	Acquisitiona

	Сус	WN	TT	OMCS	L	омс	G	М
Begun	1983	1985	1993	1999	2001	2006	1973	1992
Enterer	S	S	S	NS	NS	NS	NS	М
Interface	GUI	T	T	GUI	GUI	GUI	G	
Feedback	1				1	1	1	
Event effects	1	1	1	1		1		1
Arguments	1		1					
Disambiguated	1	1	1	F 1				

^a WN, WordNet; TT, ThoughtTreasure; OMCS, Open Mind Common Sense; L, LEARNER; OMC, Open Mind Commons; G, games; M, mining S, specialist; NS, non-specialist; GUI, graphical user interface; T, text files.

360

We would like to clearly represent, for example, that if a_1 hurts a_2 , then a_1 will feel pain and a_2 will feel pain. This is represented in the event calculus as follows:

Initiates $(Hurt(a_1, a_2), Pain(a_1), t)$ Initiates $(Hurt(a_1, a_2), Pain(a_2), t)$

The knowledge acquired by many of the later systems is not disambiguated, although another crowdsourcing system, Open Mind Word Expert (Chklovski & Mihalcea, 2002), has been used to disambiguate facts in OMCS.

19.7 HOW BIG IS HUMAN COMMON SENSE?

How much commonsense knowledge do we need to acquire? How big is human commonsense knowledge? Landauer (1986) produced estimates of the size of an adult's long-term memory ranging from 0.5×10^9 to 3.4×10^9 bits using different methods:

- 1. Several estimates were based on the rate information is added to long-term memory—1.2 bits per second for text and 2.3 bits per second for pictures, from psychological experiments—and a linear accumulation over 70 years.
- 2. Another estimate took into account forgetting.
- 3. Another estimate was based on 346 bits to define each word in a dictionary containing 10⁵ words, multiplied by 15 to take account of other domains of knowledge such as history, music, nature, personal life history, and motor skills.

Estimates ventured over the years are summarized in Table 19.2. For comparison, the KNEXT system has extracted 10⁸ factoids (J. M. Gordon, Van Durme, & Schubert, 2010, p. 10).

Table	19.2	Estimates	of the	Size of	Human	Common	Sense

Turing (1950, p. 442)	10 ⁹ bits for a 70% chance of identifying a program as not a human after 5 min of text-based questioning
von Neumann (1958, pp. 63 and 64)	2.8×10^{20} bits of "memory capacity" based on 10^{10} neurons \times 14 bits per second per neuron \times 2 \times 10 ⁹ s, assuming "there is no true forgetting in the nervous system"
Minsky (1968, p. 26)	10 ⁵ -10 ⁷ "elements of knowledge in order to behave with reasonable sensibility in ordinary situations"
Landauer (1986)	10 ⁹ bits of "information from experience"
Schwartz (1988, p. 126)	0.8×10^{17} bits of "long-term memory"
Marvin Minsky (Lenat & Guha, 1990, p. 21)	10 ⁷ entries, assuming a child acquires an entry every 10 seconds from ages 0 to 8
Kurzweil (1999, p. 119)	10 ⁸ chunks or "bits of understanding, concepts, patterns, specific skills"
Moravec (1999, p. 56)	0.8×10^{15} bits of "nervous system memory" based on 10^{14} synapses \times 1 byte per synapse
Mahoney (1999)	10 ⁹ bits for predicting "how people respond to arbitrary input during communication"

BIBLIOGRAPHIC NOTES

Manual acquisition

Cyc was originally proposed as a way of overcoming knowledge acquisition bottlenecks (Lenat, Prakash, & Shepherd, 1985). An early version of Cyc called Knoesphere is described by Lenat, Borning, McDonald, Taylor, and Weyer (1983). The development of Cyc is documented in a series of papers by Lenat, Prakash, and Shepherd (1985), Lenat, Guha, Pittman, Pratt, and Shepherd (1990), Guha and Lenat (1994), and Lenat (1995). A book-length treatment of Cyc is provided by Lenat and Guha (1990). The Cyc frame editor is mentioned by Lenat, Prakash, and Shepherd (1985, p. 73). Cyc's shift from frames to predicate logic and the evolution of CycL are discussed by Guha and Lenat (1990a, 1994) and Lenat and Guha (1991a). Lenat and Guha (1991a, p. 87) note that CycL began in 1984 as a reimplementation of the framebased Representation Language Language (RLL), which is described by Greiner and Lenat (1980). RLL was used in the EURISKO learning by discovery program (Lenat, 1984). CycL is described by Cycorp (2014c). The formalization of contexts was proposed by McCarthy (1987) and developed by Guha (1992) and McCarthy (1993). Cyc's contexts are discussed by Guha and Lenat (1994). Entry of knowledge into Cyc is discussed by Cycorp (2014c, chap. 3). Cyc's RKF tools are discussed by Cycorp (2002a, sec. 19.5), Panton et al. (2002), and Witbrock et al. (2003). KE text is described by Cycorp (2014f). KE facilitation rules are described by Cycorp (2014c, sec. 8.5). The Factivore tool is described by Belasco et al. (2004) and Witbrock et al. (2005). The Predicate Populator and the Abductive Sentence Suggestor are described by Witbrock et al. (2005). Cyc's machine learning at night is mentioned by Guha and Lenat (1990a, p. 53).

WordNet is described by Fellbaum (1998). The WordNet lexicographer file format is described in the WordNet reference manual (Trustees of Princeton University, 2006). ThoughtTreasure is described by Mueller (1998). Scripts in ThoughtTreasure are described by Mueller (2000).

Crowdsourcing

Open Mind Common Sense is described by Singh (2002) and Singh et al. (2002). Part of speech tagging and syntactic parsing are discussed by Manning and Schütze (1999) and Jurafsky and Martin (2009). Learner is described by Chklovski (2003a, 2003b). Open Mind Commons is described by Speer (2007). An early version of ConceptNet called the Concept Node Graph (30,000 nodes) is described by Liu and Lieberman (2002). Another early version called OMCSNet (140,000 items) is described by Liu (2003). ConceptNet 2 (over 300,000 nodes) is described by Liu and Singh (2004b). ConceptNet 3 (over 150,000 nodes) is described by Speer (2007) and Havasi, Speer, and Alonso (2007, 2009). ConceptNet 5 (3.9 million nodes), which pulls in DBpedia, Wiktionary, WordNet, and other sources, is described by Speer and Havasi (2012).

Analogy

Lenat, Prakash, and Shepherd (1985, pp. 66, 68-70) proposed to use analogy to suggest new concepts and rules to be added to Cyc. T. Lin (2002) and Singh

et al. (2002) discuss the generation of plausible facts using analogical inference rules. Chklovski and Fredette (2001) and Chklovski (2003b) discuss the generation of plausible facts using analogy in Learner. Latent semantic analysis is described by Deerwester, Dumais, Furnas, Landauer, and Harshman (1990). AnalogySpace is described by Speer (2007), Speer, Havasi, and Lieberman (2008), and Havasi (2009). Singular value decomposition is described by Golub and Van Loan (1996) and Watkins (2010). Truncated singular value decomposition is described by Hansen (1998). Krishnamurthy and Lieberman (2010) describe an analogy algorithm based on truncated singular value decomposition that finds analogies in ConceptNet.

Games

A description of ANIMAL and the program code are provided by Ahl (1973, p. 17). Stork and Lam (2000) created an Internet version of ANIMAL. GIOMI is described by Garcia, Havasi, and Todd (2002). Verbosity is described by von Ahn, Kedia, and Blum (2006). von Ahn and Dabbish (2008) present templates and strategies for building successful games with a purpose. Common Consensus is described by Lieberman, Smith, and Teeters (2007).

Mining

Extracting and learning information from text corpora is discussed by Zernik (1991), Armstrong (1993), Manning and Schütze (1999), and Jurafsky and Martin (2009). Hearst (1992, 1998) proposes to extract relation instances automatically from large text corpora using patterns. Hobbs (1984, p. 8) mentions a rule similar to (19.3). Richardson, Dolan, and Vanderwende (1998) describe the MindNet lexical resource, which is built by extracting relation instances from dictionaries and encyclopedias. Berland and Charniak (1999) extract instances of the part relation from text. D. Lin and Pantel (2001) learn inference rules such as "X wrote Y \approx X is the author of Y" from text. Chambers and Jurafsky (2008, 2009) learn narrative schemas (scripts) and their participants from text.

Schubert (2002) proposes to extract world knowledge from text. KNEXT and related research are described by Schubert (2002), Schubert and Tong (2003), Van Durme (2009), Schubert, Gordon, Stratos, and Rubinoff (2011), and J. M. Gordon (2014). Episodic logic is described by Schubert and Hwang (2000). Sharpening of quantifiers is discussed by J. M. Gordon and Schubert (2010). Extracting entailment rules from text is discussed by J. M. Gordon and Schubert (2011) and J. M. Gordon (2014). J. M. Gordon and Schubert (2012) also discuss learning event frequencies from text. The Penn Treebank is described by Marcus, Marcinkiewicz, and Santorini (1993). TGrep2 is described by Rohde (2005), and TTT is described by Purtee and Schubert (2012). Sil and Yates (2011) present a system that learns the preconditions and effects of 40 actions.

EXERCISES

- **19.1** Give examples in which Open Mind Common Sense analogical inference rule (19.2) succeeds. Give examples in which the rule fails.
- **19.2** Propose other analogical inference rules along the lines of Open Mind Common Sense rules (19.1) and (19.2).
- **19.3** Write a program that applies analogical inference rules to a text-based commonsense knowledge base.
- **19.4** (Research Problem) Design and implement a crowdsourcing system or game to acquire *Initiates* and *Terminates* axioms including event and fluent arguments and their sorts.
- **19.5** (Research Problem) Mine *Initiates* and *Terminates* axioms including event and fluent arguments and their sorts from text.

212.0349.43

- r a growd it ar yn ac yn caellainidd a Blight nag y ddidfweg ang ac cae a cae a 190. Taellain ach claig a lain a laigh a bae a bae a chae a

 - have the above of the control of the
- en a la francia de l'estre en l'Anna de la majori de la completa de la francia de l'estre de la francia de l' La la completa de la francia de la francia de la completa de la francia de
 - and the contract of the contra

Conclusion VIII

Constusion V. M. Moiaulono

Conclusion

This book has provided a detailed treatment of commonsense reasoning and a guide to automating commonsense reasoning using predicate logic and the event calculus. We have described general methods that can be applied to a wide range of commonsense reasoning problems. In this chapter, we summarize what has been accomplished and discuss where this work is leading.

20.1 WHAT WAS ACCOMPLISHED?

We started by describing commonsense reasoning, a common activity that people perform almost without realizing it. We then considered several examples of commonsense reasoning and presented important aspects of this activity that need to be treated by any method for automating it or any formalism for describing it. We demonstrated that all these aspects can be handled using a particular logic, the event calculus. We described the event calculus, showed how it can be used for commonsense reasoning using several reasoning programs, and presented some sample applications. We reviewed other logical and nonlogical methods for commonsense reasoning, and we described methods for acquisition of commonsense knowledge.

20.1.1 WHAT IS THE EVENT CALCULUS?

The event calculus is based on classical many-sorted predicate logic with equality. It is characterized by a set of axioms and definitions: 17 in EC and 12 in DEC. The event calculus uses reification: It treats time-varying properties and events as objects so that statements can be made about the truth values of properties at timepoints and the occurrences of events at timepoints.

The event calculus uses circumscription, or the minimization of the extensions of predicates, to allow default reasoning. The event calculus uses the default assumptions that (1) the only events that occur are those known to occur and (2) the only effects of events are those that are known. When new information becomes available, the circumscriptions can be recomputed and reasoning again performed, which may lead to new conclusions. Circumscription is defined by a formula of second-order logic, but in most cases of interest circumscriptions compile into formulas of first-order logic.

An event calculus domain description consists of an axiomatization, observations of world properties, and a narrative of known world events. Given a domain description, various types of commonsense reasoning can be performed. Temporal projection consists of predicting the results of events given an initial state. Abduction consists of determining what events might have led from an initial state to a final state. Postdiction consists of determining the initial state given events and a final state. Model finding consists of determining properties and events that agree with a given narrative and set of observations.

20.1.2 HOW IS THE EVENT CALCULUS USED?

We have discussed a number of techniques for using the event calculus to perform commonsense reasoning. How do we go about doing this? First, we create an axiomatization that will be used to solve various problems. Second, we create a domain description for any given problem we wish to solve. Third, we solve the problem using manual proof techniques or using automated reasoning programs such as the Discrete Event Calculus Reasoner or answer set programming.

The axiomatization is created as follows. The kinds of problems to be handled are considered and the areas needing formalization are determined; it is useful to work with several sample problems. Sorts, subsort relationships, and variables for each sort are defined. Predicate, function, fluent, and event symbols are defined. The symbols are then used to write the necessary axioms for the areas of interest.

The domain description for a problem is created as follows. The logical constants for the particular problem are defined. These constants are used to specify observations of time-varying properties (fluents) and a narrative of event occurrences. Temporal ordering formulas, which relate the times of properties and events, may be specified. For example, it may be known that one event occurs prior to another event. Unique names axioms for events and fluents are specified.

20.2 WHERE IS THIS LEADING?

What is the reach of the techniques described in this book? Where is this leading? What we have here is the following. Given an axiomatization of some commonsense domains and incomplete information about any given world scenario involving those domains, we can run a reasoning program to fill in missing information about that scenario. This missing information can include events, initial states, intermediate states, and final states. In sum, we have a strategy for building computer systems that understand any commonsense domains of interest. The strategy is to axiomatize the domains, represent a scenario, and then run a reasoning program. We can use this strategy to enrich countless applications with commonsense reasoning capabilities.

There are several potential obstacles to the use of commonsense reasoning. The first obstacle is computing resources. Not all commonsense reasoning problems can be solved efficiently on standard computers. There are several ways of dealing with this. We can use large computer clusters and distributed computing networks. We can continue to perform research on the efficiency of reasoning algorithms in order

to discover and implement more efficient algorithms. We can also use the knowledge gained from this research to state problems in such a way that they can be solved efficiently. For example, experiments have shown that random SAT problems are most quickly solved either when they are underconstrained so that they have many solutions, or when they are overconstrained so that they have few solutions.

Another potential obstacle is our ability to construct complete and correct axiomatizations. Although we have presented appropriate axiomatizations and techniques for a number of commonsense areas, the commonsense world is large. Considerable effort and ingenuity are required to develop good axiomatizations. To some degree the task can be eased by using acquisition techniques such as crowdsourcing and text mining.

Another potential obstacle is that of linking up the event calculus to the world. How do we transform a problem in the world into an event calculus problem? Certain problems such as those involving electronic payment systems use representations that are easily translated into the event calculus. Other problems require more extensive preprocessing. Natural language text or speech must first be processed by syntactic and semantic parsers, and images must first be treated by image processing software.

20.3 CLOSING REMARKS

This book has considered commonsense reasoning and how the event calculus can capture it. This formalization of commonsense reasoning has two main benefits: It brings us a greater understanding of the human capacity for commonsense reasoning and it allows us to build more flexible and friendly computer systems. The current situation of automated commonsense reasoning can be likened to the situation of the web in the early 1990s. Decades of research on hypertext and computer networking had finally crystallized into two simple and powerful mechanisms for sharing information online: the hypertext transfer protocol (HTTP) and the hypertext markup language (HTML). In the years following, these mechanisms allowed the online world to take off exponentially. Similarly, decades of research have now crystallized into a simple and powerful mechanism for commonsense reasoning, the event calculus. I hope that the event calculus will lead to an explosion of applications. I invite you to build them.

BIBLIOGRAPHIC NOTES

Mitchell, Selman, and Levesque (1992) study the time taken by the Davis-Putnam-Logemann-Loveland procedure (M. Davis, Logemann, & Loveland, 1962; M. Davis & Putnam, 1960) to solve randomly generated 3-SAT problems, or SAT problems whose clauses contain three literals. They vary the ratio of the number of clauses to the number of variables and find that problems with a low-clause-to-variable ratio (around 2) or a high-clause-to-variable ratio (around 8) are quickly solved. The problems with a low-clause-to-variable ratio are underconstrained—most truth

370 CHAPTER 20 Conclusion

assignments are satisfying. The problems with a high-clause-to-variable ratio are overconstrained—few if any truth assignments are satisfying. On the other hand, problems with a clause-to-variable ratio around 4.25, for which approximately half the truth assignments are satisfying, take much longer to solve. Baum (2004, pp. 22, 23, 300-302) argues that the world is overconstrained, which allows humans to develop compact and overconstrained representations, which in turn allows reasoning to proceed efficiently.

Appendices

aeoilbhagul A

Logical Foundations

This appendix discusses logical foundations: relations, inductive definitions, first-order logic, many-sorted first-order logic, second-order logic, real numbers, lists, circumscription, and the *SM* operator.

A.1 RELATIONS

Relations are used in the definitions of the semantics of first-order logic and many-sorted first-order logic, and in the section on state constraints (Section 3.4).

Definition A.1. An *n*-ary relation R on a set S is a subset of S^n .

Definition A.2. A binary relation R on a set S is a subset of $S \times S$.

Definition A.3. A binary relation $R \subseteq S \times S$ is *reflexive* if and only if, for every $a \in S$, $\langle a, a \rangle \in R$.

Definition A.4. A binary relation $R \subseteq S \times S$ is *irreflexive* if and only if, for every $a \in S$, $\langle a, a \rangle \notin R$.

Definition A.5. A binary relation $R \subseteq S \times S$ is *symmetric* if and only if, for every $a, b \in S$, whenever $\langle a, b \rangle \in R$, we have $\langle b, a \rangle \in R$.

Definition A.6. A binary relation $R \subseteq S \times S$ is *antisymmetric* if and only if, for every $a, b \in S$, whenever $\langle a, b \rangle \in R$ and $a \neq b$, we have $\langle b, a \rangle \notin R$.

Definition A.7. A binary relation $R \subseteq S \times S$ is *transitive* if and only if, for every $a, b, c \in S$, whenever $\langle a, b \rangle \in R$ and $\langle b, c \rangle \in R$, we have $\langle a, c \rangle \in R$.

Definition A.8. A binary relation $R \subseteq S \times S$ is *intransitive* if and only if, for every $a, b, c \in S$, whenever $\langle a, b \rangle \in R$ and $\langle b, c \rangle \in R$, we have $\langle a, c \rangle \notin R$.

Definition A.9. A binary relation $R \subseteq S \times S$ is *trichotomous* if and only if, for every $a, b \in S$, exactly one of the following is the case: $\langle a, b \rangle \in R$, a = b, or $\langle b, a \rangle \in R$.

Definition A.10. A binary relation $R \subseteq S \times S$ is *total* if and only if, for every $a \in S$, there is a $b \in S$ such that $\langle a, b \rangle \in R$.

Definition A.11. A binary relation $R \subseteq S \times S$ is *functional* if and only if, for every $a, b, c \in S$, whenever $\langle a, b \rangle \in R$ and $\langle a, c \rangle \in R$, we have b = c.

Definition A.12. A binary relation $R \subseteq S \times S$ is *surjective* if and only if, for every $b \in S$, there is an $a \in S$ such that $\langle a, b \rangle \in R$.

Definition A.13. A binary relation $R \subseteq S \times S$ is *injective* if and only if, for every $a, b, c \in S$, whenever $\langle a, c \rangle \in R$ and $\langle b, c \rangle \in R$, we have a = b.

374

Definition A.14. A binary relation R is an *equivalence relation* if and only if R is reflexive, symmetric, and transitive.

Definition A.15. A binary relation R is a *partial order* if and only if R is reflexive, antisymmetric, and transitive.

Definition A.16. A partial order $R \subseteq S \times S$ is a *total order* if and only if, for every $a, b \in S$, either $\langle a, b \rangle \in R$ or $\langle b, a \rangle \in R$.

A.2 INDUCTIVE DEFINITIONS

An inductive definition of a set S consists of

- basis clauses specifying objects that are in S,
- *inductive clauses* specifying how to create new objects in S given other objects in S, and
- an extremal clause (or limiting clause) specifying that the only objects in S are
 those that can be obtained by applying the basis and inductive clauses a finite
 number of times.

For example, a nonnegative integer is defined inductively as follows:

- Basis clause: 0 is a nonnegative integer.
- Inductive clause: If n is a nonnegative integer, then n + 1 is a nonnegative integer.
- Extremal clause: Nothing else is a nonnegative integer.

A.3 FIRST-ORDER LOGIC

This section discusses the syntax, semantics, and proof theory of first-order logic.

A.3.1 SYNTAX OF FIRST-ORDER LOGIC

The syntax of first-order logic is defined as follows.

Definition A.17. A *signature* σ consists of the following disjoint sets:

- A set of constants.
- For every $n \in \{1, 2, 3, ...\}$, a set of *n*-ary *function symbols*.
- For every $n \in \{0, 1, 2, ...\}$, a set of *n*-ary *predicate symbols*.

Given a signature σ and a set of *variables* disjoint from the signature, we define formulas of the language $\mathcal{L}(\sigma)$ of first-order logic with equality as follows.

Definition A.18. A *term* is defined inductively as follows:

- A constant is a term.
- A variable is a term.
- If ϕ is an *n*-ary function symbol and τ_1, \ldots, τ_n are terms, then $\phi(\tau_1, \ldots, \tau_n)$ is a term. The terms τ_1, \ldots, τ_n are the **arguments** of ϕ .
- · Nothing else is a term.

Definition A.19. A *ground term* is a term containing no variables. **Definition A.20.** An *atom* is defined inductively as follows:

- If ρ is an *n*-ary predicate symbol and τ_1, \ldots, τ_n are terms, then $\rho(\tau_1, \ldots, \tau_n)$ is an atom. The terms τ_1, \ldots, τ_n are the *arguments* of ρ .
- If ρ is a 0-ary predicate symbol, then ρ is an atom.
- If τ_1 and τ_2 are terms, then $\tau_1 = \tau_2$ is an atom.
- Nothing else is an atom.

Definition A.21. A *ground atom* is an atom containing no variables. **Definition A.22.** A *formula* is defined inductively as follows:

- · An atom is a formula.
- \perp (*false*) and \top (*true*) are formulas.
- If α is a formula, then $\neg \alpha$ is a formula, called a *negation*.
- If α and β are formulas, then $(\alpha \wedge \beta)$ is a formula, called a *conjunction*. The formulas α and β are the *conjuncts* of $(\alpha \wedge \beta)$.
- If α and β are formulas, then $(\alpha \vee \beta)$ is a formula, called a *disjunction*. The formulas α and β are the *disjuncts* of $(\alpha \vee \beta)$.
- If α and β are formulas, then (α ⇒ β) is a formula, called a *conditional* or *implication*. The formula α is the *antecedent* or *hypothesis* of (α ⇒ β), whereas β is its *consequent* or *conclusion*. ⇒ is sometimes written as → or ⊃. The implication (α ⇒ β) represents that α is a *sufficient condition* for β or that β is a *necessary condition* for α.
- If α and β are formulas, then $(\alpha \Leftrightarrow \beta)$ is a formula, called a *biconditional*, *bi-implication*, or *equivalence*. \Leftrightarrow is sometimes written as \leftrightarrow or \equiv .
- If ν is a variable and α is a formula, then $(\exists \nu \alpha)$ is a formula, called an *existential quantification*.
- If ν is a variable and α is a formula, then $(\forall \nu \alpha)$ is a formula, called a *universal* quantification.
- Nothing else is a formula.

The symbols \bot , \top , \neg , \wedge , \vee , \Rightarrow , and \Leftrightarrow are *logical connectives*. The symbols \bot and \top are *zero-place connectives*. The symbol \exists is the *existential quantifier*, and the symbol \forall is the *universal quantifier*.

Definition A.23. The *scope* of the existential quantifier \exists in the formula $(\exists v \alpha)$ is α .

Definition A.24. The *scope* of the universal quantifier \forall in the formula $(\forall \nu \alpha)$ is α .

Definition A.25. The *scope* of the logical connective $0 \in \{\land, \lor, \Rightarrow, \Leftrightarrow\}$ in the formula $(\alpha \circ \beta)$ is α and β .

Definition A.26. The *scope* of \neg in the formula $\neg \alpha$ is α .

Definition A.27. An occurrence of a variable ν is **bound** in a formula Γ if and only if the occurrence is within a formula of the form $(\exists \nu \ \alpha)$ or $(\forall \nu \ \alpha)$ in Γ .

Definition A.28. An occurrence of a variable is *free* in a formula if and only if it is not bound in the formula.

Definition A.29. A *sentence* is a formula containing no occurrences of variables that are free in the formula.

376

In order to simplify the reading and writing of first-order logic formulas and sentences, we use the following notational conventions:

- We omit unnecessary parentheses. The precedence of logical connectives and quantifier symbols, from highest to lowest, is: ¬, ∧, ∨, ⇒, ⇔.
- We use $\tau_1 \neq \tau_2$ as an abbreviation for $\neg(\tau_1 = \tau_2)$.
- We use $\exists \nu_1, \ldots, \nu_n \alpha$ as an abbreviation for $\exists \nu_1 \ldots \exists \nu_n \alpha$, and $\forall \nu_1, \ldots, \nu_n \alpha$ as an abbreviation for $\forall \nu_1 \ldots \forall \nu_n \alpha$.

(See also Section 2.1.5 for further notational conventions.)

A.3.2 SEMANTICS OF FIRST-ORDER LOGIC

The *semantics* of first-order logic is defined as follows. The meaning of a formula of first-order logic is the set of structures in which the formula is true or the set of models of the formula.

Definition A.30. A structure or interpretation S of a signature σ consists of:

- A nonempty set of objects dom(S) called the **domain**.
- A function $c^{\mathcal{S}}$ from the constants of σ to $dom(\mathcal{S})$. Given a constant a, we say that $c^{\mathcal{S}}(a)$ is the object **named** by a in \mathcal{S} .
- For each *n*-ary function symbol ϕ of σ , an *n*-ary function $\phi^{\mathcal{S}}$ from $dom(\mathcal{S})^n$ to $dom(\mathcal{S})$.
- For each *n*-ary predicate symbol ρ of σ , an *n*-ary relation $\rho^{\mathcal{S}} \subseteq dom(\mathcal{S})^n$. The set $\rho^{\mathcal{S}}$ is called the *extension* of ρ in \mathcal{S} .

If ρ is a 0-ary predicate symbol, then $\rho^{\mathcal{S}} \subseteq \{\langle \rangle \}$. The extension $\rho^{\mathcal{S}} = \{\langle \rangle \}$ represents true, and the extension $\rho^{\mathcal{S}} = \emptyset$ represents false.

Definition A.31. A *variable assignment* on a structure S is a function from variables to dom(S).

Definition A.32. If *V* is a variable assignment, ν and ν are variables, and $d \in dom(S)$, then $V[\nu/d]$ is defined as follows:

$$V[v/d](v) = \begin{cases} d & \text{if } v = v \\ V(v) & \text{otherwise} \end{cases}$$

Definition A.33. A variable assignment V on S is extended to a function \overline{V} from terms of $\mathcal{L}(\sigma)$ to dom(S) as follows:

- If v is a variable, then $\overline{V}(v) = V(v)$.
- If a is a constant, then $\overline{V}(a) = c^{S}(a)$.
- If ϕ is an *n*-ary function symbol and τ_1, \ldots, τ_n are terms, then $\overline{V}(\phi(\tau_1, \ldots, \tau_n)) = \phi^{\mathcal{S}}(\overline{V}(\tau_1), \ldots, \overline{V}(\tau_n))$.

Definition A.34. The *truth* of a formula ψ of $\mathcal{L}(\sigma)$ in a structure \mathcal{S} under variable assignment V, written $(\mathcal{S}, V) \models \psi$, is defined as follows:

• If ρ is an *n*-ary predicate symbol and τ_1, \ldots, τ_n are terms, then $(S, V) \models \rho(\tau_1, \ldots, \tau_n)$ if and only if $\langle \overline{V}(\tau_1), \ldots, \overline{V}(\tau_n) \rangle \in \rho^S$.

- If τ_1 and τ_2 are terms, then $(S, V) \models \tau_1 = \tau_2$ if and only if $\overline{V}(\tau_1) = \overline{V}(\tau_2)$.
- It is not the case that $(S, V) \models \bot$.
- It is the case that $(S, V) \models \top$.
- If α is a formula, then $(S, V) \models \neg \alpha$ if and only if it is not the case that $(S, V) \models \alpha$.
- If α and β are formulas, then $(S, V) \models (\alpha \land \beta)$ if and only if $(S, V) \models \alpha$ and $(S, V) \models \beta$.
- If α and β are formulas, then $(S, V) \models (\alpha \lor \beta)$ if and only if $(S, V) \models \alpha$ or $(S, V) \models \beta$.
- If α and β are formulas, then $(S, V) \models (\alpha \Rightarrow \beta)$ if and only if $(S, V) \models \neg \alpha$ or $(S, V) \models \beta$.
- If α and β are formulas, then $(S, V) \models (\alpha \Leftrightarrow \beta)$ if and only if $(S, V) \models (\alpha \Rightarrow \beta)$ and $(S, V) \models (\beta \Rightarrow \alpha)$.
- If ν is a variable and α is a formula, then $(S, V) \models (\exists \nu \alpha)$ if and only if $(S, V[\nu/d]) \models \alpha$ for some $d \in dom(S)$.
- If ν is a variable and α is a formula, then $(S, V) \models (\forall \nu \alpha)$ if and only if $(S, V[\nu/d]) \models \alpha$ for every $d \in dom(S)$.

Definition A.35. A formula ψ is *true* in \mathcal{S} , written $\mathcal{S} \models \psi$, if and only if, for every variable assignment V, we have $(\mathcal{S}, V) \models \psi$. In this case, we say that \mathcal{S} is a *model* of ψ , and that \mathcal{S} *satisfies* ψ .

Definition A.36. A formula ψ is *satisfiable* if and only if, for some structure S and variable assignment V, we have $(S, V) \models \psi$.

Definition A.37. A formula ψ is *valid*, written $\models \psi$, if and only if, for every structure \mathcal{S} , we have $\mathcal{S} \models \psi$. A valid formula is called a *tautology*. Some useful tautologies are shown in Table A.1.

Definition A.38. A formula ψ *entails* a formula π , written $\psi \models \pi$, if and only if, for every \mathcal{S} such that $\mathcal{S} \models \psi$, we have $\mathcal{S} \models \pi$.

A.3.3 HERBRAND STRUCTURES AND MODELS

Definition A.39. A structure or interpretation S of a signature σ is a *Herbrand structure* or *Herbrand interpretation* if and only if

- dom(S) is the set of all ground terms of $\mathcal{L}(\sigma)$,
- for every constant a of σ , $c^{\mathcal{S}}(a) = a$, and
- for every *n*-ary function symbol ϕ of σ and ground terms τ_1, \ldots, τ_n of $\mathcal{L}(\sigma)$, $\phi^{\mathcal{S}}(\tau_1, \ldots, \tau_n) = \phi(\tau_1, \ldots, \tau_n)$.

Definition A.40. A structure S is a *Herbrand model* of a formula ψ if and only if S is a Herbrand structure and S is a model of ψ .

A.3.4 PROOF THEORY

Proof theory is concerned with defining the notion of a proof.

Table A.1 Oseful Tautologies"		
Name	Tautology	
Associative laws	$((\alpha \wedge \beta) \wedge \gamma) \Leftrightarrow (\alpha \wedge (\beta \wedge \gamma))$	
	$((\alpha \vee \beta) \vee \gamma) \Leftrightarrow (\alpha \vee (\beta \vee \gamma))$	
Commutative laws	$(\alpha \wedge \beta) \Leftrightarrow (\beta \wedge \alpha)$	
	$(\alpha \vee \beta) \Leftrightarrow (\beta \vee \alpha)$	
Contraposition	$(\alpha \Rightarrow \beta) \Leftrightarrow (\neg \beta \Rightarrow \neg \alpha)$	
De Morgan's laws	$\neg(\alpha \land \beta) \Leftrightarrow (\neg\alpha \lor \neg\beta)$	
	$\neg(\alpha \vee \beta) \Leftrightarrow (\neg\alpha \wedge \neg\beta)$	
Distributive laws	$(\alpha \vee (\beta \wedge \gamma)) \Leftrightarrow ((\alpha \vee \beta) \wedge (\alpha \vee \gamma))$	
	$(\alpha \wedge (\beta \vee \gamma)) \Leftrightarrow ((\alpha \wedge \beta) \vee (\alpha \wedge \gamma))$	
Double negation	$\neg \neg \alpha \Leftrightarrow \alpha$	
Exportation and	$((\alpha \land \beta) \Rightarrow \gamma) \Leftrightarrow (\alpha \Rightarrow (\beta \Rightarrow \gamma))$	
importation	The state of the s	
Idempotence	$(\alpha \wedge \alpha) \Leftrightarrow \alpha$	
	$(\alpha \vee \alpha) \Leftrightarrow \alpha$	
Law of contradiction	$\neg(\alpha \land \neg \alpha)$	
Law of excluded middle	$\alpha \vee \neg \alpha$	
Laws for bi-implication	$(\alpha \Leftrightarrow \beta) \Leftrightarrow ((\alpha \Rightarrow \beta) \land (\beta \Rightarrow \alpha))$	
	$(\alpha \Leftrightarrow \beta) \Leftrightarrow ((\neg \alpha \lor \beta) \land (\neg \beta \lor \alpha))$	
Law for implication	$(\alpha \Rightarrow \beta) \Leftrightarrow (\neg \alpha \lor \beta)$	

Table A.1 Useful Tautologies^a

Quantifier exchange

Definition A.41. An *axiom system A* consists of a set of *logical axioms* and a set of *inference rules*. The logical axioms are formulas, and inference rules specify how a formula may be inferred from other formulas.

 $(\neg \exists \nu \alpha) \Leftrightarrow (\forall \nu \neg \alpha)$

A standard inference rule is *modus ponens*, which states that, from α and $\alpha \Rightarrow \beta$, we may infer β . This inference rule is written as

$$\frac{\alpha \quad \alpha \Rightarrow \beta}{\beta}$$

Definition A.42. A *proof* of a formula π given a formula ψ is a finite sequence of formulas such that the last formula is π and each formula is either a logical axiom, ψ , or a formula inferred from previous formulas using one of the inference rules.

Definition A.43. A formula π is *provable* from a formula ψ , written $\psi \vdash \pi$, if and only if there is a proof of π given ψ .

Definition A.44. A formula ψ is *consistent* if and only if there is no formula π such that both $\psi \vdash \pi$ and $\psi \vdash \neg \pi$.

Definition A.45. A formula is *inconsistent* if and only if it is not consistent.

 $^{^{}a}\alpha, \beta, \gamma = formulas; \nu = variable.$

Definition A.46. An axiom system A is **sound** if and only if, for all formulas ψ and π , it is the case that $\psi \vdash \pi$ implies $\psi \models \pi$.

Definition A.47. An axiom system A is *complete* if and only if, for all formulas ψ and π , it is the case that $\psi \models \pi$ implies $\psi \vdash \pi$.

Many sound and complete axiom systems exist for first-order logic.

A.4 MANY-SORTED FIRST-ORDER LOGIC

Many-sorted first-order logic is used by the event calculus to distinguish such things as events and fluents.

A.4.1 SYNTAX OF MANY-SORTED FIRST-ORDER LOGIC

In the event calculus, we write formulas such as

 $\exists e, t (Happens(e, t) \land t_1 \leq t < t_2 \land Initiates(e, f, t)).$

But consider the ground atom Happens(Lucy, Margaret). We would like to regard this as ill-formed. We would like the variable e to range only over events and the variable t to range only over timepoints. Therefore, the event calculus is based on a logic with many sorts.

Definition A.48. A *many-sorted signature* σ is a (one-sorted) signature extended with:

- A nonempty set of sorts S.
- A subsort partial order $H \subseteq S \times S$.
- · A sort associated with every constant.
- A sort associated with every function symbol (the sort of the "result of the function").
- A sort associated with every argument position of every function symbol and predicate symbol.

Given a many-sorted signature σ and a set of *variables* for each sort, we define formulas of the language $\mathcal{L}(\sigma)$ of many-sorted first-order logic with equality as follows.

Definition A.49. A sort s_1 is a *subsort* of a sort s_2 if and only if $\langle s_1, s_2 \rangle \in H$. Note that every sort is a subsort of itself because a partial order is reflexive.

Definition A.50. The sort of a term τ is defined as follows:

- If τ is a constant or variable, the sort of the term τ is the sort of the constant or variable τ.
- If τ is $\phi(\tau_1, \ldots, \tau_n)$, where ϕ is an *n*-ary function symbol, τ_1, \ldots, τ_n are terms, and for each $i \in \{1, \ldots, n\}$ the sort of τ_i is a subsort of the sort of the *i*th argument position of ϕ , then the sort of τ is the sort of ϕ .

Definition A.51. A term is defined inductively as follows:

- · A constant is a term.
- A variable is a term.
- If ϕ is an *n*-ary function symbol, τ_1, \ldots, τ_n are terms, and for each $i \in \{1, \ldots, n\}$ the sort of τ_i is a subsort of the sort of the *i*th argument position of ϕ , then $\phi(\tau_1, \ldots, \tau_n)$ is a term.
- · Nothing else is a term.

Definition A.52. An *atom* is defined inductively as follows:

- If ρ is an n-ary predicate symbol, τ₁, ..., τ_n are terms, and for each
 i ∈ {1,...,n} the sort of τ_i is a subsort of the sort of the ith argument position of
 ρ, then ρ(τ₁,..., τ_n) is an atom.
- If ρ is a 0-ary predicate symbol, then ρ is an atom.
- If τ_1 and τ_2 are terms, then $\tau_1 = \tau_2$ is an atom.
- Nothing else is an atom.

The definition of a formula is the same as for one-sorted logic.

A.4.2 SEMANTICS OF MANY-SORTED FIRST-ORDER LOGIC

Definition A.53. A *structure* or *interpretation* S of a many-sorted signature σ consists of:

- For each sort s of σ , a nonempty set of objects $dom_s(S)$ called the **domain** of s such that for every sort s' of σ , if s is a subsort of s' (that is, if $\langle s, s' \rangle \in H$), then $dom_s(S) \subseteq dom_{s'}(S)$.
- For each sort s of σ , a function $c_s^{\mathcal{S}}$ from the set of constants of σ whose sort is s to $dom_{\epsilon}(\mathcal{S})$.
- For each *n*-ary function symbol ϕ of σ , an *n*-ary function ϕ^S from $dom_{s_1}(S) \times \cdots \times dom_{s_n}(S)$ to $dom_s(S)$, where s_1, \ldots, s_n are the sorts of the argument positions of ϕ and s is the sort of ϕ .
- For each *n*-ary predicate symbol ρ of σ , an *n*-ary relation $\rho^{S} \subseteq dom_{s_1}(S) \times \cdots \times dom_{s_n}(S)$, where s_1, \ldots, s_n are the sorts of the argument positions of ρ .

The definition of truth is similar to that for one-sorted logic. Many-sorted first-order logic is reducible to one-sorted first-order logic. The usual method is to replace formulas of the form

$$\exists \nu \ \Sigma(\nu)$$
 (A.1)

with

$$\exists \nu \, (Sort(\nu) = s \Rightarrow \Sigma(\nu)) \tag{A.2}$$

where s is the sort of the variable ν . The formula (A.2) is called the relativization of (A.1). Universal quantification is treated similarly.

A.5 SECOND-ORDER LOGIC

Second-order logic extends first-order logic with quantification over predicates and functions. It is used in this book to define circumscription and the *SM* operator. Second-order logic introduces predicate variables and function variables. The definition of a term is modified to allow the use of a function variable in place of a function symbol. The definition of an atom is modified to allow the use of a predicate variable in place of a predicate symbol. The definition of a formula is modified to allow predicate variables and function variables to appear in quantifiers.

A.6 DATATYPES

Real numbers and lists are used in the event calculus and domain formalizations.

A.6.1 REAL NUMBERS

We have a real number sort R, with numeric constants such as -1, 3, and π . Function and predicate symbols are defined as in Table A.2, which also provides the abbreviations that are used. Table A.3 provides further abbreviations.

We do not provide an axiomatization of real numbers but, instead, assume a standard interpretation of the reals. That is, we assume that in all structures S:

- We have $dom_R(S) = \mathbb{R}$, where \mathbb{R} is the set of real numbers.
- For every numeric constant a that represents the real number x, we have $c_R^S(a) = x$.
- For every *n*-ary function symbol ϕ in Table A.2, we have $\phi^{\mathcal{S}}(x_1, \dots, x_n) = \phi'(x_1, \dots, x_n)$, where ϕ' is the function from \mathbb{R}^n to \mathbb{R} corresponding to ϕ . For example, $Plus^{\mathcal{S}}(x, y) = x + y$. We assume that the

Table A.2 Functions and Predicates for Real Numbers

Туре	Function/Predicate	Abbreviation
Function	Plus(x,y)	x+y
	Minus(x,y)	x-y
	Times(x,y)	$xy, x \cdot y$
	DividedBy(x,y)	X/Y
	Remainder(x, y)	
	Power(x, y)	x ^y
	Floor(x)	[X]
	Sin(x)	
	Cos(x)	
Predicate	LessThan(x,y)	X < Y

Trainbor Torritatao		
Abbreviation	Formula	
$X \leq y$	LessThan $(x, y) \lor x = y$	
X > y	$\neg LessThan(x,y) \land x \neq y$	
$X \ge y$	¬LessThan(x, y)	
\sqrt{x}	Power(x, 0.5)	
X < Y < Z	$X < Y \land Y < Z$	
$X < Y \le Z$	$X < Y \land Y \le Z$	
$X \le y < Z$	$X \le y \land y < Z$	
X < V < Z	$X < V \land V < Z$	

Table A.3 Abbreviations for Real Number Formulas

functions corresponding to *DividedBy* and *Power* are extended to total functions. For example, we may define $\frac{x}{0} = 0$ for every $x \in \mathbb{R}$.

• For every *n*-ary predicate symbol ρ in Table A.2, we have $\rho^{S} = \rho'$, where ρ' is the relation on \mathbb{R}^{n} corresponding to ρ . For example, $\langle x, y \rangle \in LessThan^{S}$ if and only if x < y.

A.6.2 LISTS

We present an axiomatization of lists based on that of Zohar Manna and Richard Waldinger. We use lists to represent plans in Section 11.1. We have a list sort, with variables l, l_1 , l_2 , We have a sort for other entities, with variables x, x_1 , x_2 ,

 $Insert(x, l_1) = l_2$: The result of inserting x at the front of list l_1 is l_2 . Head(l) = x: The head of list l is x. $Tail(l_1) = l_2$: The tail of list l_1 is list l_2 . Length(l) = n: The length of list l is n.

We also have a predicate ElementOf(x, l), which represents that x is an element of the list l, and a constant Empty, which represents the empty list.

We use $[\tau_1, \tau_2, \dots, \tau_n]$ as an abbreviation for $Insert(\tau_1, Insert(\tau_2, \dots, Insert(\tau_n, Empty) \dots))$, and we use $x \in l$ as an abbreviation for ElementOf(x, l).

Intuitively, we would like the following to be true:

We have the following functions.

Insert(A, [B, C]) = [A, B, C] Head([A, B]) = A Tail([A, B, C]) = [B, C] Length(Empty) = 0 Length([A, B, C]) = 3 $B \in [A, B, C]$ [A, B, C] = [A, B, C] $P = Q \Rightarrow [P, B] = [Q, B]$ We have the following axioms.

Axiom L1.

$$Head(Insert(x, l)) = x$$

Axiom L2.

$$Tail(Insert(x, l)) = l$$

Axiom L3.

$$Length(Empty) = 0$$

Axiom L4.

$$Length(Insert(x, l)) = 1 + Length(l)$$

Axiom L5.

$$\neg ElementOf(x, Empty)$$

Axiom L6.

$$ElementOf(x_1, Insert(x_2, l)) \Leftrightarrow x_1 = x_2 \vee ElementOf(x_1, l)$$

Axiom L7.

$$Empty \neq Insert(x, l)$$

Axiom L8.

$$Insert(x_1, l_1) = Insert(x_2, l_2) \Leftrightarrow x_1 = x_2 \wedge l_1 = l_2$$

A.7 CIRCUMSCRIPTION

Circumscription is used in the event calculus to implement default reasoning.

A.7.1 DEFINITION OF CIRCUMSCRIPTION

We start by defining some abbreviations, and then we define circumscription.

Definition A.54. If ρ_1 and ρ_2 are *n*-ary predicate symbols and ν_1, \ldots, ν_n are distinct variables of appropriate sort, then:

- $\rho_1 = \rho_2$ is an abbreviation for $\forall \nu_1, \ldots, \nu_n \rho_1(\nu_1, \ldots, \nu_n) \Leftrightarrow \rho_2(\nu_1, \ldots, \nu_n)$.
- $\rho_1 \le \rho_2$ is an abbreviation for $\forall \nu_1, \ldots, \nu_n \, \rho_1(\nu_1, \ldots, \nu_n) \Rightarrow \rho_2(\nu_1, \ldots, \nu_n)$.

Definition A.55. If ρ_1 and ρ_2 are *n*-ary predicate symbols, then $\rho_1 < \rho_2$ is an abbreviation for $(\rho_1 \le \rho_2) \land \neg (\rho_1 = \rho_2)$.

Definition A.56. If Γ is a first-order formula containing the predicate symbol ρ , then the *(basic) circumscription* of ρ in Γ , written $CIRC[\Gamma; \rho]$, is the second-order formula

$$\Gamma \wedge \neg \exists \phi (\Gamma(\phi) \wedge \phi < \rho)$$

where ϕ is a predicate variable with the same arity and argument sorts as ρ , and $\Gamma(\phi)$ is the formula obtained from Γ by replacing each occurrence of ρ with ϕ .

384

This says that, in every model of $CIRC[\Gamma; \rho]$, the extension of ρ complies with Γ and there is no proper subset of the extension of ρ that complies with Γ . That is, the extension of ρ is minimal given Γ .

A.7.2 EXAMPLE: CIRCUMSCRIPTION OF P(A)

Suppose $\Gamma = P(A)$. Then $CIRC[\Gamma; P]$ is given by the second-order formula

$$P(A) \land \neg \exists \phi (\phi(A) \land \phi < P)$$

This means that for every model \mathcal{M} of $CIRC[\Gamma; P]$, if \mathbf{A} is the object named by A in \mathcal{M} , then $\mathbf{A} \in P^{\mathcal{M}}$ and there is no proper subset Q of $P^{\mathcal{M}}$ such that $\mathbf{A} \in Q$, from which we conclude that $P^{\mathcal{M}} = \{\mathbf{A}\}$. Therefore, $CIRC[\Gamma; P]$ is equivalent to the first-order formula

$$\forall x (P(x) \Leftrightarrow x = A)$$

A.7.3 PARALLEL CIRCUMSCRIPTION

The event calculus requires circumscription of several predicates, called parallel circumscription.

Definition A.57. If Γ is a first-order formula containing the predicate symbols ρ_1, \ldots, ρ_n , then the *(parallel) circumscription* of ρ_1, \ldots, ρ_n in Γ , written $CIRC[\Gamma; \rho_1, \ldots, \rho_n]$, is the second-order formula

$$\Gamma \wedge \neg \exists \phi_1, \ldots, \phi_n \left(\Gamma(\phi_1, \ldots, \phi_n) \wedge \bigwedge_{i=1}^n \phi_i < \rho_i \right),$$

where ϕ_1, \ldots, ϕ_n are distinct predicate variables with the same arities and argument sorts as ρ_1, \ldots, ρ_n , respectively, and $\Gamma(\phi_1, \ldots, \phi_n)$ is the formula obtained from Γ by replacing each occurrence of ρ_1, \ldots, ρ_n with ϕ_1, \ldots, ϕ_n , respectively.

A.8 SM

The SM operator is used in Chapter 15 on commonsense reasoning using answer set programming. As discussed in Section 15.2.3, we assume that the logical connectives are limited to \bot (false), \land , \lor , and \Rightarrow . Other logical connectives are considered to be abbreviations.

Definition A.58. If Γ is a first-order formula containing the predicate symbols ρ_1, \ldots, ρ_n , then $SM[\Gamma; \rho_1, \ldots, \rho_n]$ is the second-order formula

$$\Gamma \wedge \neg \exists \phi_1, \ldots, \phi_n \left(\Gamma^*(\phi_1, \ldots, \phi_n) \wedge \bigwedge_{i=1}^n \phi_i < \rho_i \right)$$

where ϕ_1, \ldots, ϕ_n are distinct predicate variables with the same arities and argument sorts as ρ_1, \ldots, ρ_n , respectively, and $\Gamma^*(\phi_1, \ldots, \phi_n)$ is obtained from Γ by applying the following recursive definition:

```
• \rho_i(\tau_1,\ldots,\tau_n)^* = \phi_i(\tau_1,\ldots,\tau_n).
```

- $\alpha^* = \alpha$ for any atom α not containing any of the predicate symbols ρ_1, \ldots, ρ_n .
- $(\alpha \wedge \beta)^* = \alpha^* \wedge \beta^*$.
- $(\alpha \vee \beta)^* = \alpha^* \vee \beta^*$.
- $(\alpha \Rightarrow \beta)^* = (\alpha^* \Rightarrow \beta^*) \land (\alpha \Rightarrow \beta).$
- $(\forall \nu \alpha)^* = (\forall \nu \alpha^*).$
- $(\exists \nu \, \alpha)^* = (\exists \nu \, \alpha^*).$

Definition A.59. If Γ is a formula, then $SM[\Gamma]$ is defined as $SM[\Gamma; \rho_1, \ldots, \rho_n]$, where ρ_1, \ldots, ρ_n are all the predicate symbols occurring in Γ .

BIBLIOGRAPHIC NOTES

Inductive definitions are discussed by Kleene (1952, pp. 258-261). First-order logic is treated by Church (1956), Curry (1963), Kleene (1967), Mates (1972), Hamilton (1988), Ebbinghaus, Flum, and Thomas (1994), Mendelson (1997), Nerode and Shore (1997), Enderton (2001), Hodges (2001), and Wolf (2005). Model theory is treated in detail by Hodges (1993). The notation $(S, V) \models \psi$ is taken from Fagin, Halpern, Moses, and Vardi (1995, p. 79). Lists of tautologies are provided by Whitehead and Russell (1925), Kleene (1952, pp. 118-119, 162-163), Mates (1972, pp. 103-110, 126-130), Doherty, Łukaszewicz, and Szałas (1997, p. 301), Nerode and Shore (1997, pp. 35-36), Enderton (2001, pp. 26-27), and Wolfram (2002, p. 817). Herbrand structures and models are discussed by Ebbinghaus, Flum, and Thomas (1994, pp. 199-200). Proof theory is treated in detail by Buss (1998). Our definition of an axiom system is based on that of Fagin, Halpern, Moses, and Vardi (1995, p. 50). Proofs of soundness and completeness of axiom systems for first-order logic are given by Hamilton (1988, pp. 73-104), Ebbinghaus, Flum, and Thomas (1994, pp. 59-85), and Enderton (2001, pp. 109-146). These proofs of completeness are patterned after the one given by Henkin (1949). The completeness theorem was first proved by Gödel (1930/1967).

Our definition of many-sorted first-order logic is based on that of Enderton (2001, pp. 295-299), extended with notions from Walther (1983, 1987), and Oberschelp (1990, pp. 12-13), who add a subsort order to many-sorted first-order logic. Many-sorted logic with a subsort order is sometimes called "order-sorted logic" (Oberschelp, 1990, p. 8). Enderton (2001, pp. 296-299) reduces many-sorted first-order logic to one-sorted first-order logic. Relativization is discussed by Walther (1983, p. 883; 1987, p. 6), Oberschelp (1990, p. 10), Ebbinghaus, Flum, and Thomas (1994, p. 49), and Enderton (2001, p. 297).

In our version of many-sorted first-order logic, $\tau_1 = \tau_2$ is an atom regardless of the sorts of τ_1 and τ_2 , as in Walther (1983, p. 885). In contrast, in the many-sorted logic of Enderton (2001, pp. 295-296), each sort i may have an equality symbol $=_i$, and $\tau_1 =_i$ τ_2 is an atom if the sort of both τ_1 and τ_2 is i. An introduction to the foundations of the real number system is provided by Eves (1990, pp. 173-211). Our axiomatization of lists is based on that of Manna and Waldinger (1985, pp. 437-469). See also

Green's (1969, pp. 106-108) axiomatization of Lisp. Second-order logic is treated by Ebbinghaus, Flum, and Thomas (1994, pp. 138-142), Manzano (1996, pp. 1-68), Mendelson (1997, pp. 368-382), Enderton (2001, pp. 282-306), and van Benthem and Doets (2001, pp. 200-216). Circumscription is discussed by McCarthy (1977) and Lifschitz (1994). The *SM* operator is discussed by Ferraris, Lee, and Lifschitz (2011).

Equivalence of EC and DEC

In this appendix, we prove that EC and DEC are logically equivalent if the timepoint sort is restricted to the integers. Our proof is structured as follows: We must show that EC implies DEC and that DEC implies EC. It is easy to show that EC implies DEC. This follows by universal instantiation, substituting $t_1 + 1$ for t_2 . Showing that DEC implies EC is more difficult. We prove a number of lemmas stating that individual EC axioms follow from DEC.

Lemma B.1. If the timepoint sort is restricted to the integers, then

$$DEC \Rightarrow EC9$$

Proof. Suppose DEC. Let τ_1 and τ_2 be arbitrary integer timepoints and β be an arbitrary fluent. We must show

$$(HoldsAt(\beta, \tau_1) \land \tau_1 < \tau_2 \land$$

$$PersistsBetween(\tau_1, \beta, \tau_2) \land \neg Clipped(\tau_1, \beta, \tau_2)) \Rightarrow$$

$$HoldsAt(\beta, \tau_2)$$

$$(B.1)$$

Case 1: $\tau_1 \ge \tau_2$. (B.1) is trivially satisfied.

Case 2: $\tau_1 < \tau_2$. We proceed by mathematical induction.

Base case: We show that (B.1) is true for $\tau_2 = \tau_1 + 1$. Suppose

$$HoldsAt(\beta, \tau_1) \land PersistsBetween(\tau_1, \beta, \tau_1 + 1) \land \neg Clipped(\tau_1, \beta, \tau_1 + 1)$$

From $PersistsBetween(\tau_1, \beta, \tau_1 + 1)$ and definition EC7, we have $\neg ReleasedAt(\beta, \tau_1 + 1)$. From $\neg Clipped(\tau_1, \beta, \tau_1 + 1)$ and definition EC1, we have $\neg \exists a(Happens(a, \tau_1) \land Terminates(a, \beta, \tau_1))$. From this, $HoldsAt(\beta, \tau_1)$, $\neg ReleasedAt(\beta, \tau_1 + 1)$, and DEC5, we have $HoldsAt(\beta, \tau_1 + 1)$ as required.

Induction step: Suppose (B.1) is true for $\tau_2 = k, k > \tau_1$ (induction hypothesis):

$$(HoldsAt(\beta, \tau_1) \land \tau_1 < k \land$$

$$PersistsBetween(\tau_1, \beta, k) \land \neg Clipped(\tau_1, \beta, k)) \Rightarrow$$

$$HoldsAt(\beta, k)$$
(B.2)

We must show that (B.1) is true for $\tau_2 = k + 1$. Suppose

$$HoldsAt(\beta, \tau_1) \wedge \tau_1 < k + 1 \wedge PersistsBetween(\tau_1, \beta, k + 1) \wedge \neg Clipped(\tau_1, \beta, k + 1)$$

¹This appendix is a slightly altered version of section 3.2 of an article by Mueller (2004a) in the *Journal of Logic and Computation*, published by Oxford University Press.

From $PersistsBetween(\tau_1, \beta, k+1)$ and definition EC7, we have $PersistsBetween(\tau_1, \beta, k)$. From $\neg Clipped(\tau_1, \beta, k+1)$ and definition EC1, we have $\neg Clipped(\tau_1, \beta, k)$. From this, $HoldsAt(\beta, \tau_1)$, $\tau_1 < k$, $PersistsBetween(\tau_1, \beta, k)$, and the induction hypothesis (B.2), we have $HoldsAt(\beta, k)$. From $PersistsBetween(\tau_1, \beta, k+1)$ and definition EC7, we have $\neg ReleasedAt(\beta, k+1)$. From $\neg Clipped(\tau_1, \beta, k+1)$ and definition EC1, we have $\neg \exists a(Happens(a, k) \land Terminates(a, \beta, k))$. From this, $HoldsAt(\beta, k)$, $\neg ReleasedAt(\beta, k+1)$, and DEC5, we have $HoldsAt(\beta, k+1)$ as required.

Lemma B.2. If the timepoint sort is restricted to the integers, then

$$DEC \Rightarrow EC10$$

Proof. The proof is identical to that of Lemma B.1, except that ¬*HoldsAt* is substituted for *HoldsAt*, *Inititates* is substituted for *Terminates*, DEC6 is substituted for DEC5, *Declipped* is substituted for *Clipped*, EC2 is substituted for EC1, and EC10 is substituted for EC9. ■

Lemma B.3. If the timepoint sort is restricted to the integers, then

$$DEC \Rightarrow EC11$$

Proof. Suppose DEC. Let τ_1 and τ_2 be arbitrary integer timepoints and β be an arbitrary fluent. We must show

$$(ReleasedAt(\beta, \tau_1) \wedge \tau_1 < \tau_2 \wedge$$

$$\neg Clipped(\tau_1, \beta, \tau_2) \wedge \neg Declipped(\tau_1, \beta, \tau_2)) \Rightarrow$$

$$ReleasedAt(\beta, \tau_2)$$
(B.3)

Case 1: $\tau_1 \ge \tau_2$. (B.3) is trivially satisfied.

Case 2: $\tau_1 < \tau_2$. We proceed by mathematical induction.

Base case: We show that (B.3) is true for $\tau_2 = \tau_1 + 1$. Suppose

$$\begin{aligned} \textit{ReleasedAt}(\beta,\tau_1) \wedge \tau_1 < \tau_1 + 1 \wedge \\ \neg \textit{Clipped}(\tau_1,\beta,\tau_1+1) \wedge \neg \textit{Declipped}(\tau_1,\beta,\tau_1+1) \end{aligned}$$

From $\neg Declipped(\tau_1, \beta, \tau_1 + 1)$ and definition EC2, we have $\neg \exists a(Happens(a, \tau_1) \land Initiates(a, \beta, \tau_1))$. From $\neg Clipped(\tau_1, \beta, \tau_1 + 1)$ and definition EC1, we have $\neg \exists a(Happens(a, \tau_1) \land Terminates(a, \beta, \tau_1))$. From $ReleasedAt(\beta, \tau_1)$, $\neg \exists a(Happens(a, \tau_1) \land Initiates(a, \beta, \tau_1))$, $\neg \exists a(Happens(a, \tau_1) \land Terminates(a, \beta, \tau_1))$, and DEC7, we have $ReleasedAt(\beta, \tau_1 + 1)$ as required.

Induction step: Suppose (B.3) is true for $\tau_2 = k, k > \tau_1$ (induction hypothesis):

$$(ReleasedAt(\beta, \tau_1) \land \tau_1 < k \land \neg Clipped(\tau_1, \beta, k) \land \neg Declipped(\tau_1, \beta, k)) \Rightarrow ReleasedAt(\beta, k)$$
(B.4)

We must show that (B.3) is true for $\tau_2 = k + 1$. Suppose

$$ReleasedAt(\beta, \tau_1) \land \tau_1 < k+1 \land \neg Clipped(\tau_1, \beta, k+1) \land \neg Declipped(\tau_1, \beta, k+1)$$

From $\neg Clipped(\tau_1, \beta, k + 1)$ and definition EC1, we have $\neg Clipped(\tau_1, \beta, k)$. From $\neg Declipped(\tau_1, \beta, k + 1)$ and definition EC2, we have $\neg Declipped(\tau_1, \beta, k)$. From

this, $ReleasedAt(\beta, \tau_1)$, $\tau_1 < k$, $\neg Clipped(\tau_1, \beta, k)$, and the induction hypothesis (B.4), we have $ReleasedAt(\beta, k)$. From $\neg Declipped(\tau_1, \beta, k+1)$ and definition EC2, we have $\neg \exists a(Happens(a, k) \land Initiates(a, \beta, k))$. From $\neg Clipped(\tau_1, \beta, k+1)$ and definition EC1, we have $\neg \exists a(Happens(a, k) \land Terminates(a, \beta, k))$. From $ReleasedAt(\beta, k)$, $\neg \exists a(Happens(a, k) \land Terminates(a, \beta, k))$, and DEC7, we have $ReleasedAt(\beta, k+1)$ as required.

The following lemma is used in Theorem B.1 as well as Lemmas B.5 and B.6. Lemma B.4. If the timepoint sort is restricted to the integers, then

$$DEC \Rightarrow EC12$$

Proof. Suppose DEC. Let τ_1 and τ_2 be arbitrary integer timepoints and β be an arbitrary fluent. We must show

$$(\neg ReleasedAt(\beta, \tau_1) \land \tau_1 < \tau_2 \land \neg ReleasedBetween(\tau_1, \beta, \tau_2)) \Rightarrow \qquad (B.5)$$

$$\neg ReleasedAt(\beta, \tau_2)$$

Case 1: $\tau_1 \ge \tau_2$. (B.5) is trivially satisfied.

Case 2: $\tau_1 < \tau_2$. We proceed by mathematical induction.

Base case: We show that (B.5) is true for $\tau_2 = \tau_1 + 1$. Suppose

$$\neg ReleasedAt(\beta, \tau_1) \land \tau_1 < \tau_1 + 1 \land \neg ReleasedBetween(\tau_1, \beta, \tau_1 + 1)$$

From $\neg ReleasedBetween(\tau_1, \beta, \tau_1 + 1)$ and definition EC8, we have $\neg \exists a (Happens(a, \tau_1) \land Releases(a, \beta, \tau_1))$. From this, $\neg ReleasedAt(\beta, \tau_1)$, and DEC8, we have $\neg ReleasedAt(\beta, \tau_1 + 1)$ as required.

Induction step: Suppose (B.5) is true for $\tau_2 = k, k > \tau_1$ (induction hypothesis):

$$(\neg ReleasedAt(\beta, \tau_1) \land \tau_1 < k \land \neg ReleasedBetween(\tau_1, \beta, k)) \Rightarrow \\ \neg ReleasedAt(\beta, k)$$
(B.6)

We must show that (B.5) is true for $\tau_2 = k + 1$. Suppose

$$\neg ReleasedAt(\beta, \tau_1) \land \tau_1 < k + 1 \land \neg ReleasedBetween(\tau_1, \beta, k + 1)$$

From $\neg ReleasedBetween(\tau_1, \beta, k+1)$ and definition EC8, we have $\neg ReleasedBetween(\tau_1, \beta, k)$. From this, $\neg ReleasedAt(\beta, \tau_1)$, $\tau_1 < k$, and the induction hypothesis (B.6), we have $\neg ReleasedAt(\beta, k)$. From $\neg ReleasedBetween(\tau_1, \beta, k+1)$ and definition EC8, we have $\neg \exists a(Happens(a, k) \land Releases(a, \beta, k))$. From this, $\neg ReleasedAt(\beta, k)$, and DEC8, we have $\neg ReleasedAt(\beta, k+1)$ as required.

Lemma B.5. If the timepoint sort is restricted to the integers, then

$$DEC \Rightarrow EC14$$

Proof. Suppose DEC. Let τ_1 and τ_2 be arbitrary integer timepoints, α be an arbitrary event, and β be an arbitrary fluent. We must show

$$(Happens(\alpha, \tau_1) \land Initiates(\alpha, \beta, \tau_1) \land \tau_1 < \tau_2 \land \neg StoppedIn(\tau_1, \beta, \tau_2) \land \neg ReleasedIn(\tau_1, \beta, \tau_2)) \Rightarrow HoldsAt(\beta, \tau_2)$$
(B.7)

Case 1: $\tau_1 \ge \tau_2$. (B.7) is trivially satisfied.

Case 2: $\tau_1 < \tau_2$. We proceed by mathematical induction.

Base case: We show that (B.7) is true for $\tau_2 = \tau_1 + 1$. Suppose

$$Happens(\alpha, \tau_1) \wedge Initiates(\alpha, \beta, \tau_1) \wedge \tau_1 < \tau_1 + 1 \wedge \neg StoppedIn(\tau_1, \beta, \tau_1 + 1) \wedge \neg ReleasedIn(\tau_1, \beta, \tau_1 + 1)$$

From this and DEC9, we have $HoldsAt(\beta, \tau_1 + 1)$, as required.

Induction step: Suppose (B.7) is true for $\tau_2 = k, k > \tau_1$ (induction hypothesis):

$$(Happens(\alpha, \tau_1) \land Initiates(\alpha, \beta, \tau_1) \land \tau_1 < k \land \neg StoppedIn(\tau_1, \beta, k) \land \neg ReleasedIn(\tau_1, \beta, k)) \Rightarrow HoldsAt(\beta, k)$$
(B.8)

We must show that (B.7) is true for $\tau_2 = k + 1$. Suppose

$$Happens(\alpha, \tau_1) \land Initiates(\alpha, \beta, \tau_1) \land \tau_1 < k + 1 \land \neg StoppedIn(\tau_1, \beta, k + 1) \land \neg ReleasedIn(\tau_1, \beta, k + 1)$$

From $Happens(\alpha, \tau_1)$, $Initiates(\alpha, \beta, \tau_1)$, and DEC9, we have $HoldsAt(\beta, \tau_1 + 1)$. From $\neg StoppedIn(\tau_1, \beta, k + 1)$ and definition EC3, we have $\neg StoppedIn(\tau_1, \beta, k)$. From $\neg ReleasedIn(\tau_1, \beta, k + 1)$ and definition EC13, we have $\neg ReleasedIn(\tau_1, \beta, k)$. From $Happens(\alpha, \tau_1)$, $Initiates(\alpha, \beta, \tau_1)$, $\tau_1 < k$, $\neg StoppedIn(\tau_1, \beta, k)$, $\neg ReleasedIn(\tau_1, \beta, k)$, and the induction hypothesis (B.8), we have $HoldsAt(\beta, k)$. From $Happens(\alpha, \tau_1)$, $Initiates(\alpha, \beta, \tau_1)$, and DEC12, we have $\neg ReleasedIn(\tau_1, \beta, k + 1)$, definition EC13, and definition EC8, we have $\neg ReleasedBetween(\tau_1 + 1, \beta, k + 1)$. From $\bot ReleasedBetween(\tau_1 + 1, \beta, k + 1)$. From $\bot ReleasedBetween(\tau_1 + 1, \beta, k + 1)$, and EC12, we have $\lnot ReleasedAt(\beta, \tau_1 + 1)$, $\tau_1 + 1 < k + 1$, $\lnot ReleasedBetween(\tau_1 + 1, \beta, k + 1)$, and definition EC3, we have $\lnot ReleasedAt(\beta, k + 1)$. From $\lnot StoppedIn(\tau_1, \beta, k + 1)$ and definition EC3, we have $\lnot Happens(a, k) \land Terminates(a, \beta, k)$. From this, $HoldsAt(\beta, k)$, $\lnot ReleasedAt(\beta, k + 1)$, and DEC5, we have $HoldsAt(\beta, k + 1)$ as required.

Lemma B.6. If the timepoint sort is restricted to the integers, then

Proof. The proof is identical to that of Lemma B.5, except that $\neg HoldsAt$ is substituted for *HoldsAt*, *Terminates* is substituted for *Inititates*, DEC10 is substituted for DEC9, *StartedIn* is substituted for *StoppedIn*, EC4 is substituted for EC3, and DEC6 is substituted for DEC5.

Lemma B.7. If the timepoint sort is restricted to the integers, then

Proof. Suppose DEC. Let τ_1 and τ_2 be arbitrary integer timepoints, α be an arbitrary event, and β be an arbitrary fluent. We must show

$$(Happens(\alpha, \tau_1) \land Releases(\alpha, \beta, \tau_1) \land \tau_1 < \tau_2 \land \neg StoppedIn(\tau_1, \beta, \tau_2) \land \neg StartedIn(\tau_1, \beta, \tau_2)) \Rightarrow ReleasedAt(\beta, \tau_2)$$
(B.9)

Case 1: $\tau_1 \ge \tau_2$. (B.9) is trivially satisfied.

Case 2: $\tau_1 < \tau_2$. We proceed by mathematical induction.

Base case: We show that (B.9) is true for $\tau_2 = \tau_1 + 1$. Suppose

$$Happens(\alpha, \tau_1) \land Releases(\alpha, \beta, \tau_1) \land \tau_1 < \tau_1 + 1 \land \neg StoppedIn(\tau_1, \beta, \tau_1 + 1) \land \neg StartedIn(\tau_1, \beta, \tau_1 + 1)$$

From $Happens(\alpha, \tau_1)$, $Releases(\alpha, \beta, \tau_1)$, and DEC11, we have $ReleasedAt(\beta, \tau_1 + 1)$, as required.

Induction step: Suppose (B.9) is true for $\tau_2 = k, k > \tau_1$ (induction hypothesis):

$$(Happens(\alpha, \tau_1) \land Releases(\alpha, \beta, \tau_1) \land \tau_1 < k \land \\ \neg StoppedIn(\tau_1, \beta, k) \land \neg StartedIn(\tau_1, \beta, k)) \Rightarrow \\ ReleasedAt(\beta, k)$$
(B.10)

We must show that (B.9) is true for $\tau_2 = k + 1$. Suppose

$$Happens(\alpha, \tau_1) \land Releases(\alpha, \beta, \tau_1) \land \tau_1 < k + 1 \land \neg StoppedIn(\tau_1, \beta, k + 1) \land \neg StartedIn(\tau_1, \beta, k + 1)$$

From $Happens(\alpha, \tau_1)$, $Releases(\alpha, \beta, \tau_1)$, and DEC11, we have $ReleasedAt(\beta, \tau_1 + 1)$. From $\neg StoppedIn(\tau_1, \beta, k + 1)$ and definition EC3, we have $\neg StoppedIn(\tau_1, \beta, k)$. From $\neg StartedIn(\tau_1, \beta, k + 1)$ and definition EC4, we have $\neg StartedIn(\tau_1, \beta, k)$. From $Happens(\alpha, \tau_1)$, $Releases(\alpha, \beta, \tau_1)$, $\tau_1 < k$, $\neg StoppedIn(\tau_1, \beta, k)$, $\neg StartedIn(\tau_1, \beta, k)$, and the induction hypothesis (B.10), we have $ReleasedAt(\beta, k)$. From $\neg StoppedIn(\tau_1, \beta, k + 1)$ and definition EC3, we have $\neg \exists a(Happens(a, k) \land Terminates(a, \beta, k))$. From $\neg StartedIn(\tau_1, \beta, k + 1)$ and definition EC4, we have $\neg \exists a(Happens(a, k) \land Initiates(a, \beta, k))$. From this, $ReleasedAt(\beta, k)$, $\neg \exists a(Happens(a, k) \land Terminates(a, \beta, k))$, and DEC7, we have $ReleasedAt(\beta, k + 1)$ as required.

Lemma B.8. If the timepoint sort is restricted to the integers, then

Proof. Suppose DEC. Let τ_1 and τ_2 be arbitrary integer timepoints, α be an arbitrary event, and β be an arbitrary fluent. We must show

$$(Happens(\alpha, \tau_1) \land (Initiates(\alpha, \beta, \tau_1) \lor Terminates(\alpha, \beta, \tau_1)) \land (B.11)$$

$$\tau_1 < \tau_2 \land \neg ReleasedIn(\tau_1, \beta, \tau_2)) \Rightarrow \\ \neg ReleasedAt(\beta, \tau_2)$$

Case 1: $\tau_1 \ge \tau_2$. (B.11) is trivially satisfied.

Case 2: $\tau_1 < \tau_2$. We proceed by mathematical induction.

Base case: We show that (B.11) is true for $\tau_2 = \tau_1 + 1$. Suppose

$$Happens(\alpha, \tau_1) \wedge (Initiates(\alpha, \beta, \tau_1) \vee Terminates(\alpha, \beta, \tau_1)) \wedge$$

 $\tau_1 < \tau_1 + 1 \wedge \neg ReleasedIn(\tau_1, \beta, \tau_1 + 1)$

From $Happens(\alpha, \tau_1)$, $(Initiates(\alpha, \beta, \tau_1) \vee Terminates(\alpha, \beta, \tau_1))$, and DEC12, we have $\neg ReleasedAt(\beta, \tau_1 + 1)$, as required.

Induction step: Suppose (B.11) is true for $\tau_2 = k, k > \tau_1$ (induction hypothesis):

$$(Happens(\alpha, \tau_1) \land (Initiates(\alpha, \beta, \tau_1) \lor Terminates(\alpha, \beta, \tau_1)) \land \\ \tau_1 < k \land \neg ReleasedIn(\tau_1, \beta, k)) \Rightarrow \\ \neg ReleasedAt(\beta, k)$$
(B.12)

We must show that (B.11) is true for $\tau_2 = k + 1$. Suppose

$$Happens(\alpha, \tau_1) \land (Initiates(\alpha, \beta, \tau_1) \lor Terminates(\alpha, \beta, \tau_1)) \land \tau_1 < k + 1 \land \neg ReleasedIn(\tau_1, \beta, k + 1)$$

From $Happens(\alpha, \tau_1)$, $Initiates(\alpha, \beta, \tau_1) \vee Terminates(\alpha, \beta, \tau_1)$, and DEC12, we have $\neg ReleasedAt(\beta, \tau_1 + 1)$. From $\neg ReleasedIn(\tau_1, \beta, k + 1)$ and definition EC13, we have $\neg ReleasedIn(\tau_1, \beta, k)$. From this, $Happens(\alpha, \tau_1)$, $Initiates(\alpha, \beta, \tau_1) \vee Terminates(\alpha, \beta, \tau_1)$, $\tau_1 < k$, and the induction hypothesis (B.12), we have $\neg ReleasedAt(\beta, k)$. From $\neg ReleasedIn(\tau_1, \beta, k + 1)$ and definition EC13, we have $\neg \exists a(Happens(a, k) \wedge Releases(a, \beta, k))$. From this, $\neg ReleasedAt(\beta, k)$, and DEC8, we have $\neg ReleasedAt(\beta, k + 1)$ as required.

Now we proceed to the equivalence theorem.

Theorem B.1. If the timepoint sort is restricted to the integers, then

EC ⇔ DEC

Proof. We prove the two directions separately.

(EC \Rightarrow DEC): Suppose EC. DEC3 is identical to EC5 and DEC4 is identical to EC6. DEC5 follows from EC9 by universal instantiation, substituting $t_1 + 1$ for t_2 . Similarly, DEC6, DEC7, DEC8, DEC9, DEC10, DEC11, and DEC12 follow from EC10, EC11, EC12, EC14, EC15, EC16, and EC17, respectively, by universal instantiation, substituting $t_1 + 1$ for t_2 .

(EC \Leftarrow DEC): Suppose DEC. EC5 is identical to DEC3 and EC6 is identical to DEC4. EC9, EC10, EC11, EC12, EC14, EC15, EC16, and EC17 follow from Lemmas B.1, B.2, B.3, B.4, B.5, B.6, B.7, and B.8, respectively.

Events with Duration

In most versions of the event calculus, event occurrences are instantaneous. This appendix presents a revised version of EC that allows event occurrences with duration. A three-argument Happens predicate $Happens3(e,t_1,t_2)$ is introduced, representing that event e occurs between t_1 and t_2 . EC is revised as follows.

Definition EC1'.

$$Clipped(t_1, f, t_4) \stackrel{\text{def}}{\equiv}$$

 $\exists e, t_2, t_3 \ (Happens 3(e, t_2, t_3) \land t_1 \leq t_3 \land t_2 < t_4 \land Terminates(e, f, t_2))$

Definition EC2'.

$$Declipped(t_1, f, t_4) \stackrel{\text{def}}{\equiv}$$

 $\exists e, t_2, t_3 \ (Happens 3(e, t_2, t_3) \land t_1 \leq t_3 \land t_2 < t_4 \land Initiates(e, f, t_2))$

Definition EC3'.

$$StoppedIn(t_1, f, t_4) \stackrel{\text{def}}{\equiv}$$

 $\exists e, t_2, t_3 \ (Happens 3(e, t_2, t_3) \land t_1 < t_3 \land t_2 < t_4 \land Terminates(e, f, t_2))$

Definition EC4'.

$$StartedIn(t_1, f, t_4) \stackrel{\text{def}}{\equiv}$$

 $\exists e, t_2, t_3 \ (Happens 3(e, t_2, t_3) \land t_1 < t_3 \land t_2 < t_4 \land Initiates(e, f, t_2))$

Axiom EC5'.

$$Happens3(e, t_1, t_2) \wedge Initiates(e, f_1, t_1) \wedge 0 < t_3 \wedge$$

 $Trajectory(f_1, t_1, f_2, t_3) \wedge \neg StoppedIn(t_1, f_1, t_2 + t_3) \Rightarrow$
 $HoldsAt(f_2, t_2 + t_3)$

Axiom EC6'.

$$Happens3(e, t_1, t_2) \land Terminates(e, f_1, t_1) \land 0 < t_3 \land AntiTrajectory(f_1, t_1, f_2, t_3) \land \neg StartedIn(t_1, f_1, t_2 + t_3) \Rightarrow HoldsAt(f_2, t_2 + t_3)$$

Definition EC8'.

ReleasedBetween
$$(t_1, f, t_4) \stackrel{\text{def}}{\equiv}$$

 $\exists e, t_2, t_3 \ (Happens3(e, t_2, t_3) \land t_1 \leq t_3 \land t_2 < t_4 \land Releases(e, f, t_2))$

Definition EC13'.

$$ReleasedIn(t_1, f, t_4) \stackrel{\text{def}}{\equiv}$$

$$\exists e, t_2, t_3 \ (Happens3(e, t_2, t_3) \land t_1 < t_3 \land t_2 < t_4 \land Releases(e, f, t_2))$$

Axiom EC14'.

$$Happens3(e,t_1,t_2) \land Initiates(e,f,t_1) \land t_2 < t_3 \land \neg StoppedIn(t_1,f,t_3) \land \neg ReleasedIn(t_1,f,t_3) \Rightarrow HoldsAt(f,t_3)$$

Axiom EC15'.

$$Happens3(e, t_1, t_2) \land Terminates(e, f, t_1) \land t_2 < t_3 \land \neg StartedIn(t_1, f, t_3) \land \neg ReleasedIn(t_1, f, t_3) \Rightarrow \neg HoldsAt(f, t_3)$$

Axiom EC16'.

$$Happens3(e, t_1, t_2) \land Releases(e, f, t_1) \land t_2 < t_3 \land \neg StoppedIn(t_1, f, t_3) \land \neg StartedIn(t_1, f, t_3) \Rightarrow ReleasedAt(f, t_3)$$

Axiom EC17'.

$$Happens3(e, t_1, t_2) \land (Initiates(e, f, t_1) \lor Terminates(e, f, t_1)) \land t_2 < t_3 \land \neg ReleasedIn(t_1, f, t_3) \Rightarrow \neg ReleasedAt(f, t_3)$$

Axiom EC18.

$$Happens3(e, t_1, t_2) \Rightarrow t_1 \leq t_2$$

Definition EC7 and Axioms EC9, EC10, EC11, and EC12 remain unchanged. Two-argument *Happens* is defined in terms of three-argument *Happens* as follows. **Axiom EC19.**

$$Happens(e,t) \Leftrightarrow Happens3(e,t,t)$$

Instead of representing events with duration as events, they may be represented as fluents, as discussed in Section 7.1.2.

Once events have duration, it becomes possible to represent compound events. For example, we may represent that event E1 is a compound event that consists of event E2 immediately followed by E3 as follows:

$$Happens3(E1, t_1, t_3) \Leftrightarrow \\ \exists t_2 (t_1 < t_2 < t_3 \land Happens3(E2, t_1, t_2) \land Happens3(E3, t_2, t_3))$$

BIBLIOGRAPHIC NOTES

Three-argument *Happens* for representing event occurrences with duration and event calculus axioms for event occurrences with duration were introduced by Shanahan (1997a, 1999a) based on previous work (R. Miller & Shanahan, 1994). Shanahan (1997a, 1999a) presents examples of how to use three-argument *Happens* to represent compound events.

The Discrete Event Calculus with Branching Time

In this appendix, we present BDEC, a branching time version of the discrete event calculus. We characterize the relationship between BDEC and the linear discrete event calculus, and between BDEC and a simple version of the situation calculus.

D.1 LDEC

We start by defining LDEC, a version of the linear discrete event calculus, which facilitates comparison with BDEC. LDEC includes an axiomatization of the nonnegative integers, but does not support gradual change. The language has the constant S_0 denoting the initial situation, the function $S_L(s)$, which denotes the unique successor of situation s, and the following predicates:

- $Happens_L(e, s)$: Event e occurs at situation s.
- HoldsAt(f, s): Fluent f is true at situation s.
- ReleasedAt(f, s): Fluent f is released from the commonsense law of inertia at situation s.
- Initiates_L(e, f, s): If event e occurs at situation s, then fluent f will be true and not released from the commonsense law of inertia at the successor of s.
- $Terminates_L(e, f, s)$: If event e occurs at situation s, then fluent f will be false and not released from the commonsense law of inertia at the successor of s.
- $Releases_L(e, f, s)$: If event e occurs at situation s, then fluent f will be released from the commonsense law of inertia at the successor of s.

Let LDEC be the conjunction of the following axioms:

Axiom LDEC1.

$$S_L(s) \neq S_0$$

Axiom LDEC2.

$$S_L(s_1) = S_L(s_2) \Rightarrow s_1 = s_2$$

Axiom LDEC3.

$$\forall P ((P(S_0) \land \forall s (P(s) \Rightarrow P(S_L(s)))) \Rightarrow \forall s P(s))$$

¹Portions of this appendix are from a paper by Mueller (2007a) that appeared in a technical report published by the Association for the Advancement of Artificial Intelligence.

Axiom LDEC4.

$$HoldsAt(f, s) \land \neg ReleasedAt(f, S_L(s)) \land$$

 $\neg \exists e (Happens_L(e, s) \land Terminates_L(e, f, s)) \Rightarrow$
 $HoldsAt(f, S_L(s))$

Axiom LDEC5.

$$\neg HoldsAt(f, s) \land \neg ReleasedAt(f, S_L(s)) \land$$

 $\neg \exists e (Happens_L(e, s) \land Initiates_L(e, f, s)) \Rightarrow$
 $\neg HoldsAt(f, S_L(s))$

Axiom LDEC6.

$$ReleasedAt(f,s) \land \\ \neg \exists e \ (Happens_L(e,s) \land (Initiates_L(e,f,s) \lor Terminates_L(e,f,s))) \Rightarrow \\ ReleasedAt(f,S_L(s))$$

Axiom LDEC7.

$$\neg ReleasedAt(f, s) \land$$
 $\neg \exists e (Happens_L(e, s) \land Releases_L(e, f, s)) \Rightarrow$
 $\neg ReleasedAt(f, S_L(s))$

Axiom LDEC8.

$$Happens_L(e,s) \wedge Initiates_L(e,f,s) \Rightarrow HoldsAt(f,S_L(s))$$

Axiom LDEC9.

$$Happens_L(e,s) \land Terminates_L(e,f,s) \Rightarrow \neg HoldsAt(f,S_L(s))$$

Axiom LDEC10.

$$Happens_L(e, s) \land Releases_L(e, f, s) \Rightarrow ReleasedAt(f, S_L(s))$$

Axiom LDEC11.

$$Happens_L(e, s) \land$$

 $(Initiates_L(e, f, s) \lor Terminates_L(e, f, s)) \Rightarrow$
 $\neg ReleasedAt(f, S_L(s))$

Axioms LDEC1 through LDEC3 are the Peano axioms for the nonnegative integers. Axiom LDEC3 is a second-order axiom of induction.

D.2 BDEC

We extend LDEC to branching time as follows. We replace the function S_L with a relation S_L , and allow a situation to have zero or more successors. We add an argument to Happens, Initiates, Terminates, and Releases specifying the successor situation. It is important to add the successor situation to Initiates, Terminates, and Teleases to treat concurrent events with cumulative and canceling effects.

The language has the constant S_0 denoting the initial situation, and the following predicates:

- $S(s_1, s_2)$: Situation s_2 is a successor of situation s_1 .
- $Happens(e, s_1, s_2)$: Event e occurs between situation s_1 and situation s_2 .
- HoldsAt(f, s): Fluent f is true at situation s.
- ReleasedAt(f, s): Fluent f is released from the commonsense law of inertia at situation s.
- Initiates (e, f, s_1, s_2) : If event e occurs between situation s_1 and situation s_2 , then fluent f will be true and not released from the commonsense law of inertia at s_2 .
- Terminates (e, f, s_1, s_2) : If event e occurs between situation s_1 and situation s_2 , then fluent f will be false and not released from the commonsense law of inertia at s_2 .
- Releases (e, f, s_1, s_2) : If event e occurs between situation s_1 and situation s_2 , then fluent f will be released from the commonsense law of inertia at s_2 .

Let BDEC be the conjunction of the following axioms:

Axiom BDEC1.

$$\neg S(s, S_0)$$

Axiom BDEC2.

$$S(s_1,s) \wedge S(s_2,s) \Rightarrow s_1 = s_2$$

Axiom BDEC3.

$$\forall P ((P(S_0) \land \forall s_1, s_2 (S(s_1, s_2) \land P(s_1) \Rightarrow P(s_2))) \Rightarrow \forall s P(s))$$

Axiom BDEC4.

$$S(s_1, s_2) \land HoldsAt(f, s_1) \land \neg ReleasedAt(f, s_2) \land \neg \exists e (Happens(e, s_1, s_2) \land Terminates(e, f, s_1, s_2)) \Rightarrow HoldsAt(f, s_2)$$

Axiom BDEC5.

$$S(s_1, s_2) \land \neg HoldsAt(f, s_1) \land \neg ReleasedAt(f, s_2) \land \neg \exists e (Happens(e, s_1, s_2) \land Initiates(e, f, s_1, s_2)) \Rightarrow \neg HoldsAt(f, s_2)$$

Axiom BDEC6.

$$S(s_1, s_2) \land ReleasedAt(f, s_1) \land$$
 $\neg \exists e (Happens(e, s_1, s_2) \land$
 $(Initiates(e, f, s_1, s_2) \lor Terminates(e, f, s_1, s_2))) \Rightarrow$
 $ReleasedAt(f, s_2)$

Axiom BDEC7.

$$S(s_1, s_2) \land \neg ReleasedAt(f, s_1) \land$$

 $\neg \exists e (Happens(e, s_1, s_2) \land Releases(e, f, s_1, s_2)) \Rightarrow$
 $\neg ReleasedAt(f, s_2)$

Axiom BDEC8.

$$Happens(e, s_1, s_2) \wedge Initiates(e, f, s_1, s_2) \Rightarrow HoldsAt(f, s_2)$$

Axiom BDEC9.

$$Happens(e, s_1, s_2) \land Terminates(e, f, s_1, s_2) \Rightarrow \neg HoldsAt(f, s_2)$$

Axiom BDEC10.

$$Happens(e, s_1, s_2) \land Releases(e, f, s_1, s_2) \Rightarrow ReleasedAt(f, s_2)$$

Axiom BDEC11.

$$Happens(e, s_1, s_2) \land$$
 $(Initiates(e, f, s_1, s_2) \lor Terminates(e, f, s_1, s_2)) \Rightarrow$
 $\neg ReleasedAt(f, s_2)$

Axiom BDEC12.

$$Happens(e, s_1, s_2) \Rightarrow S(s_1, s_2)$$

Axioms BDEC1 through BDEC3 are generalized Peano axioms along the lines of Schmidt (1960) and K. L. Clark and Tärnlund (1977), which do not require each situation to have exactly one successor. BDEC3 is a second-order induction axiom similar to the one used by Reiter (1993) for the situation calculus. In any model of these axioms, situations form a tree whose root is S_0 (Manzano, 1996, p. 90; Pinto, 1994, pp. 103-105).

D.3 RELATIONSHIP OF BDEC AND LDEC

Bridging axioms are bi-implications that specify the correspondence between two vocabularies. The relationship of BDEC and LDEC can be characterized using L, which is the conjunction of the following bridging axioms:

Axiom L1.

$$S(s_1, s_2) \Leftrightarrow S_L(s_1) = s_2$$

Axiom L2.

$$Happens(e, s_1, s_2) \Leftrightarrow Happens_L(e, s_1) \wedge S_L(s_1) = s_2$$

Axiom L3.

$$Initiates(e, f, s_1, s_2) \Leftrightarrow Initiates_L(e, f, s_1)$$

Axiom L4.

$$Terminates(e, f, s_1, s_2) \Leftrightarrow Terminates_L(e, f, s_1)$$

Axiom L5.

$$Releases(e, f, s_1, s_2) \Leftrightarrow Releases_L(e, f, s_1)$$

We can show that the conjunction of BDEC and L is logically equivalent to the conjunction of LDEC and L. We first prove several lemmas.

Lemma D.1. $LDEC \wedge L \Rightarrow BDEC8$.

Proof. Suppose $LDEC \wedge L$. Let e be an arbitrary event, f be an arbitrary fluent, and s_1 and s_2 be arbitrary situations. We must show $Happens(e, s_1, s_2) \wedge Initiates(e, f, s_1, s_2) \Rightarrow HoldsAt(f, s_2)$. Suppose

$$Happens(e, s_1, s_2)$$
 (D.1)

$$Initiates(e, f, s_1, s_2)$$
 (D.2)

From (D.1) and L2, we have

$$Happens_L(e, s_1) \wedge S_L(s_1) = s_2 \tag{D.3}$$

From (D.2) and L3, we have $Initiates_L(e, f, s_1)$. From this, (D.3), and LDEC8, we have $HoldsAt(f, s_2)$, as required.

Lemma D.2. $LDEC \wedge L \Rightarrow BDEC9$.

Proof. The proof is identical to that of Lemma D.1, except that $\neg HoldsAt$ is substituted for HoldsAt, Terminates is substituted for Initiates, Terminates is substituted for Initiates, and LDEC9 is substituted for LDEC8.

Lemma D.3. $LDEC \wedge L \Rightarrow BDEC10$.

Proof. The proof is identical to that of Lemma D.1, except that *ReleasedAt* is substituted for *HoldsAt*, *Releases* is substituted for *Initiates*, *Releases*_L is substituted for *Initiates*_L, and LDEC10 is substituted for LDEC8.

Lemma D.4. $LDEC \wedge L \Rightarrow BDEC11$.

Proof. Suppose $LDEC \wedge L$. Let e be an arbitrary event, f be an arbitrary fluent, and s_1 and s_2 be arbitrary situations. We must show $Happens(e, s_1, s_2) \wedge (Initiates(e, f, s_1, s_2) \vee Terminates(e, f, s_1, s_2)) \Rightarrow \neg ReleasedAt(f, s_2)$. Suppose

$$Happens(e, s_1, s_2)$$
 (D.4)

$$Initiates(e, f, s_1, s_2) \vee Terminates(e, f, s_1, s_2)$$
 (D.5)

From (D.4) and L2, we have

$$Happens_I(e, s_1) \wedge S(s_1) = s_2 \tag{D.6}$$

From (D.5), L3, and L4, we have $Initiates_L(e, f, s_1) \vee Terminates_L(e, f, s_1)$. From this, (D.6), and LDEC11, we have $\neg ReleasedAt(f, s_2)$, as required.

Now we proceed to the equivalence results.

Theorem D.1. $BDEC \wedge L \Rightarrow LDEC$.

Proof. Suppose $BDEC \wedge L$.

LDEC1 follows from BDEC1 and L1.

LDEC2 follows from BDEC2 and L1.

LDEC3 follows from BDEC3 and L1.

LDEC4 follows from BDEC4, L1, L2, and L4.

LDEC5 follows from BDEC5, L1, L2, and L3.

LDEC6 follows from BDEC6, L1, L2, L3, and L4.

LDEC7 follows from BDEC7, L1, L2, and L5.

LDEC8 follows from BDEC8, L2, and L3.

LDEC9 follows from BDEC9, L2, and L4.

402

LDEC10 follows from BDEC10, L2, and L5. LDEC11 follows from BDEC11, L2, L3, and L4. Therefore, *LDEC*.

Theorem D.2. $LDEC \wedge L \Rightarrow BDEC$.

Proof. Suppose $LDEC \wedge L$.

BDEC1 follows from LDEC1 and L1.

BDEC2 follows from LDEC2 and L1.

BDEC3 follows from LDEC3 and L1.

BDEC4 follows from LDEC4, L1, L2, and L4.

BDEC5 follows from LDEC5, L1, L2, and L3.

BDEC6 follows from LDEC6, L1, L2, L3, and L4.

BDEC7 follows from LDEC7, L1, L2, and L5.

BDEC8 follows from Lemma D.1.

BDEC9 follows from Lemma D.2.

BDEC10 follows from Lemma D.3.

BDEC11 follows from Lemma D.4.

BDEC12 follows from L1 and L2.

Therefore, BDEC.

Corollary D.1. $BDEC \wedge L \Leftrightarrow LDEC \wedge L$.

Proof. This follows from Theorems D.1 and D.2.

D.4 RELATIONSHIP OF BDEC AND THE SITUATION CALCULUS

If BDEC is restricted appropriately, then we can show that it is equivalent to a simple version of the situation calculus. We restrict BDEC by (1) eliminating the ability to release fluents from the commonsense law of inertia and (2) disallowing multiple events between two situations.

Let BDECS be the conjunction of the following axioms:

Axiom BDECS1.

 $\neg S(s, S_0)$

Axiom BDECS2.

$$S(s_1,s) \wedge S(s_2,s) \Rightarrow s_1 = s_2$$

Axiom BDECS3.

$$\forall P((P(S_0) \land \forall s_1, s_2 (S(s_1, s_2) \land P(s_1) \Rightarrow P(s_2))) \Rightarrow \forall s P(s))$$

Axiom BDECS4.

$$S(s_1, s_2) \land HoldsAt(f, s_1) \land$$

 $\neg \exists e (Happens(e, s_1, s_2) \land Terminates(e, f, s_1, s_2)) \Rightarrow$
 $HoldsAt(f, s_2)$

Axiom BDECS5.

$$S(s_1, s_2) \land \neg HoldsAt(f, s_1) \land$$

 $\neg \exists e (Happens(e, s_1, s_2) \land Initiates(e, f, s_1, s_2)) \Rightarrow$
 $\neg HoldsAt(f, s_2)$

Axiom BDECS6.

$$Happens(e, s_1, s_2) \wedge Initiates(e, f, s_1, s_2) \Rightarrow HoldsAt(f, s_2)$$

Axiom BDECS7.

$$Happens(e, s_1, s_2) \land Terminates(e, f, s_1, s_2) \Rightarrow \neg HoldsAt(f, s_2)$$

Axiom BDECS8.

$$Happens(e, s_1, s_2) \Rightarrow S(s_1, s_2)$$

Axiom BDECS9.

$$Happens(e_1, s_1, s_2) \wedge Happens(e_2, s_1, s_2) \Rightarrow e_1 = e_2$$

Axioms BDECS1 through BDECS8 are obtained by removing mention of the predicates *ReleasedAt* and *Releases* from BDEC. Axiom BDECS9 disallows multiple events between situations.

We use a simple version of the situation calculus similar to that of Kowalski and Sadri (1997). Let SC be the conjunction of the following axioms:

Axiom SC1.

$$Do(e,s) \neq S_0$$

Axiom SC2.

$$Do(e_1, s_1) = Do(e_2, s_2) \Rightarrow e_1 = e_2 \land s_1 = s_2$$

Axiom SC3.

$$\forall P((P(S_0) \land \forall e, s(P(s) \Rightarrow P(Do(e, s)))) \Rightarrow \forall s P(s))$$

Axiom SC4.

$$HoldsAt(f, s) \land \neg Terminates_S(e, f, s) \Rightarrow HoldsAt(f, Do(e, s))$$

Axiom SC5.

$$\neg HoldsAt(f,s) \land \neg Initiates_S(e,f,s) \Rightarrow \neg HoldsAt(f,Do(e,s))$$

Axiom SC6.

$$Initiates_S(e, f, s) \Rightarrow HoldsAt(f, Do(e, s))$$

Axiom SC7.

$$Terminates_S(e, f, s) \Rightarrow \neg HoldsAt(f, Do(e, s))$$

The relationship of BDECS and SC can be characterized using S, which is the conjunction of the following bridging axioms:

Axiom S1.

$$S(s_1, s_2) \Leftrightarrow \exists e (Do(e, s_1) = s_2)$$

Axiom S2.

$$Happens(e, s_1, s_2) \Leftrightarrow Do(e, s_1) = s_2$$

Axiom S3.

$$Initiates(e, f, s_1, s_2) \Leftrightarrow Initiates_S(e, f, s_1)$$

Axiom S4.

$$Terminates(e, f, s_1, s_2) \Leftrightarrow Terminates_S(e, f, s_1)$$

We can show that the conjunction of BDECS and S is logically equivalent to the conjunction of SC and S. We start by proving a number of lemmas.

Lemma D.5. $BDECS \land S \Rightarrow SC2$.

Proof. Suppose $BDECS \wedge S$. Let e_1 and e_2 be arbitrary events and s_1 and s_2 be arbitrary situations. We must show $Do(e_1, s_1) = Do(e_2, s_2) \Rightarrow e_1 = e_2 \wedge s_1 = s_2$. Suppose

$$Do(e_1, s_1) = Do(e_2, s_2)$$
 (D.7)

Let $s_3 = Do(e_1, s_1)$. From this and S2, we have

$$Happens(e_1, s_1, s_3) \tag{D.8}$$

From $s_3 = Do(e_1, s_1)$, (D.7), and S2, we have

$$Happens(e_2, s_2, s_3) \tag{D.9}$$

From (D.8) and BDECS8, we have

$$S(s_1, s_3) \tag{D.10}$$

From (D.9) and BDECS8, we have

$$S(s_2, s_3) \tag{D.11}$$

From this, (D.10), and BDECS2, we have $s_1 = s_2$, as required. From this, (D.8), (D.9), and BDECS9, we have $e_1 = e_2$, as required.

Lemma D.6. $BDECS \land S \Rightarrow SC3$.

Proof. Suppose $BDECS \wedge S$. Let P be an arbitrary predicate. We must show $(P(S_0) \wedge \forall e, s \ (P(s) \Rightarrow P(Do(e, s)))) \Rightarrow \forall s \ P(s)$. Suppose

$$P(S_0) \tag{D.12}$$

$$\forall e, s (P(s) \Rightarrow P(Do(e, s)))$$
 (D.13)

We can show

$$\forall s_1, s_2 \left(S(s_1, s_2) \land P(s_1) \Rightarrow P(s_2) \right) \tag{D.14}$$

To see this, let s_1 and s_2 be arbitrary situations. Suppose

$$S(s_1, s_2) \tag{D.15}$$

$$P(s_1) \tag{D.16}$$

From (D.15) and S1, we have $Do(E, s_1) = s_2$ for some E. From this, (D.16), and (D.13), we have $P(s_2)$, as required.

From (D.12), (D.14), and BDECS3, we have $\forall s P(s)$, as required.

Lemma D.7. $BDECS \land S \Rightarrow SC4$.

Proof. Suppose $BDECS \land S$. Let e be an arbitrary event, f be an arbitrary fluent, and s_1 be an arbitrary situation. We must show $HoldsAt(f, s_1) \land \neg Terminates_S(e, f, s_1) \Rightarrow HoldsAt(f, Do(e, s_1))$. Suppose

$$HoldsAt(f, s_1)$$
 (D.17)

$$\neg Terminates_S(e, f, s_1)$$
 (D.18)

Let $s_2 = Do(e, s_1)$. From this and S1, we have

$$S(s_1, s_2) \tag{D.19}$$

From $s_2 = Do(e, s_1)$ and S2, we have $Happens(e, s_1, s_2)$. From this and BDECS9, we have

$$Happens(e', s_1, s_2) \Rightarrow e' = e$$
 (D.20)

From (D.18) and S4, we have $\neg Terminates(e, f, s_1, s_2)$. From this and (D.20), we have $\neg \exists e' \ (Happens(e', s_1, s_2) \land Terminates(e', f, s_1, s_2))$. From this, (D.19), (D.17), and BDECS4, we have $HoldsAt(f, s_2)$. From this and $s_2 = Do(e, s_1)$, we have $HoldsAt(f, Do(e, s_1))$, as required.

Lemma D.8. $BDECS \land S \Rightarrow SC5$.

Proof. The proof is identical to that of Lemma D.7, except that $\neg HoldsAt$ is substituted for HoldsAt, $Initiates_S$ is substituted for $Terminates_S$, Initiates is substituted for $Terminates_S$, and BDECS5 is substituted for BDECS4.

Lemma D.9. $BDECS \land S \Rightarrow SC6$.

Proof. Suppose $BDECS \wedge S$. Let e be an arbitrary event, f be an arbitrary fluent, and s_1 be an arbitrary situation. We must show $Initiates_S(e, f, s_1) \Rightarrow HoldsAt(f, Do(e, s_1))$. Suppose

$$Initiates_S(e, f, s_1)$$
 (D.21)

Let $s_2 = Do(e, s_1)$. From this and S2, we have

$$Happens(e, s_1, s_2)$$
 (D.22)

From (D.21) and S3, we have $Initiates(e, f, s_1, s_2)$. From this, (D.22), and BDECS6, we have $HoldsAt(f, s_2)$. From this and $s_2 = Do(e, s_1)$, we have $HoldsAt(f, Do(e, s_1))$, as required.

Lemma D.10. $BDECS \land S \Rightarrow SC7$.

Proof. The proof is identical to that of Lemma D.9, except that ¬*HoldsAt* is substituted for *HoldsAt*, *Terminates* is substituted for *Initiates*, *Terminates* is substituted for *Initiates*, and BDECS7 is substituted for BDECS6.

Lemma D.11. $SC \wedge S \Rightarrow BDECS2$.

Proof. Suppose $SC \wedge S$. Let s_1 , s_2 , and s be arbitrary situations. We must show $S(s_1, s) \wedge S(s_2, s) \Rightarrow s_1 = s_2$. Suppose $S(s_1, s) \wedge S(s_2, s)$. From this and S1, we have $Do(E_1, s_1) = Do(E_2, s_2)$ for some E_1 and E_2 . From this and SC2, we have $s_1 = s_2$, as required.

Lemma D.12. $SC \wedge S \Rightarrow BDECS3$.

Proof. Suppose $SC \wedge S$. Let P be an arbitrary predicate. We must show $(P(S_0) \wedge \forall s_1, s_2 (S(s_1, s_2) \wedge P(s_1) \Rightarrow P(s_2))) \Rightarrow \forall s P(s)$. Suppose

$$P(S_0) \tag{D.23}$$

$$\forall s_1, s_2 \left(S(s_1, s_2) \land P(s_1) \Rightarrow P(s_2) \right) \tag{D.24}$$

We can show

$$\forall e, s (P(s) \Rightarrow P(Do(e, s)))$$
 (D.25)

To see this, let e be an arbitrary event and s be an arbitrary situation. Suppose

$$P(s)$$
 (D.26)

Let $s_3 = Do(e, s)$. From this and S1, we have $S(s, s_3)$. From this, (D.26), and (D.24), we have $P(s_3)$. From this and $s_3 = Do(e, s)$, we have P(Do(e, s)), as required.

From (D.23), (D.25), and SC3, we have $\forall s P(s)$, as required.

Lemma D.13. $SC \wedge S \Rightarrow BDECS4$.

Proof. Suppose $SC \wedge S$. Let f be an arbitrary fluent and s_1 and s_2 be arbitrary situations. We must show $S(s_1, s_2) \wedge HoldsAt(f, s_1) \wedge \neg \exists e (Happens(e, s_1, s_2) \wedge Terminates(e, f, s_1, s_2)) \Rightarrow HoldsAt(f, s_2)$. Suppose

$$S(s_1, s_2) \tag{D.27}$$

$$HoldsAt(f, s_1)$$
 (D.28)

$$\neg \exists e (Happens(e, s_1, s_2) \land Terminates(e, f, s_1, s_2))$$
 (D.29)

From (D.29), we have

$$Happens(e, s_1, s_2) \Rightarrow \neg Terminates(e, f, s_1, s_2)$$
 (D.30)

From (D.27) and S1, we have

$$Do(E, s_1) = s_2 \tag{D.31}$$

for some E. From this and S2, we have $Happens(E, s_1, s_2)$. From this and (D.30), we have $\neg Terminates(E, f, s_1, s_2)$. From this and S4, we have $\neg Terminates(E, f, s_1)$. From this, (D.28), and SC4, we have $HoldsAt(f, Do(E, s_1))$. From this and (D.31), we have $HoldsAt(f, s_2)$, as required.

Lemma D.14. $SC \wedge S \Rightarrow BDECS5$.

Proof. The proof is identical to that of Lemma D.13, except that $\neg HoldsAt$ is substituted for HoldsAt, Initiates is substituted for Terminates, $Initiates_S$ is substituted for $Terminates_S$, and SC5 is substituted for SC4.

Lemma D.15. $SC \wedge S \Rightarrow BDECS6$.

Proof. Suppose $SC \wedge S$. Let e be an arbitrary event, f be an arbitrary fluent, and s_1 and s_2 be arbitrary situations. We must show $Happens(e, s_1, s_2) \wedge Initiates(e, f, s_1, s_2) \Rightarrow HoldsAt(f, s_2)$. Suppose

$$Happens(e, s_1, s_2)$$
 (D.32)

$$Initiates(e, f, s_1, s_2)$$
 (D.33)

From (D.33) and S3, we have

$$Initiates_S(e, f, s_1)$$
 (D.34)

From (D.32) and S2, we have $Do(e, s_1) = s_2$. From this, (D.34), and SC6, we have $HoldsAt(f, s_2)$, as required.

Lemma D.16. $SC \wedge S \Rightarrow BDECS7$.

Proof. The proof is identical to that of Lemma D.15, except that ¬*HoldsAt* is substituted for *HoldsAt*, *Terminates* is substituted for *Initiates*, *Terminates* is substituted for *Initiates*, and SC7 is substituted for SC6.

Now we proceed to the equivalence results.

Theorem D.3. $BDECS \land S \Rightarrow SC$.

Proof. Suppose $BDECS \wedge S$.

SC1 follows from BDECS1 and S1.

SC2 follows from Lemma D.5.

SC3 follows from Lemma D.6.

SC4 follows from Lemma D.7.

SC5 follows from Lemma D.8.

SC6 follows from Lemma D.9.

SC7 follows from Lemma D.10.

Therefore, SC.

Theorem D.4. $SC \wedge S \Rightarrow BDECS$.

Proof. Suppose $SC \wedge S$.

BDECS1 follows from SC1 and S1.

BDECS2 follows from Lemma D.11.

BDECS3 follows from Lemma D.12.

BDECS4 follows from Lemma D.13.

BDECS5 follows from Lemma D.14.

BDECS6 follows from Lemma D.15.

BDECS7 follows from Lemma D.16.

BDECS8 follows from S1 and S2.

BDECS9 follows from SC2 and S2.

Therefore, BDECS.

Corollary D.2. $BDECS \wedge S \Leftrightarrow SC \wedge S$.

Proof. This follows from Theorems D.3 and D.4.

BIBLIOGRAPHIC NOTES

BDEC was introduced by Mueller (2007a). Patkos and Plexousakis (2009) and Patkos (2010) use BDEC to define a theory of knowledge based on possible worlds. They use the axiom

 $HoldsAt(Knows_B(f), s) \equiv \forall s' \ K(s', s) \Rightarrow HoldsAt(f, s')$ (Patkos & Plexousakis, 2009, p. 888)

where K(s', s) represents that world or situation s' is accessible from s.

Several researchers have introduced formalisms that combine the event calculus and the situation calculus. The main difference between BDEC and the other formalisms is that BDEC considers situations and timepoints to be one and the same. Provetti (1996) associates a tree of situations with every timepoint. Kowalski and Sadri (1997) identify timepoints with both situations and transitions between situations. Van Belleghem, Denecker, and De Schreye (1997) define situations as sets of timepoints. Lévy and Quantz (1998) add a situation argument to every event calculus predicate.

BDEC is similar to the situation calculus, but it differs in several ways. Pirri and Reiter (1999) provide the following foundational axioms for the situation calculus:

$$do(a_1, s_1) = do(a_2, s_2) \supset a_1 = a_2 \land s_1 = s_2$$
 (D.35)

$$(\forall P).P(S_0) \land (\forall a, s)[P(s) \supset P(do(a, s))] \supset (\forall s)P(s) \tag{D.36}$$

$$\neg (s \sqsubset S_0) \tag{D.37}$$

$$s \sqsubset do(a, s') \equiv s = s' \lor s \sqsubset s'$$
 (D.38)

In any model of these axioms, every situation has a successor for every element of the action domain. In any model of BDEC, if an event occurs between situation s_1 and s_2 , then s_1 has s_2 as a successor—see Axiom BDEC12. Whereas BDEC allows more than one event between two situations, the situation calculus of Pirri and Reiter (1999) does not. In BDEC, we can write $Happens(E_1, S_0, S_1) \wedge Happens(E_2, S_0, S_1) \wedge E_1 \neq E_2$. The analogous situation calculus formula $S_1 = do(E_1, S_0) \wedge S_1 = do(E_2, S_0) \wedge E_1 \neq E_2$ is inconsistent with axiom (D.35).

The Event Calculus and Temporal Action Logics

In this appendix, we compare the event calculus with support for events with duration (R. Miller & Shanahan, 2002; Shanahan, 1999a) and TAL 1.0 (Doherty, 1996; Doherty, Gustafsson, Karlsson, & Kvarnström, 1998). We use the variant of TAL 1.0 in which actions are treated as first-class citizens (Doherty, Gustafsson, Karlsson, & Kvarnström, 1998, pp. 19 and 20). We start by restricting the event calculus and TAL 1.0 to integer time, inertial fluents, and relational fluents. We further restrict TAL 1.0 action type specifications to definite reassignment of a single fluent. We then prove that these restricted versions are not equivalent. We show that equivalence cannot be restored even if more general TAL action type specifications are used. We then further restrict the two formalisms to single-step actions and prove that these versions are logically equivalent.

E.1 THE EVENT CALCULUS AND TAL

How shall we go about proving logical equivalence of the event calculus with events with duration and TAL 1.0? As shown in Table E.1, the formalisms do not support the same features. In addition, the formalisms do not address indirect effects and nondeterministic effects using the same language features. Indirect effects are represented in the event calculus using causal constraints and effect constraints (Shanahan, 1999b), whereas they are represented in TAL 1.0 using dependency constraints (Doherty, Gustafsson, & Kvarnström, 1998, pp. 16-18). Nondeterministic effects are represented in the event calculus using determining fluents (Shanahan, 1999a, pp. 419 and 420), whereas they are represented in TAL 1.0 using disjunctions in reassignment operators (Doherty, 1996, pp. 35 and 36).

At this point, we have two choices. We can either extend the formalisms with their missing features, or we can restrict the formalisms to their common features. We choose the second approach. We disallow causal constraints, continuous change, continuous time, and effect constraints in the event calculus, and we disallow dependency constraints, disjunctions in reassignment operators, durational fluents, and functional fluents in TAL 1.0.

¹This appendix is based on an article by Mueller (2006) in the journal *Artificial Intelligence*, published by Elsevier.

Table E.1 Features of the Event Calculus and TAL 1.0

Feature	EC	TAL 1.0
Causal constraints	1	
Concurrent events	1	1
Context-sensitive effects	· V	✓
Continuous change	1	
Continuous time	1	
Dependency constraints		√
Disjunctions in reassignment operators		1
Durational fluents		1
Effect constraints	1	
Events with duration	1	1
Functional fluents	120	1
Inertial fluents	1	1
State constraints	1	1

In order to prove logical equivalence, we would like to characterize the event calculus and TAL 1.0 using the same classical language. TAL 1.0 domain descriptions are written in a specialized language $\mathcal{L}(ND)$ and then translated into a classical language $\mathcal{L}(FL)$. The important translation rules are provided in Section E.8. Event calculus domain descriptions are also expressed in a classical language. But TAL 1.0 $\mathcal{L}(FL)$ and the event calculus use different symbol sets. TAL 1.0 $\mathcal{L}(FL)$ uses Holds, Occurs, and Occlude, whereas the event calculus as we have restricted it uses HoldsAt, InitiallyP, InitiallyP, InitiallyP, InitiallyP, InitiallsP, InitialsP, InitialsP,

In TAL 1.0, the effects of events are specified using $\mathcal{L}(ND)$ action type specifications of the form

$$[\tau,\tau']\alpha \leadsto \beta$$

where τ and τ' are timepoints, α is an action, and β is a formula that specifies the preconditions and postconditions of α . Postconditions are defined using the R, X, and I reassignment operators. The R operator specifies that a fluent is released from the commonsense law of inertia during a time interval and is constrained to have a particular value at the end of the interval. The I operator specifies that a fluent is released from the commonsense law of inertia during a time interval and is constrained to have a particular value during the interval. The X operator specifies that a fluent is released from the commonsense law of inertia during a time interval. Note that a fluent released from the commonsense law of inertia by a reassignment operator may be further constrained by other parts of the same action type specification or by different axioms such as state constraints.

The effects of actions are often² specified using $\mathcal{L}(ND)$ action type specifications of the form

$$[\tau, \tau'] \alpha \leadsto [\tau] \gamma \to R((\tau, \tau'] (\neg) \beta)$$
 (E.1)

where τ and τ' are timepoints, α is an action, γ is a formula, and β is a fluent. This represents that, if α occurs from τ to τ' , and γ is true at τ , then β will be of indeterminate truth value from $\tau+1$ to $\tau'-1$ inclusive, and will be true (false) starting at τ' . A specification of this form is translated into an $\mathcal{L}(FL)$ formula

$$\begin{aligned} Occurs(\tau, \tau', \alpha) \rightarrow \\ (\gamma' \rightarrow (\neg) Holds(\tau', \beta) \land \forall t \, (\tau < t \land t \leq \tau' \rightarrow Occlude(t, \beta))) \end{aligned} \tag{E.2}$$

where γ' is the $\mathcal{L}(FL)$ translation of $[\tau] \gamma$. Notice that (E.2) is logically equivalent to the conjunction of the formulas:

$$\begin{aligned} \textit{Occurs}(\tau, \tau', \alpha) \land \gamma' &\rightarrow (\neg) \textit{Holds}(\tau', \beta) \\ \textit{Occurs}(\tau, \tau', \alpha) \land \gamma' \land \tau &< t \land t \leq \tau' \rightarrow \textit{Occlude}(t, \beta) \end{aligned}$$

In order to reconcile the two languages, we assume that all TAL 1.0 action type specifications are of the form (E.1). Given this assumption, we show in Sections E.2 and E.4 that the restricted TAL 1.0 is not equivalent to the restricted event calculus. We argue in Section E.5 that, even if we relax this assumption and allow more general action type specifications, we still cannot obtain equivalence.

Given this assumption we can express $[\tau, \tau'] \alpha \leadsto [\tau] \gamma \to R((\tau, \tau'] \beta)$ as $\gamma' \to Initiates(\alpha, \beta, \tau)$, and $[\tau, \tau'] \alpha \leadsto [\tau] \gamma \to R((\tau, \tau'] \neg \beta)$ as $\gamma' \to Terminates(\alpha, \beta, \tau)$, just as in the event calculus. We must then add the following domain-independent axioms to TAL:

$$Occurs(t_1, t_2, e) \land Initiates(e, f, t_1) \rightarrow Holds(t_2, f)$$
 (E.3)

$$Occurs(t_1, t_2, e) \land Terminates(e, f, t_1) \rightarrow \neg Holds(t_2, f)$$
 (E.4)

(Initiates(e,f,t₁))
$$\vee$$
 Terminates(e,f,t₁)) \wedge
Occurs(t₁,t₂,e) \wedge t₁ < t \wedge t \leq t₂ \rightarrow Occlude(t,f)

Furthermore, we treat the TAL 1.0 $\mathcal{L}(FL)$ predicates Holds(t,f), $Occurs(t_1,t_2,e)$, and Occlude(t,f), and the event calculus predicates InitiallyP(f), InitiallyN(f), $Clipped(t_1,f,t_2)$, and $Declipped(t_1,f,t_2)$ as abbreviations.

²Forty-six of the 68 unique action type specifications provided with version 2.999.910 alpha of VITAL are of this form or can be rewritten as several specifications of this form. Eight specifications are of the form $[\tau, \tau'] \alpha \rightarrow [\tau] \gamma \rightarrow I((\tau, \tau'] (\neg)\beta)$ where β is a durational fluent, 5 specifications involve $R([\tau'] (\neg)\beta)$, 3 specifications use disjunctions in reassignment operators, and the remaining 6 specifications use other combinations of reassignment operators. Current TAL domains are more complex, but have not yet been added to VITAL.

³For example, the $\mathcal{L}(FL)$ translation of $[\tau] \beta_1 \wedge \neg \beta_2$ is $Holds(\tau, \beta_1) \wedge \neg Holds(\tau, \beta_2)$. See Section E.8 for more details.

We use a many-sorted language with equality, with sorts for events, fluents, and timepoints. The domain of the timepoint sort is the integers. The language has the following predicates:

- HoldsAt(f, t): Fluent f is true at timepoint t.
- Happens3(e, t_1, t_2): Event e occurs from timepoint t_1 to timepoint t_2 .
- Initiates (e, f, t_1) : If event e occurs from timepoint t_1 to timepoint t_2 , then fluent f will be true after t_2 .
- Terminates (e, f, t_1) : If event e occurs from timepoint t_1 to timepoint t_2 , then fluent f will be false after t_2 .

E.1.1 TALA AXIOMATIZATION

We use the following axiomatization of the restricted TAL 1.0, which we call TALA. We start with definitions of *Holds* and *Occurs*.

Definition TALA1.

$$Holds(t,f) \stackrel{\text{def}}{\equiv} HoldsAt(f,t)$$

Definition TALA2.

$$Occurs(t_1, t_2, e) \stackrel{\text{def}}{=} Happens3(e, t_1, t_2 - 1)$$

Note the difference in the ending timepoint t_2 between *Occurs* and *Happens3*.

TAL uses circumscription of the *Occlude* and *Occurs* predicates (Kvarnström, 2005, p. 26), just as the event calculus uses circumscription of *Initiates*, *Terminates*, and *Happens*. We continue with a definition based on the circumscription of *Occlude* in (E.5). We compute the circumscription using Theorem 2.1, which reduces circumscription to predicate completion.

Definition TALA3.

$$Occlude(t,f) \stackrel{\text{def}}{\equiv} \exists e, t_1, t_2 ((Initiates(e, f, t_1)) \lor Terminates(e, f, t_1)) \land \\ Occurs(t_1, t_2, e) \land t_1 < t \land t \leq t_2)$$

The TAL 1.0 nochange axiom $\neg Occlude(t+1,f) \rightarrow (Holds(t+1,f) \leftrightarrow Holds(t,f))$ (Doherty, 1996, p. 30) is logically equivalent to the conjunction of the axioms TALA4 and TALA5.

Axiom TALA4.

$$Holds(t,f) \land \neg Occlude(t+1,f) \rightarrow Holds(t+1,f)$$

Axiom TALA5.

$$\neg Holds(t,f) \land \neg Occlude(t+1,f) \rightarrow \neg Holds(t+1,f)$$

We continue with formulas (E.3) and (E.4).

Axiom TALA6.

$$Occurs(t_1, t_2, e) \land Initiates(e, f, t_1) \rightarrow Holds(t_2, f)$$

Axiom TALA7.

$$Occurs(t_1, t_2, e) \land Terminates(e, f, t_1) \rightarrow \neg Holds(t_2, f)$$

413

We finish with a constraint on the starting and ending timepoints of an event occurrence.

Axiom TALA8.

$$Occurs(t_1, t_2, e) \rightarrow t_1 < t_2$$

Let TALA be the formula generated by conjoining axioms TALA4 through TALA8 and then expanding the predicates *Holds*, *Occurs*, and *Occlude* using definitions TALA1 through TALA3.

E.1.2 ECA AXIOMATIZATION

There are two versions of the event calculus that support events with duration (R. Miller & Shanahan, 2002; Shanahan, 1999a). Both are candidates for equivalence with TAL 1.0. We start by using the following axiomatization of the event calculus. It is obtained from the version of the event calculus of Shanahan (1999a, p. 416) by eliminating *Releases*, and replacing *InitiallyP*, *InitiallyN*, *Clipped*, and *Declipped* with definitions.

Definition ECA1.

$$InitiallyP(f) \stackrel{\text{def}}{\equiv} HoldsAt(f,0)$$

Definition ECA2.

$$InitiallyN(f) \stackrel{\text{def}}{=} \neg HoldsAt(f, 0)$$

Definition ECA3.

Clipped
$$(t_1, f, t_4) \stackrel{\text{def}}{\equiv} \exists e, t_2, t_3 \ (Happens 3(e, t_2, t_3) \land t_1 < t_3 \land t_2 < t_4 \land Terminates(e, f, t_2))$$

Definition ECA4.

Declipped
$$(t_1, f, t_4) \stackrel{\text{def}}{\equiv} \exists e, t_2, t_3 \ (Happens3(e, t_2, t_3) \land t_1 < t_3 \land t_2 < t_4 \land Initiates(e, f, t_2))$$

Axiom ECA5.

$$\textit{InitiallyP}(f) \land \neg \textit{Clipped}(0,f,t) \rightarrow \textit{HoldsAt}(f,t)$$

Axiom ECA6.

$$InitiallyN(f) \land \neg Declipped(0, f, t) \rightarrow \neg HoldsAt(f, t)$$

Axiom ECA7.

$$Happens3(e, t_1, t_2) \land Initiates(e, f, t_1) \land t_2 < t_3 \land \neg Clipped(t_1, f, t_3) \rightarrow HoldsAt(f, t_3)$$

Axiom ECA8.

$$Happens3(e, t_1, t_2) \land Terminates(e, f, t_1) \land t_2 < t_3 \land \neg Declipped(t_1, f, t_3) \rightarrow \neg HoldsAt(f, t_3)$$

Axiom ECA9.

$$Happens3(e, t_1, t_2) \rightarrow t_1 \leq t_2$$

Let ECA be the formula generated by conjoining axioms ECA5 through ECA9 and then expanding the predicates *InitiallyP*, *InitiallyN*, *Clipped*, and *Declipped* using definitions ECA1 through ECA4.

We can now proceed to our first result.

E.2 LACK OF EQUIVALENCE BETWEEN TALA AND ECA

In this section, we expose two differences between TALA and ECA. The first difference involves an occurrence of an event that initiates a fluent, followed by another occurrence of an event that initiates the same fluent. In TALA, the fluent is of indeterminate truth value within the durations of both event occurrences, whereas in ECA, it is only of indeterminate truth value within the duration of the first event occurrence. Within the duration of the second event occurrence, the fluent is true, because it was previously initiated and has not been clipped.

Theorem E.1. TALA $\not\models$ ECA.

Proof. Consider the following structure *S*:

Initiates =
$$\{\langle \mathbf{I}, \mathbf{F}, 1 \rangle, \langle \mathbf{I}, \mathbf{F}, 4 \rangle\}$$
 (E.5)

$$Terminates = \emptyset (E.6)$$

$$Happens3 = \{ \langle \mathbf{I}, 1, 2 \rangle, \langle \mathbf{I}, 4, 5 \rangle \}$$
 (E.7)

$$HoldsAt = \{\langle \mathbf{F}, 3 \rangle, \langle \mathbf{F}, 4 \rangle, \langle \mathbf{F}, 6 \rangle, \langle \mathbf{F}, 7 \rangle, \langle \mathbf{F}, 8 \rangle, \dots \}$$
(E.8)

We can show $S \models TALA$ but $S \not\models ECA$. It is straightforward to verify $S \models TALA$. In order to show $S \not\models ECA$, it is sufficient to show $S \not\models ECA$. Moreover, we need only show

$$S \not\models Happens3(I, 1, 2) \land Initiates(I, F, 1) \land 2 < 5 \land$$

$$\neg Clipped(1, F, 5) \rightarrow HoldsAt(F, 5)$$
(E.9)

From (E.6), we have

$$S \models \neg \exists e, t_2, t_3 \ (Happens 3(e, t_2, t_3) \land 1 < t_3 \land t_2 < 5 \land Terminates(e, F, t_2))$$

From this and definition ECA3, we have $S \models \neg Clipped(1, F, 5)$. From this, (E.7), and (E.5), we have

$$S \models Happens3(I, 1, 2) \land Initiates(I, F, 1) \land 2 < 5 \land \neg Clipped(1, F, 5)$$

But from (E.8), we have
$$S \models \neg HoldsAt(F, 5)$$
. Therefore, we have (E.9).

The second difference between TALA and ECA involves an occurrence of an event that initiates a fluent, which overlaps in time an occurrence of an event that terminates the same fluent. In TALA, the fluent is true at the end of the initiating event occurrence, whereas in ECA, the fluent is of indeterminate truth value at the end of the initiating event occurrence.

Theorem E.2. ECA $\not\models$ TALA.

Proof. Consider the following structure S:

$$Initiates = \{\langle \mathbf{I}, \mathbf{F}, 1 \rangle\}$$
 (E.10)

Terminates =
$$\{\langle \mathbf{T}, \mathbf{F}, 2 \rangle\}$$
 (E.11)

$$Happens3 = \{ \langle \mathbf{I}, 1, 2 \rangle, \langle \mathbf{T}, 2, 3 \rangle \}$$
 (E.12)

$$HoldsAt = \emptyset (E.13)$$

We can show $S \models \text{ECA}$ but $S \not\models \text{TALA}$. It is straightforward to verify $S \models \text{ECA}$. In order to show $S \not\models \text{TALA}$, it is sufficient to show $S \not\models \text{TALA6}$. Furthermore, we need only show

$$S \not\models Occurs(1,3,I) \land Initiates(I,F,1) \rightarrow Holds(3,F)$$
 (E.14)

From (E.12), definition TALA2, and (E.10), we have $Occurs(1, 3, I) \land Initiates(I, F, 1)$. But from (E.13) and definition TALA1, we have $S \models \neg Holds(3, F)$. Therefore, we have (E.14).

Thus we have lack of equivalence.

Corollary E.1. TALA is not logically equivalent to ECA.

Proof. This follows from either Theorems E.1 or E.2.

E.3 ECB AXIOMATIZATION

A second axiomatization of the event calculus that supports events with duration is provided by R. Miller and Shanahan (2002, pp. 470 and 471). After rewriting it in the style of ECA, it is as follows.

Definition ECB1.

Clipped'
$$(t_1, f, t_4) \stackrel{\text{def}}{\equiv} \exists e, t_2, t_3 \ (Happens3(e, t_2, t_3) \land t_1 \leq t_3 \land t_2 < t_4 \land Terminates(e, f, t_2))$$

Definition ECB2.

Declipped
$$'(t_1, f, t_4) \stackrel{\text{def}}{\equiv} \exists e, t_2, t_3 \ (Happens 3(e, t_2, t_3) \land t_1 \leq t_3 \land t_2 < t_4 \land Initiates(e, f, t_2))$$

Definition ECB3.

Clipped
$$(t_1, f, t_4) \stackrel{\text{def}}{\equiv} \exists e, t_2, t_3 \ (Happens3(e, t_2, t_3) \land t_1 < t_3 \land t_2 < t_4 \land Terminates(e, f, t_2))$$

Definition ECB4.

$$Declipped(t_1, f, t_4) \stackrel{\text{def}}{=} \exists e, t_2, t_3 \ (Happens 3(e, t_2, t_3) \land t_1 < t_3 \land t_2 < t_4 \land Initiates(e, f, t_2))$$

Axiom ECB5.

$$HoldsAt(f, t_1) \wedge t_1 < t_2 \wedge \neg Clipped'(t_1, f, t_2) \rightarrow HoldsAt(f, t_2)$$

Axiom ECB6.

$$\neg HoldsAt(f, t_1) \land t_1 < t_2 \land \neg Declipped'(t_1, f, t_2) \rightarrow \neg HoldsAt(f, t_2)$$

Axiom ECB7.

$$Happens3(e, t_1, t_2) \wedge Initiates(e, f, t_1) \wedge t_2 < t_3 \wedge \neg Clipped(t_1, f, t_3) \rightarrow HoldsAt(f, t_3)$$

Axiom ECB8.

$$Happens3(e, t_1, t_2) \land Terminates(e, f, t_1) \land t_2 < t_3 \land \neg Declipped(t_1, f, t_3) \rightarrow \neg HoldsAt(f, t_3)$$

Axiom ECB9.

$$Happens3(e, t_1, t_2) \rightarrow t_1 \leq t_2$$

ECB differs from ECA in the following ways:

- It eliminates the definitions of *InitiallyP* and *InitiallyN*.
- It add definitions of Clipped' and Declipped'.
- It adds the axioms of inertia ECB5 and ECB6.

Let ECB be the formula generated by conjoining axioms ECB5 through ECB9 and then expanding the predicates *Clipped'*, *Declipped'*, *Clipped*, and *Declipped* using definitions ECB1 through ECB4.

We then have our second result.

E.4 LACK OF EQUIVALENCE BETWEEN TALA AND ECB

ECB is not equivalent to TALA, for the two reasons previously given for ECA, as well as the following reason. Consider a single occurrence of an event that initiates a fluent. Within the duration of the event occurrence, the fluent is of indeterminate truth value in TALA, whereas in ECB a fluent that is true persists in each model because of the frame axiom ECB5. That is, if in a given model the fluent is true at any given timepoint within an event occurrence, then it is true for all remaining timepoints within the event occurrence.

Theorem E.3. TALA $\not\models$ ECB.

Proof. Consider the following structure S:

$$Initiates = \{\langle \mathbf{I}, \mathbf{F}, 1 \rangle\}$$
 (E.15)

$$Terminates = \emptyset (E.16)$$

$$Happens3 = \{\langle \mathbf{I}, 1, 3 \rangle\} \tag{E.17}$$

$$HoldsAt = \{\langle \mathbf{F}, 2 \rangle, \langle \mathbf{F}, 4 \rangle, \langle \mathbf{F}, 5 \rangle, \langle \mathbf{F}, 6 \rangle, \dots \}$$
 (E.18)

We can show $S \models TALA$ but $S \not\models ECB$. It is straightforward to verify $S \models TALA$. In order to show $S \not\models ECB$, it is sufficient to show $S \not\models ECB5$. Moreover, we need only show

$$S \not\models HoldsAt(F,2) \land 2 < 3 \land$$
 (E.19)
 $\neg Clipped'(2,F,3) \rightarrow HoldsAt(F,3)$

From (E.16), we have

$$S \models \neg \exists e, t_2, t_3 \ (Happens3(e, t_2, t_3) \land 2 \le t_3 \land t_2 < 3 \land Terminates(e, F, t_2))$$

From this and definition ECB1, we have $S \models \neg Clipped'(2, F, 3)$. From this and (E.18), we have

$$S \models HoldsAt(F, 2) \land 2 < 3 \land \neg Clipped'(2, F, 3)$$

But from (E.18), we have $S \models \neg HoldsAt(F, 3)$. Therefore, we have (E.19).

Corollary E.2. TALA is not logically equivalent to ECB.

Proof. This follows from Theorem E.3.

E.5 GENERAL ACTION TYPE SPECIFICATIONS

We have shown that, if TAL action type specifications are of the form (E.1), then TAL and the event calculus are not equivalent. What if we use a more general form of action type specification? Can we restore equivalence with the event calculus?

The answer is no. It is sufficient to show that the difference highlighted in the proof of Theorem E.2 cannot be erased. ECA7 (as well as ECB7, which is identical) entails that, if a fluent is not clipped during an event occurrence that initiates the fluent, then the fluent is true at the end of the event occurrence. Action type specifications of the form (E.1) entail that the fluent is always true at the end of the event. We would like to add to the action type specification the condition that the fluent is not clipped:

$$[t_1, t_2]I \sim \neg \exists t_3, t_4 [[t_3, t_4]T \wedge t_1 < t_4 - 1 \wedge t_3 < t_2] \rightarrow R([t_2]F)$$

(*I* and *T* are actions, and *F* is a fluent.) Unfortunately, the consequent of an action type specification cannot contain action occurrence statements such as $[t_3, t_4] T$ (Doherty, 1996, p. 28).

The underlying difficulty is that TAL does not have the notions of clipped and declipped. In order for TAL to emulate the event calculus with events with duration, it would have to be extended with these notions.

E.6 RESTRICTION TO SINGLE-STEP ACTIONS

We now consider what happens if we restrict TAL and the event calculus to singlestep actions. We add TALA9 to TALA:

Definition TALA1.

$$Holds(t,f) \stackrel{\text{def}}{\equiv} HoldsAt(f,t)$$

Definition TALA2.

$$Occurs(t_1, t_2, e) \stackrel{\text{def}}{\equiv} Happens3(e, t_1, t_2 - 1)$$

Definition TALA3.

$$Occlude(t,f) \stackrel{\text{def}}{\equiv} \exists e, t_1, t_2 ((Initiates(e,f,t_1) \lor Terminates(e,f,t_1)) \land \\ Occurs(t_1,t_2,e) \land t_1 < t \land t \leq t_2)$$

Axiom TALA4.

$$Holds(t,f) \land \neg Occlude(t+1,f) \rightarrow Holds(t+1,f)$$

Axiom TALA5.

$$\neg Holds(t,f) \land \neg Occlude(t+1,f) \rightarrow \neg Holds(t+1,f)$$

1 1 7 7

$$Occurs(t_1, t_2, e) \land Initiates(e, f, t_1) \rightarrow Holds(t_2, f)$$

Axiom TALA7.

Axiom TALA6.

$$Occurs(t_1, t_2, e) \land Terminates(e, f, t_1) \rightarrow \neg Holds(t_2, f)$$

Axiom TALA8.

$$Occurs(t_1, t_2, e) \rightarrow t_1 < t_2$$

Axiom TALA9.

$$Occurs(t_1, t_2, e) \rightarrow t_2 = t_1 + 1$$

Let TALAS be the formula generated by conjoining axioms TALA4 through TALA9 and then expanding the predicates *Holds*, *Occurs*, and *Occlude* using definitions TALA1 through TALA3.

For single-step actions, the version of the event calculus that appears to be the most similar to TAL is DEC. The following axiomatization is obtained from the full version of DEC by eliminating *Trajectory*, *AntiTrajectory*, *Releases*, and *ReleasedAt*. **Definition DECA1.**

$$Happens(e,t) \stackrel{\text{def}}{\equiv} Happens3(e,t,t)$$

Axiom DECA2.

$$HoldsAt(f,t) \land \neg \exists e (Happens(e,t) \land Terminates(e,f,t)) \rightarrow HoldsAt(f,t+1)$$

Axiom DECA3.

$$\neg HoldsAt(f,t) \land \neg \exists e (Happens(e,t) \land Initiates(e,f,t)) \rightarrow \neg HoldsAt(f,t+1)$$

Axiom DECA4.

$$Happens(e,t) \land Initiates(e,f,t) \rightarrow HoldsAt(f,t+1)$$

Axiom DECA5.

$$Happens(e,t) \land Terminates(e,f,t) \rightarrow \neg HoldsAt(f,t+1)$$

Axiom DECA6.

$$Happens3(e, t_1, t_2) \rightarrow t_1 = t_2$$

Let DECA be the formula generated by conjoining axioms DECA2 through DECA6 and then expanding the predicate *Happens* using definition DECA1.

We then obtain our final result.

E.7 EQUIVALENCE OF TALAS AND DECA

We can show that TALAS and DECA are logically equivalent. First, we prove a number of lemmas.

419

Lemma E.1. TALAS \models DECA2.

Proof. Suppose TALAS. Let f be an arbitrary fluent and t be an arbitrary time-point. We must show $HoldsAt(f,t) \land \neg \exists e \ (Happens(e,t) \land Terminates(e,f,t)) \rightarrow HoldsAt(f,t+1)$. Suppose

$$HoldsAt(f,t)$$
 (E.20)

$$\neg \exists e (Happens(e, t) \land Terminates(e, f, t))$$
 (E.21)

We consider two cases.

Case 1: $\exists e (Happens(e, t) \land Initiates(e, f, t)).$

From definition DECA1, TALA2, and existential instantiation, we get $Occurs(t, t+1, E) \land Initiates(E, f, t)$ for some E. From this, TALA6, and TALA1, we have HoldsAt(f, t+1), as required.

Case 2: $\neg \exists e (Happens(e, t) \land Initiates(e, f, t))$.

From (E.21), definition DECA1, and TALA2, we get

$$\neg \exists e ((Initiates(e, f, t) \lor Terminates(e, f, t)) \land Occurs(t, t + 1, e))$$

Therefore,

$$t_1 = t \wedge t_2 = t_1 + 1 \rightarrow \tag{E.22}$$

 $\neg ((Initiates(e, f, t_1) \lor Terminates(e, f, t_1)) \land Occurs(t_1, t_2, e))$

From TALA9, by contraposition, we get $t_2 \neq t_1 + 1 \rightarrow \neg Occurs(t_1, t_2, e)$. Hence,

$$t_2 \neq t_1 + 1 \rightarrow$$

 $\neg ((Initiates(e, f, t_1) \lor Terminates(e, f, t_1)) \land Occurs(t_1, t_2, e))$

From this and (E.22), we have

$$t_2 \neq t_1 + 1 \lor t_1 = t \to$$

$$\neg ((Initiates(e, f, t_1) \lor Terminates(e, f, t_1)) \land Occurs(t_1, t_2, e))$$
(E.23)

We can show

$$t_1 < t + 1 \land t + 1 \le t_2 \rightarrow t_2 \ne t_1 + 1 \lor t_1 = t$$
 (E.24)

which is logically equivalent to $t_1 < t+1 \land t+1 \le t_2 \land t_2 = t_1+1 \rightarrow t_1 = t$. To see this, suppose

$$t_1 < t + 1$$
 (E.25)

$$t + 1 \le t_2 \tag{E.26}$$

$$t_2 = t_1 + 1 (E.27)$$

From (E.26) and (E.27), we get $t \le t_1$. From this and (E.25), we have $t_1 = t$, as required.

From (E.24) and (E.23), we have

$$t_1 < t + 1 \land t + 1 \le t_2 \rightarrow$$

$$\neg ((Initiates(e, f, t_1) \lor Terminates(e, f, t_1)) \land Occurs(t_1, t_2, e))$$
(E.28)

From this and TALA3, we get $\neg Occlude(t+1,f)$. From this, (E.20), TALA1, and TALA4, we have HoldsAt(f,t+1), as required.

Lemma E.2. TALAS \models DECA3.

Proof. The proof is identical to that of Lemma E.1, except that ¬*HoldsAt* is substituted for *HoldsAt*, *Initiates* and *Terminates* are swapped, TALA7 is substituted for TALA6, and TALA5 is substituted for TALA4.

Lemma E.3. TALAS \models DECA4.

Proof. Suppose TALAS. Let e be an arbitrary event, f be an arbitrary fluent, and t be an arbitrary timepoint. We must show $Happens(e,t) \land Initiates(e,f,t) \rightarrow HoldsAt(f,t+1)$. Suppose $Happens(e,t) \land Initiates(e,f,t)$. From Happens(e,t), definition DECA1, and TALA2, we get Occurs(t,t+1,e). From this, Initiates(e,f,t), TALA6, and TALA1, we have HoldsAt(f,t+1).

Lemma E.4. TALAS ⊨ DECA5.

Proof. The proof is identical to that of Lemma E.3, except that ¬*HoldsAt* is substituted for *HoldsAt*, *Terminates* is substituted for *Initiates*, and TALA7 is substituted for TALA6.

Lemma E.5. TALAS \models DECA6.

Proof. This follows from TALA9 and TALA2.

Now we consider the other direction.

Lemma E.6. DECA \models TALA4.

Proof. Suppose DECA. Let f be an arbitrary fluent and t be an arbitrary timepoint. We must show $Holds(t,f) \wedge \neg Occlude(t+1,f) \rightarrow Holds(t+1,f)$. Suppose

$$Holds(t,f)$$
 (E.29)

 $\neg Occlude(t+1,f)$ (E.30)

From (E.30) and definition TALA3, we have

$$\neg \exists e, t_1, t_2 ((Initiates(e, f, t_1) \lor Terminates(e, f, t_1)) \land Occurs(t_1, t_2, e) \land t_1 < t + 1 \land t + 1 \le t_2)$$

Hence, $\neg \exists e \ (Terminates(e,f,t) \land Occurs(t,t+1,e))$. From this, definition TALA2, and DECA1, we get $\neg \exists e \ (Happens(e,t) \land Terminates(e,f,t))$. From this, (E.29), definition TALA1, and DECA2, we have Holds(t+1,f), as required.

Lemma E.7. DECA \models TALA5.

Proof. The proof is identical to that of Lemma E.6, except that ¬*Holds* is substituted for *Holds*, *Initiates*, and *Terminates* are swapped, and DECA3 is substituted for DECA2.

Lemma E.8. DECA \models TALA6.

Proof. Suppose DECA. Let e be an arbitrary event, f be an arbitrary fluent, and t_1 and t_2 be arbitrary timepoints. We must show $Occurs(t_1, t_2, e) \land Initiates(e, f, t_1) \rightarrow Holds(t_2, f)$. Suppose $Occurs(t_1, t_2, e) \land Initiates(e, f, t_1)$. From $Occurs(t_1, t_2, e)$ and definition TALA2, we have $Happens3(e, t_1, t_2 - 1)$. From this and DECA6, we get $t_2 = t_1 + 1$. From this, $Happens3(e, t_1, t_2 - 1)$, and DECA1, we have $Happens(e, t_1)$. From this, $Initiates(e, f, t_1)$, DECA4, and definition TALA1, we get $Holds(t_1 + 1, f)$. From this and $t_2 = t_1 + 1$, we have $Holds(t_2, f)$.

Lemma E.9. DECA \models TALA7.

Proof. The proof is identical to that of Lemma E.8, except that ¬*Holds* is substituted for *Holds*, *Terminates* is substituted for *Initiates*, and DECA5 is substituted for DECA4.

Lemma E.10. DECA \models TALA8.

Proof. This follows from definition TALA2 and DECA6.

Lemma E.11. DECA \models TALA9.

Proof. This follows from definition TALA2 and DECA6.

Now we proceed to the equivalence theorem.

Theorem E.4. TALAS is logically equivalent to DECA.

Proof. We prove the two directions separately.

 $(TALAS \models DECA)$

Suppose TALAS. Then DECA2, DECA3, DECA4, DECA5, and DECA6 follow from Lemmas E.1, E.2, E.3, E.4, and E.5, respectively.

 $(DECA \models TALAS)$

Suppose DECA. Then TALA4, TALA5, TALA6, TALA7, TALA8, and TALA9 follow from Lemmas E.6, E.7, E.8, E.9, E.10, and E.11, respectively.

E.8 TRANSLATION FROM TAL 1.0 $\mathcal{L}(ND)$ TO $\mathcal{L}(FL)$

The important translation rules from TAL 1.0 $\mathcal{L}(ND)$ to $\mathcal{L}(FL)$ are as follows (Doherty, Gustafsson, Karlsson, & Kvarnström, 1998, pp. 6-9):

- If α is an action occurrence statement, then $Trans(\alpha \leadsto \beta) = Trans(\alpha) \to Trans(\beta)$. If disjunction (\lor) is used in β , it must be in the scope of an R, I, or X reassignment operator so that circumscription of *Occlude* can be computed using predicate completion (Lifschitz, 1994).
- If α is an action, then $Trans([\tau, \tau']\alpha) = Occurs(\tau, \tau', \alpha)$.
- $Trans(R((\tau, \tau']\alpha)) = Trans(X((\tau, \tau']\alpha) \wedge [\tau']\alpha).$
- $Trans(R([\tau]\alpha)) = Trans(X([\tau]\alpha) \wedge [\tau]\alpha).$
- $Trans(I((\tau, \tau']\alpha)) = Trans(X((\tau, \tau']\alpha) \wedge (\tau, \tau']\alpha).$
- $Trans(X((\tau, \tau'] \alpha)) = \forall t (\tau < t \land t \le \tau' \rightarrow Trans(X([t] \alpha))).$
- $Trans(X([\tau] \neg \alpha)) = Trans(X([\tau] \alpha)).$
- If $\otimes \in \{\land, \lor, \to, \leftrightarrow\}$, then $Trans(X([\tau] \alpha \otimes \beta)) = Trans(X([\tau] \alpha)) \land Trans(X([\tau] \beta))$.
- If $Q \in \{\exists, \forall\}$, then $Trans(X([\tau] Q \nu [\alpha])) = Q \nu (Trans(X([\tau] \alpha)))$.
- If α is a fluent, then $Trans(X([\tau]\alpha)) = Occlude(\tau, \alpha)$.
- $Trans([\tau] \neg \alpha) = \neg Trans([\tau] \alpha).$
- If $\otimes \in \{\land, \lor, \rightarrow, \leftrightarrow\}$, then $Trans([\tau] \alpha \otimes \beta) = Trans([\tau] \alpha) \otimes Trans([\tau] \beta)$.
- If $Q \in \{\exists, \forall\}$, then $Trans([\tau] Q \nu [\alpha]) = Q \nu (Trans([\tau] \alpha))$.
- If α is a fluent, then $Trans([\tau]\alpha) = Holds(\tau, \alpha)$.

ł,																							
			4																				
										8:													

LESS OF LEAST OF AT MOTE ARMAST

See the control of th

See that makes sonomorphises in agency the

To the proof of the contract of the proof of the contract of t

California of the Stanffer Control

Contact to the Contact (Contact to property the party

The state of the s

to profine a visual

Commence of the property of the property of the commence of th

To be a supply the theory of the contract of t

Answers to Selected Exercises

CHAPTER 2

2.2. The expression U[Awake, Asleep] is an abbreviation for the conjunction of the following formulas:

$$Awake(a_1) \neq Asleep(a_2)$$

 $Awake(a_1) = Awake(a_2) \Rightarrow a_1 = a_2$
 $Asleep(a_1) = Asleep(a_2) \Rightarrow a_1 = a_2$

2.3. The following formulas are positive relative to Q:

$$Q(A)$$

$$P(x) \Rightarrow Q(x)$$

The following formulas are not positive relative to Q:

$$\neg Q(A)$$

$$P(x) \Rightarrow \neg Q(x)$$

$$Q(x) \Rightarrow P(x)$$

$$Q(x) \Leftrightarrow P(x)$$

$$Q(A) \Rightarrow Q(B)$$

CHAPTER 3

3.2. We use a positive effect axiom. The axiom states that if there exists a room such that agents 1 and 2 are in that room, agent 2 is listening to agent 1, and agent 1 tells agent 2 a fact, then agent 2 will know that fact:

$$(\exists r HoldsAt(InRoom(a_1, r), t) \land HoldsAt(InRoom(a_2, r), t)) \land HoldsAt(ListeningTo(a_2, a_1), t) \Rightarrow Initiates(Tell(a_1, a_2, f), Know(a_2, f), t)$$

We might also wish to add a state constraint that says that an agent is in one room at a time:

$$HoldsAt(InRoom(a, r_1), t) \land HoldsAt(InRoom(a, r_2), t) \Rightarrow$$

 $r_1 = r_2$

3.11. The scenario in which two agents dial one another simultaneously does not expose a bug. If the two agents pick up their respective phones and then dial one another simultaneously, they will both get busy signals. If the two agents dial one another simultaneously without first picking up their phones, then nothing happens. The scenario in which one agent dials another agent just as the other agent picks up the phone exposes a bug in the formalization. We can show *HoldsAt(Ringing(Phone1, Phone2), T)* and *HoldsAt(DialTone(Phone2), T)*, which contradict the state constraint (3.49).

CHAPTER 4

4.1. First we add an effect axiom that states that if a clock is beeping and an agent presses the clock's snooze button, then the clock's alarm time will be the current time plus 9:

$$HoldsAt(Beeping(c), t) \Rightarrow$$
 $Initiates(PressSnooze(a, c), AlarmTime(c, t + 9), t)$

Then we add an effect axiom that states that if a clock is beeping, the clock's alarm time is t_1 , and t_1 is not already the current time plus 9, then the clock's alarm time will no longer be t_1 :

$$HoldsAt(Beeping(c), t) \land$$
 $HoldsAt(AlarmTime(c, t_1), t) \land$
 $t_1 \neq t + 9 \Rightarrow$
 $Terminates(PressSnooze(a, c), AlarmTime(c, t_1), t)$

Finally, we add an effect axiom that states that if an agent presses a clock's snooze button, then the clock will not be beeping:

Terminates(PressSnooze(a, c), Beeping(c), t)

Pressing the snooze button when the clock is not beeping has no effect.

CHAPTER 5

5.3. From $CIRC[\Sigma; Initiates, Terminates, Releases]$, Theorem 2.2, and Theorem 2.1, we have

$$\begin{array}{l} \textit{Initiates}(e,f,t) \Leftrightarrow \\ \exists a,g \ (e = Load(a,g) \land f = Loaded(g)) \end{array} \tag{F.1}$$

Terminates
$$(e, f, t) \Leftrightarrow \exists a_1, a_2, g \ (e = Shoot(a_1, a_2, g) \land f = Alive(a_2) \land$$
(F.2)

$$HoldsAt(Loaded(g), t)) \lor$$

 $\exists a_1, a_2, g \ (e = Shoot(a_1, a_2, g) \land f = Loaded(g) \land$
 $HoldsAt(Loaded(g), t))$

$$\neg Releases(e, f, t)$$
 (F.3)

From $CIRC[\Delta; Happens]$ and Theorem 2.1, we have

$$Happens(e, t) \Leftrightarrow$$
 (F.4)
 $(e = Load(Nathan, Gun) \land t = 0) \lor$
 $(e = Wait(Nathan) \land t = 1) \lor$
 $(e = Shoot(Nathan, Turkey, Gun) \land t = 2)$

From (5.21) (which follows from (F.4)), (5.16) (which follows from (F.1)), and (5.10), we have

$$HoldsAt(Loaded(Gun), 1)$$
 (F.5)

From (F.4) and (F.2), we have $\neg \exists e (Happens(e, 1) \land Terminates(e, Loaded (Gun), 1))$. From this, (F.5), and (5.14), we have

From this, (5.23) (which follows from (F.4)), (5.17) (which follows from (F.2)), and (5.15), we have $\neg HoldsAt(Alive(Turkey), 3)$, as required.

5.4. From $CIRC[\Sigma; Initiates, Terminates, Releases]$, Theorem 2.2, and Theorem 2.1, we have

$$Initiates(e,f,t) \Leftrightarrow$$

$$\exists a,g \ (e = Load(a,g) \land f = Loaded(g))$$
(F.6)

Terminates
$$(e, f, t) \Leftrightarrow$$
 (F.7)
 $\exists a_1, a_2, g \ (e = Shoot(a_1, a_2, g) \land$
 $f = Alive(a_2) \land$
 $HoldsAt(Loaded(g), t)) \lor$
 $\exists a_1, a_2, g \ (e = Shoot(a_1, a_2, g) \land$
 $f = Loaded(g) \land$
 $HoldsAt(Loaded(g), t))$

$$Releases(e, f, t) \Leftrightarrow$$

$$\exists a, g \ (e = Spin(a, g) \land$$

$$f = Loaded(g) \land$$

$$HoldsAt(Loaded(g), t))$$
(F.8)

From $CIRC[\Delta; Happens]$ and Theorem 2.1, we have

$$Happens(e, t) \Leftrightarrow$$
 (F.9)
 $(e = Load(Nathan, Gun) \land t = 0) \lor$
 $(e = Spin(Nathan, Gun) \land t = 1) \lor$
 $(e = Shoot(Nathan, Turkey, Gun) \land t = 2)$

We first show (5.34). From HoldsAt(Loaded(Gun), 2), (5.23) (which follows from (F.9)), (5.17) (which follows from (F.7)), and (5.15), we have $\neg HoldsAt$ (*Alive(Turkey*), 3), as required.

Now we show (5.35). From (F.9) and (F.7), we have $\neg \exists e \ (Happens(e, 0) \land Terminates(e, Alive(Turkey), 0))$. From this, (5.19), (5.32), and (5.25), we have

$$HoldsAt(Alive(Turkey), 1)$$
 (F.10)

From (F.9) and (F.7), we have $\neg \exists e \ (Happens(e, 1) \land Terminates(e, Alive \ (Turkey), 1))$. From this, (F.10), (5.32), and (5.25), we have

$$HoldsAt(Alive(Turkey), 2)$$
 (F.11)

From (F.7) and $\neg HoldsAt(Loaded(Gun), 2)$, we have $\neg \exists e \ (Happens(e, 2) \land Terminates(e, Alive(Turkey), 2))$. From this, (F.9), (5.32), and (5.25), we have HoldsAt(Alive(Turkey), 3), as required.

CHAPTER 6

6.4. We use a counter sort with variable c and an integer sort with variables n, n_1 , and n_2 . We use the following fluents.

Count(c, n) represents that the count of counter c is n.

InputLine(c) represents that the value of the input line of c is true InputLine is always released from the commonsense law of inertia.

True(c) represents that the current value of the input line of c is true. True is subject to the commonsense law of inertia. It is set to true whenever the input line changes to true and to false whenever the input line changes to false.

We use the following events.

FalseToTrue(c) represents that the input line of counter c changes from false to true.

TrueToFalse(c) represents that the input line of counter c changes from true to false.

We have two trigger axioms. The first states that, if the current value of the input line of a counter is false and the value of the input line of the counter is true, then the input line of the counter changes from false to true:

 $\neg HoldsAt(True(c), t) \land HoldsAt(InputLine(c), t) \Rightarrow Happens(FalseToTrue(c), t)$

The second states that, if the current value of the input line of a counter is true and the value of the input line of the counter is false, then the input line of the counter changes from true to false:

```
HoldsAt(True(c), t) \land 

\neg HoldsAt(InputLine(c), t) \Rightarrow 

Happens(TrueToFalse(c), t)
```

We then have several effect axioms. If the value of the input line of a counter changes from false to true, then the current value of the input line of the counter is true:

```
Initiates(FalseToTrue(c), True(c), t)
```

If the value of the input line of a counter changes from true to false, then the current value of the input line of the counter is false:

```
Terminates(TrueToFalse(c), True(c), t)
```

If the count of a counter is n and the value of the input line of the counter changes from false to true, then the count of the counter will be n + 1 and will no longer be n:

```
HoldsAt(Count(c, n), t) \Rightarrow

Initiates(FalseToTrue(c), Count(c, n + 1), t)
```

```
HoldsAt(Count(c, n), t) \Rightarrow

Terminates(FalseToTrue(c), Count(c, n), t)
```

Last, we have a state constraint to ensure that a counter has a unique count:

```
HoldsAt(Count(c, n_1), t) \land HoldsAt(Count(c, n_2), t) \Rightarrow n_1 = n_2
```

CHAPTER 8

8.3. We use a sort for colors, with variables c, c_1 , and c_2 , and a sort for palettes with variable p. We use four effect axioms. If yellow and blue are placed on the palette simultaneously then green will be on the palette:

```
Happens(PlaceOnPalette(p, Yellow), t) \Rightarrow
Initiates(PlaceOnPalette(p, Blue), OnPalette(p, Green), t)
```

If yellow and blue are placed on the palette simultaneously and a color other than green is on the palette, then that color will no longer be on the palette:

```
Happens(PlaceOnPalette(p, Yellow), t) \land \\ HoldsAt(OnPalette(p, c), t) \land \\ c \neq Green \Rightarrow \\ Terminates(PlaceOnPalette(p, Blue), OnPalette(p, c), t)
```

If yellow and blue are not placed on the palette simultaneously and a color is placed on the palette, then that color will be on the palette:

```
\negHappens(PlaceOnPalette(p, Yellow), t) \lor

\negHappens(PlaceOnPalette(p, Blue), t) \Rightarrow

Initiates(PlaceOnPalette(p, c), OnPalette(p, c), t)
```

If yellow and blue are not placed on the palette simultaneously, color 1 is on the palette, and a color 2 that is different from color 1 is placed on the palette, then color 1 will no longer be on the palette:

```
\neg (Happens(PlaceOnPalette(p, Yellow), t) \land Happens(PlaceOnPalette(p, Blue), t)) \land HoldsAt(OnPalette(p, c_1), t) \land c_1 \neq c_2 \Rightarrow Terminates(PlaceOnPalette(p, c_2), OnPalette(p, c_1), t)
```

We use the following state constraint, which says that a unique color is on the palette:

```
HoldsAt(OnPalette(p, c_1), t) \land HoldsAt(OnPalette(p, c_2), t) \Rightarrow c_1 = c_2
```

Bibliography

- Abelson, R. P. (1981). Psychological status of the script concept. *American Psychologist*, 36(7), 715-729.
- Ahl, D. H. (Ed.). (1973). 101 BASIC computer games. Maynard, MA: Digital Equipment Corporation.
- Aho, A. V., Hopcroft, J. E., & Ullman, J. D. (1983). Data structures and algorithms. Reading, MA: Addison-Wesley.
- Aho, A. V., & Ullman, J. D. (1979). Universality of data retrieval languages. In Conference record of the sixth annual ACM symposium on principles of programming languages (pp. 110-120). New York: ACM.
- Ali, S. S., & Shapiro, S. C. (1993). Natural language processing using a propositional semantic network with structured variables. *Minds and Machines*, *3*(4), 421-451.
- Allen, J. F. (1983). Maintaining knowledge about temporal intervals. *Communications of the ACM*, 26(11), 832-843.
- Allen, J. F. (1984). Towards a general theory of action and time. Artificial Intelligence, 23, 123-154.
- Allen, J. F. (1991). Planning as temporal reasoning. In J. F. Allen, R. E. Fikes, & E. Sandewall (Eds.), Proceedings of the second international conference on principles of knowledge representation and reasoning (pp. 3-14). San Mateo, CA: Morgan Kaufmann.
- Allen, J. F. (1995). Natural language understanding (2nd ed.). Redwood City, CA: Ben-jamin/Cummings.
- Allen, J. F., Hendler, J., & Tate, A. (Eds.). (1990). *Readings in planning*. San Mateo, CA: Morgan Kaufmann.
- Alshawi, H. (Ed.). (1992). The Core Language Engine. Cambridge, MA: MIT Press.
- Antoniou, G. (1997). Nonmonotonic reasoning. Cambridge, MA: MIT Press.
- Apache. (2014). Lucene search engine. http://lucene.apache.org.
- Armstrong, S. (Ed.). (1993). Using large corpora. Cambridge, MA: MIT Press.
- Bacchus, F., Tenenberg, J., & Koomen, J. A. (1991). A non-reified temporal logic. Artificial Intelligence, 52, 87-108.
- Baillargeon, R. (1995). Physical reasoning in infancy. In M. S. Gazzaniga (Ed.), *The cognitive neurosciences* (pp. 181-204). Cambridge, MA: MIT Press.
- Baker, A. B. (1991). Nonmonotonic reasoning in the framework of situation calculus. Artificial Intelligence, 49(1-3), 5-23.
- Balint, A., Belov, A., Heule, M. J. H., & Järvisalo, M. (Eds.). (2013). *Proceedings of SAT competition 2013: Solver and benchmark descriptions*. Helsinki: University of Helsinki.
- Balzer, R. (1985). A 15 year perspective on automatic programming. *IEEE Transactions on Software Engineering*, SE-11(11), 1257-1268.
- Balzer, R., Goldman, N., & Wile, D. (1978). Informality in program specifications. *IEEE Transactions on Software Engineering*, SE-4(2), 94-103.
- Baral, C. (1995). Reasoning about actions: Non-deterministic effects, constraints, and qualification. In *Proceedings of the fourteenth international joint conference on artificial intelligence* (pp. 2017-2026). San Mateo, CA: Morgan Kaufmann.
- Baral, C. (2003). Knowledge representation, reasoning and declarative problem solving. Cambridge: Cambridge University Press.

- Baral, C., & Gelfond, M. (1997). Reasoning about effects of concurrent actions. *Journal of Logic Programming*, 31(1-3), 85-117.
- Baral, C., Tran, N., & Tuan, L.-C. (2002). Reasoning about actions in a probabilistic setting. In Proceedings of the eighteenth national conference on artificial intelligence and fourteenth conference on innovative applications of artificial intelligence (pp. 507-512). Menlo Park, CA: AAAI Press.
- Baum, E. B. (2004). What is thought? Cambridge, MA: MIT Press.
- Bayardo Jr., R. J., & Schrag, R. C. (1997). Using CSP look-back techniques to solve real world SAT instances. In Proceedings of the fourteenth national conference on artificial intelligence and ninth innovative applications of artificial intelligence conference (pp. 203-208). Menlo Park, CA: AAAI Press.
- Beale, S., Nirenburg, S., Mahesh, K., (1995). Semantic analysis in the Mikrokosmos machine translation project. In: *Proceedings of the Second Symposium on Natural Language Processing*. National Electronics and Computer Technology Center, Bangkok, Thailand, pp. 297-307.
- Beaudoin, L. (1994). *Goal processing in autonomous agents*. Doctoral dissertation. School of Computer Science, University of Birmingham, Birmingham, England.
- Belasco, A., Curtis, J., Kahlert, R. C., Klein, C., Mayans, C., & Reagan, P. (2004). Representing knowledge gaps effectively. In D. Karagiannis & U. Reimer (Eds.), *Practical aspects of knowledge management* (Vol. 3336, pp. 159-164). Berlin: Springer.
- Berland, M., & Charniak, E. (1999). Finding parts in very large corpora. In *Thirty-seventh* annual meeting of the association for computational linguistics: Proceedings of the conference (pp. 57-64). San Francisco: Morgan Kaufmann.
- Bibel, W., & Nicolas, J.-M. (1989). The role of logic for data and knowledge bases: A brief survey. In J. W. Schmidt & C. Thanos (Eds.), *Foundations of knowledge base management* (pp. 3-22). Berlin: Springer.
- Biere, A., Heule, M. J. H., van Maaren, H., & Walsh, T. (Eds.). (2009). *Handbook of satisfiability*. Amsterdam: IOS Press.
- Bihlmeyer, R., Faber, W., Ielpa, G., Lio, V., & Pfeifer, G. (2014). *DLV—User manual*. http://www.dlvsystem.com/html/DLV_User_Manual.html.
- Birnbaum, L. (1991). Rigor mortis: A response to Nilsson's "Logic and artificial intelligence". *Artificial Intelligence*, 47(1-3), 57-77.
- Blackburn, P., & Bos, J. (2005). Representation and inference for natural language: A first course in computational semantics. Stanford, CA: CSLI.
- Blum, A. L., & Furst, M. L. (1997). Fast planning through planning graph analysis. Artificial Intelligence, 90(1-2), 281-300.
- Bobrow, D. G. (1980). Editor's preface [Special issue on non-monotonic reasoning]. Artificial Intelligence, 13(1-2), 1-4.
- Bobrow, D. G., & Winograd, T. (1977). An overview of KRL, a knowledge representation language. *Cognitive Science*, 1(1), 3-46.
- Bornscheuer, S.-E., & Thielscher, M. (1996). Explicit and implicit indeterminism: Reasoning about uncertain and contradictory specifications of dynamic systems (Tech. Rep. No. TR-96-009). Berkeley, CA: International Computer Science Institute.
- Brachman, R. J., & Levesque, H. J. (2004). *Knowledge representation and reasoning*. San Francisco: Morgan Kaufmann.
- Braine, M. D. S. (1978). On the relation between the natural logic of reasoning and standard logic. *Psychological Review*, 85(1), 1-21.
- Braine, M. D. S., & O'Brien, D. P. (Eds.). (1998). *Mental logic*. Mahwah, NJ: Lawrence Erlbaum.

- Brandano, S. (2001). The event calculus assessed. In *Eighth international symposium on temporal representation and reasoning (TIME-01)* (pp. 7-12). Washington, DC: IEEE Computer Society.
- Bratman, M. E. (1987). *Intention, plans, and practical reason*. Cambridge, MA: Harvard University Press.
- Bratman, M. E., Israel, D. J., & Pollack, M. E. (1988). Plans and resource-bounded practical reasoning. *Computational Intelligence*, 4, 349-355.
- Brewka, G., Dix, J., & Konolige, K. (1997). *Nonmonotonic reasoning: An overview*. Stanford, CA: CSLI.
- Briggs, R. (1999). The snowman. New York: Random House (adapted by Michelle Knudsen; illustrated by Maggie Downer).
- Brooks, R. A. (1985). A robust layered control system for a mobile robot. A.I. Memo 864. Cambridge, MA: Artificial Intelligence Laboratory, Massachusetts Institute of Technology.
- Brooks, R. A. (1990). *The behavior language: User's guide.* A.I. Memo 1227. Cambridge, MA: Artificial Intelligence Laboratory, Massachusetts Institute of Technology.
- Brown, F. M. (Ed.). (1987). The frame problem in artificial intelligence: Proceedings of the 1987 workshop. Los Altos, CA: Morgan Kaufmann.
- Buss, S. R. (Ed.). (1998). Handbook of proof theory. Amsterdam: Elsevier.
- Cabalar, P., Pearce, D., & Valverde, A. (2005). Reducing propositional theories in equilibrium logic to logic programs. In C. Bento, A. Cardoso, & G. Dias (Eds.), *Progress in artificial intelligence, twelfth Portuguese conference on artificial intelligence* (Vol. 3808, pp. 4-17). Berlin: Springer.
- Calimeri, F., Faber, W., Gebser, M., Ianni, G., Kaminski, R., Krennwallner, T., Leone, N., Ricca, F., & Schaub, T. (2012). ASP-Core-2 input language format. https://www.mat. unical.it/aspcomp2013/files/ASP-CORE-2.03b.pdf.
- Calimeri, F., Ianni, G., & Ricca, F. (2014). The third open answer set programming competition. *Theory and Practice of Logic Programming*, 14(1), 117-135.
- Cassimatis, N. L. (2002). Polyscheme: A cognitive architecture for integrating multiple representation and inference schemes. Doctoral dissertation. Program in Media Arts and Sciences, School of Architecture and Planning, Massachusetts Institute of Technology, Cambridge, MA.
- Cassimatis, N. L. (2006). A cognitive substrate for achieving human-level intelligence. *AI Magazine*, 27(2), 45-56.
- Cassimatis, N. L., Trafton, J. G., Bugajska, M. D., & Schultz, A. C. (2004). Integrating cognition, perception and action through mental simulation in robots. *Robotics and Autonomous Systems*, 49(1-2), 13-23.
- Castilho, M. A., Gasquet, O., & Herzig, A. (1999). Formalizing action and change in modal logic I: The frame problem. *Journal of Logic and Computation*, 9(5), 701-735.
- Ceccato, S. (1966). Automatic translation of languages. In A. Ghizzetti, North Atlantic Treaty Organization, & Advanced Study Institute (Eds.), Automatic translation of languages: Papers presented at NATO summer school held in Venice, July 1962 (pp. 55-108). Oxford: Pergamon Press.
- Chambers, N., & Jurafsky, D. (2008). Unsupervised learning of narrative event chains. In K. McKeown, J. D. Moore, S. Teufel, J. Allan, & S. Furui (Eds.), Proceedings of the forty-sixth annual meeting of the association for computational linguistics (pp. 789-797). Stroudsburg, PA: Association for Computational Linguistics.
- Chambers, N., & Jurafsky, D. (2009). Unsupervised learning of narrative schemas and their participants. In K.-Y. Su, J. Su, & J. Wiebe (Eds.), Proceedings of the forty-seventh annual

- meeting of the association for computational linguistics and the fourth international joint conference on natural language processing of the AFNLP (pp. 602-610). Stroudsburg, PA: Association for Computational Linguistics.
- Charniak, E. (1972). Toward a model of children's story comprehension (Tech. Rep. No. AITR-266). Cambridge, MA: Artificial Intelligence Laboratory, Massachusetts Institute of Technology.
- Charniak, E. (2000). A maximum-entropy-inspired parser. In First meeting of the North American chapter of the association for computational linguistics: Proceedings of the conference (pp. 132-139). Stroudsburg, PA: Association for Computational Linguistics.
- Charniak, E., & McDermott, D. V. (1985). Introduction to artificial intelligence. Reading, MA: Addison-Wesley.
- Charniak, E., Riesbeck, C. K., & McDermott, D. V. (1980). Artificial intelligence programming. Hillsdale, NJ: Lawrence Erlbaum.
- Chklovski, T. (2003a). Learner: A system for acquiring commonsense knowledge by analogy. In Proceedings of the second international conference on knowledge capture (pp. 4-12). New York: ACM.
- Chklovski, T. (2003b). Using analogy to acquire commonsense knowledge from human contributors (Tech. Rep. No. AITR-2003-002). Cambridge, MA: Artificial Intelligence Laboratory, Massachusetts Institute of Technology.
- Chklovski, T., & Fredette, M. (2001). *Learner*. http://web.media.mit.edu/~timc/learner/learner-manual.pdf.
- Chklovski, T., & Mihalcea, R. (2002). Building a sense tagged corpus with Open Mind Word Expert. In Proceedings of the SIGLEX/SENSEVAL workshop on word sense disambiguation: Recent successes and future directions (pp. 116-122). Stroudsburg, PA: Association for Computational Linguistics.
- Chu-Carroll, J., Fan, J., Boguraev, B. K., Carmel, D., Sheinwald, D., & Welty, C. (2012). Finding needles in the haystack: Search and candidate generation. *IBM Journal of Research and Development*, 56(3-4), 6:1-6:12.
- Church, A. (1956). *Introduction to mathematical logic* (Vol. I). Princeton, NJ: Princeton University Press.
- Church, A. (2004). A note on the Entscheidungsproblem. In M. Davis (Ed.), *The undecidable:* Basic papers on undecidable propositions, unsolvable problems and computable functions (corrected ed., pp. 108-115). Mineola, NY: Dover (Original work published 1936)
- Cicekli, N. K., & Yildirim, Y. (2000). Formalizing workflows using the event calculus. In M. T. Ibrahim, J. Küng, & N. Revell (Eds.), *Database and expert systems applications* (Vol. 1873, pp. 222-231). Berlin: Springer.
- Clark, K. L. (1978). Negation as failure. In H. Gallaire & J. Minker (Eds.), Logic and data bases (pp. 293-322). New York: Plenum.
- Clark, K. L., & Tärnlund, S.-A. (1977). A first order theory of data and programs. In B. Gilchrist (Ed.), *Proceedings of the IFIP congress* 77 (pp. 939-944). Amsterdam: North-Holland.
- Clark, P., Harrison, P., Jenkins, T., Thompson, J. A., & Wojcik, R. H. (2005). Acquiring and using world knowledge using a restricted subset of English. In I. Russell & Z. Markov (Eds.), Proceedings of the eighteenth international Florida artificial intelligence research society conference (pp. 506-511). Menlo Park, CA: AAAI Press.
- Clark, P., & Porter, B. (2000). KM—The knowledge machine 1.4.0: KM's situation mechanism. Austin, TX: Department of Computer Science, University of Texas.

- Clark, P., & Porter, B. (2004). KM—The Knowledge Machine 2.0: Users [sic] manual. Austin, TX: Department of Computer Science, University of Texas.
- Clocksin, W. F., & Mellish, C. S. (2003). Programming in Prolog (5th ed.). Berlin: Springer.
- Cohen, P. R. (1995). Empirical methods for artificial intelligence. Cambridge, MA: MIT Press.
- Cohen, P. R., & Levesque, H. J. (1990). Intention is choice with commitment. Artificial Intelligence, 42, 213-261.
- Cohn, A. G., Bennett, B., Gooday, J., & Gotts, N. M. (1997). Representing and reasoning with qualitative spatial relations about regions. In O. Stock (Ed.), *Spatial and temporal reasoning* (pp. 97-134). Dordrecht: Kluwer.
- Collins, M. (1999). Head-driven statistical models for natural language parsing. Doctoral dissertation. Computer and Information Science, University of Pennsylvania, Philadelphia.
- Collins, M. (2003). Head-driven statistical models for natural language parsing. Computational Linguistics, 29(4), 589-637.
- Collins, A. M., & Quillian, M. R. (1969). Retrieval time from semantic memory. *Journal of Verbal Learning and Verbal Behavior*, 8, 240-247.
- Cook, S. A. (1971). The complexity of theorem-proving procedures. In *Proceedings of the third annual ACM symposium on theory of computing* (pp. 151-158). New York: ACM.
- Crawford, J. M., & Etherington, D. W. (1992). Formalizing reasoning about change: A qualitative reasoning approach. In W. R. Swartout (Ed.), *Proceedings of the tenth national conference on artificial intelligence* (pp. 577-583). Menlo Park, CA: AAAI Press.
- Crevier, D. (1993). AI: The tumultuous history of the search for artificial intelligence. New York: BasicBooks.
- Curry, H. B. (1963). Foundations of mathematical logic. New York: McGraw-Hill.
- Cycorp. (2002a). Ontological engineer's handbook version 0.7. Austin, TX: Cycorp.
- Cycorp. (2002b). OpenCyc release 0.7.0 [Computer software]. Austin, TX: Cycorp.
- Cycorp. (2002). OpenCyc selected vocabulary and upper ontology. Austin, TX: Cycorp.
- Cycorp. (2014a). *Introduction to Cyc inferencing*. http://www.cyc.com/documentation/introduction-cyc-inferencing.
- Cycorp. (2014b). Negation in CycL. http://www.cyc.com/documentation/negation-in-cycl.
- Cycorp. (2014c). Ontological engineer's handbook. http://www.cyc.com/documentation/ontological-engineering-handbook.
- Cycorp. (2014d). Resolution in CycL. http://www.cyc.com/documentation/ resolution-cycl.
- Cycorp. (2014e). The Cyc knowledge base. http://www.cyc.com/cyc/kb.
- Cycorp. (2014f). KE text. http://www.cyc.com/documentation/ke-text.
- Dahlgren, K., McDowell, J., & Stabler, E. P., Jr. (1989). Knowledge representation for commonsense reasoning with text. *Computational Linguistics* 15(3), 149-170.
- Davidson, D. (2001). The logical form of action sentences. In D. Davidson (Ed.), Essays on actions and events (2nd ed., pp. 105-148). Oxford: Oxford University Press (Original work published 1967)
- Davis, M. (1959). Lecture notes on mathematical logic. Based on student notes by Allen Weingarten, Fall 1959. New York: New York University.
- Davis, M. (1980). The mathematics of non-monotonic reasoning. Artificial Intelligence, 13(1-2), 73-80.

- Davis, E. (1990). Representations of commonsense knowledge. San Mateo, CA: Morgan Kaufmann.
- Davis, E. (1992). Axiomatizing qualitative process theory. In B. Nebel, C. Rich, & W. R. Swartout (Eds.), *Proceedings of the third international conference on principles of knowledge representation and reasoning* (pp. 177-188). San Mateo, CA: Morgan Kaufmann.
- Davis, E. (1995). A highly expressive language of spatial constraints (Tech. Rep. No. TR1995-714). New York: Computer Science Department, New York University.
- Davis, E. (1999). Guide to axiomatizing domains in first-order logic. *Electronic News Journal on Reasoning about Actions and Change*, 3(1), 25-28.
- Davis, M., Logemann, G., & Loveland, D. (1962). A machine program for theorem-proving. *Communications of the ACM*, 5(7), 394-397.
- Davis, M., & Putnam, H. (1960). A computing procedure for quantification theory. *Journal of the ACM*, 7(3), 201-215.
- DBpedia. (2014). DBpedia. http://dbpedia.org.
- de Kleer, J. (1975). *Qualitative and quantitative knowledge in classical mechanics* (Tech. Rep. No. AITR-352). Cambridge, MA: Artificial Intelligence Laboratory, Massachusetts Institute of Technology.
- de Kleer, J., & Brown, J. S. (1984). A qualitative physics based on confluences. *Artificial Intelligence*, 24(1-3), 7-83.
- de Nivelle, H. (1999). Bliksem 1.10 user manual. Saarbrücken, Germany: Max-Planck Institut für Informatik.
- Dean, T., & Boddy, M. (1988). Reasoning about partially ordered events. *Artificial Intelligence*, 36(3), 375-399.
- Dechter, R. (2003). Constraint processing. San Francisco: Morgan Kaufmann.
- Deerwester, S., Dumais, S. T., Furnas, G. W., Landauer, T. K., & Harshman, R. (1990). Indexing by latent semantic analysis. *Journal of the American Society for Information Science*, 41(6), 391-407.
- Denecker, M., Dupré, D. T., & Belleghem, K. V. (1998). An inductive definition approach to ramifications. *Linköping Electronic Articles in Computer and Information Science*, *3*(007), 1-43.
- Denecker, M., Missiaen, L., & Bruynooghe, M. (1992). Temporal reasoning with abductive event calculus. In B. Neumann (Ed.), *Proceedings of the tenth European conference on artificial intelligence* (pp. 384-388). Chichester, UK: John Wiley.
- DIMACS. (1993). Satisfiability suggested format (Tech. Rep.). Piscataway, NJ: Center for Discrete Mathematics and Theoretical Computer Science.
- Dimopoulos, Y., Kakas, A. C., & Michael, L. (2004). Reasoning about actions and change in answer set programming. In V. Lifschitz & I. Niemelä (Eds.), *Proceedings of the seventh international conference on logic programming and nonmonotonic reasoning* (Vol. 2923, pp. 61-73). Berlin: Springer.
- Doherty, P. (1994). Reasoning about action and change using occlusion. In A. G. Cohn (Ed.), *Proceedings of the eleventh European conference on artificial intelligence* (pp. 401-405). Chichester, UK: John Wiley.
- Doherty, P. (1996). pmon⁺: A fluent logic for action and change. Formal specification, version 1.0 (Tech. Rep. No. LiTH-IDA-R-96-33). Linköping, Sweden: Department of Computer and Information Science, Linköping University.
- Doherty, P., Gustafsson, J., Karlsson, L., & Kvarnström, J. (1998). TAL: Temporal Action Logics language specification and tutorial. *Linköping Electronic Articles in Computer and Information Science*, 3(015), 1-32.

- Doherty, P., & Kvarnström, J. (1997). Tackling the qualification problem using fluent dependency constraints: Preliminary report. Linköping Electronic Articles in Computer and Information Science, 2(016), 1-14.
- Doherty, P., & Łukaszewicz, W. (1994). Circumscribing features and fluents. In D. M. Gabbay & H. J. Ohlbach (Eds.), *Temporal logic* (Vol. 827, pp. 82-100). Berlin: Springer.
- Doherty, P., Łukaszewicz, W., & Szałas, A. (1997). Computing circumscription revisited: A reduction algorithm. *Journal of Automated Reasoning*, 18(3), 297-336.
- Domeshek, E., Jones, E., & Ram, A. (1999). Capturing the contents of complex narratives. In A. Ram & K. Moorman (Eds.), *Understanding language understanding: Computational models of reading* (pp. 73-105). Cambridge, MA: MIT Press.
- Dowty, D. R., Wall, R. E., & Peters, S. (1981). Introduction to Montague semantics. Dordrecht: Kluwer.
- Du, D., Gu, J., & Pardalos, P. M. (Eds.). (1997). Satisfiability problem: Theory and applications (Vol. 35). Boston, MA: American Mathematical Society.
- Dyer, M. G. (1983). In-depth understanding: A computer model of integrated processing for narrative comprehension. Cambridge, MA: MIT Press.
- Ebbinghaus, H.-D., Flum, J., & Thomas, W. (1994). *Mathematical logic* (2nd ed.). New York: Springer.
- Eiter, T. (Ed.). (2014). Proceedings of the Fourteenth International Conference on Principles of Knowledge Representation and Reasoning. Menlo Park, CA: AAAI Press.
- Elgot-Drapkin, J. J., Kraus, S., Miller, M., Nirkhe, M., & Perlis, D. (1999). *Active logics:* A unified formal approach to episodic reasoning (Tech. Rep. No. CS-TR-4072). College Park, MD: Department of Computer Science, University of Maryland.
- Elgot-Drapkin, J. J., & Perlis, D. (1990). Reasoning situated in time I: Basic concepts. *Journal of Experimental and Theoretical Artificial Intelligence*, 2(1), 75-98.
- Elkan, C. (1996). Reasoning about unknown, counterfactual, and nondeterministic actions in first-order logic. In G. McCalla (Ed.), *Advances in artificial intelligence* (Vol. 1081, pp. 54-68). Berlin: Springer.
- Enderton, H. B. (2001). A mathematical introduction to logic (2nd ed.). San Diego: Academic Press.
- Epstein, E. A., Schor, M. I., Iyer, B. S., Lally, A., Brown, E. W., & Cwiklik, J. (2012). Making Watson fast. *IBM Journal of Research and Development*, 56(3-4), 15:1-15:12.
- Ernst, M., Millstein, T. D., & Weld, D. S. (1997). Automatic SAT-compilation of planning problems. In *Proceedings of the fifteenth international joint conference on artificial* intelligence (pp. 1169-1176). San Mateo, CA: Morgan Kaufmann.
- Eshghi, K. (1988). Abductive planning with event calculus. In R. A. Kowalski & K. A. Bowen (Eds.), *Logic programming: Proceedings of the fifth international conference and symposium* (Vol. 1, pp. 562-579). Cambridge, MA: MIT Press.
- Etherington, D. W. (1988). Reasoning with incomplete information. Los Altos, CA: Morgan Kaufmann.
- Eves, H. (1990). Foundations and fundamental concepts of mathematics (3rd ed.). Mineola, NY: Dover.
- Fagin, R., Halpern, J. Y., Moses, Y., & Vardi, M. Y. (1995). Reasoning about knowledge. Cambridge, MA: MIT Press.
- Fahlman, S. E. (1974). A planning system for robot construction tasks. Artificial Intelligence, 5(1), 1-49.
- Fahlman, S. E. (1979). NETL: A system for representing and using real-world knowledge. Cambridge, MA: MIT Press.

- Falkenhainer, B. C. (1988). Learning from physical analogies: A study in analogy and the explanation process (Tech. Rep. No. UIUCDCS-R-88-1479). Urbana, IL: University of Illinois at Urbana-Champaign.
- Falkenhainer, B. C., Forbus, K. D., & Gentner, D. (1989). The structure-mapping engine: Algorithm and examples. *Artificial Intelligence*, 41(1), 1-63.
- Fellbaum, C. (Ed.). (1998). WordNet: An electronic lexical database. Cambridge, MA: MIT Press.
- Ferraris, P., Lee, J., & Lifschitz, V. (2007). A new perspective on stable models. In M. M. Veloso (Ed.), *Proceedings of the twentieth international joint conference on artificial intelligence* (pp. 372-379). Menlo Park, CA: AAAI Press.
- Ferraris, P., Lee, J., & Lifschitz, V. (2011). Stable models and circumscription. *Artificial Intelligence*, 175(1), 236-263.
- Ferrucci, D. (2012). Introduction to "This is Watson". *IBM Journal of Research and Development*, 56(3-4), 1:1-1:15.
- Ferrucci, D., & Brown, E. W. (2012). AdaptWatson: A methodology for developing and adapting Watson technology (Tech. Rep. No. RC25244). Yorktown Heights, NY: IBM Research Division.
- Ferrucci, D., Brown, E. W., Chu-Carroll, J., Fan, J., Gondek, D., Kalyanpur, A. A., Lally, A., Murdock, J. W., Nyberg, E., Prager, J. M., Schlaefer, N., & Welty, C. (2010). Building Watson: An overview of the DeepQA project. AI Magazine, 31(3), 59-79.
- Ferrucci, D., & Lally, A. (2004). Building an example application with the Unstructured Information Management Architecture. IBM Systems Journal, 43(3), 455-475.
- Ferrucci, D., Levas, A., Bagchi, S., Gondek, D., & Mueller, E. T. (2013). Watson: Beyond Jeopardy! Artificial Intelligence, 199-200, 93-105.
- Fikes, R. E., Hart, P. E., & Nilsson, N. J. (1972a). Learning and executing generalized robot plans. *Artificial Intelligence*, *3*, 251-288.
- Fikes, R. E., Hart, P. E., & Nilsson, N. J. (1972b). Some new directions in robot problem solving. In B. Meltzer & D. Michie (Eds.), *Machine intelligence* 7 (pp. 405-430). Edinburgh, Scotland: Edinburgh University Press.
- Fikes, R. E., & Nilsson, N. J. (1971). STRIPS: A new approach to the application of theorem proving to problem solving. *Artificial Intelligence*, 2, 189-208.
- Finger, J. J. (1987). Exploiting constraints in design synthesis. Doctoral dissertation. Department of Computer Science, Stanford University, Stanford, CA.
- Forbus, K. D. (1984). Qualitative process theory. Artificial Intelligence, 24(1-3), 85-168.
- Forbus, K. D. (2001). Exploring analogy in the large. In D. Gentner, K. J. Holyoak, & B. N. Kokinov (Eds.), *The analogical mind: Perspectives from cognitive science* (pp. 23-58). Cambridge, MA: MIT Press.
- Forbus, K. D., & Gentner, D. (1997). Qualitative mental models: Simulations or memories? In *Proceedings of the eleventh international workshop on qualitative reasoning* (pp. 1-8). Cortona, Italy.
- Ford, K. M., & Pylyshyn, Z. W. (Eds.). (1996). The robot's dilemma revisited: The frame problem in artificial intelligence. Norwood, NJ: Ablex.
- Frege, G. (1967). Begriffsschrift, a formula language, modeled upon that of arithmetic, for pure thought. In J. van Heijenoort (Ed.), From Frege to Gödel: A source book in mathematical logic, 1879-1931 (pp. 1-82). Cambridge, MA: Harvard University Press (Original work published 1879)
- Freud, A. (1946). *The ego and the mechanisms of defence*. New York: International Universities (Original work published 1936)

- Fuchs, N. E., & Schwertel, U. (2002). Reasoning in Attempto Controlled English (Tech. Rep. No. ifi-2002.01). Zürich: Institut für Informatik der Universität Zürich.
- Fuchs, N. E., Schwertel, U., & Schwitter, R. (1999). Attempto Controlled English (ACE) language manual version 3.0 (Tech. Rep. No. 99.03). Zürich: Institut für Informatik der Universität Zürich.
- Gabbay, D. M., & Guenthner, F. (Eds.). (2001). Handbook of philosophical logic (2nd ed.). Dordrecht: Kluwer.
- Gabbay, D. M., Hogger, C. J., & Robinson, J. A. (Eds.). (1994). Handbook of logic in artificial intelligence and logic programming (Vol. 3: Nonmonotonic reasoning and uncertain reasoning). Oxford: Oxford University Press.
- Gabbay, D. M., & Ohlbach, H. J. (1992). Quantifier elimination in second-order predicate logic. In B. Nebel, C. Rich, & W. R. Swartout (Eds.), Proceedings of the third international conference on principles of knowledge representation and reasoning (pp. 425-435). San Mateo, CA: Morgan Kaufmann.
- Garcia, D., Havasi, C., & Todd, K. (2002). Interactively improving the Open Mind database: Game for interactive Open Mind Improvement (GIOMI). http://web.media.mit.edu/~lieber/Teaching/Common-Sense-Course/Projects/Giomi/.
- Garey, M. R., & Johnson, D. S. (1979). Computers and intractability: A guide to the theory of NP-completeness. San Francisco: W. H. Freeman.
- Garnier, R., & Taylor, J. (1996). 100% mathematical proof. Chichester, UK: John Wiley.
- Gebser, M., Kaminski, R., Kaufmann, B., & Schaub, T. (2013). Answer set solving in practice. San Rafael, CA: Morgan & Claypool.
- Gebser, M., Kaminski, R., Ostrowski, M., Schaub, T., & Thiele, S. (2009). On the input language of ASP grounder Gringo. In E. Erdem, F. Lin, & T. Schaub (Eds.), *Logic programming and nonmonotonic reasoning, tenth international conference* (Vol. 5753, pp. 502-508). Berlin: Springer.
- Gebser, M., Ostrowski, M., Kaminski, R., Kaufmann, B., & Schaub, T. (2010). A user's guide to gringo, clasp, clingo, and iclingo. http://sourceforge.net/projects/potassco/files/potassco_guide/2010-10-04/guide.pdf/download.
- Geffner, H. (1990). Causal theories for nonmonotonic reasoning. In T. Dietterich & W. R. Swartout (Eds.), Proceedings of the eighth national conference on artificial intelligence (pp. 524-530). Menlo Park, CA: AAAI Press.
- Gelfond, M. (2008). Answer sets. In F. van Harmelen, V. Lifschitz, & B. Porter (Eds.), *Handbook of knowledge representation* (pp. 285-316). Amsterdam: Elsevier.
- Gelfond, M., & Kahl, Y. (2014). Knowledge representation, reasoning, and the design of intelligent agents: The answer-set programming approach. New York: Cambridge University Press.
- Gelfond, M., & Lifschitz, V. (1988). The stable model semantics for logic programming. In R. A. Kowalski & K. A. Bowen (Eds.), Logic programming: Proceedings of the fifth international conference and symposium (Vol. 2, pp. 1070-1080). Cambridge, MA: MIT Press.
- Gelfond, M., & Lifschitz, V. (1991). Classical negation in logic programs and disjunctive databases. *New Generation Computing*, 9(3-4), 365-386.
- Gelfond, M., & Lifschitz, V. (1993). Representing action and change by logic programs. *Journal of Logic Programming*, 17(2-4), 301-321.
- Gelfond, M., & Lifschitz, V. (1998). Action languages. Linköping Electronic Articles in Computer and Information Science, 3(016), 1-15.

- Gelfond, M., Lifschitz, V., & Rabinov, A. (1991). What are the limitations of the situation calculus? In R. S. Boyer (Ed.), *Automated reasoning: Essays in honor of Woody Bledsoe* (pp. 167-179). Dordrecht: Kluwer.
- Genesereth, M. R., & Nilsson, N. J. (1987). Logical foundations of artificial intelligence. Palo Alto, CA: Morgan Kaufmann.
- Gentner, D. (1983). Structure-mapping: A theoretical framework for analogy. Cognitive Science, 7(2), 155-170.
- Gentner, D., Holyoak, K. J., & Kokinov, B. N. (Eds.). (2001). The analogical mind: Perspectives from cognitive science. Cambridge, MA: MIT Press.
- Gentzen, G. (1969). Investigations into logical deduction. In M. E. Szabo (Ed.), The collected papers of Gerhard Gentzen (pp. 68-131). Amsterdam: North-Holland (Original work published 1935)
- Ghallab, M., Nau, D., & Traverso, P. (2004). Automated planning: Theory and practice. San Francisco: Morgan Kaufmann.
- Gildea, D., & Jurafsky, D. (2002). Automatic labeling of semantic roles. *Computational Linguistics*, 28(3), 245-288.
- Ginsberg, M. L. (Ed.). (1987). Readings in nonmonotonic reasoning. Los Altos, CA: Morgan Kaufmann.
- Ginsberg, M. L. (1991). Marvin Minsky, the society of mind. Artificial Intelligence, 48, 335-339.
- Ginsberg, M. L., & Smith, D. E. (1987a). Reasoning about action II: The qualification problem. In F. M. Brown (Ed.), The frame problem in artificial intelligence: proceedings of the 1987 workshop (pp. 259-287). Los Altos, CA: Morgan Kaufmann.
- Ginsberg, M. L., & Smith, D. E. (1987b). Reasoning about action I: A possible worlds approach. In F. M. Brown (Ed.), *The frame problem in artificial intelligence: proceedings of the 1987 workshop* (pp. 233-258). Los Altos, CA: Morgan Kaufmann.
- Ginsberg, M. L., & Smith, D. E. (1988a). Reasoning about action II: The qualification problem. Artificial Intelligence, 35(3), 311-342.
- Ginsberg, M. L., & Smith, D. E. (1988b). Reasoning about action I: A possible worlds approach. *Artificial Intelligence*, 35(2), 165-195.
- Giunchiglia, E., Lee, J., Lifschitz, V., McCain, N. C., & Turner, H. (2004). Nonmonotonic causal theories. Artificial Intelligence, 153, 49-104.
- Giunchiglia, E., & Lifschitz, V. (1998). An action language based on causal explanation: Preliminary report. In Proceedings of the fifteenth national conference on artificial intelligence and tenth conference on innovative applications of artificial intelligence (pp. 623-630). Menlo Park, CA: AAAI Press.
- Giunchiglia, E., & Sebastiani, R. (1999). Applying the Davis-Putnam procedure to non-clausal formulas. In *Proceedings of the sixth congress of the Italian association for artificial intelligence*. Bologna.
- Giunchiglia, F., & Ghidini, C. (1998). Local models semantics, or contextual reasoning = locality + compatibility. In A. G. Cohn, L. K. Schubert, & S. C. Shapiro (Eds.), *Proceedings of the sixth international conference on principles of knowledge representation and reasoning* (pp. 282-289). San Francisco: Morgan Kaufmann.
- Gödel, K. (1967). The completeness of the axioms of the functional calculus of logic. In J. van Heijenoort (Ed.), *From Frege to Gödel: A source book in mathematical logic, 1879-1931* (pp. 582-591). Cambridge, MA: Harvard University Press (Original work published 1930)
- Golub, G. H., & Van Loan, C. F. (1996). *Matrix computations* (3rd ed.). Baltimore and London: Johns Hopkins University Press.

439

- Gomes, C. P., Kautz, H., Sabharwal, A., & Selman, B. (2008). Satisfiability solvers. In F. van Harmelen, V. Lifschitz, & B. Porter (Eds.), *Handbook of knowledge representation* (pp. 89-134). Amsterdam: Elsevier.
- Gondek, D. C., Lally, A., Kalyanpur, A., Murdock, J. W., Duboue, P. A., Zhang, L., Pan, Y., Qiu, Z. M., & Welty, C. (2012). A framework for merging and ranking of answers in DeepQA. *IBM Journal of Research and Development*, 56(3-4), 14:1-14:12.
- Gordon, A. S. (2004). Strategy representation: An analysis of planning knowledge. Mahwah, NJ: Lawrence Erlbaum.
- Gordon, J. M. (2014). *Inferential commonsense knowledge from text*. Doctoral dissertation. Department of Computer Science, University of Rochester, Rochester, NY.
- Gordon, J. M., & Schubert, L. K. (2010). Quantificational sharpening of commonsense knowledge. In C. Havasi, D. B. Lenat, & B. D. Van Durme (Eds.), Commonsense knowledge: Papers from the AAAI fall symposium (pp. 27-32). Menlo Park, CA: AAAI Press.
- Gordon, J. M., & Schubert, L. K. (2011). Discovering commonsense entailment rules implicit in sentences. In *Proceedings of the TextInfer 2011 workshop on textual entailment* (pp. 59-63). Stroudsburg, PA: Association for Computational Linguistics.
- Gordon, J. M., & Schubert, L. K. (2012). Using textual patterns to learn expected event frequencies. In *Proceedings of the joint workshop on automatic knowledge base construc*tion and web-scale knowledge extraction (pp. 122-127). Stroudsburg, PA: Association for Computational Linguistics.
- Gordon, J. M., Van Durme, B., & Schubert, L. K. (2010). Learning from the web: Extracting general world knowledge from noisy text. In V. Nastase, R. Navigli, & F. Wu (Eds.), Collaboratively-built knowledge sources and artificial intelligence: Papers from the AAAI workshop (pp. 8-13). Menlo Park, CA: AAAI Press.
- Green, C. C. (1969). The application of theorem proving to question-answering systems. Doctoral dissertation. Department of Electrical Engineering, Stanford University, Stanford, CA.
- Green, Jr., B. F., Wolf, A. K., Chomsky, C., & Laughery, K. (1961). Baseball: An automatic question-answerer. In *Proceedings of the western joint computer conference* (pp. 219-224). New York: National Joint Computer Committee.
- Greiner, R., & Lenat, D. B. (1980). A representation language language. In R. M. Balzer (Ed.), Proceedings of the first national conference on artificial intelligence (pp. 165-169). Menlo Park, CA: AAAI Press.
- Grosof, B. (1984). Default reasoning as circumscription: A translation of default logic into circumscription or maximizing defaults is minimizing predicates. In *Proceedings* of the non-monotonic reasoning workshop (pp. 115-124). Menlo Park, CA: AAAI Press.
- Guha, R. V. (1990). The representation of defaults in Cyc (Tech. Rep. No. ACT-CYC-083-90).
 Austin, TX: Microelectronics and Computer Technology Corporation.
- Guha, R. V. (1992). Contexts: A formalization and some applications. Doctoral dissertation. Computer Science Department, Stanford University, Stanford, CA.
- Guha, R. V., & Lenat, D. B. (1990a). CYC: A midterm report. AI Magazine 11(3), 32-59.
- Guha, R. V., & Lenat, D. B. (1990b). CycL: The Cyc representation language, part 4 (Tech. Rep. No. ACT-CYC-154-90). Austin, TX: Microelectronics and Computer Technology Corporation.
- Guha, R. V., & Lenat, D. B. (1994). Enabling agents to work together. *Communications of the ACM*, 37(7), 127-142.

- Guicciardini, N. (1999). Reading the Principia: The debate on Newton's mathematical methods for natural philosophy from 1687 to 1736. Cambridge: Cambridge University Press.
- Gustafsson, J., & Doherty, P. (1996). Embracing occlusion in specifying the indirect effects of actions. In L. C. Aiello, J. Doyle, & S. C. Shapiro (Eds.), Proceedings of the fifth international conference on principles of knowledge representation and reasoning (pp. 87-98). San Francisco: Morgan Kaufmann.
- Haas, A. R. (1987). The case for domain-specific frame axioms. In F. M. Brown (Ed.), The frame problem in artificial intelligence: Proceedings of the 1987 workshop (pp. 343-348). Los Altos, CA: Morgan Kaufmann.
- Halpern, M. (1966). Foundations of the case for natural-language programming. In *AFIPS fall joint computer conference* (pp. 639-649). Washington, DC: Spartan Books.
- Halpern, J. Y. (1999). On the adequacy of modal logic. *Electronic News Journal on Reasoning About Actions and Change*, 3(3), 1-5.
- Halpern, J. Y. (2000). On the adequacy of modal logic, II: A response to McCarthy. Electronic News Journal on Reasoning About Actions and Change, 4(1), 1-3.
- Halpern, J. Y. (2003). Reasoning about uncertainty. Cambridge, MA: MIT Press.
- Halpin, H., Moore, J. D., & Robertson, J. (2004). Automatic analysis of plot for story rewriting. In D. Lin & D. Wu (Eds.), Proceedings of the 2004 conference on empirical methods in natural language processing (pp. 127-133). Barcelona, Spain.
- Hamilton, A. G. (1988). Logic for mathematicians (revised ed.). Cambridge: Cambridge University Press.
- Hanks, S., & Madigan, D. (2005). Probabilistic temporal reasoning. In M. Fisher, D. Gabbay, & L. Vila (Eds.), Handbook of temporal reasoning in artificial intelligence (Vol. 1, pp. 315-342). Amsterdam: Elsevier.
- Hanks, S., & McDermott, D. V. (1985). Temporal reasoning and default logics (Tech. Rep. No. YALE/DCS/tr430). New Haven, CT: Computer Science Department, Yale University.
- Hanks, S., & McDermott, D. V. (1986). Default reasoning, nonmonotonic logics, and the frame problem. In *Proceedings of the fifth national conference on artificial intelligence* (pp. 328-333). Los Altos, CA: Morgan Kaufmann.
- Hanks, S., & McDermott, D. V. (1987). Nonmonotonic logic and temporal projection. Artificial Intelligence, 33(3), 379-412.
- Hansen, P. C. (1998). Rank-deficient and discrete ill-posed problems. Philadelphia: SIAM.
- Harel, D. (1984). Dynamic logic. In D. M. Gabbay & F. Guenthner (Eds.), Handbook of philosophical logic (1st ed., Vol. 2, pp. 497-604). Dordrecht: Reidel.
- Havasi, C. (2009). Discovering semantic relations using singular value decomposition based techniques. Doctoral dissertation. Computer Science Department, Brandeis University, Waltham, MA.
- Havasi, C., Speer, R., & Alonso, J. B. (2007). ConceptNet 3: A flexible, multilingual semantic network for common sense knowledge. In *Recent advances in natural language processing*. Borovets, Bulgaria.
- Havasi, C., Speer, R., & Alonso, J. B. (2009). ConceptNet: A lexical resource for common sense knowledge. In N. Nicolov, G. Angelova, & R. Mitkov (Eds.), *Recent advances in natural language processing V* (pp. 269-280). Amsterdam: John Benjamins.
- Hayes, P. J. (1971). A logic of actions. In B. Meltzer & D. Michie (Eds.), Machine intelligence 6 (pp. 495-520). New York: Halsted.
- Hayes, P. J. (1973). The frame problem and related problems in artificial intelligence. In A. Elithorn & D. Jones (Eds.), Artificial and human thinking (pp. 45-59). Amsterdam: Elsevier.

- Hayes, P. J. (1977). In defence of logic. In R. Reddy (Ed.), Proceedings of the fifth international joint conference on artificial intelligence (pp. 559-565). Los Altos, CA: William Kaufmann.
- Hayes, P. J. (1979). The logic of frames. In D. Metzing (Ed.), Frame conceptions and text understanding (pp. 46-61). Berlin: Walter de Gruyter.
- Hayes, P. J. (1985). Naive physics I: Ontology for liquids. In J. R. Hobbs & R. C. Moore (Eds.), Formal theories of the commonsense world (pp. 71-107). Norwood, NJ; Ablex.
- Hearn, R. A. (2001). Building grounded abstractions for artificial intelligence programming. Master's thesis. Department of Electrical Engineering and Computer Science, Massachusetts Institute of Technology, Cambridge, MA.
- Hearst, M. A. (1992). Automatic acquisition of hyponyms from large text corpora. In C. Boitet (Ed.), Proceedings of the fifteenth [fourteenth] international conference on computational linguistics (pp. 539-545). Morristown, NJ: Association for Computational Linguistics.
- Hearst, M. A. (1998). Automated discovery of WordNet relations. In C. Fellbaum (Ed.), WordNet: An electronic lexical database (pp. 131-151). Cambridge, MA: MIT Press.
- Heider, F. (1958). The psychology of interpersonal relations. Hillsdale, NJ: Lawrence Erlbaum.
- Hendrix, G. G. (1973). Modeling simultaneous actions and continuous processes. *Artificial Intelligence*, *4*, 145-180.
- Henkin, L. (1949). The completeness of the first-order functional calculus. *Journal of Symbolic Logic*, 14(3), 159-166.
- Henle, M. (1962). On the relation between logic and thinking. *Psychological Review*, 69(4), 366-378.
- Herrmann, C. S., & Thielscher, M. (1996). Reasoning about continuous processes. In *Proceedings of the thirteenth national conference on artificial intelligence and eighth annual conference on innovative applications of artificial intelligence* (pp. 639-644). Menlo Park, CA: AAAI Press.
- Hewitt, C. (1972). Description and theoretical analysis (using schemata) of planner: A language for proving theorems and manipulating models in a robot (Tech. Rep. No. AITR-258). Cambridge, MA: Artificial Intelligence Laboratory, Massachusetts Institute of Technology.
- Hewitt, C. (1987). Metacritique of McDermott and the logicist approach. *Computational Intelligence*, *3*, 185-189.
- Hintikka, J. (1962). Knowledge and belief: An introduction to the logic of the two notions. Ithaca, NY: Cornell University Press.
- Hobbs, J. R. (1984). Sublanguage and knowledge. Technical Note 329. Menlo Park, CA: SRI International.
- Hobbs, J. R. (1985). Ontological promiscuity. In *Proceedings of the twenty-third annual meeting of the association for computational linguistics* (pp. 61-69). Morristown, NJ: Association for Computational Linguistics.
- Hobbs, J. R., & Moore, R. C. (Eds.). (1985). Formal theories of the commonsense world. Norwood, NJ: Ablex.
- Hobbs, J. R., Stickel, M. E., Appelt, D. E., & Martin, P. (1993). Interpretation as abduction. *Artificial Intelligence*, *63*, 69-142.
- Hodges, W. (1993). Model theory. Cambridge: Cambridge University Press.

- Hodges, W. (2001). Elementary predicate logic. In D. M. Gabbay & F. Guenthner (Eds.), Handbook of philosophical logic (2nd ed., Vol. 1, pp. 1-129). Dordrecht: Kluwer.
- Hoeksema, J. (1986). Monotonicity phenomena in natural language. *Linguistic Analysis*, 16(1-2), 25-40.
- Hölldobler, S., & Schneeberger, J. (1990). A new deductive approach to planning. *New Generation Computing*, 8(3), 225-244.
- Hölldobler, S., & Thielscher, M. (1995). Computing change and specificity with equational logic programs. *Annals of Mathematics and Artificial Intelligence*, 14(1), 99-133.
- Holyoak, K. J., & Thagard, P. (1989). Analogical mapping by constraint satisfaction. Cognitive Science, 13(3), 295-355.
- Hoos, H. H., & Stützle, T. (2005). Stochastic local search: Foundations and applications. San Francisco: Morgan Kaufmann.
- Horty, J. F., Thomason, R. H., & Touretzky, D. S. (1990). A skeptical theory of inheritance in nonmonotonic semantic networks. *Artificial Intelligence*, 42(2-3), 311-348.
- IMDb. (2014). Internet movie database. http://www.imdb.com.
- Israel, D. J. (1980). What's wrong with non-monotonic logic? In R. M. Balzer (Ed.), Proceedings of the first national conference on artificial intelligence (pp. 99-101). Menlo Park, CA: AAAI Press.
- Israel, D. J. (1985). A short companion to the naive physics manifesto. In J. R. Hobbs & R. C. Moore (Eds.), Formal theories of the commonsense world (pp. 427-447). Norwood, NJ: Ablex.
- Iwańska, L. M., & Shapiro, S. C. (Eds.). (2000). Natural language processing and knowledge representation. Cambridge, MA: MIT Press.
- Jackson, D. (2000). Automating first-order relational logic. In *Proceedings of the eighth international symposium on the foundations of software engineering* (pp. 130-139). New York: ACM.
- Janhunen, T., & Niemelä, I. (2011). Compact translations of non-disjunctive answer set programs to propositional clauses. In M. Balduccini & T. C. Son (Eds.), Logic programming, knowledge representation, and nonmonotonic reasoning (Vol. 6565, pp. 111-130). Berlin: Springer.
- Johnson-Laird, P. N. (1983). Mental models: Toward a cognitive science of language, inference, and consciousness. Cambridge, MA: Harvard University Press.
- Johnson-Laird, P. N. (1993). Human and machine thinking. Hillsdale, NJ: Lawrence Erlbaum.
- Jordan, P. W. (2004). Using student explanations as models for adapting tutorial dialogue. In V. Barr & Z. Markov (Eds.), Proceedings of the seventeenth international Florida artificial intelligence research society conference (pp. 905-910). Menlo Park, CA: AAAI Press.
- Jurafsky, D., & Martin, J. H. (2009). Speech and language processing: An introduction to natural language processing, computational linguistics, and speech recognition (2nd ed.). Upper Saddle River, NJ: Prentice Hall.
- Kakas, A. C. (Ed.). (2013). Eleventh international symposium on logical formalizations of commonsense reasoning. Ayia Napa, Cyprus.
- Kakas, A.C., Michael, L., Miller, R., (2005). Modular-E: an elaboration tolerant approach to the ramification and qualification problems. In: McIlraith, S., Peppas, P., Thielscher, M. (Eds.), Seventh International Symposium on Logical Formalizations of Commonsense Reasoning. Corfu, Greece. Technischen Universität Dresden, Dresden, Germany.
- Kakas, A. C., Michael, L., & Miller, R. (2011). Modular-E and the role of elaboration tolerance in solving the qualification problem. *Artificial Intelligence*, 175(1), 49-78.

- Kakas, A. C., & Miller, R. (1997a). Reasoning about actions, narratives and ramifications. Linköping Electronic Articles in Computer and Information Science, 2(012), 1-29.
- Kakas, A. C., & Miller, R. (1997b). A simple declarative language for describing narratives with actions. *Journal of Logic Programming*, 31(1-3), 157-200.
- Kamp, H., & Reyle, U. (1993). From discourse to logic: Introduction to modeltheoretic semantics of natural language, formal logic and discourse representation theory. Dordrecht: Kluwer.
- Karlsson, L., & Gustafsson, J. (1997). Reasoning about actions in a multi-agent environment. Linköping Electronic Articles in Computer and Information Science, 2(014), 1-22.
- Karlsson, L., Gustafsson, J., & Doherty, P. (1998). Delayed effects of actions. In H. Prade (Ed.), Proceedings of the thirteenth European conference on artificial intelligence (pp. 542-546). Chichester, UK: John Wiley.
- Kartha, G. N. (1994). Two counterexamples related to Baker's approach to the frame problem. *Artificial Intelligence*, 69(1-2), 379-391.
- Kartha, G. N., & Lifschitz, V. (1994). Actions with indirect effects (preliminary report). In J. Doyle, E. Sandewall, & P. Torasso (Eds.), *Proceedings of the fourth international conference on principles of knowledge representation and reasoning* (pp. 341-350). San Francisco: Morgan Kaufmann.
- Kartha, G. N., & Lifschitz, V. (1995). A simple formalization of actions using circumscription. In *Proceedings of the fourteenth international joint conference on artificial intelligence* (pp. 1970-1977). San Mateo, CA: Morgan Kaufmann.
- Kautz, H. A. (1986). The logic of persistence. In *Proceedings of the fifth national conference on artificial intelligence* (pp. 401-405). Los Altos, CA: Morgan Kaufmann.
- Kautz, H. A., & Selman, B. (1992). Planning as satisfiability. In B. Neumann (Ed.), Proceedings of the tenth European conference on artificial intelligence (pp. 359-363). Chichester, UK: John Wiley.
- Kautz, H. A., & Selman, B. (1996). Pushing the envelope: Planning, propositional logic, and stochastic search. In Proceedings of the thirteenth national conference on artificial intelligence and eighth annual conference on innovative applications of artificial intelligence (pp. 1194-1201). Menlo Park, CA: AAAI Press.
- Kautz, H. A., & Selman, B. (2003). Ten challenges redux: Recent progress in propositional reasoning and search. In F. Rossi (Ed.), *Principles and practice of constraint programming* (Vol. 2833, pp. 1-18). Berlin: Springer.
- Kim, T.-W. (2009). Format-output program. http://reasoning.eas.asu.edu/ecasp/.
- Kim, T.-W., Lee, J., & Palla, R. (2009). Circumscriptive event calculus as answer set programming. In C. Boutilier (Ed.), *Proceedings of the twenty-first international joint conference on artificial intelligence* (pp. 823-829). Menlo Park, CA: AAAI Press.
- Kleene, S. C. (1952). Introduction to metamathematics. New York: D. Van Nostrand.
- Kleene, S. C. (1967). Mathematical logic. New York: John Wiley.
- Kneale, W., & Kneale, M. (1962). The development of logic. Oxford: Oxford University Press.
- Koenderink, J. J., & van Doorn, A. J. (1979). The internal representation of solid shape with respect to vision. *Biological Cybernetics*, 32, 211-216.
- Kolaitis, P. G., & Papadimitriou, C. H. (1990). Some computational aspects of circumscription. Journal of the ACM, 37(1), 1-14.
- Kolata, G. (1982). How can computers get common sense? Science, 217(4566), 1237-1238.
- Kolodner, J. L. (1993). Case-based reasoning. San Mateo, CA: Morgan Kaufmann.

- Kowalski, R. A. (1974). Logic for problem solving. Memo No. 75. Edinburgh, Scotland: Department of Computational Logic, University of Edinburgh.
- Kowalski, R. A. (1979). Logic for problem solving. New York: North-Holland.
- Kowalski, R. A. (1986). *Database updates in the event calculus* (Tech. Rep. No. DOC 86/12). London: Imperial College of Science, Technology, and Medicine.
- Kowalski, R. A. (1992). Database updates in the event calculus. *Journal of Logic Programming*, 12, 121-146.
- Kowalski, R. A., & Sadri, F. (1994). The situation calculus and event calculus compared. In M. Bruynooghe (Ed.), Logic programming: The 1994 international symposium (pp. 539-553). Cambridge, MA: MIT Press.
- Kowalski, R. A., & Sadri, F. (1997). Reconciling the event calculus with the situation calculus. *Journal of Logic Programming*, 31(1-3), 39-58.
- Kowalski, R. A., & Sergot, M. J. (1986). A logic-based calculus of events. *New Generation Computing*, 4(1), 67-95.
- Kripke, S. A. (1963). Semantical analysis of modal logic I: Normal modal propositional calculi. *Zeitschrift für Mathematische Logik und Grundlagen der Mathematik*, 9(5-6), 67-96.
- Krishnamurthy, J., & Lieberman, H. (2010). CrossBridge: Finding analogies using dimensionality reduction. In C. Havasi, D. B. Lenat, & B. D. Van Durme (Eds.), Commonsense knowledge: Papers from the AAAI fall symposium (pp. 58-63). Menlo Park, CA: AAAI Press.
- Kuhn, T. (2014). A survey and classification of controlled natural languages. *Computational Linguistics*, 40(1), 121-170.
- Kuipers, B. (1986). Qualitative simulation. Artificial Intelligence, 29(3), 289-338.
- Kuipers, B. (1994). Qualitative reasoning: Modeling and simulation with incomplete knowledge. Cambridge, MA: MIT Press.
- Kuipers, B. (2000). The spatial semantic hierarchy. Artificial Intelligence, 119, 191-233.
- Kurzweil, R. (1999). The age of spiritual machines. New York: Viking.
- Kushmerick, N., Hanks, S., & Weld, D. S. (1995). An algorithm for probabilistic planning. *Artificial Intelligence*, 76, 239-286.
- Kvarnström, J. (2001). VITAL: Visualization and implementation of temporal action logic. Linköping, Sweden: Department of Computer and Information Science, Linköping University.
- Kvarnström, J. (2005). *TALplanner and other extensions to temporal action logic*. Doctoral dissertation. Department of Computer and Information Science, Linköping University, Linköping, Sweden.
- Kvarnström, J., & Doherty, P. (2000a). Tackling the qualification problem using fluent dependency constraints. *Computational Intelligence*, 16(2), 169-209.
- Kvarnström, J., & Doherty, P. (2000b). TALplanner: A temporal logic based forward chaining planner. *Annals of Mathematics and Artificial Intelligence*, 30(1-4), 119-169.
- Lakoff, G. (1970). Linguistics and natural logic. Synthese, 22, 151-271.
- Lally, A., Prager, J. M., McCord, M. C., Boguraev, B. K., Patwardhan, S., Fan, J., Fodor, P. & Chu-Carroll, J. (2012). Question analysis: How Watson reads a clue. *IBM Journal of Research and Development*, 56(3-4), 2:1-2:14.
- Lally, A., Bagchi, S., Barborak, M. A., Buchanan, D. W., Chu-Carroll, J., Ferrucci, D., Glass, M. R., Kalyanpur, A., Mueller, E. T., Murdock, J. W., Patwardhan, S., Prager, J.M., & Welty, C. A. (2014). WatsonPaths: Scenario-based question answering and inference over unstructured information. Research Report RC25489 (WAT1409-048), IBM Research, Yorktown Heights, NY.

- Landauer, T. K. (1986). How much do people remember? Some estimates of the quantity of learned information in long-term memory. *Cognitive Science*, 10(4), 477-493.
- Leake, D. B. (1995). Combining rules and cases to learn case adaptation. In *Proceedings of the seventeenth annual conference of the cognitive science society* (pp. 84-89). Hillsdale, NJ: Lawrence Erlbaum.
- Leake, D. B. (1996). CBR in context: The present and future. In D. B. Leake (Ed.), Case-based reasoning: Experiences, lessons, & future directions (pp. 3-30). Cambridge, MA: MIT Press.
- Lee, J., Lifschitz, V., & Palla, R. (2008). A reductive semantics for counting and choice in answer set programming. In *Proceedings of the twenty-third AAAI conference on artificial* intelligence (pp. 472-479). Menlo Park, CA: AAAI Press.
- Lee, J., Lifschitz, V., & Yang, F. (2013). Action language BC: Preliminary report. In F. Rossi (Ed.), Proceedings of the twenty-third international joint conference on artificial intelligence (pp. 983-989). Menlo Park, CA: AAAI Press.
- Lee, J., & Palla, R. (2009). System F2LP—Computing answer sets of first-order formulas. In E. Erdem, F. Lin, & T. Schaub (Eds.), *Logic programming and nonmonotonic reasoning, tenth international conference* (Vol. 5753, pp. 515-521). Berlin: Springer.
- Lee, J., & Palla, R. (2012). Reformulating the situation calculus and the event calculus in the general theory of stable models and in answer set programming. *Journal of Artificial Intelligence Research*, 43, 571-620.
- Lehnert, W. G. (1978). *The process of question answering: A computer simulation of cognition*. Hillsdale, NJ: Lawrence Erlbaum.
- Lemur Project. (2014). *Indri search engine*. http://www.lemurproject.org/indri.php. Lenat, D. B. (1984). Why AM and EURISKO appear to work. *Artificial Intelligence*, 23(3), 269-294.
- Lenat, D. B. (1995). Cyc: A large-scale investment in knowledge infrastructure. Communications of the ACM, 38(11), 33-48.
- Lenat, D. B., Borning, A., McDonald, D., Taylor, C., & Weyer, S. (1983). Knoesphere: Building expert systems with encyclopedic knowledge. In A. Bundy (Ed.), Proceedings of the eighth international joint conference on artificial intelligence (Vol. 1, pp. 167-169). Los Altos, CA: William Kaufmann.
- Lenat, D. B., & Guha, R. V. (1990). Building large knowledge-based systems: Representation and inference in the Cyc project. Reading, MA: Addison-Wesley.
- Lenat, D. B., & Guha, R. V. (1991a). The evolution of CycL, the Cyc representation language. ACM SIGART Bulletin, 2(3), 84-87.
- Lenat, D. B., & Guha, R. V. (1991b). *Ideas for applying Cyc* (Tech. Rep. No. ACT-CYC-407-91). Austin, TX: Microelectronics and Computer Technology Corporation.
- Lenat, D. B., Guha, R. V., Pittman, K., Pratt, D., & Shepherd, M. (1990). Cyc: Toward programs with common sense. *Communications of the ACM*, 33(8), 30-49.
- Lenat, D. B., Prakash, M., & Shepherd, M. (1985). CYC: Using common sense knowledge to overcome brittleness and knowledge acquisition bottlenecks. *AI Magazine*, 6(4), 65-85.
- Levesque, H. J. (1981). A formal treatment of incomplete knowledge bases. Doctoral dissertation. Department of Computer Science, University of Toronto, Toronto.
- Levin, L. A. (1973). Universal search problems. *Problemy Peredachi Informatsii [Problems of Information Transmission]*, 9(3), 265-266 (in Russian).
- Lévy, F., & Quantz, J. J. (1998). Representing beliefs in a situated event calculus. In H. Prade (Ed.), Proceedings of the thirteenth European conference on artificial intelligence (pp. 547-551). Chichester, UK: John Wiley.

- Lewin, K. (1951). Intention, will and need. In D. Rapaport (Ed.), Organization and pathology of thought (pp. 95-153). New York: Columbia University Press (Original work published 1926)
- Lieberman, H., Liu, H., Singh, P., & Barry, B. A. (2004). Beating common sense into interactive applications. AI Magazine, 25(4), 63-76.
- Lieberman, H., Smith, D.A., Teeters, A., (2007). Common consensus: a web-based game for collecting commonsense goals. In: Havasi, C., Lieberman, H. (Eds.), Workshop on Common Sense and Intelligent User Interfaces. Honolulu, Hawaii. Association for Computing Machinery, New York.
- Lifschitz, V. (1985). Computing circumscription. In Proceedings of the ninth international joint conference on artificial intelligence (pp. 121-127). Los Altos, CA: Morgan Kaufmann.
- Lifschitz, V. (1987a). Formal theories of action. In F. M. Brown (Ed.), The frame problem in artificial intelligence: Proceedings of the 1987 workshop (pp. 35-57). Los Altos, CA: Morgan Kaufmann.
- Lifschitz, V. (1987b). On the semantics of STRIPS. In M. P. Georgeff & A. L. Lansky (Eds.), Reasoning about actions and plans: Proceedings of the 1986 workshop (pp. 1-9). San Mateo, CA: Morgan Kaufmann.
- Lifschitz, V. (1987c). Pointwise circumscription. In M. L. Ginsberg (Ed.), *Readings in nonmonotonic reasoning* (pp. 179-193). Los Altos, CA: Morgan Kaufmann.
- Lifschitz, V. (1989). Benchmark problems for formal nonmonotonic reasoning: Version 2.00.
 In M. Reinfrank, J. de Kleer, M. L. Ginsberg, & E. Sandewall (Eds.), Non-monotonic reasoning, 2nd international workshop (Vol. 346, pp. 202-219). Berlin: Springer.
- Lifschitz, V. (Ed.). (1990a). Formalizing common sense: Papers by John McCarthy. Norwood, NJ: Ablex.
- Lifschitz, V. (1990b). Frames in the space of situations. Artificial Intelligence, 46(3), 365-376.
- Lifschitz, V. (1994). Circumscription. In D. M. Gabbay, C. J. Hogger, & J. A. Robinson (Eds.), *Handbook of logic in artificial intelligence and logic programming* (Vol. 3: Nonmonotonic reasoning and uncertain reasoning, pp. 298-352). Oxford: Oxford University Press.
- Lifschitz, V. (1997a). Responses to Costello and Doherty. Electronic Newsletter on Reasoning AUT About Actions and Change, 1(4), 146-147.
- Lifschitz, V. (1997b). Responses to Sandewall, Doherty, Costello, and Hayes. *Electronic Newsletter on Reasoning About Actions and Change, 1*(4), 153-155.
- Lifschitz, V. (1999). Success of default logic. In H. J. Levesque & F. Pirri (Eds.), Logical foundations for cognitive agents: Contributions in honor of Ray Reiter (pp. 208-212). Berlin: Springer.
- Lifschitz, V. (2003). *Choosing a place for dinner*. Message posted to Texas Action Group electronic mailing list, archived at http://www.cs.utexas.edu/users/vl/tag/discussions.html.
- Lifschitz, V., Tang, L. R., & Turner, H. (1999). Nested expressions in logic programs. Annals of Mathematics and Artificial Intelligence, 25(3-4), 369-389.
- Lin, D., & Pantel, P. (2001). Discovery of inference rules for question-answering. *Natural Language Engineering*, 7(4), 343-360.
- Lin, F. (1995). Embracing causality in specifying the indirect effects of actions. In *Proceedings* of the fourteenth international joint conference on artificial intelligence (pp. 1985-1993). San Mateo, CA: Morgan Kaufmann.
- Lin, F. (1996). Embracing causality in specifying the indeterminate effects of actions. In Proceedings of the thirteenth national conference on artificial intelligence and eighth

- annual conference on innovative applications of artificial intelligence (pp. 670-676). Menlo Park, CA: AAAI Press.
- Lin, F., & Reiter, R. (1994). State constraints revisited. Journal of Logic and Computation, 4(5), 655-678.
- Lin, F., & Shoham, Y. (1992). Concurrent actions in the situation calculus. In W. R. Swartout (Ed.), Proceedings of the tenth national conference on artificial intelligence (pp. 590-595). Menlo Park, CA: AAAI Press.
- Lin, F., & Shoham, Y. (1995). Provably correct theories of action. *Journal of the ACM*, 42(2), 293-320.
- Lin, T. (2002). Analogical inference over a common sense database. In Proceedings of the eighteenth national conference on artificial intelligence and fourteenth conference on innovative applications of artificial intelligence (pp. 955-956). Menlo Park, CA: AAAI Press.
- Liu, H. (2003). Unpacking meaning from words: A context-centered approach to computational lexicon design. In P. Blackburn, C. Ghidini, R. M. Turner, & F. Giunchiglia (Eds.), Modeling and using context (Vol. 2680, pp. 218-232). Berlin: Springer.
- Liu, H., Lieberman, H., (2002). Robust photo retrieval using world semantics. In: de Loupy, C. (Ed.), Proceedings of the LREC 2002 Workshop on Creating and Using Semantics for Information Retrieval and Filtering. Las Palmas, Canary Islands, Spain. European Language Resources Assocation, Paris, pp. 13-18.
- Liu, H., & Singh, P. (2004a). Commonsense reasoning in and over natural language. In M. G. Negoita, R. J. Howlett, & L. C. Jain (Eds.), Knowledge-based intelligent information and engineering systems (Vol. 3215, pp. 293-306). Berlin: Springer.
- Liu, H., & Singh, P. (2004b). ConceptNet—A practical commonsense reasoning tool-kit. BT Technology Journal, 22(4), 211-226.
- Ma, J., & Knight, B. (2001). Reified temporal logics: An overview. Artificial Intelligence Review, 15(3), 189-217.
- Ma, J., Miller, R., Morgenstern, L., & Patkos, T. (2013a). An epistemic event calculus for ASP-based reasoning about knowledge of the past, present and future. In *Nineteenth* international conference on logic for programming, artificial intelligence and reasoning. Stellenbosch, South Africa.
- Ma, J., Miller, R., Morgenstern, L., & Patkos, T. (2013b). Resources for the epistemic functional event calculus (EFEC). http://www.ucl.ac.uk/infostudies/efec/.
- MacCartney, B., & Manning, C. D. (2008). Modeling semantic containment and exclusion in natural language inference. In D. Scott & H. Uszkoreit (Eds.), *Proceedings of the twenty-second international conference on computational linguistics* (pp. 521-528). Stroudsburg, PA: Association for Computational Linguistics.
- Mahoney, M. (1999). The complexity of natural language (dissertation proposal). Florida Institute of Technology, Melbourne, FL.
- Mani, I. (2013). Computational modeling of narrative. San Rafael, CA: Morgan & Claypool.
- Manna, Z., & Waldinger, R. (1985). *The logical basis for computer programming* (Vol. 1: Deductive reasoning). Reading, MA: Addison-Wesley.
- Manning, C. D., & Schütze, H. (1999). Foundations of statistical natural language processing. Cambridge, MA: MIT Press.
- Manzano, M. (1996). Extensions of first order logic. Cambridge: Cambridge University Press.
- Marcus, M. P., Marcinkiewicz, M. A., & Santorini, B. (1993). Building a large annotated corpus of English: The Penn Treebank. Computational Linguistics 19(2), 313-330.

- Marsden, J. E. (1974). Elementary classical analysis. San Francisco: W.H. Freeman.
- Mates, B. (1972). Elementary logic (2nd ed.). New York: Oxford University Press.
- Mateus, P., Pacheco, A., & Pinto, J. A. (2002). Observations and the probabilistic situation calculus. In D. Fensel, F. Giunchiglia, D. McGuinness, & M.-A. Williams (Eds.), Proceedings of the eighth international conference on principles of knowledge representation and reasoning (pp. 327-338). San Francisco: Morgan Kaufmann.
- Max Planck Institute for Computer Science. (2014). YAGO. http://www.mpi-inf.mpg.de/yago-naga/yago/.
- Maybury, M. T. (Ed.). (2004). New directions in question answering. Menlo Park, CA: AAAI Press.
- McAllester, D. A., & Givan, R. (1989). Natural language syntax and first order inference. A.I. Memo 1176. Cambridge, MA: Artificial Intelligence Laboratory, Massachusetts Institute of Technology.
- McAllester, D. A., & Givan, R. (1992). Natural language syntax and first-order inference. Artificial Intelligence, 56(1), 1-20.
- McCain, N. C. (1997). Causality in commonsense reasoning about actions (Tech. Rep. No. CS-TR-97-25). Austin, TX: Department of Computer Sciences, University of Texas.
- McCain, N. C., & Turner, H. (1995). A causal theory of ramifications and qualifications. In *Proceedings of the fourteenth international joint conference on artificial intelligence* (pp. 1978-1984). San Mateo, CA: Morgan Kaufmann.
- McCain, N. C., & Turner, H. (1997). Causal theories of action and change. In Proceedings of the fourteenth national conference on artificial intelligence and ninth innovative applications of artificial intelligence conference (pp. 460-465). Menlo Park, CA: AAAI Press.
- McCarthy, J. (1959). Programs with common sense. In *Mechanisation of thought processes:* Proceedings of a symposium held at the national physical laboratory on 24-27 November 1958 (Vol. 1, pp. 75-91). London: Her Majesty's Stationery Office.
- McCarthy, J. (1963). Situations, actions and causal laws. Memo 2. Stanford, CA: Stanford Artificial Intelligence Project, Stanford University.
- McCarthy, J. (1968). Programs with common sense. In M. Minsky (Ed.), Semantic information processing (pp. 403-418). Cambridge, MA: MIT Press.
- McCarthy, J. (1977). Epistemological problems of artificial intelligence. In R. Reddy (Ed.), *Proceedings of the fifth international joint conference on artificial intelligence* (pp. 1038-1044). Los Altos, CA: William Kaufmann.
- McCarthy, J. (1979). First order theories of individual concepts and propositions. In J. E. Hayes, D. Michie, & L. I. Mikulich (Eds.), *Machine intelligence* 9 (pp. 129-148). Chichester, UK: Ellis Horwood.
- McCarthy, J. (1980). Circumscription—A form of non-monotonic reasoning. Artificial Intelligence, 13(1-2), 27-39.
- McCarthy, J. (1983). President's quarterly message: AI needs more emphasis on basic research. AI Magazine, 4(4), 5.
- McCarthy, J. (1984a). Applications of circumscription to formalizing common sense knowledge. In *Proceedings of the non-monotonic reasoning workshop* (pp. 295-324). Menlo Park, CA: AAAI Press.
- McCarthy, J. (1984b). Some expert systems need common sense. In H. R. Pagels (Ed.), *Computer culture: The scientific, intellectual, and social impact of the computer* (pp. 129-137). New York: New York Academy of Sciences.

- McCarthy, J. (1986). Applications of circumscription to formalizing common-sense knowledge. *Artificial Intelligence*, 28, 89-116.
- McCarthy, J. (1987). Generality in artificial intelligence. *Communications of the ACM*, 30(12), 1030-1035.
- McCarthy, J. (1988). Mathematical logic in artificial intelligence. Dædalus, 117(1), 297-311.
- McCarthy, J. (1990). An example for natural language understanding and the AI problems it raises. In V. Lifschitz (Ed.), *Formalizing common sense: Papers by John McCarthy* (pp. 70-76). Norwood, NJ: Ablex.
- McCarthy, J. (1993). Notes on formalizing context. In R. Bajcsy (Ed.), *Proceedings of the thirteenth international joint conference on artificial intelligence* (pp. 555-562). San Mateo, CA: Morgan Kaufmann.
- McCarthy, J. (1997). Modality, si! Modal logic, no! Studia Logica, 59(1), 29-32.
- McCarthy, J., (1998a). Elaboration tolerance. In Miller, R., Shanahan, M. (Eds.), *Fourth Symposium on Logical Formalizations of Commonsense Reasoning*. London. Queen Mary and Westfield College, London, pp. 198-216.
- McCarthy, J. (1998b). Making robots conscious of their mental states. In K. Furukawa, D. Michie, & S. Muggleton (Eds.), *Machine intelligence 15* (pp. 3-17). Oxford: Oxford University Press.
- McCarthy, J. (1999). Modality for robots—Responses to Halpern and Wansing. *Electronic News Journal on Reasoning About Actions and Change*, 3(5), 1-2.
- McCarthy, J. (2000). Modality for robots II—Response to Halpern. *Electronic Newsletter on Reasoning About Actions and Change*, 4(3), 1-3.
- McCarthy, J., & Hayes, P. J. (1969). Some philosophical problems from the standpoint of artificial intelligence. In B. Meltzer & D. Michie (Eds.), *Machine intelligence 4* (pp. 463-502). Edinburgh, Scotland: Edinburgh University Press.
- McCarthy, J., & Lifschitz, V. (1987). Commentary on McDermott. Computational Intelligence, 3, 196-197.
- McCarthy, J., Minsky, M., Sloman, A., Gong, L., Lau, T., Morgenstern, L., Mueller, E. T., Riecken, D., Singh, M., & Singh, P. (2002). An architecture of diversity for commonsense reasoning. *IBM Systems Journal*, *41*(3), 530-539.
- McClelland, J. L., Rumelhart, D. E., & PDP Research Group (Eds.). (1986). Parallel distributed processing: Explorations in the microstructure of cognition (Vol. 2: Psychological and biological models). Cambridge, MA: MIT Press.
- McCord, M. C. (2006a). A formal system for slot grammar (Tech. Rep. No. RC23976). Yorktown Heights, NY: IBM Research Division.
- McCord, M. C. (2006b). *The slot grammar lexical formalism* (Tech. Rep. No. RC23977). Yorktown Heights, NY: IBM Research Division.
- McCord, M. C. (2010). *Using slot grammar* (Tech. Rep. No. RC23978 revised). Yorktown Heights, NY: IBM Research Division.
- McCord, M. C., Murdock, J. W., & Boguraev, B. K. (2012). Deep parsing in Watson. *IBM Journal of Research and Development*, 56(3-4), 3:1-3:15.
- McCorduck, P. (2004). *Machines who think: A personal inquiry into the history and prospects of artificial intelligence*. Natick, MA: A K Peters (25th Anniversary Update).
- McDermott, D. V. (1982). A temporal logic for reasoning about processes and plans. Cognitive Science, 6, 101-155.
- McDermott, D. V. (1987). A critique of pure reason. Computational Intelligence, 3, 151-160.

- McDermott, D. V., & Doyle, J. (1980). Non-monotonic logic I. Artificial Intelligence, 13(1-2), 41-72.
- McMillan, K. L., & Amla, N. (2003). Automatic abstraction without counterexamples. In H. Garavel & J. Hatcliff (Eds.), Tools and algorithms for the construction and analysis of systems: TACAS 2003 (Vol. 2619, pp. 2-17). Berlin: Springer.
- Mendelson, E. (1997). Introduction to mathematical logic (4th ed.). Boca Raton, FL: Chapman & Hall.
- Miller, G. A., Galanter, E., & Pribram, K. H. (1960). *Plans and the structure of behavior*. New York: Holt, Rinehart, and Winston.
- Miller, R. (1996). A case study in reasoning about actions and continuous change. In W. Wahlster (Ed.), *Proceedings of the twelfth European conference on artificial intelligence* (pp. 624-628). Chichester, UK: John Wiley.
- Miller, R., Morgenstern, L., & Patkos, T. (2013). Reasoning about knowledge and action in an epistemic event calculus. In A. C. Kakas (Ed.), *Eleventh international symposium on logical formalizations of commonsense reasoning*. Ayia Napa, Cyprus.
- Miller, R., & Shanahan, M. (1994). Narratives in the situation calculus. *Journal of Logic and Computation*, 4(5), 513-530.
- Miller, R., & Shanahan, M. (1996). Reasoning about discontinuities in the event calculus. In L. C. Aiello, J. Doyle, & S. C. Shapiro (Eds.), *Proceedings of the fifth international conference on principles of knowledge representation and reasoning* (pp. 63-74). San Francisco: Morgan Kaufmann.
- Miller, R., & Shanahan, M. (1999). The event calculus in classical logic—Alternative axiomatisations. *Linköping Electronic Articles in Computer and Information Science*, 4(016), 1-27.
- Miller, R., & Shanahan, M. (2002). Some alternative formulations of the event calculus. In A. C. Kakas & F. Sadri (Eds.), Computational logic: Logic programming and beyond: Essays in honour of Robert A. Kowalski, part II (Vol. 2408, pp. 452-490). Berlin: Springer.
- Minker, J. (1993). An overview of nonmonotonic reasoning and logic programming. *Journal of Logic Programming*, 17(2-4), 95-126.
- Minsky, M. (1961). Descriptive languages and problem solving. In *Proceedings of the western joint computer conference* (pp. 215-218). New York: National Joint Computer Committee.
- Minsky, M. (1968). Introduction. In M. Minsky (Ed.), *Semantic information processing* (pp. 1-32). Cambridge, MA: MIT Press.
- Minsky, M. (1974). A framework for representing knowledge. A.I. Memo 306. Cambridge, MA: Artificial Intelligence Laboratory, Massachusetts Institute of Technology.
- Minsky, M. (1977). Plain talk about neurodevelopmental epistemology. In R. Reddy (Ed.), *Proceedings of the fifth international joint conference on artificial intelligence* (pp. 1083-1092). Los Altos, CA: William Kaufmann.
- Minsky, M. (1980). K-lines: A theory of memory. Cognitive Science, 4, 117-133.
- Minsky, M. (1982). Learning meaning (draft). Cambridge, MA: Artificial Intelligence Laboratory, Massachusetts Institute of Technology.
- Minsky, M. (1986). The society of mind. New York: Simon & Schuster.
- Minsky, M. (1991a). Logical versus analogical or symbolic versus connectionist or neat versus scruffy. AI Magazine, 12(2), 34-51.

- Minsky, M. (1991b). Society of Mind: a response to four reviews. Artificial Intelligence, 48, 371-396.
- Minsky, M. (1994). Negative expertise. International Journal of Expert Systems, 7(1), 13-19.
- Minsky, M. (2006). The emotion machine: Commonsense thinking, artificial intelligence, and the future of the human mind. New York: Simon & Schuster.
- Minsky, M., & Papert, S. (1972). Artificial intelligence progress report. A.I. Memo 252. Cambridge, MA: Artificial Intelligence Laboratory, Massachusetts Institute of Technology.
- Minsky, M., Singh, P., & Sloman, A. (2004). The St. Thomas common sense symposium: Designing architectures for human-level intelligence. *AI Magazine*, 25(2), 113-124.
- Mitchell, D. G., Selman, B., & Levesque, H. J. (1992). Hard and easy distributions of sat problems. In W. R. Swartout (Ed.), *Proceedings of the tenth national conference on artificial intelligence* (pp. 459-465). Menlo Park, CA: AAAI Press.
- Montague, R. (1970). Universal grammar. *Theoria*, 36(3), 373-398.
- Moore, J. D. (1995). Participating in explanatory dialogues: Interpreting and responding to questions in context. Cambridge, MA: MIT Press.
- Moore, R. C. (1980). *Reasoning about knowledge and action*. Technical Note 191. Menlo Park, CA: SRI International.
- Moore, R. C. (1982). The role of logic in knowledge representation and commonsense reasoning. In D. L. Waltz (Ed.), *Proceedings of the national conference on artificial* intelligence (pp. 428-433). Menlo Park, CA: AAAI Press.
- Moore, R. C. (1985a). A formal theory of knowledge and action. In J. R. Hobbs & R. C. Moore (Eds.), *Formal theories of the commonsense world* (pp. 319-358). Norwood, NJ: Ablex.
- Moore, R. C. (1985b). Semantical considerations on nonmonotonic logic. Artificial Intelligence, 25(1), 75-94.
- Moore, R. C. (1995). Logic and representation. Stanford, CA: CSLI.
- Moravec, H. (1999). Robot. New York: Oxford University Press.
- Morgan, B. (2013). A substrate for accountable layered systems. Doctoral dissertation. Program in Media Arts and Sciences, School of Architecture and Planning, Massachusetts Institute of Technology, Cambridge, MA.
- Morgenstern, L. (1988). Foundations of a logic of knowledge, action, and communication.

 Doctoral dissertation. Department of Computer Science, New York University, New York.
- Morgenstern, L. (2001). Mid-sized axiomatizations of commonsense problems: A case study in egg cracking. *Studia Logica*, 67, 333-384.
- Morgenstern, L., & Miller, R. (2014). Common sense problem page. http://commonsensereasoning.org/problem_page.html.
- Mueller, E. T. (1990). Daydreaming in humans and machines: A computer model of the stream of thought. Norwood, NJ: Ablex.
- Mueller, E. T. (1998). Natural language processing with ThoughtTreasure. New York: Signiform.
- Mueller, E. T. (2000). A database and lexicon of scripts for ThoughtTreasure. *Computing Research Repository*, cs.AI/0003004.
- Mueller, E. T. (2002). Story understanding. In L. Nadel (Ed.), Encyclopedia of cognitive science (Vol. 4, pp. 238-246). London: Nature Publishing Group.
- Mueller, E. T. (2003). Story understanding through multi-representation model construction.
 In G. Hirst & S. Nirenburg (Eds.), Text meaning: Proceedings of the HLT-NAACL 2003 workshop (pp. 46-53). East Stroudsburg, PA: Association for Computational Linguistics.

- Mueller, E. T. (2004a). Event calculus reasoning through satisfiability. *Journal of Logic and Computation*, 14(5), 703-730.
- Mueller, E. T. (2004b). A tool for satisfiability-based commonsense reasoning in the event calculus. In V. Barr & Z. Markov (Eds.), Proceedings of the seventeenth international Florida artificial intelligence research society conference (pp. 147-152). Menlo Park, CA: AAAI Press.
- Mueller, E. T. (2004c). Understanding script-based stories using commonsense reasoning. *Cognitive Systems Research*, 5(4), 307-340.
- Mueller, E. T. (2006). Event calculus and temporal action logics compared. *Artificial Intelligence*, 170(11), 1017-1029.
- Mueller, E. T. (2007a). Discrete event calculus with branching time. In E. Amir, V. Lifschitz, & R. Miller (Eds.), Logical formalizations of commonsense reasoning: Papers from the AAAI spring symposium (pp. 126-131). Menlo Park, CA: AAAI Press.
- Mueller, E. T. (2007b). Modelling space and time in narratives about restaurants. *Literary and Linguistic Computing*, 22(1), 67-84.
- Mueller, E. T. (2009). Automating commonsense reasoning using the event calculus. *Communications of the ACM*, 52(1), 113-117.
- Mueller, E. T., & Sutcliffe, G. (2005a). Discrete event calculus deduction using first-order automated theorem proving. In B. Konev & S. Schulz (Eds.), Proceedings of the fifth international workshop on the implementation of logics (pp. 43-56). Liverpool, UK: Department of Computer Science, University of Liverpool.
- Mueller, E. T., & Sutcliffe, G. (2005b). Reasoning in the event calculus using first-order automated theorem proving. In I. Russell & Z. Markov (Eds.), Proceedings of the eighteenth international Florida artificial intelligence research society conference (pp. 840-841). Menlo Park, CA: AAAI Press.
- Murdock, J. W. (2011). Structure mapping for Jeopardy! clues. In A. Ram & N. Wiratunga (Eds.), *Case-based reasoning research and development* (Vol. 6880, pp. 6-10). Berlin: Springer.
- Murdock, J. W., Fan, J., Lally, A., Shima, H., & Boguraev, B. K. (2012). Textual evidence gathering and analysis. *IBM Journal of Research and Development*, 56(3-4), 8:1-8:14.
- Murdock, J. W., Kalyanpur, A., Welty, C., Fan, J., Ferrucci, D., Gondek, D. C., Zhang, L., & Kanayama, H. (2012). Typing candidate answers using type coercion. *IBM Journal of Research and Development*, 56(3-4), 7:1-7:13.
- Narayanan, S. S. (1997). Knowledge-based action representations for metaphor and aspect (KARMA). Doctoral dissertation. University of California, Berkeley, Berkeley, CA.
- Nelson, M. J., & Mateas, M. (2008). Recombinable game mechanics for automated design support. In C. Darken & M. Mateas (Eds.), Proceedings of the fourth artificial intelligence and interactive digital entertainment conference (pp. 84-89). Menlo Park, CA: AAAI Press.
- Nerode, A., & Shore, R. A. (1997). Logic for applications (2nd ed.). New York: Springer.
- Newell, A., & Simon, H. A. (1961). GPS, a program that simulates human thought. In H. Billing (Ed.), *Lernende automaten* (pp. 109-124). Munich: Oldenbourgh.
- Newell, A., & Simon, H. A. (1972). *Human problem-solving*. Englewood Cliffs, NJ: Prentice-Hall.
- Newton, I. (1969). De methodis serierum et fluxionum. In D. T. Whiteside (Ed.), The mathematical papers of Isaac Newton (Vols. III: 1670-1673, pp. 32-353). Cambridge: Cambridge University Press (Original work published 1670)

- Niemelä, I., Simons, P., & Soininen, T. (1999). Stable model semantics of weight constraint rules. In M. Gelfond, N. Leone, & G. Pfeifer (Eds.), *Logic programming and nonmonotonic reasoning, fifth international conference* (Vol. 1730, pp. 317-331). Berlin: Springer.
- Nilsson, N. J. (1980). Principles of artificial intelligence. Los Altos, CA: Morgan Kaufmann.
- Nilsson, N. J. (1991). Logic and artificial intelligence. Artificial Intelligence, 47(1-3), 31-56.
- Nilsson, N. J. (1998). Artificial intelligence: A new synthesis. San Francisco: Morgan Kaufmann.
- Norvig, P. (1989). Marker passing as a weak method for text inferencing. *Cognitive Science*, 13(4), 569-620.
- Oberschelp, A. (1990). Order sorted predicate logic. In K. H. Bläsius, U. Hedtstück, & C. R. Rollinger (Eds.), *Sorts and types in artificial intelligence* (Vol. 418, pp. 8-17). Berlin: Springer.
- O'Rorke, P., & Ortony, A. (1994). Explaining emotions. Cognitive Science, 18, 283-323.
- Ortony, A., Clore, G. L., & Collins, A. M. (1988). *The cognitive structure of emotions*. Cambridge: Cambridge University Press.
- Palla, R. (2012). Bridging the gap between classical logic based formalisms and logic programs. Doctoral dissertation. Arizona State University, Tempe, AZ. http:// repository.asu.edu/items/14557.
- Palmer, M., Gildea, D., & Kingsbury, P. (2005). The Proposition Bank: An annotated corpus of semantic roles. *Computational Linguistics*, 31(1), 71-105.
- Panton, K., Miraglia, P., Salay, N., Kahlert, R. C., Baxter, D., & Reagan, R. (2002). Knowledge formation and dialogue using the KRAKEN toolset. In *Proceedings of the eighteenth* national conference on artificial intelligence and fourteenth conference on innovative applications of artificial intelligence (pp. 900-905). Menlo Park, CA: AAAI Press.
- Parmar, A. (2001). The representation of actions in KM and Cyc (Tech. Rep. No. FRG-1). Stanford, CA: Department of Computer Science, Stanford University.
- Parmar, A. (2003). Formalizing elaboration tolerance. Doctoral dissertation. Department of Computer Science, Stanford University, Stanford, CA.
- Patkos, T. (2010). A formal theory for reasoning about action, knowledge and time. Doctoral dissertation. Department of Computer Science, University of Crete, Heraklion, Greece.
- Patkos, T., & Plexousakis, D. (2009). Reasoning with knowledge, action and time in dynamic and uncertain domains. In C. Boutilier (Ed.), Proceedings of the twenty-first international joint conference on artificial intelligence (pp. 885-890). Menlo Park, CA: AAAI Press.
- Pearl, J. (1984). Heuristics: Intelligent search strategies for computer problem solving. Reading, MA: Addison-Wesley.
- Pearl, J. (1988a). On logic and probability. Computational Intelligence, 4, 99-103.
- Pearl, J. (1988b). Probabilistic reasoning in intelligent systems: Networks of plausible inference (revised second printing ed.). San Francisco: Morgan Kaufmann.
- Pearl, J. (2000). Causality: Models, reasoning, and inference. Cambridge: Cambridge University Press.
- Pednault, E. P. D. (1987). Formulating multiagent, dynamic-world problems in the classical planning framework. In M. P. Georgeff & A. L. Lansky (Eds.), *Reasoning about actions and plans: Proceedings of the 1986 workshop* (pp. 47-82). San Mateo, CA: Morgan Kaufmann.
- Pednault, E. P. D. (1989). ADL: Exploring the middle ground between STRIPS and the situation calculus. In R. J. Brachman, H. J. Levesque, & R. Reiter (Eds.), Proceedings of the first international conference on principles of knowledge representation and reasoning (pp. 324-332). San Mateo, CA: Morgan Kaufmann.
- Pinto, J. A. (1994). *Temporal reasoning in the situation calculus*. Doctoral dissertation. Graduate Department of Computer Science, University of Toronto, Toronto.

- Pinto, J. A. (1998a). Causality, indirect effects and triggers. In H. Geffner & V. Lifschitz (Eds.), Workshop on action and causality. Trento, Italy.
- Pinto, J. A. (1998b). Occurrences and narratives as constraints in the branching structure of the situation calculus. *Journal of Logic and Computation*, 8, 777-808.
- Pinto, J. A., & Reiter, R. (1993). Temporal reasoning in logic programming: A case for the situation calculus. In D. S. Warren (Ed.), *Logic programming: Proceedings of the tenth international conference* (pp. 203-221). Cambridge, MA: MIT Press.
- Pirri, F., & Reiter, R. (1999). Some contributions to the metatheory of the situation calculus. *Journal of the ACM*, 46(3), 325-361.
- Plaisted, D. A., & Greenbaum, S. (1986). A structure-preserving clause form translation. *Journal of Symbolic Computation*, 2, 293-304.
- Portinale, L. (1994). Petri net models for diagnostic knowledge representation and reasoning. Doctoral dissertation. Dipartimento di Informatica, Università di Torino, Turin, Italy.
- Portner, P. H. (2005). What is meaning? Fundamentals of formal semantics. Malden, MA: Blackwell.
- Pratt, V. R. (1976). Semantical considerations on Floyd-Hoare logic. In *Proceedings of the 17th symposium on the foundations of computer science* (pp. 109-121). Washington, DC: IEEE Computer Society.
- Priest, G. (2002). Paraconsistent logic. In D. M. Gabbay & F. Guenthner (Eds.), *Handbook of philosophical logic* (2nd ed., Vol. 6, pp. 287-393). Dordrecht: Kluwer.
- Provetti, A. (1996). Hypothetical reasoning about actions: From situation calculus to event calculus. *Computational Intelligence*, 12, 478-498.
- Punyakanok, V., Roth, D., & Yih, W.-T. (2008). The importance of syntactic parsing and inference in semantic role labeling. *Computational Linguistics*, 34(2), 257-287.
- Purdy, W. C. (1991). A logic for natural language. *Notre Dame Journal of Formal Logic*, 32(3), 409-425.
- Purtee, A., & Schubert, L. K. (2012). TTT: A tree transduction language for syntactic and semantic processing. In *Proceedings of the workshop on applications of tree automata techniques in natural language processing* (pp. 21-30). Stroudsburg, PA: Association for Computational Linguistics.
- Pylyshyn, Z. W. (Ed.). (1987). The robot's dilemma: The frame problem in artificial intelligence. Norwood, NJ: Ablex.
- Quillian, M. R. (1968). Semantic memory. In M. Minsky (Ed.), Semantic information processing (pp. 227-270). Cambridge, MA: MIT Press.
- Ram, A., & Moorman, K. (Eds.). (1999). Understanding language understanding: Computational models of reading. Cambridge, MA: MIT Press.
- Randell, D. A., Cui, Z., & Cohn, A. G. (1992). A spatial logic based on regions and connection. In B. Nebel, C. Rich, & W. R. Swartout (Eds.), Proceedings of the third international conference on principles of knowledge representation and reasoning (pp. 165-176). San Mateo, CA: Morgan Kaufmann.
- Rao, A. S., & Georgeff, M. P. (1992). An abstract architecture for rational agents. In B. Nebel, C. Rich, & W. R. Swartout (Eds.), Proceedings of the third international conference on principles of knowledge representation and reasoning (pp. 439-449). San Mateo, CA: Morgan Kaufmann.
- Reichgelt, H. (1991). Knowledge representation: An AI perspective. Norwood, NJ: Ablex. Reisig, W. (1985). Petri nets: An introduction. Berlin: Springer.

- Reiter, R. (1978). On reasoning by default. In *Proceedings of the 1978 workshop on theoretical issues in natural language processing* (pp. 210-218). New York: Association of Computing Machinery.
- Reiter, R. (1980a). Equality and domain closure in first-order databases. *Journal of the ACM*, 27(2), 235-249.
- Reiter, R. (1980b). A logic for default reasoning. Artificial Intelligence 13(1-2) 81-132.
- Reiter, R. (1982). Circumscription implies predicate completion (sometimes). In D. L. Waltz (Ed.), Proceedings of the national conference on artificial intelligence (pp. 418-420). Menlo Park, CA: AAAI Press.
- Reiter, R. (1991). The frame problem in the situation calculus: A simple solution (sometimes) and a completeness result for goal regression. In V. Lifschitz (Ed.), Artificial intelligence and mathematical theory of computation: Papers in honor of John McCarthy (pp. 359-380). San Diego: Academic Press.
- Reiter, R. (1993). Proving properties of states in the situation calculus. *Artificial Intelligence*, 64(2), 337-351.
- Reiter, R. (1996). Natural actions, concurrency and continuous time in the situation calculus. In L. C. Aiello, J. Doyle, & S. C. Shapiro (Eds.), *Proceedings of the fifth international conference on principles of knowledge representation and reasoning* (pp. 2-13). San Francisco: Morgan Kaufmann.
- Reiter, R. (2001). Knowledge in action: Logical foundations for specifying and implementing dynamical systems. Cambridge, MA: MIT Press.
- Reiter, R., & Criscuolo, G. (1981). On interacting defaults. In *Proceedings of the seventh international joint conference on artificial intelligence* (Vol. 1, pp. 270-276). Los Altos, CA: William Kaufmann.
- Remolina, E., & Kuipers, B. (2004). Towards a general theory of topological maps. *Artificial Intelligence*, 152(1), 47-104.
- Richardson, S. D., Dolan, W. B., & Vanderwende, L. (1998). MindNet: Acquiring and structuring semantic information from text. In *Proceedings of the thirty-sixth annual meeting of the association for computational linguistics and seventeenth international conference on computational linguistics: Proceedings of the conference* (pp. 1098-1102). San Mateo, CA: Morgan Kaufmann.
- Riecken, D. (1994). M: An architecture of integrated agents. *Communications of the ACM*, 37(7), 107-116, 146.
- Rips, L. J. (1983). Cognitive processes in propositional reasoning. *Psychological Review*, 90(1), 38-71.
- Rips, L. J. (1994). The psychology of proof: Deductive reasoning in human thinking. Cambridge, MA: MIT Press.
- Roberts, R. B., & Goldstein, I. P. (1977). The FRL manual. A.I. Memo 409. Cambridge, MA: Artificial Intelligence Laboratory, Massachusetts Institute of Technology.
- Robinson, J. A. (1965). A machine-oriented logic based on the resolution principle. *Journal of the ACM*, 12(1), 23-41.
- Robinson, J. A., & Voronkov, A. (2001a). *Handbook of automated reasoning* (Vol. 1). Amsterdam and Cambridge, MA: Elsevier and MIT Press.
- Robinson, J. A., & Voronkov, A. (2001b). *Handbook of automated reasoning* (Vol. 2). Amsterdam and Cambridge, MA: Elsevier and MIT Press.
- Rohde, D. L. T. (2005). TGrep2 user manual: $Version\ 1.15$. http://tedlab.mit.edu/~dr/ Tgrep2/tgrep2.pdf.

- Rosenbloom, P. S., Laird, J. E., & Newell, A. (Eds.). (1993). *The Soar papers: Research on integrated intelligence* (Vol. 1 and 2). Cambridge, MA: MIT Press.
- Rumelhart, D. E., McClelland, J. L., & PDP Research Group (Eds.). (1986). *Parallel distributed processing: Explorations in the microstructure of cognition* (Vol. 1: Foundations). Cambridge, MA: MIT Press.
- Russell, S. J., & Norvig, P. (2009). *Artificial intelligence: A modern approach* (3rd ed.). Upper Saddle River, NJ: Prentice Hall.
- Sacerdoti, E. D. (1974). Planning in a hierarchy of abstraction spaces. *Artificial Intelligence*, 5, 115-135.
- Sacerdoti, E. D. (1977). A structure for plans and behavior. New York: Elsevier.
- Sammet, J. E. (1966). The use of English as a programming language. *Communications of the ACM*, 9(3), 228-230.
- Sánchez Valencia, V. (1991). Categorial grammar and natural reasoning (Tech. Rep. No. LP-91-08). Amsterdam: Institute for Language, Logic and Information, University of Amsterdam.
- Sanders, K. E. (1989). A logic for emotions: A basis for reasoning about commonsense psychological knowledge (Tech. Rep. No. CS-89-23). Providence, RI: Department of Computer Science, Brown University.
- Sandewall, E. (1972). An approach to the frame problem, and its implementation. In B. Meltzer & D. Michie (Eds.), *Machine intelligence* 7 (pp. 195-204). Edinburgh, Scotland: Edinburgh University Press.
- Sandewall, E. (1989a). Combining logic and differential equations for describing real-world systems. In R. J. Brachman, H. J. Levesque, & R. Reiter (Eds.), Proceedings of the first international conference on principles of knowledge representation and reasoning (pp. 412-420). San Mateo, CA: Morgan Kaufmann.
- Sandewall, E. (1989b). Filter [sic] preferential entailment for the logic of action in almost continuous worlds. In N. S. Sridharan (Ed.), *Proceedings of the eleventh international joint conference on artificial intelligence* (pp. 894-899). San Mateo, CA: Morgan Kaufmann.
- Sandewall, E. (1991). Features and fluents. An agenda and logic-based framework for the representation of knowledge about dynamical systems. Review version of chapters 1 and 3-7 (Tech. Rep. No. LiTH-IDA-R-91-29). Linköping, Sweden: Department of Computer and Information Science, Linköping University.
- Sandewall, E. (1994). Features and fluents: The representation of knowledge about dynamical systems (Vol. I). Oxford: Oxford University Press.
- Sandewall, E. (1996). Assessments of ramification methods that use static domain constraints. In L. C. Aiello, J. Doyle, & S. C. Shapiro (Eds.), Proceedings of the fifth international conference on principles of knowledge representation and reasoning (pp. 99-110). San Francisco: Morgan Kaufmann.
- Sandewall, E. (1997). Response to Lifschitz. *Electronic Newsletter on Reasoning About Actions and Change*, 1(4), 147-149.
- SAT Competition. (2011). Result page for benchmark APPLICATIONS/c32sat/post-cbmc-zfcp-2.8-u2-noholes.cnf. http://www.cril.univ-artois.fr/SAT11/results/bench.php?idev=45&idbench=70953.
- Schank, R. C. (1982). Dynamic memory. Cambridge: Cambridge University Press.
- Schank, R. C., & Abelson, R. P. (1977). Scripts, plans, goals, and understanding: An inquiry into human knowledge structures. Hillsdale, NJ: Lawrence Erlbaum.

- Schank, R. C., Kass, A., & Riesbeck, C. K. (Eds.). (1994). *Inside case-based explanation*. Hillsdale, NJ: Lawrence Erlbaum.
- Schank, R. C., & Riesbeck, C. K. (Eds.). (1981). *Inside computer understanding: Five programs plus miniatures*. Hillsdale, NJ: Lawrence Erlbaum.
- Scherl, R. B., & Levesque, H. J. (2003). Knowledge, action, and the frame problem. Artificial Intelligence, 144(1-2), 1-39.
- Schmidt, J. (1960). Peano-Bäume. Zeitschrift für mathematische Logik und Grundlagen der Mathematik, 6(3-4), 225-239.
- Schubert, L. K. (1990). Monotonic solution of the frame problem in the situation calculus: An efficient method for worlds with fully specified actions. In H. E. Kyburg, Jr., R. P. Loui, & G. N. Carlson (Eds.), Knowledge representation and defeasible reasoning (pp. 23-67). Dordrecht: Kluwer.
- Schubert, L. K. (2002). Can we derive general world knowledge from texts? In M. P. Marcus (Ed.), *Proceedings of the second international conference on human language technology research* (pp. 94-97). San Francisco, CA: Morgan Kaufmann.
- Schubert, L. K., Gordon, J. M., Stratos, K., & Rubinoff, A. (2011). Towards adequate knowledge and natural inference. In P. Langley (Ed.), Advances in cognitive systems: Papers from the AAAI fall symposium (pp. 288-296). Menlo Park, CA: AAAI Press.
- Schubert, L. K., & Hwang, C. H. (1989). An episodic knowledge representation for narrative texts. In R. J. Brachman, H. J. Levesque, & R. Reiter (Eds.), Proceedings of the first international conference on principles of knowledge representation and reasoning (pp. 444-458). San Mateo, CA: Morgan Kaufmann.
- Schubert, L. K., & Hwang, C. H. (2000). Episodic Logic meets Little Red Riding Hood: A comprehensive, natural representation for language understanding. In L. M. Iwańska & S. C. Shapiro (Eds.), Natural language processing and knowledge representation (pp. 111-174). Cambridge, MA: MIT Press.
- Schubert, L. K., & Tong, M. (2003). Extracting and evaluating general world knowledge from the Brown corpus. In G. Hirst & S. Nirenburg (Eds.), *Text meaning: Proceedings* of the HLT-NAACL 2003 workshop (pp. 7-13). East Stroudsburg, PA: Association for Computational Linguistics.
- Schwartz, J. T. (1988). The new connectionism: Developing relationships between neuroscience and artificial intelligence. In S. R. Graubard (Ed.), *The artificial intelligence debate* (pp. 123-141). Cambridge, MA: MIT Press.
- Schwitter, R. (2011). Specifying events and their effects in controlled natural language. *Procedia—Social and Behavioral Sciences*, 27, 12-21.
- Selman, B., Kautz, H. A., & Cohen, B. (1993). Local search strategies for satisfiability testing. In D. S. Johnson & M. A. Trick (Eds.), Cliques, coloring, and satisfiability: Second dimacs implementation challenge (Vol. 26). Boston, MA: American Mathematical Society.
- Selman, B., Kautz, H. A., & McAllester, D. A. (1997). Ten challenges in propositional reasoning and search. In *Proceedings of the fifteenth international joint conference on* artificial intelligence (pp. 50-54). San Mateo, CA: Morgan Kaufmann.
- Shanahan, M. (1989). Prediction is deduction but explanation is abduction. In N. S. Sridharan (Ed.), Proceedings of the eleventh international joint conference on artificial intelligence (pp. 1055-1060). San Mateo, CA: Morgan Kaufmann.
- Shanahan, M. (1990). Representing continuous change in the event calculus. In L. C. Aiello (Ed.), *Proceedings of the ninth european conference on artificial intelligence* (pp. 598-603). London: Pitman.

- Shanahan, M. (1995a). A circumscriptive calculus of events. Artificial Intelligence, 77, 249-284.
- Shanahan, M. (1995b). Default reasoning about spatial occupancy. Artificial Intelligence, 74, 147-163.
- Shanahan, M. (1996). Robotics and the common sense informatic situation. In W. Wahlster (Ed.), *Proceedings of the twelfth European conference on artificial intelligence* (pp. 684-688). Chichester, UK: John Wiley.
- Shanahan, M. (1997a). Event calculus planning revisited. In S. Steel & R. Alami (Eds.), *Recent advances in AI planning* (Vol. 1348, pp. 390-402). Berlin: Springer.
- Shanahan, M. (1997b). Solving the frame problem. Cambridge, MA: MIT Press.
- Shanahan, M. (1998). A logical formalisation of Ernie Davis's egg cracking problem. In R. Miller & M. Shanahan (Eds.), Fourth symposium on logical formalizations of commonsense reasoning. London: Queen Mary and Westfield College.
- Shanahan, M. (1998). Protocol of online discussion about the article A logical account of the common sense informatic situation for a mobile robot. *Electronic News Journal on Reasoning about Actions and Change*, 2(10), 328-329.
- Shanahan, M. (1999a). The event calculus explained. In M. J. Wooldridge & M. M. Veloso (Eds.), Artificial intelligence today: Recent trends and developments (Vol. 1600, pp. 409-430). Berlin: Springer.
- Shanahan, M. (1999b). The ramification problem in the event calculus. In *Proceedings of the sixteenth international joint conference on artificial intelligence* (pp. 140-146). San Mateo, CA: Morgan Kaufmann.
- Shanahan, M. (1999c). What sort of computation mediates best between perception and action? In H. J. Levesque & F. Pirri (Eds.), *Logical foundations for cognitive agents: Contributions in honor of Ray Reiter* (pp. 352-369). Berlin: Springer.
- Shanahan, M. (2000). An abductive event calculus planner. *Journal of Logic Programming*, 44(1-3), 207-240.
- Shanahan, M. (2002). The frame problem. In L. Nadel (Ed.), *Encyclopedia of cognitive science* (Vol. 2, pp. 144-150). London: Nature Publishing Group.
- Shanahan, M. (2004). An attempt to formalise a non-trivial benchmark problem in common sense reasoning. *Artificial Intelligence*, 153, 141-165.
- Shanahan, M. (2005). Perception as abduction: Turning sensor data into meaningful representation. *Cognitive Science*, 29, 103-134.
- Shanahan, M., & Randell, D. A. (2004). A logic-based formulation of active visual perception. In D. Dubois, C. A. Welty, & M.-A. Williams (Eds.), *Proceedings of the ninth international conference on principles of knowledge representation and reasoning* (pp. 64-72). Menlo Park, CA: AAAI Press.
- Shanahan, M., & Witkowski, M. (2004). Event calculus planning through satisfiability. *Journal of Logic and Computation*, 14(5), 731-745.
- Shapiro, S. C. (1979). The SNePS semantic network processing system. In N. V. Findler (Ed.), Associative networks: Representation and use of knowledge by computers (pp. 179-203). New York: Academic Press.
- Shoham, Y. (1987). Temporal logics in AI: Semantical and ontological considerations. Artificial Intelligence, 33, 89-104.
- Shoham, Y. (1988). Reasoning about change: Time and causation from the standpoint of artificial intelligence. Cambridge, MA: MIT Press.
- Shoham, Y. (1993). Agent-oriented programming. Artificial Intelligence, 60, 51-92.

- Siklóssy, L., & Dreussi, J. (1973). An efficient robot planner which generates its own procedures. In Advance papers of the third international joint conference on artificial intelligence (pp. 423-430). Los Altos, CA: William Kaufmann.
- Sil, A., & Yates, A. (2011). Extracting STRIPS representations of actions and events. In G. Angelova, K. Bontcheva, R. Mitkov, & N. Nicolov (Eds.), Recent advances in natural language processing (pp. 1-8). Shoumen, Bulgaria: Incoma.
- Simon, H. A. (1967). Motivational and emotional controls of cognition. *Psychological Review*, 74(1), 29-39.
- Singh, P. (1998). Failure-directed reformulation. Master's thesis. Department of Electrical Engineering and Computer Science, Massachusetts Institute of Technology, Cambridge, MA.
- Singh, P. (2002). The public acquisition of commonsense knowledge. In J. Karlgren (Ed.), Acquiring (and using) linguistic (and world) knowledge for information access: Papers from 2002 AAAI spring symposium (pp. 47-52). Menlo Park, CA: AAAI Press.
- Singh, P. (2004). Examining the Society of Mind. Computing and Informatics, 22(6), 521-543.
- Singh, P. (2005). EM-ONE: An architecture for reflective commonsense thinking. Doctoral dissertation. Department of Electrical Engineering and Computer Science, Massachusetts Institute of Technology, Cambridge, MA.
- Singh, P., Barry, B. A., & Liu, H. (2004). Teaching machines about everyday life. *BT Technology Journal*, 22(4), 227-240.
- Singh, P., Lin, T., Mueller, E. T., Lim, G., Perkins, T., & Zhu, W. L. (2002). Open Mind Common Sense: Knowledge acquisition from the general public. In R. Meersman & Z. Tari (Eds.), On the move to meaningful internet systems 2002: DOA/CoopIS/ODBASE 2002 (Vol. 2519, pp. 1223-1237). Berlin: Springer.
- Singh, P., & Minsky, M. (2004). An architecture for cognitive diversity. In D. N. Davis (Ed.), Visions of mind: Architectures for cognition and affect (pp. 312-331). Hershey, PA: Idea Group.
- Singh, P., Minsky, M., & Eslick, I. (2004). Computing commonsense. *BT Technology Journal*, 22(4), 201-210.
- Sirbu, M. A., & Tygar, J. D. (1995). NetBill: An Internet commerce system optimized for network delivered services. In 40th IEEE computer society international conference (pp. 20-25). Washington, DC: IEEE Computer Society.
- Sloman, A. (2001). Beyond shallow models of emotion. *Cognitive Processing*, 2(1), 177-198. Smedslund, J. (1997). *The structure of psychological common sense*. Mahwah, NJ: Lawrence
- Erlbaum.
 Smith, T. F., & Waterman, M. S. (1981). Identification of common molecular subsequences.
- Journal of Molecular Biology, 147(1), 195-197.

 Solow, D. (2002). How to read and do proofs: An introduction to mathematical thought processes (3rd ed.). New York: John Wiley.
- Speer, R. (2007). Learning common sense knowledge from user interaction and principal component analysis. Master's thesis. Department of Electrical Engineering and Computer Science, Massachusetts Institute of Technology, Cambridge, MA.
- Speer, R., & Havasi, C. (2012). Representing general relational knowledge in ConceptNet 5. In N. Calzolari et al. (Eds.), *Proceedings of the eighth international conference on language resources and evaluation* (pp. 3679-3686). Istanbul, Turkey: European Language Resources Association.
- Speer, R., Havasi, C., & Lieberman, H. (2008). AnalogySpace: Reducing the dimensionality of common sense knowledge. In *Proceedings of the twenty-third AAAI conference on artificial* intelligence (AAAI 2008) (pp. 548-553). Menlo Park, CA: AAAI Press.

- Speer, R., Havasi, C., & Surana, H. (2010). Using verbosity: Common sense data from games with a purpose. In H. W. Guesgen & R. C. Murray (Eds.), Proceedings of the twentythird international Florida artificial intelligence research society conference (pp. 104-109). Menlo Park, CA: AAAI Press.
- Spelke, E. S., Vishton, P. M., & von Hofsten, C. (1995). Object perception, object-directed action, and physical knowledge in infancy. In M. S. Gazzaniga (Ed.), *The cognitive neurosciences* (pp. 165-179). Cambridge, MA: MIT Press.
- Stein, L. A. (1992). Resolving ambiguity in nonmonotonic inheritance hierarchies. Artificial Intelligence, 55(2-3), 259-310.
- Stein, L. A., & Morgenstern, L. (1994). Motivated action theory: a formal theory of causal reasoning. Artificial Intelligence, 71(1), 1-42.
- Stork, D. G. (1999). The Open Mind Initiative. *IEEE Intelligent Systems and their Applications*, 14(3), 19-20.
- Stork, D. G., & Lam, C. P. (2000). Open Mind Animals: Insuring the quality of data openly contributed over the world wide web. In N. Japkowicz (Ed.), *Learning from imbalanced* data sets: Papers from the AAAI workshop (pp. 4-9). Menlo Park, CA: AAAI Press.
- Strzalkowski, T., & Harabagiu, S. (Eds.). (2008). Advances in open domain question answering. Dordrecht: Springer.
- Sun, R. (1994). Integrating rules and connectionism for robust commonsense reasoning. New York: John Wiley.
- Sun, R. (1995). A new approach toward modeling causality in commonsense reasoning. International Journal of Intelligent Systems, 10, 581-616.
- Sun, R. (1996). Commonsense reasoning with rules, cases, and connectionist models: A paradigmatic comparison. Fuzzy Sets and Systems, 82(2), 187-200.
- Suppes, P. (1979). Logical inference in English: A preliminary analysis. *Studia Logica*, 38(4), 375-391.
- Suppes, P., & Warren, H. (1975). On the generation and classification of defence mechanisms. *International Journal of Psycho-Analysis*, 56, 405-414.
- Sutcliffe, G. (2013). The sixth IJCAR automated theorem proving system competition—CASC-J6. *AI Communications*, 26(2), 211-223.
- Sutcliffe, G., & Suttner, C. B. (2014). *The TPTP problem library for automated theorem proving*. Coral Gables, FL: Department of Computer Science, University of Miami. http://www.cs.miami.edu/~tptp/.
- Swartout, W. R. (1977). A digitalis therapy advisor with explanations. In R. Reddy (Ed.), *Proceedings of the fifth international joint conference on artificial intelligence* (pp. 819-825). Los Altos, CA: William Kaufmann.
- Sycara, K. (1988). Patching up old plans. In *Proceedings of the tenth annual conference of the cognitive science society* (pp. 405-411). Hillsdale, NJ: Lawrence Erlbaum.
- Synge, J. L. (1960). Classical dynamics. In S. Flügge (Ed.), Encyclopedia of physics (Vol. III/1: Principles of classical mechanics and field theory, pp. 1-225). Berlin: Springer.
- Syrjänen, T. (2000). Lparse 1.0 user's manual. http://www.tcs.hut.fi/Software/smodels/lparse.ps.gz.
- Szolovits, P., Hawkinson, L. B., & Martin, W. A. (1977). *An overview of OWL, a language for knowledge representation* (Tech. Rep. No. MIT-LCS-TM-086). Cambridge, MA: Laboratory for Computer Science, Massachusetts Institute of Technology.
- Thagard, P. (1996). Mind: Introduction to cognitive science. Cambridge, MA: MIT Press.
- Thanassas, D. (1992). The phenomenon of commonsense reasoning: Nonmonotonicity, action and information. Chichester, UK: Ellis Horwood.

- Thielscher, M. (1995). Computing ramifications by postprocessing. In *Proceedings of the fourteenth international joint conference on artificial intelligence* (pp. 1994-2000). San Mateo, CA: Morgan Kaufmann.
- Thielscher, M. (1996). Ramification and causality (Tech. Rep. No. TR-96-003). Berkeley, CA: International Computer Science Institute.
- Thielscher, M. (1997). Ramification and causality. Artificial Intelligence, 89, 317-364.
- Thielscher, M. (1999a). Fluent calculus planning with continuous change. *Linköping Electronic Articles in Computer and Information Science*, 4(011), 1-15.
- Thielscher, M. (1999b). From situation calculus to fluent calculus: State update axioms as a solution to the inferential frame problem. *Artificial Intelligence*, 111, 277-299.
- Thielscher, M. (1999c). On-line tutorial on the fluent calculus. Dresden, Germany: Technischen Universität Dresden.
- Thielscher, M. (2000). Modeling actions with ramifications in nondeterministic, concurrent, and continuous domains—And a case study. In *Proceedings of the seventeenth national conference on artificial intelligence and twelfth conference on innovative applications of artificial intelligence* (pp. 497-502). Menlo Park, CA: AAAI Press.
- Thielscher, M. (2001). The qualification problem: A solution to the problem of anomalous models. *Artificial Intelligence*, *131*, 1-37.
- Thielscher, M. (2005a). Reasoning robots: The art and science of programming robotic agents. Dordrecht: Springer.
- Thielscher, M. (2005b). FLUX: A logic programming method for reasoning agents. *Theory and Practice of Logic Programming*, 5(4-5), 533-565.
- Thielscher, M. (2008). Action programming languages. San Rafael, CA: Morgan & Claypool. Thomason, R. H. (Ed.). (1974). Formal philosophy: Selected papers of Richard Montague. New Haven, CT: Yale University Press.
- Tran, N., & Baral, C. (2004a). Encoding probabilistic causal model in probabilistic action language. In D. L. McGuinness & G. Ferguson (Eds.), Proceedings of the nineteenth national conference on artificial intelligence and sixteenth conference on innovative applications of artificial intelligence (pp. 305-310). Menlo Park, CA: AAAI Press.
- Tran, N., & Baral, C. (2004b). Reasoning about triggered actions in AnsProlog and its application to molecular interactions in cells. In D. Dubois, C. A. Welty, & M.-A. Williams (Eds.), Proceedings of the ninth international conference on principles of knowledge representation and reasoning (pp. 554-563). Menlo Park, CA: AAAI Press.
- Trustees of Princeton University. (2006). WordNet 3.0 reference manual. http://wordnet.princeton.edu/wordnet/documentation/.
- Turing, A. M. (1950). Computing machinery and intelligence. Mind, 59(236), 433-460.
- Turing, A. M. (2004). On computable numbers, with an application to the Entscheidungsproblem. In M. Davis (Ed.), *The undecidable: Basic papers on undecidable propositions, unsolvable problems and computable functions* (corrected ed., pp. 115-154). Mineola, NY: Dover (Original work published 1936)
- United States National Library of Medicine. (2014). *Unified medical language system*. http://www.nlm.nih.gov/research/umls/.
- Van Belleghem, K., Denecker, M., & De Schreye, D. (1994). Representing continuous change in the abductive event calculus. In P. V. Hentenryck (Ed.), *Logic programming: The eleventh international conference* (pp. 225-239). Cambridge, MA: MIT Press.
- Van Belleghem, K., Denecker, M., & De Schreye, D. (1997). On the relation between situation calculus and event calculus. *Journal of Logic Programming*, 31(1-3), 3-37.
- Van Durme, B. D. (2009). Extracting implicit knowledge from text. Doctoral dissertation. Department of Computer Science, University of Rochester, Rochester, NY.

- van Harmelen, F., Lifschitz, V., & Porter, B. (Eds.). (2008). Handbook of knowledge representation. Amsterdam: Elsevier.
- van Lambalgen, M., & Hamm, F. (2005). The proper treatment of events. Malden, MA: Blackwell.
- van Benthem, J. (1987). Meaning: Interpretation and inference. Synthese, 73(3), 451-470.
- van Benthem, J., & Doets, K. (2001). Higher-order logic. In D. M. Gabbay & F. Guenthner (Eds.), *Handbook of philosophical logic* (2nd ed., Vol. 1, pp. 189-243). Dordrecht: Kluwer.
- Velleman, D. J. (1994). How to prove it: A structured approach. Cambridge: Cambridge University Press.
- Veloso, M. M. (1989). Nonlinear problem solving using intelligent casual-commitment (Tech. Rep. No. CMU-CS-89-210). Pittsburgh, PA: Computer Science Department, Carnegie Mellon University.
- von Ahn, L., & Dabbish, L. (2008). Designing games with a purpose. Communications of the ACM, 51(8), 58-67.
- von Ahn, L., Kedia, M., & Blum, M. (2006). Verbosity: A game for collecting common-sense facts. In *Proceedings of the SIGCHI conference on human factors in computing systems* (pp. 75-78). New York, NY: ACM.
- von Neumann, J. (1958). The computer and the brain. New Haven, CT: Yale University Press.
- Waldinger, R. (1977). Achieving several goals simultaneously. In E. Elcock & D. Michie (Eds.), *Machine intelligence 8* (pp. 94-136). Chichester, UK: Ellis Horwood.
- Walther, C. (1983). A many-sorted calculus based on resolution and paramodulation. In A. Bundy (Ed.), Proceedings of the eighth international joint conference on artificial intelligence (Vol. 2, pp. 882-891). Los Altos, CA: William Kaufmann.
- Walther, C. (1987). A many-sorted calculus based on resolution and paramodulation. London: Pitman.
- Wansing, H. (1998). Editorial. Journal of Logic, Language and Information, 7(3), iii-vii.
- Watkins, D. S. (2010). Fundamentals of matrix computations (3rd ed.). Hoboken, NJ: Wiley.
- Watson, J. B. (1924). Behaviorism. New York: W.W. Norton.
- Weld, D. S., & de Kleer, J. (Eds.). (1990). Readings in qualitative reasoning about physical systems. San Mateo, CA: Morgan Kaufmann.
- Whitehead, A. N., & Russell, B. (1925). *Principia mathematica* (2nd ed., Vol. 1). Cambridge: Cambridge University Press.
- Wikimedia Foundation. (2014a). Wikipedia. http://www.wikipedia.org.
- Wikimedia Foundation. (2014b). Wiktionary. http://en.wiktionary.org.
- Wilensky, R. (1978). *Understanding goal-based stories* (Tech. Rep. No. YALE/DCS/tr140). New Haven, CT: Computer Science Department, Yale University.
- Wilensky, R. (1983). Planning and understanding: A computational approach to human reasoning. Reading, MA: Addison-Wesley.
- Wilk, J. (2004). *Dynamic workflow pulling the strings*. Distinguished Project (MEng). London: Department of Computing, Imperial College London.
- Williams, M.-A. (1997). Belief revision, implementing belief revision, and interconnections. In G. Antoniou (Ed.), *Nonmonotonic reasoning* (pp. 183-225). Cambridge, MA: MIT Press.
- Winikoff, M., Padgham, L., Harland, J., & Thangarajah, J. (2002). Declarative & procedural goals in intelligent agent systems. In D. Fensel, F. Giunchiglia, D. McGuinness, & M.-A. Williams (Eds.), Proceedings of the eighth international conference on principles of knowledge representation and reasoning (pp. 470-481). San Francisco: Morgan Kaufmann.

- Winograd, T. (1972). Understanding natural language. New York: Academic Press.
- Winograd, T. (1975). Frame representations and the declarative/procedural controversy. In D. G. Bobrow & A. M. Collins (Eds.), Representation and understanding: Studies in cognitive science (pp. 185-210). New York: Academic Press.
- Winston, P. H. (1970). Learning structural descriptions from examples (Tech. Rep. No. AITR-231). Cambridge, MA: Artificial Intelligence Laboratory, Massachusetts Institute of Technology.
- Winston, P. H. (1977). Artificial intelligence. Reading, MA: Addison-Wesley.
- Witbrock, M., Baxter, D., Curtis, J., Schneider, D., Kahlert, R. C., Miraglia, P., Wagner, P., Panton, K., Matthews, G., & Vizedom, A. (2003). An interactive dialogue system for knowledge acquisition in Cyc. In *Proceedings and presentations of the workshop on mixed-initiative intelligent systems* (pp. 138-145). Fairfax, VA: George Mason University Computer Science Department.
- Witbrock, M., Matuszek, C., Brusseau, A., Kahlert, R. C., Fraser, C. B., & Lenat, D. B. (2005). Knowledge begets knowledge: Steps towards assisted knowledge acquisition in Cyc. In T. Chklovski, P. Domingos, H. Lieberman, R. Mihalcea, & P. Singh (Eds.), Knowledge collection from volunteer contributors: Papers from the AAAI spring symposium (pp. 99-105). Menlo Park, CA: AAAI Press.
- Wolf, R. S. (2005). A tour through mathematical logic. Washington, DC: Mathematical Association of America.
- Wolfram, S. (2002). A new kind of science. Champaign, IL: Wolfram Media.
- Woods, W. A. (1973). Progress in natural language understanding: An application to lunar geology. In AFIPS fall joint computer conference (pp. 441-450). Montvale, NJ: AFIPS Press.
- Wooldridge, M. (2000). Reasoning about rational agents. Cambridge, MA: MIT Press.
- Workflow Management Coalition. (1999). Workflow management coalition terminology & glossary. Document Number WFMC-TC-1011. Document Status—Issue 3.0, Workflow Management Coalition, Winchester, UK.
- Yolum, P., & Singh, M. P. (2004). Reasoning about commitments in the event calculus: An approach for specifying and executing protocols. *Annals of Mathematics and Artificial Intelligence*, 42(1-3), 227-253.
- Zernik, U. (Ed.). (1991). Lexical acquisition: Exploiting on-line resources to build a lexicon. Hillsdale, NJ: Lawrence Erlbaum.

- The first state of the state of
- the good profile shape or and the strong forms are a second of the P. A. godenne are all managed profiles appropriate to some grown of the State and the strong forms of the STATE.
 - The second of the second of
- To again of callegated and the control of control of the control of the callegate of the ca
- Antonic Victor Cook of Problems And the Cook of the Cook of Control of Cooking and Cooking of Cooki
- The state of the s
 - The section of the second of t
- tin valorita uktolometus opailes viiki alpatojat kannas tresinent sõi ten läisi. Monteaki Intiitikkop – tile epiki 1984–19. Laja vari vaita jorganis toi vallegaali Kitti – til selikuse
- And the second of the second o
- and the state of t
- and the state of the

Author Index

Note: Page numbers followed by f indicate figures and t indicate tables.

Abelson, R.P., 8-9, 15, 65-66, 200, 246, 331-332, 334-335 Ahl, D.H., 362 Aho, A.V., 45, 310 Ali, S.S., 334 Allen, J.F., 43, 44, 200 Alonso, J.B., 348, 361 Alshawi, H., 246 Amla, N., 231 Antoniou, G., 44, 215-216 Appelt, D.E., 46, 246 Armstrong, S., 362 В Bacchus, F., 43 Bagchi, S., 334-335 Baillargeon, R., 13 Baker, A.B., 7, 114, 291 Balint, A., 13-14, 15-16 Balzer, R., 315-316, 333-334 Baral, C., 13, 64, 74, 112-114, 135-136, 143-144, 268, 293, 311 Barborak, M.A., 334-335 Barry, B.A., 246, 334 Baum, E.B., 370 Baxter, D., 361 Bayardo, R.J. Jr., 230-231 Beale, S., 246 Beaudoin, L., 200 Belasco, A., 361 Belleghem, K.V., 115-116, 125-126, 408 Belov, A., 237, 288 Bennett, B., 163 Berland, M., 362 Bibel, W., 237 Biere, A., 288 Bihlmeyer, R., 268 Birnbaum, L., 228, 237 Blackburn, P., 246, 334 Blum, A.L., 134, 353, 362 Blum, M., 134, 353, 362 Bobrow, D.G., 44, 212-213 Boddy, M., 46 Boguraev, B.K., 246, 334-335

Borning, A., 361

Bornscheuer, S.-E., 294 Bos, J., 246, 334 Brachman, R.J., 13, 212-213, 274t Braine, M.D.S., 13-14 Brandano, S., 293 Bratman, M.E., 199, 200 Brewka, G., 44, 215-216 Briggs, R., 241-244 Brooks, R.A., 199 Brown, E.W., 334-335 Brown, F.M., 334-335 Brown, J.S., 310 Brusseau, A., 361 Bruynooghe, M., 46 Buchanan, D.W., 334-335 Bugajska, M.D., 311-312 Buss, S.R., 385

C

Cabalar, P., 260

Calimeri, F., 15-16, 268 Carmel, D., 334-335 Cassimatis, N.L., 164, 311-312 Castilho, M.A., 296 Ceccato, S., 212-213 Chambers, N., 362 Charniak, E., 46, 212-213, 246, 274t, 355, 362 Chklovski, T., 346, 347, 360, 361–362 Chomsky, C., 334-335 Chu-Carroll, J., 334-335 Church, A., 15, 385 Cicekli, N.K., 237, 246 Clark, K.L., 44, 45, 114, 400 Clark, P., 292, 334 Clocksin, W.F., 268 Clore, G.L., 184, 185, 201 Cohen, B., 230-231 Cohen, P.R., 200, 230-231, 334-335 Cohn, A.G., 163 Collins, A.M., 213 Collins, M., 246 Cook, S.A., 288 Crawford, J.M., 87 Crevier, D., 12 Criscuolo, G., 213 Cui, Z., 163

Fahlman, S.E., 107, 113-114

Falkenhainer, B.C., 310, 311, 313, 334-335 Curry, H.B., 385 Fan. J., 334-335 Curtis, J., 361 Fellbaum, C., 15, 361 Cwiklik, J., 334-335 Ferraris, P., 256, 257, 268-269, 385-386 Ferrucci, D., 15, 321, 334-335 Fikes, R.E., 63, 111, 112, 113-114, 125, 200, Dabbish, L., 362 292, 293 Dahlgren, K., 246 Finger, J.J., 111-112 Davidson, D., 295-296 Flum, J., 385-386 Davis, E., 13, 14-15, 39, 44, 45, 64-65, 86-87, 88, Forbus, K.D., 310, 311, 313, 334-335 163, 199, 274t, 310 Ford, K.M., 86 Davis, M., 44t, 45, 370 Fraser, C.B., 361 de Kleer, J., 310 Fredette, M., 361-362 de Nivelle, H., 230-231 Frege, G., 44t De Schreye, D., 125-126, 408 Freud, A., 202 Dean, T., 46 Fuchs, N.E., 318-319, 334 Dechter, R., 15-16 Furnas, G.W., 361-362 Deerwester, S., 361-362 Furst, M.L., 134 Denecker, M., 46, 115-116, 125-126, 408 Dimopoulos, Y., 269 G Dix, J., 44, 215-216 Gabbay, D.M., 12, 44, 45 Doets, K., 385-386 Galanter, E., 200 Doherty, P., 45, 64-65, 87, 114, 210, 216-217, 276, Garcia, D., 353, 362 293, 385, 409, 412, 417, 421 Garey, M.R., 15-16 Dolan, W.B., 362 Garnier, R., 45 Domeshek, E., 246 Gasquet, O., 296 Dowty, D.R., 334 Gebser, M., 268 Doyle, J., 44 Geffner, H., 293 Dreussi, J., 15 Gelfond, M., 8t, 74, 125, 135-136, 249, 268, Du, D., 15-16 280, 289-290, 293 Duboue, P.A., 334-335 Genesereth, M.R., 15, 43, 45, 64-65, 200, Dumais, S.T., 361-362 215, 216, 274t Dupré, D.T., 115-116 Gentner, D., 310, 311, 313, 334-335 Dyer, M.G., 15, 65-66, 200-201, 246 Gentzen, G., 44t Georgeff, M.P., 200 Ghallab, M., 200, 296 Ebbinghaus, H.-D., 385-386 Ghidini, C., 46 Eiter, T., 14 Gildea, D., 246 Elgot-Drapkin, J.J., 14, 199 Ginsberg, M.L., 8t, 13-14, 44, 64-65, 112, 114 Elkan, C., 143-144 Giunchiglia, E., 46, 216, 230-231, 280, 293, 296 Enderton, H.B., 385-386 Giunchiglia, F., 46 Epstein, E.A., 334-335 Givan, R., 317, 318, 334 Ernst, M., 87, 134 Gödel, K., 15, 385 Eshghi, K., 40, 42t Goldman, N., 315-316, 333-334 Eslick, I., 311-312 Goldstein, I.P., 212-213 Etherington, D.W., 87, 215-216 Golub, G.H., 350, 351, 361-362 Eves, H., 385-386 Gomes, C.P., 15-16 Gondek, D.C., 334-335 F Gong, L., 311-312 Gooday, J., 163 Faber, W., 268 Gordon, A.S., 200 Fagin, R., 199, 385 Gordon, J.M., 355, 360, 362

Gotts, N.M., 163 Green, B.F. Jr., 334-335 Ianni, G., 15-16 Green, C.C., 63, 64-65, 111, 274t, 385-386 Ielpa, G., 268 Greenbaum, S., 230-231 Israel, D.J., 13-14, 44, 200 Greiner, R., 361 Iwańska, L.M., 334 Grosof, B., 213 Iyer, B.S., 334-335 Gu, J., 15-16 Guenthner, F., 12 Guha, R.V., 13, 46, 246, 294-296, 360t, 361 Guicciardini, N., 39 Jackson, D., 230-231 Janhunen, T., 268 Gustafsson, J., 64-65, 114, 276, 293, 409, 421 Järvisalo, M., 14, 15-16 Jenkins, T., 334 Н Johnson, D.S., 15-16 Haas, A.R., 86-87, 112 Johnson-Laird, P.N., 13-14 Halpern, J.Y., 199, 311 Jones, E., 246 Halpern, M., 315, 333-334 Jordan, P.W., 313 Hamilton, A.G., 385 Jurafsky, D., 246, 361, 362 Hamm, F., 246 Hanks, S., 8t, 46, 81-82, 88, 292, 311 K Hansen, P.C., 361-362 Kahl, Y., 268 Harabagiu, S., 334-335 Kahlert, R.C., 361 Harel, D., 296 Kakas, A.C., 14, 113, 267, 269, 293 Harland, J., 15, 170-171, 200 Kalyanpur, A.A., 334-335 Harrison, P., 334 Kaminski, R., 268 Harshman, R., 361-362 Kamp, H., 334 Hart, P.E., 63, 112, 200 Karlsson, L., 64-65, 276, 293, 409, 421 Havasi, C., 344, 348, 349, 353, 361-362 Kartha, G.N., 8t, 87, 88-89, 143-144, 293 Hawkinson, L.B., 316, 333-334 Kass, A., 246 Hayes, P.J., 7, 13-14, 15, 39, 41-43, 44, 64-65, 86, Kaufmann, B., 268 125-126, 163, 274t, 289 Kautz, H.A., 8t, 15-16, 86, 230-231 Hearn, R.A., 311-312 Kedia, M., 353, 362 Hearst, M.A., 9, 15, 354, 355, 362 Kim, T.-W., 12t, 262, 268-269 Heider, F., 200, 216-217 Kingsbury, P., 246 Hendler, J., 200 Kleene, S.C., 44t, 385 Hendrix, G.G., 15, 125 Klein, C., 361 Henkin, L., 385 Kneale, M., 12 Henle, M., 13-14 Kneale, W., 12 Herrmann, C.S., 125 Knight, B., 43 Herzig, A., 296 Koenderink, J.J., 246 Heule, M.J.H., 14, 15-16 Kokinov, B.N., 310 Hewitt, C., 14, 44 Kolaitis, P.G., 45 Hintikka, J., 199 Kolata, G., 13-14 Hobbs, J.R., 13, 46, 246, 334, 362 Kolodner, J.L., 310-311 Hodges, W., 385 Konolige, K., 44, 215-216 Hoeksema, J., 334 Koomen, J.A., 43 Hogger, C.J., 44 Kowalski, R.A., 7, 14, 40, 41-43, 42t, 74, 86, Hölldobler, S., 285, 294 113–114, 125, 274*t*, 275, 289, 403, 408 Holyoak, K.J., 310 Kraus, S., 14, 199 Hoos, H.H., 311-312 Krennwallner, T., 268 Hopcroft, J.E., 310 Kripke, S.A., 199 Horty, J.F., 212-213 Krishnamurthy, J., 361-362 Hwang, C.H., 334, 362

Kuhn, T., 334 Kuipers, B., 163-164, 310, 313 Kurzweil, R., 360t Kushmerick, N., 311 Kvarnström, J., 64-65, 210, 216-217, 276, 293, 296, 409, 412, 421 L Laird, J.E., 62-63 Lakoff, G., 334 Lally, A., 334-335 Lam. C.P., 362 Landauer, T.K., 360, 360t, 361-362 Lau, T., 311-312 Laughery, K., 334-335 Leake, D.B., 310-311 Lee, J., 12t, 46, 74, 216, 257, 258, 259, 260, 268-269, 280, 293, 296, 385-386 Lehnert, W.G., 334-335 Lenat, D.B., 13, 246, 294–296, 339, 360t, 361–362 Leone, N., 323 Levas, A., 334-335 Levesque, H.J., 13, 199, 200, 212-213, 274t, 370 Levin, L.A., 15-16 Lévy, F., 199, 408 Lewin, K., 200 Lieberman, H., 246, 349, 353-354, 361-362 Lifschitz, V., 8t, 13-15, 31, 43, 45, 46, 63, 74, 86, 87, 88–89, 113–114, 115, 125, 135, 143–144, 213, 214t, 215, 216-217, 249, 256, 257, 268-269, 280, 289–290, 291, 293, 296, 385–386, 421 Lim. G., 15, 361 Lin, D., 362 Lin, F., 64, 87, 112-113, 114, 135, 143-144, 289, 291 Lin, T., 345-346, 361-362 Lio, V., 268 Liu, H., 246, 334, 348, 361 Logemann, G., 370 Loveland, D., 370 Łukaszewicz, W., 45, 87, 216, 276, 293, 385 M Ma, J., 43, 195, 196, 199 MacCartney, B., 334

Ma, J., 43, 195, 196, 199
MacCartney, B., 334
Madigan, D., 311
Mahesh, K., 246
Mahoney, M., 360t
Mani, I., 246
Manna, Z., 382, 385–386
Manning, C.D., 246, 334–335, 361, 362

Manzano, M., 385-386, 400 Marcinkiewicz, M.A., 362 Marcus, M.P., 362 Marsden, J.E., 163-164 Martin, J.H., 361, 362 Martin, P., 46, 246 Martin, W.A., 316 Mateas, M., 246 Mates, B., 385 Mateus, P., 291 Matuszek, C., 361 Mayans, C., 361 Maybury, M.T., 334-335 McAllester, D.A., 15-16, 317, 318, 334 McCain, N.C., 46, 74, 114, 216, 280, 293, 296 McCarthy, J., 7, 12, 13-15, 30, 32, 39, 41-43, 45, 46, 63, 64-65, 86, 88-89, 125-126, 199, 202, 213, 214t, 215, 274t, 289, 294, 311-312, 361, 385-386 McClelland, J.L., 312 McCord, M.C., 246, 334-335 McCorduck, P., 12 McDermott, D.V., 8t, 13-14, 15, 43, 44, 46, 81-82, 88, 125, 212–213, 274t, 292, 296 McDonald, D., 361 McDowell, J., 246 McMillan, K.L., 231 Mellish, C.S., 268 Mendelson, E., 385-386 Michael, L., 99-100, 170-171, 249, 269, 280, 285 Mihalcea, R., 360 Miller, G.A., 200, 341 Miller, M., 14, 199 Miller, R., 7, 8t, 14, 39-40, 41, 63-64, 74, 88-89, 113, 122-123, 125-126, 136, 195, 196, 199, 267, 269, 291, 293, 313, 395, 409, 413-414, 415-416 Millstein, T.D., 87, 134 Minker, J., 44 Minsky, M., 9, 13-14, 44, 111, 212-213, 303, 304, 308, 309, 311-312, 313, 360t Miraglia, P., 361 Missiaen, L., 46 Mitchell, D.G., 370 Montague, R., 317, 334 Moore, J.D., 246 Moore, R.C., 13-14, 44, 199 Moorman, K., 246 Moravec, H., 360t

Morgan, B., 311-312, 378t

199, 200, 296

Morgenstern, L., 8t, 14-15, 41, 74, 164, 195, 196,

Moses, Y., 199, 385 Mueller, E.T., 12t, 14, 15-16, 40, 41, 42t, 87, 164-165, 200, 201, 202, 230-231, 241, 246, 311-312, 334-335, 342, 361, 397, 407, 409 Murdock, J.W., 246, 334-335

Narayanan, S.S., 231, 312 Nau, D., 200, 296 Nelson, M.J., 246 Nerode, A., 45, 385 Newell, A., 62-63, 200 Newton, I., 39 Nicolas, J.-M., 14 Niemelä, I., 254, 268 Nilsson, N.J., 13-14, 15, 43, 45, 63, 64-65, 86, 111, 112, 113-114, 125, 200, 215, 216, 274t, 292, 293 Nirenburg, S., 246 Nirkhe, M., 14, 199 Norvig, P., 12, 13, 45, 213, 246, 274t, 311-312

Oberschelp, A., 385 O'Brien, D.P., 13-14 Ohlbach, H.J., 45 O'Rorke, P., 201 Ortony, A., 184, 185, 201 Ostrowski, M., 268

Padgham, L., 15, 170-171, 200 Palla, R., 12t, 258, 259, 260, 267, 268-269 Palmer, M., 246 Pan, Y., 244 Pantel, P., 362 Panton, K., 361 Papadimitriou, C.H., 45 Papert, S., 311-312 Pardalos, P.M., 15-16 Parmar, A., 45, 295-296 Patkos, T., 8t, 41, 195, 196, 199, 407 Patwardhan, S., 334-335 Pearce, D., 260 Pearl, J., 294, 311-312 Pednault, E.P.D., 86-87, 135, 293 Perkins, T., 15, 344, 361 Perlis, D., 14, 199 Peters, S., 334 Pfeifer, G., 268 Pinto, J.A., 74, 125, 134, 135-136, 289-291, 400

Pirri, F., 43, 112-113, 289, 408 Pittman, K., 361 Plaisted, D.A., 230-231 Plexousakis, D., 407 Pollack, M.E., 200 Porter, B., 13, 292 Portinale, L., 312 Portner, P.H., 334 Prager, J.M., 334-335 Prakash, M., 361-362 Pratt, D., 361 Pratt, V.R., 44, 296 Pribram, K.H., 200 Priest, G., 14 Provetti, A., 408 Punyakanok, V., 246 Purdy, W.C., 334 Purtee, A., 362 Putnam, H., 370 Pylyshyn, Z.W., 86

Q

Quantz, J.J., 199, 408 Quillian, M.R., 212-213

Rabinov, A., 8t, 125, 135, 289-290

R

Ram, A., 246

Rubinoff, A., 357, 362

Randell, D.A., 163, 244, 246 Rao, A.S., 200 Reagan, P., 361 Reagan, R., 361 Reichgelt, H., 13 Reisig, W., 312 Reiter, R., 8t, 13, 43, 44, 45, 46, 64-65, 74, 86-87, 88, 112-113, 125-126, 135-136, 143-144, 213, 273, 274t, 275, 289-290, 291, 293, 294, 400, 408 Remolina, E., 163-164 Reyle, U., 334 Ricca, F., 15-16 Richardson, S.D., 362 Riecken, D., 311-312 Riesbeck, C.K., 15, 212-213, 246, 334-335 Rips, L.J., 14 Roberts, R.B., 212-213 Robertson, J., 246 Robinson, J.A., 15, 44, 63, 294 Rohde, D.L.T., 362 Rosenbloom, P.S., 62 Roth, D., 246

Rumelhart, D.E., 312 Russell, B., 44t, 385 Russell, S.J., 12, 13, 44t, 45, 213, 274t, 311-312 Sabharwal, A., 15-16 Sacerdoti, E.D., 112, 200 Sadri, F., 275, 289, 403, 408 Salay, N., 361 Sammet, J.E., 315, 333-334 Sánchez Valencia, V., 334 Sanders, K.E., 201 Sandewall, E., 8t, 14-15, 40-41, 87, 88-89, 125, 216, 292, 293, 310 Santorini, B., 362 Schank, R.C., 8-9, 15, 65-66, 200, 246, 331-332 Schaub, T., 268 Scherl, R.B., 199 Schmidt, J., 400 Schneeberger, J., 285, 294 Schneider, D., 361 Schor, M.I., 334-335 Schrag, R.C., 230-231 Schubert, L.K., 86-87, 112, 135, 334, 355, 356-357, 360, 362 Schultz, A.C., 311-312 Schütze, H., 246, 334-335, 361, 362 Schwartz, J.T., 360t Schwertel, U., 318-319, 334 Schwitter, R., 318-319, 334 Sebastiani, R., 230-231 Selman, B., 15-16, 86, 230-231, 370 Sergot, M.J., 7, 14, 40, 42t, 74, 125 Shanahan, M., 8t, 12t, 13, 14, 15-16, 39-40, 41, 42t, 43, 46, 58, 63–65, 86, 87, 88, 108f, 113–114, 115, 122-123, 125-126, 134, 136, 143-144, 164, 214t, 216, 230-231, 233, 246, 274t, 289, 291, 293, 313, 395, 409, 413-414, 415-416 Shapiro, S.C., 39, 334 Sheinwald, D., 334-335 Shepherd, M., 361-362 Shima, H., 334-335 Shoham, Y., 43, 44, 87, 135, 200, 201 Shore, R.A., 45, 385 Siklóssy, L., 15 Sil, A., 362 Simon, H.A., 62-63, 200 Simons, P., 254, 268 Singh, M.P., 233, 246

Singh, P., 9, 15, 233, 246, 311-312, 313, 334, 344,

361-362

Sirbu, M.A., 246

Sloman, A., 308, 311-312 Smedslund, J., 200 Smith, D.A., 8t, 64-65, 112, 327, 353-354 Smith, D.E., 362 Smith, T.F., 327 Soininen, T., 254, 268 Solow, D., 45 Speer, R., 348, 349, 353, 361-362 Spelke, E.S., 13 Stabler, E.P. Jr., 246 Stein, L.A., 212-213, 296 Stickel, M.E., 46, 246 Stork, D.G., 15, 362 Stratos, K., 357, 362 Strzalkowski, T., 334-335 Stützle, T., 311-312 Sun, R., 88, 312 Suppes, P., 202, 334 Surana, H., 353 Sutcliffe, G., 12t, 14, 15–16 Suttner, C.B., 12t Swartout, W.R., 333-334 Sycara, K., 310-311 Synge, J.L., 164 Syrjänen, T., 268 Szałas, A., 45, 385 Szolovits, P., 316, 333-334

Т Tang, L.R., 268-269 Tärnlund, S.-A., 400 Tate, A., 200 Taylor, C., 45, 361 Taylor, J., 45, 361 Teeters, A., 353-354, 362 Teichholtz, N., 352-353 Tenenberg, J., 43 Thagard, P., 13, 310 Thanassas, D., 13 Thangarajah, J., 15, 170-171, 200 Thiele, S., 268 Thielscher, M., 8t, 13, 99-100, 100f, 115, 125, 216–217, 285, 289, 294 Thomas, W., 345-346, 385-386 Thomason, R.H., 212-213, 334 Thompson, J.A., 334 Todd, K., 353, 362 Tong, M., 362 Touretzky, D.S., 212-213 Trafton, J.G., 311-312 Tran, N., 74, 311 Traverso, P., 200, 296

Tuan, L.-C., 311
Turing, A.M., 15, 360*t*Turner, H., 46, 74, 114, 216, 268–269, 280, 293, 296
Tygar, J.D., 246

U

Ullman, J.D., 45, 310

٧

Valverde, A., 260 Van Belleghem, K., 125-126, 408 van Benthem, J., 334, 385-386 van Doorn, A.J., 246 Van Durme, B.D., 355, 360, 362 van Harmelen, F., 13 van Lambalgen, M., 246 Van Loan, C.F., 350, 351, 361-362 van Maaren, H., 264 Vanderwende, L., 362 Vardi, M.Y., 199, 385 Velleman, D.J., 45 Veloso, M.M., 134 Vishton, P.M., 13 von Ahn, L., 353, 362 von Hofsten, C., 13 von Neumann, J., 360t Voronkov, A., 15

W

Waldinger, R., 63, 111, 382, 385–386 Wall, R.E., 38–39, 67, 126, 135, 334 Walsh, T., 15–16 Walther, C., 385 Wansing, H., 199

Waterman, M.S., 327 Watkins, D.S., 350, 351 Watson, J.B., 199 Weld, D.S., 87, 134, 310, 311 Welty, C., 334-335 Weyer, S., 361 Whitehead, A.N., 44t, 385 Wile, D., 46, 200, 334-335 Wilensky, R., 46, 200, 334-335 Wilk, J., 246 Williams, M.-A., 216 Winikoff, M., 200 Winograd, T., 15, 112, 212-213 Winston, P.H., 15, 112, 212-213, 274t Witbrock, M., 361 Witkowski, M., 12t, 15-16, 64, 87, 134, 230-231 Wojcik, R.H., 334 Wolf, A.K., 334-335 Wolf, R.S., 385 Wolfram, S., 385 Woods, W.A., 334-335 Wooldridge, M., 200

Υ

Yang, F., 293 Yates, A., 362 Yih, W.-T., 246 Yildirim, Y., 246 Yolum, P., 233, 246

Warren, H., 202

Z

Zernik, U., 362 Zhang, L., 334–335 Zhu, W.L., 15, 344, 361 As a mark

6-2 Str. 187

The second of th

e Verez e e

dr Towns

909 1000 - AME 1000 - AMERICAN SECURITION OF SECURITION OF

Ar nem F#

A Section of the sect

W

10 A

Subject Index

Note: Page numbers followed by f indicate figures and t indicate tables.

A Design the second	event calculus in
Abduction, 301–302	carrying book, 265-267
problem, 223–224	domain description, 261-262
reasoning types, 6	EC2ASP, 259-260
Abnormality predicate, 205–206	running and driving, 264-265
ACE. See Attempto Controlled English (ACE)	SM operator (see SM operator)
Action languages, 279, 293	solver, running, 262
C+ action language (see C + action language)	F2LP program, 267
causal theories, 282, 283–285	semantics of, 252-253
precondition axiom, 275	stable models, 253-254
probability and, 300–302	syntax, 251-252
AdaptWatson methodology, 332–333	Antitrajectory axioms, 105-107, 121-123
Agent behavior	falling object, 123-125
beliefs and knowledge, 199	hot air balloon example, 122-123
commonsense psychology, 200	Applications, commonsense reasoning
epistemic functional event calculus, 195–199	business systems (see Business systems)
axioms, 197–199	natural language, understanding, 240-244
FEC axiomatization, 196–197	story understanding problem, 240-244
possible worlds approach, 197	vision component, 244-245
predicates and functions of FEC, 196	Arithmetic symbols, 251
formalization, 168–170	Atemporal default reasoning, 205-206
goal-driven, 167–168	Atom, answer set program, 251
goals and plans, 167–184, 200	Atomic formula, Montagovian syntax, 317
human emotions, 200–201	Attempto Controlled English (ACE), 318-31
emotion theory, 184–185	Axioms
formalization, 185–193	action precondition, 58
lottery example, 193–195	agent behavior, 196-199
hungry cat scenario, 170–184	antitrajectory, 105-107, 121-123
reactive behavior, 167, 199	falling object, 123-125
society of mind theory, 303	hot air balloon example, 122-123
Analogical processing, 298–300, 310	disjunctive event, 142-143
AnalogySpace, 349, 361–362	epistemic functional event calculus,
deep similarity, 351–352	196–199
flat similarity, 351	fluent precondition axioms, 58
generation of plausible facts, 351	modified effect, 130
knowledge base, 350	positive and negative effect, 49-56,
singular value decomposition, 350	91–94, 113
truncated singular value decomposition, 350–351	advantage and disadvantage, 94
AND-join, workflow modeling, 237–239	agent picks up a book, 91-93
AND-split, workflow modeling, 237–239	initiates and terminates predicate, 49
ANIMAL program, commonsense knowledge,	phone behavior, 50-56
352–353, 362	precondition axiom, 275
Answer merging phase, Watson, 330	situation calculus effect, 274
Answer set programming, 249, 250–251	trajectory
\mathcal{E} action language, 267–268	falling object, 117-118
choice rules 254 255	Trajectory predicate, 121

Axioms (Continued)	example, 384
trigger	methods based on, 213-216
alarm clock, 67-69, 424	parallel, 384
definition, 67	SM operator and, 257
Shanahan's circuit with delays, 107-111, 108f	Class expression, Montagovian syntax, 317
Thielscher's circuit with delays, 105-107	Classical logic event calculus, 287–288
	Common analysis structure (CAS), 321
В	Common Consensus, commonsense knowledge 353–354
Bank account service fee example, 70–73	Commonsense knowledge, 359t
Baseballs colliding example, 154–160	AnalogySpace, 349-352, 361-362
Base phase, Watson, 329	ANIMAL program, 352-353, 362
Bayesian networks, 302–303	Common Consensus, 353–354
BDEC, 398–400	comparison, 359-360
and LDEC, 400-402	ConceptNet, 348-349
and situation calculus, 402-407	Cyc, 339-341, 361
Benchmark problems, 213	event calculus reasoning, 357-359
Business systems	GIOMI, 353, 362
payment protocols, 233–237	human, 360
workflow modeling, 237–239	Learner system, 346–348
Bus ride scenario, 8t	OMCS, 344-346, 348-349, 361
	text mining, 354-357, 362
C A Section of the Control of the Co	ThoughtTreasure, 342-344
C+ action language, 280–285	Verbosity, 353
to causal theories, 283–285	WordNet, 341-342, 361
formula, 280, 281	Commonsense law of inertia, 4, 5, 77-81, 88
syntax of, 280-282	classical frame axiom, 78, 86-88
Candidate generation, Watson, 324	explanation closure axiom, 78-79
Candidate inferences, SME, 299	frame problem, 77–78, 86
CAS. See Common analysis structure (CAS)	initiates predicate, 79-80
Case-based reasoning (CBR), 310-311	minimize event effects, 80
Causal constraints, indirect effects, 99-105, 115	minimize event occurrences, 79
primitive and derived fluents, 100-101	release axiom, 85
Thielscher's circuit, 102-105	representation of release
Causal theory	explanation closure axioms, 83
C+ to, 283–285	Releases and ReleasedAt predicates,
reduction to propositional logic, 283	82–83, 88–89
semantics of, 282	restoring inertia, 83
syntax of, 282	Russian turkey scenario, 84
CBR. See Case-based reasoning (CBR)	Yale shooting scenario, 81–82, 88,
CC, for event calculus reasoning, 264f	424–426
Chessboard scenario, 8t	terminates predicate, 80
Choice rules, of answer set programming, 254–255	Commonsense reasoning
Circumscription	automated reasoning, 15
conjunctions of, 215	benchmark problems, 14–15
default reasoning, 213–216	book-length treatments of, 13
definition, 383–384	declarative/procedural distinction, 15
event calculus, 30-32, 45, 383-384	description, 1
computing circumscription, 31, 423	formalization benefits, 369
of happens, 31–32	issues of
of initiates, 32	abduction, 6
nonmonotonic reasoning, 30-32, 44-45	commonsense law of inertia, 4, 5

concurrent events, 3	intersection, 61
context-sensitive effects, 3	irreflexive and antisymmetric relation, 59
default reasoning, 5–6	negation, 60
delayed effects and continuous change, 4	qualification constraint, 59-60
effects of events, 2–3	telephone axiomatization, 61-62, 423-424
events and time, 2	Context-dependent answer scoring, 326
indirect effects, 3	Context-independent answer scoring, 328
mental states, 6	Contexts, 339
nondeterministic effects, 3	Continuous change
object identity, 2	antitrajectory axioms, 121–123
objects and properties, 2	falling object, 123–125
postdiction, 6	hot air balloon example, 122–123
preconditions of actions/events, 3–4	trajectory axioms
reasoning/inference, 2	falling object, 117–118
representation, 2	Trajectory predicate, 121
space, 3	Critic-selector model, 309
temporal projection/prediction, 6	Cumulative and canceling effects
triggered events, 5	camera with flash unit example, 130-131
logical methods, 7, 14	modified effect axioms, 130
logic-based artificial intelligence, 13-14	moving robot example, 131-134
nonlogical methods, 8-9, 15	Cyc, 294-296, 339, 361
potential obstacles, 368-369	knowledge acquisition, 340
psychology, 200	Rapid Knowledge Formation tools, 340-341
satisfiability, 15–16	
unstructured information	
definition, 315	D
natural language (see Natural language)	Datatypes
OWL system, 316	lists, 382–383
SAFE system, 315–316	real numbers, 381–382, 381 <i>t</i> , 382 <i>t</i>
WatsonPaths for, 331–332	DEC, 26
Commuter scenario, 8t	Declarative knowledge, acquisition of,
Comparative predicates, 251	342–343
ConceptNet, 348–349	
•	Deduction problem, 222–223
Concurrent event occurrences	Default reasoning, 5–6
cumulative and canceling effects	atemporal, 205–206
camera with a flash unit example, 130–131	benchmark problems, 213
modified effect axioms, 130	circumscription, 213–216
moving robot example, 131–134	events, 211–212
restrictions	frames and inheritance networks, 212–213
event occurrence constraints, 128–129	logic-based methods for, 213
state constraints, 127–128	method for, 207–208
Conjunctions, of circumscriptions, 215	properties, 212
Connectionism approach, 312	and qualification problem, 208-211
Constraints, 250–251	broken device, 210
answer set program, 252	device revisited, 208–209
causal constraints, indirect effects, 99-105, 115	erratic device, 210-211
primitive and derived fluents, 100-101	strong and weak qualifications, 210
Thielscher's circuit, 102–105	temporal, 206–207
effect, 98-99, 115	Deliberative critics, EM-ONE, 308
state constraints, event effects, 64-65	Determining fluent, 139–142, 210–211
exactly one, 61–62	DFL. See Discrete fluent logic (DFL)
functional and total relation, 59–60	Discourse representation structure, 319, 320
	2 o representation structure, 517, 520

Discrete event calculus	English Slot Grammar (ESG), 322
BDEC, 398-400, 402-407	Epistemic functional event calculus (EFEC),
event calculus and, 263f, 387, 388, 389, 390, 391,	195–199
392	axioms, 197-199
LDEC, 397-398, 400-402	FEC axiomatization, 196-197
and SAT, 222	possible worlds approach, 197
Discrete Event Calculus Reasoner program	predicates and functions of FEC, 196
abduction, 223–224	ε action language, 267–268
architecture, 221, 222f	Event calculus, 206–207, 368
deduction, 222–223	action languages (see Action languages)
formula symbols, 230t	in answer set programming
language, 229–230	carrying book, 265–267
model-finding, 225	domain description, 261-262
postdiction, 224–225	EC2ASP, 259-260
SAT problems, encoding, 221–222	running and driving, 264-265
statements, 230t	SM operator (see SM operator)
story understanding, 240–241	solver, running, 262
telephone example, 226–229	automated reasoning, 11–12
Discrete fluent logic (DFL), 276	axiomatizations, 413–414
Disjunctive event axioms, 142–143	DEC, 26–27
Domain description	EC, 23–25
event calculus, 32–36, 367–368	basics and axioms, 39–41
elaboration tolerant, 32	business systems, 233
event occurrence formula, 32	CC for, 264f
HoldsAt and ReleasedAt formulas, 32–34	circumscription, 30–32, 45, 383–384
	computing circumscription, 31, 423
inconsistency, 36	of happens, 31–32
sleep event, 34–36	of initiates, 32
temporal ordering formula, 34	nonmonotonic reasoning, 30–32,
writing, 261–262	44–45
Domain theory, 216	and commonsense knowledge, 357–359
Door latch scenario, 294	conditions, 29–30
Driving, answer set programming, 264–265	default assumptions, 367
Durational fluent, 279	and discrete event calculus, 263f, 387, 388, 389
	390, 391, 392
E	domain description, 32-36, 367-368
EC, 23	elaboration tolerant, 32
EC2ASP, 259–260	event occurrence formula, 32
correctness of, 260	HoldsAt and ReleasedAt formulas, 32-34
event calculus in answer set programming,	inconsistency, 36
259–260	sleep event, 34–36
Effect axioms, 234, 235, 236, 237-239, 244-245	temporal ordering formula, 34
positive and negative, 49-56, 91-94, 113	with duration, 393-394
advantage and disadvantage, 94	equivalence, 418-421
agent picks up a book, 91-93	events of, 9–10
initiates and terminates predicate, 49	features of, 410t
phone behavior, 50–56	first-order logic
situation calculus, 274	many-sorted first-order logic, 20
Effect interaction problem, 135–136	notational conventions, 21
Elaboration tolerance, 32, 45, 215	proof theory, 20
Electrical circuit, 74	semantics, 20
EM-ONE architecture/system, 308-310	syntax, 19

fluent, 9–10	irreflexive and antisymmetric relation, 59
calculus (see Fluent calculus)	negation, 60
states, 23	qualification constraint, 59-60
lists datatype, 382–383	telephone axiomatization, 61–62, 423–424
natural language, understanding, 240–244	STRIPS, 63
payment protocols, 233–237	temporal default reasoning, 207
and PENG Light, 319–320	
predicates, 22–23	Exogenous, C + action language, 281
real numbers, 381–382	
	Fig. 1. The second seco
reasoning types, 46	Fact, answer set program, 252
abduction and planning, 37	Falling object
deduction/temporal projection, 37	antitrajectory axioms, 123-125
model finding, 39	trajectory axioms
postdiction, 38–39	with events, 118-121
sleep abduction, 37–38	without air resistance, 117-118
reification, 28-29, 41-43, 367	Feature merging process, Watson, 328–329
situation calculus (see Situation calculus)	Ferryboat connection scenario, 292
and society of mind theory, 304	Finite state machine (FSM), 233–234
sorts, 22	First-order logic
story understanding problem, 240-244	
TAL (see Temporal action logics (TAL))	many-sorted first-order logic, 20
three-argument Happens, 394	notational conventions, 21
time intervals, 43–44	abbreviations, 21
timepoints, 9–10	case conventions, 21
unique names axioms, 29	conjunctions and disjunctions, 21
vision component, 244–245	implicit universal quantification, 21
workflow modeling, 237–239	running exclusive/(XOR) notation, 21
working principle, 10–11	proof theory, 20
writing proofs, 45	semantics of, 20, 373–374, 376–377
Event effects	syntax, 19, 374–376
GPS, 62–63	F2LP program, 267, 267 <i>t</i>
idioms	Fluent calculus, 294
	concurrent actions, 286-287
flipping, 56	nondeterministic effects, 286
functional modification, 57	plus and minus macros, 286
many-to-many mapping, 57	states, 285
selection, 56–57	state update axioms, 286
setting and resetting, 56	Fluent formula, C+ action language, 280, 281
inconsistency, 63–64	Fluent logic language $\mathcal{L}(FL)$, 277–279
positive and negative effect axiom, 49-56	FOL-representation, 256, 257
initiates and terminates predicate, 49	Forced separation, 216
phone behavior, 50–56	Formalization, 234–236
preconditions, 57–59, 64	Frame, 212–213
action precondition axiom, 58	axioms, 86–88
fluent precondition axioms, 58	problem, 77–78, 86
qualification problem, 57, 58	society of mind theory, 303
walk through door, 59	Frame-array, 303
QA3, 63	Functional event calculus (FEC). See also
qualification problem, 64	
state constraints, 64-65	Epistemic functional event calculus (EFEC)
exactly one, 61-62	axiomatization, 196–197
functional and total relation, 59-60	predicates and functions, 196
intersection, 61	Functional fluent, 273, 275–276
	Function symbols, 251

G Game for Interactive Open Mind Improvement (GIOMI), 353, 362 Global mappings, SME, 298-299 GPS, 62-63 Ground atom, answer set program, 252 Ground program, answer set program, 252 Ground rule, answer set program, 252 Ground term, answer set program, 251

Н

Herbrand structures/interpretation, 377 Higher-level vision component, 244-245 Hitlist normalization phase, Watson, 329 Hot air balloon example, 122-123 Human emotions, agent behavior, 200-201 emotion theory, 184-185 formalization, 185-193 lottery example, 193-195 Hungry cat scenario, 170-184

Idioms, event effects flipping, 56 functional modification, 57 many-to-many mapping, 57 selection, 56-57 setting and resetting, 56 Indirect effects, events causal constraints, 99-105, 115 primitive and derived fluents, 100-101 Thielscher's circuit, 102-105 effect constraints, 98-99, 115 positive and negative effect axioms, 91-94, 113 advantage and disadvantage, 94 agent picks up a book, 91-93 primitive and derived fluents, 94-96, 113-114 ramification problems, 111-113 release axioms and state constraints, 96-98 trigger axioms Shanahan's circuit with delays, 107-111, 108f Thielscher's circuit with delays, 105-107 walking turkey scenario, 114 Indri search engines, 323, 324-325 Inductive definitions, 374 Inferential frame problem, 294 Inhabited dynamical systems (IDS), 292 Inheritance axioms, cancellation of, 215-216 Inheritance networks, 212-213 Inverse document frequency (idf), 326

K

Kitchen sink scenario, 4, 6, 8t, 15 K-line, society of mind theory, 304 Knext system, 355 extracting logical forms, 356 sharpening quantifiers, 356-357 Knowledge acquisition, commonsense knowledge. See Commonsense knowledge Knowledge entry (KE) text, 340 Knowledge machine (KM), 292

Learner system, 346 computing similarity, 348 follow-up questions generation, 347 sentences representation, 347-348 Lexical answer type (LAT), 322 Lexicographer files, 341 Lifting a table, 135 Linear discrete event calculus (LDEC) BDEC and, 400-402 description, 397-398 Liquids, ontology for, 163 Literal, Montagovian syntax, 317 Logical form answer candidate scorer (LFACS), 327-329 Logical foundations circumscription, 383-384 first-order logic, 374-379 Herbrand structures, 377 inductive definitions, 374 lists, 382-383 many-sorted first-order logic, 379-380 proof theory, 377-379 real numbers, 381-382, 381t, 382t relations, 380 second-order logic, 381 SM operator, 384-385 Logic-based methods, for default reasoning, 213 Logic program, answer set program, 252 Logistic regression models, Watson, 329 Low-level vision component, 244 Lucene search engines, 323

M

Machine learning phases, Watson, 329-330 Macros, plus and minus, 286 Many-sorted first-order logic semantics of, 373-374, 380 syntax, 379-380 Metacritics, EM-ONE, 309

Metric space, 153–160	Postdiction, 6, 302
MICRO PAM program, 331–332	Discrete Event Calculus Reasoner program,
Microtheories, 339	224–225
Minus macros, fluent calculus, 286	event calculus reasoning, 38-39
Missionaries and cannibals problem, 64	problem, 224–225
Model-finding problem, 225	Precondition interaction problem, 135
Montagovian syntax, 317–318	Preconditions of effects, 57–59, 64
	action precondition axiom, 58
N	fluent precondition axioms, 58
Narrative description language $\mathcal{L}(ND)$, 277–279	qualification problem, 57, 58
Natural actions, 290-291	walk through door, 59
Natural language	Predicates
OWL, 316	abnormality, 205–206
PENG Light, 319-320	comparative, 251
as programming language, 315–316	event calculus, 22–23
reasoning with, 320, 333t	initiates and terminates, 49
restricted, 316–320	prototypical, 213
SAFE system, 315–316	symbols, 251 trajectory, 121
understanding, 240–244	Prevents, 213
Watson (see Watson)	Primitive and derived fluents, 94–96, 113–114
NetBill protocol, 234	Probabilistic reasoning, 311
Neural networks approach, 312	Bayesian networks, 302–303
Nixon diamond, 213, 214–215	probability and action, 300–302
Nondeterministic effects	Probability, and action, 300–302
determining fluent, 139–142	Procedural knowledge, acquisition of, 343–344
disjunctive event axioms, 142–143	Prolog language, 249, 319
	Prototypical predicates, 213
0	
Object identity, space, 160–163	Q
one screen scenario, 160–162	QA3, 63
two screen scenario, 162–163	QSIM, 297–298
Open Mind Common Sense (OMCS), 361	Qualification problem
extracting structured knowledge, 346	defaults reasoning and
free-form activities, 345	broken device, 210
generation of plausible facts, 345–346	device revisited, 208–209
template-based activities, 344	erratic device, 210–211
OWL system, 316	strong and weak qualifications, 210
D	definition, 57
P	event effects, 64
Paranome, society of mind theory, 304	preconditions of effects, 57, 58
Passage term match scorer, 326–327	Qualitative differential equation (QDE), 297
Payment protocols, 233–234	Qualitative reasoning, 297-298, 310
formalization, 234–236	Quantifiers, sharpening, 356–357
NetBill protocol, 234	Question analysis, Watson, 322-323
scenario, 236–237	
PENG Light language, 319–320	R
Plus macros, fluent calculus, 286	Ramification problems, 111–113
Pointwise minimization of occlusion with nochange premises (PMON), 276	Rapid Knowledge Formation (RKF) tools, 340–341
POLYSCHEME cognitive architecture/system, 306–308	Reactive critics, EM-ONE, 308

275-276

Real numbers, 381-382 Skip-bigram scorer, 327 abbreviations, 382t SME. See Structure-mapping engine functions and predicates, 381t (SME) Reflective critics, EM-ONE, 308-309 SM operator, 256, 384-385 REFORMULATOR, 320, 333 and circumscription, 257 for event calculus reasoning, 258-259 Region connection calculus (RCC), 163 and stable models, 256-257 Relational fluent, situation calculus, 273 Relational space, 147 Society of mind theory, 303, 304, 311-312 EM-ONE, 308-310 basic representation, 147-148 event calculus and, 304 extended representation, 148-150 moving a newspaper and box example, 150-153 POLYSCHEME, 306-308 Release axioms and state constraints, 96-98 ThoughtTreasure, 304-306 Solver, answer set, 262 Restricting concurrency event occurrence constraints, 128-129 Soup bowl scenario, 8t, 135-136 conflicting actions of one agents, 129 Space metric space, 153-160 conflicting actions of two agents, 128, 129 object identity, 160-163 totally ordered plan, 128 state constraints, 127-128 one screen scenario, 160-162 Roulette wheel example, 139-142 two screen scenario, 162-163 Rule, answer set program, 252 relational space, 147 Running basic representation, 147-148 extended representation, 148-150 answer set programming, 264-265 and driving example, 142-143 moving newspaper and box example, Russian turkey scenario, 8t, 84 150-153 Spatial semantic hierarchy, 163-164 Stable models S of answer set programming, 253-254 SAFE system, 315-316 semantics, 249 Satisfiability (SAT) problems, 221-222 SM operator and, 256-257 Second-order logic, 381 State constraints, event effects, 64-65 Sequence, workflow modeling, 237 exactly one, 61-62 Shanahan's circuit, 107-111, 108f functional and total relation, 59-60 Shopping outlet scenario, 8t, 195, 196 intersection, 61 Signature irreflexive and antisymmetric relation, 59 answer set program, 251 negation, 60 C+ action language, 280 qualification constraint, 59-60 Situation calculus, 275-276, 287, 289 telephone axiomatization, 61-62, 423-424 actions, 273-274 States, fluent calculus, 285 effects, 274 State update axioms, fluent calculus, 286 preconditions, 275 Stockholm delivery scenario, 292 actual situations and events, 290 Stolen car scenario, 8t assessing logics, 292-293 Story understanding problem, 240-244 BDEC and, 402-407 STRIPS, 63 concurrent events, 291 Structured information, 315 continuous change, 289-290, 291 Structured Knowledge Base (SKB), 324 and event calculus, 275 Structure-mapping engine (SME), 298 inertia, 291 candidate inferences, 299 knowledge machine, 292 example, 299-300 narrative time line, 291 global mappings, 298-299 nondeterminism, 291 score, 299 notational variants, 274t Stuffy room scenario, 8t relational and functional fluents, 273, Syntactic-semantic graph, 327

1	trigger axiom
TACS. See Textual alignment candidate scorer	alarm clock, 67–69, 424
(TACS)	definition, 67
Temporal action logics (TAL), 276-279, 293	Triggered fluents, 74
axiomatization, 412-413	Tweety example, 213
durational fluent, 279	to your second or the property of
equivalence, 418-421	U
event calculus and, 409-414	Unstructured information
action type specifications, 417	definition, 315
equivalence, 414-415, 416-417	natural language (see Natural language
restriction to single-step actions, 417-418	OWL system, 316
features of, 410t	SAFE system, 315-316
observation statements, 277	Unstructured Information Management
occurrences and effects, 277-279	Architecture (UIMA), 321
scenario descriptions, 279	
translation, 421	V
Temporal default reasoning, 206-207	Verbosity, 353
Temporal projection, 301	Vision component, 244–245
Term	vision component, 244–243
answer set program, 251	14/
matching, Watson, 325-326	W
weighting, Watson, 326	Walking turkey scenario, 8t, 114
Text mining, commonsense knowledge, 354-357,	Watson
362	AdaptWatson methodology, 332–333
Textual alignment candidate scorer	answer lookup, 324
(TACS), 327	candidate generation, 324
TGrep2 pattern, 357	context-dependent answer
Thielscher's circuit, 8t, 100f, 102-105, 115	scoring, 326
causal constraints, 102-105	context-independent answer
fluent calculus, 115	scoring, 328
trigger axioms, with delays, 105-107	English Slot Grammar, 322
ThoughtTreasure	feature merging process, 328–329
commonsense reasoning, 304–306	lexical answer type, 322
declarative knowledge acquisition, 342-343	logical form answer candidate scorer,
procedural knowledge acquisition, 343-344	327–328
Traditional program, answer set program, 252	logistic regression models, 329
Traditional rule, answer set program, 252	machine learning phases, 329–330
Trajectory axioms, 125	passage term match scorer, 326–327
falling object	primary search, 323
with events, 118–121	question analysis, 322–323
without air resistance, 117–118	question answering system, 321
Trajectory predicate, 121	skip-bigram scorer, 327
Transframe, society of mind theory, 303	standardized features, 329
Trigger axioms, 105–111, 234, 237–239,	Structured Knowledge Base, 324
241–244	supporting evidence retrieval, 324–325
alarm clock, 67-69, 424	syntactic-semantic graph, 327
definition, 67	term matching, 325–326
Shanahan's circuit with delays,	term weighting, 326
107–111, 108 <i>f</i>	textual alignment candidate
Thielscher's circuit with delays, 105–107	scorer, 327
Triggered event	Unstructured Information Management
prayant rangeted triggaring 70, 72	Architecture 321

482 Subject Index

WatsonPaths, 330–331 algorithm, 330–331 for commonsense reasoning, 331–332 Winograd Schema Challenge, 14 WordNet, commonsense knowledge, 341–342, 361 Workflow Management Coalition, 237 Workflow modeling, 237–239

XOR-join, workflow modeling, 237–239 XOR-split, workflow modeling, 237–239

Yale shooting scenario, 8t, 81-82, 88, 213, 424-426